Sociology

Understanding and Changing the Social World

Open Education North Carolina (OENC) is an NC LIVE initiative that aims to reduce the cost of higher education for North Carolina students by providing free, open textbooks for the most frequently taught courses across NC's 2- and 4-year colleges and universities.

The Open Education North Carolina initiative is partially supported by grant funds from the Institute of Museum and Library Services under the provisions of the federal Library Services and Technology Act as administered by the State Library of North Carolina, a division of the Department of Natural and Cultural Resources (IMLS grant number LS-00-18-0034-18).

Sociology: Understanding and Changing the Social World

This book was adapted from a University of Minnesota Libraries publishing edition (2013) which was adapted from a work (2010) originally produced by a publisher who requested it not receive attribution. This book was produced using Pressbooks.com, and PDF rendering was done by PrinceXML.

Sociology is licensed under a Creative Commons Attribution-NonCommercial-ShareAlike 4.0 International (CC BY-NC-SA 4.0) license, except where otherwise noted.

This Open Education North Carolina edition has a doi of:
https://doi.org/10.5149/9781469659299_UniversityofMinnesotaLibrariesPublishing

ISBN 978-1-4696-5928-2 (pbk: alk. paper)
ISBN 978-1-4696-5929-9 (pdf: ebook)

Published by NC LIVE
www.nclive.org/oenc

Print version distributed by the University of North Carolina Press
www.uncpress.org

Contents

Chapter 15: The Family

Chapter 16: Education

Chapter 17: Religion

Chapter 18: Health and Medicine

Chapter 19: Population and Urbanization

Chapter 20: Social Change and the Environment

Chapter 21: Collective Behavior and Social Movements

Chapter 22: Conclusion: Understanding and Changing the Social World

Publisher Information

Sociology: Understanding and Changing the Social World is adapted from a work produced and distributed under a Creative Commons license (CC BY-NC-SA) in 2010 by a publisher who has requested that they and the original author not receive attribution. This adapted edition is produced by the University of Minnesota Libraries Publishing through the eLearning Support Initiative.

This adaptation has reformatted the original text, and replaced some images and figures to make the resulting whole more shareable. This adaptation has not significantly altered or updated the original 2010 text. This work is made available under the terms of a Creative Commons Attribution-NonCommercial-ShareAlike license.

About the Author

Sociology: Understanding and Changing the Social World is adapted from a work produced by a publisher who has requested that they and the original author not receive attribution. This adapted edition is produced by the University of Minnesota Libraries Publishing through the eLearning Support Initiative. Though the publisher has requested that they and the original author not receive attribution, this adapted edition reproduces all original text and sections of the book, except for publisher and author name attribution.

Unnamed Author is a professor of sociology at the University of Maine. He is the author of several other textbooks: (1) *Discovering Sociology: An Introduction Using MicroCase ExplorIt*, second edition (Wadsworth); (2) *Criminology: A Sociological Understanding*, fifth edition (Prentice Hall); (3) *Law and Society: An Introduction* (Prentice Hall); (4) *Collective Violence*, second edition (with Lynne Snowden; Sloan Publishing); and (5) *Fundamentals of Criminal Justice*, second edition (with George Bryjak; Jones and Bartlett). He has also authored more than 30 journal articles and book chapters in sources such as the *American Sociological Review*; *Journal for the Scientific Study of Religion*; *Journal of Research in Crime and Delinquency*; *Justice Quarterly*; *Mobilization*; *Review of Religious Research*; *Social Forces*; *Social Problems*; *Social Science Quarterly*; and *Sociological Forum*.

Professor Unnamed Author is past president of the Society for the Study of Social Problems and is currently in his 17th year (fortunately, not all consecutive) as chair of his department. He has received an Outstanding Faculty Award from the College of Liberal Arts and Sciences at UMaine. A native of Philadelphia, Pennsylvania, Professor Unnamed Author has lived in Maine for the past 32 years. He received his PhD in sociology from the State University of New York at Stony Brook and his BA in sociology from Trinity College (Hartford, Connecticut), where he began to learn how to think like a sociologist and also to appreciate the value of a sociological perspective for understanding and changing society. He sincerely hopes that instructors and students enjoy reading this book in the format of their choice.

Acknowledgments

As always in my books, I express my personal and professional debt to two sociologists, Norman Miller and Forrest Dill. Norman Miller was my first sociology professor in college and led me in his special way into a discipline and profession that became my life's calling. Forrest Dill was my adviser in graduate school and helped me in ways too numerous to mention. His untimely death shortly after I began my career robbed the discipline of a fine sociologist and took away a good friend.

My professional life since graduate school has been at the University of Maine, where my colleagues over the years have nurtured my career and provided a wonderful working environment. I trust they will see their vision of sociology reflected in the pages that follow. Thanks to them all for being who they are.

Special thanks go to Michael Boezi, Vanessa Gennarelli, and Gina Huck Siegert, who all worked tirelessly to make this book the best it could be. My efforts also benefited greatly from the many sociologists who reviewed some or all of the text. These reviewers were tough but fair, and I hope they are pleased with the result. They include the following:

- Velmarie Albertini, Southeastern University
- Marcia Andrejevich, Purdue University North Central Campus
- Kathleen Angco-Vieweg, American International College
- Sharon Arnold, Lebanon Valley College
- Grace Auyang, University of Cincinnati
- Melissa Bonstead-Bruns, University of Wisconsin–Eau Claire
- David Briscoe, University of Arkansas at Little Rock
- Clifford Broman, Michigan State University
- Jennifer Brougham, Arizona State University
- Benjamin Brown, University of New Hampshire
- Thomas Busnarda, Niagara College, Welland, Ontario
- Derral Cheatwood, University of Texas at San Antonio
- Alan Dahl, University of Kentucky
- Wenqian Dai, University of South Dakota
- Keri Diggins, Scottsdale Community College
- Scott Dolan, University at Albany–SUNY
- Charles Faupel, Auburn University
- Fang Gong, Ball State University

- Gayle Gordon Bouzard, Texas State University–San Marcos
- Mark Gottdiener, University at Buffalo–SUNY
- Gaetano Guzzo, Wright State University
- Kellie Hagewen, University of Nebraska
- Rahime-Malik Howard, Collin College/El Centro College
- Jay Irwin, University of Nebraska at Omaha
- Kristin Joos, University of Florida
- Yoshinori Kamo, Louisiana State University
- Todd Krohn, University of Georgia
- Linda Kaye Larrabee, Texas Tech University
- Jason Leiker, Utah State University
- Royal Loresco, South Texas College
- Suzanne Macaluso, Purdue University
- Donald Mack, Tarrant County College
- Stephanie Malin, Utah State University
- William Martin, Binghamton University
- Richard McMillan, University at Albany–SUNY
- Joan Morris, University of Central Florida Cocoa Campus
- Timothy O'Boyle, Kutztown University
- Takamitsu Ono, University of Illinois
- Romana Pires, San Bernadino Valley College
- Antonia Randolph, University of Delaware
- Fernando Rivera, University of Central Florida
- Joseph Scimecca, George Mason University
- Glenn Sims, Glendale Community College
- Irena Stepanikova, University of South Carolina
- Eric Strayer, Hartnell College
- Chris Sutcliff, Lewis and Clark Community College
- Ronald Thrasher, Oklahoma State University
- William Tinney, University of South Carolina
- Linda Vang, Fresno City College
- Jesse Weiss, University of the Ozarks

- Susan Wortmann, University of Nebraska–Lincoln
- Jun Xu, Ball State University
- Yih-Jin Young, Nassau Community College

Authors usually save the best for last in their acknowledgments, and that is the family members to whom they owe so much. Barbara Tennent and our sons David and Joel have once again shared with me the joy and exhaustion of writing a textbook, and their patience has certainly been a virtue. I know they will share the gratitude I will feel when students read this text for free or at relatively low cost.

I have saved two family members for the very last, and they are my late parents, Morry and Sylvia Barkan. They have been gone many years, but whatever I have achieved in my personal and professional life, I owe to them.

Preface

Welcome to this new introduction to sociology text! According to recent news stories, thousands of college students are applying for jobs in AmeriCorps, Teach for America, the Peace Corps, and other national, local, and international service programs. Reports on college students find growing interest in voluntarism. Like generations before them, today's students want to make a difference in their society.

The founders of sociology in the United States also wanted to make a difference. A central aim of sociologists in the early 20th century at the University of Chicago and elsewhere was to use sociological knowledge to benefit society. A related aim of sociologists like Jane Addams, W. E. B. Du Bois, Ida B. Wells-Barnett, and others since was to use sociological knowledge to understand and alleviate gender, racial, and class inequality.

It is no accident that many sociology instructors and students are first drawn to sociology because they want to learn a body of knowledge that can help them make a difference in the world at large. This new text is designed for this audience. As its subtitle implies, it aims to present not only a sociological understanding of society but also a sociological perspective on how to improve society. In this regard, the text responds to the enthusiasm that "public sociology" has generated after serving as the theme of the 2004 annual meeting of the American Sociological Association, and it demonstrates sociology's relevance for today's students who want to make a difference in the world beyond them.

Several pedagogical features of the book convey this theme:

- Most chapters begin with a "Social Issues in the News" story taken from recent media coverage that recounts an event related to the chapter's topic and uses it as a starting point for the chapter's discussion. Additional material at the end of the chapter discusses promising strategies for addressing the social issues presented in the news story and in the chapter as a whole. The inclusion and discussion of "Social Issues in the News" will help students appreciate the relevance of sociology for newsworthy events and issues.
- Three types of boxes in almost every chapter reflect the U.S. founders' emphasis on sociology and social justice. The first box, "Sociology Making a Difference," discusses a social issue related to the chapter's topic and shows how sociological insights and findings have been used, or could be used, to address the issue. The second box, "Learning From Other Societies," discusses the experience in another nation(s) regarding a social issue related to the chapter; this box helps students appreciate what has worked and not worked in other nations regarding the issue and thus better understand how social reform might be achieved in the United States. The third box, "What Sociology Suggests," summarizes social policies grounded in sociological theory and research that hold strong potential for addressing issues discussed in the chapter. In addition, many chapters contain tables called "Theory Snapshots." These tables provide a quick reference tool for students to understand the various theoretical approaches to the sociological topic that the chapter is discussing.
- Most chapters end with a "Using Sociology" vignette that presents a hypothetical scenario concerning an issue or topic from the chapter and asks students to use the chapter's discussion in a decision-

making role involving social change. These vignettes help students connect the chapter's discussion with real-life situations and, in turn, better appreciate the relevance of sociological knowledge for social reform.

- Drawing on these features and other discussions throughout the book, a unique final chapter, Chapter 22 "Conclusion: Understanding and Changing the Social World", summarizes what students have learned about the potential of sociology to achieve social reform and includes further discussion of the relevance of sociological knowledge for addressing important social issues.

In this innovative spirit, *Sociology: Understanding and Changing the Social World* makes sociology relevant for today's students by using a fresh approach that, ironically, takes them back to sociology's American roots in the use of sociological knowledge to benefit society.

Chapter 1: Sociology and the Sociological Perspective

1.1 The Sociological Perspective

Learning Objectives

1. Define the sociological perspective.
2. Provide examples of how Americans may not be as "free" as they think.
3. Explain what is meant by considering individuals as "social beings."

Most Americans probably agree that we enjoy a great amount of freedom. And yet perhaps we have less freedom than we think, because many of our choices are influenced by our society in ways we do not even realize. Perhaps we are not as distinctively individualistic as we believe we are.

For example, consider the right to vote. The secret ballot is one of the most cherished principles of American democracy. We vote in secret so that our choice of a candidate is made freely and without fear of punishment. That is all true, but it is also possible to guess the candidate for whom any one individual will vote if enough is known about the individual. This is because our choice of a candidate is affected by many aspects of our social backgrounds and, in this sense, is not made as freely as we might think.

To illustrate this point, consider the 2008 presidential election between Democrat Barack Obama and Republican John McCain. Suppose a room is filled with 100 randomly selected voters from that election. Nothing is known about them except that they were between 18 and 24 years of age when they voted. Because exit poll data found that Obama won 66% of the vote from people in this age group (http://abcnews.go.com/PollingUnit/ExitPolls), a prediction that each of these 100 individuals voted for Obama would be correct about 66 times and incorrect only 34 times. Someone betting $1 on each prediction would come out $32 ahead ($66 – $34 = $32), even though the only thing known about the people in the room is their age.

Young people were especially likely to vote for Barack Obama in 2008, while white men tended, especially in Wyoming and several other states, to vote for John McCain. These patterns illustrate the influence of our social backgrounds on many aspects of our lives.

Wikimedia Commons – CC BY 3.0; Wikimedia Commons – public domain.

Now let's suppose we have a room filled with 100 randomly selected white men from Wyoming who voted in 2008. We know only three things about them: their race, gender, and state of residence. Because exit poll data found that 67% of white men in Wyoming voted for McCain, a prediction can be made with fairly good accuracy that these 100 men tended to have voted for McCain. Someone betting $1 that each man in the room voted for McCain would be right about 67 times and wrong only 33 times and would come out $34 ahead ($67 – $33 = $34). Even though young people in the United States and white men from Wyoming had every right and freedom under our democracy to vote for whomever they wanted in 2008, they still tended to vote for a particular candidate because of the influence of their age (in the case of the young people) or of their gender, race, and state of residence (white men from Wyoming).

Yes, Americans have freedom, but our freedom to think and act is constrained at least to some degree by society's standards and expectations and by the many aspects of our social backgrounds. This is true for the kinds of important beliefs and behaviors just discussed, and it is also true for less important examples. For instance, think back to the last class you attended. How many of the women wore evening gowns? How many of the men wore skirts? Students are "allowed" to dress any way they want in most colleges and universities, but notice how few students, if any, dress in the way just mentioned. They do not dress that way because of the strange looks and even negative reactions they would receive.

Think back to the last time you rode in an elevator. Why did you not face the back? Why did you not sit on the floor? Why did you not start singing? Children can do these things and "get away with it," because they look cute doing so, but adults risk looking odd. Because of that, even though we are "allowed" to act strangely in an elevator, we do not.

The basic point is that society shapes our attitudes and behavior even if it does not determine them altogether. We still have freedom, but that freedom is limited by society's expectations. Moreover, our views and behavior depend to some degree on our social location in society—our gender, race, social class, religion, and so forth. Thus society as a whole and our own social backgrounds affect our attitudes and behaviors. Our social backgrounds also affect one other important part of our lives, and that is our **life chances**—our chances (whether we have a good chance or little chance) of being healthy, wealthy, and well educated and, more generally, of living a good, happy life.

The influence of our **social environment** in all of these respects is the fundamental understanding that **sociology**—the scientific study of social behavior and social institutions—aims to present. At the heart of sociology is the **sociological perspective**, the view that our social backgrounds influence our attitudes, behavior, and life chances. In this regard, we are not just individuals but rather *social beings* deeply enmeshed in society. Although we all differ from one another in many respects, we share with many other people basic aspects of our social backgrounds, perhaps especially gender, race and ethnicity, and social class. These shared qualities make us more similar to each other than we would otherwise be.

Does **society** totally determine our beliefs, behavior, and life chances? No. Individual differences still matter, and disciplines such as psychology are certainly needed for the most complete understanding of human action and beliefs. But if individual differences matter, so do society and the social backgrounds from which we come. Even the most individual attitudes and behaviors, such as the voting decisions discussed earlier, are influenced to some degree by our social backgrounds and, more generally, by the society to which we belong.

In this regard, consider what is perhaps the most personal decision one could make: the decision to take one's own life. What could be more personal and individualistic than this fatal decision? When individuals commit suicide, we usually assume that they were very unhappy, even depressed. They may have been troubled by a crumbling romantic relationship, bleak job prospects, incurable illness, or chronic pain. But not all people in these circumstances commit suicide; in fact, few do. Perhaps one's chances of committing suicide depend at least in part on various aspects of the person's social background.

In this regard, consider suicide rates—the percentage of a particular group of people who commit suicide, usually taken as, say, eight suicides for every 100,000 people in that group. Different groups have different suicide rates. As just one example, men are more likely than women to commit suicide (Figure 1.1 "Gender and Suicide Rate, 2006"). Why is this? Are men more depressed than women? No, the best evidence indicates that women are more depressed than men (Klein, Corwin, & Ceballos, 2006) and that women try to commit suicide more often than men (Centers for Disease Control and Prevention, 2008). If so, there must be something about being a man that makes it more likely that males' suicide attempts will result in death. One of these "somethings" is that males are more likely than females to try to commit suicide with a firearm, a far more lethal method than, say, taking an overdose of sleeping pills (Miller & Hemenway, 2008). If this is true, then it is fair to say that gender influences our chances of committing suicide, even if suicide is perhaps the most personal of all acts.

Figure 1.1 Gender and Suicide Rate, 2006

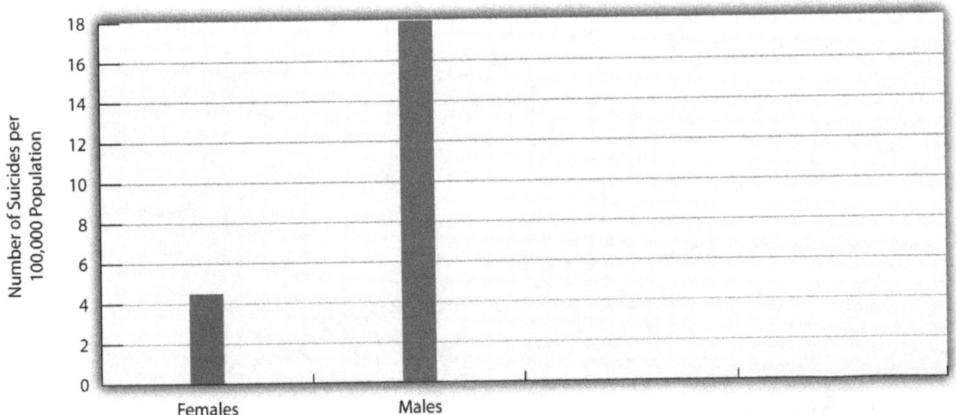

Source: Data from U.S. Census Bureau. (2010). *Statistical abstract of the United States: 2010*. Washington, DC: U.S. Government Printing Office. Retrieved from http://www.census.gov/compendia/statab.

In the United States, suicide rates are generally higher west of the Mississippi River than east of it (Figure 1.2 "U.S. Suicide Rates, 2000–2006 (Number of Suicides per 100,000 Population)"). Is that because people out west are more depressed than those back east? No, there is no evidence of this. Perhaps there is something else about the western states that helps lead to higher suicide rates. For example, many of these states are sparsely populated compared to their eastern counterparts, with people in the western states living relatively far from one another. Because we know that social support networks help people deal with personal problems and deter possible suicides (Stack, 2000), perhaps these networks are weaker in the western states, helping lead to higher suicide rates. Then too, membership in organized religion is lower out west than back east (Finke & Stark, 2005). Because religious beliefs help us deal with personal problems, perhaps suicide rates are higher out west in part because religious belief is weaker. Thus a depressed person out west is, all other things being equal, at least a little more likely than a depressed person back east to commit suicide.

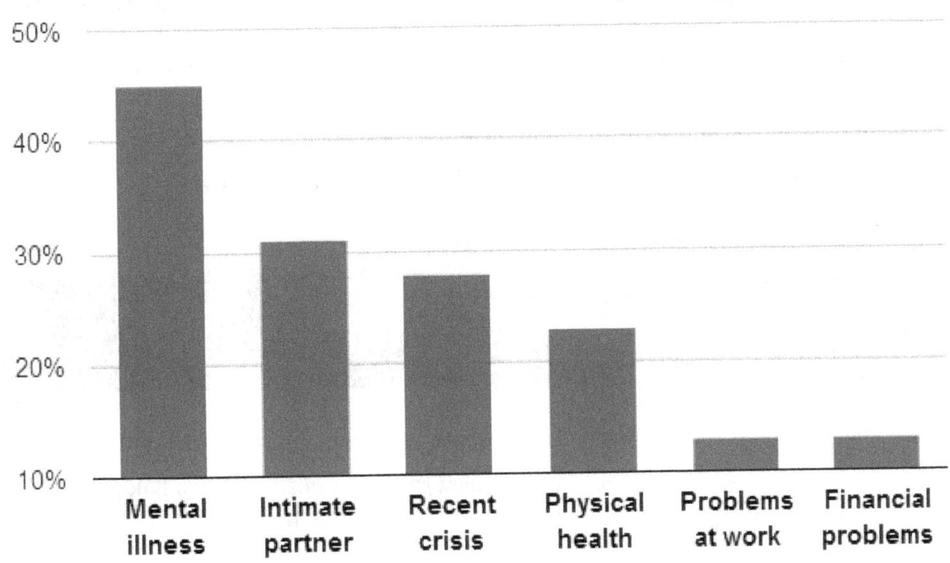

Although suicide is popularly considered to be a very individualistic act, it is also true that individuals' likelihood of committing suicide depends at least partly on various aspects of their social backgrounds.

Wikimedia Commons – CC BY-SA 2.0.

Figure 1.2 U.S. Suicide Rates, 2000–2006 (Number of Suicides per 100,000 Population)

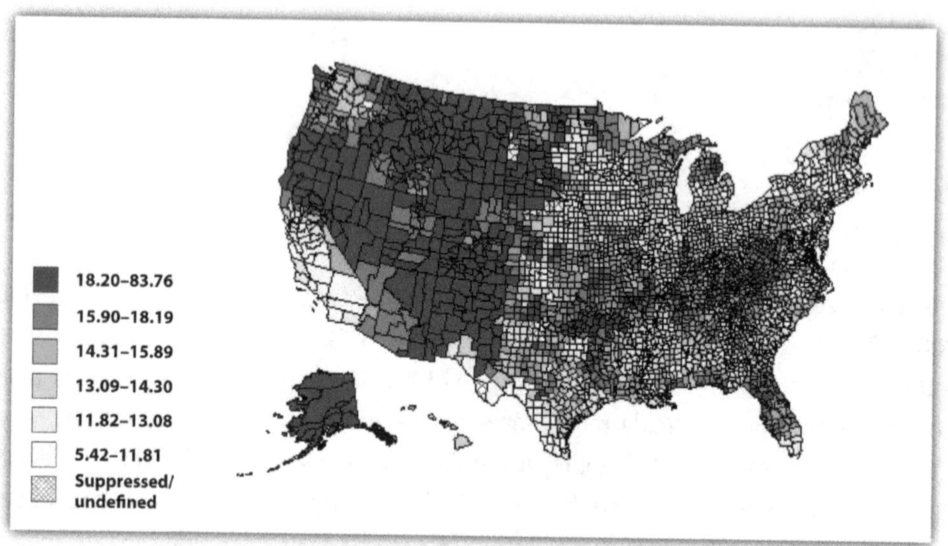

Source: Adapted from Centers for Disease Control and Prevention, National Center for Injury Prevention and Control, Division of Violence Prevention. (2009). National suicide statistics at a glance. Retrieved from http://www.cdc.gov/violenceprevention/suicide/statistics/suicide_map.html.

Key Takeaways

- According to the sociological perspective, social backgrounds influence attitudes, behavior, and life chances.
- Social backgrounds influence but do not totally determine attitudes and behavior.
- Americans may be less "free" in their thoughts and behavior than they normally think they are.

For Your Review

1. Do you think that society constrains our thoughts and behaviors as the text argues? Why or why not?
2. Describe how one aspect of your own social background has affected an important attitude you hold, a behavior in which you have engaged, or your ability to do well in life (life chances).

References

Centers for Disease Control and Prevention. (2008). Suicide: Facts at a glance. Retrieved from http://www.cdc.gov/ViolencePrevention/pdf/Suicide-DataSheet-a.pdf.

Finke, R., & Stark, S. (2005). *The churching of America: Winners and losers in our religious economy* (2nd ed.). New Brunswick, NJ: Rutgers University Press.

Klein, L. C., Corwin, E. J., & Ceballos, R. M. (2006). The social costs of stress: How sex differences in stress responses can lead to social stress vulnerability and depression in women. In C. L. M. Keyes & S. H. Goodman (Eds.), *Women and depression: A handbook for the social, behavioral, and biomedical sciences* (pp. 199–218). New York, NY: Cambridge University Press.

Miller, M., & Hemenway. D. (2008). Guns and suicide in the United States. *New England Journal of Medicine, 359*, 989–991.

Stack, S. (2000). Sociological research into suicide. In D. Lester (Ed.), *Suicide prevention: Resources for the millennium* (pp. 17–30). New York, NY: Routledge.

1.2 Understanding Society

Learning Objectives

1. Explain the debunking motif.
2. Define the sociological imagination.
3. Explain what is meant by the blaming-the-victim ideology.

We have just seen that sociology regards individuals as social beings influenced in many ways by their social environment and perhaps less free to behave and think than Americans ordinarily assume. If this insight suggests to you that sociology might have some other surprising things to say about the social world, you are certainly correct. Max Weber (1864–1920), a founder of sociology, wrote long ago that a major goal of sociology was to reveal and explain "inconvenient facts" (Gerth & Mills, 1946, p. 147). These facts include the profound influence of society on the individual and also, as we shall see throughout this book, the existence and extent of social inequality.

In line with Weber's observation, as sociologists use the sociological perspective in their theory and research, they often challenge conventional understandings of how society works and of controversial social issues. This emphasis is referred to as the *debunking motif*, to which we now turn.

The Debunking Motif

As Peter L. Berger (1963, pp. 23–24) noted in his classic book *Invitation to Sociology*, "The first wisdom of sociology is this—things are not what they seem." Social reality, he said, has "many layers of meaning," and a goal of sociology is to help us discover these multiple meanings. He continued, "People who like to avoid shocking discoveries…should stay away from sociology."

As Berger was emphasizing, sociology helps us see through conventional understandings of how society works. He referred to this theme of sociology as the **debunking motif**. By "looking for levels of reality other than those given in the official interpretations of society" (p. 38), Berger said, sociology looks beyond on-the-surface understandings of social reality and helps us recognize the value of alternative understandings. In this manner, sociology often challenges conventional understandings about social reality and social institutions.

For example, suppose two people meet at a college dance. They are interested in getting to know each other. What would be an on-the-surface understanding and description of their interaction over the next few minutes? What do they say? If they are like a typical couple who just met, they will ask questions like, What's your name? Where are you from? What dorm do you live in? What's your major? Now, such a description of their interaction is OK as far as it goes, but what is *really* going on here? Does either of the two people really care that much about the other person's answers to these questions? Isn't each one more concerned about how the other person is responding, both verbally and nonverbally, during this brief interaction? For example, is the other person paying attention and smiling? Isn't this kind of understanding a more complete analysis of these few minutes of interaction than an understanding based solely on the answers to questions like, What's your major? For the most complete understanding of this brief encounter, then, we must look beyond the rather superficial things the two people are telling each other to uncover the true meaning of what is going on.

As another example, consider the power structure in a city or state. To know who has the power to make decisions, we would probably consult a city or state charter or constitution that spells out the powers of the branches of government. This written document would indicate who makes decisions and has power, but what would it *not* talk about? To put it another way, who or what else has power to influence the decisions elected officials make? Big corporations? Labor unions? The media? Lobbying groups representing all sorts of interests? The city or state charter or constitution may indicate who has the power to make decisions, but this understanding would be limited unless one looks beyond these written documents to get a deeper, more complete understanding of how power really operates in the setting being studied.

Social Structure and the Sociological Imagination

One way sociology achieves a more complete understanding of social reality is through its focus on the importance of the social forces affecting our behavior, attitudes, and life chances. This focus involves an emphasis on **social structure**, the social patterns through which a society is organized. Social structure can be both horizontal or vertical. **Horizontal social structure** refers to the social relationships and the social and physical characteristics of communities to which individuals belong. Some people belong to many networks of social relationships, including groups like the PTA and the Boy or Girl Scouts, while other people have fewer such networks. Some people grew up on streets where the houses were crowded together, while other people grew up in areas where the homes were much farther apart. These are examples of the sorts of factors constituting the horizontal social structure that forms such an important part of our social environment and backgrounds.

The other dimension of social structure is vertical. **Vertical social structure**, more commonly called **social inequality**, refers to ways in which a society or group ranks people in a hierarchy, with some more “equal” than others. In the United States and most other industrial societies, such things as wealth, power, race and ethnicity, and gender help determine one's social ranking, or position, in the vertical social structure. Some people are at the top of society, while many more are in the middle or at the bottom. People's positions in society's hierarchy in turn often have profound consequences for their attitudes, behaviors, and life chances, both for themselves and for their children.

In recognizing the importance of social structure, sociology stresses that individual problems are often rooted in problems stemming from the horizontal and vertical social structures of society. This key insight informed C. Wright Mills's (1959) classic distinction between **personal troubles** and **public issues**. *Personal troubles* refer to a problem affecting individuals that the affected individual, as well as other members of society, typically blame on the individual's own failings. Examples include such different problems as eating disorders, divorce, and unemployment. *Public issues*, whose source lies in the social structure and culture of a society, refer to social problems affecting many individuals. Thus problems in society help account for problems that individuals experience. Mills felt that many problems ordinarily considered private troubles are best understood as public issues, and he coined the term **sociological imagination** to refer to the ability to appreciate the structural basis for individual problems.

To illustrate Mills's viewpoint, let's use our sociological imaginations to understand some important contemporary social problems. We will start with unemployment, which Mills himself discussed. If only a few people were unemployed, Mills wrote, we could reasonably explain their unemployment by saying they were lazy, lacked good work habits, and so forth. If so, their unemployment would be their own personal trouble. But when millions of people are out of work, unemployment is best understood as a public issue because, as Mills (1959, p. 9) put it, "the very structure of opportunities has collapsed. Both the correct statement of the problem and the range of possible solutions require us to consider the economic and political institutions of the society, and not merely the personal situation and character of a scatter of individuals."

The growing unemployment rate stemming from the severe economic downturn that began in 2008 provides a telling example of the point Mills was making. Millions of people lost their jobs through no fault of their own. While some individuals are undoubtedly unemployed because they are lazy or lack good work habits, a more structural explanation focusing on lack of opportunity is needed to explain why so many people were out of work as this book went to press. If so, unemployment is best understood as a public issue rather than a personal trouble.

Another contemporary problem is crime, which we explore further in Chapter 7 "Deviance, Crime, and Social Control". If crime were only a personal trouble, then we could blame crime on the moral failings of individuals, and some explanations of crime do precisely this. But such an approach ignores the fact that crime is a public issue, because structural factors such as inequality and the physical characteristics of communities contribute to high crime rates among certain groups in American society. As an illustration, consider identical twins separated at birth. One twin grows up in a wealthy suburb or rural area, while the other twin grows up in a blighted neighborhood in a poor, urban area. Twenty years later, which twin will be more likely to have a criminal record? You probably answered the twin growing up in the poor, rundown urban neighborhood. If so, you recognize that there is something about growing up in that type of neighborhood that increases the chances of a person becoming prone to crime. That "something" is the structural factors just mentioned. Criminal behavior is a public issue, not just a personal trouble.

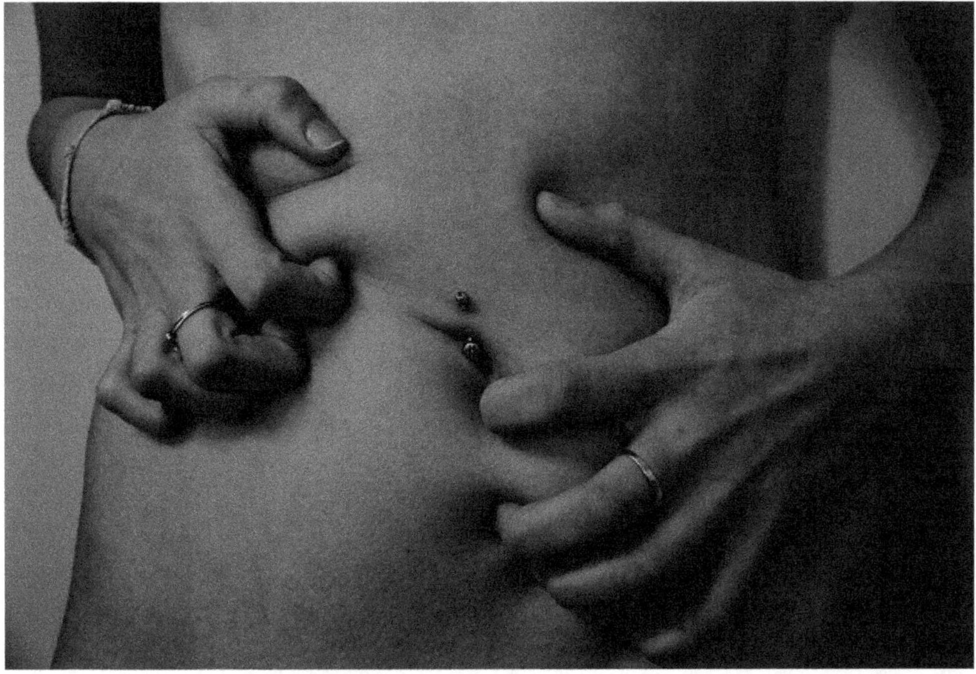

Although eating disorders often stem from personal problems, they also may reflect a cultural emphasis for women to have slender bodies.

Christy McKenna – grab – CC BY-SA 2.0.

A third problem is eating disorders. We usually consider a person's eating disorder to be a personal trouble that stems from a lack of control, low self-esteem, or another personal problem. This explanation may be OK as far as it goes, but it does not help us understand why so many people have the personal problems that lead to eating disorders. Perhaps more important, this belief also neglects the larger social and cultural forces that help explain such disorders. For example, most Americans with eating disorders are women, not men. This gender difference forces us to ask what it is about being a woman in American society that makes eating disorders so much more common. To begin to answer this question, we need to look to the standard of beauty for women that emphasizes a slender body (Whitehead & Kurz, 2008). If this cultural standard did not exist, far fewer American women would suffer from eating disorders than do now. Even if every girl and woman with an eating disorder were cured, others would take their places unless we could somehow change the cultural standard of female slenderness. To the extent this explanation makes sense, eating disorders are best understood as a public issue, not just as a personal trouble.

Picking up on Mills's insights, William Ryan (1976) pointed out that Americans typically think that social problems such as poverty and unemployment stem from personal failings of the people experiencing these problems, not from structural problems in the larger society. Using Mills's terms, Americans tend to think of social problems as personal troubles rather than public issues. As Ryan put it, they tend to believe in **blaming the victim** rather than **blaming the system.**

To help us understand a blaming-the-victim ideology, let's consider why poor children in urban areas often learn very little in their schools. A blaming-the-victim approach, according to Ryan, would say that the children's parents do not care about their learning, fail to teach them good study habits, and do not encourage them to take school seriously. This type of explanation may apply to some parents, in Ryan's opinion, but it ignores a much more important reason: the sad shape of America's urban schools, which are decrepit structures housing old textbooks and out-of-date equipment. To improve the schooling of children in urban areas, he wrote, we must improve the schools themselves, and not just try to "improve" the parents.

As this example suggests, a blaming-the-victim approach points to solutions to social problems such as poverty and illiteracy that are very different from those suggested by a more structural approach that "blames the system." If we blame the victim, we would spend our limited dollars to address the personal failings of individuals who suffer from poverty, illiteracy, poor health, eating disorders, and other difficulties. If instead we blame the system, we would focus our attention on the various social conditions (decrepit schools, cultural standards of female beauty, and the like) that account for these difficulties. A sociological perspective suggests that the latter approach is ultimately needed to help us deal successfully with the social problems facing us today.

Sociology and Social Reform: Public Sociology

This book's subtitle is "understanding and changing the social world." The last several pages were devoted to the subtitle's first part, *understanding*. Our discussion of Mills's and Ryan's perspectives in turn points to the implications of a sociological understanding for *changing* the social world. This understanding suggests the need to focus on the various aspects of the social environment that help explain both social issues and private troubles, to recall Mills's terms.

The use of sociological knowledge to achieve social reform was a key theme of sociology as it developed in the United States after emerging at the University of Chicago in the 1890s (Calhoun, 2007). The early Chicago sociologists aimed to use their research to achieve social reform and, in particular, to reduce poverty and its related effects. They worked closely with Jane Addams (1860–1935), a renowned social worker who founded Hull House (a home for the poor in Chicago) in 1899 and won the Nobel Peace Prize in 1931. Addams gained much attention for her analyses of poverty and other social problems of the time, and her book *Twenty Years at Hull House* remains a moving account of her work with the poor and ill in Chicago (Deegan, 1990).

About the same time, W. E. B. Du Bois (1868–1963), a sociologist and the first African American to obtain a PhD from Harvard University, wrote groundbreaking books and articles on race in American society and, more specifically, on the problems facing African Americans (Morris, 2007). One of these works was his 1899 book *The Philadelphia Negro: A Social Study*, which attributed the problems facing Philadelphia blacks to racial prejudice among whites. Du Bois also helped found the National Association for the Advancement of Colored People (NAACP). A contemporary of Du Bois was Ida B. Wells-Barnett (1862–1931), a former slave who became an activist for women's rights and worked tirelessly to improve the conditions of African Americans. She wrote several studies of lynching and joined Du Bois in helping to found the NAACP (Bay, 2009).

American sociology has never fully lost its early calling, but by the 1940s and 1950s many sociologists had developed a more scientific, professional orientation that disregarded social reform (Calhoun, 2007). In 1951, a group of sociologists who felt that sociology had abandoned the discipline's early social reform orientation formed a new national association, the Society for the Study of Social Problems (SSSP). SSSP's primary aim today remains the use of sociological knowledge to achieve social justice (http://sssp1.org). During the 1960s, a new wave of young sociologists, influenced by the political events and social movements of that tumultuous period, took up the mantle of social reform and clashed with their older colleagues. A healthy tension has existed since then between sociologists who see social reform as a major goal of their work and those who favor sociological knowledge for its own sake.

In 2004, the president of the American Sociological Association, Michael Burawoy, called for "public sociology," or the use of sociological insights and findings to address social issues and achieve social change (Burawoy, 2005). His call ignited much excitement and debate, as public sociology became the theme or prime topic of several national and regional sociology conferences and of special issues or sections of major sociological journals. Several sociology departments began degree programs or concentrations in public sociology, and a Google search of "public sociology" in November 2010 yielded 32,000 results. In the spirit of public sociology, the chapters that follow aim to show the relevance of sociological knowledge for social reform.

Key Takeaways

- The debunking motif involves seeing beyond taken-for-granted assumptions of social reality.
- According to C. Wright Mills, the sociological imagination involves the ability to recognize that private troubles are rooted in public issues and structural problems.
- Early U.S. sociologists emphasized the use of sociological research to achieve social reform, and today's public sociology reflects the historical roots of sociology in this regard.

For Your Review

1. Select an example of a "private trouble" and explain how and why it may reflect a structural problem in society.
2. Do you think it is important to emphasize the potential use of sociological research to achieve social reform? Why or why not?

References

Bay, M. (2009). *To tell the truth freely: The life of Ida B. Wells*. New York, NY: Hill and Wang.

Berger, P. L. (1963). *Invitation to sociology: A humanistic perspective*. Garden City, NY: Anchor Books.

Burawoy, M. (2005). 2004 presidential address: For public sociology. *American Sociological Review, 70*, 4–28.

Calhoun, C. (2007). Sociology in America: An introduction. In C. Calhoun (Ed.), *Sociology in America: A history* (pp. 1–38). Chicago, IL: University of Chicago Press.

Deegan, M. J. (1990). *Jane Addams and the men of the Chicago school, 1892–1918*. New Brunswick, NJ: Transaction.

Gerth, H., & Mills, C. W. (Eds.). (1946). *From Max Weber: Essays in sociology*. New York, NY: Oxford University Press.

Mills, C. W. (1959). *The sociological imagination*. London, England: Oxford University Press.

Morris, A. D. (2007). Sociology of race and W. E. B. Du Bois: The path not taken. In C. Calhoun (Ed.), *Sociology in America: A history* (pp. 503–534). Chicago, IL: University of Chicago Press.

Ryan, W. (1976). *Blaming the victim*. New York, NY: Vintage Books.

Whitehead, K., & Kurz, T. (2008). Saints, sinners and standards of femininity: Discursive constructions of anorexia nervosa and obesity in women's magazines. *Journal of Gender Studies, 17,* 345–358.

1.3 Theoretical Perspectives in Sociology

Learning Objectives

1. Distinguish macro approaches in sociology from micro approaches.
2. Summarize the most important beliefs and assumptions of functionalism and conflict theory.
3. Summarize the most important beliefs and assumptions of symbolic interactionism and exchange theory.

We have talked repeatedly about "a" sociological perspective, as if all sociologists share the same beliefs on how society works. This implication is misleading. Although all sociologists would probably accept the basic premise that social backgrounds affect people's attitudes, behavior, and life chances, their views as sociologists differ in many other ways.

Macro and Micro Approaches

Although this may be overly simplistic, sociologists' views basically fall into two camps: **macrosociology** and **microsociology**. Macrosociologists focus on the big picture, which usually means such things as social structure, social institutions, and social, political, and economic change. They look at the large-scale social forces that change the course of human society and the lives of individuals. Microsociologists, on the other hand, study social interaction. They look at how families, coworkers, and other small groups of people interact; why they interact the way they do; and how they interpret the meanings of their own interactions and of the social settings in which they find themselves. Often macro- and microsociologists look at the same phenomena but do so in different ways. Their views taken together offer a fuller understanding of the phenomena than either approach can offer alone.

Microsociologists examine the interaction of small groups of people, such as the two women conversing here. These sociologists examine how and why individuals interact and interpret the meanings of their interaction.

Piero Fissore – CC BY-NC-ND 2.0.

The different but complementary nature of these two approaches can be seen in the case of armed robbery. Macrosociologists would discuss such things as why robbery rates are higher in poorer communities and whether these rates change with changes in the national economy. Microsociologists would instead focus on such things as why individual robbers decide to commit a robbery and how they select their targets. Both types of approaches give us a valuable understanding of robbery, but together they offer an even richer understanding.

Within the broad macro camp, two perspectives dominate: functionalism and conflict theory. Within the micro camp, two other perspectives exist: symbolic interactionism and utilitarianism (also called rational choice theory or exchange theory) (Collins, 1994). We now turn to these four theoretical perspectives, which are summarized in Table 1.1 "Theory Snapshot".

Table 1.1 Theory Snapshot

Theoretical perspective	Major assumptions
Functionalism	Social stability is necessary to have a strong society, and adequate socialization and social integration are necessary to achieve social stability. Society's social institutions perform important functions to help ensure social stability. Slow social change is desirable, but rapid social change threatens social order. Functionalism is a macro theory.
Conflict theory	Society is characterized by pervasive inequality based on social class, gender, and other factors. Far-reaching social change is needed to reduce or eliminate social inequality and to create an egalitarian society. Conflict theory is a macro theory.
Symbolic interactionism	People construct their roles as they interact; they do not merely learn the roles that society has set out for them. As this interaction occurs, individuals negotiate their definitions of the situations in which they find themselves and socially construct the reality of these situations. In so doing, they rely heavily on symbols such as words and gestures to reach a shared understanding of their interaction. Symbolic interactionism is a micro theory.
Utilitarianism (rational choice theory or exchange theory)	People act to maximize their advantages in a given situation and to reduce their disadvantages. If they decide that benefits outweigh disadvantages, they will initiate the interaction or continue it if it is already under way. If they instead decide that disadvantages outweigh benefits, they will decline to begin interacting or stop the interaction if already begun. Social order is possible because people realize it will be in their best interests to cooperate and to make compromises when necessary. Utilitarianism is a micro theory.

Functionalism

Functionalism, also known as the functionalist perspective, arose out of two great revolutions of the 18th and 19th centuries. The first was the French Revolution of 1789, whose intense violence and bloody terror shook Europe to its core. The aristocracy throughout Europe feared that revolution would spread to their own lands, and intellectuals feared that social order was crumbling.

The Industrial Revolution of the 19th century reinforced these concerns. Starting first in Europe and then in the United States, the Industrial Revolution led to many changes, including the rise and growth of cities as people left their farms to live near factories. As the cities grew, people lived in increasingly poor, crowded, and decrepit conditions. One result of these conditions was mass violence, as mobs of the poor roamed the streets of European and American cities. They attacked bystanders, destroyed property, and generally wreaked havoc. Here was additional evidence, if European intellectuals needed it, of the breakdown of social order.

In response, the intellectuals began to write that a strong society, as exemplified by strong social bonds and rules and effective socialization, was needed to prevent social order from disintegrating (Collins, 1994). In this regard, their view was similar to that of the 20th-century novel *Lord of the Flies* by William Golding (1954), which many college students read in high school. Some British boys are stranded on an island after a plane crash. No longer supervised by adults and no longer in a society as they once knew it, they are not sure how to proceed and come up with new rules for their behavior. These rules prove ineffective, and the boys slowly become savages, as the book calls them, and commit murder. However bleak, Golding's view echoes that of the conservative intellectuals writing in the aftermath of the French and Industrial Revolutions. Without a strong society and effective socialization, they warned, social order breaks down, and violence and other signs of social disorder result.

This general framework reached fruition in the writings of Émile Durkheim (1858–1917), a French scholar largely responsible for the sociological perspective as we now know it. Adopting the conservative intellectuals' view of the need for a strong society, Durkheim felt that human beings have desires that result in chaos unless society limits them. He wrote, "To achieve any other result, the passions first must be limited.…But since the individual has no way of limiting them, this must be done by some force exterior to him" (Durkheim, 1897/1952, p. 274). This force, Durkheim continued, is the moral authority of society.

How does society limit individual aspirations? Durkheim emphasized two related social mechanisms: socialization and social integration. Socialization helps us learn society's rules and the need to cooperate, as people end up generally agreeing on important norms and values, while social integration, or our ties to other people and to social institutions such as religion and the family, helps socialize us and integrate us into society and reinforce our respect for its rules. In general, Durkheim added, society comprises many types of social facts, or forces external to the individual, that affect and constrain individual attitudes and behavior. The result is that socialization and social integration help establish a strong set of social rules—or, as Durkheim called it, a strong **collective conscience**—that is needed for a stable society. By so doing, society "creates a kind of cocoon around the individual, making him or her less individualistic, more a member of the group" (Collins, 1994, p. 181). Weak rules or social ties weaken this "moral cocoon" and lead to social disorder. In all of these respects, says Randall Collins (1994, p. 181), Durkheim's view represents the "core tradition" of sociology that lies at the heart of the sociological perspective.

Émile Durkheim was a founder of sociology and largely responsible for the sociological perspective as we now know it.

https://www.marxists.org/glossary/people/d/pics/durkheim.jpg – public domain.

Durkheim used suicide to illustrate how social disorder can result from a weakening of society's moral cocoon. Focusing on group rates of suicide, he felt they could not be explained simply in terms of individual unhappiness and instead resulted from external forces. One such force is **anomie**, or normlessness, which results from situations, such as periods of rapid social change, when social norms are weak and unclear or social ties are weak.

When anomie sets in, people become more unclear about how to deal with problems in their life. Their aspirations are no longer limited by society's constraints and thus cannot be fulfilled. The frustration stemming from anomie leads some people to commit suicide (Durkheim, 1897/1952).

To test his theory, Durkheim gathered suicide rate data and found that Protestants had higher suicide rates than Catholics. To explain this difference, he rejected the idea that Protestants were less happy than Catholics and instead hypothesized that Catholic doctrine provides many more rules for behavior and thinking than does Protestant doctrine. Protestants' aspirations were thus less constrained than Catholics' desires. In times of trouble, Protestants also have fewer norms on which to rely for comfort and support than do Catholics. He also thought that Protestants' ties to each other were weaker than those among Catholics, providing Protestants fewer social support networks to turn to when troubled. In addition, Protestant belief is ambivalent about suicide, while Catholic doctrine condemns it. All of these properties of religious group membership combine to produce higher suicide rates among Protestants than among Catholics.

Today's functionalist perspective arises out of Durkheim's work and that of other conservative intellectuals of the 19th century. It uses the human body as a model for understanding society. In the human body, our various organs and other body parts serve important functions for the ongoing health and stability of our body. Our eyes help us see, our ears help us hear, our heart circulates our blood, and so forth. Just as we can understand the body by describing and understanding the functions that its parts serve for its health and stability, so can we understand society by describing and understanding the functions that its "parts"—or, more accurately, its social institutions—serve for the ongoing health and stability of society. Thus functionalism emphasizes the importance of social institutions such as the family, religion, and education for producing a stable society. We look at these institutions in later chapters.

Similar to the view of the conservative intellectuals from which it grew, functionalism is skeptical of rapid social change and other major social upheaval. The analogy to the human body helps us understand this skepticism. In our bodies, any sudden, rapid change is a sign of danger to our health. If we break a bone in one of our legs, we have trouble walking; if we lose sight in both our eyes, we can no longer see. Slow changes, such as the growth of our hair and our nails, are fine and even normal, but sudden changes like those just described are obviously troublesome. By analogy, sudden and rapid changes in society and its social institutions are troublesome according to the functionalist perspective. If the human body evolved to its present form and functions because these made sense from an evolutionary perspective, so did society evolve to its present form and functions because these made sense. Any sudden change in society thus threatens its stability and future. By taking a skeptical approach to social change, functionalism supports the status quo and is thus often regarded as a conservative perspective.

Conflict Theory

In many ways, **conflict theory** is the opposite of functionalism but ironically also grew out of the Industrial Revolution, thanks largely to Karl Marx (1818–1883) and his collaborator, Friedrich Engels (1820–1895). Whereas conservative intellectuals feared the mass violence resulting from industrialization, Marx and Engels deplored the conditions they felt were responsible for the mass violence and the capitalist society they felt was responsible for these conditions. Instead of fearing the breakdown of social order that mass violence represented, they felt that revolutionary violence was needed to eliminate capitalism and the poverty and misery they saw as its inevitable result (Marx, 1867/1906; Marx & Engels, 1848/1962).

Karl Marx and his collaborator Friedrich Engels were intense critics of capitalism. Their work inspired the later development of conflict theory in sociology.

Wikimedia Commons – public domain.

According to Marx and Engels, every society is divided into two classes based on the ownership of the means of production (tools, factories, and the like). In a capitalist society, the **bourgeoisie**, or ruling class, owns the means of production, while the **proletariat**, or working class, does not own the means of production and instead is oppressed and exploited by the bourgeoisie. This difference creates an automatic conflict of interests between the two groups. Simply put, the bourgeoisie is interested in maintaining its position at the top of society, while the proletariat's interest lies in rising up from the bottom and overthrowing the bourgeoisie to create an egalitarian society.

In a capitalist society, Marx and Engels wrote, revolution is inevitable because of structural contradictions arising from the very nature of capitalism. Because profit is the main goal of capitalism, the bourgeoisie's interest lies in maximizing profit. To do so, capitalists try to keep wages as low as possible and to spend as little money as possible on working conditions. This central fact of capitalism, said Marx and Engels, eventually prompts the rise among workers of **class consciousness**, or an awareness of the reasons for their oppression. Their class consciousness in turn leads them to revolt against the bourgeoisie to eliminate the oppression and exploitation they suffer.

Over the years, Marx and Engels's views on the nature of capitalism and class relations have greatly influenced social, political, and economic theory and also inspired revolutionaries in nations around the world. However, history has not supported their prediction that capitalism will inevitably result in a revolution of the proletariat. For example, no such revolution has occurred in the United States, where workers never developed the degree of class consciousness envisioned by Marx and Engels. Because the United States is thought to be a free society where everyone has the opportunity to succeed, even poor Americans feel that the system is basically just. Thus various aspects of American society and ideology have helped minimize the development of class consciousness and prevent the revolution that Marx and Engels foresaw.

Despite this shortcoming, their basic view of conflict arising from unequal positions held by members of society lies at the heart of today's conflict theory. This theory emphasizes that different groups in society have different interests stemming from their different social positions. These different interests in turn lead to different views on important social issues. Some versions of the theory root conflict in divisions based on race and ethnicity, gender, and other such differences, while other versions follow Marx and Engels in seeing conflict arising out of different positions in the economic structure. In general, however, conflict theory emphasizes that the various parts of society contribute to ongoing inequality, whereas functionalist theory, as we have seen, stresses that they contribute to the ongoing stability of society. Thus, while functionalist theory emphasizes the benefits of the various parts of society for ongoing social stability, conflict theory favors social change to reduce inequality. In this regard, conflict theory may be considered a progressive perspective.

Feminist theory has developed in sociology and other disciplines since the 1970s and for our purposes will be considered a specific application of conflict theory. In this case, the conflict concerns gender inequality rather than the class inequality emphasized by Marx and Engels. Although many variations of feminist theory exist, they all emphasize that society is filled with gender inequality such that women are the subordinate sex in many dimensions of social, political, and economic life (Tong, 2009). Liberal feminists view gender inequality as arising out of gender differences in socialization, while Marxist feminists say that this inequality is a result of the rise of capitalism, which made women dependent on men for economic support. On the other hand, radical feminists view gender inequality as present in all societies, not just capitalist ones. Chapter 11 "Gender and Gender Inequality" examines some of the arguments of feminist theory at great length.

Symbolic Interactionism

Whereas the functionalist and conflict perspectives are macro approaches, **symbolic interactionism** is a micro approach that focuses on the interaction of individuals and on how they interpret their interaction. Its roots lie in the work in the early 1900s of American sociologists, social psychologists, and philosophers who were interested in human consciousness and action. Herbert Blumer (1969), a sociologist at the University of Chicago, built on their writings to develop symbolic interactionism, a term he coined. This view remains popular today, in part because many sociologists object to what they perceive as the overly deterministic view of human thought and action and passive view of the individual inherent in the sociological perspective derived from Durkheim.

Drawing on Blumer's work, symbolic interactionists feel that people do not merely learn the roles that society has set out for them; instead they construct these roles as they interact. As they interact, they "negotiate" their definitions of the situations in which they find themselves and socially construct the reality of these situations. In so doing, they rely heavily on symbols such as words and gestures to reach a shared understanding of their interaction.

An example is the familiar symbol of shaking hands. In the United States and many other societies, shaking hands is a symbol of greeting and friendship. This simple act indicates that you are a nice, polite person with whom someone should feel comfortable. To reinforce this symbol's importance for understanding a bit of interaction, consider a situation where someone *refuses* to shake hands. This action is usually intended as a sign of dislike or as an insult, and the other person interprets it as such. Their understanding of the situation and subsequent interaction will be very different from those arising from the more typical shaking of hands.

Now let's say that someone does not shake hands, but this time the reason is that the person's right arm is broken. Because the other person realizes this, no snub or insult is inferred, and the two people can then proceed to have a comfortable encounter. Their definition of the situation depends not only on whether they shake hands but also, if they do not shake hands, on why they do not. As the term *symbolic interactionism* implies, their understanding of this encounter arises from what they do when they interact and their use and interpretation of the various symbols included in their interaction. According to symbolic interactionists, social order is possible because people learn what various symbols (such as shaking hands) mean and apply these meanings to different kinds of situations. If you visited a society where sticking your right hand out to greet someone was interpreted as a threatening gesture, you would quickly learn the value of common understandings of symbols.

Utilitarianism

Utilitarianism is a general view of human behavior that says people act to maximize their pleasure and to reduce their pain. It originated in the work of such 18th-century thinkers as the Italian economist Cesare Beccaria (1738–1794) and the English philosopher Jeremy Bentham (1748–1832). Both men thought that people act rationally and decide before they act whether their behavior will cause them more pleasure or pain. Applying their views to crime, they felt the criminal justice system in Europe at the time was far harsher than it needed to be to deter criminal behavior. Another 18th-century utilitarian thinker was Adam Smith, whose book *The Wealth of Nations* (1776/1910) laid the foundation for modern economic thought. Indeed, at the heart of economics is the view that sellers and buyers of goods and services act rationally to reduce their costs and in this and other ways to maximize their profits.

In sociology, utilitarianism is commonly called **exchange theory** or **rational choice theory** (Coleman, 1990; Homans, 1961). No matter what name it goes under, this view emphasizes that when people interact, they seek to maximize the benefits they gain from the interaction and to reduce the disadvantages. If they decide that the interaction's benefits outweigh its disadvantages, they will initiate the interaction or continue it if it is already under way. If they instead decide that the interaction's disadvantages outweigh its benefits, they will decline to begin interacting or stop the interaction if already begun. Social order is possible because people realize it will be in their best interests to cooperate and to make compromises when necessary.

A familiar application of exchange theory would be a dating relationship. Each partner in a dating relationship gives up a bit of autonomy in return for love and other benefits of being close to someone. Yet every relationship has its good and bad moments, and both partners make frequent compromises to ensure the relationship will endure. As long as the couple feels the good moments outweigh the bad moments, the relationship will continue. But once one or both partners decide the reverse is true, the relationship will end.

Comparing Macro and Micro Perspectives

This brief presentation of the four major theoretical perspectives in sociology is necessarily incomplete but should at least outline their basic points. Each perspective has its proponents, and each has its detractors. All four offer a lot of truth, and all four oversimplify and make other mistakes. We will return to them in many of the chapters ahead, but a brief critique is in order here.

A major problem with functionalist theory is that it tends to support the status quo and thus seems to favor existing inequalities based on race, social class, and gender. By emphasizing the contributions of social institutions such as the family and education to social stability, functionalist theory minimizes the ways in which these institutions contribute to social inequality.

Conflict theory also has its problems. By emphasizing inequality and dissensus in society, conflict theory overlooks the large degree of consensus on many important issues. And by emphasizing the ways in which social institutions contribute to social inequality, conflict theory minimizes the ways in which these institutions are necessary for society's stability.

Neither of these two macro perspectives has very much to say about social interaction, one of the most important building blocks of society. In this regard, the two micro perspectives, symbolic interactionism and utilitarianism, offer significant advantages over their macro cousins. Yet their very micro focus leads them to pay relatively little attention to the reasons for, and possible solutions to, such broad and fundamentally important issues as poverty, racism, sexism, and social change, which are all addressed by functionalism and conflict theory. In this regard, the two macro perspectives offer significant advantages over their micro cousins. In addition, one of the micro perspectives, rational choice theory, has also been criticized for ignoring the importance of emotions, altruism, and other values for guiding human interaction (Lowenstein, 1996).

These criticisms aside, all four perspectives taken together offer a more comprehensive understanding of social phenomena than any one perspective can offer alone. To illustrate this, let's return to our armed robbery example. A functionalist approach might suggest that armed robbery and other crimes actually serve positive functions for society. As one function, fear of crime ironically strengthens social bonds by uniting the law-abiding public against the criminal elements in society. As a second function, armed robbery and other crimes create many jobs for police officers, judges, lawyers, prison guards, the construction companies that build prisons, and the various businesses that provide products the public buys to help protect against crime.

To explain armed robbery, symbolic interactionists focus on how armed robbers decide when and where to rob a victim and on how their interactions with other criminals reinforce their own criminal tendencies.

Geoffrey Fairchild – The Robbery – CC BY 2.0.

Conflict theory would take a very different but no less helpful approach to understanding armed robbery. It might note that most street criminals are poor and thus emphasize that armed robbery and other crimes are the result of the despair and frustration of living in poverty and facing a lack of jobs and other opportunities for economic and social success. The roots of street crime, from the perspective of conflict theory, thus lie in society at least as much as they lie in the individuals committing such crime.

In explaining armed robbery, symbolic interactionism would focus on how armed robbers make such decisions as when and where to rob someone and on how their interactions with other criminals reinforce their own criminal tendencies. Exchange or rational choice theory would emphasize that armed robbers and other criminals are rational actors who carefully plan their crimes and who would be deterred by a strong threat of swift and severe punishment.

Now that you have some understanding of the major theoretical perspectives in sociology, we will discuss in Chapter 2 "Eye on Society: Doing Sociological Research" how sociologists conduct their research.

Key Takeaways

- Sociological theories may be broadly divided into macro approaches and micro approaches.
- Functionalism emphasizes the importance of social institutions for social stability and implies that far-reaching social change will be socially harmful.
- Conflict theory emphasizes social inequality and suggests that far-reaching social change is needed to achieve a just society.
- Symbolic interactionism emphasizes the social meanings and understandings that individuals derive from their social interaction.
- Utilitarianism emphasizes that people act in their self-interest by calculating whether potential behaviors will be more advantageous than disadvantageous.

For Your Review

1. In thinking about how you view society and individuals, do you consider yourself more of a macro thinker or a micro thinker?
2. At this point in your study of sociology, which one of the four sociological traditions sounds most appealing to you? Why?

References

Blumer, H. (1969). *Symbolic interactionism: Perspective and method*. Englewood Cliffs, NJ: Prentice Hall.

Coleman, J. S. (1990). *Foundations of social theory*. Cambridge, MA: Harvard University Press; Homans, G. (1961). *Social behavior: Its elementary forms*. Orlando, FL: Harcourt Brace Jovanovich.

Collins, R. (1994). *Four sociological traditions*. New York, NY: Oxford University Press.

Durkheim, É. (1952). *Suicide*. New York, NY: Free Press. (Original work published 1897).

Golding, W. (1954). *Lord of the flies*. London, England: Coward-McCann.

Lowenstein, G. (1996). Out of control: Visceral influences on behavior. *Organizational Behavior and Human Decision Processes, 65*, 272–292.

Marx, K. 1906. *Capital*. New York, NY: Random House. (Original work published 1867)

Marx, K., & Engels, F. (1962). The communist manifesto. In *Marx and Engels: Selected works* (pp. 21–65). Moscow, Russia: Foreign Language Publishing House. (Original work published 1848).

Smith, A. (1910). *The wealth of nations*. London, England: J. M. Dent & Sons; New York, NY: E. P. Dutton. (Original work published 1776).

Tong, R. (2009). *Feminist thought: A more comprehensive introduction*. Boulder, CO: Westview Press.

1.4 End-of-Chapter Material

Summary

1. Although Americans enjoy much freedom of thought and action, society constrains their views and behaviors.
2. The sociological perspective emphasizes that our social backgrounds influence our attitudes, behaviors, and life chances. The chances of committing even an individual act such as suicide depend to some degree on the group backgrounds from which we come.
3. Because sociology deals in generalizations and not laws, people don't always behave and think in the patterns sociologists predict. For every sociological generalization, there are many exceptions.
4. Personal experience, common sense, and the media are all valuable sources of knowledge about various aspects of society, but they often present a limited or distorted view of these aspects.
5. A theme of sociology is the debunking motif. This means that sociological knowledge aims to look beyond on-the-surface understandings of social reality.
6. According to C. Wright Mills, the sociological imagination involves the ability to realize that personal troubles are rooted in problems in the larger social structure. The sociological imagination thus supports a blaming-the-system view over a blaming-the-victim view.
7. Theoretical perspectives in sociology generally divide into macro and micro views. Functionalism emphasizes the functions that social institutions serve to ensure the ongoing stability of society, while conflict theory focuses on the conflict among different racial, ethnic, social class, and other groups and emphasizes how social institutions help ensure inequality. Two micro perspectives, symbolic interactionism and utilitarianism, focus on interaction among individuals. Symbolic interactionism focuses on how individuals interpret the meanings of the situations in which they find themselves, while utilitarianism emphasizes that people are guided in their actions by a desire to maximize their benefits and to minimize their disadvantages.

Chapter 2: Eye on Society: Doing Sociological Research

Social Issues in the News

In the late 1990s, Oregon had one of the highest rates of hunger among the 50 states, and a higher rate than would have been expected from its more average level of poverty. Sociologist Mark S. Edwards of Oregon State University investigated the reasons for the high hunger rate and found problems in the way the state was distributing food stamps and making food available at food banks. In one county, for example, the food bank was located in an upper-class community, and hungry residents from elsewhere in the county were embarrassed to be seen at the food bank. Edwards's research "assisted advocacy groups and legislators in improving the state's efforts to enroll low income families in food stamp programs," according to his department's Web site (http://oregonstate.edu/cla/sociology/research), and the changes based on his findings were credited with lowering the state's hunger rate before the deep economic recession began in 2008.
After the recession hit the nation, officials and news media outlets in Oregon and elsewhere turned to Edwards for advice on dealing with the growing hunger and food insecurity that resulted. Edwards was gratified that his research had helped make a difference. "I've chosen to do projects that are not high-powered, big academic projects," he said, "but are simple research projects that are trying to deal with social justice questions in our state." (Blome & Kravitz, 2006; Govier, 2010; Herring, 2008; E. Lindsey, 2009)

Some sociologists do research for its own sake, and some sociologists, such as Mark Edwards, do research to try to benefit society. Whatever the goals of their research, sociologists follow the scientific method as they gather information that they then analyze. This chapter examines the research process in sociology. It first discusses sociology as a social science and the different ways that people ordinarily try to understand social reality. It then examines the primary methods that sociologists use in their research and the practical and ethical issues they sometimes encounter.

References

Blome, C., & Kravitz, J. (2006, May 11). Stamping out food insecurity: More people in Benton County could be using food stamps. *The Daily Barometer.* Retrieved from http://media.barometer.orst.edu/media/storage/paper854/news/2006/2005/2011/News/Stamping.Out.Food.Insecurity-2291747.shtml.

Govier, G. (2010, June 14). InterVarsity alumni—Mark Edwards. *InterVarsity News.* Retrieved from http://www.intervarsity.org/news/intervarsity-alumni-mark-edwards-.

Herring, P. (2008, November 17). New report on hunger identifies Oregon as one of the worst. *Extension Service News.* Retrieved from http://extension.oregonstate.edu/news/story.php?S_No=614&storyType=news.

Lindsey, E. (2009, November 17). Oregon's recession means many in state go hungry. *Oregon Public Broadcasting*. Retrieved from http://news.opb.org/article/6220-oregons-recession-means-many-state-go-hungry

2.1 Sociology as a Social Science

Learning Objectives

1. Explain what is meant by saying that sociology is a social science.
2. Describe the difference between a generalization and a law in scientific research.
3. List the sources of knowledge on which people rely for their understanding of social reality and explain why the knowledge gained from these sources may sometimes be faulty.
4. List the basic steps of the scientific method.

Like anthropology, economics, political science, and psychology, sociology is a social science. All these disciplines use research to try to understand various aspects of human thought and behavior. Although this chapter naturally focuses on sociological research methods, much of the discussion is also relevant for research in the other social and behavioral sciences.

When we say that sociology is a social science, we mean that it uses the scientific method to try to understand the many aspects of society that sociologists study. An important goal is to yield **generalizations**—general statements regarding trends among various dimensions of social life. We discussed many such generalizations in Chapter 1 "Sociology and the Sociological Perspective": men are more likely than women to commit suicide, young people were more likely to vote for Obama than McCain in 2008, and so forth. A generalization is just that: a statement of a tendency, rather than a hard-and-fast law. For example, the statement that men are more *likely* than women to commit suicide does not mean that every man commits suicide and no woman commits suicide. It means only that men have a higher suicide rate, even though most men, of course, do not commit suicide. Similarly, the statement that young people were more likely to vote for Obama than for McCain in 2008 does not mean that all young people voted for Obama; it means only that they were more likely than not to do so.

A generalization regarding the 2008 election is that young people were more likely to vote for Barack Obama than for John McCain. This generalization does not mean that every young person voted for Obama and no young person voted for McCain; it means only that they were more likely than not to vote for Obama.

Wikimedia Commons – CC BY 2.0.

Many people will not fit the pattern of such a generalization, because people are shaped but not totally determined by their social environment. That is both the fascination and the frustration of sociology. Sociology is fascinating because no matter how much sociologists are able to predict people's behavior, attitudes, and life chances, many people will not fit the predictions. But sociology is frustrating for the same reason. Because people can never be totally explained by their social environment, sociologists can never completely understand the sources of their behavior, attitudes, and life chances.

In this sense, sociology as a social science is very different from a discipline such as physics, in which known laws exist for which no exceptions are possible. For example, we call the law of gravity a law because it describes a physical force that exists on the earth at all times and in all places and that always has the same result. If you were to pick up the book you are now reading—or the computer or other device on which you are reading or listening to—and then let go, the object you were holding would definitely fall to the ground. If you did this a second time, it would fall a second time. If you did this a billion times, it would fall a billion times. In fact, if there were even one time out of a billion that your book or electronic device did not fall down, our understanding of the physical world would be totally revolutionized, the earth could be in danger, and you could go on television and make a lot of money.

People's attitudes, behavior, and life chances are influenced but not totally determined by many aspects of their social environment.

redjar – Cheering – CC BY-SA 2.0.

For better or worse, people are less predictable than this object that keeps falling down. Sociology can help us understand the social forces that affect our behavior, beliefs, and life chances, but it can only go so far. That limitation conceded, sociological understanding can still go fairly far toward such an understanding, and it can help us comprehend who we are and what we are by helping us first understand the profound yet often subtle influence of our social backgrounds on so many things about us.

Although sociology as a discipline is very different from physics, it is not as different as one might think from this and the other "hard" sciences. Like these disciplines, sociology as a social science relies heavily on systematic research that follows the standard rules of the scientific method. We return to these rules and the nature of sociological research later in this chapter. Suffice it to say here that careful research is essential for a sociological understanding of people, social institutions, and society.

At this point a reader might be saying, "I already know a lot about people. I could have told you that young people voted for Obama. I already had heard that men have a higher suicide rate than women. Maybe our social backgrounds do influence us in ways I had not realized, but what beyond that does sociology have to tell me?"

Students often feel this way because sociology deals with matters already familiar to them. Just about everyone has grown up in a family, so we all know something about it. We read a lot in the media about topics like divorce and health care, so we all already know something about these, too. All this leads some students to wonder if they will learn anything in their introduction to sociology course that they do not already know.

How Do We Know What We Think We Know?

Let's consider this issue a moment: how do we know what we think we know? Our usual knowledge and understanding of social reality come from at least five sources: (a) personal experience; (b) common sense; (c) the media (including the Internet); (d) "expert authorities," such as teachers, parents, and government officials; and (e) tradition. These are all important sources of our understanding of how the world "works," but at the same time their value can often be very limited.

Personal Experience

Let's look at these sources separately by starting with personal experience. Although personal experiences are very important, not everyone has the same personal experience. This fact casts some doubt on the degree to which our personal experiences can help us understand everything about a topic and the degree to which we can draw conclusions from them that necessarily apply to other people. For example, say you grew up in Maine or Vermont, where more than 98% of the population is white. If you relied on your personal experience to calculate how many people of color live in the country, you would conclude that almost everyone in the United States is also white, which certainly is not true. As another example, say you grew up in a family where your parents had the proverbial perfect marriage, as they loved each other deeply and rarely argued. If you relied on your personal experience to understand the typical American marriage, you would conclude that most marriages were as good as your parents' marriage, which, unfortunately, also is not true. Many other examples could be cited here, but the basic point should be clear: although personal experience is better than nothing, it often offers only a very limited understanding of social reality other than our own.

Common Sense

If personal experience does not help that much when it comes to making predictions, what about common sense? Although common sense can be very helpful, it can also contradict itself. For example, which makes more sense, *haste makes waste* or *he or she who hesitates is lost*? How about *birds of a feather flock together* versus *opposites attract*? Or *two heads are better than one* versus *too many cooks spoil the broth*? Each of these common sayings makes sense, but if sayings that are opposite of each other both make sense, where does the truth lie? Can common sense always be counted on to help us understand social life? Slightly more than five centuries ago, everyone "knew" the earth was flat—it was just common sense that it had to be that way. Slightly more than a century ago, some of the leading physicians in the United States believed that women should not go to college because the stress of higher education would disrupt their menstrual cycles (Ehrenreich & English, 1979). If that bit of common sense(lessness) were still with us, many of the women reading this book would not be in college.

During the late 19th century, a common belief was that women should not go to college because the stress of higher education would disrupt their menstrual cycles. This example shows that common sense is often incorrect.

Steven Depolo – Female Black College Graduates Cap Gown – CC BY 2.0.

Still, perhaps there are some things that make so much sense they just have to be true; if sociology then tells us that they are true, what have we learned? Here is an example of such an argument. We all know that older people—those 65 or older—have many more problems than younger people. First, their health is generally worse. Second, physical infirmities make it difficult for many elders to walk or otherwise move around. Third, many have seen their spouses and close friends pass away and thus live lonelier lives than younger people. Finally, many are on fixed incomes and face financial difficulties. All of these problems indicate that older people should be less happy than younger people. If a sociologist did some research and then reported that older people are indeed less happy than younger people, what have we learned? The sociologist only confirmed the obvious.

The trouble with this confirmation of the obvious is that the "obvious" turns out not to be true after all. In the 2008 General Social Survey, which was given to a random sample of Americans, respondents were asked, "Taken all together, how would you say things are these days? Would you say that you are very happy, pretty happy, or not too happy?" Respondents aged 65 or older were actually slightly more likely than those younger than 65 to say they were very happy! About 40% of older respondents reported feeling this way, compared with only 30% of younger respondents (see Figure 2.1 "Age and Happiness"). What we all "knew" was obvious from common sense turns out not to have been so obvious after all.

Figure 2.1 Age and Happiness

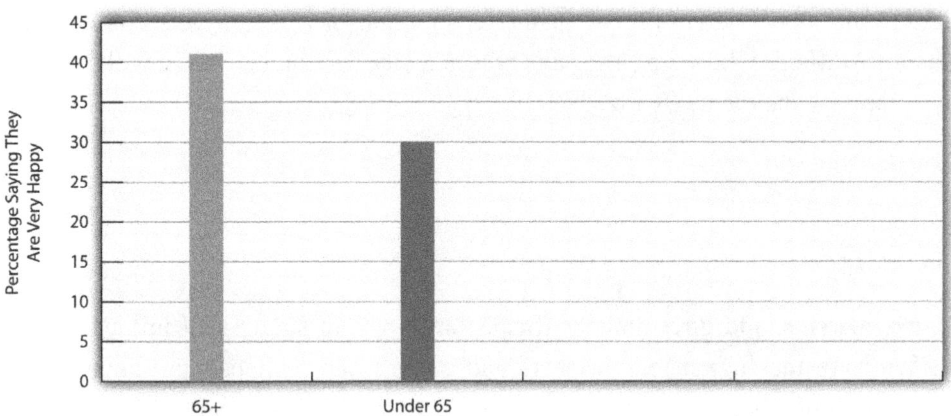

Source: Data from General Social Survey, 2008.

The Media

The news media often oversimplify complex topics and in other respects provide a misleading picture of social reality. As one example, news coverage sensationalizes violent crime and thus suggests that such crime is more common than it actually is.

Wikiemedia Commons – CC BY-SA 2.0.

If personal experience and common sense do not always help that much, how about the media? We learn a lot about current events and social and political issues from the Internet, television news, newspapers and magazines, and other media sources. It is certainly important to keep up with the news, but media coverage may oversimplify complex topics or even distort what the best evidence from systematic research seems to be telling us. A good example here is crime. Many studies show that the media sensationalize crime and suggest there is much more violent crime than there really is. For example, in the early 1990s, the evening newscasts on the major networks increased their coverage of murder and other violent crimes, painting a picture of a nation where crime was growing rapidly. The reality was very different, however, as crime was actually declining. The view that crime was growing was thus a myth generated by the media (Kurtz, 1997).

Expert Authorities

Expert authorities, such as teachers, parents, and government officials, are a fourth source that influences our understanding of social reality. We learn much from our teachers and parents and perhaps from government officials, but, for better or worse, not all of what we learn from these sources about social reality is completely accurate. Teachers and parents do not always have the latest research evidence at their fingertips, and various biases may color their interpretation of any evidence with which they are familiar. As many examples from U.S. history illustrate, government officials may simplify or even falsify the facts. We should perhaps always listen to our teachers and parents and maybe even to government officials, but that does not always mean they give us a true, complete picture of social reality.

Tradition

A final source that influences our understanding of social reality is tradition, or long-standing ways of thinking about the workings of society. Tradition is generally valuable, because a society should always be aware of its roots. However, traditional ways of thinking about social reality often turn out to be inaccurate and incomplete. For example, traditional ways of thinking in the United States once assumed that women and people of color were biologically and culturally inferior to men and whites. Although some Americans continue to hold these beliefs, these traditional assumptions have given way to more egalitarian assumptions. As we shall also see in later chapters, most sociologists certainly do not believe that women and people of color are biologically and culturally inferior.

If we cannot always trust personal experience, common sense, the media, expert authorities, and tradition to help us understand social reality, then the importance of systematic research gathered by sociology and the other social sciences becomes apparent.

The Scientific Method

As noted earlier, because sociology is a social science, sociologists follow the rules of the **scientific method** in their research. Most readers probably learned these rules in science classes in high school, college, or both. The scientific method is followed in the natural, physical, and social sciences to help yield the most accurate and reliable conclusions possible, especially ones that are free of bias or methodological errors. An overriding principle of the scientific method is that research should be conducted as objectively as possible. Researchers are often passionate about their work, but they must take care not to let the findings they expect and even hope to uncover affect how they do their research. This in turn means that they must not conduct their research in a manner that "helps" achieve the results they expect to find. Such bias can happen unconsciously, and the scientific method helps reduce the potential for this bias as much as possible.

This potential is arguably greater in the social sciences than in the natural and physical sciences. The political views of chemists and physicists typically do not affect how an experiment is performed and how the outcome of the experiment is interpreted. In contrast, researchers in the social sciences, and perhaps particularly in sociology, often have strong feelings about the topics they are studying. Their social and political beliefs may thus influence how they perform their research on these topics and how they interpret the results of this research. Following the scientific method helps reduce this possible influence.

Figure 2.2 The Scientific Method

Measuring and Gathering Data -> Analyzing Data -> Drawing a Conclusion" style="max-width: 497px;"/>

As you probably learned in a science class, the scientific method involves these basic steps: (a) formulating a hypothesis, (b) measuring and gathering data to test the hypothesis, (c) analyzing these data, and (d) drawing appropriate conclusions (see Figure 2.2 "The Scientific Method"). In following the scientific method, sociologists are no different from their colleagues in the natural and physical sciences or the other social sciences, even though their research is very different in other respects. The next section discusses the stages of the sociological research process in more detail.

Key Takeaways

- As a social science, sociology presents generalizations, or general statements regarding trends among various dimensions of social life. There are always many exceptions to any generalization, because people are not totally determined by their social environment.
- Our knowledge and understanding of social reality usually comes from five sources: (a) personal experience, (b) common sense, (c) the media, (d) expert authorities, and (e) tradition. Sometimes and perhaps often, the knowledge gained from these sources is faulty.
- Like research in other social sciences, sociological research follows the scientific method to ensure the most accurate and reliable results possible. The basic steps of the scientific method include (a) formulating a hypothesis, (b) measuring and gathering data to test the hypothesis, (c) analyzing these data, and (d) drawing appropriate conclusions.

For Your Review

1. Think of a personal experience you have had that might have some sociological relevance. Write a short essay in which you explain how this experience helped you understand some aspect of society. Your essay should also consider whether the understanding gained from your personal experience is generalizable to other people and situations.
2. Why do you think the media sometimes provide a false picture of social reality? Does this problem result from honest mistakes, or is the media's desire to attract more viewers, listeners, and readers to blame?

References

Ehrenreich, B., & English, D. (1979). *For her own good: 150 years of the experts' advice to women*. Garden City, NY: Anchor Books.

Kurtz, H. (1997, August 12). The crime spree on network news. *The Washington Post*, p. D1.

2.2 Stages in the Sociological Research Process

Learning Objectives

1. List the major stages of the sociological research process.
2. Describe the different types of units of analysis in sociology.
3. Explain the difference between an independent variable and a dependent variable.

Sociological research consists of several stages. The researcher must first choose a topic to investigate and then become familiar with prior research on the topic. Once appropriate data are gathered and analyzed, the researcher can then draw appropriate conclusions. This section discusses these various stages of the research process.

Choosing a Research Topic

The first step in the research process is choosing a topic. There are countless topics from which to choose, so how does a researcher go about choosing one? Many sociologists choose a topic based on a *theoretical interest* they may have. For example, Émile Durkheim's interest in the importance of social integration motivated his monumental study of suicide that Chapter 1 "Sociology and the Sociological Perspective" discussed. Many sociologists since the 1970s have had a theoretical interest in gender, and this interest has motivated a huge volume of research on the difference that gender makes for behavior, attitudes, and life chances. The link between theory and research lies at the heart of the sociological research process, as it does for other social, natural, and physical sciences. Accordingly, this book discusses many examples of studies motivated by sociologists' varied theoretical interests.

Many sociologists, such as the two pictured here, have a theoretical interest in gender that leads them to investigate the importance of gender for many aspects of the social world.

Francisco Osorio – CL Society 31: Sociologists – CC BY 2.0.

Many sociologists also choose a topic based on a *social policy interest* they may have. For example, sociologists concerned about poverty have investigated its effects on individuals' health, educational attainment, and other outcomes during childhood, adolescence, and adulthood. Sociologists concerned about racial prejudice and discrimination have carried out many studies documenting their negative consequences for people of color. As Chapter 1 "Sociology and the Sociological Perspective" discussed and as this book emphasizes, the roots of sociology in the United States lie in the use of sociological knowledge to achieve social reform, and many sociologists today continue to engage in numerous research projects because of their social policy interests. The news story that began this chapter discussed an important example of this type of research. The "Sociology Making a Difference" box further discusses research of this type.

Sociology Making a Difference

Survey Research to Help the Poor

The Community Service Society (CSS) of New York City is a nonprofit organization that, according to its Web site (http://www.cssny.org), "engages in advocacy, research and direct service" to help low-income residents of the city. It was established about 160 years ago and has made many notable accomplishments over the years, including aiding the victims of the *Titanic* disaster in 1912, helping initiate the free school lunch program that is now found around the United States, and establishing the largest senior volunteer program in the nation.

A key component of the CSS's efforts today involves gathering much information about the lives of poor New Yorkers through an annual survey of random samples of these residents. Because the needs of the poor are so often neglected and their voices so often unheard, the CSS calls this effort the Unheard Third survey, as the poor represent about one-third of the New York City population. The Unheard Third survey asks respondents their opinions about many issues affecting their lives and also asks them many questions about such matters as their health and health care needs, employment status and job satisfaction, debt, and housing. The CSS then uses all this information in reports about the needs of the poor and near-poor in New York that it prepares for city and state officials, the news media, and key individuals in the private sector. In these ways, the CSS uses survey research in the service of society. As its Web site (http://www.cssny.org/research) states, "research is a critical tool we use to increase our understanding of conditions that drive poverty as we advocate for public policy and programs that will improve the economic standing of low-income New Yorkers."

A third source of inspiration for research topics is *personal experience*. Like other social scientists (and probably also natural and physical scientists), many sociologists have had various experiences during childhood, adolescence, or adulthood that lead them to study a topic from a sociological standpoint. For example, a sociologist whose parents divorced while the sociologist was in high school may become interested in studying the effects of divorce on children. A sociologist who was arrested during college for a political protest may become interested in studying how effective protest might be for achieving the aims of a social movement. A sociologist who acted in high school plays may choose a dissertation during graduate school that focuses on a topic involving social interaction. Although the exact number will never be known, many research studies in sociology are undoubtedly first conceived because personal experience led the author to become interested in the theory or social policy addressed by the study.

Conducting a Literature Review

Whatever topic is chosen, the next stage in the research process is a review of the literature. A researcher who begins a new project typically reads a good number of studies that have already been published on the topic that the researcher wants to investigate. In sociology, most of these studies are published in journals, but many are also published as books. The government and private research organizations also publish reports that researchers consult for their literature reviews.

Regardless of the type of published study, a literature review has several goals. First, the researcher needs to determine that the study she or he has in mind has not already been done. Second, the researcher needs to determine how the proposed study will add to what is known about the topic of the study. How will the study add to theoretical knowledge of the topic? How will the study improve on the methodology of earlier studies? How will the study aid social policy related to the topic? Typically, a research project must answer at least one of these questions satisfactorily for it to have a chance of publication in a scholarly journal, and a thorough literature review is necessary to determine the new study's possible contribution. A third goal of a literature review is to see how prior studies were conducted. What research design did they use? From where did their data come? How did they measure key concepts and variables? A thorough literature review enhances the methodology of the researcher's new study and enables the researcher to correct any possible deficiencies in the methodology of prior studies.

In "the old days," researchers would conduct a literature review primarily by going to an academic library, consulting a printed index of academic journals, trudging through shelf after shelf of printed journals, and photocopying articles they found or taking notes on index cards. Those days are long gone, and thankfully so. Now researchers use any number of electronic indexes and read journal articles online or download a PDF version to read later. Literature reviews are still a lot of work, but the time they take is immeasurably shorter than just a decade ago.

Formulating a Hypothesis

After the literature review has been completed, it is time to formulate the hypothesis that will guide the study. As you might remember from a science class, a **hypothesis** is a statement of the relationship between two variables concerning the units of analysis the researcher is studying. To understand this definition, we must next define *variable* and *unit of analysis*. Let's start with **unit of analysis**, which refers to the type of entity a researcher is studying. As we discuss further in a moment, the most common unit of analysis in sociology is a person, but other units of analysis include organizations and geographical locations. A **variable** is any feature or factor that may differ among the units of analysis that a researcher is studying. Key variables in sociological studies of people as the units of analysis include gender, race and ethnicity, social class, age, and any number of attitudes and behaviors. Whatever unit of analysis is being studied, sociological research aims to test relationships between variables or, more precisely, to test whether one variable affects another variable, and a hypothesis outlines the nature of the relationship that is to be tested.

Suppose we want to test the hypothesis that women were more likely than men to have voted for Obama in 2008. The first variable in this hypothesis is gender, whether someone is a woman or a man. (As Chapter 11 "Gender and Gender Inequality" discusses, gender is actually more complex than this, but let's keep things simple for now.) The second variable is voting preference—for example, whether someone voted for Obama or McCain. In this example, gender is the independent variable and voting preference is the dependent variable. An **independent variable** is a variable we think can affect another variable. This other variable is the **dependent variable**, or the variable we think is affected by the independent variable (see Figure 2.3 "Causal Path for the Independent and Dependent Variable"). When sociological research tests relationships between variables, it normally is testing whether an independent variable affects a dependent variable.

Figure 2.3 Causal Path for the Independent and Dependent Variable

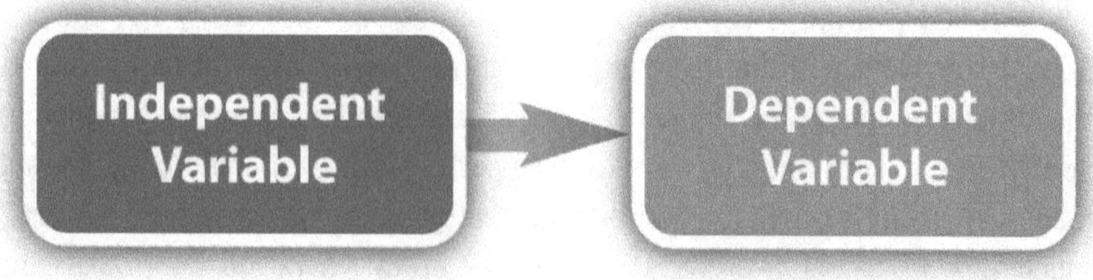

Many hypotheses in sociology involve variables concerning people, but many also involve variables concerning organizations and geographical locations. As this statement is meant to suggest, sociological research is conducted at different levels, depending on the unit of analysis chosen. As noted earlier, the most common unit of analysis in sociology is the *person*; this is probably the type of research with which you are most familiar. If we conduct a national poll to see how gender influences voting decisions or how race influences views on the state of the economy, we are studying characteristics, or variables, involving people, and the person is the unit of analysis. Another common unit of analysis in sociology is the *organization*. Suppose we conduct a study of hospitals to see whether the patient-to-nurse ratio (the number of patients divided by the number of nurses) is related to the average number of days that patients stay in the hospital. In this example, the patient-to-nurse ratio and the average number of days patients stay are both characteristics of the hospital, and the hospital is the unit of analysis. A third unit of analysis in sociology is the *geographical location*, whether it is cities, states, regions of a country, or whole societies. In the United States, for example, large cities generally have higher violent crime rates than small cities. In this example, the city is the unit of analysis.

Figure 2.4

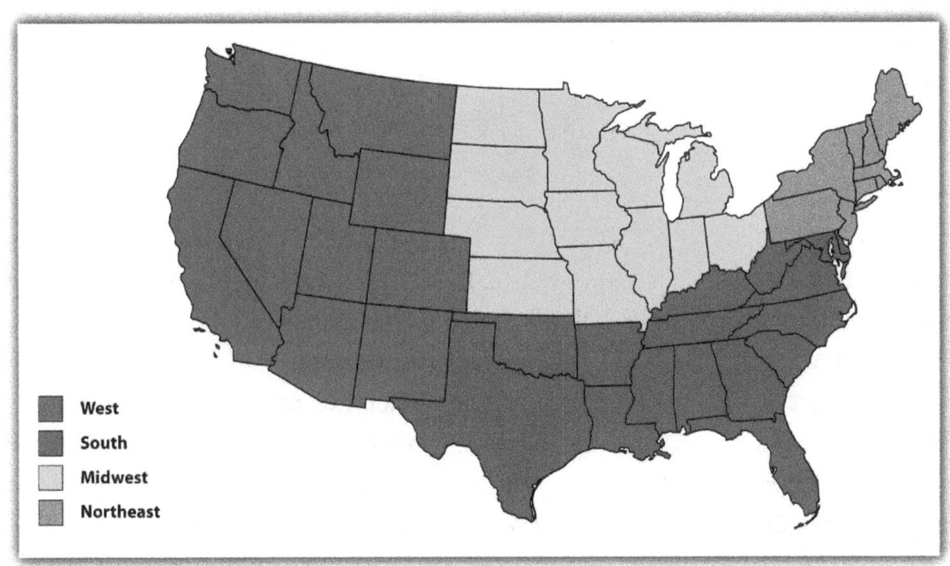

One of the units of analysis in sociological research is the geographical location. The major regions of the United States are often compared on various characteristics. In one notable finding, the South has the highest regional homicide rate.

Source: Adapted from http://commons.wikimedia.org/wiki/File:Blank_US_Map.svg.

Measuring Variables and Gathering Data

After the hypothesis has been formulated, the sociologist is now ready to begin the actual research. Data must be gathered via one or more of the research designs examined later in this chapter, and variables must be measured. Data can either be *quantitative* (numerical) or *qualitative* (nonnumerical). Data gathered through a questionnaire are usually quantitative. The answers a *respondent* gives to a questionnaire are coded for computer analysis. For example, if a question asks whether respondents consider themselves to be politically conservative, moderate, or liberal, those who answer "conservative" might receive a "1" for computer analysis; those who choose "moderate" might receive a "2"; and those who say "liberal" might receive a "3."

Data gathered through observation and/or intensive interviewing, research designs discussed later in this chapter, are usually qualitative. If a researcher interviews college students at length to see what they think about dating violence and how seriously they regard it, the researcher may make simple comparisons, such as "most" of the interviewed students take dating violence very seriously, but without really statistically analyzing the in-depth responses from such a study. Instead, the goal is to make sense of what the researcher observes or of the in-depth statements that people provide to an interviewer and then to relate the major findings to the hypothesis or topic the researcher is investigating.

The measurement of variables is a complex topic and lies far beyond the scope of this discussion. Suffice it to say that accurate measurement of variables is essential in any research project. In a questionnaire, for example, a question should be worded clearly and unambiguously. Take the following question, which has appeared in national surveys: "Do you ever drink more than you think you should?" This question is probably meant to measure whether the respondent has an alcohol problem. But some respondents might answer yes to this question even if they only have a few drinks per year if, for example, they come from a religious background that frowns on alcohol use; conversely, some respondents who drink far too much might answer no because they do not think they drink too much. A researcher who interpreted a yes response from the former respondents as an indicator of an alcohol problem or a no response from the latter respondents as an indicator of no alcohol problem would be in error.

As another example, suppose a researcher hypothesizes that younger couples are happier than older couples. Instead of asking couples how happy they are through a questionnaire, the researcher decides to observe couples as they walk through a shopping mall. Some interesting questions of measurement arise in this study. First, how does the researcher know who is a couple? Second, how sure can the researcher be of the approximate age of each person in the couple? The researcher might be able to distinguish people in their 20s or early 30s from those in their 50s and 60s, but age measurement beyond this gross comparison might often be in error. Third, how sure can the researcher be of the couple's degree of happiness? Is it really possible to determine how happy a couple is by watching them for a few moments in the mall? What exactly does being happy look like, and do all people look this way when they are happy? These and other measurement problems in this particular study might be so severe that the study should not be done, at least if the researcher hopes to publish it.

Sampling

After any measurement issues have been resolved, it is time to gather the data. For the sake of simplicity, let's assume the unit of analysis is the person. A researcher who is doing a study "from scratch" must decide which people to study. Because it is certainly impossible to study everybody, the researcher only studies a **sample**, or subset of the population of people in whom the researcher is interested. Depending on the purpose of the study, the population of interest varies widely: it can be the adult population of the United States, the adult population of a particular state or city, all young women aged 13–18 in the nation, or countless other variations.

Many researchers who do survey research (discussed in a later section) study people selected for a **random sample** of the population of interest. In a random sample, everyone in the population (whether it be the whole U.S. population or just the population of a state or city, all the college students in a state or city or all the students at just one college, and so forth) has the same chance of being included in the survey. The ways in which random samples are chosen are too complex to fully discuss here, but suffice it to say the methods used to determine who is in the sample are equivalent to flipping a coin or rolling some dice. The beauty of a random sample is that it allows us to generalize the results of the sample to the population from which the sample comes. This means that we can be fairly sure of the attitudes of the whole U.S. population by knowing the attitudes of just 400 people randomly chosen from that population.

Other researchers use *nonrandom* samples, in which members of the population do not have the same chance of being included in the study. If you ever filled out a questionnaire after being approached in a shopping mall or campus student center, it is very likely that you were part of a nonrandom sample. While the results of the study (marketing research or social science research) for which you were interviewed might have been interesting, they could not necessarily be generalized to all students or all people in a state or in the nation because the sample for the study was not random.

High school classes often are used as a convenience sample in sociological and other social science research.

NWABR – 2009 Student Fellows – CC BY 2.0.

A specific type of nonrandom sample is the **convenience sample**, which refers to a nonrandom sample that is used because it is relatively quick and inexpensive to obtain. If you ever filled out a questionnaire during a high school or college class, as many students have done, you were very likely part of a convenience sample—a researcher can simply go into class, hand out a survey, and have the data available for coding and analysis within a few minutes. Convenience samples often include students, but they also include other kinds of people. When prisoners are studied, they constitute a convenience sample, because they are definitely not going anywhere. Partly because of this fact, convenience samples are also sometimes called *captive-audience samples*.

Another specific type of nonrandom sample is the **quota sample**. In this type of sample, a researcher tries to ensure that the makeup of the sample resembles one or more characteristics of the population as closely as possible. For example, on a campus of 10,000 students where 60% of the students are women and 40% are men, a researcher might decide to study 100 students by handing out a questionnaire to those who happen to be in the student center building on a particular day. If the researcher decides to have a quota sample based on gender, the researcher will select 60 women students and 40 male students to receive the questionnaire. This procedure might make the sample of 100 students more representative of all the students on campus than if it were not used, but it still does not make the sample entirely representative of all students. The students who happen to be in the student center on a particular day might be very different in many respects from most other students on the campus.

As we shall see later when research design is discussed, the choice of a design is very much related to the type of sample that is used. Surveys lend themselves to random samples, for example, while observation studies and experiments lend themselves to nonrandom samples.

Analyzing Data

After all data have been gathered, the next stage is to analyze the data. If the data are quantitative, the analysis will almost certainly use highly sophisticated statistical techniques beyond the scope of this discussion. Many statistical analysis software packages exist for this purpose, and sociologists learn to use one or more of these packages during graduate school. If the data are qualitative, researchers analyze their data (what they have observed and/or what people have told them in interviews) in ways again beyond our scope. Many researchers now use qualitative analysis software that helps them uncover important themes and patterns in the qualitative data they gather. However qualitative or quantitative data are analyzed, it is essential that the analysis be as accurate as possible. To go back to a point just made, this means that variable measurement must also be as accurate as possible, because even expert analysis of inaccurate data will yield inaccurate results. As a phrase from the field of computer science summarizes this problem, "garbage in, garbage out." Data analysis can be accurate only if the data are accurate to begin with.

Criteria of Causality

As researchers analyze their data, they naturally try to determine whether their analysis supports their hypothesis. As noted above, when we test a hypothesis, we want to be able to conclude that an independent variable affects a dependent variable. Four criteria must be satisfied before we can conclude this (see Table 2.1 "Criteria of Causality").

Table 2.1 Criteria of Causality

1. The independent variable and dependent variable must be statistically related.
2. The independent variable must precede the dependent variable in time and/or in logic.
3. The relationship between the independent variable and dependent variable must not be spurious.
4. No better explanation exists for the relationship between the independent variable and the dependent variable.

First, the independent variable and the dependent variable must be *statistically related*. That means that the independent variable makes a statistical difference for where one ranks on the dependent variable. Suppose we hypothesize that age was related to voting preference in the 2008 presidential election. Here age is clearly the independent variable and voting preference the dependent variable. (It is possible for age to affect voting preference, but it is not possible for voting preference to affect age.) Exit poll data indicate that 66% of 18- to 24-year-olds voted for Obama in 2008, while only 45% of those 65 and older voted for him. The two variables are thus statistically related, as younger voters were more likely than older voters to prefer Obama.

The second criterion is called the *causal order* (or chicken-and-egg) problem and reflects the familiar saying that "correlation does not mean causation." Just because an independent and a dependent variable are related does not automatically mean that the independent variable affects the dependent variable. It might well be that the dependent variable is affecting the independent. To satisfy this criterion, the researcher must be sure that the independent variable precedes the dependent variable in time or in logic. In the example just discussed, age might affect voting preference, but voting preference definitely cannot affect age. However, causal order is not as clear in other hypotheses. For example, suppose we find a statistical relationship between marital happiness and job satisfaction: the more happy people are in their marriage, the more satisfied they are with their jobs. Which makes more sense, that having a happy marriage leads you to like your job more, or that being satisfied with your work leads you to have a happier marriage? In this example, causal order is not very clear, and thus the second criterion is difficult to satisfy.

The third criterion involves **spurious relationships**. A relationship between an independent variable and dependent variable is spurious if a third variable accounts for the relationship because it affects both the independent and dependent variables. Although this sounds a bit complicated, an example or two should make it clear. If you did a survey of Americans 18 and older, you would find that people who attend college have worse acne than people who do not attend college. Does this mean that attending college causes worse acne? Certainly not. You would find this statistical relationship only because a third variable, age, affects both the likelihood of attending college and the likelihood of having acne: young people are more likely than older people to attend college, and also more likely—for very different reasons—to have acne. Controlling for age makes it clear that the original relationship between attending college and having acne was spurious. Figure 2.5 "Diagram of a Spurious Relationship" diagrams this particular spurious relationship; notice that there is no causal arrow between the attending college and having acne variables.

Figure 2.5 Diagram of a Spurious Relationship

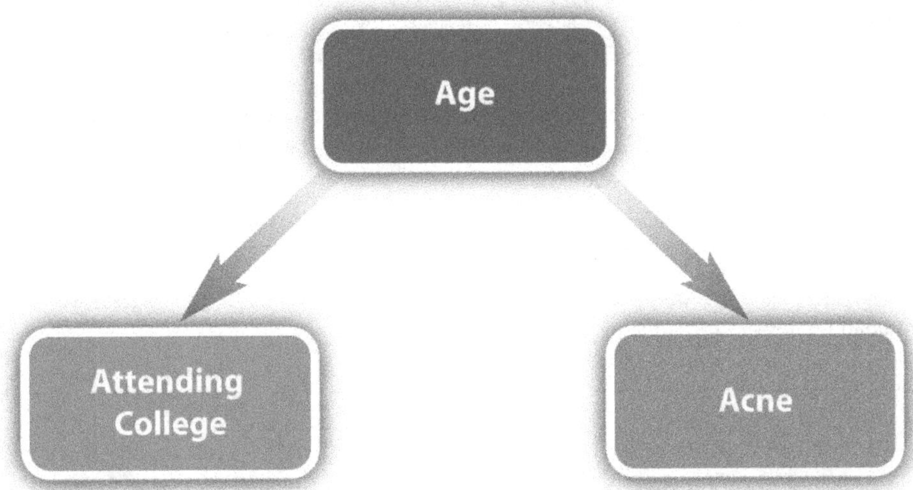

In another example, the more fire trucks at a fire, the more damage the fire causes. Does that mean that fire trucks somehow make fires worse, as the familiar saying "too many cooks spoil the broth" might suggest? Of course not! The third variable here is the intensity of the fire: the more intense the fire, the more fire trucks respond to fight it, and the more intense the fire, the more damage it causes. The relationship between number of fire trucks and damage the fire causes is spurious.

The final criterion of causality is that our explanation for the relationship between the independent and dependent variables is the *best explanation*. Even if the first three criteria are satisfied, that does not necessarily mean the two variables are in fact related. For example, the U.S. crime rate dropped in the early 1980s, and in 1984 the reelection campaign of President Ronald Reagan took credit for this drop. This relationship satisfied the first three criteria: the crime rate fell after President Reagan took office in 1981, the drop in the crime rate could not have affected the election of this president, and there was no apparent third variable that influenced both why Reagan was elected and why the crime rate fell. However, social scientists pointed to another reason that accounted for the crime rate decrease during the 1980s: a drop in the birth rate some 15–20 years earlier, which led to a decrease during the early 1980s of the number of U.S. residents in the high-crime ages of 15–30 (Steffensmeier & Harer, 1991). The relationship between the election of Ronald Reagan and the crime rate drop was thus only a coincidence.

Drawing a Conclusion

Once the data are analyzed, the researcher finally determines whether the data analysis supports the hypothesis that has been tested, taking into account the criteria of causality just discussed. Whether or not the hypothesis is supported, the researcher (if writing for publication) typically also discusses what the results of the present research imply for both prior and future studies on the topic. If the primary purpose of the project has been to test or refine a particular theory, the conclusion will discuss the implications of the results for this theory. If the primary purpose has been to test or advance social policy, the conclusion will discuss the implications of the results for policy making relevant to the project's subject matter.

Key Takeaways

- Several stages compose the sociological research process. These stages include (a) choosing a research topic, (b) conducting a literature review, (c) measuring variables and gathering data, (d) analyzing data, and (e) drawing a conclusion.
- Sociologists commonly base their choice of a research topic on one or more of the following: (a) a theoretical interest, (b) a social policy interest, and (c) one or more personal experiences.
- Accurate measurement of variables is essential for sound sociological research. As a minimum, measures should be as clear and unambiguous as possible.

For Your Review

1. Consider the following question from a survey: "Generally speaking, are you very happy, somewhat happy, or not too happy?" Write a brief essay in which you evaluate how well this question measures happiness.
2. Think of a personal experience you have had that lends itself to a possible research project. Write a brief essay in which you describe the experience and discuss the hypothesis that the research project based on the experience would address.

References

Steffensmeier, D., & Harer, M. D. (1991). Did crime rise or fall during the Reagan presidency? The effects of an "aging" U.S. population on the nation's crime rate. *Journal of Research in Crime and Delinquency, 28*(3), 330–359.

2.3 Research Design in Sociology

Learning Objective

1. List the major advantages and disadvantages of surveys, experiments, and observational studies.

We now turn to the major methods that sociologists use to gather the information they analyze in their research. Table 2.2 "Major Sociological Research Methods" summarizes the advantages and disadvantages of each method.

Table 2.2 Major Sociological Research Methods

Method	Advantages	Disadvantages
Survey	Many people can be included. If given to a random sample of the population, a survey's results can be generalized to the population.	Large surveys are expensive and time consuming. Although much information is gathered, this information is relatively superficial.
Experiments	If random assignment is used, experiments provide fairly convincing data on cause and effect.	Because experiments do not involve random samples of the population and most often involve college students, their results cannot readily be generalized to the population.
Observation (field research)	Observational studies may provide rich, detailed information about the people who are observed.	Because observation studies do not involve random samples of the population, their results cannot readily be generalized to the population.
Existing data	Because existing data have already been gathered, the researcher does not have to spend the time and money to gather data.	The data set that is being analyzed may not contain data on all the variables in which a sociologist is interested or may contain data on variables that are not measured in ways the sociologist prefers.

Types of Sociological Research

Surveys

The survey is the most common method by which sociologists gather their data. The Gallup Poll is perhaps the best-known example of a survey and, like all surveys, gathers its data with the help of a questionnaire that is given to a group of respondents. The Gallup Poll is an example of a survey conducted by a private organization, but it typically includes only a small range of variables. It thus provides a good starting point for research but usually does not include enough variables for a full-fledged sociological study. Sociologists often do their own surveys, as does the government and many organizations in addition to Gallup.

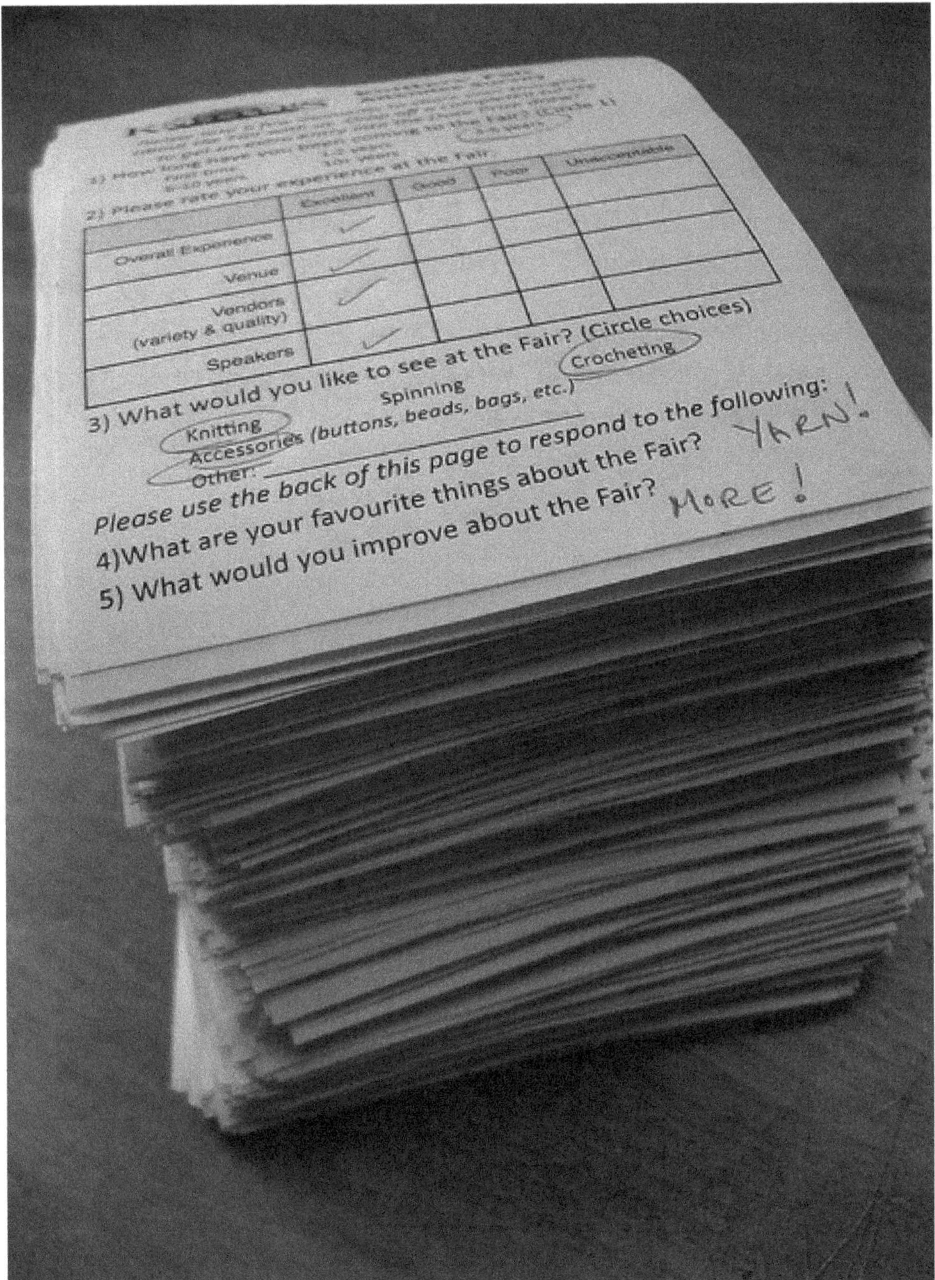

The survey is the most common research design in sociological research. Respondents either fill out questionnaires themselves or provide verbal answers to interviewers asking them the questions.

The Bees – Surveys to compile – CC BY-NC 2.0.

The General Social Survey, described earlier, is an example of a face-to-face survey, in which interviewers meet with respondents to ask them questions. This type of survey can yield a lot of information, because interviewers typically will spend at least an hour asking their questions, and a high **response rate** (the percentage of all people in the sample who agree to be interviewed), which is important to be able to generalize the survey's results to the entire population. On the downside, this type of survey can be very expensive and time-consuming to conduct.

Because of these drawbacks, sociologists and other researchers have turned to telephone surveys. Most Gallup Polls are conducted over the telephone. Computers do random-digit dialing, which results in a random sample of all telephone numbers being selected. Although the response rate and the number of questions asked are both lower than in face-to-face surveys (people can just hang up the phone at the outset or let their answering machine take the call), the ease and low expense of telephone surveys are making them increasingly popular.

Mailed surveys, done by mailing questionnaires to respondents, are still used, but not as often as before. Compared with face-to-face surveys, mailed questionnaires are less expensive and time consuming but have lower response rates, because many people simply throw out the questionnaire along with other junk mail.

Whereas mailed surveys are becoming less popular, surveys done over the Internet are becoming more popular, as they can reach many people at very low expense. A major problem with Web surveys is that their results cannot necessarily be generalized to the entire population, because not everyone has access to the Internet.

Experiments

Experiments are the primary form of research in the natural and physical sciences, but in the social sciences they are for the most part found only in psychology. Some sociologists still use experiments, however, and they remain a powerful tool of social research.

The major advantage of experiments is that the researcher can be fairly sure of a cause-and-effect relationship because of the way the experiment is set up. Although many different experimental designs exist, the typical experiment consists of an **experimental group** and a **control group**, with subjects *randomly assigned* to either group. The researcher makes a change to the experimental group that is not made to the control group. If the two groups differ later in some variable, then it is safe to say that the condition to which the experimental group was subjected was responsible for the difference that resulted.

Experiments are very common in the natural and physical sciences and in sociology. A major advantage of experiments is that they are very useful for establishing cause-and-effect-relationships.

biologycorner – Science Experiment – CC BY-NC 2.0.

Most experiments take place in the laboratory, which for psychologists may be a room with a one-way mirror, but some experiments occur in "the field," or in a natural setting. In Minneapolis, Minnesota, in the early 1980s, sociologists were involved in a much-discussed field experiment sponsored by the federal government. The researchers wanted to see whether arresting men for domestic violence made it less likely that they would commit such violence again. To test this hypothesis, the researchers had police do one of the following after arriving at the scene of a domestic dispute: they either arrested the suspect, separated him from his wife or partner for several hours, or warned him to stop but did not arrest or separate him. The researchers then determined the percentage of men in each group who committed repeated domestic violence during the next 6 months and found that those who were arrested had the lowest rate of recidivism, or repeat offending (Sherman & Berk, 1984). This finding led many jurisdictions across the United States to adopt a policy of mandatory arrest for domestic violence suspects. However, replications of the Minneapolis experiment in other cities found that arrest sometimes reduced recidivism for domestic violence but also sometimes increased it, depending on which city was being studied and on certain characteristics of the suspects, including whether they were employed at the time of their arrest (Sherman, 1992).

As the Minneapolis study suggests, perhaps the most important problem with experiments is that their results are not generalizable beyond the specific subjects studied. The subjects in most psychology experiments, for example, are college students, who are not typical of average Americans: they are younger, more educated, and more likely to be middle class. Despite this problem, experiments in psychology and other social sciences have given us very valuable insights into the sources of attitudes and behavior.

Observational Studies and Intensive Interviewing

Observational research, also called field research, is a staple of sociology. Sociologists have long gone into the field to observe people and social settings, and the result has been many rich descriptions and analyses of behavior in juvenile gangs, bars, urban street corners, and even whole communities.

Observational studies consist of both **participant observation** and **nonparticipant observation**. Their names describe how they differ. In participant observation, the researcher is part of the group that she or he is studying. The researcher thus spends time with the group and might even live with them for a while. Several classical sociological studies of this type exist, many of them involving people in urban neighborhoods (Liebow, 1967, 1993; Whyte, 1943). Participant researchers must try not to let their presence influence the attitudes or behavior of the people they are observing. In nonparticipant observation, the researcher observes a group of people but does not otherwise interact with them. If you went to your local shopping mall to observe, say, whether people walking with children looked happier than people without children, you would be engaging in nonparticipant observation.

A related type of research design is *intensive interviewing*. Here a researcher does not necessarily observe a group of people in their natural setting but rather sits down with them individually and interviews them at great length, often for one or two hours or even longer. The researcher typically records the interview and later transcribes it for analysis. The advantages and disadvantages of intensive interviewing are similar to those for observational studies: intensive interviewing provides much information about the subjects being interviewed, but the results of such interviewing cannot necessarily be generalized beyond the subjects.

A classic example of field research is Kai T. Erikson's *Everything in Its Path* (1976), a study of the loss of community bonds in the aftermath of a flood in a West Virginia mining community, Buffalo Creek. The flood occurred when an artificial dam composed of mine waste gave way after days of torrential rain. The local mining company had allowed the dam to build up in violation of federal law. When it broke, 132 million gallons of water broke through and destroyed several thousand homes in seconds while killing 125 people. Some 2,500 other people were rendered instantly homeless. Erikson was called in by the lawyers representing the survivors to document the sociological effects of their loss of community, and the book he wrote remains a moving account of how the destruction of the Buffalo Creek way of life profoundly affected the daily lives of its residents.

Intensive interviewing can yield in-depth information about the subjects who are interviewed, but the results of this research design cannot necessarily be generalized beyond these subjects.

Fellowship of the Rich – Interview – CC BY-NC-ND 2.0.

Similar to experiments, observational studies cannot automatically be generalized to other settings or members of the population. But in many ways they provide a richer account of people's lives than surveys do, and they remain an important method of sociological research.

Existing Data

Sometimes sociologists do not gather their own data but instead analyze existing data that someone else has gathered. The U.S. Census Bureau, for example, gathers data on all kinds of areas relevant to the lives of Americans, and many sociologists analyze census data on such topics as poverty, employment, and illness. Sociologists interested in crime and the legal system may analyze data from court records, while medical sociologists often analyze data from patient records at hospitals. Analysis of existing data such as these is called **secondary data analysis.** Its advantage to sociologists is that someone else has already spent the time and money to gather the data. A disadvantage is that the data set being analyzed may not contain data on all the variables in which a sociologist may be interested or may contain data on variables that are not measured in ways the sociologist might prefer.

Nonprofit organizations often analyze existing data, usually gathered by government agencies, to get a better understanding of the social issue with which an organization is most concerned. They then use their analysis to help devise effective social policies and strategies for dealing with the issue. The "Learning From Other Societies" box discusses a nonprofit organization in Canada that analyzes existing data for this purpose.

Learning From Other Societies

Social Research and Social Policy in Canada

In several nations beyond the United States, nonprofit organizations often use social science research, including sociological research, to develop and evaluate various social reform strategies and social policies. Canada is one of these nations. Information on Canadian social research organizations can be found at http://www.canadiansocialresearch.net/index.htm.

The Canadian Research Institute for Social Policy (CRISP) at the University of New Brunswick is one of these organizations. According to its Web site (http://www.unb.ca/crisp/index.php), CRISP is "dedicated to conducting policy research aimed at improving the education and care of Canadian children and youth…and supporting low-income countries in their efforts to build research capacity in child development." To do this, CRISP analyzes data from large data sets, such as the Canadian National Longitudinal Survey of Children and Youth, and it also evaluates policy efforts at the local, national, and international levels.

A major concern of CRISP has been developmental problems in low-income children and teens. These problems are the focus of a CRISP project called Raising and Leveling the Bar: A Collaborative Research Initiative on Children's Learning, Behavioral, and Health Outcomes. This project at the time of this writing involved a team of five senior researchers and almost two dozen younger scholars. CRISP notes that Canada may have the most complete data on child development in the world but that much more research with these data needs to be performed to help inform public policy in the area of child development. CRISP's project aims to use these data to help achieve the following goals, as listed on its Web site: (a) safeguard the healthy development of infants, (b) strengthen early childhood education, (c) improve schools and local communities, (d) reduce socioeconomic segregation and the effects of poverty, and (e) create a family enabling society (http://www.unb.ca/crisp/rlb.html). This project has written many policy briefs, journal articles, and popular press articles to educate varied audiences about what the data on children's development suggest for child policy in Canada.

Key Takeaways

- The major types of sociological research include surveys, experiments, observational studies, and the use of existing data.
- Surveys are very common and allow for the gathering of much information on respondents that is relatively superficial. The results of surveys that use random samples can be generalized to the population that the sample represents.
- Observational studies are also very common and enable in-depth knowledge of a small group of people. Because the samples of these studies are not random, the results cannot necessarily be generalized to a population.
- Experiments are much less common in sociology than in psychology. When field experiments are conducted in sociology, they can yield valuable information because of their experimental design.

For Your Review

1. Write a brief essay in which you outline the various kinds of surveys and discuss the advantages and disadvantages of each type.
2. Suppose you wanted to study whether gender affects happiness. Write a brief essay that describes how you would do this either with a survey or with an observational study.

References

Erikson, K. T. (1976). *Everything in its path: Destruction of community in the Buffalo Creek flood.* New York, NY: Simon and Schuster.

Liebow, E. (1967). *Tally's corner*. Boston, MA: Little, Brown.

Liebow, E. (1993). *Tell them who I am: The lives of homeless women*. New York, NY: Free Press.

Sherman, L W. (1992). *Policing domestic violence: Experiments and dilemmas*. New York, NY: Free Press.

Sherman, L. W., & Berk, R. A. (1984). The specific deterrent effects of arrest for domestic assault. *American Sociological Review, 49*, 261–272.

Whyte, W. F. (1943). *Street corner society: The social structure of an Italian slum*. Chicago, IL: University of Chicago Press.

2.4 Ethical Issues in Sociological Research

Learning Objective

1. Describe two kinds of ethical issues and/or guidelines that characterize sociological research.

Research involving human subjects must follow certain ethical standards to make sure the subjects are not harmed. Such harm can be quite severe in medical research unless certain precautions are taken. For example, in 1932 the U.S. Public Health Service began studying several hundred poor, illiterate African American men in Tuskegee, Alabama. The men had syphilis, for which no cure then existed, and were studied to determine its effects. After scientists found a decade later that penicillin could cure this disease, the government scientists decided not to give penicillin to the Tuskegee men because doing so would end their research. As a result, several of the men died from their disease, and some of their wives and children came down with it. The study did not end until the early 1970s, when the press finally disclosed the experiment. Several observers likened it to experiments conducted by Nazi scientists. If the subjects had been white and middle class, they said, the government would have ended the study once it learned that penicillin could cure syphilis (Jones, 1981).

In a study that began in 1932 of syphilis among African American men in Tuskegee, Alabama, government physicians decided not to give penicillin to the men after it was found that this drug would cure syphilis.

Wikimedia Commons – public domain.

Fortunately, sociological research does not have this potential for causing death or serious illness, but it still can cause other kinds of harm and thus must follow ethical standards. The federal government has an extensive set of standards for research on human subjects, and the major sociology professional society, the American Sociological Association, has a code of ethics for sociological research.

One of the most important ethical guidelines in sociological and other human-subject research concerns privacy and confidentiality. When they do research, sociologists should protect the privacy and confidentiality of their subjects. When a survey is used, the data must be coded (prepared for computer analysis) anonymously, and in no way should it be possible for any answers to be connected with the respondent who gave them. In field research, anonymity must also be maintained, and aliases (fake names) should normally be used when the researcher reports what she or he has been observing.

Some sociologists consider the privacy and confidentiality of subjects so important that they have risked imprisonment when they have refused to violate confidentiality. In one example, a graduate student named Mario Brajuha had been doing participant observation as a restaurant waiter on Long Island, New York, when the restaurant burned down. When the police suspected arson, they asked Brajuha to turn over his field notes. When Brajuha refused, he was threatened with imprisonment. Meanwhile, two suspects in the case also demanded his field notes for their legal defense, but again Brajuha refused. The controversy ended 2 years later when the suspects died and the prosecutor's office abandoned its effort to obtain the notes (Brajuha & Hallowell, 1986).

In another case, a graduate student named Rik Scarce refused to turn over his field notes on radical environmentalists after one of the groups he was studying vandalized a university laboratory. Scarce was jailed for contempt of court when he refused to tell a grand jury what he had learned about the group and spent several months behind bars (Monaghan, 1993).

A third example aroused much discussion among sociologists when it came to light. Laud Humphreys studied male homosexual sex that took place in public bathrooms. He did so by acting as the lookout in several encounters where two men had sex; the men did not know Humphreys was a researcher. He also wrote down their license plates and obtained their addresses and a year later disguised himself and interviewed the men at their homes. Many sociologists and other observers later criticized Humphreys for acting so secretly and for violating his subjects' privacy. Humphreys responded that he protected the men's names and that their behavior was not private, as it was conducted in a public setting (Humphreys, 1975).

The requirement of informed consent becomes an ethical issue when prisoners are studied, because prisoners may feel pressured to participate in the study.

Kim Daram – prison – CC BY-NC 2.0.

Another ethical issue concerns *consent*. Before a researcher can begin obtaining data, the subjects of the research must normally sign an *informed consent* form. This form summarizes the aims of the study and the possible risks of being a subject. If researchers want to study minors (under age 18), they normally must obtain a signature from a parent or legal guardian. Informed consent is a requirement for most "real" research these days, but ethical issues arise over the meaning of "consent." For consent to have any real meaning, potential research subjects must have the right to refuse to take part in a research project without any penalties whatsoever. Otherwise, they may feel pressured to participate in the project without really wanting to do so. This result would violate what "consent" is supposed to mean in the research process. Sometimes subjects are promised a small reward (often between $5 and $20) for taking part in a research project, but they are still utterly free to refuse to do so, and this small inducement is not considered to be undue pressure to participate.

Informed consent becomes a particular problem when a researcher wants to include certain populations in a study. Perhaps the clearest example of such a problem is when a study involves prisoners. When prisoners are asked to be interviewed or to fill out a questionnaire, they certainly can refuse to do so, but they may feel pressured to participate. They realize that if they do participate, they may be more likely to be seen as a "model" prisoner, which helps them win "good time" that reduces their sentence or helps them win a release decision from a parole board. Conversely, if they refuse to participate, they not only lose these advantages but also may be seen as a bit of a troublemaker and earn extra scrutiny from prison guards. Scholarly societies continue to debate the ethical issues involved in studies of prisoners and other vulnerable populations (e.g., offenders in juvenile institutions, patients in mental institutions), and there are no easy answers to the ethical questions arising in such studies.

As all these examples of ethical issues demonstrate, it is not always easy to decide whether a particular research project is ethically justifiable. Partly for this reason, colleges and universities have committees that review proposed human-subject research to ensure that federal guidelines are followed.

Key Takeaways

- Potential ethical issues in sociological research are normally not as serious as those in medical research, but sociologists must still take care to proceed in an ethical manner in their research.
- The guideline that informed consent must be obtained from potential research subjects is a special issue for vulnerable populations such as prisoners.

For Your Review

1. Do you think it is appropriate to ask prisoners to take part in a research study? Why or why not?
2. If you were a researcher and police demanded to see notes you had taken as part of your research, would you turn the notes over to the police, or would you refuse to do so at the risk of being arrested? Explain your answer.

References

Brajuha, M., & Hallowell, L. (1986). Legal intrusion and the politics of fieldwork: The impact of the Brajuha case. *Urban Life, 14,* 454–478.

Humphreys, L. (1975). *Teamroom trade: Impersonal sex in public places*. Chicago, IL: Aldine.

Jones, J. H. (1981). *Bad blood: The Tuskegee syphilis experiment*. New York, NY: Free Press.

Monaghan, P. (1993). Sociologist is jailed for refusing to testify about research subject. *Chronicle of Higher Education, 39,* 10.

2.5 Sociological Research in the Service of Society

Should the primary aim of sociological research be to help improve society, or should its primary aim be to discover social knowledge for its own sake? There is no right or wrong answer to this question. However, following in the spirit of the early American sociologists, this book hopes to show the relevance of sociological knowledge and insights, as derived from sound, objective research, for addressing many of the social issues facing American society and various nations around the world.

Although sociological research findings may be relevant for many social issues, this certainly does not guarantee that these findings will actually be marshaled to address these issues. For this to happen, elected officials and other policymakers must be open to the implications of research findings, and an informed public must make its desire for addressing these issues known. For many readers, the introduction to sociology course they are now taking might be the only sociology course they ever take; other readers will take more sociology courses and may even become a sociology major. Regardless of how many sociology courses you do take, and regardless of whether you become an elected official or policymaker or you remain a member of the informed public, this book hopes to help you think like a sociologist as social issues continue and emerge in the many years ahead.

2.6 End-of-Chapter Material

Summary

1. Because sociology deals in generalizations and not laws, people don't always behave and think in the patterns sociologists predict. For every sociological generalization, there are many exceptions.
2. Personal experience, common sense, the media, expert opinion, and tradition are all valuable sources of knowledge about various aspects of society, but they often present a limited or erroneous view of these aspects.
3. Sociological research follows the scientific method. A major goal is to test hypotheses suggesting how an independent variable influences a dependent variable. Hypotheses can concern several units of analysis: the person, the organization, and the geographical region.
4. The major stages of sociological research include (a) choosing a topic, (b) conducting a literature review, (c) formulating a hypothesis, (d) measuring variables and gathering data, (e) analyzing data, and (f) drawing a conclusion.
5. The major sociological methods for gathering data are surveys, experiments, field research, and existing data. Surveys are the most common research method in sociology, but field research provides richer and more detailed information. Experiments are rather uncommon in sociology, but field experiments may provide very valuable information. Sociologists also analyze existing data gathered by government agencies and other sources, and nonprofit organizations often use existing data to shed light on the social issues with which they are concerned.
6. To be sure that an independent variable affects a dependent variable, we must be certain that the two variables are statistically related, that the independent variable precedes the dependent variable in time, and that the relationship between the two variables is not spurious.
7. Several ethical standards guide sociological research. Among the most important of these are the rights to privacy and confidentiality and to freedom from harm. Some sociologists have risked imprisonment to protect these rights. Such vulnerable populations as prisoners raise special issues in regard to informed consent.

Using Sociology

Imagine that you are the mayor of a city of about 100,000 residents. Similar to many other cities, yours has a mixture of rich and poor neighborhoods. Because you and one of your key advisers were sociology majors in college, you both remember that the type of neighborhoods in which children grow up can influence many aspects of their development. Your adviser suggests that you seek a large federal grant to conduct a small field experiment to test the effects of neighborhoods in your city. In this experiment, 60 families from poor neighborhoods would be recruited to volunteer. Half of these families would be randomly selected to move to middle-class neighborhoods with their housing partially subsidized (the experimental group), and the other 30 families would remain where they are (the control group). A variety of data would then be gathered about the children in both groups of families over the next decade to determine whether living in middle-class neighborhoods improved the children's cognitive and social development.

You recognize the potential value of this experiment, but you also wonder whether it is entirely ethical, as it would be virtually impossible to maintain the anonymity of the families in the experimental group and perhaps even in the control group. You also worry about the political problems that might result if the people already in the middle-class neighborhoods object to the new families moving into their midst. Do you decide to apply for the federal grant? Why or why not?

Chapter 3: Culture

Social Issues in the News

"Cows With Gas," the headline said. In India, cows are considered sacred by that nation's major religion, Hinduism. They are also an important source of milk and fertilizer. It is no surprise that India has almost 300 million cows, the highest number in the world, and that they roam freely in Indian cities and towns. But one problem of this abundance of cows is the methane gas they excrete as they burp and belch. They emit so much methane that scientists think Indian cows, along with some 180 million sheep and goats, are a significant cause of global warming. One reason Indian livestock emit so much methane, aside from their sheer numbers, is that they are underfed and undernourished; better diets would reduce their methane emission. However, India is such a poor country that the prospect of a better diet for livestock remains years away, and the problem of cows with gas will continue for some time to come. (Singh, 2009)

The idea of cows with too much gas, or any gas at all, roaming city streets is probably not very appealing, but cow worship is certainly a part of India's culture. This news story provides just one of many examples of the importance of cultural differences for beliefs and behaviors.

Although kissing certainly seems like a very normal and natural act, anthropological evidence indicates that culture affects whether people kiss and whether they like kissing.

Yulia Volodina – kiss – CC BY-NC-ND 2.0.

Here is a more pleasing example. When you are in love, what can be more natural and enjoyable than kissing? This simple act is the highlight of countless movies and television shows where two people meet each other, often not liking each other at first, but then slowly but surely fall madly in love and have their first magical kiss. What we see on the screen reflects our own interest in kissing. When we reach puberty, many of us yearn for our first kiss. That kiss is as much a part of growing up as almost anything else we can think of, and many of us can remember when, where, and with whom our first kiss occurred.

Kissing certainly seems a natural, enjoyable act to most of us, but evidence from some societies indicates kissing might not be so natural after all. In traditional societies such as the Balinese and Tinguian of Oceania, the Chewa and Thonga of Africa, and the Siriono of South America, kissing is unknown, as the people there think it is unhealthy and disgusting. When the Thonga first saw Europeans kissing, they retorted, "Look at them—they eat each other's saliva and dirt" (Ford & Beach, 1972, p. 49). Even in industrial societies, kissing is not always considered desirable. Until fairly recently, the Japanese abhorred kissing and did not even have a word for it until they created *kissu* from the English kiss, and even today older Japanese frown on kissing in public. Reflecting the traditional Japanese view, when Rodin's famous statue *The Kiss* arrived in Japan in the 1920s as part of a European art show, the Japanese hid it behind a curtain. In other societies, people do kiss, but their type of kissing differs greatly from what we are used to. In one of these, people kiss the mouth and the nose simultaneously, while people in a few other societies kiss only by sucking the lips of their partners (Tanikawa, 1995; Tiefer, 1995).

References

Ford, C. S., & Beach, F. A. (1972). *Patterns of sexual behavior*. New York, NY: Harper and Row.

Singh, M. (2009, April 11). Cows with gas: India's global-warming problem. *Time*. Retrieved from http://www.time.com/time/world/article/0,8599,1890646,00.html.

Tanikawa, M. (1995, May 28). Japan's young couples discover the kiss. *The New York Times*, p. 39.

Tiefer, L. (1995). *Sex is not a natural act and other essays*. Boulder, CO: Westview Press.

3.1 Culture and the Sociological Perspective

Learning Objectives

1. Describe examples of how culture influences behavior.
2. Explain why sociologists might favor cultural explanations of behavior over biological explanations.

As this evidence on kissing suggests, what seems to us a very natural, even instinctual act turns out not to be so natural and biological after all. Instead, kissing seems best understood as something we learn to enjoy from our **culture**, or the symbols, language, beliefs, values, and artifacts (material objects) that are part of a society. Because society, as defined in Chapter 1 "Sociology and the Sociological Perspective", refers to a group of people who live in a defined territory and who share a culture, it is obvious that culture is a critical component of any society.

If the culture we learn influences our beliefs and behaviors, then culture is a key concept to the sociological perspective. Someone who grows up in the United States differs in many ways, some of them obvious and some of them not so obvious, from someone growing up in China, Sweden, South Korea, Peru, or Nigeria. Culture influences not only language but the gestures we use when we interact, how far apart we stand from each other when we talk, and the values we consider most important for our children to learn, to name just a few. Without culture, we could not have a society.

The profound impact of culture becomes most evident when we examine behaviors or conditions that, like kissing, are normally considered biological in nature. Consider morning sickness and labor pains, both very familiar to pregnant women before and during childbirth, respectively. These two types of discomfort have known biological causes, and we are not surprised that so many pregnant women experience them. But we *would* be surprised if the husbands of pregnant women woke up sick in the morning or experienced severe abdominal pain while their wives gave birth. These men are neither carrying nor delivering a baby, and there is no logical—that is, biological—reason for them to suffer either type of discomfort.

And yet scholars have discovered several traditional societies in which men about to become fathers experience precisely these symptoms. They are nauseous during their wives' pregnancies, and they experience labor pains while their wives give birth. The term *couvade* refers to these symptoms, which do not have any known biological origin. Yet the men feel them nonetheless, because they have learned from their culture that they *should* feel these types of discomfort (Doja, 2005). And because they should feel these symptoms, they actually do so. Perhaps their minds are playing tricks on them, but that is often the point of culture. As sociologists William I. and Dorothy Swaine Thomas (1928) once pointed out, if things are perceived as real, then they are real in their consequences. These men learn how they should feel as budding fathers, and thus they feel this way. Unfortunately for them, the perceptions they learn from their culture are real in their consequences.

The example of drunkenness further illustrates how cultural expectations influence a behavior that is commonly thought to have biological causes. In the United States, when people drink too much alcohol, they become intoxicated and their behavior changes. Most typically, their inhibitions lower and they become loud, boisterous, and even rowdy. We attribute these changes to alcohol's biological effect as a drug on our central nervous system, and scientists have documented how alcohol breaks down in our body to achieve this effect.

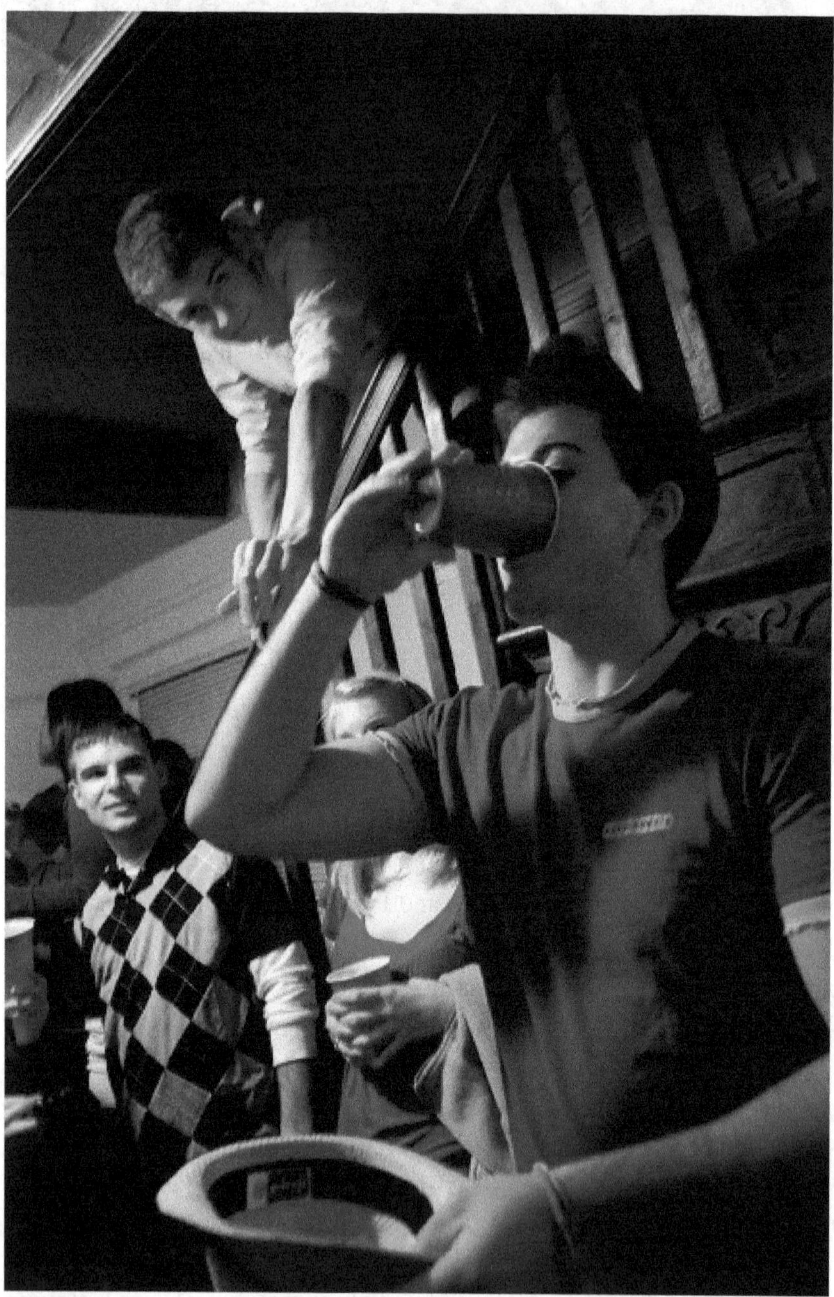

Culture affects how people respond when they drink alcohol. Americans often become louder and lose their sexual inhibitions when they drink, but people in some societies studied by anthropologists often respond very differently, with many never getting loud or not even enjoying themselves.

Melissa Wang – bp tourney – CC BY-SA 2.0.

This explanation of alcohol's effect is OK as far as it goes, but it turns out that *how* alcohol affects our behavior depends on our culture. In some small, traditional societies, people drink alcohol until they pass out, but they never get loud or boisterous; they might not even appear to be enjoying themselves. In other societies, they drink lots of alcohol and get loud but not rowdy. In some societies, including our own, people lose sexual inhibitions as they drink, but in other societies they do not become more aroused. The cross-cultural evidence is very clear: alcohol as a drug does affect human behavior, but culture influences the types of effects that occur. We learn from our culture how to behave when drunk just as we learn how to behave when sober (McCaghy, Capron, Jamieson, & Carey, 2008).

Culture and Biology

These examples suggest that human behavior is more the result of culture than it is of biology. This is not to say that biology is entirely unimportant. As just one example, humans have a biological need to eat, and so they do. But humans are much less under the control of biology than any other animal species, including other primates such as monkeys and chimpanzees. These and other animals are governed largely by biological instincts that control them totally. A dog chases any squirrel it sees because of instinct, and a cat chases a mouse for the same reason. Different breeds of dogs do have different personalities, but even these stem from the biological differences among breeds passed down from one generation to another. Instinct prompts many dogs to turn around before they lie down, and it prompts most dogs to defend their territory. When the doorbell rings and a dog begins barking, it is responding to ancient biological instinct.

Because humans have such a large, complex central nervous system, we are less controlled by biology. The critical question then becomes, how much does biology influence our behavior? Predictably, scholars in different disciplines answer this question in different ways. Most sociologists and anthropologists would probably say that culture affects behavior much more than biology does. In contrast, many biologists and psychologists would give much more weight to biology. Advocating a view called **sociobiology**, some scholars say that several important human behaviors and emotions, such as competition, aggression, and altruism, stem from our biological makeup. Sociobiology has been roundly criticized and just as staunchly defended, and respected scholars continue to debate its premises (Freese, 2008).

Why do sociologists generally favor culture over biology? Two reasons stand out. First, and as we have seen, many behaviors differ dramatically among societies in ways that show the strong impact of culture. Second, biology cannot easily account for why groups and locations differ in their rates of committing certain behaviors. For example, what biological reason could explain why suicide rates west of the Mississippi River are higher than those east of it, to take a difference discussed in Chapter 2 “Eye on Society: Doing Sociological Research”, or why the U.S. homicide rate is so much higher than Canada’s? Various aspects of culture and social structure seem much better able than biology to explain these differences.

Many sociologists also warn of certain implications of biological explanations. First, they say, these explanations implicitly support the status quo. Because it is difficult to change biology, any problem with biological causes cannot be easily fixed. A second warning harkens back to a century ago, when perceived biological differences were used to justify forced sterilization and mass violence, including genocide, against certain groups. As just one example, in the early 1900s, some 70,000 people, most of them poor and many of them immigrants or African Americans, were involuntarily sterilized in the United States as part of the **eugenics** movement, which said that certain kinds of people were biologically inferior and must not be allowed to reproduce (Lombardo, 2008). The Nazi Holocaust a few decades later used a similar eugenics argument to justify its genocide against Jews, Catholics, gypsies, and gays (Kuhl, 1994). With this history in mind, some scholars fear that biological explanations of human behavior might still be used to support views of biological inferiority (York & Clark, 2007).

Key Takeaways

- Culture refers to the symbols, language, beliefs, values, and artifacts that are part of any society.
- Because culture influences people's beliefs and behaviors, culture is a key concept to the sociological perspective.
- Many sociologists are wary of biological explanations of behavior, in part because these explanations implicitly support the status quo and may be used to justify claims of biological inferiority.

For Your Review

1. Have you ever traveled outside the United States? If so, describe one cultural difference you remember in the nation you visited.
2. Have you ever traveled within the United States to a very different region (e.g., urban versus rural, or another part of the country) from the one in which you grew up? If so, describe one cultural difference you remember in the region you visited.
3. Do you share the concern of many sociologists over biological explanations of behavior? Why or why not?

References

Doja, A. (2005). Rethinking the *couvade*. *Anthropological Quarterly, 78,* 917–950.

Freese, J. (2008). Genetics and the social science explanation of individual outcomes [Supplement]. *American Journal of Sociology, 114,* S1–S35.

Kuhl, S. (1994). *The Nazi connection: Eugenics, American racism, and German national socialism.* New York, NY: Oxford University Press.

Lombardo, P. A. (2008). *Three generations, no imbeciles: Eugenics, the Supreme Court, and Buck v. Bell.* Baltimore, MD: Johns Hopkins University Press.

McCaghy, C. H., Capron, T. A., Jamieson, J. D., & Carey, S. H. (2008). *Deviant behavior: Crime, conflict, and interest groups.* Boston, MA: Allyn & Bacon.

Thomas, W. I., & Thomas, D. S. (1928). *The child in America: Behavior problems and programs*. New York, NY: Knopf.

York, R., & Clark, B. (2007). Gender and mathematical ability: The toll of biological determinism. *Monthly Review, 59*, 7–15.

3.2 The Elements of Culture

Learning Objectives

1. Distinguish material culture and nonmaterial culture.
2. List and define the several elements of culture.
3. Describe certain values that distinguish the United States from other nations.

Culture was defined earlier as the symbols, language, beliefs, values, and artifacts that are part of any society. As this definition suggests, there are two basic components of culture: ideas and symbols on the one hand and artifacts (material objects) on the other. The first type, called **nonmaterial culture**, includes the values, beliefs, symbols, and language that define a society. The second type, called **material culture**, includes all the society's physical objects, such as its tools and technology, clothing, eating utensils, and means of transportation. These elements of culture are discussed next.

Symbols

Every culture is filled with **symbols**, or things that stand for something else and that often evoke various reactions and emotions. Some symbols are actually types of nonverbal communication, while other symbols are in fact material objects. As the symbolic interactionist perspective discussed in Chapter 1 "Sociology and the Sociological Perspective" emphasizes, shared symbols make social interaction possible.

Let's look at nonverbal symbols first. A common one is shaking hands, which is done in some societies but not in others. It commonly conveys friendship and is used as a sign of both greeting and departure. Probably all societies have nonverbal symbols we call **gestures**, movements of the hands, arms, or other parts of the body that are meant to convey certain ideas or emotions. However, the same gesture can mean one thing in one society and something quite different in another society (Axtell, 1998). In the United States, for example, if we nod our head up and down, we mean yes, and if we shake it back and forth, we mean no. In Bulgaria, however, nodding means no, while shaking our head back and forth means yes! In the United States, if we make an "O" by putting our thumb and forefinger together, we mean "OK," but the same gesture in certain parts of Europe signifies an obscenity. "Thumbs up" in the United States means "great" or "wonderful," but in Australia it means the same thing as extending the middle finger in the United States. Certain parts of the Middle East and Asia would be offended if they saw you using your left hand to eat, because they use their left hand for bathroom hygiene.

The meaning of a gesture may differ from one society to another. This familiar gesture means "OK" in the United States, but in certain parts of Europe it signifies an obscenity. An American using this gesture might very well be greeted with an angry look.

d Wang – ok – CC BY-NC-ND 2.0.

Some of our most important symbols are objects. Here the U.S. flag is a prime example. For most Americans, the flag is not just a piece of cloth with red and white stripes and white stars against a field of blue. Instead, it is a symbol of freedom, democracy, and other American values and, accordingly, inspires pride and patriotism. During the Vietnam War, however, the flag became to many Americans a symbol of war and imperialism. Some burned the flag in protest, prompting angry attacks by bystanders and negative coverage by the news media.

Other objects have symbolic value for religious reasons. Three of the most familiar religious symbols in many nations are the cross, the Star of David, and the crescent moon, which are widely understood to represent Christianity, Judaism, and Islam, respectively. Whereas many cultures attach no religious significance to these shapes, for many people across the world they evoke very strong feelings of religious faith. Recognizing this, hate groups have often desecrated these symbols.

As these examples indicate, shared symbols, both nonverbal communication and tangible objects, are an important part of any culture but also can lead to misunderstandings and even hostility. These problems underscore the significance of symbols for social interaction and meaning.

Language

Perhaps our most important set of symbols is language. In English, the word *chair* means something we sit on. In Spanish, the word *silla* means the same thing. As long as we agree how to interpret these words, a shared language and thus society are possible. By the same token, differences in languages can make it quite difficult to communicate. For example, imagine you are in a foreign country where you do not know the language and the country's citizens do not know yours. Worse yet, you forgot to bring your dictionary that translates their language into yours, and vice versa, and your iPhone battery has died. You become lost. How will you get help? What will you do? Is there any way to communicate your plight?

As this scenario suggests, language is crucial to communication and thus to any society's culture. Children learn language from their culture just as they learn about shaking hands, about gestures, and about the significance of the flag and other symbols. Humans have a capacity for language that no other animal species possesses. Our capacity for language in turn helps make our complex culture possible.

Language is a key symbol of any culture. Humans have a capacity for language that no other animal species has, and children learn the language of their society just as they learn other aspects of their culture.

Bill Benzon – IMGP3639 – talk – CC BY-SA 2.0.

In the United States, some people consider a common language so important that they advocate making English the official language of certain cities or states or even the whole country and banning bilingual education in the public schools (Ray, 2007). Critics acknowledge the importance of English but allege that this movement smacks of anti-immigrant prejudice and would help destroy ethnic subcultures. In 2009, voters in Nashville, Tennessee, rejected a proposal that would have made English the city's official language and required all city workers to speak in English rather than their native language (R. Brown, 2009).

Language, of course, can be spoken or written. One of the most important developments in the evolution of society was the creation of written language. Some of the preindustrial societies that anthropologists have studied have written language, while others do not, and in the remaining societies the "written" language consists mainly of pictures, not words. Figure 3.1 "The Presence of Written Language (Percentage of Societies)" illustrates this variation with data from 186 preindustrial societies called the Standard Cross-Cultural Sample (SCCS), a famous data set compiled several decades ago by anthropologist George Murdock and colleagues from information that had been gathered on hundreds of preindustrial societies around the world (Murdock & White, 1969). In Figure 3.1 "The Presence of Written Language (Percentage of Societies)", we see that only about one-fourth of the SCCS societies have a written language, while about equal proportions have no language at all or only pictures.

Figure 3.1 The Presence of Written Language (Percentage of Societies)

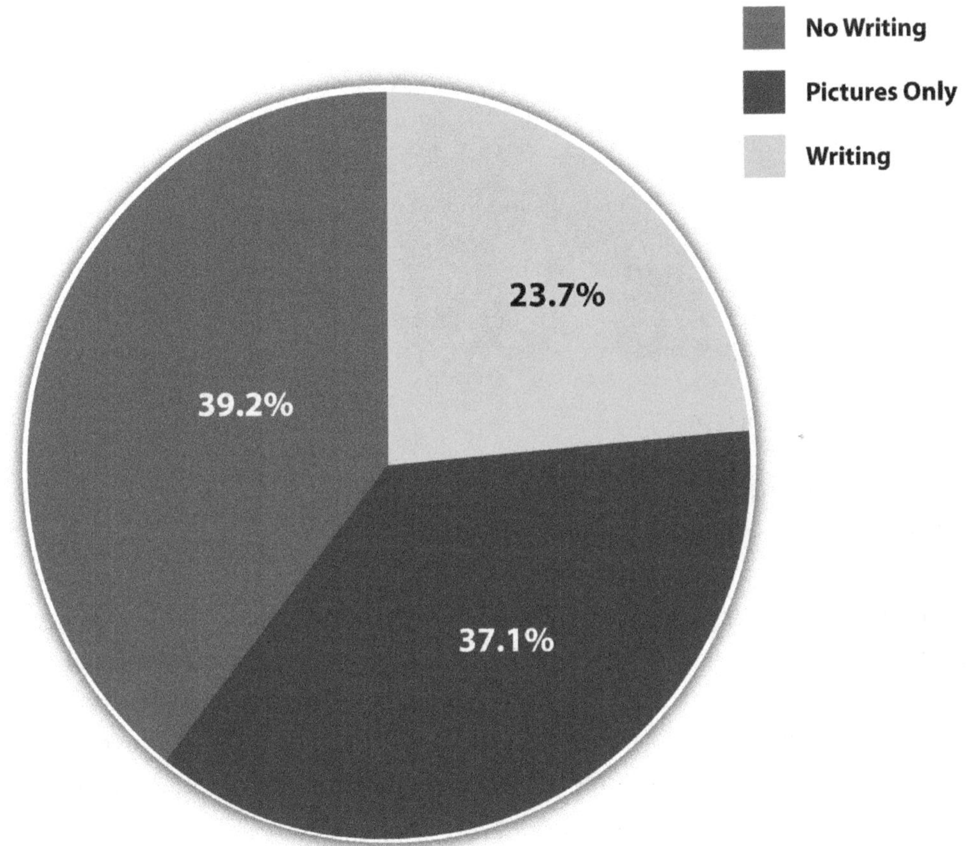

Source: Data from Standard Cross-Cultural Sample.

To what extent does language influence how we think and how we perceive the social and physical worlds? The famous but controversial **Sapir-Whorf hypothesis**, named after two linguistic anthropologists, Edward Sapir and Benjamin Lee Whorf, argues that people cannot easily understand concepts and objects unless their language contains words for these items (Whorf, 1956). Language thus influences how we understand the world around us. For example, people in a country such as the United States that has many terms for different types of kisses (e.g. buss, peck, smack, smooch, and soul) are better able to appreciate these different types than people in a country such as Japan, which, as we saw earlier, only fairly recently developed the word *kissu* for kiss.

Another illustration of the Sapir-Whorf hypothesis is seen in sexist language, in which the use of male nouns and pronouns shapes how we think about the world (Miles, 2008). In older children's books, words like fire*man* and mail*man* are common, along with pictures of men in these jobs, and critics say they send a message to children that these are male jobs, not female jobs. If a teacher tells a second-grade class, "Every student should put his books under his desk," the teacher obviously means students of both sexes but may be sending a subtle message that boys matter more than girls. For these reasons, several guidebooks promote the use of nonsexist language

(Maggio, 1998). Table 3.1 "Examples of Sexist Terms and Nonsexist Alternatives" provides examples of sexist language and nonsexist alternatives.

Table 3.1 Examples of Sexist Terms and Nonsexist Alternatives

Term	Alternative
Businessman	Businessperson, executive
Fireman	Fire fighter
Chairman	Chair, chairperson
Policeman	Police officer
Mailman	Letter carrier, postal worker
Mankind	Humankind, people
Man-made	Artificial, synthetic
Waitress	Server
He (as generic pronoun)	He or she; he/she; s/he
"A professor should be devoted to his students"	"Professors should be devoted to their students"

The use of racist language also illustrates the Sapir-Whorf hypothesis. An old saying goes, "Sticks and stones may break my bones, but names will never hurt me." That may be true in theory but not in reality. Names can hurt, especially names that are racial slurs, which African Americans growing up before the era of the civil rights movement routinely heard. According to the Sapir-Whorf hypothesis, the use of these words would have affected how whites perceived African Americans. More generally, the use of racist terms may reinforce racial prejudice and racial stereotypes.

Sociology Making a Difference

Overcoming Cultural and Ethnic Differences

People from many different racial and ethnic backgrounds live in large countries such as the United States. Because of cultural differences and various prejudices, it can be difficult for individuals from one background to interact with individuals from another background. Fortunately, a line of research, grounded in *contact theory* and conducted by sociologists and social psychologists, suggests that interaction among individuals from different backgrounds can indeed help overcome tensions arising from their different cultures and any prejudices they may hold. This happens because such contact helps disconfirm stereotypes that people may hold of those from different backgrounds (Dixon, 2006; Pettigrew & Tropp, 2005).

Recent studies of college students provide additional evidence that social contact can help overcome cultural differences and prejudices. Because many students are randomly assigned to their roommates when they enter college, interracial roommates provide a "natural" experiment for studying the effects of social interaction on racial prejudice. Studies of such roommates find that whites with black roommates report lowered racial prejudice and greater numbers of interracial friendships with other students (Laar, Levin, Sinclair, & Sidanius, 2005; Shook & Fazio, 2008).

It is not easy to overcome cultural differences and prejudices, and studies also find that interracial college roommates often have to face many difficulties in overcoming the cultural differences and prejudices that existed before they started living together (Shook & Fazio, 2008). Yet the body of work supporting contact theory suggests that efforts that increase social interaction among people from different cultural and ethnic backgrounds in the long run will reduce racial and ethnic tensions.

Norms

Cultures differ widely in their **norms**, or standards and expectations for behaving. We already saw that the nature of drunken behavior depends on society's expectations of how people should behave when drunk. Norms of drunken behavior influence how we behave when we drink too much.

Norms are often divided into two types, **formal norms** and **informal norms**. Formal norms, also called *mores* (MOOR-ayz) and *laws*, refer to the standards of behavior considered the most important in any society. Examples in the United States include traffic laws, criminal codes, and, in a college context, student behavior codes addressing such things as cheating and hate speech. Informal norms, also called *folkways* and *customs*, refer to standards of behavior that are considered less important but still influence how we behave. Table manners are a common example of informal norms, as are such everyday behaviors as how we interact with a cashier and how we ride in an elevator.

Many norms differ dramatically from one culture to the next. Some of the best evidence for cultural variation in norms comes from the study of sexual behavior (Edgerton, 1976). Among the Pokot of East Africa, for example, women are expected to enjoy sex, while among the Gusii a few hundred miles away, women who enjoy sex are considered deviant. In Inis Beag, a small island off the coast of Ireland, sex is considered embarrassing and even disgusting; men feel that intercourse drains their strength, while women consider it a burden. Even nudity is considered terrible, and people on Inis Beag keep their clothes on while they bathe. The situation is quite different in Mangaia, a small island in the South Pacific. Here sex is considered very enjoyable, and it is the major subject of songs and stories.

While many societies frown on homosexuality, others accept it. Among the Azande of East Africa, for example, young warriors live with each other and are not allowed to marry. During this time, they often have sex with younger boys, and this homosexuality is approved by their culture. Among the Sambia of New Guinea, young males live separately from females and engage in homosexual behavior for at least a decade. It is felt that the boys would be less masculine if they continued to live with their mothers and that the semen of older males helps young boys become strong and fierce (Edgerton, 1976).

Although many societies disapprove of homosexuality, other societies accept it. This difference illustrates the importance of culture for people's attitudes.

philippe leroyer – Lesbian & Gay Pride – CC BY-NC-ND 2.0.

Other evidence for cultural variation in norms comes from the study of how men and women are expected to behave in various societies. For example, many traditional societies are simple hunting-and-gathering societies. In most of these, men tend to hunt and women tend to gather. Many observers attribute this gender difference to at least two biological differences between the sexes. First, men tend to be bigger and stronger than women and are thus better suited for hunting. Second, women become pregnant and bear children and are less able to hunt. Yet a different pattern emerges in some hunting-and-gathering societies. Among a group of Australian aborigines called the Tiwi and a tribal society in the Philippines called the Agta, both sexes hunt. After becoming pregnant, Agta women continue to hunt for most of their pregnancy and resume hunting after their child is born (Brettell & Sargent, 2009).

Some of the most interesting norms that differ by culture govern how people stand apart when they talk with each other (Hall & Hall, 2007). In the United States, people who are not intimates usually stand about three to four feet apart when they talk. If someone stands more closely to us, especially if we are of northern European heritage, we feel uncomfortable. Yet people in other countries—especially Italy, France, Spain, and many of the nations of Latin America and the Middle East—would feel uncomfortable if they were standing three to four feet apart. To them, this distance is too great and indicates that the people talking dislike each other. If a U.S. native of British or Scandinavian heritage were talking with a member of one of these societies, they might well have trouble interacting, because at least one of them will be uncomfortable with the physical distance separating them.

Rituals

Different cultures also have different **rituals**, or established procedures and ceremonies that often mark transitions in the life course. As such, rituals both reflect and transmit a culture's norms and other elements from one generation to the next. Graduation ceremonies in colleges and universities are familiar examples of time-honored rituals. In many societies, rituals help signify one's gender identity. For example, girls around the world undergo various types of initiation ceremonies to mark their transition to adulthood. Among the Bemba of Zambia, girls undergo a month-long initiation ceremony called the *chisungu,* in which girls learn songs, dances, and secret terms that only women know (Maybury-Lewis, 1998). In some cultures, special ceremonies also mark a girl's first menstrual period. Such ceremonies are largely absent in the United States, where a girl's first period is a private matter. But in other cultures the first period is a cause for celebration involving gifts, music, and food (Hathaway, 1997).

Boys have their own initiation ceremonies, some of them involving circumcision. That said, the ways in which circumcisions are done and the ceremonies accompanying them differ widely. In the United States, boys who are circumcised usually undergo a quick procedure in the hospital. If their parents are observant Jews, circumcision will be part of a religious ceremony, and a religious figure called a *moyel* will perform the circumcision. In contrast, circumcision among the Maasai of East Africa is used as a test of manhood. If a boy being circumcised shows signs of fear, he might well be ridiculed (Maybury-Lewis, 1998).

Are rituals more common in traditional societies than in industrial ones such as the United States? Consider the Nacirema, studied by anthropologist Horace Miner more than 50 years ago (Miner, 1956). In this society, many rituals have been developed to deal with the culture's fundamental belief that the human body is ugly and in danger of suffering many diseases. Reflecting this belief, every household has at least one shrine in which various rituals are performed to cleanse the body. Often these shrines contain magic potions acquired from medicine men. The Nacirema are especially concerned about diseases of the mouth. Miner writes, "Were it not for the rituals of the mouth, they believe that their teeth would fall out, their gums bleed, their jaws shrink, their friends desert them, and their lovers reject them" (p. 505). Many Nacirema engage in "mouth-rites" and see a "holy-mouth-man" once or twice yearly.

Spell Nacirema backward and you will see that Miner was describing American culture. As his satire suggests, rituals are not limited to preindustrial societies. Instead, they function in many kinds of societies to mark transitions in the life course and to transmit the norms of the culture from one generation to the next.

Changing Norms and Beliefs

Our examples show that different cultures have different norms, even if they share other types of practices and beliefs. It is also true that norms change over time within a given culture. Two obvious examples here are hairstyles and clothing styles. When the Beatles first became popular in the early 1960s, their hair barely covered their ears, but parents of teenagers back then were aghast at how they looked. If anything, clothing styles change even more often than hairstyles. Hemlines go up, hemlines go down. Lapels become wider, lapels become narrower. This color is in, that color is out. Hold on to your out-of-style clothes long enough, and eventually they may well end up back in style.

Some norms may change over time within a given culture. In the early 1960s, the hair of the four members of the Beatles barely covered their ears, but many parents of U.S. teenagers were very critical of the length of their hair.

U.S. Library of Congress – public domain.

A more important topic on which norms have changed is abortion and birth control (Bullough & Bullough, 1977). Despite the controversy surrounding abortion today, it was very common in the ancient world. Much later, medieval theologians generally felt that abortion was not murder if it occurred within the first several weeks after conception. This distinction was eliminated in 1869, when Pope Pius IX declared abortion at any time to be murder. In the United States, abortion was not illegal until 1828, when New York state banned it to protect women from unskilled abortionists, and most other states followed suit by the end of the century. However, the sheer number of unsafe, illegal abortions over the next several decades helped fuel a demand for repeal of abortion laws that in turn helped lead to the *Roe v. Wade* Supreme Court decision in 1973 that generally legalized abortion during the first two trimesters.

Contraception was also practiced in ancient times, only to be opposed by early Christianity. Over the centuries, scientific discoveries of the nature of the reproductive process led to more effective means of contraception and to greater calls for its use, despite legal bans on the distribution of information about contraception. In the early 1900s, Margaret Sanger, an American nurse, spearheaded the growing birth-control movement and helped open a birth-control clinic in Brooklyn in 1916. She and two other women were arrested within 10 days, and Sanger and one other defendant were sentenced to 30 days in jail. Efforts by Sanger and other activists helped to change views on contraception over time, and finally, in 1965, the U.S. Supreme Court ruled in *Griswold v. Connecticut* that contraception information could not be banned. As this brief summary illustrates, norms about contraception changed dramatically during the last century.

Other types of cultural beliefs also change over time (Figure 3.2 "Percentage of People Who Say They Would Vote for a Qualified African American for President" and Figure 3.3 "Percentage of People Who Agree Women Should Take Care of Running Their Homes"). Since the 1960s, the U.S. public has changed its views about some important racial and gender issues. Figure 3.2 "Percentage of People Who Say They Would Vote for a Qualified African American for President", taken from several years of the General Social Survey (GSS), shows that the percentage of Americans who would vote for a qualified black person as president rose almost 20 points from the early 1970s to the middle of 1996, when the GSS stopped asking the question. If beliefs about voting for an African American had not changed, Barack Obama would almost certainly not have been elected in 2008. Figure 3.3 "Percentage of People Who Agree Women Should Take Care of Running Their Homes", also taken from several years of the GSS, shows that the percentage saying that women should take care of running their homes and leave running the country to men declined from almost 36% in the early 1970s to only about 15% in 1998, again, when the GSS stopped asking the question. These two figures depict declining racial and gender prejudice in the United States during the past quarter-century.

Figure 3.2 Percentage of People Who Say They Would Vote for a Qualified African American for President

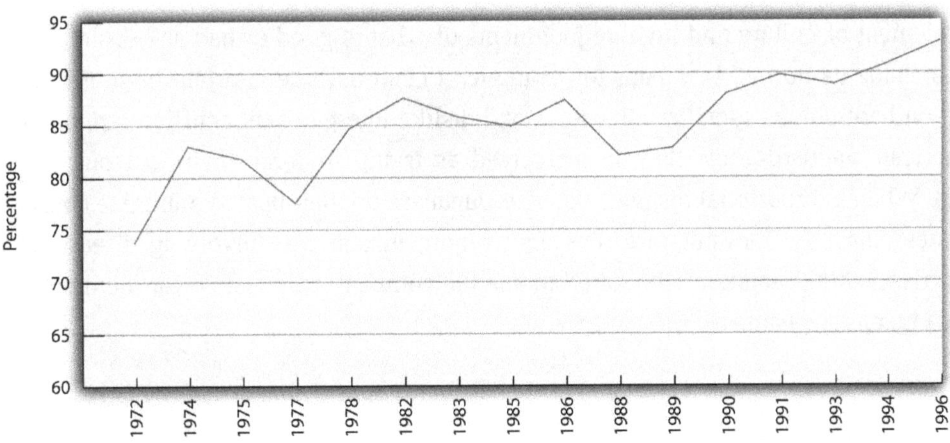

Source: Data from General Social Surveys, 1972–1996.

Figure 3.3 Percentage of People Who Agree Women Should Take Care of Running Their Homes

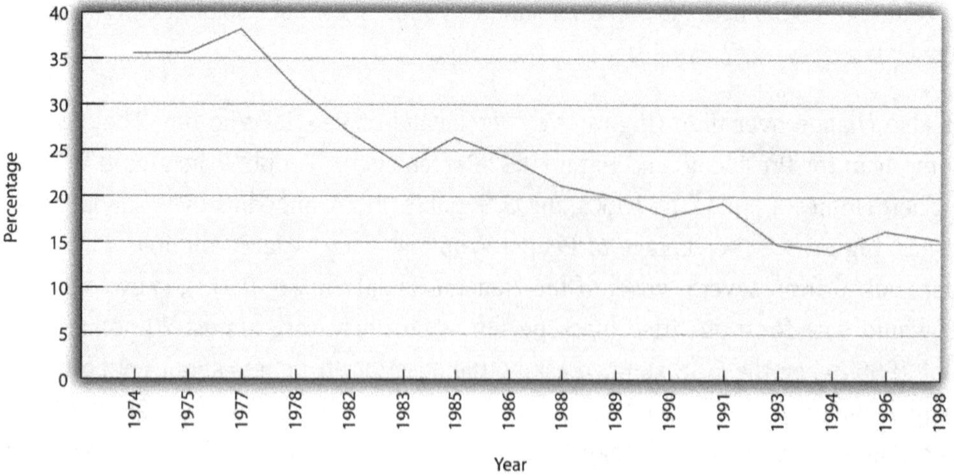

Source: Data from General Social Surveys, 1974–1998.

Values

Values are another important element of culture and involve judgments of what is good or bad and desirable or undesirable. A culture's values shape its norms. In Japan, for example, a central value is group harmony. The Japanese place great emphasis on harmonious social relationships and dislike interpersonal conflict. Individuals are fairly unassertive by American standards, lest they be perceived as trying to force their will on others (Schneider & Silverman, 2010). When interpersonal disputes do arise, Japanese do their best to minimize conflict by trying to resolve the disputes amicably. Lawsuits are thus uncommon; in one case involving disease and death from a mercury-polluted river, some Japanese who dared to sue the company responsible for the mercury poisoning were considered bad citizens (Upham, 1976).

Individualism in the United States

American culture promotes competition and an emphasis on winning in the sports and business worlds and in other spheres of life. Accordingly, lawsuits over frivolous reasons are common and even expected.

Clyde Robinson – Courtroom – CC BY 2.0.

In the United States, of course, the situation is quite different. The American culture extols the rights of the individual and promotes competition in the business and sports worlds and in other areas of life. Lawsuits over the most frivolous of issues are quite common and even expected. Phrases like "Look out for number one!" abound. If the Japanese value harmony and group feeling, Americans value competition and individualism. Because the Japanese value harmony, their norms frown on self-assertion in interpersonal relationships and on lawsuits to correct perceived wrongs. Because Americans value and even thrive on competition, our norms promote assertion in relationships and certainly promote the use of the law to address all kinds of problems.

Figure 3.4 "Percentage of People Who Think Competition Is Very Beneficial" illustrates this difference between the two nations' cultures with data from the 2002 World Values Survey (WVS), which was administered to random samples of the adult populations of more than 80 nations around the world. One question asked in these nations was, "On a scale of one ('competition is good; it stimulates people to work hard and develop new ideas') to ten ('competition is harmful; it brings out the worst in people'), please indicate your views on competition." Figure 3.4 "Percentage of People Who Think Competition Is Very Beneficial" shows the percentages of Americans and Japanese who responded with a "one" or "two" to this question, indicating they think competition is very beneficial. Americans are about three times as likely as Japanese to favor competition.

Figure 3.4 Percentage of People Who Think Competition Is Very Beneficial

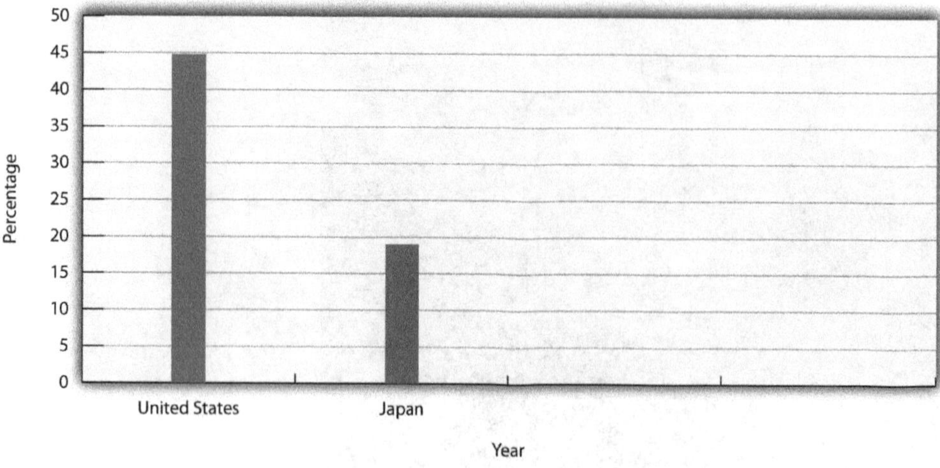

Source: Data from World Values Survey, 2002.

The Japanese value system is a bit of an anomaly, because Japan is an industrial nation with very traditional influences. Its emphasis on group harmony and community is more usually thought of as a value found in traditional societies, while the U.S. emphasis on individuality is more usually thought of as a value found in industrial cultures. Anthropologist David Maybury-Lewis (1998, p. 8) describes this difference as follows: “The heart of the difference between the modern world and the traditional one is that in traditional societies people are a valuable resource and the interrelations between them are carefully tended; in modern society things are the valuables and people are all too often treated as disposable.” In industrial societies, continues Maybury-Lewis, individualism and the rights of the individual are celebrated and any one person’s obligations to the larger community are weakened. Individual achievement becomes more important than values such as kindness, compassion, and generosity.

Other scholars take a less bleak view of industrial society, where they say the spirit of community still lives even as individualism is extolled (Bellah, Madsen, Sullivan, Swidler, & Tipton, 1985). In American society, these two simultaneous values sometimes create tension. In Appalachia, for example, people view themselves as rugged individuals who want to control their own fate. At the same time, they have strong ties to families, relatives, and their neighbors. Thus their sense of independence conflicts with their need for dependence on others (Erikson, 1976).

The Work Ethic

Another important value in the American culture is the work ethic. By the 19th century, Americans had come to view hard work not just as something that had to be done but as something that was morally good to do (Gini, 2000). The commitment to the work ethic remains strong today: in the 2008 General Social Survey, 72% of respondents said they would continue to work even if they got enough money to live as comfortably as they would like for the rest of their lives.

Cross-cultural evidence supports the importance of the work ethic in the United States. Using earlier World Values Survey data, Figure 3.5 “Percentage of People Who Take a Great Deal of Pride in Their Work” presents the percentage of people in United States and three other nations from different parts of the world—Mexico, Poland,

and Japan—who take "a great deal of pride" in their work. More than 85% of Americans feel this way, compared to much lower proportions of people in the other three nations.

Figure 3.5 Percentage of People Who Take a Great Deal of Pride in Their Work

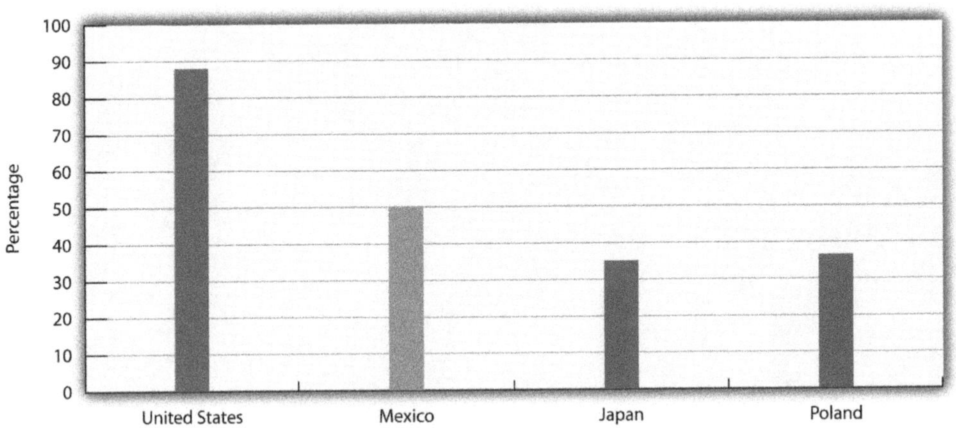

Source: Data from World Values Survey, 1993.

Closely related to the work ethic is the belief that if people work hard enough, they will be successful. Here again the American culture is especially thought to promote the idea that people can pull themselves up by their "bootstraps" if they work hard enough. The WVS asked whether success results from hard work or from luck and connections. Figure 3.6 "Percentage of People Who Think Hard Work Brings Success" presents the proportions of people in the four nations just examined who most strongly thought that hard work brings success. Once again we see evidence of an important aspect of the American culture, as U.S. residents were especially likely to think that hard work brings success.

Figure 3.6 Percentage of People Who Think Hard Work Brings Success

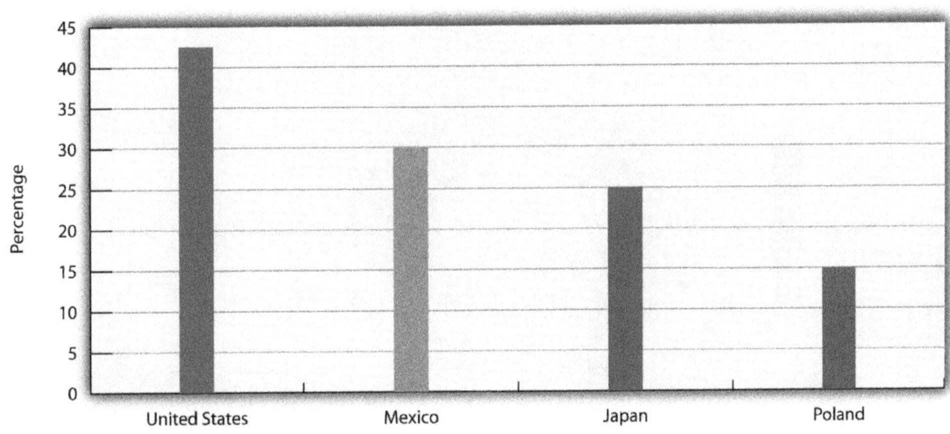

Source: Data from World Values Survey, 1997.

If Americans believe hard work brings success, then they should be more likely than people in most other nations to believe that poverty stems from not working hard enough. True or false, this belief is an example of the blaming-the-victim ideology introduced in Chapter 1 "Sociology and the Sociological Perspective". Figure 3.7 "Percentage of People Who Attribute Poverty to Laziness and Lack of Willpower" presents WVS percentages of respondents who said the most important reason people are poor is "laziness and lack of willpower." As expected, Americans are much more likely to attribute poverty to not working hard enough.

Figure 3.7 Percentage of People Who Attribute Poverty to Laziness and Lack of Willpower

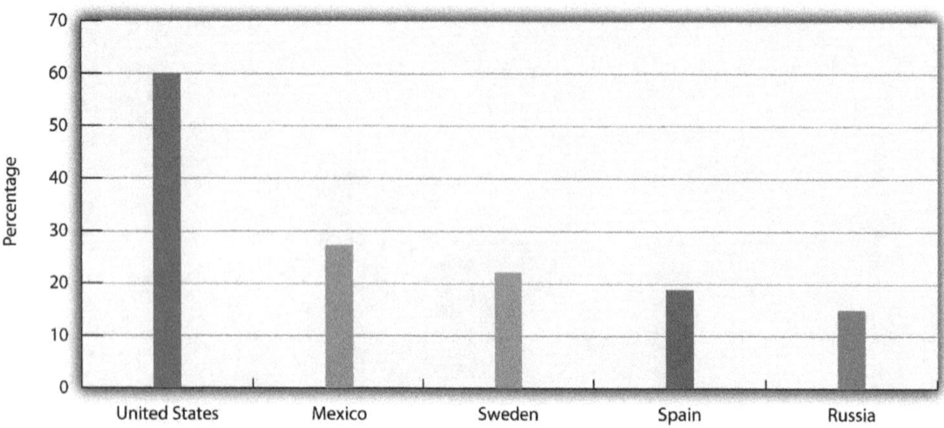

Source: Data from World Values Survey, 1997.

We could discuss many other values, but an important one concerns how much a society values women's employment outside the home. The WVS asked respondents whether they agree that "when jobs are scarce men should have more right to a job than women." Figure 3.8 "Percentage of People Who Disagree That Men Have More Right to a Job Than Women When Jobs Are Scarce" shows that U.S. residents are more likely than those in nations with more traditional views of women to *disagree* with this statement.

Figure 3.8 Percentage of People Who Disagree That Men Have More Right to a Job Than Women When Jobs Are Scarce

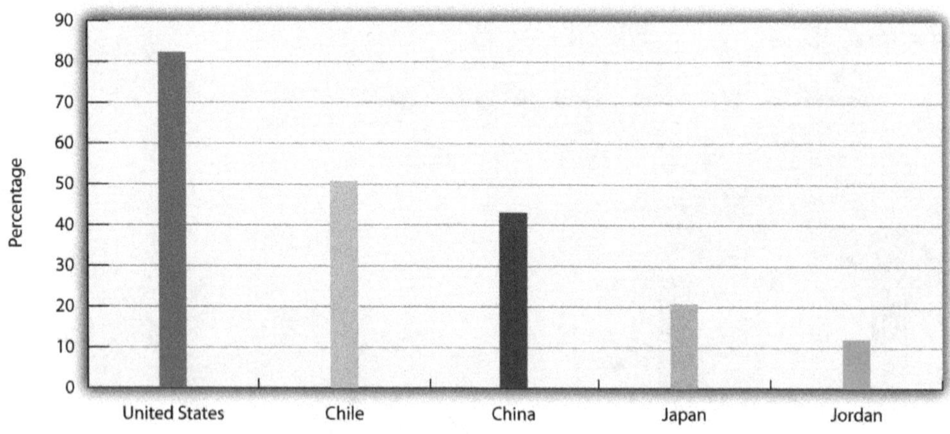

Source: Data from World Values Survey, 2002.

Artifacts

The last element of culture is the **artifacts**, or material objects, that constitute a society's material culture. In the most simple societies, artifacts are largely limited to a few tools, the huts people live in, and the clothing they wear. One of the most important inventions in the evolution of society was the wheel. Figure 3.9 "Primary Means of Moving Heavy Loads" shows that very few of the societies in the SCCS use wheels to move heavy loads over land, while the majority use human power and about one-third use pack animals.

Figure 3.9 Primary Means of Moving Heavy Loads

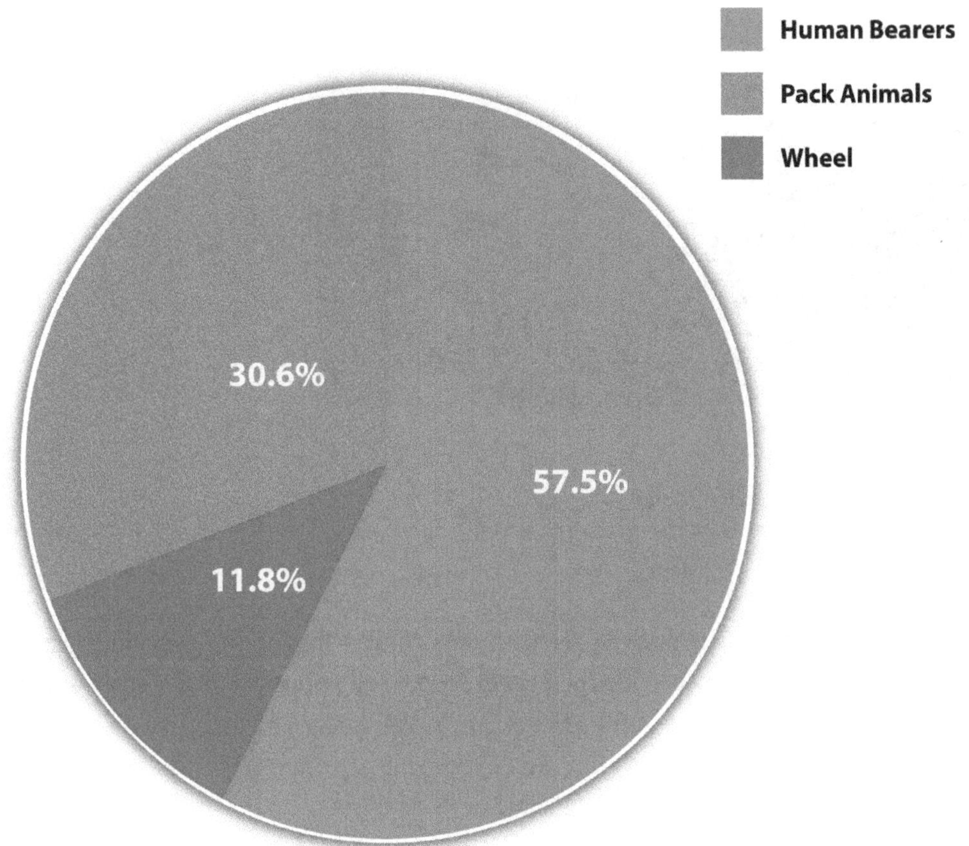

Source: Data from Standard Cross-Cultural Sample.

Although the wheel was a great invention, artifacts are much more numerous and complex in industrial societies. Because of technological advances during the past two decades, many such societies today may be said to have a *wireless* culture, as smartphones, netbooks and laptops, and GPS devices now dominate so much of modern life. The artifacts associated with this culture were unknown a generation ago. Technological development created these artifacts and new language to describe them and the functions they perform. Today's wireless artifacts in turn help reinforce our own commitment to wireless technology as a way of life, if only because children are now growing up with them, often even before they can read and write.

The iPhone is just one of the many notable cultural artifacts in today's wireless world. Technological development created these artifacts and new language to describe them and their functions—for example, "There's an app for that!"

Philip Brooks – iPhone – CC BY-NC-ND 2.0.

Sometimes people in one society may find it difficult to understand the artifacts that are an important part of another society's culture. If a member of a tribal society who had never seen a cell phone, or who had never even used batteries or electricity, were somehow to visit the United States, she or he would obviously have no idea of what a cell phone was or of its importance in almost everything we do these days. Conversely, if we were to visit that person's society, we might not appreciate the importance of some of its artifacts.

In this regard, consider once again India's cows, discussed in the news article that began this chapter. As the article mentioned, people from India consider cows holy, and they let cows roam the streets of many cities. In a nation where hunger is so rampant, such cow worship is difficult to understand, at least to Americans, because a ready source of meat is being ignored.

Anthropologist Marvin Harris (1974) advanced a practical explanation for India's cow worship. Millions of Indians are peasants who rely on their farms for their food and thus their existence. Oxen and water buffalo, not tractors, are the way they plow their fields. If their ox falls sick or dies, farmers may lose their farms. Because, as Harris observes, oxen are made by cows, it thus becomes essential to preserve cows at all costs. In India, cows also act as an essential source of fertilizer, to the tune of 700 million tons of manure annually, about half of which is used for fertilizer and the other half of which is used as fuel for cooking. Cow manure is also mixed with water and used as flooring material over dirt floors in Indian households. For all of these reasons, cow worship is not so puzzling after all, because it helps preserve animals that are very important for India's economy and other aspects of its way of life.

According to anthropologist Marvin Harris, cows are worshipped in India because they are such an important part of India's agricultural economy.

Francisco Martins – Cow in Mumbai – CC BY-NC 2.0.

If Indians exalt cows, many Jews and Muslims feel the opposite about pigs: they refuse to eat any product made from pigs and so obey an injunction from the Old Testament of the Bible and from the Koran. Harris thinks this injunction existed because pig farming in ancient times would have threatened the ecology of the Middle East. Sheep and cattle eat primarily grass, while pigs eat foods that people eat, such as nuts, fruits, and especially grains. In another problem, pigs do not provide milk and are much more difficult to herd than sheep or cattle. Next, pigs do not thrive well in the hot, dry climate in which the people of the Old Testament and Koran lived. Finally, sheep and cattle were a source of food back then because beyond their own meat they provided milk, cheese, and manure, and cattle were also used for plowing. In contrast, pigs would have provided only their own meat. Because sheep and cattle were more "versatile" in all of these ways, and because of the other problems pigs would have posed, it made sense for the eating of pork to be prohibited.

In contrast to Jews and Muslims, at least one society, the Maring of the mountains of New Guinea, is characterized by "pig love." Here pigs are held in the highest regard. The Maring sleep next to pigs, give them names and talk to them, feed them table scraps, and once or twice every generation have a mass pig sacrifice that is intended to ensure the future health and welfare of Maring society. Harris explains their love of pigs by noting that their climate is ideally suited to raising pigs, which are an important source of meat for the Maring. Because too many pigs would overrun the Maring, their periodic pig sacrifices help keep the pig population to manageable levels. Pig love thus makes as much sense for the Maring as pig hatred did for people in the time of the Old Testament and the Koran.

Key Takeaways

- The major elements of culture are symbols, language, norms, values, and artifacts.
- Language makes effective social interaction possible and influences how people conceive of concepts and objects.
- Major values that distinguish the United States include individualism, competition, and a commitment to the work ethic.

For Your Review

1. How and why does the development of language illustrate the importance of culture and provide evidence for the sociological perspective?
2. Some people say the United States is too individualistic and competitive, while other people say these values are part of what makes America great. What do you think? Why?

References

Axtell, R. E. (1998). *Gestures: The do's and taboos of body language around the world*. New York, NY: Wiley.

Bellah, R. N., Madsen, R., Sullivan, W. M., Swidler, A., & Tipton, S. M. (1985). *Habits of the heart: Individualism and commitment in American life*. Berkeley: University of California Press.

Brettell, C. B., & Sargent, C. F. (Eds.). (2009). *Gender in cross-cultural perspective* (5th ed.). Upper Saddle River, NJ: Prentice Hall.

Brown, R. (2009, January 24). Nashville voters reject a proposal for English-only. *The New York Times*, p. A12.

Bullough, V. L., & Bullough, B. (1977). *Sin, sickness, and sanity: A history of sexual attitudes*. New York, NY: New American Library.

Dixon, J. C. (2006). The ties that bind and those that don't: Toward reconciling group threat and contact theories of prejudice. *Social Forces, 84*, 2179–2204.

Edgerton, R. (1976). *Deviance: A cross-cultural perspective*. Menlo Park, CA: Cummings.

Erikson, K. T. (1976). *Everything in its path: Destruction of community in the Buffalo Creek flood*. New York, NY: Simon and Schuster.

Gini, A. (2000). *My job, my self: Work and the creation of the modern individual*. New York, NY: Routledge.

Hall, E. T., & Hall, M. R. (2007). The sounds of silence. In J. M. Henslin (Ed.), *Down to earth sociology: Introductory readings* (pp. 109–117). New York, NY: Free Press.

Harris, M. (1974). *Cows, pigs, wars, and witches: The riddles of culture*. New York, NY: Vintage Books.

Hathaway, N. (1997). Menstruation and menopause: Blood rites. In L. M. Salinger (Ed.), *Deviant behavior 97/98* (pp. 12–15). Guilford, CT: Dushkin.

Laar, C. V., Levin, S., Sinclair, S., & Sidanius, J. (2005). The effect of university roommate contact on ethnic attitudes and behavior. *Journal of Experimental Social Psychology, 41*, 329–345.

Maggio, R. (1998). *The dictionary of bias-free usage: A guide to nondiscriminatory language*. Phoenix, AZ: Oryx Press.

Maybury-Lewis, D. (1998). Tribal wisdom. In K. Finsterbusch (Ed.), *Sociology 98/99* (pp. 8–12). Guilford, CT: Dushkin/McGraw-Hill.

Miles, S. (2008). *Language and sexism*. New York, NY: Cambridge University Press.

Miner, H. (1956). Body ritual among the Nacirema. *American Anthropologist, 58*, 503–507.

Murdock, G. P., & White, D. R. (1969). Standard cross-cultural sample. *Ethnology, 8*, 329–369.

Pettigrew, T. F., & Tropp, L. R. (2005). Allport's intergroup contact hypothesis: Its history and influence. In J. F. Dovidio, P. S. Glick, & L. A. Rudman (Eds.), *On the nature of prejudice: Fifty years after Allport* (pp. 262–277). Malden, MA: Blackwell.

Ray, S. (2007). Politics over official language in the United States. *International Studies, 44*, 235–252.

Schneider, L., & Silverman, A. (2010). *Global sociology: Introducing five contemporary societies* (5th ed.). New York, NY: McGraw-Hill.

Shook, N. J., & Fazio, R. H. (2008). Interracial roommate relationships: An experimental test of the contact hypothesis. *Psychological Science, 19*, 717–723.

Shook, N. J., & Fazio, R. H. (2008). Roommate relationships: A comparison of interracial and same-race living situations. *Group Processes & Intergroup Relations, 11*, 425–437.

Upham, F. K. (1976). Litigation and moral consciousness in Japan: An interpretive analysis of four Japanese pollution suits. *Law and Society Review, 10*, 579–619.

Whorf, B. (1956). *Language, thought and reality*. Cambridge, MA: MIT Press.

3.3 Cultural Diversity

Learning Objectives

1. Define subculture and counterculture and give one example of each.
2. Distinguish cultural relativism and ethnocentrism.

These cow and pig examples remind us that material and nonmaterial cultures often make sense only in the context of a given society. If that is true, then it is important for outsiders to become familiar with other societies and to appreciate their cultural differences. These differences are often referred to as **cultural diversity**. Cultural diversity also occurs within a single society, where subcultures and countercultures can both exist.

Learning From Other Societies

Saving Dogs and Cats in South Korea

Sometimes citizens can make a difference. Dog ownership has recently been increasing in South Korea, a nation in which dogs have traditionally been preferred more as a source of food than as pets. Two individuals who can claim credit for the more humane treatment of dogs there are Kyenan Kum and Haesun Park, two women who founded the Korea Animal Protection and Education Society (KAPES; http://www.koreananimals.org/index.htm) in 2007.

The mission of KAPES is to educate South Koreans about the humane treatment of dogs and cats and to promote compassionate treatment of these pets. Kyenan Kum had previously founded the International Aid for Korean Animals (IAKA) organization in 1997, to achieve the same goals. During the next 10 years, IAKA advocated for the more humane treatment of pets and publicized their plight to other nations to help bring international pressure to bear on South Korea. In 2007, IAKA's efforts proved successful when the Korean government strengthened its Animal Protection Law. With stronger legal protections for pets in place, Kum and Park decided it was now time to focus on convincing the public that pets should be treated humanely, and they founded KAPES to achieve this goal. In December 2008, Park received an award from the Ministry of Agriculture for her efforts, which have included the holding of animal protection festivals and advocating for government funding for animal shelters.

It is not easy to confront a deeply embedded cultural practice as Kyenan Kum and Haesun Park have done. Their example offers inspiration to Americans and other citizens who also dedicate their lives to various kinds of social reforms.

The Amish in the United States are a subculture that shuns electricity and many other modern conveniences.

Shinya Suzuki – Amish – CC BY-ND 2.0.

A **subculture** refers to a group that shares the central values and beliefs of the larger culture but still retains certain values, beliefs, and norms that make it distinct from the larger culture. A good example of a U.S. subculture is the Amish, who live primarily in central Pennsylvania and parts of Ohio and shun electricity and other modern conveniences, including cars, tractors, and telephones. Their way of life is increasingly threatened by the expansion of non-Amish businesses and residences into Amish territory (Rifkin, 2009). Since the 1970s, development has cost Lancaster County, Pennsylvania—where many Amish live—thousands of acres of farming land. Some Amish families have moved to other states or left farming to start small businesses, where some do use cell phones and computers. Despite these concessions to modern development, for the most part the Amish live the way they always have. Most still do not drive cars or even ride bikes. The case of the Amish dramatically illustrates the persistence of an old-fashioned subculture and its uneasy fit with the larger, dominant culture.

A **counterculture** is a group whose values and beliefs directly oppose those of the larger culture and even reject it. Perhaps the most discussed example of a counterculture is the so-called youth counterculture of the 1960s, often referred to as the hippies but also comprising many other young people who did not fit the "tuned-out" image of the hippies and instead were politically engaged against U.S. government policy in Vietnam and elsewhere (Roszak, 1969). A contemporary example of a U.S. counterculture is the survivalists, whose extreme antigovernment views and hoarding of weapons fit them into the counterculture category (Mitchell, 2002).

Cultural Relativism and Ethnocentrism

The fact of cultural diversity raises some important but difficult questions of cultural relativism and ethnocentrism. **Cultural relativism** refers to the belief that we should not judge any culture as superior or inferior to another culture. In this view, all cultures have their benefits and disadvantages, and we should not automatically assume that our own culture is better and "their" culture is worse. **Ethnocentrism**, the opposite view, refers to the tendency to judge another culture by the standards of our own and to the belief that our own culture is indeed superior to another culture. When we think of cow worship in India, it is easy to be amused by it and even to make fun of it. That is why anthropologist Marvin Harris's analysis was so important, because it suggests that cow worship is in fact very important for the Indian way of life.

Some scholars think cultural relativism is an absolute, that we should never judge another culture's beliefs and practices as inferior to our own. Other scholars think cultural relativism makes sense up to a point, but that there are some practices that should be condemned, even if they are an important part of another culture, because they violate the most basic standards of humanity. For example, a common practice in areas of India and Pakistan is *dowry deaths*, where a husband and his relatives murder the husband's wife because her family has not provided the dowry they promised when the couple got married (Kethineni & Srinivasan, 2009). Often they burn the wife in her kitchen with cooking oil or gasoline and make it look like an accident. The number of such dowry deaths is estimated to be at least several hundred every year and perhaps as many as several thousand. Should we practice cultural relativism and not disapprove of dowry deaths? Or is it fair to condemn this practice, even if it is one that many people in those nations accept?

Dowry deaths are relatively common in certain parts of India and Pakistan. Should we practice cultural relativism and not disapprove of dowry deaths? Or is it fair to condemn this practice, even if it is one that many people in these nations accept?

Owen Young – Bishnoi grandmother – CC BY 2.0.

Because dowry death is so horrible, you might be sure we should not practice cultural relativism for this example. However, other cultural practices such as cow worship might sound odd to you but are not harmful, and you would probably agree we should accept these practices on their own terms. Other practices lie between these two extremes. Consider the eating of dog meat, which was mentioned in the "Learning From Other Societies" box. In China, South Korea, and other parts of Asia, dog meat is considered a delicacy, and people sometimes kill dogs to eat them (Dunlop, 2008). As one observer provocatively asked about eating dog meat, "For a Westerner, eating it can feel a little strange, but is it morally different from eating, say, pork? The dogs brought to table in China are not people's pets, but are raised as food, like pigs. And pigs, of course, are also intelligent and friendly" (Dunlop, 2008). Should we accept the practice of eating dog meat on its own terms? Is it any worse than eating pork or slaughtering cattle in order to eat beef? If an Asian immigrant killed and ate a dog in the United States, should that person be arrested for engaging in a practice the person grew up with? Cultural relativism and ethnocentrism certainly raise difficult issues in today's increasingly globalized world.

Key Takeaways

- Subcultures and countercultures are two types of alternative cultures that may exist amid the dominant culture.
- Cultural relativism and ethnocentrism are often in tension, and it is sometimes difficult to determine whether it is appropriate to condemn behaviors that one's own culture finds repugnant but that another culture considers appropriate.

For Your Review

1. This section discussed the eating of dog meat in some other cultures. Many Americans and Europeans condemn this practice. Do you think it is appropriate to condemn eating dog meat, or do you think such criticism violates cultural relativism and is thus inappropriate? Explain your answer.

References

Dunlop, F. (2008, August 4). It's too hot for dog on the menu. *The New York Times*, p. A19.

Kethineni, S., & Srinivasan, M. (2009). Police handling of domestic violence cases in Tamil Nadu, India. *Journal of Contemporary Criminal Justice, 25*, 202–213.

Mitchell, R. G., Jr. (2002). *Dancing at Armageddon: Survivalism and chaos in modern times*. Chicago, IL: University of Chicago Press.

Rifkin, G. (2009, January 8). The Amish flock from farms to small businesses. *The New York Times*, p. B3.

Roszak, T. (1969). *The making of a counterculture*. Garden City, NY: Doubleday.

3.4 End-of-Chapter Material

Summary

1. Culture involves the symbols, language, norms, values, and artifacts that characterize any society and that shape the thoughts, behaviors, and attitudes of the members of the society.
2. Scholars continue to debate the relative importance of biology and culture for human behavior. Sociologists favor culture over biology for several reasons, including the cultural variations existing around the world, the inability of biological explanations to account for many differences in groups' rates of behavior, and the support of biological explanations of behavior for the status quo.
3. Symbols are an important part of culture and help members of a society interact. They include both objects and nonverbal means of communication. Failure to understand the meanings of symbols can make it difficult to interact.
4. Language is another important element of culture and fundamental to communication. If the Sapir-Whorf hypothesis is correct, language shapes the thoughts and perceptions of society's members.
5. A culture's norms and values influence how people behave. When we look around the world, we see several dramatic illustrations of cross-cultural variation in norms and values. In Japan, for example, harmony is a central value, while in the United States individualism and competition prevail.
6. Artifacts are the final element of culture and may prove puzzling to people outside a given culture. However, artifacts often make much sense from the perspective of the people living amid a given culture.
7. Cultural relativism and ethnocentrism are two sides of the same coin in the issue of cultural diversity. Many societies have cultural practices that may surprise and even dismay us, and it's often difficult to decide whether we should accept or instead condemn these practices.

Using Sociology

Suppose you meet a young woman from Pakistan in one of your classes, and you gradually become friends with her. One day she tells you that after she receives her degree in sociology, she is supposed to go back to her native country to marry a man in a marriage arranged by her parents and the man's parents. She has only met this man once and is not in love with him, she tells you, but arranged marriages are part of her country's culture. Having lived in the United States for more than a year, she is beginning to dread the prospect of marrying a man she does not know and does not love. You sympathize with her plight but also remember from your introduction to sociology course that Americans should not be ethnocentric by condemning out of hand cultural practices in other nations. What, if anything, do you say to your new friend? Explain your answer.

Chapter 4: Socialization

Social Issues in the News

"Lessons from Charlie Howard's Death," the headline of the op-ed column said. On July 7, 2009, Bangor, Maine, marked the 25th anniversary of the death of Charlie Howard, an openly gay, 23-year-old man who was beaten and thrown off a bridge into a river by three teenagers on July 7, 1984. Howard could not swim and drowned. His three assailants eventually pleaded guilty to manslaughter and were sentenced to a juvenile correction center. One of the lessons of his death, wrote the columnist, a theology professor, is the need to challenge the hateful mindset that underlies homophobia. "The three youth who killed Charlie Howard were not social rebels acting out against societal norms and values," he wrote, but instead "were social conformists who thought they would be rewarded for acting in conformity to this community's norms. In fact, when the three boys returned to Bangor High School, they were cheered as heroes by their peers and some adults." (Ellison, 2009)

Why did three teenagers in a small town beat a gay man and hurl him to his death a quarter-century ago? We may never know, but it seems obvious that they had learned to hate gays from community norms back then and perhaps also from some of the many people with whom they interacted every day. This was not the first hate crime against a gay man or other individual, nor was it the last, but it nonetheless illustrates one of the ugly aspects of the many things we learn from our culture and from the people around us. We learn many good things, all necessary to have a society, but we can also learn to accept some very harmful beliefs and to practice very harmful behaviors.

The stories of Sarah Patton Boyle and Lillian Smith illustrate this all too well. Sarah Patton Boyle was born in 1906 to one of the leading families of Virginia. A great-grandfather had been a prominent attorney and acting governor of the state; both her grandfathers led illustrious military careers; her father was a respected Episcopalian minister. She was raised on the plantation on which her ancestors had once owned slaves, and her family employed several African American servants.

It was in this setting that little Sarah learned to be racially prejudiced. She was forbidden to visit the servants' rooms, which, she was told, were filthy and ridden with disease. The servants themselves were not allowed to use the family's bathroom or china, lest they spread disease from the germs they were assumed to harbor. Sarah's mother loved her servants the same way she loved the family's pets, "without the slightest feeling that they were much like herself," and taught Sarah that African Americans "belonged to a lower order of man than we" (Boyle, 1962, p. 14). When Sarah turned 12, she was told to stop playing with the servants' children because she was now too old to be "familiar" with black youngsters, and she then endured a "dreadful training period" in which she was scolded if she forgot her new, standoffish role. She was socialized during the next few years to treat whites better than blacks. When Sarah's adolescence ended, she was "as close to a typical Southern lady as anyone ever is to a typical anything" (Boyle, 1962, pp. 14, 29). Her racial views stayed with her for many years.

Whites like Sarah Patton Boyle and Lillian Smith, who grew up in the South before the 1960s civil rights movement, learned to be racially prejudiced toward African Americans.

U.S. Library of Congress – public domain.

Lillian Smith learned similar beliefs after her birth, a few years before Sarah's, to a wealthy family in Florida. She learned about taboos and manners in race relations just as she learned her games, prayers, and other childhood practices. A central lesson was that "I was better than a Negro, that all black folks have their place and must be kept in it…that a terrifying disaster would befall the South if ever I treated a Negro as my social equal" (Smith, 1949, p. 17). Her parents played a prime role in this learning process: "The mother who taught me what I know of tenderness and love and compassion taught me also the bleak rituals of keeping Negroes in their place. The father who…reminding me that 'all men are brothers,' trained me in the steel-rigid decorums I must demand of every colored male. They…taught me also to split my conscience from my acts and Christianity from Southern tradition" (Smith, 1949, pp. 17–18). These racial views also stayed with her for many years.

Thanks to the civil rights movement, the South is much different, of course, from when Sarah Patton Boyle and Lillian Smith were growing up, but their poignant descriptions and Charlie Howard's death remind us that children and adolescents learn all sorts of things, good or bad, without formal instruction. They learn these things from their parents, their friends, and other parts of their social environment. The things they learn constitute their culture: norms, values, and symbols. **Socialization** is the term sociologists use to describe the process by which people learn their culture. Socialization occurs in societies big and small, simple and complex, preindustrial and industrial. It happens in the United States, in Brazil, in Saudi Arabia, and in Indonesia. Without socialization we would not learn our culture, and, as Chapter 3 "Culture" indicated, without culture we could not have a society. Socialization, then, is an essential process for any society to be possible.

This chapter examines several aspects of socialization. In so doing, it continues developing the sociological perspective addressed by the previous chapters, as we will again see the ways in which our social environment shapes our thoughts, actions, and life chances.

References

Boyle, S. P. (1962). *The desegregated heart: A Virginian's stand in time of transition.* New York, NY: William Morrow.

Ellison, M. M. (2009, July 7). Lessons from Charlie Howard's death. *Bangor Daily News.* Retrieved from http://www.bangordailynews.com/detail/110121.html.

Smith, L. (1949). *Killers of the dream.* New York, NY: W. W. Norton.

4.1 The Importance of Socialization

Learning Objective

1. Describe why socialization is important for being fully human.

We have just noted that socialization is how culture is learned, but socialization is also important for another important reason. To illustrate this importance, let's pretend we find a 6-year-old child who has had almost no human contact since birth. After the child was born, her mother changed her diapers and fed her a minimal diet but otherwise did not interact with her. The child was left alone all day and night for years and never went outside. We now find her at the age of 6. How will her behavior and actions differ from those of the average 6-year-old? Take a moment and write down all the differences you would find.

In no particular order, here is the list you probably wrote. First, the child would not be able to speak; at most, she could utter a few grunts and other sounds. Second, the child would be afraid of us and probably cower in a corner. Third, the child would not know how to play games and interact with us. If we gave her some food and utensils, she would eat with her hands and not know how to use the utensils. Fourth, the child would be unable to express a full range of emotions. For example, she might be able to cry but would not know how to laugh. Fifth, the child would be unfamiliar with, and probably afraid of, our culture's material objects, including cell phones and televisions. In these and many other respects, this child would differ dramatically from the average 6-year-old youngster in the United States. She would *look* human, but she would not *act* human. In fact, in many ways she would act more like a frightened animal than like a young human being, and she would be less able than a typical dog to follow orders and obey commands.

As this example indicates, socialization makes it possible for us to fully function as human beings. Without socialization, we could not have our society and culture. And without social interaction, we could not have socialization. Our example of a socially isolated child was hypothetical, but real-life examples of such children, often called **feral** children, have unfortunately occurred and provide poignant proof of the importance of social interaction for socialization and of socialization for our ability to function as humans.

One of the most famous feral children was Victor of Aveyron, who was found wandering in the woods in southern France in 1797. He then escaped custody but emerged from the woods in 1800. Victor was thought to be about age 12 and to have been abandoned some years earlier by his parents; he was unable to speak and acted much more like a wild animal than a human child. Victor first lived in an institution and then in a private home. He never learned to speak, and his cognitive and social development eventually was no better than a toddler's when he finally died at about age 40 (Lane, 1976).

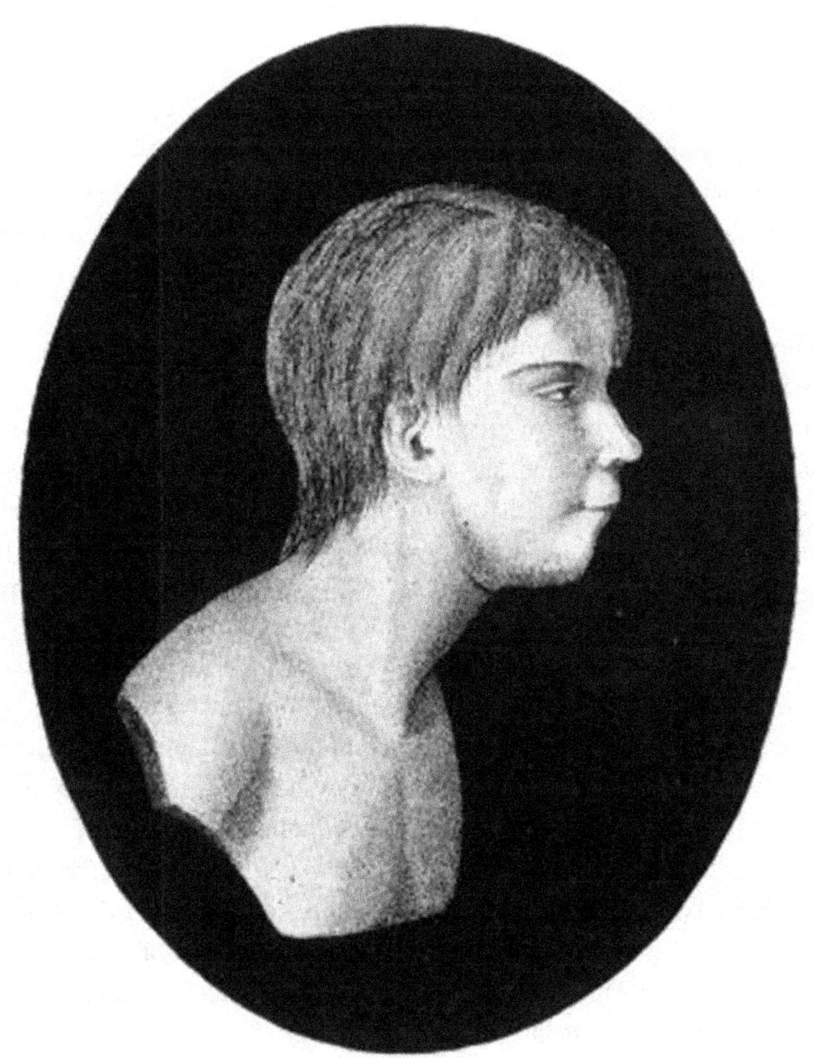

Der Wilde von Aveyron.

In rare cases, children have grown up in extreme isolation and end up lacking several qualities that make them fully human. This is a photo of Victor of Aveyron, who emerged from the woods in southern France in 1800 after apparently being abandoned by his parents some years earlier. He could not speak, and his cognitive and social skills never advanced beyond those of a small child before he died at the age of 40.

Wikimedia Commons – public domain.

Another such child, found more than about a half-century ago, was called Anna, who "had been deprived of normal contact and had received a minimum of human care for almost the whole of her first six years of life" (Davis, 1940, p. 554). After being shuttled from one residence to another for her first 5 months, Anna ended up living with her mother in her grandfather's house and was kept in a small, airless room on the second floor because the grandfather was so dismayed by her birth out of wedlock that he hated seeing her. Because her mother worked all day and would go out at night, Anna was alone almost all the time and lived in filth, often barely alive. Her only food in all those years was milk.

When Anna was found at the age of 6, she could not talk or walk or "do anything that showed intelligence" (Davis, 1940, p. 554). She was also extremely undernourished and emaciated. Two years later, she had learned to walk, understand simple commands, feed herself, and remember faces, but she could not talk and in these respects resembled a 1-year-old infant more than the 7-year-old child she really was. By the time she died of jaundice at about age 9, she had acquired the speech of a 2-year-old.

Shortly after Anna was discovered, another girl, called Isabelle, was found in similar circumstances at age 6. She was also born out of wedlock and lived alone with her mother in a dark room isolated from the rest of the mother's family. Because her mother was mute, Isabelle did not learn to speak, although she did communicate with her mother via some simple gestures. When she was finally found, she acted like a wild animal around strangers, and in other respects she behaved more like a child of 6 months than one of more than 6 years. When first shown a ball, she stared at it, held it in her hand, and then rubbed an adult's face with it. Intense training afterward helped Isabelle recover, and 2 years later she had reached a normal speaking level for a child her age (Davis, 1940).

These cases of feral children show that extreme isolation—or, to put it another way, lack of socialization—deprives children of the obvious and not-so-obvious qualities that make them human and in other respects retards their social, cognitive, and emotional development. A series of famous experiments by psychologists Harry and Margaret Harlow (1962) reinforced the latter point by showing it to be true of monkeys as well. The Harlows studied rhesus monkeys that had been removed from their mothers at birth; some were raised in complete isolation, while others were given fake mothers made of cloth and wire with which to cuddle. Neither group developed normally, although the monkeys cuddling with the fake mothers fared somewhat better than those that were totally isolated. In general, the monkeys were not able to interact later with other monkeys, and female infants abused their young when they became mothers. The longer their isolation, the more the monkeys' development suffered. By showing the dire effects of social isolation, the Harlows' experiment reinforced the significance of social interaction for normal development. Combined with the tragic examples of feral children, their experiments remind us of the critical importance of socialization and social interaction for human society.

Key Takeaways

- Socialization is the process through which individuals learn their culture and become fully human.
- Unfortunate examples of extreme human isolation illustrate the importance of socialization for children's social and cognitive development.

For Your Review

1. Do you agree that effective socialization is necessary for an individual to be fully human? Could this assumption imply that children with severe developmental disabilities, who cannot undergo effective socialization, are not fully human?

2. Do you know anyone with negative views in regard to race and ethnicity, sexual orientation, or religious preference? If so, how do you think this person acquired these views?

References

Davis, K. (1940). Extreme social isolation of a child. *American Journal of Sociology, 45,* 554–565.

Harlow, H. F., & Harlow, M. K. (1962). Social deprivation in monkeys. *Scientific American, 207,* 137–146.

Lane, H. L. (1976). *The wild boy of Aveyron*. Cambridge, MA: Harvard University Press.

4.2 Explaining Socialization

Learning Objective

1. Describe the theories of Cooley, Mead, Freud, Piaget, Kohlberg, Gilligan, and Erikson.

Because socialization is so important, scholars in various fields have tried to understand how and why it occurs, with different scholars looking at different aspects of the process. Their efforts mostly focus on infancy, childhood, and adolescence, which are the critical years for socialization, but some have also looked at how socialization continues through the life course. Let's examine some of the major theories of socialization, which are summarized in Table 4.1 "Theory Snapshot".

Table 4.1 Theory Snapshot

Theory	Major figure(s)	Major assumptions
Looking-glass self	Charles Horton Cooley	Children gain an impression of how people perceive them as the children interact with them. In effect, children "see" themselves when they interact with other people, as if they are looking in a mirror. Individuals use the perceptions that others have of them to develop judgments and feelings about themselves.
Taking the role of the other	George Herbert Mead	Children pretend to be other people in their play and in so doing learn what these other people expect of them. Younger children take the role of significant others, or the people, most typically parents and siblings, who have the most contact with them; older children when they play sports and other games take on the roles of other people and internalize the expectations of the generalized other, or society itself.
Psychoanalytic	Sigmund Freud	The personality consists of the id, ego, and superego. If a child does not develop normally and the superego does not become strong enough to overcome the id, antisocial behavior may result.
Cognitive development	Jean Piaget	Cognitive development occurs through four stages. The final stage is the formal operational stage, which begins at age 12 as children begin to use general principles to resolve various problems.
Moral development	Lawrence Kohlberg, Carol Gilligan	Children develop their ability to think and act morally through several stages. If they fail to reach the conventional stage, in which adolescents realize that their parents and society have rules that should be followed because they are morally right to follow, they might well engage in harmful behavior. Whereas boys tend to use formal rules to decide what is right or wrong, girls tend to take personal relationships into account.
Identity development	Erik Erikson	Identity development encompasses eight stages across the life course. The fifth stage occurs in adolescence and is especially critical because teenagers often experience an identity crisis as they move from childhood to adulthood.

Sociological Explanations: The Development of the Self

One set of explanations, and the most sociological of those we discuss, looks at how the **self**, or one's identity, self-concept, and self-image, develops. These explanations stress that we learn how to interact by first interacting with others and that we do so by using this interaction to gain an idea of who we are and what they expect of us.

Charles Horton Cooley

Among the first to advance this view was Charles Horton Cooley (1864–1929), who said that by interacting with other people we gain an impression of how they perceive us. In effect, we "see" ourselves when we interact with other people, as if we are looking in a mirror when we are with them. Cooley (1902) developed his famous concept of the **looking-glass self** to summarize this process. Cooley said we first imagine how we appear to others and then imagine how they think of us and, more specifically, whether they are evaluating us positively or negatively. We then use these perceptions to develop judgments and feelings about ourselves, such as pride or embarrassment.

Sometimes errors occur in this complex process, as we may misperceive how others regard us and develop misguided judgments of our behavior and feelings. For example, you may have been in a situation where someone laughed at what you said, and you thought they were mocking you, when in fact they just thought you were being funny. Although you should have interpreted their laughter positively, you interpreted it negatively and probably felt stupid or embarrassed.

Charles Horton Cooley wrote that we gain an impression of ourselves by interacting with other people. By doing so, we "see" ourselves as if we are looking in a mirror when we are with them. Cooley developed his famous concept of the looking-glass self to summarize this process.

Helena Perez García – The Looking Glass – CC BY-NC-ND 2.0.

Whether errors occur or not, the process Cooley described is especially critical during childhood and adolescence, when our self is still in a state of flux. Imagine how much better children on a sports team feel after being cheered for making a great play or how children in the school band feel after a standing ovation at the end of the band's performance. If they feel better about themselves, they may do that much better next time. For better or worse, the reverse is also true. If children do poorly on the sports field or in a school performance and the applause they hoped for does not occur, they may feel dejected and worse about themselves and from frustration or anxiety perform worse the next time around.

Yet it is also true that the looking-glass-self process affects us throughout our lives. By the time we get out of late adolescence and into our early adult years, we have very much developed our conception of our self, yet this development is never complete. As young, middle-aged, or older adults, we continue to react to our perceptions of how others view us, and these perceptions influence our conception of our self, even if this influence is often less than was true in our younger years. Whether our social interaction is with friends, relatives, coworkers, supervisors, or even strangers, our self continues to change.

George Herbert Mead

Another scholar who discussed the development of the self was George Herbert Mead (1863–1931), a founder of the field of symbolic interactionism discussed in Chapter 1 "Sociology and the Sociological Perspective". Mead's (1934) main emphasis was on children's playing, which he saw as central to their understanding of how people should interact. When they play, Mead said, children **take the role of the other**. This means they pretend to be other people in their play and in so doing learn what these other people expect of them. For example, when children play house and pretend to be their parents, they treat their dolls the way they think their parents treat them. In so doing, they get a better idea of how they are expected to behave. Another way of saying this is that they internalize the expectations other people have of them.

Younger children, said Mead, take the role of **significant others**, or the people, most typically parents and siblings, who have the most contact with them. Older children take on the roles of other people and learn society's expectations as a whole. In so doing, they internalize the expectations of what Mead called the **generalized other**, or society itself.

This whole process, Mead wrote, involves several stages. In the *imitation* stage, infants can only imitate behavior without really understanding its purposes. If their parents rub their own bellies and laugh, 1-year-olds may do likewise. After they reach the age of 3, they are in the *play* stage. Here most of their play is by themselves or with only one or two other children, and much of it involves pretending to be other people: their parents, teachers, superheroes, television characters, and so forth. In this stage they begin taking the role of the other. Once they reach age 6 or 7, or roughly the time school begins, the *games* stage begins, and children start playing in team sports and games. The many players in these games perform many kinds of roles, and they must all learn to anticipate the actions of other members of their team. In so doing, they learn what is expected of the roles all team members are supposed to play and by extension begin to understand the roles society wants us to play, or to use Mead's term, the expectations of the generalized other.

Mead felt that the self has two parts, the *I* and the *me*. The *I* is the creative, spontaneous part of the self, while the *me* is the more passive part of the self stemming from the internalized expectations of the larger society. These two parts are not at odds, he thought, but instead complement each other and thus enhance the individual's contributions to society. Society needs creativity, but it also needs at least some minimum of conformity. The development of both these parts of the self is important not only for the individual but also for the society to which the individual belongs.

Social-Psychological Explanations: Personality and Cognitive and Moral Development

A second set of explanations is more psychological, as it focuses on the development of personality, cognitive ability, and morality.

Sigmund Freud and the Unconscious Personality

Whereas Cooley and Mead focused on interaction with others in explaining the development of the self, the great psychoanalyst Sigmund Freud (1856–1939) focused on unconscious, biological forces that he felt shape individual personality. Freud (1933) thought that the personality consists of three parts: the **id**, **ego**, and **superego**. The id is the selfish part of the personality and consists of biological instincts that all babies have, including the need for food and, more generally, the demand for immediate gratification. As babies get older, they learn that not all their needs can be immediately satisfied and thus develop the ego, or the rational part of the personality. As children get older still, they internalize society's norms and values and thus begin to develop their superego, which represents society's conscience. If a child does not develop normally and the superego does not become strong enough, the individual is more at risk for being driven by the id to commit antisocial behavior.

Sigmund Freud believed that the personality consists of three parts: the id, ego, and superego. The development of these biological forces helps shape an individual's personality.

Wikimedia Commons – public domain.

Freud's basic view that an individual's personality and behavior develop largely from within differs from sociology's emphasis on the social environment. That is not to say his view is wrong, but it is to say that it neglects the many very important influences highlighted by sociologists.

Piaget and Cognitive Development

Children acquire a self and a personality but they also learn how to think and reason. How they acquire such *cognitive development* was the focus of research by Swiss psychologist Jean Piaget (1896–1980). Piaget (1954) thought that cognitive development occurs through four stages and that proper maturation of the brain and socialization were necessary for adequate development.

The first stage is the *sensorimotor* stage, in which infants cannot really think or reason and instead use their hearing, vision, and other senses to discover the world around them. The second stage is the *preoperational* stage, lasting from about age 2 to age 7, in which children begin to use symbols, especially words, to understand objects and simple ideas. The third stage is the *concrete operational* stage, lasting from about age 7 to age 11 or 12, in which children begin to think in terms of cause and effect but still do not understand underlying principles of fairness, justice, and related concepts. The fourth and final stage is the *formal operational* stage, which begins about the age of 12. Here children begin to think abstractly and use general principles to resolve various problems.

Recent research supports Piaget's emphasis on the importance of the early years for children's cognitive development. Scientists have found that brain activity develops rapidly in the earliest years of life. Stimulation from a child's social environment enhances this development, while a lack of stimulation impairs it. Children whose parents or other caregivers routinely play with them and talk, sing, and read to them have much better neurological and cognitive development than other children (Riley, San Juan, Klinkner, & Ramminger, 2009). By providing a biological basis for the importance of human stimulation for children, this research underscores both the significance of interaction and the dangers of social isolation. For both biological and social reasons, socialization is not fully possible without extensive social interaction.

Kohlberg, Gilligan, and Moral Development

An important part of children's reasoning is their ability to distinguish right from wrong and to decide on what is morally correct to do. Psychologist Lawrence Kohlberg (1927–1987) said that children develop their ability to think and act morally through several stages. In the *preconventional* stage, young children equate what is morally right simply to what keeps them from getting punished. In the *conventional* stage, adolescents realize that their parents and society have rules that should be followed because they are morally right to follow, not just because disobeying them leads to punishment. At the *postconventional* stage, which occurs in late adolescence and early adulthood, individuals realize that higher moral standards may supersede those of their own society and even decide to disobey the law in the name of these higher standards. If people fail to reach at least the conventional stage, Kohlberg (1969) said, they do not develop a conscience and instead might well engage in harmful behavior if they think they will not be punished. Incomplete moral development, Kohlberg concluded, was a prime cause of antisocial behavior.

Carol Gilligan believes that girls take personal relationships into account during their moral development.

Vladimir Pustovit – Girls – CC BY 2.0.

One limitation of Kohlberg's research was that he studied only boys. Do girls go through similar stages of moral development? Carol Gilligan (1982) concluded that they do not. Whereas boys tend to use formal rules to decide what is right or wrong, she wrote, girls tend to take personal relationships into account. If people break a rule because of some important personal need or because they are trying to help someone, then their behavior may not be wrong. Put another way, males tend to use impersonal, *universalistic* criteria for moral decision making, whereas females tend to use more individual, *particularistic* criteria.

An example from children's play illustrates the difference between these two forms of moral reasoning. If boys are playing a sport, say basketball, and a player says he was fouled, they may disagree—sometimes heatedly—over how much contact occurred and whether it indeed was enough to be a foul. In contrast, girls in a similar situation may decide in the interest of having everyone get along to call the play a "do-over."

Erikson and Identity Development

We noted earlier that the development of the self is not limited to childhood but instead continues throughout the life span. More generally, although socialization is most important during childhood and adolescence, it, too, continues throughout the life span. Psychologist Erik Erikson (1902–1990) explicitly recognized this central fact in his theory of *identity development* (Erikson, 1980). This sort of development, he said, encompasses eight stages of life across the life course. In the first four stages, occurring in succession from birth to age 12, children ideally learn trust, self-control, and independence and also learn how to do tasks whose complexity increases with their age. If all this development goes well, they develop a positive identity, or self-image.

The fifth stage occurs in adolescence and is especially critical, said Erikson, because teenagers often experience an *identity crisis*. This crisis occurs because adolescence is a transition between childhood and adulthood: adolescents are leaving childhood but have not yet achieved adulthood. As they try to work through all the complexities of adolescence, teenagers may become rebellious at times, but most eventually enter young adulthood with their identities mostly settled. Stages 6, 7, and 8 involve young adulthood, middle adulthood, and late adulthood, respectively. In each of these stages, people's identity development is directly related to their family and work roles. In late adulthood, people reflect on their lives while trying to remain contributing members of society. Stage 8 can be a particularly troubling stage for many people, as they realize their lives are almost over.

Erikson's research helped stimulate the further study of socialization past adolescence, and today the study of socialization during the years of adulthood is burgeoning. We return to adulthood in Chapter 4 "Socialization", Section 4.4 "Socialization Through the Life Course" and address it again in the discussion of age and aging in Chapter 12 "Aging and the Elderly".

Key Takeaways

- Cooley and Mead explained how one's self-concept and self-image develop.
- Freud focused on the need to develop a proper balance among the id, ego, and superego.
- Piaget wrote that cognitive development among children and adolescents occurs from four stages of social interaction.
- Kohlberg wrote about stages of moral development and emphasized the importance of formal rules, while Gilligan emphasized that girls' moral development takes into account personal relationships.
- Erikson's theory of identity development encompasses eight stages, from infancy through old age.

For Your Review

1. Select one of the theories of socialization in this section, and write about how it helps you to understand your own socialization.
2. Gilligan emphasized that girls take social relationships into account in their moral development, while boys tend to stress the importance of formal rules. Do you agree with her argument? Why or why not?

References

Cooley, C. H. (1902). *Social organization*. New York, NY: Scribner's.

Erikson, E. H. (1980). *Identity and the life cycle*. New York, NY: Norton.

Freud, S. (1933). *New introductory lectures on psycho-analysis*. New York, NY: Norton.

Gilligan, C. (1982). *In a different voice: Psychological theory and women's development*. Cambridge, MA: Harvard University Press.

Kohlberg, L. (1969). *States in the development of moral thought and action*. New York, NY: Holt, Rinehart and Winston.

Mead, G. H. (1934). *Mind, self, and society*. Chicago, IL: University of Chicago Press.

Piaget, J. (1954). *The construction of reality in the child*. New York, NY: Basic Books.

Riley, D., San Juan, R. R., Klinkner, J., & Ramminger, A. (2009). *Intellectual development: Connecting science and practice in early childhood settings*. St. Paul, MN: Redleaf Press.

4.3 Agents of Socialization

Learning Objectives

1. Identify five agents of socialization.
2. Describe positive and negative aspects of the socialization these agents produce.

Several institutional and other sources of socialization exist and are called *agents of socialization*. The first of these, the family, is certainly the most important agent of socialization for infants and young children.

The Family

The family is perhaps the most important agent of socialization for children. Parents' values and behavior patterns profoundly influence those of their daughters and sons.

Randen Pederson – Family – CC BY 2.0.

Should parents get the credit when their children turn out to be good kids and even go on to accomplish great things in life? Should they get the blame if their children turn out to be bad? No parent deserves all the credit or blame for their children's successes and failures in life, but the evidence indicates that our parents do affect us profoundly. In many ways, we even end up resembling our parents in more than just appearance.

Sociology Making a Difference

Understanding Racial Socialization

In a society that is still racially prejudiced, African American parents continue to find it necessary to teach their children about African American culture and to prepare them for the bias and discrimination they can expect to encounter. Scholars in sociology and other disciplines have studied this process of *racial socialization*. One of their most interesting findings is that African American parents differ in the degree of racial socialization they practice: some parents emphasize African American identity and racial prejudice to a considerable degree, while other parents mention these topics to their children only minimally. The reasons for these differences have remained unclear.

Sociologist Jason E. Shelton (2008) analyzed data from a national random sample of African Americans to determine these reasons, in what he called "one of the most comprehensive analyses to date of racial socialization strategies among African Americans" (p. 237). Among other questions, respondents were asked whether "in raising your children, have you done or told them things to help them know what it means to be Black." They were also asked whether "there are any other things you've done or told your children to help them know how to get along with White people."

In his major results, Shelton found that respondents were more likely to practice racial socialization if they were older, female, and living outside the South; if they perceived that racial discrimination was a growing problem and were members of civil rights or other organization aimed at helping African Americans; and if they had higher incomes.

These results led Shelton to conclude that "African Americans are not a culturally monolithic group," as they differ in "the parental lessons they impart to their children about race relations" (2008, p. 253). Further, the parents who do practice racial socialization "do so in order to demystify and empower their offspring to seize opportunities in the larger society" (p. 253).

Shelton's study helps us to understand the factors accounting for differences in racial socialization by African American parents, and it also helps us understand that the parents who do attempt to make their children aware of U.S. race relations are merely trying, as most parents do, to help their children get ahead in life. By increasing our understanding of these matters, Shelton's research has helped make a difference.

The reason we turn out much like our parents, for better or worse, is that our families are such an important part of our socialization process. When we are born, our primary caregivers are almost always one or both of our parents. For several years we have more contact with them than with any other adults. Because this contact occurs in our most formative years, our parents' interaction with us and the messages they teach us can have a profound impact throughout our lives, as indicated by the stories of Sarah Patton Boyle and Lillian Smith presented earlier.

The ways in which our parents socialize us depend on many factors, two of the most important of which are our parents' social class and our own biological sex. Melvin Kohn (1965, 1977) found that working-class and middle-class parents tend to socialize their children very differently. Kohn reasoned that working-class parents tend to hold factory and other jobs in which they have little autonomy and instead are told what to do and how to do it. In such jobs, obedience is an important value, lest the workers be punished for not doing their jobs correctly. Working-class parents, Kohn thought, should thus emphasize obedience and respect for authority as they raise their children, and they should favor spanking as a primary way of disciplining their kids when they disobey. In contrast, middle-class parents tend to hold white-collar jobs where autonomy and independent judgment are valued and workers get ahead by being creative. These parents should emphasize independence as they raise their children and should be less likely than working-class parents to spank their kids when they disobey.

If parents' social class influences how they raise their children, it is also true that the sex of their children affects how they are socialized by their parents. Many studies find that parents raise their daughters and sons quite differently as they interact with them from birth. We will explore this further in Chapter 11 "Gender and Gender

Inequality", but suffice it to say here that parents help their girls learn how to act and think "like girls," and they help their boys learn how to act and think "like boys." That is, they help their daughters and sons learn their gender (Wood, 2009). For example, they are gentler with their daughters and rougher with their sons. They give their girls dolls to play with, and their boys guns. Girls may be made of "sugar and spice and everything nice" and boys something quite different, but their parents help them greatly, for better or worse, turn out that way. To the extent this is true, our gender stems much more from socialization than from biological differences between the sexes, or so most sociologists probably assume. To return to a question posed earlier, if Gilligan is right that boys and girls reach moral judgments differently, socialization matters more than biology for how they reach these judgments.

As the "Learning From Other Societies" box illustrates, various cultures socialize their children differently. We can also examine cross-cultural variation in socialization with data from the World Values Survey, which was administered to almost six dozen nations. Figure 4.1 "Percentage Believing That Obedience Is Especially Important for a Child to Learn" shows the percentage of people in several countries who think it is "especially important for children to learn obedience at home." Here we see some striking differences in the value placed on obedience, with the United States falling somewhat in between the nations in the figure.

Learning From Other Societies

Children and Socialization in Japan

This chapter ends with the observation that American children need to be socialized with certain values in order for our society to be able to address many of the social issues, including hate crimes and violence against women, facing it. As we consider the socialization of American children, the experience of Japan offers a valuable lesson.

Recall from Chapter 2 "Eye on Society: Doing Sociological Research" that Japan's culture emphasizes harmony, cooperation, and respect for authority. Socialization in Japan is highly oriented toward the teaching of the values just listed, with much of it stressing the importance of belonging to a group and dependence, instead of individual autonomy and independence. This is especially true in Japanese schools, which, as two sociologists write, "stress the similarity of all children, and the importance of the group" (Schneider & Silverman, 2010, p. 24). Let's see how this happens (Hendry, 1987; Schwalb & Schwalb, 1996).

From the time they begin school, Japanese children learn to value their membership in their homeroom, or *kumi*, and they spend several years in the same *kumi*. Each *kumi* treats its classroom as a "home away from home," as the children arrange the classroom furniture, bring in plants and other things from their own homes, and clean the classroom every day. At recess one *kumi* will play against another. In an interesting difference from standard practice in the United States, a *kumi* in junior high school will stay in its classroom while the teachers for, say, math and social science move from one classroom to another. In the United States, of course, the opposite is true: teachers stay in their classrooms, and students move from one room to another.

Other practices in Japanese schools further the learning of Japanese values. Young schoolchildren wear the same uniforms. Japanese teachers use constant drills to teach them how to bow, and they have the children repeatedly stand up and sit down as a group. These practices help students learn respect for authority and help enhance the sense of group belonging that the *kumi* represents. Whereas teachers in the United States routinely call on individual students to answer a question, Japanese teachers rarely do this. Rather than competing with each other for a good grade, Japanese schoolchildren are evaluated according to the performance of the *kumi* as a whole. Because decision making within the *kumi* is done by consensus, the children learn the need to compromise and to respect each other's feelings.

Because the members of a *kumi* spend so much time together for so many years, they develop extremely close friendships and think of themselves more as members of the *kumi* than as individuals. They become very loyal to the *kumi* and put its interests above their own individual interests. In these and other ways, socialization in Japanese schools helps the children and adolescents there learn the Japanese values of harmony, group loyalty, and respect for authority. If American children learned these values to a greater degree, it would be easier to address violence and other issues facing the United States.

Figure 4.1 Percentage Believing That Obedience Is Especially Important for a Child to Learn

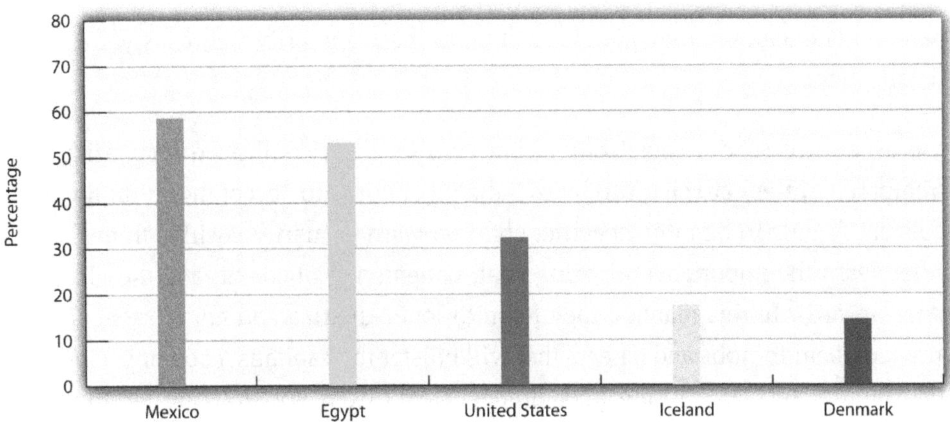

Source: Data from World Values Survey, 2002.

Schools

Schools socialize children by teaching them their formal curricula but also a hidden curriculum that imparts the cultural values of the society in which the schools are found. One of these values is the need to respect authority, as evidenced by these children standing in line.

Wikimedia Commons – public domain.

Schools socialize children in several ways. First, students learn a formal curriculum, informally called the "three Rs": reading, writing, and arithmetic. This phase of their socialization is necessary for them to become productive members of their society. Second, because students interact every day at school with their peers, they ideally strengthen their social interaction skills. Third, they interact with authority figures, their teachers, who are not their parents. For children who have not had any preschooling, their teachers are often the first authority figures they have had other than their parents. The learning they gain in relating to these authority figures is yet another important component of their socialization.

Functional theorists cite all these aspects of school socialization, but conflict theorists instead emphasize that schools in the United States also impart a **hidden curriculum** by socializing children to accept the cultural values of the society in which the schools are found. To be more specific, children learn primarily positive things about the country's past and present; they learn the importance of being neat, patient, and obedient; and they learn to compete for good grades and other rewards. In this manner, they learn to love America and not to recognize its faults, and they learn traits that prepare them for jobs and careers that will bolster the capitalist economy. Children are also socialized to believe that failure, such as earning poor grades, stems from not studying hard enough and, more generally, from not trying hard enough (Booher-Jennings, 2008; Bowles & Gintis, 1976). This process reinforces the blaming-the-victim ideology discussed in Chapter 1 "Sociology and the Sociological Perspective". Schools are also a significant source of gender socialization, as even in this modern day, teachers and curricula send out various messages that reinforce the qualities traditionally ascribed to females and males, and students engage in recess and other extracurricular activities that do the same thing (Booher-Jennings, 2008; Thorne, 1993).

Peers

When you were a 16-year-old, how many times did you complain to your parent(s), "All of my friends are [doing so and so]. Why can't I? It isn't fair!" As this all-too-common example indicates, our friends play a very important role in our lives. This is especially true during adolescence, when peers influence our tastes in music, clothes, and so many other aspects of our lives, as the now-common image of the teenager always on a cell phone reminds us. But friends are important during other parts of the life course as well. We rely on them for fun, for emotional comfort and support, and for companionship. That is the upside of friendships.

Our peers also help socialize us and may even induce us to violate social norms.

Tony – Peer Pressure – CC BY-SA 2.0.

The downside of friendships is called *peer pressure*, with which you are undoubtedly familiar. Suppose it is Friday night, and you are studying for a big exam on Monday. Your friends come by and ask you to go with them to get a pizza and a drink. You would probably agree to go with them, partly because you really dislike studying on a Friday night, but also because there is at least some subtle pressure on you to do so. As this example indicates, our friends can influence us in many ways. During adolescence, their interests can affect our own interests in film, music, and other aspects of popular culture. More ominously, adolescent peer influences have been implicated in underage drinking, drug use, delinquency, and hate crimes, such as the killing of Charlie Howard, recounted at the beginning of this chapter (Agnew, 2007) (see Chapter 5 "Social Structure and Social Interaction").

After we reach our 20s and 30s, our peers become less important in our lives, especially if we get married. Yet even then our peers do not lose all their importance, as married couples with young children still manage to get out with friends now and then. Scholars have also begun to emphasize the importance of friendships with coworkers for emotional and practical support and for our continuing socialization (Elsesser & Peplau, 2006; Marks, 1994).

The Mass Media

The mass media are another agent of socialization. Television shows, movies, popular music, magazines, Web sites, and other aspects of the mass media influence our political views; our tastes in popular culture; our views of women, people of color, and gays; and many other beliefs and practices.

In an ongoing controversy, the mass media are often blamed for youth violence and many other of our society's ills. The average child sees thousands of acts of violence on television and in the movies before reaching young adulthood. Rap lyrics often seemingly extol very ugly violence, including violence against women. Commercials can greatly influence our choice of soda, shoes, and countless other products. The mass media also reinforce racial and gender stereotypes, including the belief that women are sex objects and suitable targets of male violence. In the General Social Survey (GSS), about 28% of respondents said that they watch four or more hours of television every day, while another 46% watch two to three hours daily (see Figure 4.2 "Average Number of Hours of Television Watched Daily"). The mass media certainly are an important source of socialization unimaginable a half-century ago.

Figure 4.2 Average Number of Hours of Television Watched Daily

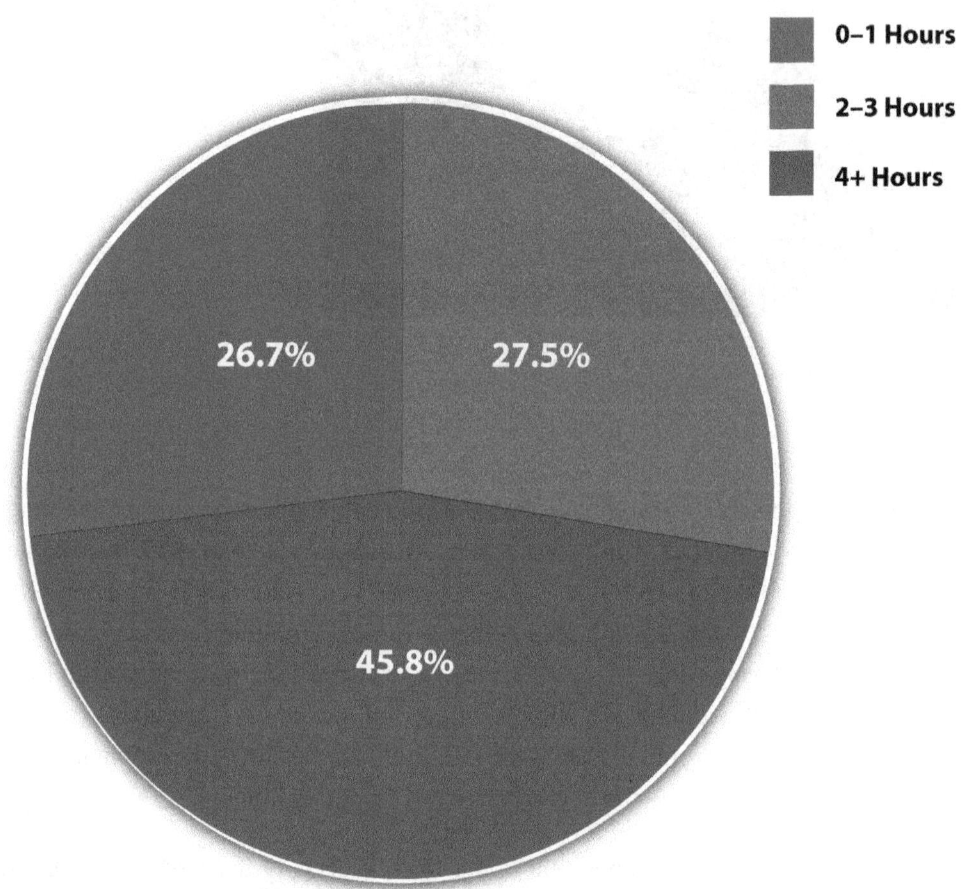

Source: Data from General Social Survey, 2008.

As the mass media socialize children, adolescents, and even adults, a key question is the extent to which media violence causes violence in our society (Surette, 2011). Studies consistently uncover a strong correlation between watching violent television shows and movies and committing violence. However, this does not necessarily mean that watching the violence actually causes violent behavior: perhaps people watch violence because they are already interested in it and perhaps even committing it. Scholars continue to debate the effect of media violence on youth violence. In a free society, this question is especially important, as the belief in this effect has prompted calls for monitoring the media and the banning of certain acts of violence. Civil libertarians argue that such calls smack of censorship that violates the First Amendment to the Constitution, whole others argue that they fall within the

First Amendment and would make for a safer society. Certainly the concern and debate over mass media violence will continue for years to come.

Religion

One final agent of socialization is religion, discussed further in Chapter 12 “Aging and the Elderly”. Although religion is arguably less important in people’s lives now than it was a few generations ago, it still continues to exert considerable influence on our beliefs, values, and behaviors.

Here we should distinguish between *religious preference* (e.g., Protestant, Catholic, or Jewish) and *religiosity* (e.g., how often people pray or attend religious services). Both these aspects of religion can affect your values and beliefs on religious and nonreligious issues alike, but their particular effects vary from issue to issue. To illustrate this, consider the emotionally charged issue of abortion. People hold very strong views on abortion, and many of their views stem from their religious beliefs. Yet which aspect of religion matters the most, religious preference or religiosity? General Social Survey data help us answer this question (Figure 4.3 “Religious Preference, Religiosity, and Belief That Abortion Should Be Legal for Any Reason”). It turns out that religious preference, if we limit it for the sake of this discussion to Catholics versus Protestants, does not matter at all: Catholics and Protestants in the GSS exhibit roughly equal beliefs on the abortion issue, as about one-third of each group thinks abortion should be allowed for any reason. (The slight difference shown in the table is not statistically significant.) However, religiosity matters a lot: GSS respondents who pray daily are only about half as likely as those who rarely or never pray to think abortion should be allowed.

Figure 4.3 Religious Preference, Religiosity, and Belief That Abortion Should Be Legal for Any Reason

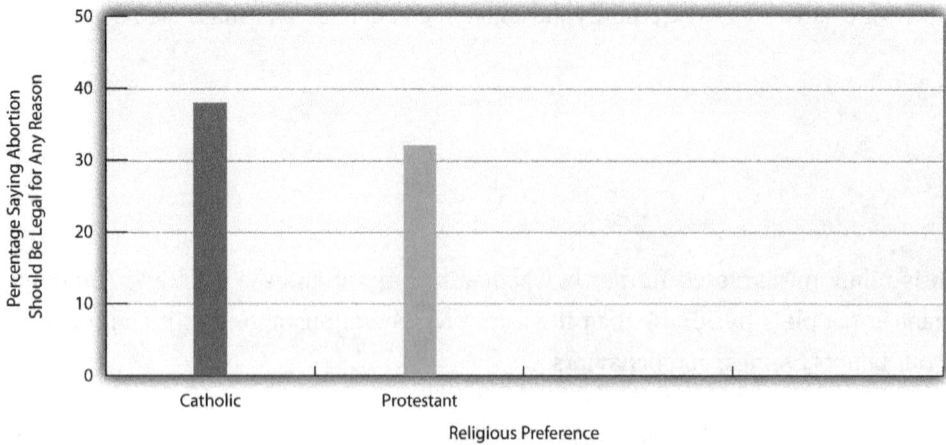

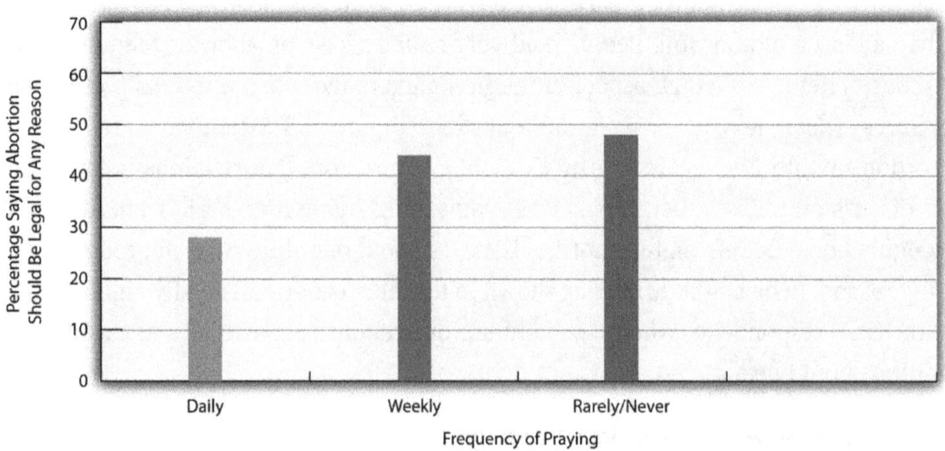

Source: Data from General Social Survey, 2008.

Key Takeaways

- The ways in which parents socialize children depend in part on the parents' social class and on their child's biological sex.
- Schools socialize children by teaching them both the formal curriculum and a hidden curriculum.
- Peers are an important source of emotional support and companionship, but peer pressure can induce individuals to behave in ways they might ordinarily regard as wrong.
- The mass media are another important agent of socialization, and scholars debate the effect the media have on violence in society.
- In considering the effects of religion on socialization, we need to distinguish between religious preference and religiosity.

For Your Review

1. Describe one important value or attitude you have that is the result of socialization by your parent(s).
2. Do you agree that there is a hidden curriculum in secondary schools? Explain your answer.
3. Briefly describe one example of how peers influenced you or someone you know in a way that you now regard as negative.

References

Agnew, R. (2007). *Pressured into crime: An overview of general strain theory*. New York, NY: Oxford University Press.

Booher-Jennings, J. (2008). Learning to label: Socialisation, gender, and the hidden curriculum of high-stakes testing. *British Journal of Sociology of Education, 29*, 149–160.

Bowles, S., & Gintis, H. (1976). *Schooling in capitalist America: Educational reforms and the contradictions of economic life*. New York, NY: Basic Books.

Elsesser, K., & Peplau, L. A. (2006). The glass partition: Obstacles to cross-sex friendships at work. *Human Relations, 59*, 1077–1100.

Hendry, J. (1987). *Understanding Japanese society*. London, England: Croom Helm.

Kohn, M. (1977). *Class and conformity*. Homewood, IL: Dorsey.

Kohn, M. (1965). Social class and parent-child relationships: An interpretation. *American Journal of Sociology, 68*, 471–480.

Marks, S. R. (1994). Intimacy in the public realm: The case of co-workers. *Social Forces, 72*, 843–858.

Schneider, L., & Silverman, A. (2010). *Global sociology: Introducing five contemporary societies* (5th ed.). New York, NY: McGraw-Hill.

Schwalb, D. W., & Schwalb, B. J. (Eds.). (1996). *Japanese childrearing: Two generations of scholarship*. New York, NY: Guilford Press.

Shelton, J. E. (2008). The investment in blackness hypothesis: Toward greater understanding of who teaches what during racial socialization. *Du Bois Review: Social Science Research on Race*, 5(2), 235–257.

Surette, R. (2011). *Media, crime, and criminal justice: Images, realities, and policies* (4th ed.). Belmont, CA: Wadsworth.

Thorne, B. (1993). *Gender play: Girls and boys in school*. New Brunswick, NJ: Rutgers University Press.

Wood, J. T. (2009). *Gendered lives: Communication, gender, and culture*. Belmont, CA: Wadsworth.

4.4 Socialization Through the Life Course

Learning Objectives

1. List the major changes of the life course.
2. Provide an example of how events during childhood may have a lifelong impact.

As you probably realize by now, most theories and discussions of socialization concern childhood. However, socialization continues throughout the several stages of the life course, most commonly categorized as childhood, adolescence, adulthood, and old age. Within each of these categories, scholars further recognize subcategories, such as early adolescence and late adolescence, early adulthood and middle adulthood, and so forth. This section sketches some important aspects of the major life course stages.

Childhood

Despite increasing recognition of the entire life course, childhood (including infancy) certainly remains the most important stage of most people's lives for socialization and for the cognitive, emotional, and physiological development that is so crucial during the early years of anyone's life. We have already discussed what can happen if an infant does not receive "normal" socialization from at least one adult, and feral children are a sad reminder that socialization is necessary to produce an entity that not only looks human but really is human in the larger sense of the word.

Beyond this basic importance of childhood, however, lies an ugly truth. In regard to education, health, and other outcomes, many children do not fare well during childhood. Moreover, how well they do fare often depends on their social location—their social class, their race and ethnicity, and their gender. The Federal Interagency Forum on Child and Family Statistics regularly publishes a report called *America's Children: Key National Indicators of Well-Being* (including a shorter version in some years). This report provides an annual update of how children are faring on more than three dozen measures. The Forum's latest report, published in July 2010, provided some disturbing facts about children's well-being, and it also showed the difference that social location makes for their well-being (Federal Interagency Forum on Child and Family Statistics, 2010).

In one important finding, only about 55% of children aged 3–5 and not in kindergarten had a family member read to them daily. This figure varied by income level. Only 40% of children in families below the poverty level profited in this way, compared to 64% of children whose families' incomes were at least twice as high as the poverty level.

About 55% of children aged 3–5 who are not in kindergarten have a family member read to them every day. Social class affects the likelihood of reading to children: only 40% of children in families below the poverty level are read to daily, compared to 64% of children in families with incomes twice the poverty level or higher.

Neeta Lind – IMG_3646 – CC BY 2.0.

In other important findings, about one-fifth of U.S. children lived in poverty in 2008, a figure that rose to more than 30% of African American and Latino children. As well, slightly more than one-fifth of children were in families that sometimes were "food insecure," meaning they had trouble providing food for at least one family member. More than 40% of households with children in 2007 were characterized by crowded or physically inadequate conditions.

What happens during childhood can have lifelong consequences. Traumatic experiences during childhood—being neglected or abused, witnessing violence, being seriously injured, and so forth—put youngsters at much greater risk for many negative outcomes. They are more likely to commit serious delinquency during adolescence, and, throughout the life course, they are more likely to experience various psychiatric problems, learning disorders, and substance abuse. They are also less likely to graduate high school or attend college, to get married or avoid divorce if they do marry, and to gain and keep a job (Adams, 2010). The separate stages of the life course are really not that separate after all.

Adolescence

As many readers may remember, adolescence can be a very challenging time. Teenagers are no longer mere children, but they are not yet full adults. They want their independence, but parents and teachers keep telling them what to do. Peer pressure during adolescence can be enormous, and tobacco, alcohol, and other drug use become a serious problem for many teens.

These are all social aspects of adolescence, but adolescence also is a time of great biological change—namely, puberty. Puberty obviously has noticeable physiological consequences and, for many adolescents, at least one very important behavioral consequence—sexual activity. But *early* puberty also seems to have two additional effects: among both boys and girls, it increases the likelihood of delinquency and also the likelihood of becoming a victim of violence (Schreck, Burek, Stewart, & Miller, 2007). These twin consequences are thought to happen for at least two reasons. First, early puberty leads to stress, and stress leads to antisocial behavior (which can also result in violence against the teen committing the behavior). Second, teens experiencing early puberty (*early maturers*) are more likely to hang out with older teens, who tend to be more delinquent because they are older. Because their influence "rubs off," early maturers get into trouble more often and are again more likely to also become victims of violence.

Romantic relationships, including the desire to be in such a relationship, also matter greatly during adolescence. Wishful thinking, unrequited love, and broken hearts are common. Dating multiple partners is thought to contribute to delinquency and substance abuse, in part because dating occurs at parties and in other unsupervised settings where delinquency and drug use can occur, and in part because the emotional problems sometimes accompanying dating may result in delinquency, drug use, or both (Seffrin, Giordano, Manning, & Longmore, 2009).

As the discussion on childhood suggested, social class, race and ethnicity, and gender continue to affect the experiences of individuals during adolescence. Adolescence can certainly be an interesting stage of the life course, but how we fare during adolescence is often heavily influenced by these three fundamental aspects of our social location.

Adulthood

Adulthood is usually defined as the 18–64 age span. Obviously, 18-year-olds are very different from 64-year-olds, which is why scholars often distinguish young adults from middle-age adults. In a way, many young adults, including most readers of this book, delay entrance into "full" adulthood by going to college after high school and, for some, then continuing to be a student in graduate or professional school. By the time the latter obtain their advanced degree, many are well into their 30s, and they finally enter the labor force full time perhaps a dozen years after people who graduate high school but do not go on to college. These latter individuals may well marry, have children, or both by the time they are 18 or 19, while those who go to college and especially those who get an advanced degree may wait until their late 20s or early to mid-30s to take these significant steps.

Marriage and parenthood are "turning points" in many young adults' lives that help them to become more settled and to behave better than they might have behaved during adolescence.

Blaise Alleyne – Husband and Wife exit the Church – CC BY-SA 2.0.

One thing is clear from studies of young adulthood: people begin to "settle down" as they leave their teenage years, and their behavior generally improves. At least two reasons account for this improvement. First, as scientists are increasingly recognizing, the teenaged brain is not yet fully mature physiologically. For example, the frontal lobe, the region of the brain that governs reasoning and the ability to consider the consequences of one's actions, is not yet fully formed, leaving teenagers more impulsive. As the brain matures into the mid- and late 20s, impulsiveness declines and behavior improves (Ruder, 2008).

Second, as sociologists recognize, young adulthood is a time when people's "stakes" in society and conformity become stronger. Many get married, some have children, and most obtain their first full-time job. These "turning points," as they are called, instill a sense of responsibility and also increase the costs of misbehavior. If you are married, your spouse might not be very happy to have you go barhopping every weekend night or even more often; if you are employed full time, your employer might not be very happy to have you show up hung over. Marriage and employment as turning points thus help account for the general improvement in behavior that occurs after people reach adulthood (Laub, Sampson, & Sweeten, 2006).

Social class, race and ethnicity, and gender continue to affect how people fare during adulthood. Chapter 8 "Social Stratification" through Chapter 11 "Gender and Gender Inequality" and sections in some subsequent chapters discuss this important but discouraging fact of our social world.

Old Age

This stage of the life course unofficially begins at age 65. Once again, scholars make finer distinctions—such as "young-old" and "old-old"—because of the many differences between people who are 65 or 66 and those who are 85, 86, or even older. Chapter 12 "Aging and the Elderly" is devoted entirely to this period of the life course. Here we will just indicate that old age can be a fulfilling time of life for some people but one filled with anxiety and problems for other people, with social location (social class, race and ethnicity, and gender) once again often making a considerable difference. These problems are compounded by the negative views and even prejudice that many Americans have toward old age and toward people who are old. Because we all want to be old someday, the discussion of aging and the elderly in Chapter 12 "Aging and the Elderly" should be of special interest.

Key Takeaways

- The four stages of the life course are childhood, adolescence, adulthood, and old age. Socialization continues throughout all these stages.
- What happens during childhood may have lifelong consequences. Traumatic experiences and other negative events during childhood may impair psychological well-being in adolescence and beyond and lead to various behavioral problems.
- Social location in society—social class, race and ethnicity, and gender—affects how well people fare during the stages of the life course.

For Your Review

1. Think of a time some sort of socialization occurred for you since you started college. Write a brief essay in which you discuss the socialization you experienced.
2. Compared to when you were in high school, has your behavior generally improved, worsened, or stayed about the same? How do you think your behavior might change 10 years from now?

References

Adams, E. J. (2010). *Healing invisible wounds: Why investing in trauma-informed care for children makes sense.* Washington, DC: Justice Policy Institute.

America's children in brief: Key national indicators of well-being, 2010. Washington, DC: U.S. Government Printing Office.

Laub, J. H., Sampson, R. J., & Sweeten, G. A. (2006). Assessing Sampson and Laub's life-course theory of crime. In F. T. Cullen (Ed.), *Taking stock: The status of criminological theory* (vol. 15, pp. 313–333). New Brunswick, NJ: Transaction.

Ruder, D. B. (2008). The teen brain: A work in progress. *Harvard Magazine, 111*(1), 8–10.

Schreck, C. J., Burek, M. W., Stewart, E. A., & Miller, J. M. (2007). Distress and violent victimization among young adolescents. *Journal of Research in Crime & Delinquency, 44*(4), 381–405.

Seffrin, P. M., Giordano, P. C., Manning, W. D., & Longmore, M. A. (2009). The influence of dating relationships on friendship networks, identity development, and delinquency. *Justice Quarterly, 26*(2), 238–267.

4.5 Resocialization and Total Institutions

Learning Objectives

1. Discuss what is meant by resocialization.
2. List any two characteristics of a total institution.

Some people live in settings where their lives are so controlled that their values and beliefs change drastically. This change is so drastic, in fact, that these people are in effect resocialized. Such **resocialization** occurs in what Erving Goffman (1961) called **total institutions**. As their name implies, these institutions have total control over the lives of the people who live in them.

A boot camp is an example of a total institution.

dualdflipflop – Marine Corps Boot Camp – CC BY-ND 2.0.

Several types of total institutions exist: mental asylums, Nazi concentration camps, military boot camps, convents, and monasteries. Some scholars would also say that criminal prisons are total institutions, as they exhibit some of the same processes found in the other types. As this list implies, total institutions can be used for good or bad purposes, and so can resocialization.

Whether we are talking about total institutions that are good or bad, they all share certain processes and procedures that make them total institutions. The most important characteristic is that they have total control over the lives of their inmates, patients, or whatever the people who live in them are called. These residents, to use a generic term, have no freedom or autonomy. They are told what to do and when to do it, and punishment for rule infraction can be quite severe. In Nazi concentration camps, punishment was torture or death; in religious cloisters, it may be banishment; in boot camp, it may be a court-martial; in mental asylums, it may be solitary confinement in a straitjacket.

Second, total institutions take away the identity of their residents in an effort to weaken their self-identity and ensure conformity to the institutions' rules. Their residents typically wear uniforms and often have their heads shaved and, depending on the institution, may be known by a number or a new name. These procedures make everyone look more similar to each other than they otherwise would and help weaken the residents' self-identity. Whether these outcomes are good or bad depends again on which total institution we have in mind.

Third, total institutions subject their residents to harsh treatment and, quite often, abuse, although the nature of this abuse, and whether it occurs at all, obviously depends on which total institution we have in mind. Nazis starved concentration camp inmates, tortured them, stripped them naked, conducted hideous experiments on them, and, of course, exterminated millions (Gigliotti & Lang, 2005). Literature on mental asylums is filled with examples of abuses of the patients living there (Goffman, 1961). Drill sergeants have also been known for harshly treating new recruits: some observers defend this practice as necessary for military discipline and readiness, while others consider it to be unjustified abuse.

Resocialization is often accompanied via a **degradation ceremony**, an encounter in which a total institution's resident is humiliated, often in front of the institution's other residents or officials (Goffman, 1961). A drill sergeant may call a physically unconditioned male recruit a "girl" or "lady" and question his manhood in front of other recruits. In a mental asylum or prison, an inmate may be stripped naked and checked in their private areas for lice and other vermin. Shaving the heads of new military recruits or prison inmates is another example of a degradation ceremony.

Resocialization also occurs in groups that are not in institutional settings. Alcoholics Anonymous is one such group, as it tries to change the alcoholics' value system by having them internalize several principles about how to live one's life. The goal here, of course, is to have the alcoholic stop drinking and to continue to refrain from drinking (Davis & Jansen, 1998). Some religious cults also resocialize their members and continue to spark much controversy in today's society (Cowan & Bromley, 2008).

Key Takeaways

- Resocialization involves far-reaching changes in an individual's values, beliefs, and behavior.
- Total institutions exert total control over the lives of their residents. They typically try to eliminate the individual identity of their residents and often subject them to harsh treatment.

For Your Review

1. Do you know anyone who has spent time in a total institution of any kind? If so, describe how this person's experience there changed the person to the best of your knowledge.

References

Cowan, D. E., & Bromley, D. G. (2008). *Cults and new religions: A brief history*. Malden, MA: Blackwell.

Davis, D. R., & Jansen, G. G. (1998). Making meaning of Alcoholics Anonymous for social workers: Myths, metaphors, and realities. *Social Work, 43*, 169–182.

Gigliotti, S., & Lang, B. (Eds.). (2005). *The Holocaust: A reader*. Malden, MA: Blackwell.

Goffman, E. (1961). *Asylums: Essays on the social situation of mental patients and other inmates*. Garden City, NY: Anchor Books.

4.6 Socialization Practices and Improving Society

Learning Objective

1. Explain why new patterns of socialization might help address certain social issues in American society.

This chapter began with a news story about the beating and killing of a gay man and proceeded with the stories of two women who grew up in the South when it was racially segregated. These stories illustrate the power of socialization, which can have both good and bad consequences. Socialization into one's culture is necessary for any society to exist, and socialization is also necessary for any one individual to be "human" in the social sense of the term, as our discussion of feral children indicated. Yet socialization can also result in attitudes and behaviors that most of us would rightly condemn. Socialization created the homophobic mentality that led three teenagers to beat Charlie Howard and throw him into a river, and it also created the racist mentality that Sarah Patton Boyle and Lillian Smith described in their accounts of growing up in the South. Most of us are socialized to become good, cooperative members of society, but some of us are socialized to hold very negative views of certain groups in society.

For many of the social issues confronting the United States today—hate crimes, other crimes, violence against women, sexism, racism, and so forth—it might not be an exaggeration to say that new patterns of socialization are ultimately necessary if our society wants to be able to address these issues effectively. Parents of young children and adolescents bear a major responsibility for making sure our children do not learn to hate and commit harm to others, but so do our schools, mass media, and religious bodies. No nation is perfect, but nations like Japan have long been more successful than the United States in raising their children to be generous and cooperative. Their examples hold many good lessons for the United States.

Key Takeaway

- New socialization practices might be necessary to address many of the social ills facing the United States and other societies.

For Your Review

1. If you were in charge of our society, what socialization practice would you most try to change to help improve our society? Explain your answer.

4.7 End-of-Chapter Material

Summary

1. Socialization is important for at least two reasons. First, it is the process by which people learn the culture of their society. Second, it is the process by which they become fully human in terms of behavior, emotions, and cognitive ability. The unfortunate examples of feral children reinforce the importance of socialization in these respects.
2. Charles Horton Cooley and George Herbert Mead both theorized about how the self develops through socialization. Cooley's concept of the looking-glass self recognized that we see ourselves when we interact with other people and through this process develop our self-image. Mead's concept of "taking the role of the other" stressed that children play at various roles and so learn what others expect of them.
3. Sigmund Freud's psychoanalytic theory of personality development stressed the role of unconscious forces. Every individual is born with a selfish id and will achieve a normal personality if the individual's ego and superego develop properly. If the id, ego, and superego are in the wrong balance, the individual may engage in antisocial or other mentally disordered behavior.
4. Jean Piaget theorized that people go through several stages of cognitive development, while Lawrence Kohlberg said the same for moral development. Carol Gilligan argued that boys and girls engage in different types of moral reasoning, with the boys' type resting on formal rules and the girls' resting more on social relationships.
5. Erik Erikson discussed identity development throughout the life span while calling attention to adolescence as a stage in which many individuals experience an identity crisis.
6. Several agents of socialization exist. The most important one is arguably the family, as parents socialize their children in any number of ways; children end up resembling their parents not only biologically but also sociologically. Schools, peers, the mass media, and, to some extent, religion all also play important roles in socializing not only children but also older individuals.
7. Socialization continues throughout the several stages of the life course. What happens during childhood can often have lifelong effects. Social class, race and ethnicity, and gender all affect how people fare during the various stages of the life course.
8. Resocialization involves a dramatic change in an individual's values, beliefs, and behavior. It is often the goal of total institutions, such as military boot camp, convents and monasteries, mental institutions, and prisons, as it was with the Nazi death camps. Total institutions often exercise arbitrary power and in many ways try to achieve total control over the individual and remove their sense of individual identity.

Using Sociology

Imagine that you are sitting with two friends in a dining hall or cafeteria on your campus. An openly gay student you know walks by on his way out the door and you wave to him. As he exits the room, you hear someone at a table behind you utter an antigay remark. Angered by this slur, you feel that you need to say something, but you also are not ordinarily the type of person to raise a ruckus. Do you decide to do or say something, or do you remain silent? Explain your answer.

Chapter 5: Social Structure and Social Interaction

Social Issues in the News

"He's Not a Patient, but Plays One for Class," the headline said. For 12 days in July 2010, a 24-year-old medical student named Matt entered a nursing home in Chelsea, Massachusetts, to play the role of an 85-year-old man bound to a wheelchair and suffering from several serious health problems. He and five other medical students were staying in the facility to get a better idea of how to care for the elderly.

Matt kept a daily journal and wrote regularly of the problems of using his wheelchair, among other topics. One day he wrote, "I never really noticed how hard it is to live like this. I just always thought of old people as grumpy people who are easily upset." He had trouble reaching a TV remote control or reading a notice that was posted too high. When he first showered in his wheelchair, he was unable to turn it to be able to wash the right side of his body. He was so embarrassed to ask for help in going to the bathroom that he tried to spread out his bathroom trips so that the same nurse would not have to help him twice in a row.

The experience taught Matt a lot about how to care not only for older patients but also for patients in general. The emotional bonds he developed with other patients during his time in the nursing home particularly made him realize how he should interact with patients. As Matt wrote in his journal, "There is a face and story behind every patient. The patient should not be viewed by the conditions that ail them, but by the person beneath the disease." (Wu, 2010)

The status of an 85-year-old man bound to a wheelchair is very different from that of a medical student. So are our views of people in each status and our expectations of their behavior. Matt quickly learned what life in a wheelchair is like and realized that his stereotypical views of older people could easily complicate his medical interactions with them. The setting in which he played the role of a very old man was an institutional setting, but this setting was also one tiny component of the vast social institution that sociologists call medicine.

In all these ways, Matt's brief experience in the nursing home illuminates important aspects of social structure and social interaction in today's society. The statuses we occupy and the roles we play in these statuses shape our lives in fundamental ways and affect our daily interactions with other people. The many social institutions that are so important in modern society affect our lives profoundly from the moment we are born. This chapter examines major aspects of social structure and social interaction. As with Chapter 3 "Culture" and Chapter 4 "Socialization", this chapter should help you further understand yourself as a social being and not just as an individual. This in turn means it should further help you understand how and why you came to be the person you are.

References

Wu, J. Q. (2010, July 19). He's not a patient, but plays one for class. *The Boston Globe*, p. B1.

5.1 Social Structure: The Building Blocks of Social Life

Learning Objectives

1. Describe the difference between a status and a role.
2. Understand the difference between an ascribed status, an achieved status, and a master status.
3. List the major social institutions.

Social life is composed of many levels of building blocks, from the very micro to the very macro. These building blocks combine to form the *social structure*. As Chapter 1 "Sociology and the Sociological Perspective" explained, **social structure** refers to the social patterns through which a society is organized and can be horizontal or vertical. To recall, *horizontal social structure* refers to the social relationships and the social and physical characteristics of communities to which individuals belong, while *vertical social structure*, more commonly called **social inequality**, refers to ways in which a society or group ranks people in a hierarchy. This chapter's discussion of social structure focuses primarily on horizontal social structure, while Chapter 8 "Social Stratification" through Chapter 12 "Aging and the Elderly", as well as much material in other chapters, examine dimensions of social inequality. The (horizontal) social structure comprises several components, to which we now turn, starting with the most micro and ending with the most macro. Our discussion of social interaction in the second half of this chapter incorporates several of these components.

Statuses

Status has many meanings in the dictionary and also within sociology, but for now we will define it as the position that someone occupies in society. This position is often a job title, but many other types of positions exist: student, parent, sibling, relative, friend, and so forth. It should be clear that *status* as used in this way conveys nothing about the prestige of the position, to use a common synonym for status. A physician's job is a status with much prestige, but a shoeshiner's job is a status with no prestige.

Any one individual often occupies several different statuses at the same time, and someone can simultaneously be a banker, Girl Scout troop leader, mother, school board member, volunteer at a homeless shelter, and spouse. This someone would be very busy! We call all the positions an individual occupies that person's **status set** (see Figure 5.1 "Example of a Status Set").

Figure 5.1 Example of a Status Set

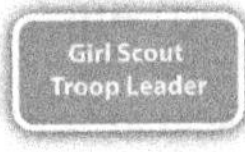

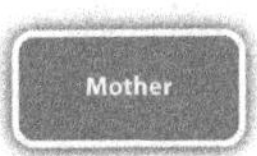

Sociologists usually speak of three types of statuses. The first type is **ascribed status**, which is the status that someone is born with and has no control over. There are relatively few ascribed statuses; the most common ones are our biological sex, race, parents' social class and religious affiliation, and biological relationships (child, grandchild, sibling, and so forth).

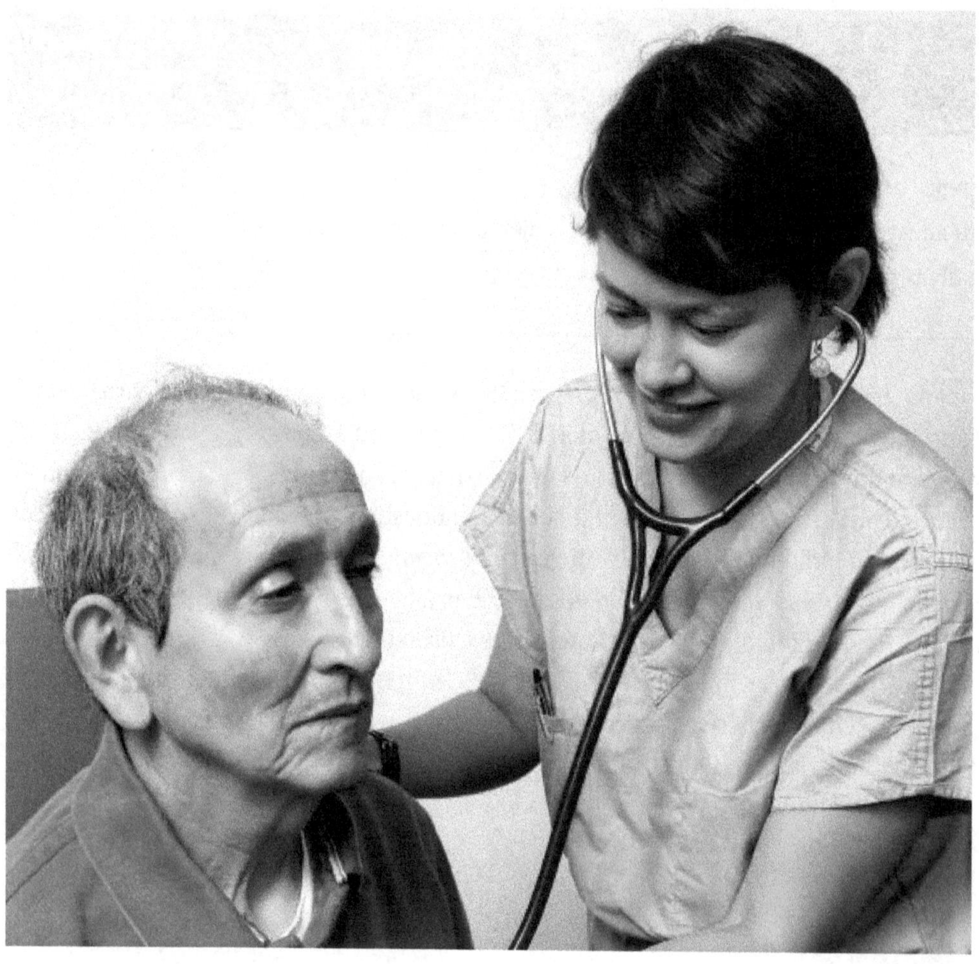

Status refers to the position an individual occupies. Used in this way, a person's status is not related to the prestige of that status. The jobs of physician and shoeshiner are both statuses, even though one of these jobs is much more prestigious than the other job.

Public Domain Images – CC0 public domain.

The second kind of status is called **achieved status**, which, as the name implies, is a status you achieve, at some point after birth, sometimes through your own efforts and sometimes because good or bad luck befalls you. The status of student is an achieved status, as is the status of restaurant server or romantic partner, to cite just two of the many achieved statuses that exist.

Two things about achieved statuses should be kept in mind. First, our ascribed statuses, and in particular our sex, race and ethnicity, and social class, often affect our ability to acquire and maintain many achieved statuses (such as college graduate). Second, achieved statuses can be viewed positively or negatively. Our society usually views achieved statuses such as physician, professor, or college student positively, but it certainly views achieved statuses such as burglar, prostitute, and pimp negatively.

The third type of status is called a **master status**. This is a status that is so important that it overrides other statuses you may hold. In terms of people's reactions, master statuses can be either positive or negative for an individual depending on the particular master status they hold. Barack Obama now holds the positive master status of president of the United States: his status as president overrides all the other statuses he holds (husband, father, and so forth), and millions of Americans respect him, whether or not they voted for him or now favor his policies, because of this status. Many other positive master statuses exist in the political and entertainment worlds and in other spheres of life.

Some master statuses have negative consequences. To recall the medical student and nursing home news story that began this chapter, a physical disability often becomes such a master status. If you are bound to a wheelchair, for example, this fact becomes more important than the other statuses you have and may prompt people to perceive and interact with you negatively. In particular, they perceive you more in terms of your master status (someone bound to a wheelchair) than as the "person beneath" the master status, to cite Matt's words. For similar reasons, gender, race, and sexual orientation may also be considered master statuses, as these statuses often subject women, people of color, and gays and lesbians, respectively, to discrimination and other problems, no matter what other statuses they may have.

Whatever status we occupy, certain objects signify any particular status. These objects are called **status symbols**. In popular terms, *status symbol* usually means something like a Rolls-Royce or BMW that shows off someone's wealth or success, and many status symbols of this type exist. But sociologists use the term more generally than that. For example, the wheelchair that Matt the medical student rode for 12 days was a status symbol that signified his master status of someone with a (feigned) disability. If someone is pushing a stroller, the stroller is a status symbol that signifies that the person pushing it is a parent or caretaker of a young child.

Roles

Whatever its type, every status is accompanied by a **role**, which is the behavior expected of someone—and in fact *everyone*—with a certain status. You and most other people reading this book are students. Despite all the other differences among you, you have at least this one status in common. As such, there is a role expected of you as a student (at least by your professors); this role includes coming to class regularly, doing all the reading assigned from this textbook, and studying the best you can for exams. Roles for given statuses existed long before we were born, and they will continue long after we are no longer alive. A major dimension of socialization is learning the roles our society has and then behaving in the way a particular role demands.

Roles help us interact because we are familiar with the behavior associated with roles. Because shoppers and cashiers know what to expect of each other, their social interaction is possible.

David Tan – Cashier – CC BY-NC-ND 2.0.

Because roles are the behavior expected of people in various statuses, they help us interact because we are familiar with the roles in the first place, a point to which the second half of this chapter returns. Suppose you are shopping in a department store. Your status is a shopper, and the role expected of you as a shopper—and of all shoppers—involves looking quietly at various items in the store, taking the ones you want to purchase to a checkout line, and paying for them. The person who takes your money is occupying another status in the store that we often call a cashier. The role expected of that cashier—and of all cashiers not only in that store but in every other store—is to accept your payment in a businesslike way and put your items in a bag. Because shoppers and cashiers all have these mutual expectations, their social interaction is possible.

Social Networks

Modern life seems increasingly characterized by social networks. A **social network** is the totality of relationships that link us to other people and groups and through them to still other people and groups. As Facebook and other social media show so clearly, social networks can be incredibly extensive. Social networks can be so large, of course, that an individual in a network may know little or nothing of another individual in the network (e.g., a friend of a friend of a friend of a friend). But these "friends of friends" can sometimes be an important source of practical advice and other kinds of help. They can "open doors" in the job market, they can introduce you to a potential romantic partner, they can pass through some tickets to the next big basketball game. As a key building block of social structure, social networks receive a fuller discussion in Chapter 6 "Groups and Organizations".

Groups and Organizations

Groups and organizations are the next component of social structure. Because Chapter 6 "Groups and Organizations" discusses groups and organizations extensively, here we will simply define them and say one or two things about them.

A **social group** (hereafter just *group*) consists of two or more people who regularly interact on the basis of mutual expectations and who share a common identity. To paraphrase John Donne, the 17th-century English poet, no one is an island; almost all people are members of many groups, including families, groups of friends, and groups of coworkers in a workplace. Sociology is sometimes called the study of group life, and it is difficult to imagine a modern society without many types of groups and a small, traditional society without at least some groups.

In terms of size, emotional bonding, and other characteristics, many types of groups exist, as Chapter 6 "Groups and Organizations" explains. But one of the most important types is the **formal organization** (also just *organization*), which is a large group that follows explicit rules and procedures to achieve specific goals and tasks. For better and for worse, organizations are an essential feature of modern societies. Our banks, our hospitals, our schools, and so many other examples are all organizations, even if they differ from one another in many respects. In terms of their goals and other characteristics, several types of organizations exist, as Chapter 6 "Groups and Organizations" will again discuss.

Social Institutions

Yet another component of social structure is the **social institution**, or patterns of beliefs and behavior that help a society meet its basic needs. Modern society is filled with many social institutions that all help society meet its needs and achieve other goals and thus have a profound impact not only on the society as a whole but also on virtually every individual in a society. Examples of social institutions include the family, the economy, the polity (government), education, religion, and medicine. Chapter 13 "Work and the Economy" through Chapter 18 "Health and Medicine" examine each of these social institutions separately.

As those chapters will show, these social institutions all help the United States meet its basic needs, but they also have failings that prevent the United States from meeting all its needs. A particular problem is social inequality, to recall the vertical dimension of social structure, as our social institutions often fail many people because of their social class, race, ethnicity, gender, or all four. These chapters will also indicate that American society could better fulfill its needs if it followed certain practices and policies of other democracies that often help their societies "work" better than our own.

Societies

The largest component of social structure is, of course, **society** itself. Chapter 1 "Sociology and the Sociological Perspective" defined society as a group of people who live within a defined territory and who share a culture. Societies certainly differ in many ways; some are larger in population and some are smaller, some are modern and some are less modern. Since the origins of sociology during the 19th century, sociologists have tried to understand how and why modern, industrial society developed. Part of this understanding involves determining the differences between industrial societies and traditional ones.

One of the key differences between traditional and industrial societies is the emphasis placed on the community versus the emphasis placed on the individual. In traditional societies, community feeling and group commitment are usually the cornerstones of social life. In contrast, industrial society is more individualistic and impersonal. Whereas the people in traditional societies have close daily ties, those in industrial societies have many relationships in which one person barely knows the other person. Commitment to the group and community become less important in industrial societies, and individualism becomes more important.

Sociologist Ferdinand Tönnies (1887/1963) long ago characterized these key characteristics of traditional and industrial societies with the German words *Gemeinschaft* and *Gesellschaft*. **Gemeinschaft** means human community, and Tönnies said that a sense of community characterizes traditional societies, where family, kin, and community ties are quite strong. As societies grew and industrialized and as people moved to cities, Tönnies said, social ties weakened and became more impersonal. Tönnies called this situation **Gesellschaft** and found it dismaying. Chapter 5 "Social Structure and Social Interaction", Section 5.2 "The Development of Modern Society" discusses the development of societies in more detail.

Key Takeaways

- The major components of social structure are statuses, roles, social networks, groups and organizations, social institutions, and society.
- Specific types of statuses include the ascribed status, achieved status, and master status. Depending on the type of master status, an individual may be viewed positively or negatively because of a master status.

For Your Review

1. Take a moment and list every status that you now occupy. Next to each status, indicate whether it is an ascribed status, achieved status, or master status.
2. Take a moment and list every group to which you belong. Write a brief essay in which you comment on which of the groups are more meaningful to you and which are less meaningful to you.

References

Tönnies, F. (1963). *Community and society*. New York, NY: Harper and Row. (Original work published 1887).

5.2 The Development of Modern Society

Learning Objectives

1. List the major types of societies that have been distinguished according to their economy and technology.
2. Explain why social development produced greater gender and wealth inequality.

To help understand how modern society developed, sociologists find it useful to distinguish societies according to their type of economy and technology. One of the most useful schemes distinguishes the following types of societies: *hunting-and-gathering, horticultural, pastoral, agricultural,* and *industrial* (Nolan & Lenski, 2009). Some scholars add a final type, *postindustrial,* to the end of this list. We now outline the major features of each type in turn. Table 5.1 "Summary of Societal Development" summarizes these features.

Table 5.1 Summary of Societal Development

Type of society	Key characteristics
Hunting-and-gathering	These are small, simple societies in which people hunt and gather food. Because all people in these societies have few possessions, the societies are fairly egalitarian, and the degree of inequality is very low.
Horticultural and pastoral	Horticultural and pastoral societies are larger than hunting-and-gathering societies. Horticultural societies grow crops with simple tools, while pastoral societies raise livestock. Both types of societies are wealthier than hunting-and-gathering societies, and they also have more inequality and greater conflict than hunting-and-gathering societies.
Agricultural	These societies grow great numbers of crops, thanks to the use of plows, oxen, and other devices. Compared to horticultural and pastoral societies, they are wealthier and have a higher degree of conflict and of inequality.
Industrial	Industrial societies feature factories and machines. They are wealthier than agricultural societies and have a greater sense of individualism and a somewhat lower degree of inequality that still remains substantial.
Postindustrial	These societies feature information technology and service jobs. Higher education is especially important in these societies for economic success.

Hunting-and-Gathering Societies

Beginning about 250,000 years ago, **hunting-and-gathering societies** are the oldest ones we know of; few of them remain today, partly because modern societies have encroached on their existence. As the name *hunting-and-gathering* implies, people in these societies both hunt for food and gather plants and other vegetation. They have few possessions other than some simple hunting-and-gathering equipment. To ensure their mutual survival, everyone is expected to help find food and also to share the food they find. To seek their food, hunting-and-gathering peoples often move from place to place. Because they are nomadic, their societies tend to be quite small, often consisting of only a few dozen people.

Beyond this simple summary of the type of life these societies lead, anthropologists have also charted the nature of social relationships in them. One of their most important findings is that hunting-and-gathering societies are fairly egalitarian. Although men do most of the hunting and women most of the gathering, perhaps reflecting the biological differences between the sexes discussed earlier, women and men in these societies are roughly equal. Because hunting-and-gathering societies have few possessions, their members are also fairly equal in terms of wealth and power, as virtually no wealth exists.

Horticultural and Pastoral Societies

Horticultural and pastoral societies both developed about 10,000–12,000 years ago. In **horticultural societies**, people use hoes and other simple hand tools to raise crops. In **pastoral societies**, people raise and herd sheep, goats, camels, and other domesticated animals and use them as their major source of food and also, depending on the animal, as a means of transportation. Some societies are either primarily horticultural or pastoral, while other societies combine both forms. Pastoral societies tend to be at least somewhat nomadic, as they often have to move to find better grazing land for their animals. Horticultural societies, on the other hand, tend to be less nomadic, as they are able to keep growing their crops in the same location for some time. Both types of societies often manage to produce a surplus of food from vegetable or animal sources, respectively, and this surplus allows them to trade their extra food with other societies. It also allows them to have a larger population size than hunting-and-gathering societies that often reaches several hundred members.

Horticultural societies often produce an excess of food that allows them to trade with other societies and also to have more members than hunting-and-gathering societies.

Jorge Quinteros – Horticulture – CC BY-NC-ND 2.0.

Accompanying the greater complexity and wealth of horticultural and pastoral societies is greater inequality in terms of gender and wealth than is found in hunting-and-gathering societies. In pastoral societies, wealth stems from the number of animals a family owns, and families with more animals are wealthier and more powerful than families with fewer animals. In horticultural societies, wealth stems from the amount of land a family owns, and families with more land are wealthier and more powerful.

One other side effect of the greater wealth of horticultural and pastoral societies is greater conflict. As just mentioned, sharing of food is a key norm in hunting-and-gathering societies. In horticultural and pastoral societies, however, wealth (and more specifically, the differences in wealth) leads to disputes and even fighting over land and animals. Whereas hunting-and-gathering peoples tend to be very peaceful, horticultural and pastoral peoples tend to be more aggressive.

Agricultural Societies

Agricultural societies developed some 5,000 years ago in the Middle East, thanks to the invention of the plow. When pulled by oxen and other large animals, the plow allowed for much more cultivation of crops than the simple tools of horticultural societies permitted. The wheel was also invented about the same time, and written language and numbers began to be used. The development of agricultural societies thus marked a watershed in the development of human society. Ancient Egypt, China, Greece, and Rome were all agricultural societies, and India and many other large nations today remain primarily agricultural.

We have already seen that the greater food production of horticultural and pastoral societies led them to become larger than hunting-and-gathering societies and to have more trade and greater inequality and conflict. Agricultural societies continue all these trends. First, because they produce so much more food than horticultural and pastoral societies, they often become quite large, with their numbers sometimes reaching into the millions. Second, their huge food surpluses lead to extensive trade, both within the society itself and with other societies. Third, the surpluses and trade both lead to degrees of wealth unknown in the earlier types of societies and thus to unprecedented inequality, exemplified in the appearance for the first time of peasants, people who work on the land of rich landowners. Finally, agricultural societies' greater size and inequality also produce more conflict. Some of this conflict is internal, as rich landowners struggle with each other for even greater wealth and power, and peasants sometimes engage in revolts. Other conflict is external, as the governments of these societies seek other markets for trade and greater wealth.

If gender inequality becomes somewhat greater in horticultural and pastoral societies than in hunting-and-gathering ones, it becomes very pronounced in agricultural societies. An important reason for this is the hard, physically taxing work in the fields, much of it using large plow animals, that characterizes these societies. Then, too, women are often pregnant in these societies, because large families provide more bodies to work in the fields and thus more income. Because men do more of the physical labor in agricultural societies—labor on which these societies depend—they have acquired greater power over women (Brettell & Sargent, 2009). In the Standard

Cross-Cultural Sample, agricultural societies are much more likely than hunting-and-gathering ones to believe men should dominate women (see Figure 5.2 "Type of Society and Presence of Cultural Belief That Men Should Dominate Women").

Figure 5.2 Type of Society and Presence of Cultural Belief That Men Should Dominate Women

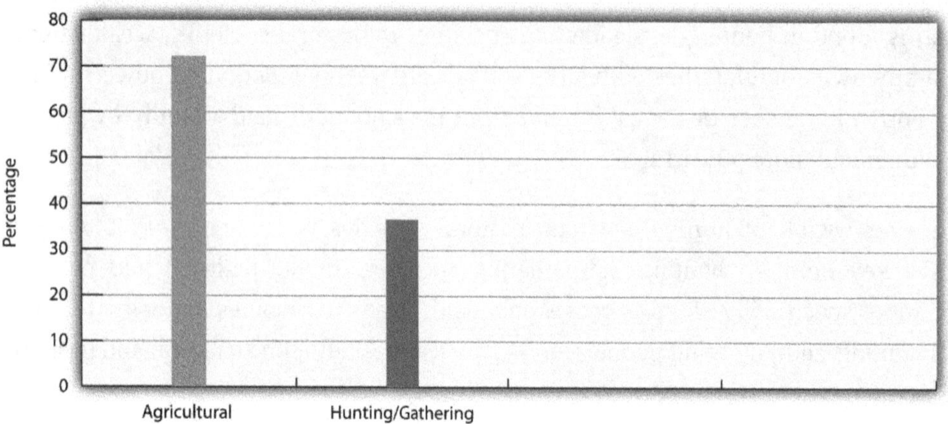

Source: Data from Standard Cross-Cultural Sample.

Industrial Societies

Industrial societies emerged in the 1700s as the development of machines and then factories replaced the plow and other agricultural equipment as the primary mode of production. The first machines were steam- and water-powered, but eventually, of course, electricity became the main source of power. The growth of industrial societies marked such a great transformation in many of the world's societies that we now call the period from about 1750 to the late 1800s the Industrial Revolution. This revolution has had enormous consequences in almost every aspect of society, some for the better and some for the worse.

On the positive side, industrialization brought about technological advances that improved people's health and expanded their life spans. As noted earlier, there is also a greater emphasis in industrial societies on individualism, and people in these societies typically enjoy greater political freedom than those in older societies. Compared to agricultural societies, industrial societies also have lowered economic and gender inequality. In industrial societies, people do have a greater chance to pull themselves up by their bootstraps than was true in earlier societies, and rags-to-riches stories continue to illustrate the opportunity available under industrialization. That said, we will see in later chapters that economic and gender inequality remains substantial in many industrial societies.

On the negative side, industrialization meant the rise and growth of large cities and concentrated poverty and degrading conditions in these cities, as the novels of Charles Dickens poignantly remind us. This urbanization changed the character of social life by creating a more impersonal and less traditional *Gesellschaft* society. It also led to riots and other urban violence that, among other things, helped fuel the rise of the modern police force and forced factory owners to improve workplace conditions. Today industrial societies consume most of the world's resources, pollute its environment to an unprecedented degree, and have compiled nuclear arsenals that could undo thousands of years of human society in an instant.

Postindustrial Societies

We are increasingly living in what has been called the *information technology age* (or just *information age*), as wireless technology vies with machines and factories as the basis for our economy. Compared to industrial economies, we now have many more service jobs, ranging from housecleaning to secretarial work to repairing computers. Societies in which this transition is happening are moving from an industrial to a postindustrial phase of development. In **postindustrial societies**, then, information technology and service jobs have replaced machines and manufacturing jobs as the primary dimension of the economy (Bell, 1999). If the car was the sign of the economic and social times back in the 1920s, then the smartphone or netbook/laptop is the sign of the economic and social future in the early years of the 21st century. If the factory was the dominant workplace at the beginning of the 20th century, with workers standing at their positions by conveyor belts, then cell phone, computer, and software companies are dominant industries at the beginning of the 21st century, with workers, almost all of them much better educated than their earlier factory counterparts, huddled over their wireless technology at home, at work, or on the road. In short, the Industrial Revolution has been replaced by the Information Revolution, and we now have what has been called an *information society* (Hassan, 2008).

As part of postindustrialization in the United States, many manufacturing companies have moved their operations from U.S. cities to overseas sites. Since the 1980s, this process has raised unemployment in cities, many of whose residents lack the college education and other training needed in the information sector. Partly for this reason, some scholars fear that the information age will aggravate the disparities we already have between the "haves" and "have-nots" of society, as people lacking a college education will have even more trouble finding gainful employment than they do now (W. J. Wilson, 2009). In the international arena, postindustrial societies may also have a leg up over industrial or, especially, agricultural societies as the world moves ever more into the information age.

Key Takeaways

- The major types of societies historically have been hunting-and-gathering, horticultural, pastoral, agricultural, industrial, and postindustrial.
- As societies developed and grew larger, they became more unequal in terms of gender and wealth and also more competitive and even warlike with other societies.
- Postindustrial society emphasizes information technology but also increasingly makes it difficult for individuals without college educations to find gainful employment.

For Your Review

1. Explain why societies became more unequal in terms of gender and wealth as they developed and became larger.
2. Explain why societies became more individualistic as they developed and became larger.
3. Describe the benefits and disadvantages of industrial societies as compared to earlier societies.

References

Bell, D. (Ed.). (1999). *The coming of post-industrial society: A venture in social forecasting*. New York, NY: Basic Books.

Brettell, C. B., & Sargent, C. F. (Eds.). (2009). *Gender in cross-cultural perspective* (5th ed.). Upper Saddle River, NJ: Prentice Hall.

Hassan, R. (2008). *The information society: Cyber dreams and digital nightmares*. Malden, MA: Polity.

Nolan, P., & Lenski, G. (2009). *Human societies: An introduction to macrosociology* (11th ed.). Boulder, CO: Paradigm.

Wilson, W. J. (2009). The economic plight of inner-city black males. In E. Anderson (Ed.), *Against the wall: Poor, young, black, and male* (pp. 55–70). Philadelphia: University of Pennsylvania Press.

5.3 Social Interaction in Everyday Life

Learning Objectives

1. Describe what is meant by dramaturgy and by impression management.
2. Provide one example of role conflict or role strain.
3. List one or two gender differences in nonverbal communication.

A fundamental feature of social life is **social interaction**, or the ways in which people act with other people and react to how other people are acting. To recall our earlier paraphrase of John Donne, no one is an island. This means that all individuals, except those who choose to live truly alone, interact with other individuals virtually every day and often many times in any one day. For social order, a prerequisite for any society, to be possible, effective social interaction must be possible. Partly for this reason, sociologists interested in microsociology have long tried to understand social life by analyzing how and why people interact they way they do. This section draws on their work to examine various social influences on individual behavior. As you read this section, you will probably be reading many things relevant to your own social interaction.

Social interaction is a fundamental feature of social life. For social order to be possible, effective social interaction must also be possible.

Martina – Friends – CC BY-NC-ND 2.0.

Chapter 4 "Socialization" emphasized that socialization results from our social interaction. The reverse is also true: we learn how to interact from our socialization. We have seen many examples of this process in earlier chapters. Among other things, we learn from our socialization how far apart to stand when talking to someone else, we learn to enjoy kissing, we learn how to stand and behave in an elevator, and we learn how to behave when we are drunk. Perhaps most important for the present discussion, we especially learn our society's roles, outlined earlier as a component of social structure. The importance of roles for social interaction merits further discussion here.

Roles and Social Interaction

Our earlier discussion of roles defined them as the behaviors expected of people in a certain status. Regardless of our individual differences, if we are in a certain status, we are all expected to behave in a way appropriate to that status. Roles thus help make social interaction possible.

As our example of shoppers and cashiers was meant to suggest, social interaction based on roles is usually very automatic, and we often perform our roles without thinking about them. This, in fact, is why social interaction is indeed possible: if we always had to think about our roles before we performed them, social interaction would be slow, tedious, and fraught with error. (Analogously, if actors in a play always had to read the script before performing their lines, as an understudy sometimes does, the play would be slow and stilted.) It is when people violate their roles that the importance of roles is thrown into sharp relief. Suppose you were shopping in a department store, and while you were in the checkout line the cashier asked you how your sex life has been! Now, you might expect such an intimate question from a very close friend, because discussions of intimate matters are part of the roles close friends play, but you would definitely *not* expect it from a cashier you do not know.

As this example suggests, effective social interaction rests on shared **background assumptions**, or our understanding of the roles expected of people in a given encounter, that are easily violated if one has the nerve to do so. If they are violated, social order might well break down, as you would quickly find if you dared to ask your cashier how her or his sex life has been, or if two students sitting in class violated their student role by kissing each other passionately. Sociologist Harold Garfinkel (1967) argued that unexpected events like these underscore how fragile social order is and remind us that people are constantly constructing the social reality of the situations in which they find themselves. To illustrate his point, he had his students perform a series of experiments, including acting like a stranger in their parents' home. Not surprisingly, their parents quickly became flustered and wondered what college was doing to their daughters and sons!

These examples indicate that social reality is to a large extent socially constructed. It is what we make of it, and individuals who interact help construct the reality of the situation in which they interact. Sociologists refer to this process as the **social construction of reality** (Berger & Luckmann, 1963). Although we usually come into a situation with shared understandings of what is about to happen, as the interaction proceeds the actors continue to define the situation and thus to construct its reality. This view lies at the heart of the symbolic interactionist perspective and helps us understand how and why roles (or to be more precise, our understanding of what behavior is expected of someone in a certain status) make social interaction possible.

Roles and Personalities

Roles help us interact and help make social order possible, but they may even shape our personalities. The idea here is that if we assume a new role, the expectations of that role can change how we interact with others and even the way we think about ourselves. In short, roles can *change* our personalities.

Roles can shape personalities. When individuals become police officers, the nature of their job can prompt them to act and think in a more authoritarian manner.

United States Forces Iraq – Pat down practice – CC BY-NC-ND 2.0.

A telling example of this effect comes from the story of a criminal justice professor from Florida named George Kirkham. In his classes, Kirkham would be critical of the harshness with which police treated suspects and other citizens. One day, some police officers in one of his classes said Kirkham could not begin to understand what it was like being a police officer, and they challenged him to become one. He took up the challenge by gaining admission to a police academy and going through the regular training program for all recruits. Kirkham (1984) later recounted what happened on his first few days on the job. In one episode, he and his veteran partner went into a bar where an intoxicated patron had been causing trouble. Kirkham politely asked the patron to go with him outside. Evidently surprised by this new police officer's politeness, the man instead swung at Kirkham and landed a blow. Kirkham could not believe this happened and was forced to subdue his assailant. In another episode, Kirkham and his partner were checking out the driver of a double-parked car. An ugly crowd soon gathered and began making threats. Alarmed, Kirkham opened up his car's trunk and pulled out a shotgun to keep the crowd away. In recounting this episode, Kirkham wrote that as a professor he quickly would have condemned the police officer he had now become. In a few short days, he had turned from a polite, kind professor into a gruff, angry police officer. His role had changed and, along with it, his personality.

Role Problems

Roles help our interactions run smoothly and automatically and, for better or worse, shape our personalities. But roles can also cause various kinds of problems. One such problem is **role conflict**, which occurs when the roles of our many statuses conflict with each other. For example, say you are a student and also a parent. Your 3-year-old child gets sick. You now have a conflict between your role as a parent and your role as a student. To perform your role as a parent, you should stay home with your sick child. To perform your role as a student, you should go to your classes and take the big exam that had been scheduled weeks ago. What do you do?

Figure 5.3 Example of a Role Conflict

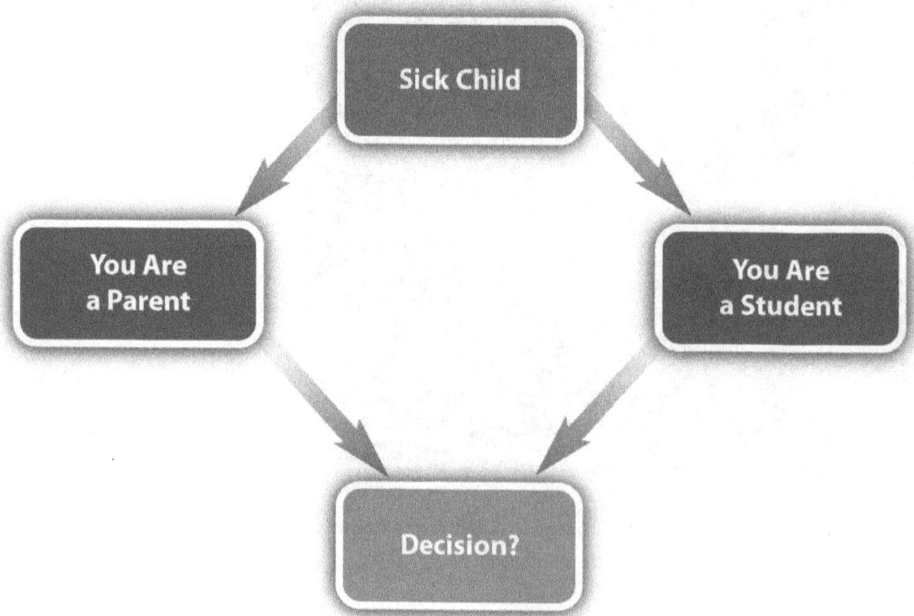

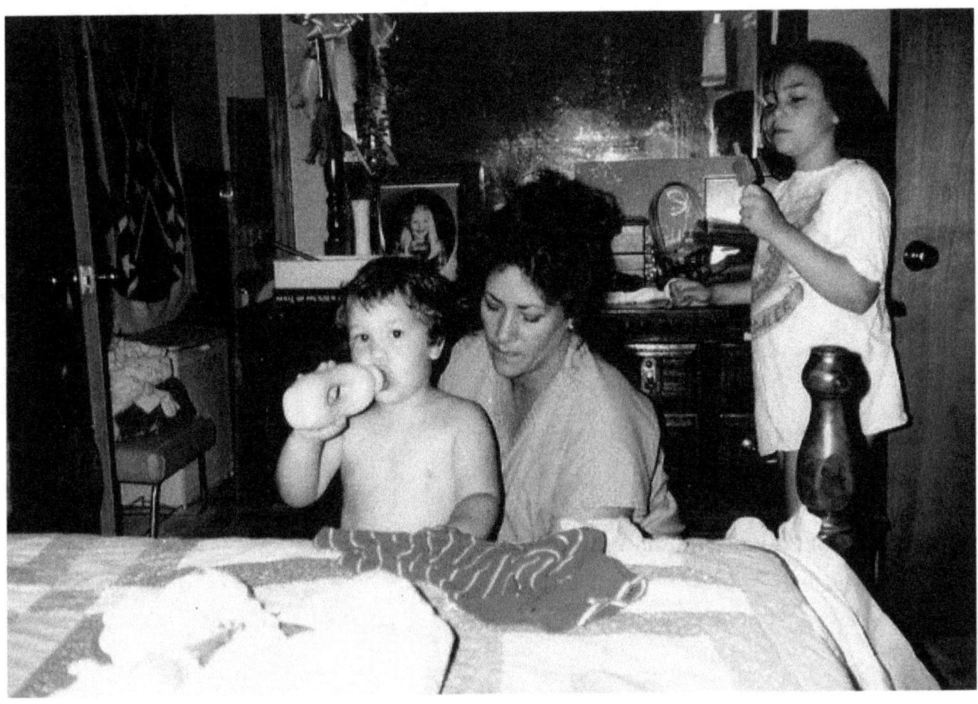

Parents can often experience role conflict stemming from the fact that they have both parental responsibilities and work responsibilities.

Lindsey Turner – working mom – CC BY 2.0.

One thing is clear: you cannot perform both roles at the same time. To resolve role conflict, we ordinarily have to choose between one role and the other, which is often a difficult choice to make. In this example, if you take care of your child, you miss your classes and exam; if you go to your classes, you have to leave your child at home alone, an unacceptable and illegal option. Another way to resolve role conflict is to find some alternative that would meet the needs of your conflicting roles. In our sick child example, you might be able to find someone to watch your child until you can get back from classes. It is certainly desirable to find such alternatives, but, unfortunately, they are not always forthcoming. If role conflict becomes too frequent and severe, a final option is to leave one of your statuses altogether. In our example, if you find it too difficult to juggle your roles as parent and student, you could stop being a parent—hardly likely!—or, more likely, take time off from school until your child is older. Most of us in these circumstances would try our best to avoid having to do this.

Another role-related problem is called **role strain**. Here you have one status, and a role associated with it, that is causing problems because of all the demands coming to you from people in other statuses with which your own status is involved. Suppose you were a high school principal. In your one role as a principal, you come into contact with people in several different statuses: teachers, students, custodial and support staff, the superintendent, school board members, the community as a whole, and the news media. These statuses may make competing demands on you in your one role as a principal. If your high school has a dress code, for example, the students may want you to abolish it, the teachers and superintendent may want you to keep it, and maybe the school board would agree with the students. As you try to please all these competing factions, you certainly might experience some role strain!

A third type of role problem occurs when we occupy a status whose role demands a certain type of personality that differs from the one we actually have. Can you imagine a police officer who was afraid of guns? An athlete who was not competitive? A flight attendant who did not like helping people or was afraid of flying? Although most people avoid this type of role problem by not taking on a role to which their personality is ill suited, such problems occur nonetheless. For example, some people who dislike children and do not have the patience to be good parents end up being parents anyway. In another example, your author once knew a new professor who was woefully nervous lecturing in front of students. You might wonder why he became a professor in the first place, but he probably just loved the subject matter so much that he thought he would overcome his nervousness. He did not.

Dramaturgy and Impression Management

From a sociological standpoint, much of our social interaction can be understood by likening it to a performance in a play. As with so many things, Shakespeare said it best when he wrote,

All the world's a stage,
And all the men and women merely players.
They have their exits and their entrances;
And one man in his time plays many parts. (As You Like It, Act II, Scene 7)

From this perspective, each individual has many parts or roles to play in society, and many of these roles specify how we should interact in any given situation. These roles exist before we are born, and they continue long after we die. The culture of society is thus similar to the script of a play. Just as actors in a play learn what lines to say, where to stand on the stage, how to position their bodies, and so many other things, so do we learn as members of society the roles that specify how we should interact.

This fundamental metaphor was developed and popularized by sociologist Erving Goffman (1959) in what he called a **dramaturgical approach**. By this he meant that we can understand social interaction as if it were a theatrical performance. People who interact are actors on a stage, the things they say and do are equivalent to the parts actors play, and any people who observe their interaction are equivalent to the audience at a play. As sociologists Jonathan H. Turner and Jan E. Stets (2006, p. 26) summarize this approach, "Individuals are, in essence, dramatic actors on a stage playing parts dictated by culture, and, like all theater, they are given some dramatic license in how they play roles, as long as they do not deviate too far from the emotional script provided by culture."

Erving Goffman's dramaturgical approach likened social interaction to acting in a theatrical performance.

Manolis Skantzakis – "with regar to Mr Alexandros" – CC BY-NC-ND 2.0.

Beyond these aspects of his theatrical analogy, Goffman also stressed that the *presentation of self* guides social interaction just as it guides behavior in a play. Actors in a play, he wrote, aim to act properly, which at a minimum means they need to say their lines correctly and in other ways carry out their parts as they were written. They try to convey the impression of their character the playwright had in mind when the play was written and the director has in mind when the play is presented.

Such **impression management**, Goffman wrote, also guides social interaction in everyday life. When people interact, they routinely try to convey a positive impression of themselves to the people with whom they interact. Our behavior in a job interview differs dramatically (pun intended) from our behavior at a party. The key dimension of social interaction, then, involves trying to manage the impressions we convey to the people with whom we interact. We usually do our best, consciously or unconsciously, to manage the impressions we convey to others and so to evoke from them reactions that will please us.

Goffman wrote about other aspects of social interaction that affect our efforts to manage these impressions. Again using his dramaturgical metaphor, he said that some interaction occurs in the "frontstage," or front region, while other interaction occurs in the "backstage," or back region (Goffman, 1959, p. 128). In a play, of course, the frontstage is what the audience sees and is obviously the location in which the actors are performing their lines. Backstage, they can do whatever they want, and the audience will have no idea of what they are doing (as long as they are quiet). Much of our everyday interaction is on the frontstage, where an audience can see everything we do and hear everything we say. But we also spend a lot of time on the backstage, by ourselves, when we can do and say things in private (such as singing in the shower) that we would not dare do or say in public.

Social interaction involves impression management. How a student behaves with a professor is probably very different from how the same student behaves when out on the town with friends.

UNH Manchester – Aspirations in Computing Studies – CC BY 2.0.

How we dress is also a form of impression management. You are the same person regardless of what clothes you wear, but if you dress for a job interview as you would dress for a party (to use our earlier example), the person interviewing you would get an impression you might not want to convey. If you showed up for a medical visit and your physician were wearing a bathing suit, wouldn't you feel just a bit uneasy?

Sociology Making a Difference

Impression Management and Job Interviewing

Erving Goffman's (1959) concept of impression management, discussed in the text, is one of the key sociological insights for the understanding of social interaction. One reason the concept has been so useful, and one reason that it interests many college students, is that impression management has so much practical relevance. Anyone who has gone out on a first date or had a job interview can immediately recognize that impression management is something we all do and can immediately realize the importance of *effective* impression management.

Impression management is important in many settings and situations but perhaps especially important in the job interview. Many scholarly publications and job-hunting manuals emphasize the importance of proper impression management during a job interview, especially an interview for a full-time, well-paying job, as opposed to a fast-food job or something similar (Van Iddekinge, McFarland, & Raymark, 2007). The strategies they discuss include impression management involving dress, body language, and other dimensions of social interaction. Interviewing tips they recommend include (a) dressing professionally, (b) showing up early for the interview, (c) shaking hands firmly while smiling and looking the interviewer in the eye, (d) sitting with a comfortable but erect posture without crossing one's arms, (e) maintaining eye contact with the interviewer throughout the interview, and (f) shaking hands at the end of the interview and saying thank you.

These strategies and tips are probably more familiar to college students from wealthy backgrounds than to working-class people who have not gone to college. Sociologists emphasize the importance of *cultural capital*, or attitudes, skills, and knowledge that enable people to achieve a higher social status (Bourdieu & Passeron, 1990). People who grow up in poverty or near-poverty, including disproportionate numbers of people of color, are less likely than those who grow up in much wealthier circumstances to possess cultural capital. The attitudes, skills, and knowledge that many college students have and take for granted, including how to conduct oneself during a job interview, are much less familiar to individuals who grow up without cultural capital. To use some sociological language, they know much less about how to manage their impressions during a job interview should they get one and thus are less likely to be hired after an interview.

For this reason, many public and private agencies in poor and working-class communities around the country regularly hold workshops on job interviewing skills. These workshops emphasize strategies similar to those outlined earlier. One of the many organizations that offer these workshops and provides related services is the Los Angeles Urban League (http://www.laul.org/milken-family-literacy-and-youth-training-center) through its Milken Family Literacy and Youth Training Center. According to its Web site, this center "provides a comprehensive system of services of programs and services to assist youth and adults in developing the skills to compete for and obtain meaningful employment." Much of what the youth and adults who attend its workshops and other programs are learning is impression-management skills that help them find employment. Goffman's concept is helping make a difference.

Individuals engage in impression management, but so do groups and organizations. Consider the medical visit just mentioned. A physician's office usually "looks" a certain way. It is clean, it has carpeting, it has attractive furniture, and it has magazines such as *People*, *Time*, and *Sports Illustrated*. Such an office assures patients by conveying the impression that the physician and staff are competent professionals. Imagine that you entered a physician's office and saw torn carpeting, some broken furniture, and magazines such as *Maxim* and *Playboy*. What would be your instant reaction? How soon would you turn around and leave the office? As this fanciful example illustrates, impression management is critically important for groups and organizations as well as for individuals.

Impression management occurs with physical settings. These two eating establishments convey very different impressions of the quality of food and service that diners can expect.

AILAFM – Eaton Centre Food Hall – CC BY-NC-ND 2.0; Laura Henderson – Restaurant – CC BY-ND 2.0.

Life is filled with impression management. Compare the decor of your favorite fast-food restaurant with that of a very expensive restaurant with which you might be familiar. Compare the appearance, dress, and demeanor of the servers and other personnel in the two establishments. The expensive restaurant is trying to convey an image that the food will be wonderful and that the time you spend there will be memorable and well worth the money. The fast-food restaurant is trying to convey just the opposite impression. In fact, if it looked too fancy, you would probably think it was too expensive.

Some people go to great efforts to manage the impressions they convey. You have probably done so in a job interview or on a date. In New York City, the capital of book publishing, editors of large publishing companies and "superagents" for authors are very conscious of the impressions they convey, because much of the publishing industry depends on gossip, impressions, and the development of rapport. Editors and agents often dine together in one of a few very expensive "power" restaurants, where their presence is certain to be noted. Publishers or senior editors who dine at these restaurants will eat only with celebrity authors, other senior editors or publishers, or important agents. Such agents rarely dine with junior editors, who are only "allowed" to eat with junior agents. To eat with someone "beneath" your standing would convey the wrong impression (Arnold, 1998).

Emotions and Social Interaction

When we interact with others, certain **emotions**—feelings that begin with a stimulus and that often involve psychological changes and a desire to engage in specific actions—often come into play. To understand social interaction, it is helpful to understand how these emotions emerge and how they affect and are affected by social interaction.

Not surprisingly, evolutionary biologists and sociologists differ in their views on the origins of emotions. Many evolutionary biologists think that human emotions exist today because they conferred an evolutionary advantage when human civilization began eons ago (Plutchik, 2001). In this way of thinking, an emotion such as fear would help prehistoric humans (as well as other primates and organisms) survive by enabling them to recognize and avoid dangerous situations. Humans who could feel and act on fear were thus more likely to survive than those who could not. In this way, fear became a biological instinct and part of our genetic heritage. The fact that emotions such as anger, fear, hate, joy, love, and sadness are found across the world and in every culture suggests that emotions are indeed part of our biological makeup as humans.

In contrast to the evolutionary approach, a sociological approach emphasizes that emotions are *socially constructed* (Turner & Stets, 2006). To recall our earlier discussion of the social construction of reality, this means that people learn from their culture and from their social interactions which emotions are appropriate to display in which situations. In particular, statuses and the roles associated with them involve expectations of specific emotions that are appropriate or inappropriate for a given status in a given social setting. Someone attending a wedding is expected to look and be happy for the couple about to be married. Someone attending a funeral is expected to look and be mournful. Emotions are socially constructed because they arise out of the roles we play and the situations in which we find ourselves.

Sociologists emphasize that emotions are socially constructed, as they arise out of expectations for specific roles in specific settings. Because we expect people to have very different emotions at weddings and funerals, they usually end up having these emotions.

Elliot Harmon – Wedding – CC BY-SA 2.0; spazbot29 – Funeral – CC BY-SA 2.0.

The origins of emotions aside, emotions still play an essential role in social interaction, and social interaction gives rise to emotions. Accordingly, sociologists have discussed many aspects of emotions and social interaction (Turner & Stets, 2006), a few of which we outline here. One important aspect is that *insincere* displays of emotion can be used to manipulate a situation. For example, a child or adult may cry to win some sympathy, a display popularly called "crocodile tears." A staple of many novels and films is to pretend to be sorry that a rich, elderly relative is very ill in order to win a place in the relative's will. By the same token, though, people who display inappropriate emotions risk social disapproval. If you are attending a funeral of someone you did not really know that well and, out of boredom, think of a recent episode of *The Simpsons* that makes you chuckle, the glares you get will make it very clear that your emotional display is quite inappropriate.

As this example suggests, a second aspect of emotions is that we often find ourselves in situations that "demand" certain emotions we simply do not feel. This discrepancy forces most of us to *manage* our emotions to avoid social disapproval, a process called *emotion work* (Hochschild, 1983). Having to engage in emotion work in turn often leads us to feel other emotions such as anger or frustration.

A third aspect is that gender influences the emotions we feel and display. In sociology, work on gender and emotions often falls under the larger topic of femininity and masculinity as expressions of gender roles, which Chapter 11 "Gender and Gender Inequality" examines at greater length. Suffice it to say here, though at the risk of sounding stereotypical, that certain gender differences in emotions and the display of emotions do exist. For example, women cry more often and more intensely than men, and men outwardly express anger much more often than women. A key question is whether gender differences in emotions (as well as other gender differences) stem more from biology or more from culture, socialization, and other social origins. Chapter 11 "Gender and Gender Inequality" again has more to stay about this basic debate in the study of gender.

According to sociologist Jonathan Turner, positive emotions are found more often among the wealthy, while negative emotions are found more often among the poor.

Eva Rinaldi – Paris Hilton – CC BY-SA 2.0; alessandro isnotaurelio – homeless – CC BY 2.0.

A final aspect is that emotions differ across the social classes. Jonathan Turner (2010) notes that some emotions, such as happiness and trust, are positive emotions, while other emotions, such as anger, fear, and sadness, are negative emotions. Positive emotions, he says, lead to more successful social interaction and help gain needed resources (e.g., a cheerful demeanor and self-confidence can help win a high-paying job or attract a romantic partner), while negative emotions have the opposite effect. He adds that positive emotions are more often found among the upper social classes, while negative emotions are more often found among the poorer social classes. Emotion is thus "a valued resource that is distributed unequally" (Turner, 2010, pp. 189–190). The upper classes benefit from their positive emotions, while the lower classes suffer various problems because of their negative emotions. In this manner, the social class difference in positive versus negative emotions helps reinforce social inequality.

Nonverbal Social Interaction

Social interaction is both verbal and nonverbal. As Chapter 3 "Culture" discussed, culture greatly influences **nonverbal communication**, or ways of communicating that do not involve talking. Nonverbal communication includes the gestures we use and how far apart we stand when we talk with someone. When we do talk with someone, much more nonverbal interaction happens beyond gestures and standing apart. We might smile, laugh, frown, grimace, or engage in any number of other facial expressions (with or without realizing we are doing so) that let the people with whom we interact know how we feel about what we are saying or they are saying. Often how we act nonverbally is at least as important, and sometimes more important, than what our mouths are saying.

Body posture is another form of nonverbal communication, and one that often combines with facial expressions to convey how a person feels. People who are angry may cross their arms or stand with their hands on their hips and glare at someone. Someone sitting slouched in a chair looks either very comfortable or very bored, and neither posture is one you would want to use at an interview for a job you really wanted to get. Men and women may engage in certain postures while they are flirting with someone. Consciously or not, they sit or stand in certain ways that convey they are romantically interested in a particular person and hopeful that the person will return this interest.

Learning From Other Societies

Personal Space and Standing Apart: Why People From Other Countries Think Americans Are Cold and Distant

As the text discusses, one aspect of nonverbal interaction involves how far we stand apart from someone with whom we are talking. To amplify on a point first mentioned in Chapter 2 "Eye on Society: Doing Sociological Research", Americans and the citizens of Great Britain and the northern European nations customarily stand about three to four feet apart from someone who is a stranger or acquaintance. If we are closer to this person without having to be closer—that is, we're not in a crowded elevator, bar, or other setting in which it is impossible to be farther apart—we feel uncomfortable.

In contrast, people in many parts of the world—South and Central America, Africa, the Middle East, and Western European nations such as France, Spain, and Italy—stand much closer to someone with whom they are talking. In these nations, people stand only about 9 to 15 inches apart when they talk. If someone for some reason wanted to stand another two feet away, a member of one of these nations would view this person as unfriendly and might well feel insulted (Ting-Toomey, 1999; Samovar, Porter, & McDaniel, 2010).

Your author once found himself in this situation in Maine. I was talking to a professor from a Middle Eastern nation who was standing very close to me. To feel more comfortable, I moved back a step or two, without really realizing it. The professor moved forward, evidently to feel more comfortable himself, and then I moved back. He again moved forward, and I again moved back. Within a few minutes, we had moved about 20 to 30 feet!

When Americans travel abroad, anecdotal evidence indicates that they often think that people in other nations are pushy and demanding and that these citizens view Americans as cold and aloof (Ellsworth, 2005). Although there are many cultural differences between Americans and people in other lands, personal space is one of the most important differences. This fact yields an important lesson for any American who travels abroad, and it also illustrates the significance of culture for behavior and thus the value of the sociological perspective.

As with emotions, gender appears to influence how people communicate nonverbally (Hall, 2006). For example, a number of studies find that women are more likely than men to smile, to nod, and to have more expressive faces. Once again, biologists and social scientists disagree over the origins of these and other gender differences in nonverbal communication, with social scientists attributing the differences to gender roles, culture, and socialization.

Research finds that women tend to smile more often than men. Biologists and social scientists disagree over the origins of this gender difference in nonverbal communication.

mhobl – colourful and smiling – CC BY-NC-ND 2.0.

Gender differences also exist in two other forms of nonverbal interaction: eye contact and touching. Women tend more than men to look directly into the eyes of people with whom they interact, a process called *gazing*. Such gazing is meant to convey interest in the interaction and to be nonthreatening. On the other hand, men are more likely than women to *stare* at someone in a way that is indeed threatening. A man might stare at a man because he resents something the other man said or did; a man might stare at a woman because he eyes her as a sexual object. In touching, men are more likely than women to touch someone, especially when that someone is a woman; as he guides her through a doorway, for example, he might put his arm behind her arm or back. On the other hand, women are more likely than men to touch themselves when they are talking with someone, a process called *self-touching*. Thus if a woman is saying "I think that…," she might briefly touch the area just below her neck to refer to herself. Men are less likely to refer to themselves in this manner.

Key Takeaways

- A dramaturgical approach likens social interaction to a dramatic production.
- Individuals ordinarily try to manage the impression they make when interacting with others. Social interaction can be understood as a series of attempts at impression management.
- Various kinds of role strains and problems often occur as individuals try to perform the roles expected of

them from the many statuses they occupy.

- Emotions and nonverbal communication are essential components of social interaction. Sociologists and biologists disagree on the origins of gender differences in these two components.

For Your Review

1. Describe a recent example of how you tried to manage the impression you were conveying in a social interaction.
2. Describe a recent example of a role problem that you experienced and what you did, if anything, to reduce this problem.
3. If you were in charge of our society, what socialization practice would you most try to change to help improve our society? Explain your answer.

Enhancing Social Interaction: What Sociology Suggests

If a goal of this book is to help you understand more about yourself and the social world around you, then a sociological understanding of social interaction should help your own social interaction and also that of other people.

We see evidence of the practical value of a sociological understanding in the "Sociology Making a Difference" and "Learning From Other Societies" boxes in this chapter. The "Sociology Making a Difference" box discussed the impact that Goffman's concept of impression management has made in job hunting in general and particularly in efforts to improve the employment chances of the poor and people of color. The "Learning From Other Societies" box discussed why Americans sometimes have trouble interacting with people abroad. Differences in personal space can lead to hurt feelings between Americans and people in other nations.

If we are aware, then, of the importance of impression management, we can be more conscious of the impressions we are making in our daily interactions, whether they involve talking with a professor, interviewing for a job, going out on a first date, or speaking to a police officer who has pulled you over. By the same token, if we are aware of the importance of personal space, we can improve our interactions with people with different cultural backgrounds. Thus, if we are Americans of northern European ancestry and are interacting with people from other nations, we can be aware that physical distance matters and perhaps stand closer to someone than we might ordinarily feel comfortable doing to help the other person feel more comfortable and like us more. Conversely, readers who are not Americans of northern European ancestry might move back a step or two to accomplish the same goals.

To illustrate the importance of enhancing social interaction among people from different cultural backgrounds, the federal government has prepared a document called "Developing Cultural Competence in Disaster Mental Health Programs: Guiding Principles and Recommendations" (http://mentalhealth. samhsa.gov/publications/allpubs/sma03-3828/sectiontwo.asp). The document is designed to help mental-health professionals who are assisting victims of natural disasters in other countries or within the United States. It warns professionals that cultural differences may impede their efforts to help victims: "Both verbal and nonverbal communication can be barriers to providing effective disaster crisis counseling when survivors and workers are from different cultures. Culture influences how people express their feelings as well as what feelings are appropriate to express in a given situation. The inability to communicate can make both parties feel alienated and helpless." It also advises professionals to be aware of the personal space needs of the people they are trying to help: "A person from one subculture might touch or move closer to another as a friendly gesture, whereas someone from a different culture might consider such behavior invasive. Disaster-crisis counselors must look for clues to a survivor's need for space. Such clues may include, for example, moving the chair back or stepping closer." As this document makes clear, if we can draw on a sociological understanding to enhance our social interaction skills, we can help not only ourselves but also people who come from other cultures.

References

Arnold, M. (1998, June 11). Art of foreplay at the table. *The New York Times*, p. B3.

Berger, P., & Luckmann, T. (1963). *The social construction of reality*. New York, NY: Doubleday.

Bourdieu, P., & Passeron, J.-C. (1990). *Reproduction in education, society and culture*. Newbury Park, CA: Sage.

Ellsworth, M. (2005, December 12). Crossing cultures—Personal space. *ExPatFacts*. Retrieved from http://www.expatfacts.com/2005/12/crossing_cultures_personal_spa.html.

Garfinkel, H. (1967). *Studies in ethnomethodology*. Cambridge, England: Polity Press.

Goffman, E. (1959). *The presentation of self in everyday life*. Garden City, NY: Doubleday.

Hall, J. A. (2006). Women's and men's nonverbal communication: Similarities, differences, stereotypes, and origins. In V. Manusov & M. L. Patterson (Eds.), *The Sage handbook of nonverbal communication* (pp. 201–218). Thousand Oaks, CA: Sage.

Hochschild, A. R. (1983). *The managed heart: Commercialization of human feeling*. Berkeley: University of California Press.

Kirkham, G. L. (1984). A professor's "street lessons." In R. G. Culbertson (Ed.), *"Order under law": Readings in criminal justice* (pp. 77–89). Prospect Heights, IL: Waveland Press.

Plutchik, R. (2001). The nature of emotions. *American Scientist, 89*, 344–350.

Ting-Toomey, S. (1999). *Communicating across cultures*. New York, NY: Guilford Press; Samovar, L. A., Porter, R. E., & McDaniel, E. R. (2010). *Communication between cultures* (7th ed.). Boston, MA: Wadsworth.

Turner, J. H., & Stets, J. E. (2006). Sociological theories of human emotions. *Annual Review of Sociology, 32*, 25–52.

Turner, J. H. (2010). The stratification of emotions: Some preliminary generalizations. *Sociological Inquiry, 80*, 168–199.

Van Iddekinge, C. H., McFarland, L. A., & Raymark, P. H. (2007). Antecedents of impression management use and effectiveness in a structured interview. *Journal of Management, 33*, 752–773.

5.4 End-of-Chapter Material

Summary

1. The major components of social structure are statuses, roles, groups and organizations, and social institutions.
2. As societies moved beyond the hunting-and-gathering stage, they became larger and more impersonal and individualistic and were characterized by increasing inequality and conflict.
3. Industrial societies developed about 250 years ago after several inventions allowed work to become more mechanized. The Industrial Revolution has had important consequences, some good and some bad, in virtually every area of society. Postindustrial societies have begun in the last few decades with the advent of the computer and an increasing number of service jobs. While it's too soon to know the consequences of the advent of postindustrialization, there are signs it will have important implications for the nature of work and employment in modern society
4. Erving Goffman used a theatrical metaphor called dramaturgy to understand social interaction, which he likened to behavior on a stage in a play. More generally, many sociologists stress the concept of roles in social interaction. Although we usually play our roles automatically, social order occasionally breaks down when people don't play their roles. This breakdown illustrates the fragility of social order.
5. Although roles help us interact, they can also lead to problems such as role conflict and role strain. In another problem, some individuals may be expected to carry out a role that demands a personality they do not have.
6. Emotions play an important role in social interaction. They influence how social interaction proceeds, and they are also influenced by social interaction. Sociologists emphasize that emotions are socially constructed, as they arise from the roles we play and the situations in which we find ourselves.
7. Nonverbal communication is an essential part of social interaction. The sexes differ in several forms of nonverbal communication. Biologists and sociologists differ on the origins of these differences.

Using Sociology

Suppose you are working in a financial services firm and are married with a 2-year-old daughter. Your spouse is out of town at a conference, and you have an important meeting to attend shortly after lunch where you are scheduled to make a key presentation. As you are reviewing your PowerPoint slides while you eat lunch at your desk, you get a call from your daughter's day care center. Your daughter is not feeling well and has a slight temperature, and the day care center asks you to come pick her up. What do you do?

Chapter 6: Groups and Organizations

Social Issues in the News

"Arrests Made in Vandalism Spree," the headline said. In March 2010, three high school students, two juveniles and one 18-year-old, allegedly spray-painted obscenities on cars, homes, and an elementary school in Muncie, Indiana. A police captain said, "I think they just started out to do a friend's house. The thing kind of carried away after that and went nuts through the rest of the neighborhood." The estimated damage was in the thousands of dollars and was so extensive that the 18-year-old suspect was charged with a felony. The police captain said the boys felt sorry for their vandalism. "They probably wish they could take it back, but it happened and it's a lot of damage." (Werner, 2010)

This news story depicts an unusual group activity, spray-painting. It is likely that none of these teens would have done the spray-painting by himself. If so, this news story reminds us of the importance of the many groups to which people typically belong. To recall Chapter 5 "Social Structure and Social Interaction", the English poet John Donne (1573–1631) once wrote, "No man is an island, entire of itself; Every man is a piece of the continent, a part of the main" (Donne, 1839, pp. 574–575). Obviously meant to apply to both sexes, Donne's passage reminds us that we are all members of society. At the more micro level, we are all members of social groups and categories. As we have seen in previous chapters, sociologists look at us more as members of groups and less as individuals, and they try to explain our attitudes and behavior in terms of the many groups and social backgrounds from which we come. For these reasons, sociology is often considered the study of group life, group behavior, and group processes. This chapter discusses the importance of many types of groups for understanding our behavior and attitudes and for understanding society itself. We will see that groups are necessary for many of our needs and for society's functioning but at the same time can often lead to several negative consequences, as the story of vandalism in Muncie illustrates.

References

Donne, J. (1839). Meditation XVII. In H. Alford (Ed.), *The works of John Donne* (Vol. III, pp. 574–575). London, England: John W. Parker.

Werner, N. (2010, April 2). Arrests made in vandalism spree. *The Star Press*. Retrieved from http://pqasb.pqarchiver.com/thestarpress/access/2000011861.html?FMT=ABS&date=Apr+02%2C+2010.

6.1 Social Groups

Learning Objectives

1. Describe how a social group differs from a social category or social aggregate.
2. Distinguish a primary group from a secondary group.
3. Define a reference group and provide one example of such a group.
4. Explain the importance of networks in a modern society.

A **social group** consists of two or more people who regularly interact on the basis of mutual expectations and who share a common identity. It is easy to see from this definition that we all belong to many types of social groups: our families, our different friendship groups, the sociology class and other courses we attend, our workplaces, the clubs and organizations to which we belong, and so forth. Except in rare cases, it is difficult to imagine any of us living totally alone. Even people who live by themselves still interact with family members, coworkers, and friends and to this extent still have several group memberships.

It is important here to distinguish social groups from two related concepts: social categories and social aggregates. A **social category** is a collection of individuals who have at least one attribute in common but otherwise do not necessarily interact. *Women* is an example of a social category. All women have at least one thing in common, their biological sex, even though they do not interact. *Asian Americans* is another example of a social category, as all Asian Americans have two things in common, their ethnic background and their residence in the United States, even if they do not interact or share any other similarities. As these examples suggest, gender, race, and ethnicity are the basis for several social categories. Other common social categories are based on our religious preference, geographical residence, and social class.

Falling between a social category and a social group is the **social aggregate**, which is a collection of people who are in the same place at the same time but who otherwise do not necessarily interact, except in the most superficial of ways, or have anything else in common. The crowd at a sporting event and the audience at a movie or play are common examples of social aggregates. These collections of people are not a social category, because the people are together physically, and they are also not a group, because they do not really interact and do not have a common identity unrelated to being in the crowd or audience at that moment.

A social aggregate is a collection of people who are in the same place at the same time but who otherwise have nothing else in common. A crowd at a sporting event and the audience at a movie or play are examples of social aggregates.

Eliud Gil Samaniego – Art – Aguilas de Mexicali – CC BY-NC-ND 2.0.

With these distinctions laid out, let's return to our study of groups by looking at the different types of groups sociologists have delineated.

Primary and Secondary Groups

A common distinction is made between primary groups and secondary groups. A **primary group** is usually small, is characterized by extensive interaction and strong emotional ties, and endures over time. Members of such groups care a lot about each other and identify strongly with the group. Indeed, their membership in a primary group gives them much of their social identity. Charles Horton Cooley, whose looking-glass-self concept was discussed in Chapter 5 "Social Structure and Social Interaction", called these groups *primary*, because they are the first groups we belong to and because they are so important for social life. The family is the primary group that comes most readily to mind, but small peer friendship groups, whether they are your high school friends, an urban street gang, or middle-aged adults who get together regularly, are also primary groups.

Although a primary group is usually small, somewhat larger groups can also act much like primary groups. Here athletic teams, fraternities, and sororities come to mind. Although these groups are larger than the typical family or small circle of friends, the emotional bonds their members form are often quite intense. In some workplaces, coworkers can get to know each other very well and become a friendship group in which the members discuss personal concerns and interact outside the workplace. To the extent this happens, small groups of coworkers can become primary groups (Elsesser & Peplau, 2006; Marks, 1994).

Our primary groups play significant roles in so much that we do. Survey evidence bears this out for the family. Figure 6.1 "Percentage of Americans Who Say Their Family Is Very Important, Quite Important, Not Too Important, or Not at All Important in Their Lives" shows that an overwhelming majority of Americans say their family is "very important" in their lives. Would you say the same for your family?

Figure 6.1 Percentage of Americans Who Say Their Family Is Very Important, Quite Important, Not Too Important, or Not at All Important in Their Lives

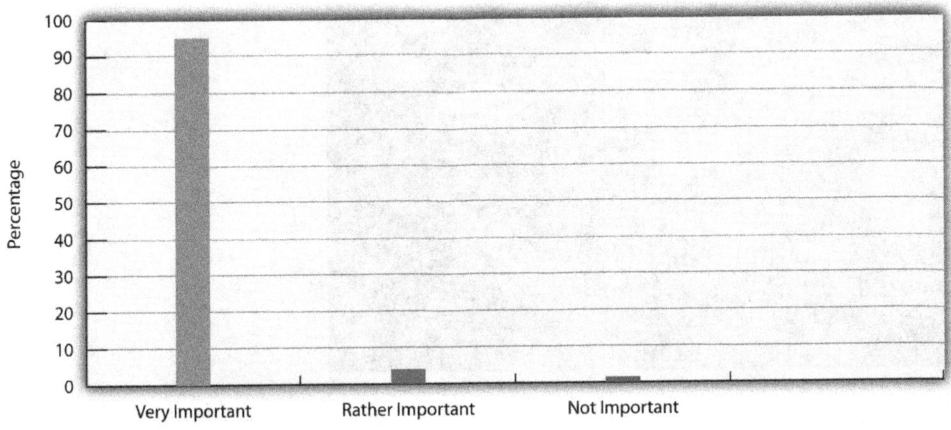

Source: Data from World Values Survey, 2002.

Ideally, our primary groups give us emotional warmth and comfort in good times and bad and provide us an identity and a strong sense of loyalty and belonging. Our primary group memberships are thus important for such things as our happiness and mental health. Much research, for example, shows rates of suicide and emotional problems are lower among people involved with social support networks such as their families and friends than among people who are pretty much alone (Maimon & Kuhl, 2008). However, our primary group relationships may also not be ideal, and, if they are negative ones, they may cause us much mental and emotional distress. In this regard, the family as a primary group is the setting for much physical and sexual violence committed against women and children (Gosselin, 2010) (see Chapter 11 "Gender and Gender Inequality").

A secondary group is larger and more impersonal than a primary group and may exist for a relatively short time to achieve a specific purpose. The students in any one of your college courses constitute a secondary group.

Jeremy Wilburn – Students in Classrooms at UIS – CC BY-NC-ND 2.0.

Although primary groups are the most important ones in our lives, we belong to many more **secondary groups**, which are groups that are larger and more impersonal and exist, often for a relatively short time, to achieve a specific purpose. Secondary group members feel less emotionally attached to each other than do primary group members and do not identify as much with their group nor feel as loyal to it. This does not mean secondary groups are unimportant, as society could not exist without them, but they still do not provide the potential emotional benefits for their members that primary groups ideally do. The sociology class for which you are reading this book is an example of a secondary group, as are the clubs and organizations on your campus to which you might belong. Other secondary groups include religious, business, governmental, and civic organizations. In some of these groups, members get to know each other better than in other secondary groups, but their emotional ties and intensity of interaction generally remain much weaker than in primary groups.

Reference Groups

Primary and secondary groups can act both as our **reference groups** or as groups that set a standard for guiding our own behavior and attitudes. The family we belong to obviously affects our actions and views, as, for example, there were probably times during your adolescence when you decided not to do certain things with your friends to avoid disappointing or upsetting your parents. On the other hand, your friends regularly acted during your adolescence as a reference group, and you probably dressed the way they did or did things with them, even against your parents' wishes, precisely because they were your reference group. Some of our reference groups are groups to which we do not belong but to which we nonetheless *want* to belong. A small child, for example, may dream of becoming an astronaut and dress like one and play like one. Some high school students may not belong to the "cool" clique in school but may still dress like the members of this clique, either in hopes of being accepted as a member or simply because they admire the dress and style of its members.

Samuel Stouffer and colleagues (Stouffer, Suchman, DeVinney, Star, & Williams, 1949) demonstrated the importance of reference groups in a well-known study of American soldiers during World War II. This study sought to determine why some soldiers were more likely than others to have low morale. Surprisingly, Stouffer found that the actual, "objective" nature of their living conditions affected their morale less than whether they felt other soldiers were better or worse off than they were. Even if their own living conditions were fairly good, they were likely to have low morale if they thought other soldiers were doing better. Another factor affecting their morale was whether they thought they had a good chance of being promoted. Soldiers in units with high promotion rates were, paradoxically, more pessimistic about their own chances of promotion than soldiers in units with low promotion rates. Evidently the former soldiers were dismayed by seeing so many other men in their unit getting promoted and felt worse off as a result. In each case, Stouffer concluded, the soldiers' views were shaped by their perceptions of what was happening in their reference group of other soldiers. They *felt* deprived relative to the experiences of the members of their reference group and adjusted their views accordingly. The concept of *relative deprivation* captures this process.

In-Groups and Out-Groups

Members of primary and some secondary groups feel loyal to those groups and take pride in belonging to them. We call such groups **in-groups**. Fraternities, sororities, sports teams, and juvenile gangs are examples of in-groups. Members of an in-group often end up competing with members of another group for various kinds of rewards. This other group is called an **out-group**. The competition between in-groups and out-groups is often friendly, as among members of intramural teams during the academic year when they vie in athletic events. Sometimes, however, in-group members look down their noses at out-group members and even act very hostilely toward them. Rival fraternity members at several campuses have been known to get into fights and trash each other's houses. More seriously, street gangs attack each other, and hate groups such as skinheads and the Ku Klux Klan have committed violence against people of color, Jews, and other individuals they consider members of out-groups. As these examples make clear, in-group membership can promote very negative attitudes toward the out-groups with which the in-groups feel they are competing. These attitudes are especially likely to develop in times of rising unemployment and other types of economic distress, as in-group members are apt to blame out-group members for their economic problems (Olzak, 1992).

Social Networks

These days in the job world we often hear of "networking," or taking advantage of your connections with people who have connections to other people who can help you land a job. You do not necessarily know these "other people" who ultimately can help you, but you *do* know the people who know them. Your ties to the other people are weak or nonexistent, but your involvement in this network may nonetheless help you find a job.

Modern life is increasingly characterized by such **social networks**, or the totality of relationships that link us to other people and groups and through them to still other people and groups. Some of these relationships involve strong bonds, while other relationships involve weak bonds (Granovetter, 1983). Facebook and other Web sites have made possible networks of a size unimaginable just a decade ago. Social networks are important for many things, including getting advice, borrowing small amounts of money, and finding a job. When you need advice or want to borrow $5 or $10, to whom do you turn? The answer is undoubtedly certain members of your social networks—your friends, family, and so forth.

The indirect links you have to people through your social networks can help you find a job or even receive better medical care. For example, if you come down with a serious condition such as cancer, you would probably first talk with your primary care physician, who would refer you to one or more specialists whom you do not know and who have no connections to you through other people you know. That is, they are not part of your social network. Because the specialists do not know you and do not know anyone else who knows you, they are likely to treat you very professionally, which means, for better or worse, impersonally.

A social network is the totality of relationships that link us to other people and groups and through them to still other people and groups. Our involvement in certain networks can bring certain advantages, including better medical care if one's network includes a physician or two.

Gavin Llewellyn – My social networks – CC BY 2.0.

Now suppose you have some nearby friends or relatives who are physicians. Because of their connections with other nearby physicians, they can recommend certain specialists to you and perhaps even get you an earlier appointment than your primary physician could. Because these specialists realize you know physicians they know, they may treat you more personally than otherwise. In the long run, you may well get better medical care from your network through the physicians you know. People lucky enough to have such connections may thus be better off medically than people who do not.

But let's look at this last sentence. What kinds of people have such connections? What kinds of people have friends or relatives who are physicians? All other things being equal, if you had two people standing before you, one employed as a vice president in a large corporation and the other working part time at a fast-food restaurant, which person do you think would be more likely to know a physician or two personally? Your answer is probably the corporate vice president. The point is that factors such as our social class and occupational status, our race and ethnicity, and our gender affect how likely we are to have social networks that can help us get jobs, good medical care, and other advantages. As just one example, a study of three working-class neighborhoods in New York City—one white, one African American, and one Latino—found that white youths were more involved through their parents and peers in job-referral networks than youths in the other two neighborhoods and thus were better able to find jobs, even if they had been arrested for delinquency (Sullivan, 1989). This study suggests that even if we look at people of different races and ethnicities in roughly the same social class, whites have an advantage over people of color in the employment world.

Gender also matters in the employment world. In many businesses, there still exists an "old boys' network," in which male executives with job openings hear about male applicants from male colleagues and friends. Male employees already on the job tend to spend more social time with their male bosses than do their female counterparts. These related processes make it more difficult for females than for males to be hired and promoted (Barreto, Ryan, & Schmitt, 2009). To counter these effects and to help support each other, some women form networks where they meet, talk about mutual problems, and discuss ways of dealing with these problems. An example of such a network is The Links, Inc., a community service group of 12,000 professional African American women whose name underscores the importance of networking (http://www.linksinc.org/index.shtml). Its members participate in 270 chapters in 42 states; Washington, DC; and the Bahamas. Every two years, more than 2,000 Links members convene for a national assembly at which they network, discuss the problems they face as professional women of color, and consider fund-raising strategies for the causes they support.

Key Takeaways

- Groups are a key building block of social life but can also have negative consequences.
- Primary groups are generally small and include intimate relationships, while secondary groups are larger and more impersonal.
- Reference groups provide a standard for guiding and evaluating our attitudes and behaviors.
- Social networks are increasingly important in modern life, and involvement in such networks may have favorable consequences for many aspects of one's life.

For Your Review

1. Briefly describe one reference group that has influenced your attitudes or behavior, and explain why it had

this influence on you.

2. Briefly describe an example of when one of your social networks proved helpful to you (or describe an example when a social network helped someone you know).
3. List at least five secondary groups to which you now belong and/or to which you previously belonged.

References

Barreto, M., Ryan, M. K., & Schmitt, M. T. (Eds.). (2009). *The glass ceiling in the 21st century: Understanding barriers to gender equality*. Washington, DC: American Psychological Association.

Elsesser, K., & Peplau L. A. (2006). The glass partition: Obstacles to cross-sex friendships at work. *Human Relations, 59,* 1077–1100.

Gosselin, D. K. (2010). *Heavy hands: An introduction to the crimes of family violence* (4th ed.). Upper Saddle River, NJ: Prentice Hall.

Granovetter, M. (1983). The strength of weak ties: A network theory revisited. *Sociological Theory, 1,* 201–233.

Maimon, D., & Kuhl, D. C. (2008). Social control and youth suicidality: Situating Durkheim's ideas in a multilevel framework. *American Sociological Review, 73,* 921–943.

Marks, S. R. (1994). Intimacy in the public realm: The case of co-workers. *Social Forces, 72,* 843–858.

Olzak, S. (1992). *The dynamics of ethnic competition and conflict*. Stanford, CA: Stanford University Press.

Stouffer, S. A., Suchman, E. A., DeVinney, L. C., Star, S. A., & Williams, R. M., Jr. (1949). *The American soldier: Adjustment during army life* (Studies in Social Psychology in World War II, Vol. 1). Princeton, NJ: Princeton University Press.

Sullivan, M. (1989). *Getting paid: Youth crime and work in the inner city*. Ithaca, NY: Cornell University Press.

6.2 Group Dynamics and Behavior

Learning Objectives

1. Explain how and why group dynamics change as groups grow in size.
2. Describe the different types of leaders and leadership styles.
3. Be familiar with experimental evidence on group conformity.
4. Explain how groupthink develops and why its development may lead to negative consequences.

Social scientists have studied how people behave in groups and how groups affect people's behavior, attitudes, and perceptions (Gastil, 2009). Their research underscores the importance of groups for social life, but it also points to the dangerous influence groups can sometimes have on their members.

The Importance of Group Size

The distinction made earlier between small primary groups and larger secondary groups reflects the importance of group size for the functioning of a group, the nature of its members' attachments, and the group's stability. If you have ever taken a very small class, say fewer than 15 students, you probably noticed that the class atmosphere differed markedly from that of a large lecture class you may have been in. In the small class, you were able to know the professor better, and the students in the room were able to know each other better. Attendance in the small class was probably more regular than in the large lecture class.

Over the years, sociologists and other scholars have studied the effects of group size on group dynamics. One of the first to do so was German sociologist Georg Simmel (1858–1918), who discussed the effects of groups of different sizes. The smallest group, of course, is the two-person group, or **dyad**, such as a married couple or two people engaged to be married or at least dating steadily. In this smallest of groups, Simmel noted, relationships can be very intense emotionally (as you might know from personal experience) but also very unstable and short lived: if one person ends the relationship, the dyad ends as well.

The smallest group is the two-person group, or dyad. Dyad relationships can be very intense emotionally but also unstable and short lived. Why is this so?

erin m – 2 couples – CC BY-NC 2.0.

A **triad**, or three-person group, involves relationships that are still fairly intense, but it is also more stable than a dyad. A major reason for this, said Simmel, is that if two people in a triad have a dispute, the third member can help them reach some compromise that will satisfy all the triad members. The downside of a triad is that two of its members may become very close and increasingly disregard the third member, reflecting the old saying that "three's a crowd." As one example, some overcrowded college dorms are forced to house students in triples, or three to a room. In such a situation, suppose that two of the roommates are night owls and like to stay up very late, while the third wants lights out by 11:00 p.m. If majority rules, as well it might, the third roommate will feel very dissatisfied and may decide to try to find other roommates.

As groups become larger, the intensity of their interaction and bonding decreases, but their stability increases. The major reason for this is the sheer number of relationships that can exist in a larger group. For example, in a dyad only one relationship exists, that between the two members of the dyad. In a triad (say composed of members A, B, and C), three relationships exist: A-B, A-C, and B-C. In a four-person group, the number of relationships rises to six: A-B, A-C, A-D, B-C, B-D, and C-D. In a five-person group, 10 relationships exist, and in a seven-person group, 21 exist (see Figure 6.2 "Number of Two-Person Relationships in Groups of Different Sizes"). As the number of possible relationships rises, the amount of time a group member can spend with any other group member must decline, and with this decline comes less intense interaction and weaker emotional bonds. But as group size increases, the group also becomes more stable because it is large enough to survive any one member's departure from the group. When you graduate from your college or university, any clubs, organizations, or sports teams to which you belong will continue despite your exit, no matter how important you were to the group, as the remaining members of the group and new recruits will carry on in your absence.

Figure 6.2 Number of Two-Person Relationships in Groups of Different Sizes

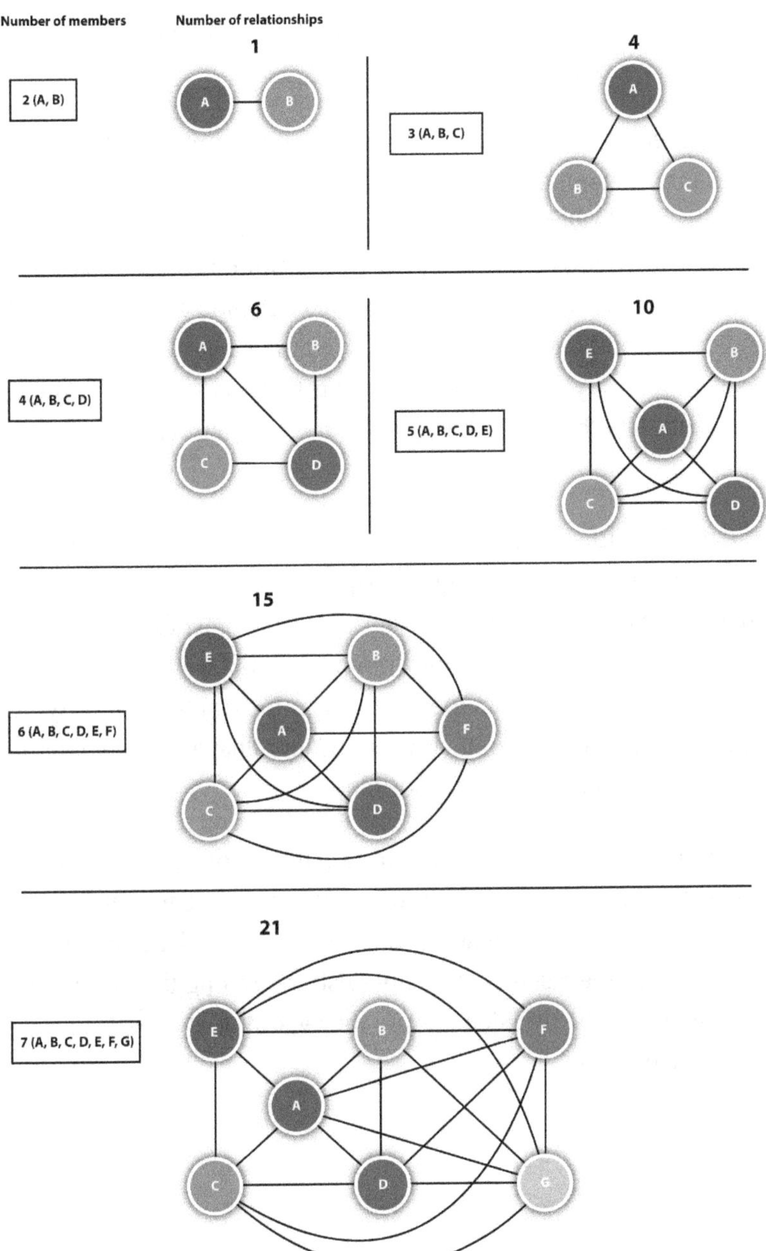

Group Leadership and Decision Making

Most groups have leaders. In the family, of course, the parents are the leaders, as much as their children sometimes might not like that. Even some close friendship groups have a leader or two who emerge over time. Virtually all secondary groups have leaders. These groups often have a charter, operations manual, or similar document that stipulates how leaders are appointed or elected and what their duties are.

Sociologists commonly distinguish two types of leaders, instrumental and expressive. An **instrumental leader** is a leader whose main focus is to achieve group goals and accomplish group tasks. Often instrumental leaders try to carry out their role even if they alienate other members of the group. The second type is the **expressive**

leader, whose main focus is to maintain and improve the quality of relationships among group members and more generally to ensure group harmony. Some groups may have both types of leaders.

Related to the leader types is leadership *style*. Three such styles are commonly distinguished. The first, **authoritarian leadership**, involves a primary focus on achieving group goals and on rigorous compliance with group rules and penalties for noncompliance. Authoritarian leaders typically make decisions on their own and tell other group members what to do and how to do it. The second style, **democratic leadership**, involves extensive consultation with group members on decisions and less emphasis on rule compliance. Democratic leaders still make the final decision but do so only after carefully considering what other group members have said, and usually their decision will agree with the views of a majority of the members. The final style is **laissez-faire leadership**. Here the leader more or less sits back and lets the group function on its own and really exerts no leadership role.

When a decision must be reached, laissez-faire leadership is less effective than the other two in helping a group get things done. Whether authoritarian or democratic leadership is better for a group depends on the group's priorities. If the group values task accomplishment more than anything else, including how well group members get along and how much they like their leader, then authoritarian leadership is preferable to democratic leadership, as it is better able to achieve group goals quickly and efficiently. But if group members place their highest priority on their satisfaction with decisions and decision making in the group, then they would want to have a lot of input in decisions. In this case, democratic leadership is preferable to authoritarian leadership.

Some small groups shun leadership and instead try to operate by *consensus*. In this model of decision making popularized by Quakers (T. S. Brown, 2009), no decision is made unless all group members agree with it. If even one member disagrees, the group keeps discussing the issue until it reaches a compromise that satisfies everyone. If the person disagreeing does not feel very strongly about the issue or does not wish to prolong the discussion, she or he may agree to "stand aside" and let the group make the decision despite the lack of total consensus. But if this person refuses to stand aside, no decision may be possible.

Some small groups operate by consensus instead of having a leader guiding or mandating their decision making. This model of decision making was popularized by the Society of Friends (Quakers).

John – All Are Welcome – CC BY 2.0.

A major advantage of the consensus style of decision making is psychic. Because everyone has a chance to voice an opinion about a potential decision, and no decisions are reached unless everyone agrees with them, group members will ordinarily feel good about the eventual decision and also about being in the group. The major disadvantage has to do with time and efficiency. When groups operate by consensus, their discussions may become long and tedious, as no voting is allowed and discussion must continue until everyone is satisfied with the outcome. This means the group may well be unable to make decisions quickly and efficiently.

One final issue is how gender influences leadership styles. Although the evidence indicates that women and men are equally capable of being good leaders, their leadership styles do tend to differ. Women are more likely to be democratic leaders, while men are more likely to be authoritarian leaders (Eagly & Carli, 2007). Because of this difference, women leaders sometimes have trouble securing respect from their subordinates and are criticized for being too soft. Yet if they respond with a more masculine, or authoritarian, style, they may be charged with acting too much like a man and be criticized in ways a man would not be.

Groups, Roles, and Conformity

We have seen in this and previous chapters that groups are essential for social life, in large part because they play an important part in the socialization process and provide emotional and other support for their members. As sociologists have emphasized since the origins of the discipline during the 19th century, the influence of groups on individuals is essential for social stability. This influence operates through many mechanisms, including the roles that group members are expected to play. Secondary groups such as business organizations are also fundamental to complex industrial societies such as our own.

Social stability results because groups induce their members to conform to the norms, values, and attitudes of the groups themselves and of the larger society to which they belong. As the chapter-opening news story about teenage vandalism reminds us, however, conformity to the group, or peer pressure, has a downside if it means that people might adopt group norms, attitudes, or values that are bad for some reason to hold and may even result in harm to others. Conformity is thus a double-edged sword. Unfortunately, bad conformity happens all too often, as several social-psychological experiments, to which we now turn, remind us.

Solomon Asch and Perceptions of Line Lengths

Several decades ago Solomon Asch (1958) conducted one of the first of these experiments. Consider the pair of cards in Figure 6.3 "Examples of Cards Used in Asch's Experiment". One of the lines (A, B, or C) on the right card is identical in length to the single line in the left card. Which is it? If your vision is up to par, you undoubtedly answered Line B. Asch showed several students pairs of cards similar to the pair in Figure 6.3 "Examples of Cards Used in Asch's Experiment" to confirm that it was very clear which of the three lines was the same length as the single line.

Figure 6.3 Examples of Cards Used in Asch's Experiment

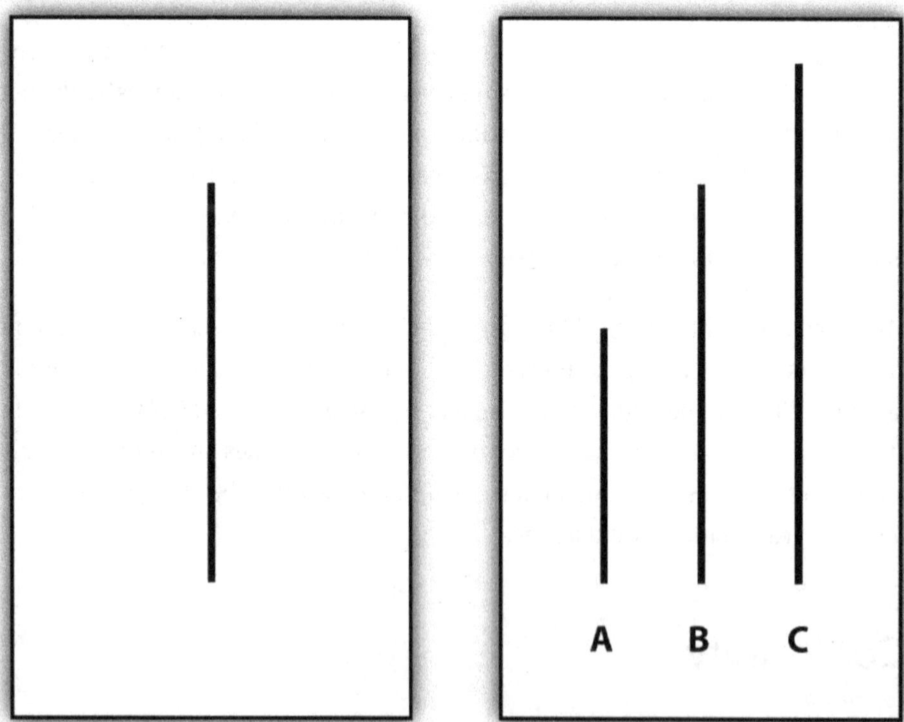

Next, he had students meet in groups of at least six members and told them he was testing their visual ability. One by one he asked each member of the group to identify which of the three lines was the same length as the single line. One by one each student gave a wrong answer. Finally, the last student had to answer, and about one-third of the time the final student in each group also gave the wrong answer that everyone else was giving.

Unknown to these final students, all the other students were confederates or accomplices, to use some experimental jargon, as Asch had told them to give a wrong answer on purpose. The final student in each group was thus a naive subject, and Asch's purpose was to see how often the naive subjects in all the groups would give the wrong answer that everyone else was giving, even though it was *very* clear it was a wrong answer.

After each group ended its deliberations, Asch asked the naive subjects who gave the wrong answers why they did so. Some replied that they knew the answer was wrong but they did not want to look different from the other people in the group, even though they were strangers before the experiment began. But other naive subjects said *they had begun to doubt their own visual perception*: they decided that if everyone else was giving a different answer, then somehow they were seeing the cards incorrectly.

Asch's experiment indicated that groups induce conformity for at least two reasons. First, members feel pressured to conform so as not to alienate other members. Second, members may decide their own perceptions or views are wrong because they see other group members perceiving things differently and begin to doubt their own perceptive abilities. For either or both reasons, then, groups can, for better or worse, affect our judgments and our actions.

Stanley Milgram and Electric Shock

Although the type of influence Asch's experiment involved was benign, other experiments indicate that individuals can conform in a very harmful way. One such very famous experiment was conducted by Yale University psychologist Stanley Milgram (1974), who designed it to address an important question that arose after World War II and the revelation of the murders of millions of people during the Nazi Holocaust. This question was, "How was the Holocaust possible?" Many people blamed the authoritarian nature of German culture and the so-called authoritarian personality that it inspired among German residents, who, it was thought, would be quite ready to obey rules and demands from authority figures.

Milgram wanted to see whether Germans would indeed be more likely than Americans to obey unjust authority. He devised a series of experiments and found that his American subjects were quite likely to give potentially lethal electric shocks to other people. During the experiment, a subject, or "teacher," would come into a laboratory and be told by a man wearing a white lab coat to sit down at a table housing a machine that sent electric shocks to a "learner." Depending on the type of experiment, this was either a person whom the teacher never saw and heard only over a loudspeaker, a person sitting in an adjoining room whom the teacher could see through a window and hear over the loudspeaker, or a person sitting right next to the teacher.

The teacher was then told to read the learner a list of word pairs, such as mother-father, cat-dog, and sun-moon. At the end of the list, the teacher was then asked to read the first word of the first word pair—for example, "mother" in our list—and to read several possible matches. If the learner got the right answer ("father"), the teacher would move on to the next word pair, but if the learner gave the wrong answer, the teacher was to administer an electric shock to the learner. The initial shock was 15 volts (V), and each time a wrong answer was given, the shock would be increased, finally going up to 450 V, which was marked on the machine as "Danger: Severe Shock." The learners often gave wrong answers and would cry out in pain as the voltage increased. In the 200-V range, they would scream, and in the 400-V range, they would say nothing at all. As far as the teachers knew, the learners had lapsed into unconsciousness from the electric shocks and even died. In reality, the learners were not actually being shocked. Instead, the voice and screams heard through the loudspeaker were from a tape recorder, and the learners that some teachers saw were only pretending to be in agony.

Before his study began, Milgram consulted several psychologists, who assured him that no sane person would be willing to administer lethal shock in his experiments. He thus was shocked (pun intended) to find that more than half the teachers went all the way to 450 V in the experiments, where they could only hear the learner over a loudspeaker and not see him. Even in the experiments where the learner was sitting next to the teacher, some teachers still went to 450 V by forcing a hand of the screaming, resisting, but tied-down learner onto a metal plate that completed the electric circuit.

Milgram concluded that people are quite willing, however reluctantly, to obey authority even if it means inflicting great harm on others. If that could happen in his artificial experiment situation, he thought, then perhaps the Holocaust was not so incomprehensible after all, and it would be too simplistic to blame the Holocaust just on the authoritarianism of German culture. Instead, perhaps its roots lay in the very conformity to roles and group norms that makes society possible in the first place. The same processes that make society possible may also make tragedies like the Holocaust possible.

The Third Wave

In 1969, concern about the Holocaust prompted Ron Jones, a high school teacher from Palo Alto, California, to conduct a real-life experiment that reinforced Milgram's findings by creating a Nazi-like environment in the school in just a few short days (Jones, 1979). He began by telling his sophomore history class about the importance of discipline and self-control. He had his students sit at attention and repeatedly stand up and sit down in quiet unison and saw their pride as they accomplished this task efficiently. All of a sudden everyone in the class seemed to be paying rapt attention to what was going on.

The next day, Jones began his class by talking about the importance of community and of being a member of a team or a cause. He had his class say over and over, "Strength through discipline, strength through community." Then he showed them a new class salute, made by bringing the right hand near the right shoulder in a curled position. He called it the Third Wave salute, because a hand in this position resembled a wave about to topple over. Jones then told the students they had to salute each other outside the classroom, which they did so during the next few days. As word of what was happening in Jones's class spread, students from other classes asked if they could come into his classroom.

On the third day of the experiment, Jones gave membership cards to every student in his class, which had now gained several new members. He told them they had to turn in the name of any student who was disobeying the class's rules. He then talked to them about the importance of action and hard work, both of which enhanced discipline and community. Jones told his students to recruit new members and to prevent any student who was not a Third Wave member from entering the classroom. During the rest of the day, students came to him with reports of other students not saluting the right way or of some students criticizing the experiment. Meanwhile, more than 200 students had joined the Third Wave.

On the fourth day of the experiment, more than 80 students squeezed into Jones's classroom. Jones informed them that the Third Wave was in fact a new political movement in the United States that would bring discipline, order, and pride to the country and that his students were among the first in the movement. The next day, Jones said, the Third Wave's national leader, whose identity was still not public, would be announcing a grand plan for action on national television at noon.

At noon the next day, more than 200 students crowded into the school auditorium to see the television speech. When Jones gave them the Third Wave salute, they saluted back. They chanted, "Strength through discipline, strength through community," over and over, and then sat in silent anticipation as Jones turned on a large television in front of the auditorium. The television remained blank. Suddenly Jones turned on a movie projector and showed scenes from a Nazi rally and the Nazi death camps. As the crowd in the auditorium reacted with shocked silence, the teacher told them there was no Third Wave movement and that almost overnight they had developed a Nazi-like society by allowing their regard for discipline, community, and action to warp their better judgment. Many students in the auditorium sobbed as they heard his words.

The Third Wave experiment was designed to help high school students in Palo Alto, California, understand how the Nazi Holocaust (represented by this photo of the Auschwitz concentration camp) could have happened. The experiment illustrated that normal group processes that make social life possible can also lead people to conform to objectionable standards.

George Olcott – Auschwitz Fence – CC BY-NC 2.0.

The Third Wave experiment once again indicates that the normal group processes that make social life possible also can lead people to conform to standards—in this case fascism—that most of us would reject. It also helps us understand further how the Holocaust could have happened. As Jones (1979, pp. 509–10) told his students in the auditorium, "You thought that you were the elect. That you were better than those outside this room. You bargained your freedom for the comfort of discipline and superiority. You chose to accept the group's will and the big lie over your own conviction.…Yes, we would all have made good Germans."

Zimbardo's Prison Experiment

In 1971, Stanford University psychologist Philip Zimbardo (1972) conducted an experiment to see what accounts for the extreme behaviors often seen in prisons: does this behavior stem from abnormal personalities of guards and prisoners or, instead, from the social structure of prisons, including the roles their members are expected to play? His experiment remains a compelling illustration of how roles and group processes can prompt extreme behavior.

Zimbardo advertised for male students to take part in a prison experiment and screened them out for histories of mental illness, violent behavior, and drug use. He then assigned them randomly to be either guards or prisoners in the experiment to ensure that any behavioral differences later seen between the two groups would have to stem from their different roles and not from any preexisting personality differences had they been allowed to volunteer.

The guards were told that they needed to keep order. They carried no weapons but did dress in khaki uniforms and wore reflector sunglasses to make eye contact impossible. On the first day of the experiment, the guards had the prisoners, who wore gowns and stocking caps to remove their individuality, stand in front of their cells (converted laboratory rooms) for the traditional prison "count." They made the prisoners stand for hours on end and verbally abused those who complained. A day later the prisoners refused to come out for the count, prompting the guards to respond by forcibly removing them from their cells and sometimes spraying them with an ice-cold fire extinguisher to expedite the process. Some prisoners were put into solitary confinement. The guards also intensified their verbal abuse of the prisoners.

By the third day of the experiment, the prisoners had become very passive. The guards, several of whom indicated before the experiment that they would have trouble taking their role seriously, now were quite serious. They continued their verbal abuse of the prisoners and became quite hostile if their orders were not followed exactly. What had begun as somewhat of a lark for both guards and prisoners had now become, as far as they were concerned, a real prison.

Shortly thereafter, first one prisoner and then a few more came down with symptoms of a nervous breakdown. Zimbardo and his assistants could not believe this was possible, as they had planned for the experiment to last for two weeks, but they allowed the prisoners to quit the experiment. When the first one was being "released," the guards had the prisoners chant over and over that this prisoner was a bad prisoner and that they would be punished for his weakness. When this prisoner heard the chants, he refused to leave the area because he felt so humiliated. The researchers had to remind him that this was only an experiment and that he was not a real prisoner. Zimbardo had to shut down the experiment after only six days.

Zimbardo (1972) later observed that if psychologists had viewed the behaviors just described in a real prison, they would likely have attributed them to preexisting personality problems in both guards and prisoners. As already noted, however, his random assignment procedure invalidated this possibility. Zimbardo thus concluded that the guards' and prisoners' behavioral problems must have stemmed from the social structure of the prison experience and the roles each group was expected to play. Zimbardo (2008) later wrote that these same processes help us understand "how good people turn evil," to cite the subtitle of his book, and thus help explain the torture and abuse committed by American forces at the Abu Ghraib prison in Iraq after the United States invaded and occupied that country in 2003. Once again we see how two of the building blocks of social life—groups and roles—contain within them the seeds of regrettable behavior and attitudes.

Groupthink

Groupthink may prompt people to conform with the judgments or behavior of a group because they do not want to appear different. Because of pressures to reach a quick verdict, jurors may go along with the majority opinion even if they believe otherwise. Have you ever been in a situation where groupthink occurred?

Brian DeWitt – Wolf Law Courtroom – CC BY-NC-ND 2.0.

As these examples suggest, sometimes people go along with the desires and views of a group against their better judgments, either because they do not want to appear different or because they have come to believe that the group's course of action may be the best one after all. Psychologist Irving Janis (1972) called this process **groupthink** and noted it has often affected national and foreign policy decisions in the United States and elsewhere. Group members often quickly agree on some course of action without thinking completely of alternatives. A well-known example here was the decision by President John F. Kennedy and his advisers in 1961 to aid the invasion of the Bay of Pigs in Cuba by Cuban exiles who hoped to overthrow the government of Fidel Castro. Although several advisers thought the plan ill advised, they kept quiet, and the invasion was an embarrassing failure (Hart, Stern, & Sundelius, 1997).

Groupthink is also seen in jury decision making. Because of the pressures to reach a verdict quickly, some jurors may go along with a verdict even if they believe otherwise. In juries and other small groups, groupthink is less likely to occur if at least one person expresses a dissenting view. Once that happens, other dissenters feel more comfortable voicing their own objections (Gastil, 2009).

Key Takeaways

- Leadership in groups and organizations involves instrumental and expressive leaders and several styles of leadership.
- Several social-psychological experiments illustrate how groups can influence the attitudes, behavior, and perceptions of their members. The Milgram and Zimbardo experiments showed that group processes can produce injurious behavior.

For Your Review

1. Think of any two groups to which you now belong or to which you previously belonged. Now think of the leader(s) of each group. Were these leaders more instrumental or more expressive? Provide evidence to support your answer.
2. Have you ever been in a group where you or another member was pressured to behave in a way that you considered improper? Explain what finally happened.

References

Asch, S. E. (1958). Effects of group pressure upon the modification and distortion of judgments. In E. E. Maccoby, T. M. Newcomb, & E. L. Hartley (Eds.), *Readings in social psychology*. New York, NY: Holt, Rinehart and Winston.

Brown, T. S. (2009). *When friends attend to business*. Philadelphia, PA: Philadelphia Yearly Meeting. Retrieved from http://www.pym.org/pm/comments.php?id=1121_0_178_0_C.

Eagly, A. H., & Carli, L. L. (2007). *Through the labyrinth: The truth about how women become leaders*. Boston, MA: Harvard Business School Press.

Gastil, J. (2009). *The group in society*. Thousand Oaks, CA: Sage.

Hart, P. T., Stern E. K., & Sundelius B., (Eds.). (1997). *Beyond groupthink: Political group dynamics and foreign policy-making*. Ann Arbor, MI: University of Michigan Press.

Janis, I. L. (1972). *Victims of groupthink*. Boston, MA: Houghton Mifflin.

Jones, R. (1979). The third wave: A classroom experiment in fascism. In J. J. Bonsignore, E. Karsh, P. d'Errico,

R. M. Pipkin, S. Arons, & J. Rifkin (Eds.), *Before the law: An introduction to the legal process* (pp. 503–511). Dallas, TX: Houghton Mifflin.

Milgram, S. (1974). *Obedience to authority*. New York, NY: Harper and Row.

Zimbardo, P. G. (2008). *The Lucifer effect: Understanding how good people turn evil*. New York, NY: Random House Trade Paperbacks.

Zimbardo, P. G. (1972). Pathology of imprisonment. *Society, 9*, 4–8.

6.3 Formal Organizations

Learning Objectives

1. Describe the three types of formal organizations.
2. List the defining characteristics of bureaucracies.
3. Discuss any two disadvantages of bureaucracies.
4. Explain Michels's iron law of oligarchy.

Modern societies are filled with **formal organizations**, or large secondary groups that follow explicit rules and procedures to achieve specific goals and tasks. Max Weber (1864–1920), one of the founders of sociology, recognized long ago that as societies become more complex, their procedures for accomplishing tasks rely less on traditional customs and beliefs and more on *rational* (which is to say rule-guided and impersonal) methods of decision making. The development of formal organizations, he emphasized, allowed complex societies to accomplish their tasks in the most efficient way possible (Weber, 1921/1978). Today we cannot imagine how any modern, complex society could run without formal organizations such as businesses and health-care institutions.

Types of Formal Organizations

Sociologist Amitai Etzioni (1975) developed a popular typology of organizations based on how they induce people to join them and keep them as members once they do join. His three types are utilitarian, normative, and coercive organizations.

Utilitarian organizations (also called *remunerative organizations*) provide an income or some other personal benefit. Business organizations, ranging from large corporations to small Mom-and-Pop grocery stores, are familiar examples of utilitarian organizations. Colleges and universities are utilitarian organizations not only for the people who work at them but also for their students, who certainly see education and a diploma as important tangible benefits they can gain from higher education.

Sociology Making a Difference

Big-Box Stores and the McDonaldization of Society

In many towns across the country during the last decade or so, activists have opposed the building of Wal-Mart and other "big-box" stores. They have had many reasons for doing so: the stores hurt local businesses; they do not treat their workers well; they are environmentally unfriendly. No doubt some activists also think the stores are all the same and are a sign of a distressing trend in the retail world.

Sociologist George Ritzer (2008) coined the term *McDonaldization* to describe this trend involving certain kinds of utilitarian organizations, to use a term from the chapter. His insights help us understand its advantages and disadvantages and thus help us to evaluate the arguments of big-box critics and the counterarguments of their proponents.

You have certainly eaten, probably too many times, at McDonald's, Burger King, Subway, KFC, and other fast-food restaurants. Ritzer says that these establishments share several characteristics that account for their popularity but that also represent a disturbing trend.

First, the food at all McDonald's restaurants is the same, as is the food at all Burger King restaurants or at any other fast-food chain. If you go to McDonald's in Maine, you can be very sure that you will find the same food that you would find at a McDonald's in San Diego on the other side of the country. You can also be sure that the food will taste the same, even though the two McDonald's are more than 3,000 miles apart. Ritzer uses the terms *predictability* and *uniformity* to refer to this similarity of McDonald's restaurants across the country.

Second, at any McDonald's the food is exactly the same size and weight. Before it was cooked, the burger you just bought was the same size and weight as the burger the person in front of you bought. This ensures that all McDonald's customers receive the identical value for their money. Ritzer calls this identical measurement of food *calculability*.

Third, McDonald's and other restaurants like it are fast. They are fast because they are efficient. As your order is taken, it is often already waiting for you while keeping warm. Moreover, everyone working at McDonald's has a specific role to play, and this division of labor contributes to the *efficiency* of McDonald's, as Ritzer characterized its operations.

Fourth and last, McDonald's is *automated* as much as possible. Machines help McDonald's employees make and serve shakes, fries, and the other food. If McDonald's could use a robot to cook its burgers and fries, it probably would.

To Ritzer, McDonald's is a metaphor for the overrationalization of society, and he fears that *the McDonaldization of society*, as he calls it, is occurring. This means that society is becoming increasingly uniform, predictable, calculable, efficient, and automated beyond the fast-food industry. For example, just 50 years ago there were no shopping malls and few national chain stores other than Sears, JCPenney, and a few others. Now we have malls across the country, and many of them have the same stores. We also have national drugstore chains, such as Rite Aid or Walgreens, that look fairly similar across the country.

This uniformity has its advantages. For example, if you are traveling and enter a McDonald's or Rite Aid, you already know exactly what you will find and probably even where to find it. But uniformity also has its disadvantages. To take just one problem, the national chains have driven out small, locally owned businesses that are apt to offer more personal attention. And if you want to buy a product that a national chain does not carry, it might be difficult to find it.

The McDonaldization of society, then, has come at a cost of originality and creativity. Ritzer says that we have paid a price for our devotion to uniformity, calculability, efficiency, and automation. Like Max Weber before him, he fears that the increasing rationalization of society will deprive us of human individuality and also reduce the diversity of our material culture. What do you think? Does his analysis change what you thought about fast-food restaurants and big-box stores?

In contrast, **normative organizations** (also called **voluntary organizations** or voluntary associations) allow people to pursue their moral goals and commitments. Their members do not get paid and instead contribute their time or money because they like or admire what the organization does. The many examples of normative organizations include churches and synagogues, Boy and Girl Scouts, the Kiwanis Club and other civic groups, and groups with political objectives, such as the National Council of La Raza, the largest advocacy organization for Latino civil rights. Alexis de Tocqueville (1835/1994) observed some 175 years ago that the United States was a nation of joiners, and contemporary research finds that Americans indeed rank above average among democratic nations in membership in voluntary associations (Curtis, Baer, & Grabb, 2001).

Some people end up in organizations involuntarily because they have violated the law or been judged to be mentally ill. Prisons and state mental institutions are examples of such **coercive organizations**, which, as total institutions (see Chapter 3 "Culture"), seek to control all phases of their members' lives. Our chances of ending up in coercive organizations depend on various aspects of our social backgrounds. For prisons one of these aspects is geographical. Figure 6.4 "Census Regions and Imprisonment Rates, 2009 (Number of Inmates per 100,000 Residents)" examines the distribution of imprisonment in the United States and shows the imprisonment rate (number of inmates per 100,000 residents) for each of the four major census regions. This rate tends to be highest in the South and in the West. Do you think this pattern exists because crime rates are highest in these regions or instead because these regions are more likely than other parts of the United States to send convicted criminals to prisons?

Figure 6.4 Census Regions and Imprisonment Rates, 2009 (Number of Inmates per 100,000 Residents)

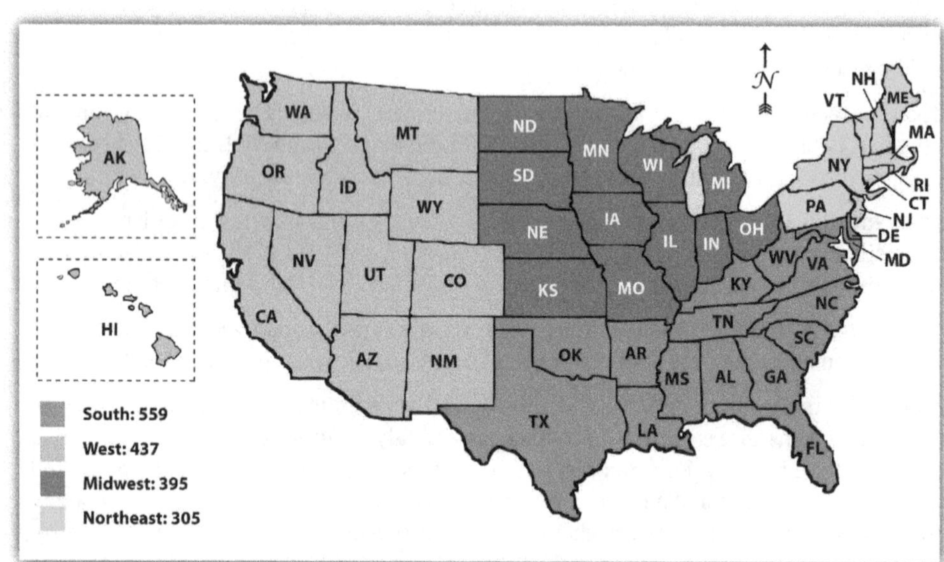

Source: Data from H. C. West (2010). *Prison inmates at midyear 2009—Statistical tables*. Washington, DC: Bureau of Justice Statistics, U.S. Department of Justice.

Bureaucracies: The Good, the Bad, and the Ugly

As discussed earlier, Max Weber emphasized that modern societies increasingly depend on formal organizations to accomplish key tasks. He particularly had in mind **bureaucracies**, or formal organizations with certain organizational features designed to achieve goals in the most efficient way possible. He said that the ideal type of bureaucracy is characterized by several features that together maximize the efficiency and effectiveness of organizational decision making and goal accomplishment:

Max Weber emphasized bureaucracies as a feature of modern life. Key aspects of bureaucracies include specialization, hierarchy, written rules and regulations, impartiality and impersonality, and record keeping.

Christian Schnettelker – Bureaucracy – CC BY 2.0.

1. **Specialization.** By specialization Weber meant a division of labor in which specific people have certain tasks—and only those tasks—to do. Presumably they are most skilled at these tasks and less skilled at others. With such specialization, the people who are best suited to do various tasks are the ones who work on them, maximizing the ability of the organization to have these tasks accomplished.
2. **Hierarchy.** Equality does not exist in a bureaucracy. Instead its structure resembles a pyramid, with a few positions at the top and many more lower down. The chain of command runs from the top to the bottom, with the persons occupying the positions at the top supervising those below them. The higher you are in the hierarchy, the fewer people to whom you have to report. Weber thought a hierarchical structure maximizes efficiency because it reduces decision-making time and puts the authority to make the most important decisions in the hands of the people at the top of the pyramid who presumably are the best qualified to make them.
3. **Written rules and regulations.** For an organization to work efficiently, everyone must know what to do and when to do it. This means their actions must be predictable. To ensure predictability, their roles and the organization's operating procedures must be written in a manual or handbook, with everyone in the organization expected to be familiar with its rules. Much of the communication among members of bureaucracies is written in the form of memos and e-mail rather than being verbal. This written communication leaves a paper trail so that accountability for individual behavior can later be determined.
4. **Impartiality and impersonality.** The head of a small, nonbureaucratic organization might prefer to hire people she or he knows and promote them on the same basis. Weber thought that impartiality in hiring, promotion, and firing would be much better for a large organization, as it guarantees people

will advance through a firm based on their skills and knowledge, not on whom they know. Clients should also be treated impersonally, as an organization in the long run would be less effective if it gave favorable treatment to clients based on whom they know or on their nice personalities. As Weber recognized, the danger is that employees and clients alike become treated like numbers or cogs in a machine, with their individual needs and circumstances ignored in the name of organizational efficiency.

5. **Record keeping.** As you probably know from personal experience, bureaucracies keep all kinds of records, especially in today's computer age. A small enterprise, say a Mom-and-Pop store, might keep track of its merchandise and the bills its customers owe with some notes scribbled here and there, even in the information technology age, but a large organization must have much more extensive record keeping to keep track of everything.

The Disadvantages of Bureaucracy

Taking all of these features into account, Weber (1921/1978) thought bureaucracies were the most efficient and effective type of organization in a large, complex society. At the same time, he despaired over their impersonality, which he saw reflecting the growing dehumanization that accompanies growing societies. As social scientists have found since his time, bureaucracies have other problems that undermine their efficiency and effectiveness:

1. **Impersonality and alienation.** The first problem is the one just mentioned: bureaucracies can be very alienating experiences for their employees and clients alike. A worker without any sick leave left who needs to take some time off to care for a sick child might find a supervisor saying no, because the rules prohibit it. A client who stands in a long line might find herself turned away when she gets to the front because she forgot to fill out every single box in a form. We all have stories of impersonal, alienating experiences in today's large bureaucracies.
2. **Red tape.** A second disadvantage of bureaucracy is "red tape," or, as sociologist Robert Merton (1968) called it, **bureaucratic ritualism**, a greater devotion to rules and regulations than to organizational goals. Bureaucracies often operate by slavish attention to even the pickiest of rules and regulations. If every *t* isn't crossed and every *i* isn't dotted, then someone gets into trouble, and perhaps a client is not served. Such bureaucratic ritualism contributes to the alienation already described.
3. **Trained incapacity.** If an overabundance of rules and regulations and overattention to them lead to bureaucratic ritualism, they also lead to an inability of people in an organization to think creatively and to act independently. In the late 1800s, Thorstein Veblen (1899/1953) called this problem *trained incapacity*. When unforeseen problems arise, trained incapacity may prevent organizational members from being able to handle them.
4. **Bureaucratic incompetence.** Two popular writers have humorously pointed to special problems in bureaucracies that undermine their effectiveness. The first of these, popularly known as Parkinson's law after its coiner, English historian C. Northcote Parkinson (1957), says that work expands to fill the time available for it. To put it another way, the more time you have to do something, the longer it takes. The second problem is called the Peter Principle, also named after its founder, Canadian author Laurence J. Peter (1969), and says that people will eventually be promoted to their level of

incompetence. In this way of thinking, someone who does a good job will get promoted and then get promoted again if she or he continues doing a good job. Eventually such people will be promoted to a job for which they are not well qualified, impeding organizational efficiency and effectiveness. Have you ever worked for someone who illustrated the Peter Principle?

5. **Goal displacement and self-perpetuation.** Sometimes bureaucracies become so swollen with rules and personnel that they take on a life of their own and lose sight of the goals they were originally designed to achieve. People in the bureaucracy become more concerned with their job comfort and security than with helping the organization accomplish its objectives. To the extent this happens, the bureaucracy's efficiency and effectiveness are again weakened.

Michels's Iron Law of Oligarchy

Several decades ago Robert Michels (1876–1936), a German activist and scholar, published his famous **iron law of oligarchy**, by which he meant that large organizations inevitably develop an oligarchy, or the undemocratic rule of many people by just a few people (Michels, 1911/1949). He said this happens as leaders increasingly monopolize knowledge because they have more access than do other organizational members to information and technology. They begin to think they are better suited than other people to lead their organizations, and they also do their best to stay in their positions of power, which they find very appealing. This latter goal becomes more important than helping the organization achieve its objectives and than serving the interests of the workers further down the organizational pyramid. Drawing on our earlier discussion of group size, it is also true that as an organization becomes larger, it becomes very difficult to continue to involve all group members in decision making, which almost inevitably becomes monopolized by the relatively few people at the top of the organization. Michels thought oligarchization happens not only in bureaucracies but also in a society's political structures and said that the inevitable tendency to oligarchy threatens democracy by concentrating political decision-making power in the hands of a few. As his use of the term *iron law* suggests, Michels thought the development of oligarchies was inevitable, and he was very pessimistic about democracy's future.

Has our society as a whole lost some of its democracy in the ways Michels predicted? Some evidence supports his prediction. For example, many large organizations, including corporations, labor unions, political parties, and colleges and universities, do resemble the types of oligarchies over which Michels despaired. In most of these organizations, at least according to their critics, decision making is indeed concentrated in the hands of a few people who often work for their own interests. On the other hand, organizational and political leaders do not work always for themselves and often have the interests of their organizations and the public in mind. Michels's law might not be so ironclad after all, but it does remind us to be on the alert for the undemocratic processes he predicted.

Gender, Race, and Formal Organizations

We previously outlined three types of organizations: utilitarian, normative, and coercive. What does the evidence indicate about the dynamics of gender and race in these organizations?

We have already seen that women in utilitarian organizations such as businesses have made striking inroads but remain thwarted by a glass ceiling and the refusal of some subordinates to accept their authority. The workforce as a whole remains segregated by sex, as many women work in a relatively few occupations such as clerical and secretarial work. This fact contributes heavily to the lower pay that women receive compared to men. Turning to race, effective federal and state laws against racial discrimination in the workplace arose in the aftermath of the Southern civil rights movement of the 1960s. Although these laws have helped greatly, people of color are still worse off than whites in hiring, promotion, and salaries, affirmative action efforts notwithstanding. Chapter 7 "Deviance, Crime, and Social Control" and Chapter 8 "Social Stratification" will further discuss the experiences of people of color and of women, respectively, in the workplace.

Learning From Other Societies

Japan's Formal Organizations: Benefits and Disadvantages of Traditional Ways

Although Japan possesses one of the world's most productive industrial economies, its culture remains very traditional in several ways. As we saw in the previous two chapters, for example, the Japanese culture continues to value harmony and cooperation and to frown on public kissing. Interestingly, Japan's traditional ways are reflected in its formal (utilitarian) organizations even as they produce much of the world's output of cars, electronics, and other products and provide some lessons for our own society.

One of these lessons concerns the experiences of women in the Japanese workplace, as this experience reflects Japan's very traditional views on women's social roles (Schneider & Silverman, 2010). Japan continues to think a woman's place is first and foremost in the home and with her children. Accordingly, women there have much fewer job opportunities than do men and in fact have few job prospects beyond clerical work and other blue-collar positions. Many young women seek to become "office ladies," whose main role in a business is to look pretty, do some filing and photocopying, and be friendly to visitors. They are supposed to live at home before marrying and typically must quit their jobs when they do marry. Women occupy only about 10% of managerial positions in Japan's business and government, compared to 43% of their U.S. counterparts (Fackler, 2007).

For these reasons, men are the primary subjects of studies on life in Japanese corporations. Here we see some striking differences from how U.S. corporations operate (Jackson & Tomioka, 2004). For example, the emphasis on the group in Japanese schools (see Chapter 3 "Culture") also characterizes corporate life. Individuals hired at roughly the same time by a Japanese corporation are evaluated and promoted collectively, not individually, although some corporations have tried to conduct more individual assessment. Just as Japanese schools have their children engage in certain activities to foster group spirit, so do Japanese corporations have their workers engage in group exercises and other activities to foster a community feeling in the workplace. The companies sponsor many recreational activities outside the workplace for the same reason. In another difference from their American counterparts, Japanese companies have their workers learn several different jobs within the same companies so that they can discover how the various jobs relate to each other. Perhaps most important, leadership in Japanese corporations is more democratic and less authoritarian than in their American counterparts. Japanese workers meet at least weekly in small groups to discuss various aspects of their jobs and of corporate goals and to give their input to corporate managers.

Japan's traditional organizational culture, then, has certain benefits but also one very important disadvantage, at least from an American perspective (Levin, 2006). Its traditional, group-oriented model seems to generate higher productivity and morale than the more individualistic American model. On the other hand, its exclusion of women from positions above the clerical level deprives Japanese corporations of women's knowledge and talents and would no doubt dismay many Americans. As the United States tries to boost its own economy, it may well make sense to adopt some elements of Japan's traditional organizational model, as some U.S. information technology companies have done, but it would certainly not make sense to incorporate its views of women and the workplace.

The church has been a significant type of normative organization for many African Americans. During the 1960s, black churches served as an important venue for the civil rights movement's organizing and fund-raising.

Wikimedia Commons – CC BY-SA 3.0.

Much less research exists on gender and race in normative organizations. But we do know that many women are involved in many types of these voluntary associations, especially those having to do with children and education and related matters. These associations allow them to contribute to society and are a source of self-esteem and, more practically, networking (Blackstone, 2004; Daniels, 1988). Many people of color have also been involved in normative organizations, especially those serving various needs of their communities. One significant type of normative organization is the church, which has been extraordinarily important in the African-American community over the decades and was a key locus of civil rights activism in the South during the 1960s (Morris, 1984).

Turning to coercive organizations, we know much about prisons and the race and gender composition of their inmates. Men, African Americans, and Latinos are overrepresented in prisons and jails. This means that they constitute much higher percentages of all inmates than their numbers in the national population would suggest. Although men make up about 50% of the national population, for example, they account for more than 90% of all prisoners. Similarly, although African Americans are about 13% of the population, they account for more than 40% of all prisoners. The corresponding percentages for Latinos are about 15% and almost 20%, respectively (Federal Bureau of Investigation, 2010).

Why these patterns exist is unclear. Do they reflect discrimination against African Americans, Latinos, and men, or do they reflect higher offending rates by these groups? Chapter 7 "Deviance, Crime, and Social Control" explores this issue as part of its broader treatment of deviance and crime.

Key Takeaways

- The major types of formal organizations include those that are utilitarian, normative, and coercive.
- As one type of formal organization, the bureaucracy has several defining characteristics, including specialization, hierarchy, written rules and regulations, impartiality and impersonality, and record keeping.
- Bureaucracies also include some negative characteristics, such as alienation and red tape.
- Michels's iron law of oligarchy assumes that large organizations inevitably develop undemocratic rule.

For Your Review

1. Think of any bureaucracy with which you have had some experience. Describe evidence that it was characterized by any three of the defining characteristics of bureaucracies.
2. Do you share Max Weber's view that bureaucracies must be impersonal and alienating? Explain your answer.

References

Blackstone, A. (2004). "It's just about being fair": Activism and the politics of volunteering in the breast cancer movement. *Gender and Society, 18*, 350–368.

Curtis, J. E., Baer, D. E., & Grabb, E. G. (2001). Nations of joiners: Explaining voluntary association membership in democratic societies. *American Sociological Review, 66*, 783–805.

Daniels, A. K. (1988). *Invisible careers: Women civic leaders from the volunteer world*. Chicago, IL: University of Chicago Press.

Etzioni, A. (1975). *A comparative analysis of complex organizations*. New York, NY: Free Press.

Fackler, M. (2007, August 6). Career women in Japan find a blocked path. *The New York Times*, p. A1.

Federal Bureau of Investigation. (2010). *Crime in the United States, 2009*. Washington, DC: Author.

Jackson, K., & Tomioka, M. (2004). *The changing face of Japanese management*. New York, NY: Routledge.

Levin, H. M. (2006). Worker democracy and worker productivity. *Social Justice Research, 19*, 109–121.

Merton, R. K. (1968). *Social theory and social structure*. New York, NY: Free Press.

Michels, R. (1949). *Political parties*. Glencoe, IL: Free Press. (Original work published 1911).

Morris, A. (1984). *The origins of the civil rights movement: Black communities organizing for change*. New York, NY: Free Press.

Parkinson, C. N. (1957). *Parkinson's law and other studies in administration*. New York, NY: Ballantine Books.

Peter, L. J., & Hull R. (1969). *The Peter principle: Why things always go wrong*. New York, NY: William Morrow.

Ritzer, G. (2008). *The McDonaldization of society*. Thousand Oaks, CA: Pine Forge Press.

Schneider, L., & Silverman, A. (2010). *Global sociology: Introducing five contemporary societies* (5th ed.). New York, NY: McGraw-Hill.

Tocqueville, A. (1994). *Democracy in America*. New York, NY: Knopf. (Original work published 1835).

Veblen, T. (1953). *The theory of the leisure class: An economic study of institutions*. New York, NY: New American Library. (Original work published 1899).

Weber, M. (1978). *Economy and society: An outline of interpretive sociology* (G. Roth & C. Wittich, Eds.). Berkeley: University of California Press. (Original work published 1921).

6.4 Groups, Organizations, and Social Change

Learning Objectives

1. Describe the two ways in which groups and organizations play an important role in social change.
2. Discuss how whistle-blowing is relevant to a discussion of groups, organizations, and social change.

As we consider ways to try to improve our society, the role of groups and organizations becomes very important. This section briefly considers this importance.

Vehicles for Social Change

One individual can certainly make a difference, but it is much more common for any difference to be made by individuals acting together—that is, by a group. In this regard, it is very clear that groups of many types have been and will continue to be vehicles for social reform and social change of many kinds. Many of the rights and freedoms Americans enjoy today were the result of committed efforts by social reform groups and social movements of years past: the abolitionist movement, the women's suffrage movement and contemporary women's movement, the labor movement, the civil rights movement, the gay rights movement, and the environmental movement, to name just a few (see Chapter 14 "Politics and Government"). Their experience reflects the wisdom of anthropologist Margaret Mead's famous quote that we should "never doubt that a small group of thoughtful, committed citizens can change the world. Indeed, it is the only thing that ever has."

Groups have often served as vehicles for many types of social reform and social change. Many of the rights and freedoms Americans enjoy today are the result of efforts by social reform groups of years past.

Wikimedia Commons – public domain.

In today's world, there are innumerable social service and social advocacy groups that are attempting to bring about changes to benefit a particular constituency or the greater society, and you might well belong to one of these groups on your campus or in your home community. All such groups, past, present, and future, are vehicles for social reform and social change, or at least have the potential for becoming such vehicles.

Obstacles to Social Change

Groups can bring about social reform and social change, but they can also thwart efforts to achieve a just society. For every social change and social reform effort that so many groups and organizations undertake, other groups and organizations try to block such efforts. Groups may be the building blocks of social reform and social change, but they are also the building blocks for the status quo. If the study of sociology can be said to be the study of group life, as noted earlier, the study of social reform and social change can also be said to be the study of what groups and organizations do to try to bring about social reform or to maintain the status quo.

Changing Groups and Organizations From Within

Groups and organizations are typically set in their ways and do not often change their dynamics, goals, or other key aspects. This is especially true of the formal organizations we call bureaucracies, which, as we saw, are so committed and even "stuck" to certain procedures that they become inefficient and even alienating. Groupthink can also set in and stifle creativity and keep group and organizational members from raising concerns about certain practices and/or goals.

Whistle-blowing is now the common term for raising such concerns, especially when the concern involves illegal and/or potentially harmful behavior (Alford, 2007; Schwartz, 2009). It is not easy to be a whistle-blower, and several individuals who have "blown the whistle" have been harassed, fired, or sued for doing so. In response to such reprisals, various federal and state laws have been passed to protect whistle-blowers (http://whistleblowerlaws.com/index.php). Still, it takes a certain amount of courage and no small amount of perseverance to be a whistle-blower. It is almost certain that some readers of this book will one day find themselves in a position where they, too, might have to decide whether to become a whistle-blower when they perceive some violation of the law and/or harmful behavior to be occurring. If so, they will have great potential for changing a group or an organization from within while performing a social good for the larger society.

Key Takeaways

- Groups can be vehicles for social change and social reform, but they can also be vehicles for thwarting social change and social reform.
- Whistle-blowing aims at exposing illegal and/or harmful behavior of corporations and other groups and organizations.

For Your Review

1. Have you ever disapproved of a policy, behavior, or goal of a group to which you belonged? If so what, if anything, did you do? Explain your answer.
2. Do you think an employee for a corporation has the responsibility to become a whistle-blower if the corporation is engaging in illegal and/or harmful behavior? Explain your answer.

References

Alford, C. F. (2007). Whistle-blower narratives: The experience of choiceless choice. *Social Research, 74*, 223–248.

Schwartz, J. (2009, July 9). Justice dept. whistle-blower in Alabama case is fired. *The New York Times*, p. A20.

6.5 End-of-Chapter Material

Summary

1. Social groups are the building blocks of social life, and it is virtually impossible to imagine a society without groups and difficult to imagine individuals not being involved with many types of groups. They are distinguished from social categories and social aggregates by the degree of interaction among their members and the identification of their members with the group.
2. Primary groups are small and involve strong emotional attachments, while secondary groups are larger and more impersonal. Some groups become in-groups and vie, sometimes hostilely, with people they identify as belonging to out-groups. Reference groups provide standards by which we judge our attitudes and behavior and can influence how we think and act.
3. Social networks connect us through the people we know to other people they know. They are increasingly influential for successful employment but are also helpful for high-quality health care and other social advantages.
4. The size of groups is a critical variable for their internal dynamics. Compared to large groups, small groups involve more intense emotional bonds but are also more unstable. These differences stem from the larger number of relationships that can exist in a larger group than in a smaller one.
5. Instrumental and expressive leaders take different approaches in exercising leadership. Instrumental leaders focus more on solving tasks, even at the risk of alienating group members, while expressive leaders focus more on group relations. Of the three major styles of leadership—authoritarian, democratic, and laissez-faire—laissez-faire leadership seems the least effective in helping a group achieve its goals.
6. Women and men are equally effective as leaders but exhibit different leadership styles. Women tend to be expressive leaders, while men tend to be more authoritarian leaders. Women leaders still face problems in securing the respect of the group members they seek to lead.
7. Processes of group conformity are essential for any society and for the well-being of its many individuals but also can lead to reprehensible norms and values. People can be influenced by their group membership and the roles they're expected to play to engage in behaviors most of us would condemn. Laboratory experiments by Asch, Milgram, and Zimbardo illustrate how this can happen, while a real-life classroom experiment called the Third Wave dramatized how a fascist atmosphere could develop from everyday group processes.
8. Formal organizations are commonly delineated according to the motivations of the people who join them. According to Etzioni's popular typology, three types of formal organizations exist: utilitarian, normative, and coercive.
9. Max Weber outlined several characteristics of bureaucracy that he felt make them the most efficient and effective type of large formal organization possible. At the same time, other scholars have pointed to several disadvantages of bureaucracies that limit their efficiency and effectiveness and thus thwart organizational goals.
10. Robert Michels hypothesized that the development of oligarchies in formal organizations and political structures is inevitable. History shows that such "oligarchization" does occur but that society remains more democratic than Michels foresaw.
11. Women and people of color have long been involved in normative organizations and continue to expand their numbers in utilitarian organizations, but in the latter they lag behind white men in rank and salary. In a major type of coercive organization, prisons, people of color and men are overrepresented. The chapter

closes with the question of whether the reason for this overrepresentation is the offending rates of these two groups or, instead, discrimination against them in criminal justice processing.

Using Sociology

Suppose that in 2025 you are working as a middle-level manager at a U.S. corporation that makes baby products. You and four other managers in your unit begin to hear reports from parents that two of your company's products, one particular crib and one particular stroller, have apparently caused injuries to their children after both products collapsed as toddlers were bouncing in them. There have been a dozen reports so far, eight for the stroller and four for the crib. The other four managers and you suspect that a hinge in both products might be to blame, but you also realize that several thousand cribs and strollers have been sold in the last year with this particular hinge, with only a dozen apparent injuries resulting. The other four managers decide to keep quiet about the parents' reports for two reasons. First, the number of reports is very few compared to the number of cribs and strollers that have been sold. Second, they worry that if they bring the reports to the attention of upper management, their jobs may be at risk.

Having learned about groupthink in your introduction to sociology course, you recognize that groupthink may be operating in your present situation in a way that could lead to further injuries of toddlers across the country. Yet you also think the two reasons the other managers have for remaining silent make some sense. What, if anything, do you do? Explain your answer.

Chapter 7: Deviance, Crime, and Social Control

Social Issues in the News

"Attack Leaves Voter, 73, in Pain and Fear," the headline said. A 73-year-old woman had just voted in the primary election in Boston, Massachusetts. As she walked home, two men rushed up, grabbed her purse, and knocked her down. She later said, "In this situation, you don't think too much. Only, you get scared when people try to take everything from you." A neighbor who came to the victim's aid recalled, "I heard a woman in distress, screaming for help. I just jumped out of bed and looked out the window. And I could see an elderly person on her knees, crying." The police later arrested a 19-year-old suspect for robbery and assault and battery. The city's district attorney said of the crime, "It's despicable. Only a coward would attack a 73-year-old woman from behind. He's brought shame to himself and his family, and he can count on an extremely aggressive prosecution." (Ellement, 2008)

This terrible crime was just one of millions that occur in the United States each year. A central message of this book so far is that society is possible because people conform to its norms, values, and roles. As the sad story of the 73-year-old Boston voter illustrates, this chapter has a different message: that people often violate their society's norms and are sometimes punished for doing so. Why do they commit deviance and crime? What influences their chances of being punished? How do behaviors come to be defined as deviant or criminal? Recalling this book's emphasis on changing society, how can crime and deviance be reduced? These are questions that sociologists have long tried to answer, and we explore possible answers in the pages that follow.

References

Ellement, J. R. (2008, September 18). Attack leaves voter, 73, in pain and fear. *The Boston Globe*, p. B1.

7.1 Social Control and the Relativity of Deviance

Learning Objectives

1. Define deviance, crime, and social control.
2. Understand why Émile Durkheim said deviance is normal.
3. Understand what is meant by the relativity of deviance.

Deviance is behavior that violates social norms and arouses negative social reactions. Some behavior is considered so harmful that governments enact written laws that ban the behavior. **Crime** is behavior that violates these laws and is certainly an important type of deviance that concerns many Americans.

The fact that both deviance and crime arouse negative social reactions reminds us that every society needs to ensure that its members generally obey social norms in their daily interaction. **Social control** refers to ways in which a society tries to prevent and sanction behavior that violates norms. Just as a society like the United States has informal and formal norms (see Chapter 2 "Eye on Society: Doing Sociological Research"), so does it have informal and formal social control. Generally, *informal social control* is used to control behavior that violates informal norms, and *formal social control* is used to control behavior that violates formal norms. We typically decline to violate informal norms, if we even think of violating them in the first place, because we fear risking the negative reactions of other people. These reactions, and thus examples of informal social control, include anger, disappointment, ostracism, and ridicule. Formal social control in the United States typically involves the legal system (police, judges and prosecutors, corrections officials) and also, for businesses, the many local, state, and federal regulatory agencies that constitute the regulatory system.

Social control is never perfect, and so many norms and people exist that there are always some people who violate some norms. In fact, Émile Durkheim (1895/1962), a founder of sociology discussed in Chapter 1 "Sociology and the Sociological Perspective", stressed that a society *without* deviance is impossible for at least two reasons. First, the collective conscience (see Chapter 1 "Sociology and the Sociological Perspective") is never strong enough to prevent *all* rule breaking. Even in a "society of saints," such as a monastery, he said, rules will be broken and negative social reactions aroused. Second, because deviance serves several important functions for society (which we discuss later in this chapter), any given society "invents" deviance by defining certain behaviors as deviant and the people who commit them as deviants. Because Durkheim thought deviance was inevitable for these reasons, he considered it a *normal* part of every healthy society.

Informal social control, such as the anger depicted here, is used to control behavior that violates informal norms.

gordonramsaysubmissions – gordon-ramsay-15 – CC BY 2.0.

Although deviance is normal in this regard, it remains true that some people are more likely than others to commit it. It is also true that some locations within a given society have higher rates of deviance than other locations; for example, U.S. cities have higher rates of violent crime than do rural areas. Still, Durkheim's monastery example raises an important point about the **relativity** of deviance: whether a behavior is considered deviant depends on the circumstances in which the behavior occurs and not on the behavior itself. Although talking might be considered deviant in a monastery, it would certainly be considered very normal elsewhere. If an assailant, say a young male, murders someone, he faces arrest, prosecution, and, in many states, possible execution. Yet if a soldier kills someone in wartime, he may be considered a hero. Killing occurs in either situation, but the context and reasons for the killing determine whether the killer is punished or given a medal.

Deviance is also relative in two other ways. First, it is *relative in space*: a given behavior may be considered deviant in one society but acceptable in another society. Recall the discussion of sexual behavior in Chapter 3 "Culture", where we saw that sexual acts condemned in some societies are often practiced in others. Second, deviance is *relative in time*: a behavior in a given society may be considered deviant in one time period but acceptable many years later; conversely, a behavior may be considered acceptable in one time period but deviant many years later. In the late 1800s, many Americans used cocaine, marijuana, and opium, because they were common components of over-the-counter products for symptoms like depression, insomnia, menstrual cramps, migraines, and toothaches. Coca-Cola originally contained cocaine and, perhaps not surprisingly, became an instant hit when it went on sale in 1894 (Goode, 2008). Today, of course, all three drugs are illegal.

The relativity of deviance in all these ways is captured in a famous statement by sociologist Howard S. Becker (1963, p. 9), who wrote several decades ago that deviance is not a quality of the act the person commits, but rather a consequence of the application by others of rules or sanctions to an "offender." The deviant is one to whom that label has been successfully applied; deviant behavior is behavior that people so label.

This insight raises some provocative possibilities for society's response to deviance and crime. First, harmful behavior committed by corporations and wealthy individuals may not be considered deviant, perhaps because "respectable" people engage in them. Second, prostitution and other arguably less harmful behaviors may be considered very deviant because they are deemed immoral or because of bias against the kinds of people (poor and nonwhite) thought to be engaging in them. These considerations yield several questions that need to be answered in the study of deviance. First, why are some individuals more likely than others to commit deviance? Second, why do rates of deviance differ within social categories such as gender, race, social class, and age? Third, why are some locations more likely than other locations to have higher rates of deviance? Fourth, why are some behaviors more likely than others to be considered deviant? Fifth, why are some individuals and those from certain social backgrounds more likely than other individuals to be considered deviant and punished for deviant behavior? Sixth and last but certainly not least, what can be done to reduce rates of violent crime and other serious forms of deviance? The sociological study of deviance and crime aims to answer all of these questions.

Key Takeaways

- Deviance is behavior that violates social norms and arouses negative social reactions.
- Crime is behavior that is considered so serious that it violates formal laws prohibiting such behavior.
- Social control refers to ways in which a society tries to prevent and sanction behavior that violates norms.
- Émile Durkheim believed that deviance is a normal part of every society.
- Whether a behavior is considered deviant depends on the circumstances under which it occurs. Considerations of certain behaviors as deviant also vary from one society to another and from one era to another within a given society.

For Your Review

1. In what ways is deviance considered relative?
2. Why did Durkheim consider deviance a normal part of society?

References

Becker, H. S. (1963). *Outsiders: Studies in the sociology of deviance*. New York, NY: Free Press.

Durkheim, É. (1962). *The rules of sociological method* (Ed. S. Lukes). New York, NY: Free Press. (Original work published 1895).

Goode, E. (2008). *Drugs in American society*. New York, NY: McGraw-Hill.

7.2 Explaining Deviance

Learning Objective

1. State the major arguments and assumptions of the various sociological explanations of deviance.

If we want to reduce violent crime and other serious deviance, we must first understand why it occurs. Many sociological theories of deviance exist, and together they offer a more complete understanding of deviance than any one theory offers by itself. Together they help answer the questions posed earlier: why rates of deviance differ within social categories and across locations, why some behaviors are more likely than others to be considered deviant, and why some kinds of people are more likely than others to be considered deviant and to be punished for deviant behavior. As a whole, sociological explanations highlight the importance of the social environment and of social interaction for deviance and the commision of crime. As such, they have important implications for how to reduce these behaviors. Consistent with this book's public sociology theme, a discussion of several such crime-reduction strategies concludes this chapter.

We now turn to the major sociological explanations of crime and deviance. A summary of these explanations appears in Table 7.1 "Theory Snapshot: Summary of Sociological Explanations of Deviance and Crime".

Table 7.1 Theory Snapshot: Summary of Sociological Explanations of Deviance and Crime

Major theory	Related explanation	Summary of explanation
Functionalist	Durkheim's views	Deviance has several functions: (a) it clarifies norms and increases conformity, (b) it strengthens social bonds among the people reacting to the deviant, and (c) it can help lead to positive social change.
	Social ecology	Certain social and physical characteristics of urban neighborhoods contribute to high crime rates. These characteristics include poverty, dilapidation, population density, and population turnover.
	Strain theory	According to Robert Merton, deviance among the poor results from a gap between the cultural emphasis on economic success and the inability to achieve such success through the legitimate means of working. According to Richard Cloward and Lloyd Ohlin, differential access to illegitimate means affects the type of deviance in which individuals experiencing strain engage.
	Deviant subcultures	Poverty and other community conditions give rise to certain subcultures through which adolescents acquire values that promote deviant behavior. Albert Cohen wrote that lack of success in school leads lower-class boys to join gangs whose value system promotes and rewards delinquency. Walter Miller wrote that delinquency stems from focal concerns, a taste for trouble, toughness, cleverness, and excitement. Marvin Wolfgang and Franco Ferracuti argued that a subculture of violence in inner-city areas promotes a violent response to insults and other problems.
	Social control theory	Travis Hirschi wrote that delinquency results from weak bonds to conventional social institutions such as families and schools. These bonds include attachment, commitment, involvement, and belief.
Conflict		People with power pass laws and otherwise use the legal system to secure their position at the top of society and to keep the powerless on the bottom. The poor and minorities are more likely because of their poverty and race to be arrested, convicted, and imprisoned.
	Feminist perspectives	Inequality against women and antiquated views about relations between the sexes underlie rape, sexual assault, intimate partner violence, and other crimes against women. Sexual abuse prompts many girls and women to turn to drugs and alcohol use and other antisocial behavior. Gender socialization is a key reason for large gender differences in crime rates.
Symbolic interactionism	Differential association theory	Edwin H. Sutherland argued that criminal behavior is learned by interacting with close friends and family members who teach us how to commit various crimes and also about the values, motives, and rationalizations we need to adopt in order to justify breaking the law.
	Labeling theory	Deviance results from being labeled a deviant; nonlegal factors such as appearance, race, and social class affect how often labeling occurs.

Functionalist Explanations

Several explanations may be grouped under the functionalist perspective in sociology, as they all share this perspective's central view on the importance of various aspects of society for social stability and other social needs.

Émile Durkheim: The Functions of Deviance

As noted earlier, Émile Durkheim said deviance is normal, but he did not stop there. In a surprising and still controversial twist, he also argued that deviance serves several important functions for society.

First, Durkheim said, deviance clarifies social norms and increases conformity. This happens because the discovery and punishment of deviance reminds people of the norms and reinforces the consequences of violating them. If your class were taking an exam and a student was caught cheating, the rest of the class would be instantly reminded of the rules about cheating and the punishment for it, and as a result they would be less likely to cheat.

A second function of deviance is that it strengthens social bonds among the people reacting to the deviant. An example comes from the classic story *The Ox-Bow Incident* (Clark, 1940), in which three innocent men are accused of cattle rustling and are eventually lynched. The mob that does the lynching is very united in its frenzy against the men, and, at least at that moment, the bonds among the individuals in the mob are extremely strong.

A final function of deviance, said Durkheim, is that it can help lead to positive social change. Although some of the greatest figures in history—Socrates, Jesus, Joan of Arc, Mahatma Gandhi, and Martin Luther King Jr. to name just a few—were considered the worst kind of deviants in their time, we now honor them for their commitment and sacrifice.

Émile Durkheim wrote that deviance can lead to positive social change. Many Southerners had strong negative feelings about Dr. Martin Luther King Jr. during the civil rights movement, but history now honors him for his commitment and sacrifice.

U.S. Library of Congress – public domain.

Sociologist Herbert Gans (1996) pointed to an additional function of deviance: deviance creates jobs for the segments of society—police, prison guards, criminology professors, and so forth—whose main focus is to deal with deviants in some manner. If deviance and crime did not exist, hundreds of thousands of law-abiding people in the United States would be out of work!

Although deviance can have all of these functions, many forms of it can certainly be quite harmful, as the story of the mugged voter that began this chapter reminds us. Violent crime and property crime in the United States victimize millions of people and households each year, while crime by corporations has effects that are even more harmful, as we discuss later. Drug use, prostitution, and other "victimless" crimes may involve willing participants, but these participants often cause themselves and others much harm. Although deviance according to Durkheim is inevitable and normal and serves important functions, that certainly does not mean the United States and other nations should be happy to have high rates of serious deviance. The sociological theories we discuss point to certain aspects of the social environment, broadly defined, that contribute to deviance and crime and that should be the focus of efforts to reduce these behaviors.

Social Ecology: Neighborhood and Community Characteristics

An important sociological approach, begun in the late 1800s and early 1900s by sociologists at the University of Chicago, stresses that certain social and physical characteristics of urban neighborhoods raise the odds that people growing up and living in these neighborhoods will commit deviance and crime. This line of thought is now called the **social ecology approach** (Mears, Wang, Hay, & Bales, 2008). Many *criminogenic* (crime-causing) neighborhood characteristics have been identified, including high rates of poverty, population density, dilapidated housing, residential mobility, and single-parent households. All of these problems are thought to contribute to **social disorganization**, or weakened social bonds and social institutions, that make it difficult to socialize children properly and to monitor suspicious behavior (Mears, Wang, Hay, & Bales, 2008; Sampson, 2006).

Sociology Making a Difference

Improving Neighborhood Conditions Helps Reduce Crime Rates

One of the sociological theories of crime discussed in the text is the social ecology approach. To review, this approach attributes high rates of deviance and crime to the neighborhood's social and physical characteristics, including poverty, high population density, dilapidated housing, and high population turnover. These problems create social disorganization that weakens the neighborhood's social institutions and impairs effective child socialization.

Much empirical evidence supports social ecology's view about negative neighborhood conditions and crime rates and suggests that efforts to improve these conditions will lower crime rates. Some of the most persuasive evidence comes from the Project on Human Development in Chicago Neighborhoods (directed by sociologist Robert J. Sampson), in which more than 6,000 children, ranging in age from birth to 18, and their parents and other caretakers were studied over a 7-year period. The social and physical characteristics of the dozens of neighborhoods in which the subjects lived were measured to permit assessment of these characteristics' effects on the probability of delinquency. A number of studies using data from this project confirm the general assumptions of the social ecology approach. In particular, delinquency is higher in neighborhoods with lower levels of "collective efficacy," that is, in neighborhoods with lower levels of community supervision of adolescent behavior.

The many studies from the Chicago project and data in several other cities show that neighborhood conditions greatly affect the extent of delinquency in urban neighborhoods. This body of research in turn suggests that strategies and programs that improve the social and physical conditions of urban neighborhoods may well help decrease the high rates of crime and delinquency that are so often found there. (Bellair & McNulty, 2009; Sampson, 2006)

Strain Theory

Failure to achieve the American dream lies at the heart of Robert Merton's (1938) famous **strain theory** (also called anomie theory). Recall from Chapter 1 "Sociology and the Sociological Perspective" that Durkheim attributed high rates of suicide to anomie, or normlessness, that occurs in times when social norms are unclear or weak. Adapting this concept, Merton wanted to explain why poor people have higher deviance rates than the nonpoor. He reasoned that the United States values economic success above all else and also has norms that specify the approved means, working, for achieving economic success. Because the poor often cannot achieve the American dream of success through the conventional means of working, they experience a gap between the goal of economic success and the means of working. This gap, which Merton likened to Durkheim's anomie because of the resulting lack of clarity over norms, leads to strain or frustration. To reduce their frustration, some poor people resort to several adaptations, including deviance, depending on whether they accept or reject the goal of economic success and the means of working. Table 7.2 "Merton's Anomie Theory" presents the logical adaptations of the poor to the strain they experience. Let's review these briefly.

Table 7.2 Merton's Anomie Theory

Adaptation	Goal of economic success	Means of working
I. Conformity	+	+
II. Innovation	+	–
III. Ritualism	–	+
IV. Retreatism	–	–
V. Rebellion	±	±
+ means accept, – means reject, ± means reject and work for a new society		

Despite their strain, most poor people continue to accept the goal of economic success and continue to believe they should work to make money. In other words, they continue to be good, law-abiding citizens. They conform to society's norms and values, and, not surprisingly, Merton calls their adaptation *conformity*.

Faced with strain, some poor people continue to value economic success but come up with new means of achieving it. They rob people or banks, commit fraud, or use other illegal means of acquiring money or property. Merton calls this adaptation *innovation*.

Other poor people continue to work at a job without much hope of greatly improving their lot in life. They go to work day after day as a habit. Merton calls this third adaptation *ritualism*. This adaptation does not involve deviant behavior but is a logical response to the strain poor people experience.

One of Robert Merton's adaptations in his strain theory is retreatism, in which poor people abandon society's goal of economic success and reject its means of employment to reach this goal. Many of today's homeless people might be considered retreatists under Merton's typology.

Franco Folini – Homeless woman with dogs – CC BY-SA 2.0.

In Merton's fourth adaptation, *retreatism*, some poor people withdraw from society by becoming hobos or vagrants or by becoming addicted to alcohol, heroin, or other drugs. Their response to the strain they feel is to reject both the goal of economic success and the means of working.

Merton's fifth and final adaptation is *rebellion*. Here poor people not only reject the goal of success and the means of working but work actively to bring about a new society with a new value system. These people are the radicals and revolutionaries of their time. Because Merton developed his strain theory in the aftermath of the Great Depression, in which the labor and socialist movements had been quite active, it is not surprising that he thought of rebellion as a logical adaptation of the poor to their lack of economic success.

Although Merton's theory has been popular over the years, it has some limitations. Perhaps most important, it overlooks deviance such as fraud by the middle and upper classes and also fails to explain murder, rape, and other crimes that usually are not done for economic reasons. It also does not explain why some poor people choose one adaptation over another.

Merton's strain theory stimulated other explanations of deviance that built on his concept of strain. **Differential opportunity theory**, developed by Richard Cloward and Lloyd Ohlin (1960), tried to explain why the poor choose one or the other of Merton's adaptations. Whereas Merton stressed that the poor have *differential access to legitimate means* (working), Cloward and Ohlin stressed that they have *differential access to illegitimate means.*

For example, some live in neighborhoods where organized crime is dominant and will get involved in such crime; others live in neighborhoods rampant with drug use and will start using drugs themselves.

In a more recent formulation, two sociologists, Steven F. Messner and Richard Rosenfeld (2007), expanded Merton's view by arguing that in the United States crime arises from several of our most important values, including an overemphasis on economic success, individualism, and competition. These values produce crime by making many Americans, rich or poor, feel they never have enough money and by prompting them to help themselves even at other people's expense. Crime in the United States, then, arises ironically from the country's most basic values.

In yet another extension of Merton's theory, Robert Agnew (2007) reasoned that adolescents experience various kinds of strain in addition to the economic type addressed by Merton. A romantic relationship may end, a family member may die, or students may be taunted or bullied at school. Repeated strain-inducing incidents such as these produce anger, frustration, and other negative emotions, and these emotions in turn prompt delinquency and drug use.

Deviant Subcultures

Some sociologists stress that poverty and other community conditions give rise to certain subcultures through which adolescents acquire values that promote deviant behavior. One of the first to make this point was Albert K. Cohen (1955), whose **status frustration theory** says that lower-class boys do poorly in school because schools emphasize middle-class values. School failure reduces their status and self-esteem, which the boys try to counter by joining juvenile gangs. In these groups, a different value system prevails, and boys can regain status and self-esteem by engaging in delinquency. Cohen had nothing to say about girls, as he assumed they cared little about how well they did in school, placing more importance on marriage and family instead, and hence would remain nondelinquent even if they did not do well. Scholars later criticized his disregard for girls and assumptions about them.

Another sociologist, Walter Miller (1958), said poor boys become delinquent because they live amid a lower-class subculture that includes several **focal concerns**, or values, that help lead to delinquency. These focal concerns include a taste for trouble, toughness, cleverness, and excitement. If boys grow up in a subculture with these values, they are more likely to break the law. Their deviance is a result of their socialization. Critics said Miller exaggerated the differences between the value systems in poor inner-city neighborhoods and wealthier, middle-class communities (Akers & Sellers, 2008).

A very popular subcultural explanation is the so-called **subculture of violence** thesis, first advanced by Marvin Wolfgang and Franco Ferracuti (1967). In some inner-city areas, they said, a subculture of violence promotes a violent response to insults and other problems, which people in middle-class areas would probably ignore. The subculture of violence, they continued, arises partly from the need of lower-class males to "prove" their masculinity in view of their economic failure. Quantitative research to test their theory has failed to show that the urban poor are more likely than other groups to approve of violence (Cao, Adams, & Jensen, 1997). On the other hand, recent ethnographic (qualitative) research suggests that large segments of the urban poor do adopt a "code" of toughness and violence to promote respect (Anderson, 1999). As this conflicting evidence illustrates, the subculture of violence view remains controversial and merits further scrutiny.

Social Control Theory

Travis Hirschi (1969) argued that human nature is basically selfish and thus wondered why people do *not* commit deviance. His answer, which is now called **social control theory** (also known as *social bonding theory*), was that their bonds to conventional social institutions such as the family and the school keep them from violating social norms. Hirschi's basic perspective reflects Durkheim's view that strong social norms reduce deviance such as suicide.

Hirschi outlined four types of bonds to conventional social institutions: attachment, commitment, involvement, and belief.

1. *Attachment* refers to how much we feel loyal to these institutions and care about the opinions of people in them, such as our parents and teachers. The more attached we are to our families and schools, the less likely we are to be deviant.
2. *Commitment* refers to how much we value our participation in conventional activities such as getting a good education. The more committed we are to these activities and the more time and energy we have invested in them, the less deviant we will be.
3. *Involvement* refers to the amount of time we spend in conventional activities. The more time we spend, the less opportunity we have to be deviant.
4. *Belief* refers to our acceptance of society's norms. The more we believe in these norms, the less we deviate.

Travis Hirschi's social control theory stresses the importance of bonds to social institutions for preventing deviance. His theory emphasized the importance of attachment to one's family in this regard.

More Good Foundation – Mormon Family Dinner – CC BY-NC 2.0.

Hirschi's theory has been very popular. Many studies find that youths with weaker bonds to their parents and schools are more likely to be deviant. But the theory has its critics (Akers & Sellers, 2008). One problem centers on the chicken-and-egg question of causal order. For example, many studies support social control theory by finding that delinquent youths often have worse relationships with their parents than do nondelinquent youths. Is that because the bad relationships prompt the youths to be delinquent, as Hirschi thought? Or is it because the youths' delinquency worsens their relationship with their parents? Despite these questions, Hirschi's social control theory continues to influence our understanding of deviance. To the extent it is correct, it suggests several strategies for preventing crime, including programs designed to improve parenting and relations between parents and children (Welsh & Farrington, 2007).

Conflict and Feminist Explanations

Explanations of crime rooted in the conflict perspective reflect its general view that society is a struggle between the "haves" at the top of society with social, economic, and political power and the "have-nots" at the bottom. Accordingly, they assume that those with power pass laws and otherwise use the legal system to secure their position at the top of society and to keep the powerless on the bottom (Bohm & Vogel, 2011). The poor and minorities are more likely because of their poverty and race to be arrested, convicted, and imprisoned. These explanations also blame street crime by the poor on the economic deprivation and inequality in which they live rather than on any moral failings of the poor.

Some conflict explanations also say that capitalism helps create street crime by the poor. An early proponent of this view was Dutch criminologist Willem Bonger (1916), who said that capitalism as an economic system involves competition for profit. This competition leads to an emphasis in a capitalist society's culture on *egoism*, or self-seeking behavior, and *greed*. Because profit becomes so important, people in a capitalist society are more likely than those in noncapitalist ones to break the law for profit and other gains, even if their behavior hurts others.

Not surprisingly, conflict explanations have sparked much controversy (Akers & Sellers, 2008). Many scholars dismiss them for painting an overly critical picture of the United States and ignoring the excesses of noncapitalistic nations, while others say the theories overstate the degree of inequality in the legal system. In assessing the debate over conflict explanations, a fair conclusion is that their view on discrimination by the legal system applies more to victimless crime (discussed in a later section) than to conventional crime, where it is difficult to argue that laws against such things as murder and robbery reflect the needs of the powerful. However, much evidence supports the conflict assertion that the poor and minorities face disadvantages in the legal system (Reiman & Leighton, 2010). Simply put, the poor cannot afford good attorneys, private investigators, and the other advantages that money brings in court. As just one example, if someone much poorer than O. J. Simpson, the former football player and media celebrity, had been arrested, as he was in 1994, for viciously murdering two people, the defendant would almost certainly have been found guilty. Simpson was able to afford a defense costing hundreds of thousands of dollars and won a jury acquittal in his criminal trial (Barkan, 1996). Also in accordance with conflict theory's views, corporate executives, among the most powerful members of society, often break the law without fear of imprisonment, as we shall see in our discussion of white-collar crime later in this chapter. Finally, many studies support conflict theory's view that the roots of crimes by poor people lie in social inequality and economic deprivation (Barkan, 2009).

Feminist Perspectives

Feminist perspectives on crime and criminal justice also fall into the broad rubric of conflict explanations and have burgeoned in the last two decades. Much of this work concerns rape and sexual assault, intimate partner violence, and other crimes against women that were largely neglected until feminists began writing about them in the 1970s (Griffin, 1971). Their views have since influenced public and official attitudes about rape and domestic violence, which used to be thought as something that girls and women brought on themselves. The feminist approach instead places the blame for these crimes squarely on society's inequality against women and antiquated views about relations between the sexes (Renzetti, 2011).

Another focus of feminist work is gender and legal processing. Are women better or worse off than men when it comes to the chances of being arrested and punished? After many studies in the last two decades, the best answer is that we are not sure (Belknap, 2007). Women are treated a little more harshly than men for minor crimes and a little less harshly for serious crimes, but the gender effect in general is weak.

A third focus concerns the gender difference in serious crime, as women and girls are much less likely than men and boys to engage in violence and to commit serious property crimes such as burglary and motor vehicle theft. Most sociologists attribute this difference to gender socialization. Simply put, socialization into the male gender role, or masculinity, leads to values such as competitiveness and behavioral patterns such as spending more time away from home that all promote deviance. Conversely, despite whatever disadvantages it may have, socialization into the female gender role, or femininity, promotes values such as gentleness and behavior patterns such as spending more time at home that help limit deviance (Chesney-Lind & Pasko, 2004). Noting that males commit so much crime, Kathleen Daly and Meda Chesney-Lind (1988, p. 527) wrote,

> A large price is paid for structures of male domination and for the very qualities that drive men to be successful, to control others, and to wield uncompromising power.…Gender differences in crime suggest that crime may not be so normal after all. Such differences challenge us to see that in the lives of women, men have a great deal more to learn.

Gender socialization helps explain why females commit less serious crime than males. Boys are raised to be competitive and aggressive, while girls are raised to be more gentle and nurturing.

Philippe Put – Fight – CC BY 2.0.

Two decades later, that challenge still remains.

Symbolic Interactionist Explanations

Because symbolic interactionism focuses on the means people gain from their social interaction, symbolic interactionist explanations attribute deviance to various aspects of the social interaction and social processes that normal individuals experience. These explanations help us understand why some people are more likely than others living in the same kinds of social environments. Several such explanations exist.

Differential Association Theory

One popular set of explanations, often called *learning theories*, emphasizes that deviance is learned from interacting with other people who believe it is OK to commit deviance and who often commit deviance themselves. Deviance, then, arises from normal socialization processes. The most influential such explanation is Edwin H. Sutherland's (1947) **differential association theory**, which says that criminal behavior is learned by interacting with close friends and family members. These individuals teach us not only how to commit various crimes but also the values, motives, and rationalizations that we need to adopt in order to justify breaking the law. The earlier in our life that we associate with deviant individuals and the more often we do so, the more likely we become deviant ourselves. In this way, a normal social process, socialization, can lead normal people to commit deviance.

Sutherland's theory of differential association was one of the most influential sociological theories ever. Over the years much research has documented the importance of adolescents' peer relationships for their entrance into the world of drugs and delinquency (Akers & Sellers, 2008). However, some critics say that not all deviance results from the influences of deviant peers. Still, differential association theory and the larger category of learning theories it represents remain a valuable approach to understanding deviance and crime.

Labeling Theory

If we arrest and imprison someone, we hope they will be "scared straight," or deterred from committing a crime again. **Labeling theory** assumes precisely the opposite: it says that labeling someone deviant increases the chances that the labeled person will continue to commit deviance. According to labeling theory, this happens because the labeled person ends up with a deviant self-image that leads to even more deviance. Deviance is the result of being labeled (Bohm & Vogel, 2011).

This effect is reinforced by how society treats someone who has been labeled. Research shows that job applicants with a criminal record are much less likely than those without a record to be hired (Pager, 2009). Suppose you had a criminal record and had seen the error of your ways but were rejected by several potential employers. Do you think you might be just a little frustrated? If your unemployment continues, might you think about committing a crime again? Meanwhile, you want to meet some law-abiding friends, so you go to a singles bar. You start talking with someone who interests you, and in response to this person's question, you say you are between jobs. When your companion asks about your last job, you reply that you were in prison for armed robbery. How do you think your companion will react after hearing this? As this scenario suggests, being labeled deviant can make it difficult to avoid a continued life of deviance.

Labeling theory also asks whether some people and behaviors are indeed more likely than others to acquire a deviant label. In particular, it asserts that nonlegal factors such as appearance, race, and social class affect how often official labeling occurs.

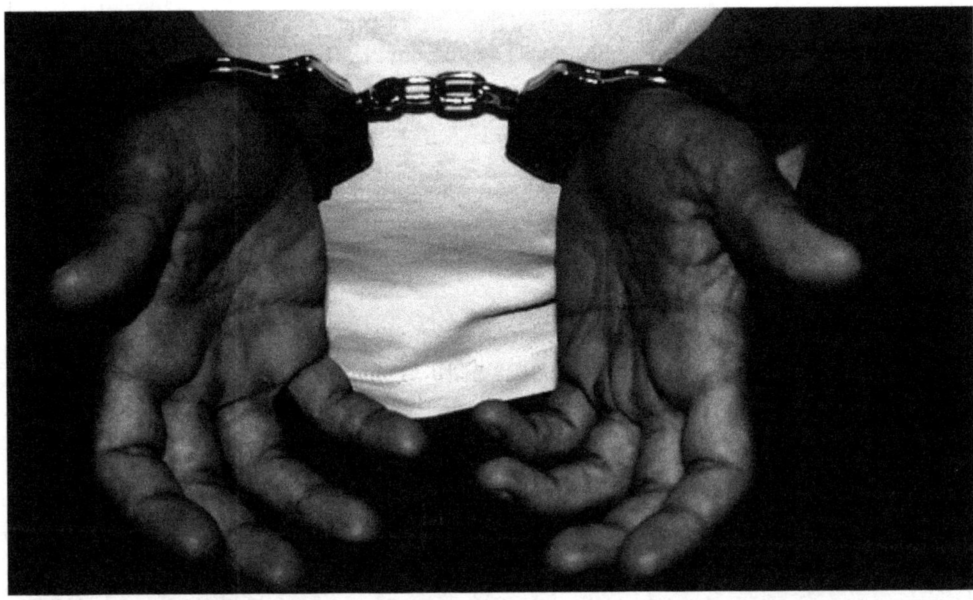

Labeling theory assumes that someone who is labeled deviant will be more likely to commit deviance as a result. One problem that ex-prisoners face after being released back into society is that potential employers do not want to hire them. This fact makes it more likely that they will commit new offenses.

Victor – Handcuffs – CC BY 2.0.

William Chambliss's (1973) classic analysis of the "Saints" and the "Roughnecks" is an excellent example of this argument. The Saints were eight male high-school students from middle-class backgrounds who were very delinquent, while the Roughnecks were six male students in the same high school who were also very delinquent but who came from poor, working-class families. Although the Saints' behavior was arguably more harmful than the Roughnecks', their actions were considered harmless pranks, and they were never arrested. After graduating from high school, they went on to college and graduate and professional school and ended up in respectable careers. In contrast, the Roughnecks were widely viewed as troublemakers and often got into trouble for their behavior. As adults they either ended up in low-paying jobs or went to prison.

Labeling theory's views on the effects of being labeled and on the importance of nonlegal factors for official labeling remain controversial. Nonetheless, the theory has greatly influenced the study of deviance and crime in the last few decades and promises to do so for many years to come.

Key Takeaways

- Both biological and psychological explanations assume that deviance stems from problems arising inside the individual.
- Sociological explanations attribute deviance to various aspects of the social environment.
- Several functionalist explanations exist. Durkheim highlighted the functions that deviance serves for society. Merton's strain theory assumed that deviance among the poor results from their inability to achieve the economic success so valued in American society. Other explanations highlight the role played by the social and physical characteristics of urban neighborhoods, of deviant subcultures, and of weak bonds to social institutions.
- Conflict explanations assume that the wealthy and powerful use the legal system to protect their own interests and to keep the poor and racial minorities subservient. Feminist perspectives highlight the importance of gender inequality for crimes against women and of male socialization for the gender difference in criminality.
- Interactionist explanations highlight the importance of social interaction in the commitment of deviance and in reactions to deviance. Labeling theory assumes that the labeling process helps ensure that someone will continue to commit deviance, and it also assumes that some people are more likely than others to be labeled deviant because of their appearance, race, social class, and other characteristics.

For Your Review

1. In what important way do biological and psychological explanations differ from sociological explanations?
2. What are any two functions of deviance according to Durkheim?
3. What are any two criminogenic social or physical characteristics of urban neighborhoods?
4. What are any two assumptions of feminist perspectives on deviance and crime?
5. According to labeling theory, what happens when someone is labeled as a deviant?

References

Agnew, R. (2007). *Pressured into crime: An overview of general strain theory*. Los Angeles, CA: Roxbury.

Akers, R. L., & Sellers, C. S. (2008). *Criminological theories: Introduction, evaluation, and application*. New York, NY: Oxford University Press.

Anderson, E. (1999). *Code of the street: Decency, violence, and the moral life of the inner city*. New York, NY: W. W. Norton.

Barkan, S. E. (1996). The social science significance of the O. J. Simpson case. In G. Barak (Ed.), *Representing O. J.: Murder, criminal justice and mass culture* (pp. 36–42). Albany, NY: Harrow and Heston.

Barkan, S. E. (2009). The value of quantitative analysis for a critical understanding of crime and society. *Critical Criminology, 17,* 247–259.

Belknap, J. (2007). *The invisible woman: Gender, crime, and justice.* Belmont, CA: Wadsworth.

Bellair, P. E., & McNulty, T. L. (2009). Gang membership, drug selling, and violence in neighborhood context. *Justice Quarterly, 26,* 644–669.

Bohm, R. M., & Vogel, B. (2011). *A Primer on crime and delinquency theory* (3rd ed.). Belmont, CA: Wadsworth.

Bonger, W. (1916). *Criminality and economic conditions* (H. P. Horton, Trans.). Boston, MA: Little, Brown.

Cao, L., Adams, A., & Jensen, V. J. (1997). A test of the black subculture of violence thesis: A research note. *Criminology, 35,* 367–379.

Chambliss, W. J. (1973). The saints and the roughnecks. *Society, 11,* 24–31.

Chesney-Lind, M., & Pasko, L. (2004). *The female offender: Girls, women, and crime*. Thousand Oaks, CA: Sage.

Clark, W. V. T. (1940). *The ox-bow incident*. New York, NY: Random House.

Cloward, R. A., & Ohlin, L. E. (1960). *Delinquency and opportunity: A theory of delinquent gangs*. New York, NY: Free Press.

Cohen, A. K. (1955). *Delinquent boys: The culture of the gang*. New York, NY: Free Press.

Daly, K., & Chesney-Lind, M. (1988). Feminism and criminology. *Justice Quarterly, 5,* 497–538.

Gans, H. J. (1996). *The war against the poor: The underclass and antipoverty policy*. New York, NY: Basic Books.

Griffin, S. (1971, September). Rape: The all-American crime. *Ramparts, 10,* 26–35.

Hirschi, T. (1969). *Causes of delinquency*. Berkeley: University of California Press.

Mears, D. P., Wang, X., Hay, C., & Bales, W. D. (2008). Social ecology and recidivism: Implications for prisoner reentry. *Criminology, 46,* 301–340.

Merton, R. K. (1938). Social structure and anomie. *American Sociological Review, 3,* 672–682.

Messner, S. F., & Rosenfeld, R. (2007). *Crime and the American dream*. Belmont, CA: Wadsworth.

Miller, W. B. (1958). Lower class culture as a generating milieu of gang delinquency. *Journal of Social Issues, 14,* 5–19.

Pager, D. (2009). *Marked: Race, crime, and finding work in an era of mass incarceration*. Chicago, IL: University of Chicago Press.

Reiman, J., & Leighton, P. (2010). *The rich get richer and the poor get prison: Ideology, class, and criminal justice* (9th ed.). Boston, MA: Allyn & Bacon.

Renzetti, C. (2011). *Feminist criminology*. Manuscript submitted for publication.

Sampson, R. J. (2006). How does community context matter? Social mechanisms and the explanation of crime rates. In P.-O. H. Wikström & R. J. Sampson (Eds.), *The explanation of crime: Context, mechanisms, and development* (pp. 31–60). New York, NY: Cambridge University Press.

Sutherland, E. H. (1947). *Principles of criminology*. Philadelphia, PA: J. P. Lippincott.

Welsh, B. C., & Farrington, D. P. (Eds.). (2007). *Preventing crime: What works for children, offenders, victims and places*. New York, NY: Springer.

Wolfgang, M. E., & Ferracuti, F. (1967). *The subculture of violence*. London, England: Social Science Paperbacks.

7.3 Crime and Criminals

Learning Objectives

1. Describe how gender and race affect public opinion about crime.
2. Explain problems in the accurate measurement of crime.
3. Describe the demographic backgrounds (race, gender, age, location) of conventional criminals.
4. Be familiar with examples of white-collar crime and with the various harms of such crime.
5. Explain the arguments over laws prohibiting victimless crime.

We now turn our attention from theoretical explanations of deviance and crime to certain aspects of crime and the people who commit it. What do we know about crime and criminals in the United States?

Crime and Public Opinion

One thing we know is that the American public is very concerned about crime. In a 2009 Gallup Poll, about 55% said crime is an "extremely" or "very" serious problem in the United States, and in other national surveys, about one-third of Americans said they would be afraid to walk alone in their neighborhoods at night (Maguire & Pastore, 2009; Saad, 2008).

Recall that according to the sociological perspective, our social backgrounds affect our attitudes, behavior, and life chances. Do gender and race affect our fear of crime? Figure 7.1 "Gender and Fear of Crime" shows that gender has quite a large effect. About 46% of women are afraid to walk alone at night, compared to only 17% of men. Because women are less likely than men to be victims of crime other than rape, their higher fear of crime reflects their heightened fear of rape and other types of sexual assault (Warr, 2000).

Figure 7.1 Gender and Fear of Crime

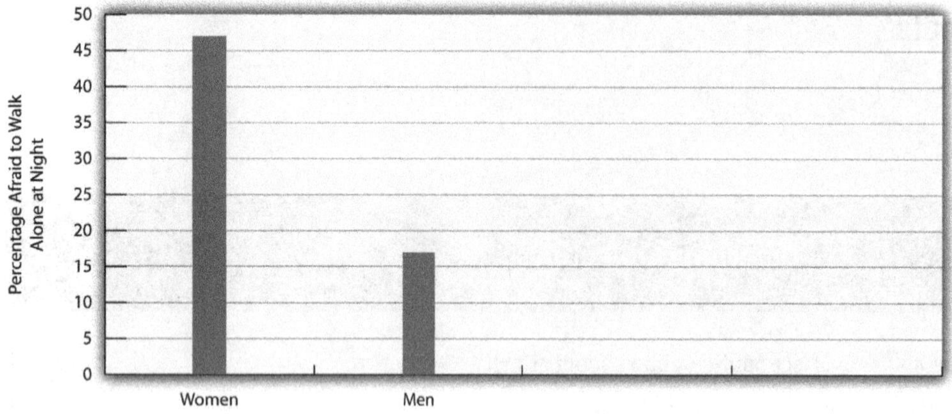

Source: Data from General Social Survey, 2008.

Race also makes a difference. Figure 7.2 "Race and Fear of Crime" shows that African Americans are more afraid than whites of walking near their homes alone at night. This difference reflects the fact that African Americans are more likely than whites to live in large cities with high crime rates and to live in higher crime neighborhoods within these cities (Peterson & Krivo, 2009).

Figure 7.2 Race and Fear of Crime

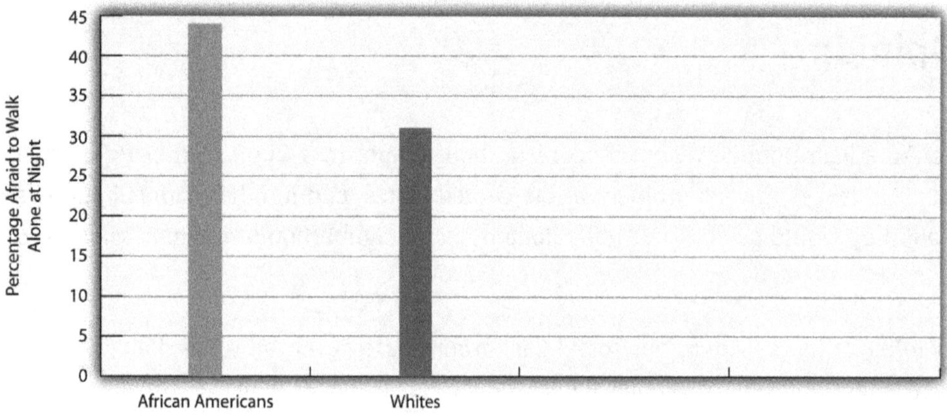

Source: Data from General Social Survey, 2008.

Race also affects views about the criminal justice system. For example, African Americans are much less likely than whites to favor the death penalty (Figure 7.3 "Race and Support for the Death Penalty"), in part because they perceive that the death penalty and criminal justice system in general are racially discriminatory (Johnson, 2008).

Figure 7.3 Race and Support for the Death Penalty

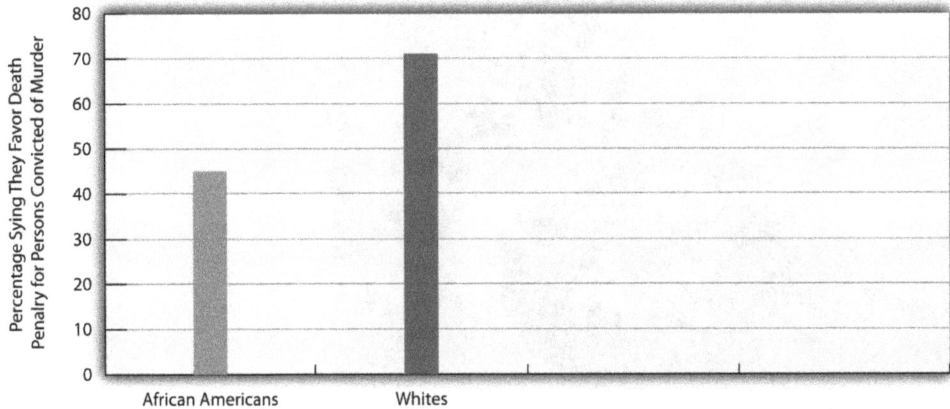

Source: Data from General Social Survey, 2008.

The Measurement of Crime

It is surprisingly difficult to know how much crime occurs. Crime is not like the weather, when we all can see whether it is raining, snowing, or sunny. Usually when crime occurs, only the criminal and the victim, and sometimes an occasional witness, know about it. Although we have an incomplete picture of the crime problem, because of various data sources we still have a fairly good understanding of how much crime exists and of who is most likely to do it and be victimized by it.

The government's primary source of crime data is the **Uniform Crime Reports (UCR)**, published annually by the Federal Bureau of Investigation. The FBI gathers its data from police departments around the country, who inform the FBI about crimes that have come to their attention. The police also tell the FBI whether someone is arrested for the crime and, if so, the person's age, gender, and race. The FBI gathers all of these UCR data and reports them in an annual volume called *Crime in the United States*.

Most UCR data concern the so-called **Part I Offenses**, eight felonies that the FBI considers the most serious. Four of these are violent crimes: homicide, rape, aggravated assault, and robbery; four are property crimes: burglary, larceny (e.g., shoplifting, pickpocketing, purse snatching), motor vehicle theft, and arson.

According to the FBI, in 2008 almost 1.4 million violent crimes and 9.8 million property crimes occurred, for a total of almost 11.2 million serious crimes, or 3,667 for every 100,000 Americans. This is the nation's official crime rate, and by any standard it is a lot of crime. However, this figure is in fact much lower than the actual crime rate because, according to surveys of random samples of crime victims, *more than half of all crime victims do not report their crimes to the police*, leaving the police unaware of the crimes. (Reasons for nonreporting include the belief that police will not be able to find the offender and fear of retaliation by the offender.) The true crime problem is therefore much greater than suggested by the UCR.

When a crime occurs, the police do not usually find out about it unless the victim or a witness informs the police about the crime.

Wikimedia Commons – public domain.

This underreporting of crime represents a major problem for the UCR's validity. Several other problems exist (Lynch & Addington, 2007). First, the UCR omits crime by corporations and thus diverts attention away from their harm (see a little later in this chapter). Second, police practices affect the UCR. For example, the police do not record every report they hear from a citizen as a crime. Sometimes they have little time to do so, sometimes they do not believe the citizen, and sometimes they deliberately fail to record a crime to make it seem that they are doing a good job of preventing crime. If they do not record the report, the FBI does not count it as a crime. If the police start recording every report, the official crime rate will rise, even though the actual number of crimes has not changed. In a third problem, if crime victims become more likely to report their crimes to the police, which might have happened after the 911 emergency number became common, the official crime rate will again change, even if the actual number of crimes has not changed.

To get a more accurate picture of crime, the federal government began in the early 1970s to administer a survey, now called the **National Crime Victimization Survey (NCVS)**, to tens of thousands of randomly selected U.S. households. People in the households are asked whether they or their residence has been the victim of several different types of crimes in the past half year. Their responses are then extrapolated to the entire U.S. population to yield fairly accurate estimates of the actual number of crimes occurring in the nation. Still, the NCVS's estimates are not perfect. Among other problems, some respondents decline to tell NCVS interviewers about victimizations they have suffered, and the NCVS's sample excludes some segments of the population, such as the homeless, whose victimizations therefore go uncounted.

Table 7.3 "Number of Crimes: Uniform Crime Reports and National Crime Victimization Survey, 2009" lists the number of violent and property crimes as reported by the UCR (see earlier) and estimated by the NCVS. Note that these two crime sources do not measure exactly the same crimes. For example, the NCVS excludes commercial crimes such as shoplifting, while the UCR includes them. The NCVS includes simple assaults (where someone receives only a minor injury), while the UCR excludes them. These differences notwithstanding, we can still see that the NCVS estimates about twice as many crimes as the UCR reports to us.

Table 7.3 Number of Crimes: Uniform Crime Reports and National Crime Victimization Survey, 2009

Type of crime	UCR	NCVS
Violent crime	1,318,398	4,343,450
Property crime	9,320,971	15,713,720
Total	10,639,369	20,057,170

Source: Data from Pastore, A. L., & Maguire, K. (2010). *Sourcebook of criminal justice statistics*. Retrieved from http://www.albany.edu/sourcebook.

A third source of crime information is the **self-report survey**. Here subjects, usually adolescents, are given an anonymous questionnaire and asked to indicate whether and how often they committed various offenses in a specific time period, usually the past year. They also answer questions about their family relationships, school performance, and other aspects of their backgrounds. Although these respondents do not always report every offense they committed, self-report studies yield valuable information about delinquency and explanations of crime. Like the NCVS, they underscore how much crime is committed that does not come to the attention of the police.

The Types and Correlates of Crime and Victimization

The three data sources just discussed give us a fairly good understanding of the types of crime, of who does them and who is victimized by them, and of why the crimes are committed. We have already looked at the "why" question when we reviewed the many theories of deviance. Let's look now at the various types of crime and highlight some important things about them.

Conventional Crime

Rates of violent crime victimization are higher in urban areas than in rural areas.

Aurelien Guichard – New York City – CC BY-SA 2.0.

By **conventional crime** we mean the violent and property offenses listed previously that worry average citizens more than any other type of crime. As Table 7.3 "Number of Crimes: Uniform Crime Reports and National Crime Victimization Survey, 2009" indicated, more than 20 million violent and property victimizations occurred in the United States in 2009. These offenses included some 15,240 murders; 126,000 rapes and sexual assaults; 534,000 robberies; and 823,000 aggravated assaults. Even more property crime occurs: 3.1 million burglaries, 11.8 million larcenies, and 736,000 motor vehicle thefts (Pastore & Maguire, 2010). The NCVS estimates that the crimes it measures cost their victims almost $20 billion each year in property losses, medical expenses, and time lost from work.

Generally, African Americans and other people of color are more likely than whites to be victims of conventional crime, poor people more likely than wealthy people, men more likely than women (excluding rape and sexual assault), and urban residents more likely than rural residents. To illustrate these differences, Figure 7.4 "Correlates of Violent Crime Victimization, 2008" presents some relevant comparisons for violent crime victimization.

Figure 7.4 Correlates of Violent Crime Victimization, 2008

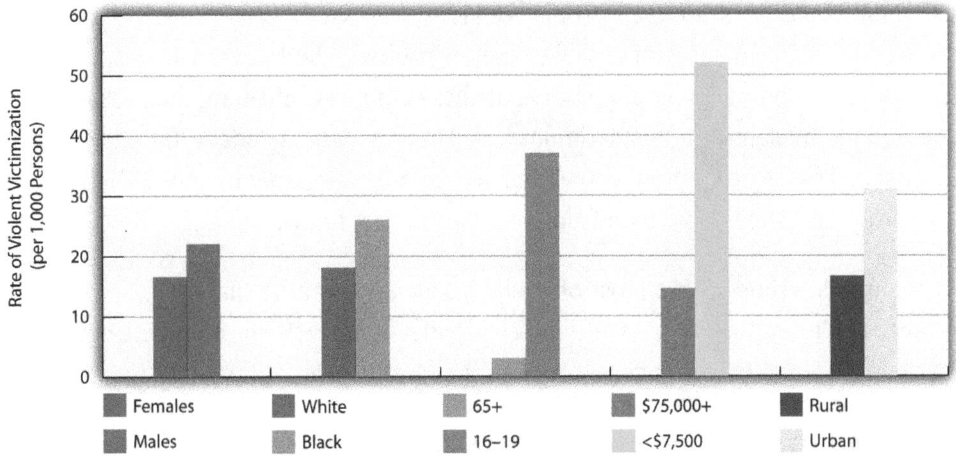

Note: Income data are for 2007; rural and urban data are for 2005.

Source: Data from Maston, C. T., & Klaus, P. (2010). *Criminal victimization in the United States, 2007—Statistical tables*. Washington, DC: Bureau of Justice Statistics, U.S. Department of Justice; Rand, M. R. (2009). *Criminal victimization, 2008*. Washington, DC: Bureau of Justice Statistics, U.S. Department of Justice.

As this figure illustrates, violent crime is more common in urban areas than in rural areas. It varies geographically in at least one other respect, and that is among the regions of the United States. In general, violent crime is more common in the South and West than in the Midwest or Northeast. Figure 7.5 "U.S. Homicide Rates, 2008" depicts this variation for homicide rates. Louisiana has the highest homicide rate, 14.24 homicides per 100,000 residents, and New Hampshire has the lowest rate, 1.1 per 100,000 residents. Although homicide is thankfully a rare occurrence, it is much more common in Louisiana than in New Hampshire, and it is generally more common in the South and West than in other regions. Scholars attribute the South's high rate of homicide and other violent crime to several factors, among them a subculture of violence, its history of slavery and racial violence, and its high levels of poverty (Lee, Bankston, Hayes, & Thomas, 2007).

Figure 7.5 U.S. Homicide Rates, 2008

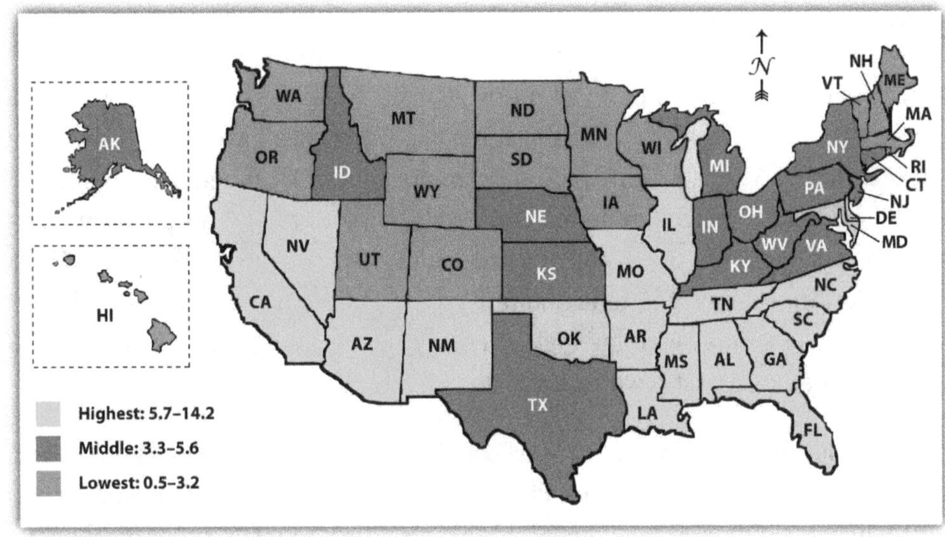

Source: Data from U.S. Census Bureau. (2010). *Statistical abstract of the United States: 2010*. Washington, DC: U.S. Government Printing Office. Retrieved from http://www.census.gov/compendia/statab.

When it comes to crime, we fear strangers much more than people we know, but NCVS data suggest our fear is somewhat misplaced (Truman & Rand, 2010). In cases of assault, rape, or robbery, the NCVS asks respondents whether they knew the offender. Strangers commit only about 42% of these offenses, meaning that 58% of the offenses, or well over half, are committed by someone the victim knows. There is also a gender difference in this area: 68% of women victims are attacked by someone they know (usually a man), compared to only 45% of male victims. Women have more to fear from men they know than from men they do not know.

Another important fact about conventional crime is that most of it is *intraracial*, meaning that the offender and victim are usually of the same race. For example, 84% of all single offender–single victim homicides in 2009 involved persons who were either both white or both African American (Federal Bureau of Investigation, 2010).

Who is most likely to commit conventional crime? As noted earlier, males are more likely than females to commit it (see Figure 7.6 "Gender and Arrest, 2008") because of gender differences in socialization. Opportunity may also matter, as during adolescence boys have more freedom than girls to be outside the home and to get into trouble.

Figure 7.6 Gender and Arrest, 2008

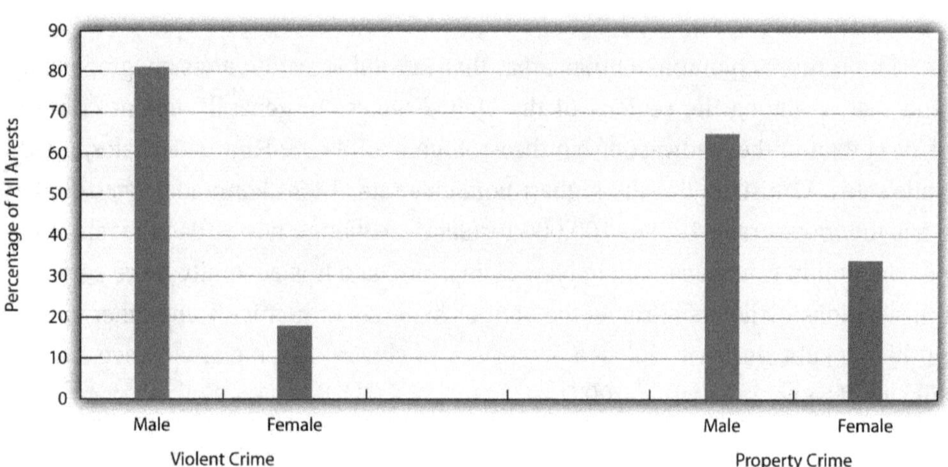

Source: Data from Federal Bureau of Investigation. (2010). *Crime in the United States, 2009*. Washington, DC: Author.

Despite much controversy over what racial differences in arrest mean, African Americans have higher rates of arrest than whites for conventional crime. Criminologists generally agree that these rates indicate higher rates of offending (Walker, Spohn, & DeLone, 2007). Although African Americans are about 13% of the U.S. population, they accounted for about 39% of all arrests for violent crime in 2009 and 30% of all arrests for property crime (Federal Bureau of Investigation, 2010). Much of these higher crime rates stem from the fact that African Americans are much poorer than whites on average and much more likely to live in the large cities with high crime rates and in the neighborhoods in these cities with the highest crime rates (McNulty & Bellair, 2003). If whites lived under the same conditions, their crime rates would be much higher as well.

Social class also makes a difference in conventional crime rates. Most people arrested for conventional crime have low education and low incomes. Such class differences in arrest can be explained by several of the explanations of deviance already discussed, including strain theory. Note, however, that wealthier people commit most white-collar crimes. If the question is whether social class affects crime rates, the answer depends on what kind of crime we have in mind.

One final factor affecting conventional crime rates is age. The evidence is very clear that conventional crime is disproportionately committed by people 30 and under. For example, people in the 10–24 age group are about 22% of the U.S. population but account for about 45% of all arrests (Federal Bureau of Investigation, 2010). During adolescence and young adulthood, peer influences are especially strong and "stakes in conventional activities," to use some sociological jargon, are weak. Once we start working full time and get married, our stakes in society become stronger and our sense of responsibility grows. We soon realize that breaking the law might prove more costly than when we were 15.

White-Collar Crime

White-collar crime is crime committed as part of one's occupation. It ranges from fraudulent repairs by auto repair shops to corruption in the high-finance industry to unsafe products and workplaces in some of our largest corporations. It also includes employee theft of objects and cash. Have you ever taken something without permission from a place where you worked? Whether or not you have, many people steal from their employees, and the National Retail Federation estimates that employee theft involves some $20 billion annually (National Retail Federation, 2007). White-collar crime also includes health-care fraud, which is estimated to cost some $100 billion a year as, for example, physicians and other health-care providers bill Medicaid for exams and tests that were never done or were unnecessary (Rosoff, Pontell, & Tillman, 2010). And it also involves tax evasion: the IRS estimates that tax evasion costs the government some $300 billion annually, a figure many times greater than the cost of all robberies and burglaries (Montgomery, 2007).

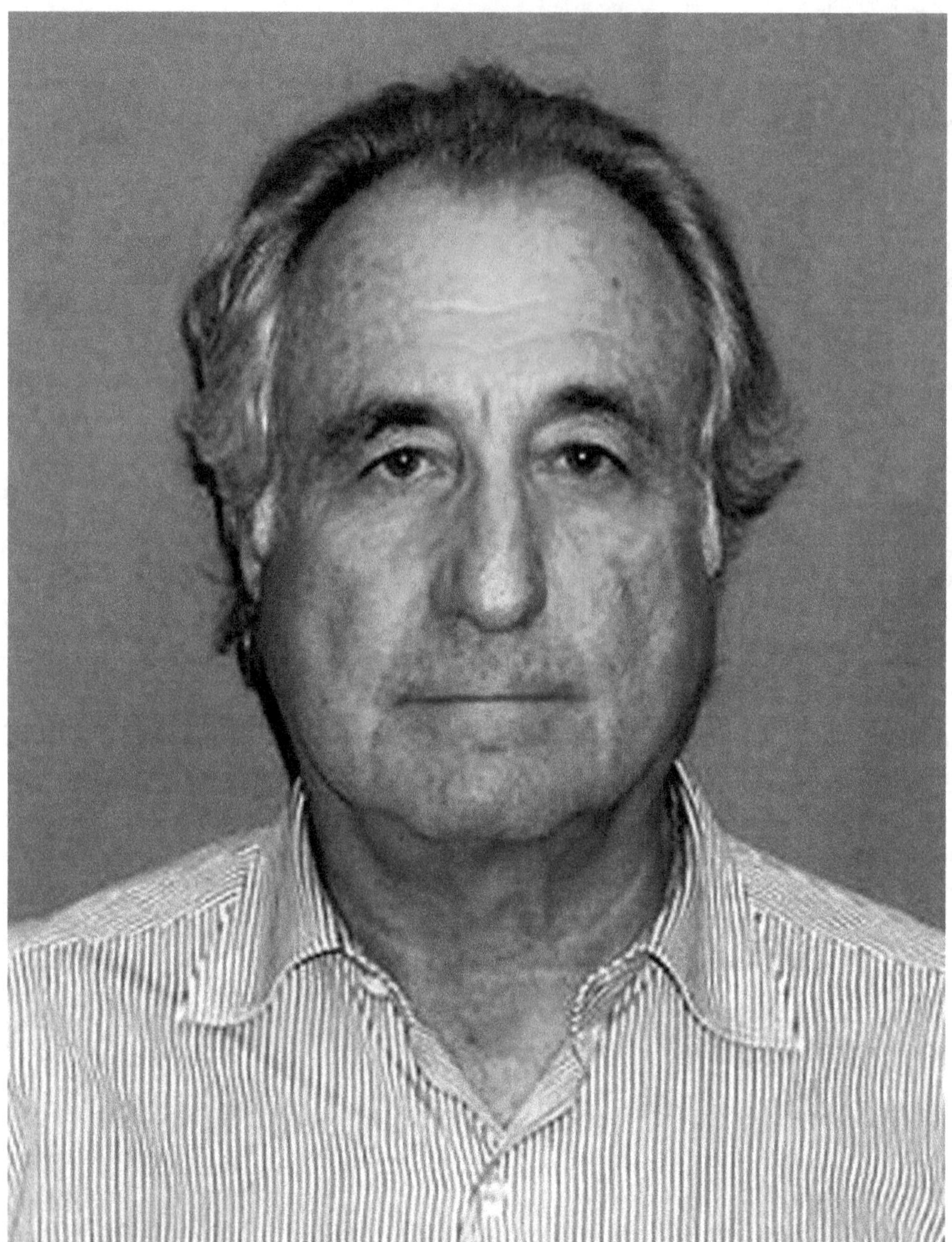

In June 2009, investment expert Bernard Madoff was sentenced to 150 years in prison for defrauding thousands of investors of tens of billions of dollars. This was the largest such crime in U.S. history.

Wikimedia Commons – public domain.

One of the most serious recent examples of white-collar crime came to light in December 2008, when it was discovered that 70-year-old investment expert Bernard Madoff had engaged in a Ponzi scheme (in which new investments are used to provide the income for older investments) since the early 1990s in which he defrauded thousands of investors of an estimated $50 billion, the largest such scandal in U.S. history (Creswell & Thomas, 2009). Madoff pleaded guilty in February 2009 to 11 felonies, including securities fraud and money laundering, and was sentenced to 150 years in prison (Henriques & Healy, 2009).

Some of the worst crime is committed by our major corporations (*corporate crime*). As just one example, price fixing in the corporate world costs the U.S. public about $60 billion a year (Simon, 2006). Even worse, an estimated 50,000 workers die each year from workplace-related illnesses and injuries that could have been prevented if companies had obeyed regulatory laws and followed known practices for safe workplaces (AFL-CIO, 2007). A tragic example of this problem occurred in April 2010, when an explosion in a mining cave in West Virginia killed 29 miners. It was widely thought that a buildup of deadly gases had caused the explosion, and the company that owned the mine had been cited many times during the prior year for safety violations related to proper gas ventilation (Urbina, 2010).

Corporations also make deadly products. In the 1930s the asbestos industry first realized their product was dangerous but hid the evidence of its danger, which was not discovered until 40 years later. In the meantime thousands of asbestos workers came down with deadly asbestos-related disease, and the public was exposed to asbestos that was routinely put into buildings until its danger came to light. It is estimated that more than 200,000 people will eventually die from asbestos (Lilienfeld, 1991).

Asbestos is not the only unsafe product. The Consumer Product Safety Commission and the U.S. Centers for Disease Control and Prevention estimate that about 10,000 Americans die annually from dangerous products, including cars, drugs, and food (U.S. Consumer Product Safety Commission, 2003; Petersen & Drew, 2003). In perhaps the most notorious case, Ford Motor Company marketed the Pinto even though company officials knew the gas tank could catch fire and explode when hit from the rear end at low speeds. Ford had determined it could fix each car's defect for $11 but that doing so would cost it more money than the amount of lawsuits it would eventually pay to the families of dead and burned Pinto victims if it did not fix the defect. Because Ford decided not to fix the defect, many people—estimates range from two dozen up to 500—people died in Pinto accidents (Cullen, Maakestad, & Cavender, 2006). In a more recent example involving a motor vehicle company, Toyota was fined $16.4 million by the federal government in April 2010 for allegedly suppressing evidence that its vehicles were at risk for sudden acceleration. The government's announcement asserted that Toyota "knowingly hid a dangerous defect for months from U.S. officials and did not take action to protect millions of drivers and their families" (Maynard, 2010, p. A1).

Corporations also damage the environment, as the BP oil spill that began in April 2010 reminds us. Because federal laws are lax or nonexistent, corporations can and do pollute the environment with little fear of serious consequences. According to one report, one-fifth of U.S. landfills and incinerators and one-half of wastewater treatment plants violate health regulations (Armstrong, 1999). It is estimated that between 50,000 and 100,000 Americans and 300,000 Europeans die every year from the side effects (including heart disease, respiratory problems, and cancer) of air pollution (BBC News, 2005); many of these deaths would not occur if corporations followed the law and otherwise did not engage in unnecessary pollution of the air, water, and land. Critics also assert that laws against pollution are relatively weak and that government enforcement of these laws is often lax.

Is white-collar crime worse than conventional crime? The evidence seems to say yes. A recent estimate put the number of deaths from white-collar crime annually at about 110,000, compared to "only" 16,000 to 17,000 from homicide. The financial cost of white-collar crime to the public was also estimated at about $565 billion annually, compared to about $18 billion from conventional crime (Barkan, 2012). Although we worry about conventional crime much more than white-collar crime, the latter harms the public more in terms of death and financial costs.

Victimless Crime

Victimless crime is illegal behavior in which people willingly engage and in which there are no unwilling victims. The most common examples are drug use, prostitution, pornography, and gambling. Many observers say these crimes are not really victimless, even if people do engage in them voluntarily. For example, many drug users hurt themselves and members of their family from their addiction and the physical effects of taking drugs. Prostitutes put themselves at risk for sexually transmitted disease and abuse by pimps and customers. Illegal gamblers can lose huge sums of money. Although none of these crimes is truly victimless, the fact that the people involved in them are not *unwilling* victims makes victimless crime different from conventional crime.

Victimless crime raises controversial philosophical and sociological questions. The philosophical question is this: should people be allowed to engage in behavior that hurts themselves (Meier & Geis, 2007)? For example, our society lets adults smoke cigarettes, even though tobacco use kills several hundred thousand people every year. We also let adults gamble legally in state lotteries, at casinos and racetracks, and in other ways. We obviously let people of all ages eat "fat food" such as hamburgers, candy bars, and ice cream. Few people would say we should prohibit these potentially harmful behaviors. Why, then, prohibit the behaviors we call victimless crime? Some scholars say that any attempt to decide which behaviors are so unsafe or immoral that they should be banned is bound to be arbitrary, and they call for these bans to be lifted. Others say that the state does indeed have a legitimate duty to ban behavior the public considers unsafe or immoral and that the present laws reflect public opinion on which behaviors should be banned.

Laws against illegal drug use and other victimless crimes raise several philosophical and sociological questions, including whether the laws do more harm than good.

Blind Nomad – marijuana wars – weeds a stimulant – CC BY 2.0.

The sociological question is just as difficult to resolve: do laws against victimless crimes do more harm than good

(Meier & Geis, 2007)? Some scholars say these laws in fact do much more harm than good, and they call for the laws to be abolished or at least reconsidered for several reasons: the laws are ineffective even though they cost billions of dollars to enforce, and they lead to police and political corruption and greater profits for organized crime. Laws against drugs further lead to extra violence, as youth gangs and other groups fight each other to corner the market for the distribution of drugs in various neighborhoods. The opponents of victimless crime laws commonly cite the example of Prohibition during the 1920s, where the banning of alcohol led to all of these problems, which in turn forced an end to Prohibition by the early 1930s. If victimless crimes were made legal, opponents add, the government could tax the behaviors now banned and collect billions of additional tax dollars.

Those in favor of laws against victimless crimes cite the danger these behaviors pose for the people engaging in them and for the larger society. If we made drugs legal, they say, even more people would use them, and even more death and illness would occur. Removing the bans against behaviors such as drug use and prostitution, these proponents add, would imply that these behaviors are acceptable in a civil society.

The debate over victimless crimes and victimless crime laws will not end soon, as both sides have several good points to make. One thing that is clear is that our current law enforcement approach is not working. More than 1 million people are arrested annually for drug use and trafficking and other victimless crimes, but there is little evidence that using the law in this manner has lowered people's willingness to take part in victimless crime behavior (Meier & Geis, 2007). Perhaps it is not too rash to say that a serious national debate needs to begin on the propriety of the laws against victimless crimes to determine what course of action makes the most sense for American society.

Learning From Other Societies

Crime and Punishment in Denmark and the Netherlands

As the text notes, since the 1970s the United States has used a get-tough approach to fight crime; a key dimension of this approach is mandatory sentencing and long prison terms and, as a result, a huge increase in the number of people in prison and jail. Many scholars say this approach has not reduced crime to a great degree and has cost hundreds of billions of dollars.

The experience of Denmark and the Netherlands suggests a different way of treating criminals and dealing with crime. Those nations, like most others in Western Europe, think prison makes most offenders worse and should be used only as a last resort for the most violent and most incorrigible offenders. They also recognize that incarceration is very expensive and much more costly than other ways of dealing with offenders. These concerns have led Denmark, the Netherlands, and other Western European nations to favor alternatives to imprisonment for the bulk of their offenders. These alternatives include the widespread use of probation, community service, and other kinds of community-based corrections. Studies indicate that these alternatives may be as effective as incarceration in reducing recidivism (repeat offending) and cost much less than incarceration. If so, an important lesson from Denmark, the Netherlands, and other nations in Western Europe is that it is possible to keep society safe from crime without using the costly get-tough approach that has been the hallmark of the U.S. criminal justice system since the 1970s. (Bijleveld & Smit, 2005; Dammer & Fairchild, 2006)

Key Takeaways

- The public is very concerned about crime. At the same time, race and gender influence public perceptions of crime.

- Accurate measurement of crime is difficult to achieve for many reasons, including the fact that many crime victims do not report their victimization to their police.
- Conventional crime is disproportionately committed by the young, by persons of color, by men, and by urban residents. The disproportionate involvement of African Americans in crime arises largely from their poverty and urban residence.
- White-collar crime is more costly in terms of personal and financial harm than conventional crime.
- For several reasons, laws against victimless crime may do more harm than good.

For Your Review

1. Why are African Americans more likely than whites to fear walking around their homes at night?
2. Why is it difficult to measure crime accurately? Why is measurement of crime by the FBI inaccurate?
3. Do you think any victimless crimes should be made legal? Why or why not? In what ways is deviance considered relative?

References

AFL-CIO. (2007). *Death on the job: The toll of neglect*. Washington, DC: AFL-CIO.

Armstrong, D. (1999, November 16). U.S. lagging on prosecutions. *The Boston Globe*, p. A1.

Barkan, S. E. (2012). *Criminology: A sociological understanding* (5th ed.). Upper Saddle River, NJ: Prentice Hall.

BBC News. (2005, February 21). Air pollution causes early deaths. Retrieved from http://news.bbc.co.uk/2/hi/health/4283295.stm.

Bijleveld, C. C. J. H., & Smit, P. R. (2005). Crime and punishment in the Netherlands, 1980–1999. *Crime and Justice: A Review of Research, 33*, 161–211.

Creswell, J., & Thomas, L., Jr. (2009, January 25). The talented Mr. Madoff. *The New York Times*, p. BU1.

Cullen, F. T., Maakestad, W. J., & Cavender, G. (2006). *Corporate crime under attack: The fight to criminalize business violence*. Cincinnati, OH: Anderson.

Dammer, H. R., & Fairchild, E. (2006). *Comparative criminal justice systems*. Belmont, CA: Wadsworth.

Federal Bureau of Investigation. (2009). *Crime in the United States, 2008*. Washington, DC: Author.

Henriques, D. B., & Healy, J. (2009, March 13). Madoff goes to jail after guilty pleas. *The New York Times*, p. A1.

Johnson, D. (2008). Racial prejudice, perceived injustice, and the black–white gap in punitive attitudes. *Journal of Criminal Justice, 36,* 198–206.

Lee, M. R., Bankston, W. B., Hayes, T. C., & Thomas, S. A. (2007). Revisiting the Southern subculture of violence. *The Sociological Quarterly, 48,* 253–275.

Lilienfeld, D. E. (1991). The silence: The asbestos industry and early occupational cancer research—a case study. *American Journal of Public Health, 81,* 791–800.

Lynch, J. P., & Addington, L. A. (2007). *Understanding crime statistics: Revisiting the divergence of the NCVS and the UCR.* New York, NY: Cambridge University Press.

Maguire, K., & Pastore, A. L. (2009). *Sourcebook of criminal justice statistics.* Retrieved from http://www.albany.edu/sourcebook.

Maynard, M. (2010, April 6). U.S. is seeking a fine of $16.4 million against Toyota. *The New York Times,* p. A1.

McNulty, T. L., & Bellair, P. E. (2003). Explaining racial and ethnic differences in serious adolescent violent behavior. *Criminology, 41,* 709–748.

Meier, R. F., & Geis, G. (2007). *Criminal justice and moral issues.* New York, NY: Oxford University Press.

Montgomery, L. (2007, April 16). Unpaid taxes tough to recover. *The Washington Post,* p. A1.

National Retail Federation. (2007, June 11). Retail losses hit $41.6 billion last year, according to National Retail Security Survey [Press release]. Retrieved from http://www.nrf.com/modules.php?name=News&op=viewlive&sp_id=318.

Pastore, A. L., & Maguire, K. (2010). *Sourcebook of criminal justice statistics.* Retrieved from http://www.albany.edu/sourcebook.

Petersen, M., & Drew, C. (2003, October 9). New safety rules fail to stop tainted meat. *The New York Times,* p. A1.

Peterson, R. D., & Krivo, L. J. (2009). Segregated spatial locations, race-ethnic composition, and neighborhood violent crime. *The ANNALS of the American Academy of Political and Social Science, 623,* 93–107.

Rosoff, S. M., Pontell, H. N., & Tillman, R. (2010). *Profit without honor: White collar crime and the looting of America* (5th ed.). Upper Saddle River, NJ: Prentice Hall.

Saad, L. (2008). Perceptions of crime problem remain curiously negative. Retrieved from http://www.gallup.com/poll/102262/Perceptions-Crime-Problem-Remain-Curiously-Negative.aspx.

Simon, D. R. (2006). *Elite deviance.* Boston, MA: Allyn & Bacon.

Truman, J. L., & Rand, M. R. (2010). *Criminal victimization, 2009.* Washington, DC: Bureau of Justice Statistics, U.S. Department of Justice.

U.S. Consumer Product Safety Commission. (2003). *Annual report to Congress, 2002*. Washington, DC: Author

Urbina, I. (2010, April 10). No survivors found after West Virginia mine disaster. *The New York Times,* p. A1.

Walker, S., Spohn, C., & DeLone, M. (2007). *The color of justice: Race, ethnicity, and crime in America*. Belmont, CA: Wadsworth.

Warr, M. (2000). Public perceptions of and reactions to crime. In J. F. Sheley (Ed.), *Criminology: A contemporary handbook* (3rd ed., pp. 13–31). Belmont, CA: Wadsworth.

7.4 The Get-Tough Approach: Boon or Bust?

Learning Objective

1. Explain the get-tough approach to conventional crime, and describe its disadvantages according to several scholars.

It would be presumptuous to claim to know exactly how to reduce crime, but a sociological understanding of its causes and dynamics points to several directions that show strong crime-reduction potential. Before sketching these directions, we first examine the get-tough approach, a strategy the United States has used to control crime since the 1970s.

Harsher law enforcement, often called the *get-tough approach*, has been the guiding strategy for the U.S. criminal justice system since the 1970s. This approach has involved increased numbers of arrests and, especially, a surge in incarceration, which has quintupled since the 1970s. Reflecting this surge, the United States now has the highest incarceration rate by far in the world. Many scholars trace the beginnings of the get-tough approach to efforts by the Republican Party to win the votes of whites by linking crime to African Americans. These efforts increased public concern about crime and pressured lawmakers of both parties to favor more punitive treatment of criminals to avoid looking soft on crime (Beckett & Sasson, 2004; Pratt, 2008). According to these scholars, the incarceration surge stems much more from political decisions and pronouncements, many of them racially motivated, by lawmakers than from trends in crime rates. As Beckett and Sasson (2004, pp. 104, 128) summarize this argument,

> Crime-related issues rise to the top of the popular agenda in response to political and media activity around crime—not the other way around. By focusing on violent crime perpetrated by racial minorities…politicians and the news media have amplified and intensified popular fear and punitiveness.…Americans have become most alarmed about crime and drugs on those occasions when national political leaders and, by extension, the mass media have spotlighted these issues.

The get-tough approach since the 1970s has greatly increased the number of prisoners. Scholars question whether this approach has reduced crime effectively and cost efficiently.

Tony Fischer – Have You Seen This Man? – CC BY 2.0.

Today more than 2.3 million Americans are incarcerated in jail or prison at any one time, compared to only about one-fourth that number 30 years ago (Warren, 2009). This increase in incarceration has cost the nation hundreds of billions of dollars since then.

Despite this very large expenditure, criminologists question whether it has helped lower crime significantly (Piquero & Blumstein, 2007; Raphael & Stoll, 2009). Although crime fell by a large amount during the 1990s as incarceration rose, scholars estimate that the increased use of incarceration accounted for at most only 10%–25% of the crime drop during this decade. They conclude that this result was not cost effective and that the billions of dollars spent on incarceration would have had a greater crime-reduction effect had they been spent on crime-prevention efforts. They also point to the fact that the heavy use of incarceration today means that some 700,000 prisoners are released back to their communities every year, creating many kinds of problems (Clear, 2007). A wide variety of evidence, then, indicates that the get-tough approach has been more bust than boon.

Recognizing this situation, several citizens' advocacy groups have formed since the 1980s to call attention to the many costs of the get-tough approach and to urge state and federal legislators to reform harsh sentencing practices and to provide many more resources for former inmates. One of the most well-known and effective such groups is the Sentencing Project (http://www.sentencingproject.org), which describes itself as "a national organization working for a fair and effective criminal justice system by promoting reforms in sentencing law and practice, and alternatives to incarceration." The Sentencing Project was founded in 1986 and has since sought "to bring national attention to disturbing trends and inequities in the criminal justice system with a successful formula that includes the publication of groundbreaking research, aggressive media campaigns and strategic advocacy for policy reform." The organization's Web site features a variety of resources on topics such as racial disparities in incarceration, women in the criminal justice system, and drug policy.

Key Takeaways

- The get-tough approach to crime has not proven effective even though it has cost billions of dollars and led to other problems.
- Racialized politics are thought to have led to the surge in incarceration that has been the highlight of this approach.

For Your Review

1. Why did the get-tough approach begin during the 1970s, and why has it continued since then?
2. Do you think the expense of the get-tough approach has been worth it? Why or why not?

What Sociology Suggests

Not surprisingly, many sociologists and other social scientists think it makes more sense to try to prevent crime than to wait until it happens and then punish the people who commit it. That does not mean abandoning all law enforcement, of course, but it does mean paying more attention to the sociological causes of crime as outlined earlier in this chapter and to institute programs and other efforts to address these causes.

Several insights for (conventional) crime reduction may be gleaned from the sociological explanations of deviance and crime discussed earlier. For example, the social ecology approach suggests paying much attention to the social and physical characteristics of urban neighborhoods that are thought to generate high rates of crime. These characteristics include, but are not limited to, poverty, joblessness, dilapidation, and overcrowding. Strain theory suggests paying much attention to poverty, while explanations regarding deviant subcultures and differential association remind us of the need to focus on peer influences. Social control theory calls attention to the need to focus on family interaction in general and especially on children in families marked by inadequate parenting, stress, and disharmony. Despite mixed support for its assumptions, labeling theory reminds us of the strong possibility that harsh punishment may do more harm than good, and feminist explanations remind us that much deviance and crime is rooted in masculinity. In sum a sociological understanding of deviance and crime reminds us that much conventional crime is ultimately rooted in poverty, in negative family functioning and negative peer relationships, in criminogenic physical and social conditions of urban neighborhoods, and in the "macho" socialization of boys.

With this backdrop in mind, a sociological understanding suggests the potential of several strategies and policies for reducing conventional crime (Currie, 1998; Greenwood, 2006; Jacobson, 2005; Welsh & Farrington, 2007). Such efforts would include, at a minimum, the following:

1. Establish good-paying jobs for the poor in urban areas.
2. Establish youth recreation programs and in other ways strengthen social interaction in urban neighborhoods.

3. Improve living conditions in urban neighborhoods.
4. Change male socialization practices.
5. Establish early childhood intervention programs to help high-risk families raise their children.
6. Improve the nation's schools by establishing small classes and taking other measures.
7. Provide alternative corrections for nondangerous prisoners in order to reduce prison crowding and costs and to lessen the chances of repeat offending.
8. Provide better educational and vocational services and better services for treating and preventing drug and alcohol abuse for ex-offenders.

This is not a complete list, but it does point the way to the kinds of strategies that would help get at the roots of conventional crime and, in the long run, help greatly to reduce it. Although the United States has been neglecting this crime-prevention approach, programs and strategies such as those just mentioned would in the long run be more likely than our current get-tough approach to create a safer society. For this reason, sociological knowledge on crime and deviance can indeed help us make a difference in our larger society.

What about white-collar crime? Although we have not stressed the point, the major sociological explanations of deviance and crime, especially those stressing poverty, the conditions of poor urban neighborhoods, and negative family functioning, are basically irrelevant for understanding why white-collar crime occurs and, in turn, do not suggest very much at all about ways to reduce it. Instead, scholars attribute the high level of white-collar crime, and especially of corporate crime, to one or more of the following: (a) greed arising from our society's emphasis on economic success, (b) the absence of strong regulations governing corporate conduct and a severe lack of funding for the federal and state regulatory agencies that police such conduct, and/or (c) weak punishment of corporate criminals when their crimes are detected (Cullen, Maakestad, & Cavender, 2006; Leaf, 2002; Rosoff, Pontell, & Tillman, 2010). Drawing on this understanding, many scholars think that more effective corporate regulation and harsher punishment of corporate criminals (that is, imprisonment in addition to the fines that corporations typically receive when they are punished) may help deter corporate crime. As a writer for *Fortune* magazine observed, corporate crime "will not go away until white-collar thieves face a consequence they're actually scared of: time in jail" (Leaf, 2002, p. 62).

References

Beckett, K., & Sasson, T. (2004). *The politics of injustice: Crime and punishment in America*. Thousand Oaks, CA: Sage.

Clear, T. R. (2007). *Imprisoning communities: How mass incarceration makes disadvantaged neighborhoods worse*. New York, NY: Oxford University Press.

Cullen, F. T., Maakestad, W. J., & Cavender, G. (2006). *Corporate crime under attack: The fight to criminalize business violence*. Cincinnati, OH: Anderson.

Currie, E. (1998). *Crime and punishment in America*. New York, NY: Henry Holt.

Greenwood, P. W. (2006). *Changing lives: Delinquency prevention as crime-control policy*. Chicago, IL: University of Chicago Press.

Jacobson, M. (2005). *Downsizing prisons: How to reduce crime and end mass incarceration*. New York, NY: New York University Press.

Leaf, C. (2002, March 18). Enough is enough. *Fortune*, pp. 60–68.

Piquero, A. R., & Blumstein, A. (2007). Does incapacitation reduce crime? *Journal of Quantitative Criminology, 23*, 267–285.

Pratt, T. C. (2008). *Addicted to incarceration: Corrections policy and the politics of misinformation in the United States*. Thousand Oaks, CA: Sage.

Raphael, S., & Stoll, M. A. (2009). Why are so many Americans in prison? In S. Raphael & M. A. Stoll (Eds.), *Do prisons make us safer? The benefits and costs of the prison boom* (pp. 27–72). New York, NY: Russell Sage Foundation.

Rosoff, S. M., Pontell, H. N., & Tillman, R. (2010). *Profit without honor: White collar crime and the looting of America* (5th ed.). Upper Saddle River, NJ: Prentice Hall.

Warren, J. (2009). *One in 31: The long reach of American corrections*. Washington, DC: Pew Center on the States.

Welsh, B. C., & Farrington, D. P. (Eds.). (2007). *Preventing crime: What works for children, offenders, victims and places*. New York, NY: Springer.

7.5 End-of-Chapter Material

Summary

1. Deviance is behavior that violates social norms and arouses negative reactions. What is considered deviant depends on the circumstances in which it occurs and varies by location and time period.
2. Durkheim said deviance performs several important functions for society. It clarifies social norms, strengthens social bonds, and can lead to beneficial social change.
3. Biological explanations of deviance assume that deviants differ biologically from nondeviants. Psychological explanations of deviance assume that deviants have a psychological problem that produces their deviance.
4. Sociological theories emphasize different aspects of the social environment as contributors to deviance and crime.
5. Crime in the United States remains a serious problem that concerns the public. Public opinion about crime does not always match reality and is related to individuals' gender and race among other social characteristics. Women and African Americans are especially likely to be afraid of crime.
6. Crime is difficult to measure, but the Uniform Crime Reports (UCR), National Crime Victimization Survey (NCVS), and self-report studies give us a fairly accurate picture of the amount of crime and of its correlates.
7. Several types of crime exist. Conventional crime includes violent and property offenses and worries Americans more than any other type of crime. Such crime tends to be intraracial, and a surprising amount of violent crime is committed by people known by the victim. White-collar crime is more harmful than conventional crime in terms of personal harm and financial harm. Victimless crime is very controversial, as it involves behavior by consenting adults. Scholars continue to debate whether the nation is better or worse off with laws against victimless crimes.
8. To reduce crime, most criminologists say that a law-enforcement approach is not enough and that more efforts aimed at crime prevention are needed. These efforts include attempts to improve schools and living conditions in inner cities and programs aimed at improving nutrition and parenting for the children who are at high risk for impairment to their cognitive and social development.

Using Sociology

Imagine that you are a member of your state legislature. As a sociology major in college, you learned that the get-tough approach to crime, involving harsher criminal sentencing and the increased use of incarceration, costs much money and is not very effective in reducing crime. A bill comes before the legislature that would double the minimum prison term for several types of violent crime. You realize that this change in policy would probably do little to reduce the crime rate and eventually cost millions of dollars in increased incarceration costs, but you also recognize that if you vote against the bill, your opponent in the upcoming election will charge that you are soft on crime. Do you vote for or against the bill? Why? Regardless of your vote, what else would you do as a state legislator to try to reduce the crime rate? How would your efforts relate to a sociological understanding of crime and deviance?

Chapter 8: Social Stratification

Social Issues in the News

"More Wichita Kids Go Hungry," the headline said. As the United States was in a deep recession, poverty-stricken parents in Wichita, Kansas, increasingly worried about how they would be able to feed their children. As a state official explained, "We see a lot of children who regularly wonder where their next meal is coming from. Churches that used to do food drives once every two to three months are now doing them once a month." The number of children eating at one of Wichita's major food pantries had climbed by one-third from a year earlier, and the number of children classified as homeless had increased by 90% from 1,000 to 1,900. A sixth-grade girl gave life to these numbers when she wrote of her own family's situation. "My mom works very hard to support our family," she said, "[but] some days we would eat only once a day. Then Mom got her paycheck and we were really happy but then the bills started coming and we couldn't buy food because a house was more important. We would rather have a house to live in and we needed a car." (Wenzl, 2009)

This story of hunger in America's heartland reminds us that poverty is far from unknown in the richest nation in the world, especially since the severe economic recession began in 2008. The United States has long been considered a land of opportunity, but research by sociologists and other social scientists shows again and again that people differ dramatically in their opportunity to realize the American dream.

To illustrate this, imagine that you and four other people are about to begin playing the popular board game Monopoly. Following the rules, each player begins with $1,500. You start the game, go around the board, buy properties or land on someone else's properties, and sometimes end up in Jail or Free Parking. Like life itself, whether you eventually win or lose the game is a matter of both luck and skill.

But if Monopoly were *more* like real life, each player would *not* begin with $1,500. Instead, they would begin with very different amounts, because in real life some people are richer than others, and some are much poorer. In fact, reflecting the unequal distribution of wealth in the United States, one player, the richest, would begin with $6,352 of the $7,500 distributed to the five players combined. The next richest player would have $848. The third player would start with $285, while the next would have $52. The fifth and poorest player would actually begin $38 in debt! Figure 8.1 "Distribution of Starting Cash If Monopoly Were More Like Real Life" depicts this huge disparity in money at the beginning of the game.

Figure 8.1 Distribution of Starting Cash If Monopoly Were More Like Real Life

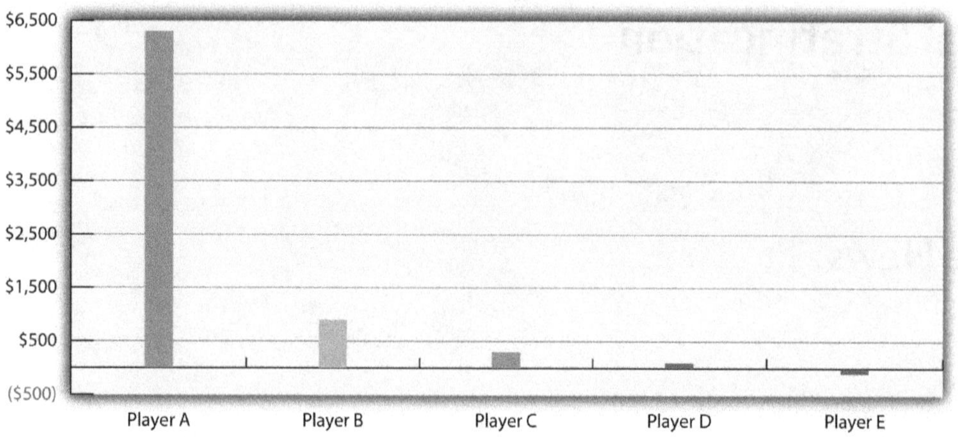

Source: Based on distribution of wealth data from Mishel, L., Bernstein, J., & Shierholz, H. (2009). *The state of working America 2008/2009*. Ithaca, NY: ILR Press [An imprint of Cornell University Press].

Now suppose you are the player starting $38 in debt. How would you feel? You can hardly afford to buy Park Place or Boardwalk. Even landing on a couple of "pay" spaces like a utility the first time you go around the board would virtually force you out of the game. If you landed in Jail, you could not afford to get out. What are your chances of winning the game? Yes, you have a chance to win, but how likely is this? The second, third, and fourth players have a better chance of winning than you do, but in the long run they certainly will not win nearly as often as the richest player, who, after all, starts out with about 85% of all the money distributed at the beginning.

Unlike most games, real life is filled with differences in wealth and other resources a society values. Sociologists refer to rankings based on these differences as **social stratification**. Except for the simplest preindustrial societies, every society is stratified to some extent, and some societies are more stratified than others. Another way of saying this is that some societies have more *economic inequality*, or a greater difference between the best-off and the worst-off, than others. In modern society, stratification is usually determined by income and other forms of wealth, such as stocks and bonds, but resources such as power and prestige matter, too. No matter what determines it, a society's stratification has significant consequences for its members' attitudes, behavior, and, perhaps most important of all, **life chances**—how well people do in such areas as education, income, and health. We will see examples of these consequences in the pages ahead and end with a discussion of some promising policies and programs for reducing inequality and poverty.

References

Wenzl, R. (2009, July 5). More Wichita kids go hungry. *The Wichita Eagle*. Retrieved from http://www.kansas.com/news/featured/story/879754.html.

8.1 Systems of Stratification

Learning Objectives

1. Explain the difference between open and closed societies.
2. Define the several systems of stratification.
3. Understand how Max Weber and Karl Marx differed in their view of class societies.

When we look around the world and through history, we see different types of stratification systems. These systems vary on their degree of **vertical mobility**, or the chances of rising up or falling down the stratification ladder. In some so-called *closed* societies, an individual has virtually no chance of moving up or down. *Open* societies have more vertical mobility, as some people, and perhaps many people, can move up or even down. That said, a key question is how much vertical mobility really exists in these societies. Let's look at several systems of stratification, moving from the most closed to the most open.

Slavery

The most closed system is **slavery**, or the ownership of people, which has been quite common in human history (Ennals, 2007). Slavery is thought to have begun 10,000 years ago, after agricultural societies developed, as people in these societies made prisoners of war work on their farms. Many of the ancient lands of the Middle East, including Babylonia, Egypt, and Persia, also owned slaves, as did ancient China and India. Slavery especially flourished in ancient Greece and Rome, which used thousands of slaves for their trade economies. Most slaves in ancient times were prisoners of war or debtors. As trade died down during the Middle Ages, so did slavery.

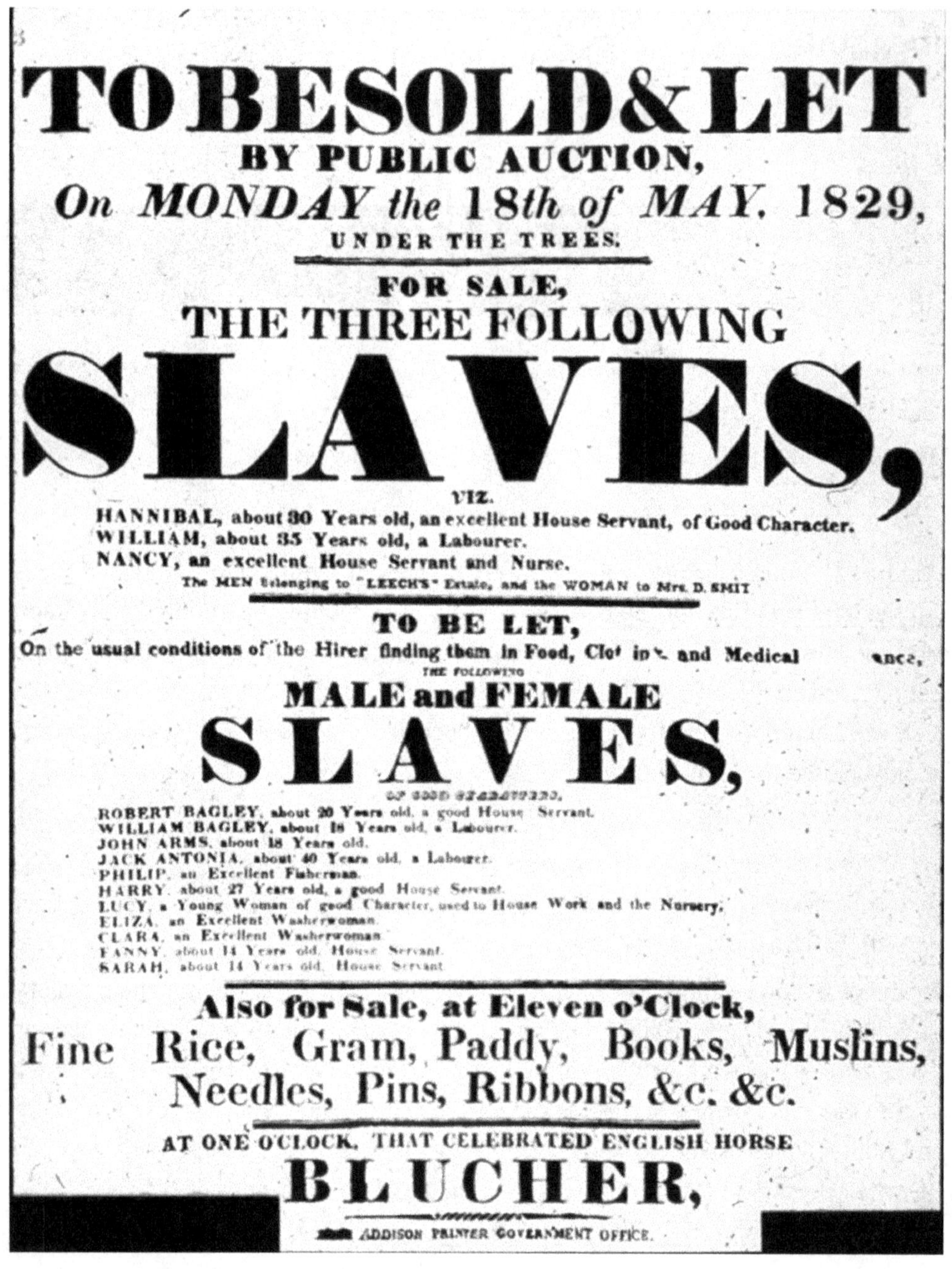

Slavery is the most closed system of stratification. Although U.S. slavery, depicted here, ended with the Civil War, slavery still exists today in parts of Africa, Asia, and South America.

Wikimedia Commons – public domain.

But once Europeans began exploring the Western Hemisphere in the 1500s, slavery regained its popularity. Portuguese and Spanish colonists who settled in Brazil and Caribbean islands made slaves of thousands of Indians already living there. After most of them died from disease and abuse, the Portuguese and Spaniards began bringing slaves from Africa. In the next century, the English, the French, and other Europeans also began bringing African slaves into the Western Hemisphere, and by the 1800s they had captured and shipped to the New World some 10–12 million Africans, almost 2 million of whom died along the way (Thornton, 1998).

The United States, of course, is all too familiar with slavery, which remains perhaps the most deplorable experience in American history and continues to have repercussions for African Americans and the rest of American society. It increasingly divided the new nation after it won its independence from Britain and helped lead to the Civil War eight decades later. The cruel treatment of slaves was captured in Harriet Beecher Stowe's classic but controversial book *Uncle Tom's Cabin*, which ignited passions on both sides of the slavery debate.

Slavery still exists in parts of Africa, Asia, and South America, with some estimates putting the number of slaves in the tens of millions. Today's slaves include (a) men first taken as prisoners of war in ethnic conflicts; (b) girls and women captured in wartime or kidnapped from their neighborhoods and used as prostitutes or sex slaves; (c) children sold by their parents to become child laborers; and (d) workers paying off debts who are abused and even tortured and too terrified to leave (Bales, 2007; Batstone, 2007).

Estate Systems

Estate systems are characterized by control of land and were common in Europe and Asia during the Middle Ages and into the 1800s. In these systems, two major estates existed: the landed gentry or nobility and the peasantry or serfs. The landed gentry owned huge expanses of land on which serfs toiled. The serfs had more freedom than slaves had but typically lived in poverty and were subject to arbitrary control by the nobility (Kerbo, 2009).

Estate systems thrived in Europe until the French Revolution in 1789 violently overturned the existing order and inspired people in other nations with its cries for freedom and equality. As time went on, European estate systems slowly gave way to class systems of stratification (discussed a little later). After the American colonies won their independence from Britain, the South had at least one characteristic of an estate system, the control of large plots of land by a relatively few wealthy individuals and their families, but it used slaves rather than serfs to work the land.

Much of Asia, especially China and Japan, also had estate systems. For centuries, China's large population lived as peasants in abject conditions and frequently engaged in peasant uprisings. These escalated starting in the 1850s after the Chinese government raised taxes and charged peasants higher rents for the land on which they worked. After many more decades of political and economic strife, Communists took control of China in 1949 (DeFronzo, 2007).

Caste Systems

In a **caste system**, people are born into unequal groups based on their parents' status and remain in these groups for the rest of their lives. For many years, the best-known caste system was in India, where, supported by Hindu beliefs emphasizing the acceptance of one's fate in life, several major castes dictated one's life chances from the moment of birth, especially in rural areas (Kerbo, 2009). People born in the lower castes lived in abject poverty throughout their lives. Another caste, the *harijan*, or *untouchables*, was considered so low that technically it was not thought to be a caste at all. People in this caste were called the untouchables because they were considered unclean and were prohibited from coming near to people in the higher castes. Traditionally, caste membership in India almost totally determined an individual's life, including what job you had and whom you married; for example, it was almost impossible to marry someone in another caste. After India won its independence from Britain in 1949, its new constitution granted equal rights to the untouchables. Modern communication and migration into cities further weakened the caste system, as members of different castes now had more contact with each other. Still, caste prejudice remains a problem in India and illustrates the continuing influence of its traditional system of social stratification.

A country that used to have a caste system is South Africa. In the days of apartheid, from 1950 to 1990, a small group of white Afrikaners ruled the country. Black people constituted more than three-quarters of the nation's population and thus greatly outnumbered Afrikaners, but they had the worst jobs, could not vote, and lived in poor, segregated neighborhoods. Afrikaners bolstered their rule with the aid of the South African police, which used terror tactics to intimidate blacks (I. Berger, 2009).

Many observers believe a caste system existed in the U.S. South until the civil rights movement ended legal racial segregation.

U.S. Library of Congress – public domain.

Many observers believe a caste system also existed in the South in the United States after Reconstruction and until the civil rights movement of the 1960s ended legal segregation. A segregated system called Jim Crow dominated the South, and even though African Americans had several rights, including the right to vote, granted to them by the 13th, 14th, and 15th Amendments to the Constitution, these rights were denied in practice. Lynchings were common for many decades, and the Southern police system bolstered white rule in the South just as the South African police system bolstered white rule in that country (Litwack, 2009).

Class Systems

Many societies, including all industrial ones, have **class systems**. In this system of stratification, a person is born into a social ranking but can move up or down from it much more easily than in caste systems or slave societies.

This movement in either direction is primarily the result of a person's own effort, knowledge, and skills or lack of them. Although these qualities do not aid upward movement in caste or slave societies, they often do enable upward movement in class societies. Of the three systems of stratification discussed so far, class systems are by far the most open, meaning they have the most vertical mobility. We will look later at social class in the United States and discuss the extent of vertical mobility in American society.

Sociologist Max Weber, whose work on organizations and bureaucracies was discussed in Chapter 6 "Groups and Organizations", also had much to say about class systems of stratification. Such systems, he wrote, are based on three dimensions of stratification: class (which we will call *wealth*), power, and prestige. **Wealth** is the total value of an individual or family, including income, stocks, bonds, real estate, and other assets; **power** is the ability to influence others to do your bidding, even if they do not want to; and **prestige** refers to the status and esteem people hold in the eyes of others.

In discussing these three dimensions, Weber disagreed somewhat with Karl Marx, who said our ranking in society depends on whether we own the means of production. Marx thus felt that the primary dimension of stratification in class systems was economic. Weber readily acknowledged the importance of this economic dimension but thought power and prestige also matter. He further said that although wealth, power, and prestige usually go hand-in-hand, they do not always overlap. For example, although the head of a major corporation has a good deal of wealth, power, and prestige, we can think of many other people who are high on one dimension but not on the other two. A professional athlete who makes millions of dollars a year has little power in the political sense that Weber meant it. An organized crime leader might also be very wealthy but have little prestige outside the criminal underworld. Conversely, a scientist or professor may enjoy much prestige but not be very wealthy.

Classless Societies

Although, as noted earlier, all societies except perhaps for the simplest ones are stratified, some large nations have done their best to eliminate stratification by developing **classless societies**. Marx, of course, predicted that one day the proletariat would rise up and overthrow the bourgeoisie and create a communist society, by which he meant a classless one in which everyone had roughly the same amount of wealth, power, and prestige. In Russia, China, and Cuba, revolutions inspired by Marx's vision occurred in the 20th century. These revolutions resulted in societies not only with less economic inequality than in the United States and other class systems but also with little or no political freedom. Moreover, governing elites in these societies enjoyed much more wealth, power, and prestige than the average citizen. Overall, the communist experiments in Russia, China, and Cuba failed to achieve Marx's vision of an egalitarian society.

Some Western European nations, such as Sweden and Denmark, have developed *social democracies* based on fairly socialist economies. Although a few have nominal monarchies, these nations have much political freedom and less economic inequality than the United States and other class societies. They also typically rank much higher than the United States on various social and economic indicators. Although these nations are not truly classless, they indicate it is possible, if not easy, to have a society that begins to fulfill Marx's egalitarian vision but where political freedom still prevails (Sandbrook, Edelman, Heller, & Teichman, 2007).

Key Takeaways

- Systems of stratification vary in their degree of vertical social mobility. Some societies are more open in this regard, while some are more closed.
- The major systems of stratification are slavery, estate systems, caste systems, and class systems.
- Some Western European nations are not classless but still have much less economic inequality than class societies such as the United States.

For Your Review

1. What, if anything, should the United States and the United Nations try to do about the slavery that still exists in today's world?
2. Why do you think some class societies have more vertical social mobility than other class societies?

References

Bales, K. (2007). *Ending slavery: How we free today's slaves*. Berkeley: University of California Press.

Batstone, D. (2007). *Not for sale: The return of the global slave trade—and how we can fight it*. New York, NY: HarperOne.

Berger, I. (2009). *South Africa in world history*. New York, NY: Oxford University Press.

DeFronzo, J. (2007). *Revolutions and revolutionary movements* (3rd ed.). Boulder, CO: Westview Press.

Ennals, R. (2007). *From slavery to citizenship*. Hoboken, NJ: John Wiley.

Kerbo, H. R. (2009). *Social stratification and inequality*. New York, NY: McGraw-Hill.

Litwack, L. F. (2009). *How free is free? The long death of Jim Crow*. Cambridge, MA: Harvard University Press.

Sandbrook, R., Edelman, M., Heller, P., & Teichman, J. (2007). *Social democracy in the global periphery: Origins, challenges, prospects*. New York, NY: Cambridge University Press.

Thornton, J. K. (1998). *Africa and Africans in the making of the Atlantic world, 1400–1800* (2nd ed.). Cambridge, England: Cambridge University Press.

8.2 Explaining Stratification

Learning Objectives

1. Outline the assumptions of the functionalist explanation of stratification.
2. Outline the assumptions of the conflict theory explanation of stratification.
3. Understand how symbolic interactionism views stratification.

Why is stratification so common? Is it possible to have a society without stratification? Sociologists trying to answer these questions have developed two very different macro explanations of stratification, while symbolic interactionists have examined the differences that stratification produces for everyday interaction. Table 8.1 "Theory Snapshot" summarizes these three approaches.

Table 8.1 Theory Snapshot

Theoretical perspective	Major assumptions
Functionalism	Stratification is necessary to induce people with special intelligence, knowledge, and skills to enter the most important occupations. For this reason, stratification is necessary and inevitable.
Conflict	Stratification results from lack of opportunity and from discrimination and prejudice against the poor, women, and people of color. It is neither necessary nor inevitable.
Symbolic interactionism	Stratification affects people's beliefs, lifestyles, daily interaction, and conceptions of themselves.

The Functionalist View

Recall from Chapter 1 "Sociology and the Sociological Perspective" that functionalist theory assumes that the various structures and processes in society exist because they serve important functions for society's stability and continuity. In line with this view, functionalist theorists in sociology assume that stratification exists because it also serves important functions for society. This explanation was developed more than 60 years ago by Kingsley Davis and Wilbert Moore (Davis & Moore, 1945) in the form of several logical assumptions that imply stratification is both necessary and inevitable. When applied to American society, their assumptions would be as follows:

1. **Some jobs are more important than other jobs.** For example, the job of a brain surgeon is more important than the job of shoe-shining.
2. **Some jobs require more skills and knowledge than other jobs.** To stay with our example, it takes

more skills and knowledge to do brain surgery than to shine shoes.

3. **Relatively few people have the ability to acquire the skills and knowledge that are needed to do these important, highly skilled jobs.** Most of us would be able to do a decent job of shining shoes, but very few of us would be able to become brain surgeons.
4. **To induce the people with the skills and knowledge to do the important, highly skilled jobs, society must promise them higher incomes or other rewards.** If this is true, some people automatically end up higher in society's ranking system than others, and stratification is thus necessary and inevitable. To illustrate this, say we have a society where shining shoes and doing brain surgery both give us incomes of $150,000 per year. (This example is *very* hypothetical, but please keep reading.) If you decide to shine shoes, you can begin making this money at age 16, but if you decide to become a brain surgeon, you will not start making this same amount until about age 35, as you first must go to college and medical school and then acquire several more years of medical training. While you have spent 19 additional years beyond age 16 getting this education and training and taking out tens of thousands of dollars in student loans, you could have spent these 19 years shining shoes and making $150,000 a year, or $2.85 million overall. Which job would you choose?

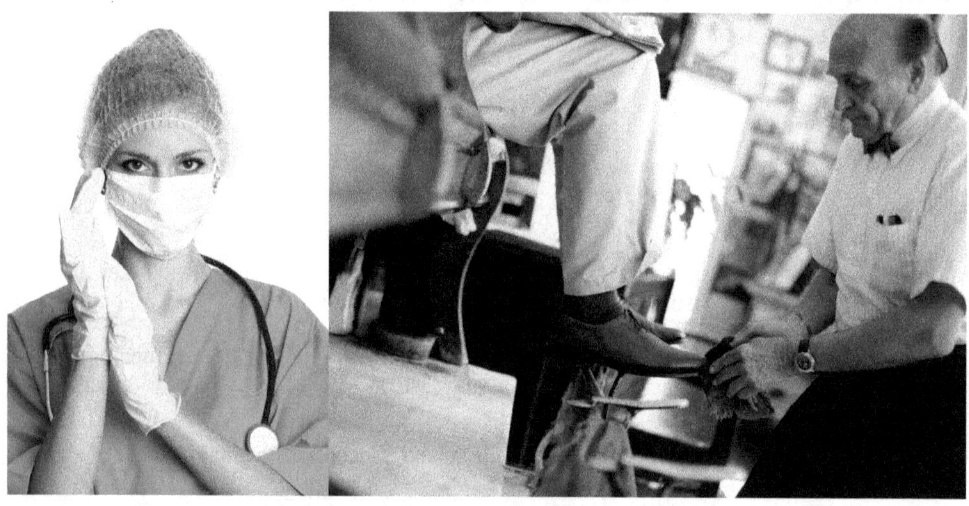

Functional theory argues that the promise of very high incomes is necessary to induce talented people to pursue important careers such as surgery. If physicians and shoe shiners made the same high income, would enough people decide to become physicians?

Public Domain Images – CC0 public domain.

As this example suggests, many people might not choose to become brain surgeons unless considerable financial and other rewards awaited them. By extension, we might not have enough people filling society's important jobs unless they know they will be similarly rewarded. If this is true, we must have stratification. This all sounds very logical, but a few years after Davis and Moore published their functionalist theory of stratification, other sociologists pointed out some serious problems in their argument (Tumin, 1953; Wrong, 1959).

First, it is difficult to compare the importance of many types of jobs. For example, which is more important, doing brain surgery or mining coal? Although you might be tempted to answer "brain surgery," if no coal were mined, much of our society could not function. In another example, which job is more important, attorney or professor? (Be careful how you answer this one!)

Second, the functionalist explanation implies that the most important jobs have the highest incomes and the least important jobs the lowest incomes, but many examples, including the ones just mentioned, counter this view. Coal miners make much less money than physicians, and professors, for better or worse, earn much less on the average than lawyers. A professional athlete making millions of dollars a year earns many times the income of the president of the United States, but who is more important to the nation? Elementary school teachers do a very important job in our society, but their salaries are much lower than those of sports agents, advertising executives, and many other people whose jobs are far less essential.

Third, the functionalist view also implies that people move up the economic ladder based on their abilities, skills, knowledge, and, more generally, their merit. If this is true, another implication is that if they do not move up the ladder, they lack the necessary merit. This view ignores the fact that much of our stratification stems from lack of equal opportunity, as our Monopoly example at the beginning of the chapter made clear. Because of their race, ethnicity, gender, and class standing at birth, some people have less opportunity than others to acquire the skills and training they need to fill the types of jobs addressed by the functionalist approach.

Finally, the functionalist explanation might make sense up to a point, but it does not justify the extremes of wealth and poverty found in the United States and other nations. Even if we do have to promise higher incomes to get enough people to become physicians, does that mean we also need the amount of poverty we have? Do CEOs of corporations really need to make millions of dollars per year to get enough qualified people to become CEOs? Don't people take on a CEO job or other high-paying job at least partly because of the challenge, working conditions, and other positive aspects they offer? The functionalist view does not answer these questions adequately.

The Conflict View

Conflict theory's explanation of stratification draws on Karl Marx's view of class societies and incorporates the critique of the functionalist view just discussed. Many different explanations grounded in conflict theory exist, but they all assume that stratification stems from a fundamental conflict between the needs and interests of the powerful, or "haves," in society and those of the weak, or "have-nots" (Kerbo, 2009). The former take advantage of their position at the top of society to stay at the top, even if it means oppressing those at the bottom. At a minimum, they can heavily influence the law, the media, and other institutions in a way that maintains society's class structure.

Ideology and Stratification

In explaining stratification, conflict theory emphasizes **ideology**, or a set of ideas that justifies the status quo. This emphasis goes back to the work of Marx, who said the ruling class shapes and even controls the ruling ideas of a society. It tries to shape these ideas so that they justify the existing order and decrease the chances that the poor will challenge it. The key goal of the ruling class here is to prevent the poor from achieving **class consciousness**, or an awareness of their oppression and the true reasons for it (Marx & Engels, 1947). If the poor instead do not recognize their interests as a class that does not control the means of production, they suffer from **false consciousness**.

As an example, Marx called religion the "opiate of the masses." By this he meant that religious beliefs influence the poor to feel that their fate in life is God's will or a test of their belief in God. If they hold such beliefs, they will neither blame their poverty on the rich nor rebel against them. Religious beliefs help create false consciousness.

Ideological beliefs bolster every system of stratification and domination. In slave societies, the dominant ideology, and one that at least some slaves accepted, was that slaves are inferior to their masters and deserve no better fate in life. When U.S. slavery existed in the South, it was commonly thought that blacks were biologically inferior and suited only to be slaves. Caste societies, as we noted earlier, have similar beliefs that justify the existence and impact of the caste system. Hitler's "final solution" likewise rested on the belief that Jews and other groups he targeted were biologically inferior and deserving of extermination.

Because he was born in a log cabin and later became president, Abraham Lincoln's life epitomizes the American Dream, the belief that people born into poverty can become successful through hard work. The popularity of this belief leads many Americans to blame poor people for their poverty.

U.S. Library of Congress – public domain.

Ideological beliefs in class societies are more subtle and complex but nonetheless influential. One of the most important beliefs in the United States is the American Dream, epitomized by the story of Abraham Lincoln. According to this belief, people born into poverty can lift themselves up by the bootstraps and become successful if they work hard enough. By implication, if people remain poor, they are not trying hard enough or have other personal deficiencies keeping them in poverty. This ideology prompts many Americans to take a blaming-the-victim approach (see Chapter 1 "Sociology and the Sociological Perspective") by blaming poverty on laziness and other problems in the poor rather than on discrimination and the lack of opportunity in society. To the extent that people accept such ideological beliefs, they are less likely to criticize the existing system of stratification. Marx did not foresee the extent to which these beliefs would impede the development of class consciousness in the United States.

International data underline this American ideology. We saw in Chapter 3 "Culture" that about 60% of Americans attribute poverty to laziness and lack of willpower, compared to less than half that in Mexico, Russia, Spain, and Sweden. Belief in the American Dream evidently helps lead to a blaming-the-victim ideology that blames the poor for their own fate.

Conflict theory assumes that class position influences our perceptions of social and political life, even if not to the degree envisioned by Marx. Some national survey data support this assumption. A General Social Survey question asks whether it is the government's responsibility to "reduce income differences between the rich and poor." As Figure 8.2 "Annual Family Income and Belief That Government "Should Reduce Income Differences Between the Rich and Poor"" shows, low-income people are much more likely than high-income people to think the government has this responsibility.

Figure 8.2 Annual Family Income and Belief That Government "Should Reduce Income Differences Between the Rich and Poor"

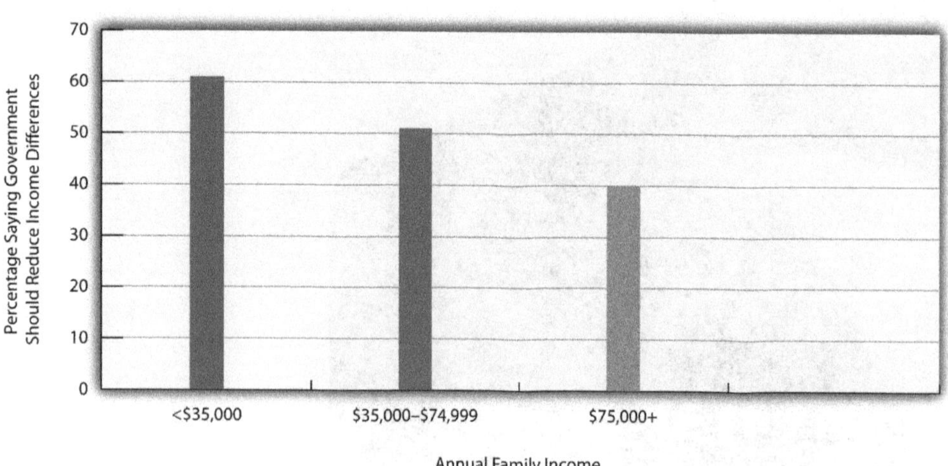

Source: Data from General Social Survey, 2006.

Symbolic Interactionism

Consistent with its micro orientation, symbolic interactionism tries to understand stratification by looking at people's interaction and understandings in their daily lives. Unlike the functionalist and conflict views, it does not try to explain why we have stratification in the first place. Rather, it examines the differences that stratification makes for people's lifestyles and their interaction with other people.

One of the most insightful analyses of stratification that fits into a symbolic interactionist framework was Thorstein Veblin's (1899/1953) famous discussion of *conspicuous consumption*, or the acquisition and display by the wealthy of lavish products that show off their wealth. The very rich do not need mansions or other very opulent homes, and neither do they need a motor vehicle costing upward of $100,000 or more or jewelry costing thousands and thousands of dollars. Yet they purchase these products to show off their wealth and to feel better about themselves. The lifestyles of the rich are featured in classic novels by writers such as F. Scott Fitzgerald and in classic films such as *The Philadelphia Story*, starring the formidable trio of Katharine Hepburn, Cary Grant, and James Stewart. Although one message of many of these cultural works is that money does not always bring happiness, it remains true, as Fitzgerald once wrote, "Let me tell you about the very rich. They are different from you and me."

Examples of the symbolic interactionist framework are also seen in the many literary works and films that portray the difficulties that the rich and poor have in interacting on the relatively few occasions when they do interact. For example, in the film *Pretty Woman*, Richard Gere plays a rich businessman who hires a prostitute, played by Julia Roberts, to accompany him to swank parties and other affairs. Roberts has to buy a new wardrobe and learn how to dine and behave in rich social settings, and much of the film's humor and poignancy come from her awkwardness in learning the lifestyle of the rich.

If there are many dramatic and humorous accounts of the "lifestyles of the rich and famous," there are also many sociological and other accounts of lives of the poor. Poverty is discussed later in this chapter, but for now it is sufficient to say that the poor often lead lives of quiet desperation and must find many ways of coping with the fact of being poor. Studies of the poor, too, reflect the symbolic interactionist perspective.

Key Takeaways

- According to the functionalist view, stratification is a necessary and inevitable consequence of the need to use the promise of financial reward to induce talented people to pursue important jobs and careers.
- According to conflict theory, stratification results from lack of opportunity and discrimination against the poor and people of color.
- According to symbolic interactionism, social class affects how people interact in everyday life and how they view certain aspects of the social world.

For Your Review

1. In explaining stratification in the United States, which view, functionalist or conflict, makes more sense to you? Why?
2. Suppose you could wave a magic wand and invent a society where everyone had about the same income no matter which job he or she performed. Do you think it would be difficult to persuade enough people to become physicians or to pursue other important careers? Explain your answer.

References

Davis, K., & Moore, W. (1945). Some principles of stratification. *American Sociological Review, 10*, 242–249.

Kerbo, H. R. (2009). *Social stratification and inequality*. New York, NY: McGraw-Hill.

Marx, K., & Engels, F. (1947). *The German ideology*. New York, NY: International Publishers.

Tumin, M. M. (1953). Some principles of stratification: A critical analysis. *American Sociological Review, 18,* 387–393.

Veblen, T. (1953). *The theory of the leisure class: An economic study of institutions*. New York, NY: New American Library. (Original work published 1899).

Wrong, D. H. (1959). The functional theory of stratification: Some neglected considerations. *American Sociological Review, 24,* 772–782.

8.3 Social Class in the United States

Learning Objectives

1. Distinguish objective and subjective measures of social class.
2. Outline the functionalist view of the American class structure.
3. Outline the conflict view of the American class structure.
4. Discuss whether the United States has much vertical social mobility.

There is a surprising amount of disagreement among sociologists on the number of social classes in the United States and even on how to measure social class membership. We first look at the measurement issue and then discuss the number and types of classes sociologists have delineated.

Measuring Social Class

We can measure social class either *objectively* or *subjectively*. If we choose the objective method, we classify people according to one or more criteria, such as their occupation, education, and/or income. The researcher is the one who decides which social class people are in based on where they stand in regard to these variables. If we choose the subjective method, we ask people what class *they think* they are in. For example, the General Social Survey asks, "If you were asked to use one of four names for your social class, which would you say you belong in: the lower class, the working class, the middle class, or the upper class?" Figure 8.3 "Subjective Social Class Membership" depicts responses to this question. The trouble with such a subjective measure is that some people say they are in a social class that differs from what objective criteria might indicate they are in. This problem leads most sociologists to favor objective measures of social class when they study stratification in American society.

Figure 8.3 Subjective Social Class Membership

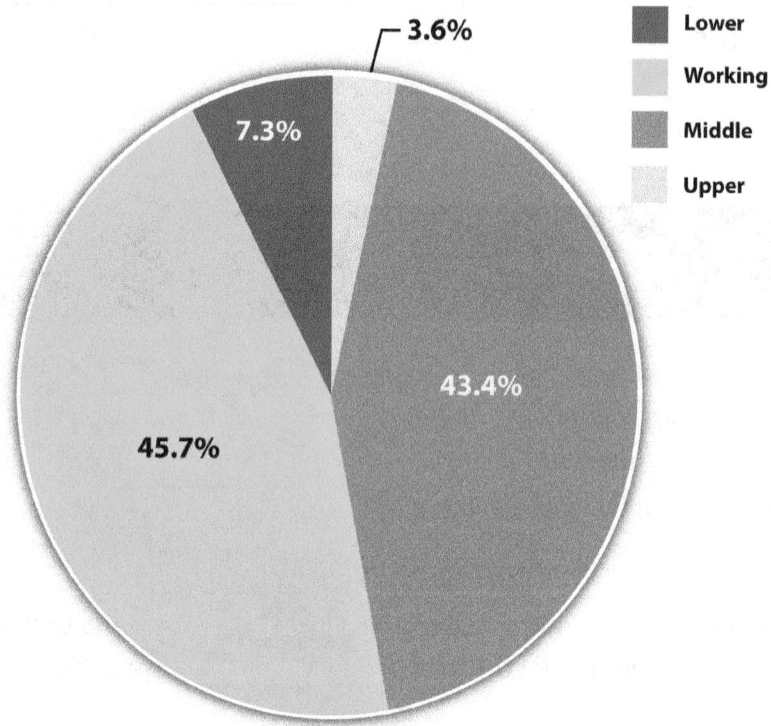

Source: Data from General Social Survey, 2008.

Yet even here there is disagreement between functionalist theorists and conflict theorists on which objective measures to use. Functionalist sociologists rely on measures of **socioeconomic status (SES)**, such as education, income, and occupation, to determine someone's social class. Sometimes one of these three variables is used by itself to measure social class, and sometimes two or all three of the variables are combined (in ways that need not concern us) to measure social class. When occupation is used, sociologists often rely on standard measures of occupational prestige. Since the late 1940s, national surveys have asked Americans to rate the prestige of dozens of occupations, and their ratings are averaged together to yield prestige scores for the occupations (Hodge, Siegel, & Rossi, 1964). Over the years these scores have been relatively stable. Here are some average prestige scores for various occupations: physician, 86; college professor, 74; elementary school teacher, 64; letter carrier, 47; garbage collector, 28; and janitor, 22.

Despite SES's usefulness, conflict sociologists prefer different, though still objective, measures of social class that take into account ownership of the means of production and other dynamics of the workplace. These measures are closer to what Marx meant by the concept of class throughout his work, and they take into account the many types of occupations and workplace structures that he could not have envisioned when he was writing during the 19th century.

For example, corporations have many upper-level managers who do not own the means of production but still determine the activities of workers under them. They thus do not fit neatly into either of Marx's two major classes, the bourgeoisie or the proletariat. Recognizing these problems, conflict sociologists delineate social class on the basis of several factors, including the ownership of the means of production, the degree of autonomy workers enjoy in their jobs, and whether they supervise other workers or are supervised themselves (Wright, 2000).

The American Class Structure

As should be evident, it is not easy to determine how many social classes exist in the United States. Over the decades, sociologists have outlined as many as six or seven social classes based on such things as, once again, education, occupation, and income, but also on lifestyle, the schools people's children attend, a family's reputation in the community, how "old" or "new" people's wealth is, and so forth (Coleman & Rainwater, 1978; Warner & Lunt, 1941). For the sake of clarity, we will limit ourselves to the four social classes included in Figure 8.3 "Subjective Social Class Membership": the upper class, the middle class, the working class, and the lower class. Although subcategories exist within some of these broad categories, they still capture the most important differences in the American class structure (Gilbert, 2011). The annual income categories listed for each class are admittedly somewhat arbitrary but are based on the percentage of households above or below a specific income level.

The Upper Class

Depending on how it is defined, the upper class consists of about 4% of the U.S. population and includes households with annual incomes (2009 data) of more than $200,000 (DeNavas-Walt, Proctor, & Smith, 2010). Some scholars would raise the ante further by limiting the upper class to households with incomes of at least $500,000 or so, which in turn reduces this class to about 1% of the population, with an average wealth (income, stocks and bonds, and real estate) of several million dollars. However it is defined, the upper class has much wealth, power, and influence (Kerbo, 2009).

The upper class in the United States consists of about 4% of all households and possesses much wealth, power, and influence.

Steven Martin – Highland Park Mansion – CC BY-NC-ND 2.0.

Members of the *upper-upper* class have “old” money that has been in their families for generations; some boast of their ancestors coming over on the *Mayflower*. They belong to exclusive clubs and live in exclusive neighborhoods; have their names in the *Social Register*; send their children to expensive private schools; serve on the boards of museums, corporations, and major charities; and exert much influence on the political process and other areas of life from behind the scenes. Members of the *lower-upper* class have “new” money acquired through hard work, lucky investments, and/or athletic prowess. In many ways their lives are similar to those of their old-money counterparts, but they do not enjoy the prestige that old money brings. Bill Gates, the founder of Microsoft and the richest person in the United States in 2009, would be considered a member of the lower-upper class because his money is too “new.” Because he does not have a long-standing pedigree, upper-upper class members might even be tempted to disparage his immense wealth, at least in private.

The Middle Class

Many of us like to think of ourselves in the middle class, as Figure 8.3 “Subjective Social Class Membership” showed, and many of us are. The middle class includes the 46% of all households whose annual incomes range from $50,000 to $199,999. As this very broad range suggests, the middle class includes people with many different levels of education and income and many different types of jobs. It is thus helpful to distinguish the *upper-middle* class from the *lower-middle* class on the upper and lower ends of this income bracket, respectively. The upper-middle class has household incomes from about $150,000 to $199,000, amounting to about 4.4% of all households. People in the upper-middle class typically have college and, very often, graduate or professional degrees; live in the suburbs or in fairly expensive urban areas; and are bankers, lawyers, engineers, corporate managers, and financial advisers, among other occupations.

The upper-middle class in the United States consists of about 4.4% of all households, with incomes ranging from $150,000 to $199,000.

Alyson Hurt – Back Porch – CC BY-NC 2.0.

The lower-middle class has household incomes from about $50,000 to $74,999, amounting to about 18% of all families. People in this income bracket typically work in white-collar jobs as nurses, teachers, and the like. Many have college degrees, usually from the less prestigious colleges, but many also have 2-year degrees or only a high school degree. They live somewhat comfortable lives but can hardly afford to go on expensive vacations or buy expensive cars and can send their children to expensive colleges only if they receive significant financial aid.

The Working Class

The working class in the United States consists of about 25% of all households, whose members work in blue-collar jobs and less skilled clerical positions.

Lisa Risager – Ebeltoft – CC BY-SA 2.0.

Working-class households have annual incomes between about $25,000 and $49,999 and constitute about 25% of all U.S. households. They generally work in blue-collar jobs such as factory work, construction, restaurant serving, and less skilled clerical positions. People in the working class typically do not have 4-year college degrees, and some do not have high school degrees. Although most are not living in official poverty, their financial situation is very uncomfortable. A single large medical bill or expensive car repair would be almost impossible to pay without going into considerable debt. Working-class families are far less likely than their wealthier counterparts to own their own homes or to send their children to college. Many of them live at risk for unemployment as their companies downsize by laying off workers even in good times, and hundreds of thousands began to be laid off when the U.S. recession began in 2008.

The Lower Class

The lower class or poor in the United States constitute about 25% of all households. Many poor individuals lack high school degrees and are unemployed or employed only part time.

Chris Hunkeler – Trailer Homes – CC BY-SA 2.0.

Although lower class is a common term, many observers prefer a less negative-sounding term like the poor, which is the term used here. The poor have household incomes under $25,000 and constitute about 25% of all U.S. households. Many of the poor lack high school degrees, and many are unemployed or employed only part time in semiskilled or unskilled jobs. When they do work, they work as janitors, house cleaners, migrant laborers, and shoe shiners. They tend to rent apartments rather than own their own homes, lack medical insurance, and have inadequate diets. We will discuss the poor further when we focus later in this chapter on inequality and poverty in the United States.

Social Mobility

Regardless of how we measure and define social class, what are our chances of moving up or down within the American class structure? As we saw earlier, the degree of vertical social mobility is a key distinguishing feature of systems of stratification. Class systems such as in the United States are thought to be open, meaning that social mobility is relatively high. It is important, then, to determine how much social mobility exists in the United States.

Here we need to distinguish between two types of vertical social mobility. **Intergenerational mobility** refers to mobility from one generation to the next within the same family. If children from poor parents end up in high-paying jobs, the children have experienced upward intergenerational mobility. Conversely, if children of college professors end up hauling trash for a living, these children have experienced downward intergenerational mobility. **Intragenerational mobility** refers to mobility within a person's own lifetime. If you start out as an administrative assistant in a large corporation and end up as an upper-level manager, you have experienced upward intragenerational mobility. But if you start out from business school as an upper-level manager and get laid off 10 years later because of corporate downsizing, you have experienced downward intragenerational mobility.

Sociologists have conducted a good deal of research on vertical mobility, much of it involving the movement of males up or down the occupational prestige ladder compared to their fathers, with the earliest studies beginning in the 1960s (Blau & Duncan, 1967; Featherman & Hauser, 1978). For better or worse, the focus on males occurred because the initial research occurred when many women were still homemakers and also because women back then were excluded from many studies in the social and biological sciences. The early research on males found that about half of sons end up in higher-prestige jobs than their fathers had but that the difference between the sons' jobs and their fathers' was relatively small. For example, a child of a janitor may end up running a hardware store but is very unlikely to end up as a corporate executive. To reach that lofty position, it helps greatly to have parents in jobs much more prestigious than a janitor's. Contemporary research also finds much less mobility among African Americans and Latinos than among non-Latino whites with the same education and family backgrounds, suggesting an important negative impact of racial and ethnic discrimination (see Chapter 7 "Deviance, Crime, and Social Control").

A college education is a key step toward achieving upward social mobility. However, the payoff of education is often higher for men than for women and for whites than for people of color.

Nazareth College – Commencement 2013 – CC BY 2.0.

A key vehicle for upward mobility is formal education. Regardless of the socioeconomic status of our parents, we are much more likely to end up in a high-paying job if we attain a college degree or, increasingly, a graduate or professional degree. Figure 8.4 "Education and Median Earnings of Year-Round, Full-Time Workers, 2007" vividly shows the difference that education makes for Americans' median annual incomes. Notice, however, that for a given level of education, men's incomes are greater than women's. Figure 8.4 "Education and Median Earnings of Year-Round, Full-Time Workers, 2007" thus suggests that the payoff of education is higher for men than for women, and many studies support this conclusion (Green & Ferber, 2008). The reasons for this gender difference are complex and will be discussed further in Chapter 11 "Gender and Gender Inequality". To the extent vertical social mobility exists in the United States, then, it is higher for men than for women and higher for whites than for people of color.

Figure 8.4 Education and Median Earnings of Year-Round, Full-Time Workers, 2007

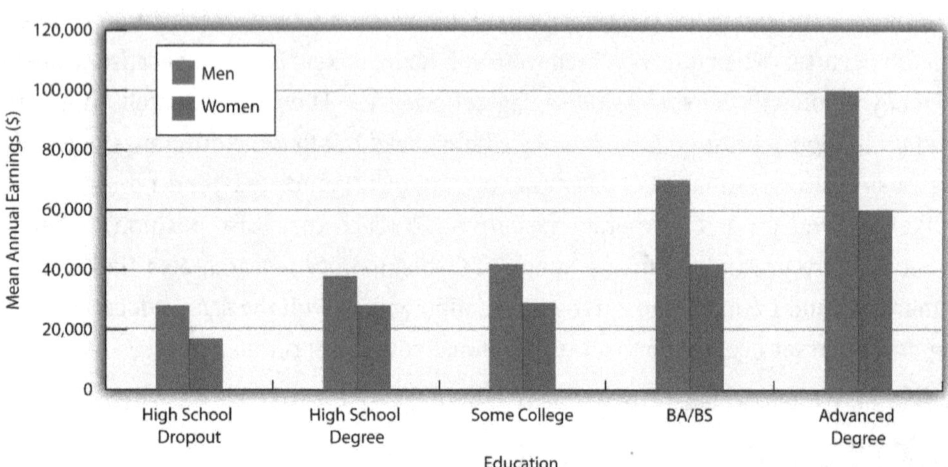

Source: Data from U.S. Census Bureau. (2010). *Statistical abstract of the United States: 2010.* Washington, DC: U.S. Government Printing Office. Retrieved from http://www.census.gov/compendia/statab.

Certainly the United States has upward social mobility, even when we take into account gender and racial discrimination. Whether we conclude the United States has *a lot of* vertical mobility or *just a little* is the key question, and the answer to this question depends on how the data are interpreted. People can and do move up the socioeconomic ladder, but their movement is fairly limited. Hardly anyone starts at the bottom of the ladder and ends up at the top. As we see later in this chapter, recent trends in the U.S. economy have made it more difficult to move up the ladder and have even worsened the status of some people.

One way of understanding the issue of U.S. mobility is to see how much parents' education affects the education their children attain. Figure 8.5 "Parents' Education and Percentage of Respondents Who Have a College Degree" compares how General Social Survey respondents with parents of different educational backgrounds fare in attaining a college (bachelor's) degree. For the sake of clarity, the figure includes only those respondents whose parents had the same level of education as each other: they either both dropped out of high school, both were high school graduates, or both were college graduates.

Figure 8.5 Parents' Education and Percentage of Respondents Who Have a College Degree

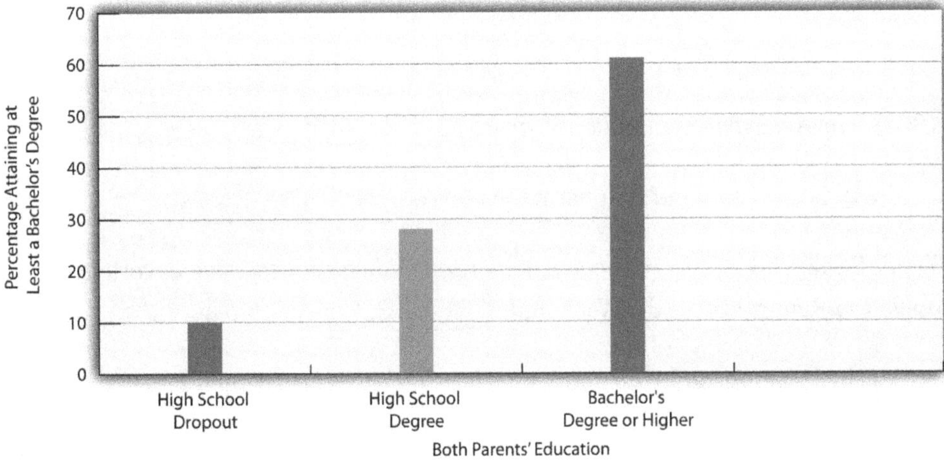

Source: Data from General Social Survey, 2008.

As Figure 8.5 "Parents' Education and Percentage of Respondents Who Have a College Degree" indicates, we are much more likely to get a college degree if our parents had college degrees themselves. The two bars for respondents whose parents were high school graduates or dropouts, respectively, do represent upward mobility, because the respondents are graduating from college even though their parents did not. But the three bars taken together also show that our chances of going to college depend heavily on our parents' education (and presumably their income and other aspects of our family backgrounds). The American Dream does exist, but it is much more likely to remain *only* a dream unless we come from advantaged backgrounds. In fact, there is less vertical mobility in the United States than in other Western democracies. As a recent analysis summarized the evidence, "There is considerably more mobility in most of the other developed economies of Europe and Scandinavia than in the United States" (Mishel, Bernstein, & Shierholz, 2009, p. 108).

Key Takeaways

- Several ways of measuring social class exist. Functionalist and conflict sociologists disagree on which objective criteria to use in measuring social class. Subjective measures of social class, which rely on people rating their own social class, may lack some validity.
- Sociologists disagree on the number of social classes in the United States, but a common view is that the United States has four classes: upper, middle, working, and lower. Further variations exist within the upper and middle classes.
- The United States has some vertical social mobility, but not as much as several nations in Western Europe.

For Your Review

1. Which way of measuring social class do you prefer, objective or subjective? Explain your answer.
2. Which objective measurement of social class do you prefer, functionalist or conflict? Explain your answer.

References

Blau, P. M., & Duncan, O. D. (1967). *The American occupational structure.* New York, NY: Wiley.

Coleman, R. P., & Rainwater, L. (1978). *Social standing in America*. New York, NY: Basic Books.

DeNavas-Walt, C., Proctor, B. D., & Smith, J. C. (2010). *Income, poverty, and health insurance coverage in the United States: 2009* (Current Population Report P60-238). Washington, DC: U.S. Census Bureau.

Featherman, D. L., & Hauser, R. M. (1978). *Opportunity and change*. New York, NY: Academic Press.

Gilbert, D. (2011). *The American class structure in an age of growing inequality* (8th ed.). Thousand Oaks, CA: Pine Forge Press.

Green, C. A., & Ferber, M. A. (2008). The long-term impact of labor market interruptions: How crucial is timing? *Review of Social Economy, 66*, 351–379.

Hodge, R. W., Siegel, P., & Rossi, P. (1964). Occupational prestige in the United States, 1925–63. *American Journal of Sociology, 70*, 286–302.

Kerbo, H. R. (2009). *Social stratification and inequality*. New York, NY: McGraw-Hill.

Mishel, L., Bernstein, J., & Shierholz, H. (2009). *The state of working America 2008/2009*. Ithaca, NY: ILR Press [An imprint of Cornell University Press].

Warner, W. L., & Lunt, P. S. (1941). *The social life of a modern community*. New Haven, CT: Yale University Press.

Wright, E. O. (2000). *Class counts: Comparative studies in class analysis*. New York, NY: Cambridge University Press.

8.4 Economic Inequality and Poverty in the United States

Learning Objectives

1. Understand trends in U.S. inequality.
2. Explain the social distribution of U.S. poverty.
3. Distinguish the structural and individual explanations of poverty.
4. List the major effects of poverty.

In his classic book *The Other America*, Michael Harrington (1962) brought the reality of poverty home to many Americans. In chapter after chapter, he discussed the troubled lives of the poor in rural Appalachia, in our urban centers, and in other areas of the country, and he indicted the country for not helping the poor. His book helped kindle interest in the White House and Congress in aiding the poor and deeply affected its thousands of readers. Almost five decades later, we know much more about poverty than we used to. Despite initial gains in fighting poverty in the 1960s (Schwartz, 1984), poverty is still with us and has worsened since the early 2000s, especially since the onset of the serious economic recession that began in 2008. What do we know about the extent of poverty, the reasons for it, and its consequences?

Economic Inequality

Let's start by discussing **economic inequality**, which refers to the extent of the economic difference between the rich and the poor. Because most societies are stratified, there will always be some people who are richer or poorer than others, but the key question is *how much* richer or poorer they are. When the gap between them is large, we say that much economic inequality exists; when the gap between them is small, we say that relatively little economic inequality exists.

Considered in this light, the United States has a very large degree of economic inequality. A common way to examine inequality is to rank the nation's families by income from lowest to highest and then to divide this distribution into *fifths*. Thus, we have the poorest fifth of the nation's families (or the 20% of families with the lowest family incomes), a second fifth with somewhat higher incomes, and so on until we reach the richest fifth of families, or the 20% with the highest incomes. We then can see what percentage each fifth has of the nation's *entire* income. Figure 8.6 "Share of National Income Going to Income Fifths, 2009" shows such a calculation for the United States. The poorest fifth enjoys only 3.4% of the nation's income, while the richest fifth enjoys 50.3%. Another way of saying this is that the richest 20% of the population have as much income as the remaining 80% of the population.

Figure 8.6 Share of National Income Going to Income Fifths, 2009

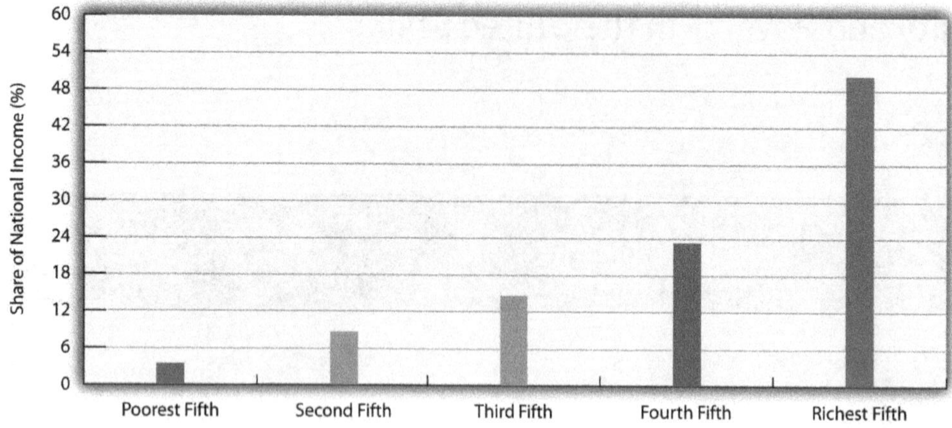

Source: Data from DeNavas-Walt, C., Proctor, B. D., & Smith, J. C. (2010). *Income, poverty, and health insurance coverage in the United States: 2009* (Current Population Report P60-238). Washington, DC: U.S. Census Bureau.

This degree of inequality is the largest in the industrialized world. Figure 8.7 "Income Inequality Around the World" compares the inequality among several industrialized nations by dividing the median income of households in the 90th percentile (meaning they have more income than 90% of all households) by the median income of households in the 10th percentile (meaning they have more income than only 10% of all households); the higher the resulting ratio, the greater a nation's inequality. The ratio for the United States, 4.86, far exceeds that for any other nation.

Figure 8.7 Income Inequality Around the World

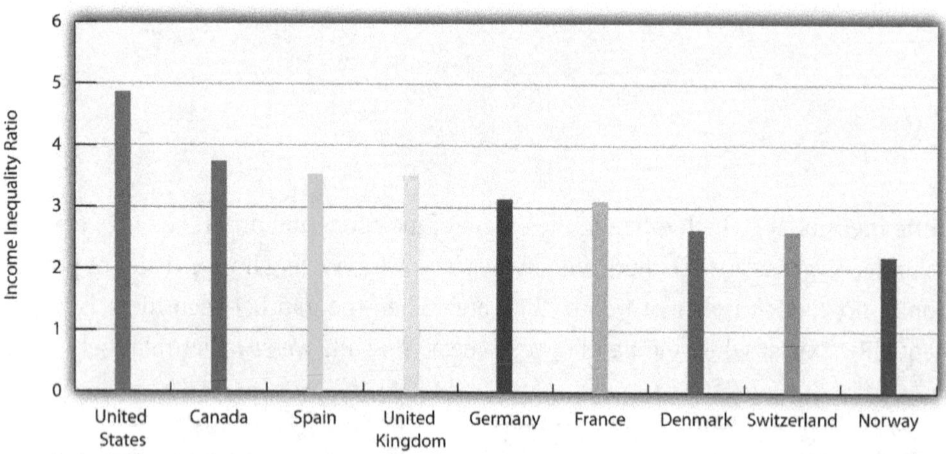

Ratio of median income of richest 10% in each nation to that of poorest 10%.

Source: Data from Mishel, L., Bernstein, J., & Shierholz, H. (2009). *The state of working America 2008/2009*. Ithaca, NY: ILR Press [An imprint of Cornell University Press].

Economic inequality in the United States has increased during the last two decades. The loss of manufacturing jobs and changes in taxation and income distribution policies since the early 1980s have favored the rich and hurt the economic standing of the middle class and the poor (Barlett & Steele, 2002; Wilson, 2009). After adjusting for inflation, the post-tax income of the nation's wealthiest families grew by a much greater amount than that for the poorest families from 1979 to 2005. It grew by only 6% for the poorest fifth but by 80% for the wealthiest fifth, and it also grew by a whopping 228% for families in the top 1% of the nation's families (Mishel, Bernstein, &

Shierholz, 2009). As the saying goes, the rich get richer. To recall our earlier discussion, to be upwardly mobile, it helps to be well-off to begin with.

Poverty

Measuring Poverty

When U.S. officials became concerned about poverty during the 1960s, they quickly realized they needed to find out how much poverty we had. To do so, a measure of official poverty, or a **poverty line**, was needed. This line was first calculated in 1963 by multiplying the cost of a very minimal diet by three, as a 1955 government study had determined that the typical American family spent one-third of its income on food. Thus a family whose income is lower than three times the cost of a very minimal diet is considered officially poor.

The measure of official poverty began in 1963 and stipulates that a family whose income is lower than three times the cost of a minimal diet is considered officially poor. This measure has not changed since 1963 even though family expenses have risen greatly in many areas.

Bill Herndon – Katrina Leftovers 1 – CC BY-NC-ND 2.0.

This way of calculating the poverty line has not changed since 1963, even though many other things, such as energy, child care, and health care, now occupy a greater percentage of the typical family's budget than was true in 1963. As a national measure, the poverty line also fails to take into account regional differences in the cost of living. For all of these reasons, many experts think the official measurement of poverty is highly suspect. As a recent report observed, "Most poverty analysts strongly believe that the official poverty statistics are inadequate to the task of determining who is poor in America" (Mishel, Bernstein, & Shierholz, 2009, p. 298).

The poverty line is adjusted annually for inflation and takes into account the number of people in a family: the larger the family size, the higher the poverty line. In 2009, the poverty line for a nonfarming family of four (two adults, two children) was $21,756. A four-person family earning even one more dollar than $21,756 in 2009 was not officially poor, even though its "extra" income hardly lifted it out of dire economic straits. Policy experts have calculated a no-frills budget that enables a family to meet its basic needs in food, clothing, shelter, and so forth; this budget is about twice the poverty line. Families with incomes between the poverty line and twice the poverty line are barely making ends meet, but they are not considered officially poor. When we talk here about the poverty level, keep in mind that we are talking only about *official* poverty and that there are many families and individuals living in near-poverty who have trouble meeting their basic needs, especially when they face unusually high medical or motor vehicle expenses or the like. For this reason, some analyses use "twice-poverty" data (i.e., family incomes below twice the poverty line) to provide a more accurate understanding of how many Americans face serious financial difficulties.

The Extent and Social Distribution of Poverty

With this caveat in mind, how many Americans are poor, and who are they? The U.S. Census Bureau gives us some answers. In 2009, 14.3% of the U.S. population, or almost 44 million Americans, lived in (official) poverty (DeNavas-Walt, Proctor, & Smith, 2010). This percentage represented a decline from the early 1990s but was higher than the rate in the late 1960s (see Figure 8.8 "U.S. Poverty, 1959–2009"). If we were winning the war on poverty in the 1960s, since then poverty has fought us to a standstill.

Figure 8.8 U.S. Poverty, 1959–2009

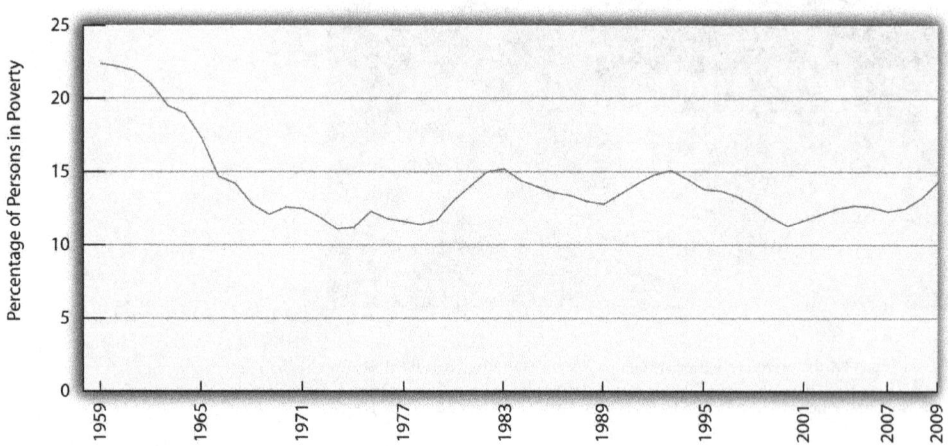

Source: Data from U.S. Census Bureau. (2010). Historical poverty tables: People. Retrieved from http://www.census.gov/hhes/www/poverty/data/historical/people.html.

Another way of understanding the extent of poverty is to consider **episodic poverty**, defined by the Census Bureau as being poor for at least 2 consecutive months in some time period. From 2004 to 2007, the last years for which data are available, almost one-third of the U.S. public, equal to about 95 million people, were poor for at least 2 consecutive months, although only 2.2% were poor for all 3 years (DeNavas-Walt, Proctor, & Smith, 2010). As these figures indicate, people go into and out of poverty, but even those who go out of it do not usually move very far from it.

Learning From Other Societies

Poverty and Poverty Policy in Other Western Democracies

To compare international poverty rates, scholars commonly use a measure of the percentage of households in a nation that receive less than half of the nation's median household income after taxes and cash transfers from the government. In 2000, the latest date for which data are available, 17% of U.S. households lived in poverty as defined by this measure (Mishel, Bernstein, & Shierholz, 2009). By comparison, selected other Western democracies had the following rates (Mishel, Bernstein, & Shierholz, 2009, p. 384):

Canada	11.4%
Denmark	9.2%
France	8.0%
Germany	8.3%
Norway	6.4%
Spain	14.3%
Sweden	6.5%
United Kingdom	12.4%

The average poverty rate of Western democracies excluding the United States is 9.8%. The U.S. rate is thus 1.73 times greater than this average.

Why is there so much more poverty in the United States than in its Western counterparts? Several differences between the United States and the other nations stand out. First, other Western nations have higher minimum wages and stronger unions than the United States has, and these lead to incomes that help push people above poverty. Second, the other nations spend a much greater proportion of their gross domestic product on social expenditures (income support and social services such as child care subsidies and housing allowances) than does the United States. As a recent analysis concluded,

> Other peer countries are much more likely than the United States to step in where markets have failed to live their most disadvantaged citizens out of poverty. This suggests that the relatively low expenditures on social welfare are at least partially implicated in the high poverty rates in the United States. (Mishel, Bernstein, & Shierholz, 2009, p. 387)
> In short, the United States has so much more poverty than other democracies in part because it spends so much less than they do on helping the poor. The United States certainly has the wealth to follow their example, but it has chosen not to do so, and a high poverty rate is the unfortunate result.

Who are the poor? Contrary to popular images, the most typical poor person in the United States is *white*: approximately 44% of poor people are white (non-Latino), 29% are Latino, 23% are black, and 4% are Asian (see Figure 8.9 "Racial and Ethnic Composition of the Poor, 2009 (Percentage of Poor Persons in Each Group)"). At the same time, race and ethnicity affect the chances of being poor: while only 9.4% of non-Latino whites are poor, 25.8% of African Americans, 12.5% of Asians, and 25.3% of Latinos (who may be of any race) are poor (see Figure 8.10 "Race, Ethnicity, and Poverty, 2009 (Percentage of Each Group That Is Poor)"). Thus African Americans and Latinos are almost three times as likely as non-Latino whites to be poor. (Because there are so many non-Latino whites in the United States, the plurality of poor people are non-Latino white, even if the percentage of whites who are poor is relatively low.) Chapter 10 "Race and Ethnicity" further discusses the link between poverty and race and ethnicity.

Figure 8.9 Racial and Ethnic Composition of the Poor, 2009 (Percentage of Poor Persons in Each Group)

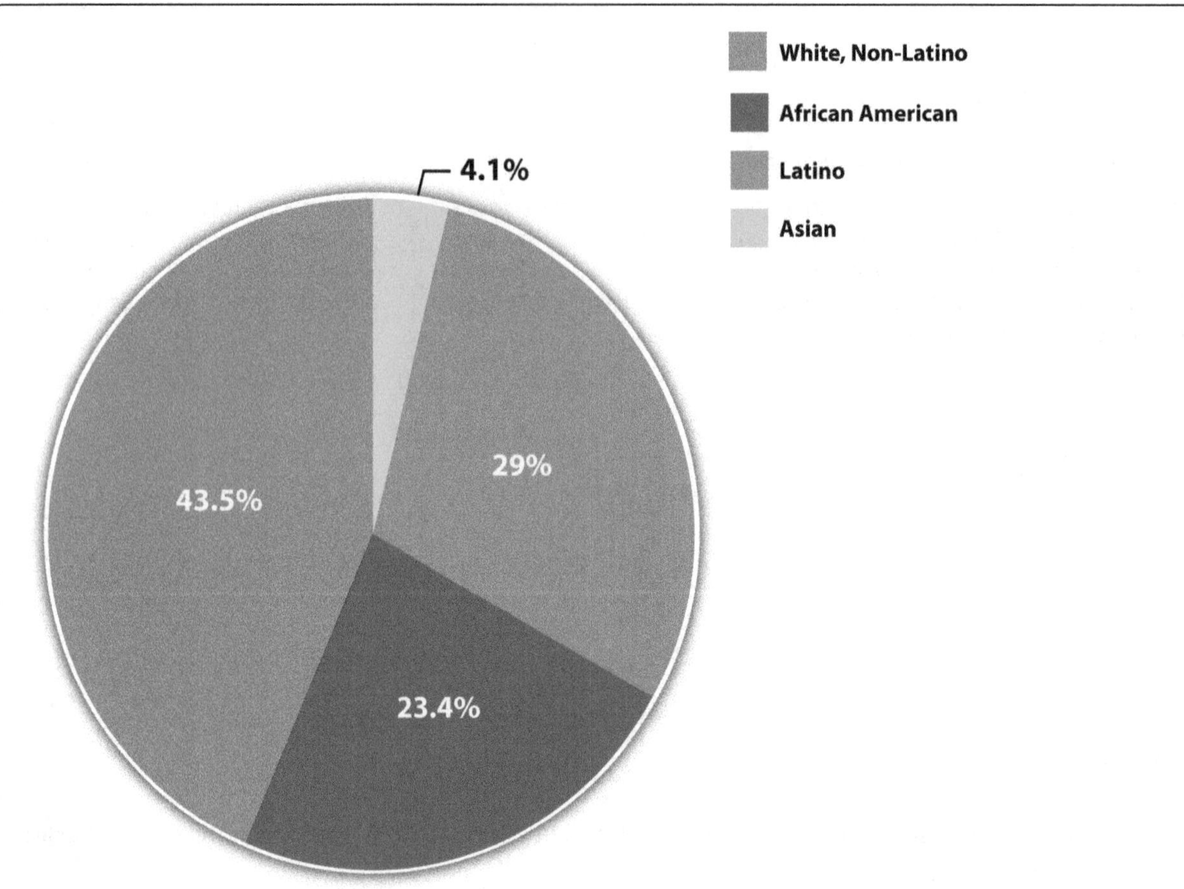

Source: Data from DeNavas-Walt, C., Proctor, B. D., & Smith, J. C. (2010). *Income, poverty, and health insurance coverage in the United States: 2009* (Current Population Report P60-238). Washington, DC: U.S. Census Bureau.

Figure 8.10 Race, Ethnicity, and Poverty, 2009 (Percentage of Each Group That Is Poor)

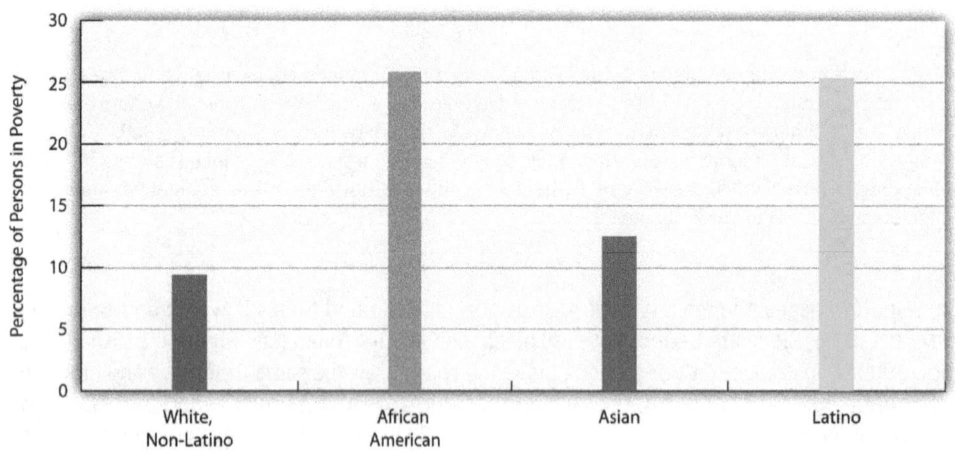

Source: Data from U.S Census Bureau Current Population Survey. (2008). POV01: Age and sex of all people, family members and unrelated individuals iterated by income-to-poverty ratio and race. Retrieved from http://www.census.gov/hhes/www/macro/032008/pov/new01_100.htm.

Turning to age, almost 21% of children under age 18 are poor (amounting to more than 15 million children), including 35.7% of African American children and 33.1% of Latino children (DeNavas-Walt, Proctor, & Smith, 2010). The poverty rate for U.S. children is the highest in the Western world and 1.5 to 9 times greater than the corresponding rates in Canada and Western Europe (Mishel, Bernstein, & Shierholz, 2009). At the other end of the age distribution, 8.9% of people aged 65 or older are poor (amounting to about 3.4 million seniors). Turning around these U.S. figures, about 36% of all poor people in the United States are children, and about 8% of the poor are 65 or older. Thus some 44% of Americans living in poverty are children or the elderly.

The poverty rate for U.S. children is the highest in the Western world.

Wikimedia Commons – CC BY-SA 3.0.

The type of family structure also makes a difference: whereas only 8.5% of children living with married parents live in poverty, 43% of those living with only their mother live in poverty (2007 data). This latter figure is about 32% for Asian children and for non-Latino white children and rises to slightly more than 50% for African American children and Latino children (Moore, Redd, Burkhauser, Mbawa, & Collins, 2009). As these latter numbers indicate, families headed by a single woman are much more likely to be poor. Poverty thus has a female face.

Explaining Poverty

Explanations of poverty focus on problems either within the poor themselves or in the society in which they live (Iceland, 2006). The first type of explanation follows logically from the functional theory of stratification and may be considered an "individual" explanation. The second type of explanation follows from conflict theory and is a structural explanation that focuses on problems in American society that produce poverty. As the "Sociology Making a Difference" box discusses, the explanation of poverty people favor affects how sympathetic they are to the poor.

According to the individual explanation, the poor have personal problems and deficiencies that are responsible for their poverty. In the past, the poor were thought to be biologically inferior, a view that has not entirely faded, but today the much more common belief is that they lack the ambition and motivation to work hard and to achieve. According to the World Values Survey, 60% of Americans believe that people are poor "because they are lazy and lack will power." This percentage reflects the tendency of Americans to favor individual explanations of poverty (Davidson, 2009).

A more sophisticated version of this type of explanation is called the *culture of poverty* theory (Banfield, 1974; O. Lewis, 1966). According to this theory, the poor generally have beliefs and values that differ from those of the nonpoor and that doom them to continued poverty. For example, they are said to be impulsive and to live for the present rather than the future. Critics say this view exaggerates the degree to which the poor and nonpoor do in fact hold different values and ignores discrimination and other problems in American society (Iceland, 2006).

According to the second, structural explanation, U.S. poverty stems from problems in American society that lead to lack of equal opportunity. These problems include (a) racial, ethnic, gender, and age discrimination; (b) lack of good schooling and adequate health care; and (c) structural changes in the American economic system, such as the departure of manufacturing companies from American cities in the 1980s and 1990s (Iceland, 2003). These problems help create a vicious cycle of poverty in which children of the poor are often fated to end up in poverty or near-poverty themselves as adults.

Sociology Making a Difference

Attributions for Poverty and Public Education Campaigns

The text discusses two general explanations for poverty. The first attributes poverty to lack of willpower and other problems among the poor themselves, while the second attributes poverty to structural obstacles and lack of opportunity in the larger society. As the text notes, Americans tend to favor the first explanation more than the second explanation. They also tend to disagree that the government should do more to help the poor. Could these two sets of views be linked? If so, what would such a link imply for poverty policy?

Sociological research finds that the explanation we favor for poverty—the attribution for poverty we hold—affects whether we want the government to take an active role in helping the poor (Bradley & Cole, 2002). People who attribute poverty to problems in the larger society are much more likely than those who attribute it to deficiencies among the poor to believe that the government should take such a role. The attribution for poverty we hold presumably affects the amount of sympathy we have for the poor, and our sympathy, or lack of sympathy, in turn affects our views about the government's role in helping the poor. As sociologist Theresa C. Davidson (2009) observes, "Beliefs about the causes of poverty shape attitudes toward the poor."

This body of research strongly suggests that public support for government aid for the poor is weak because so much of the public attributes poverty to failings among the poor themselves. If so, the public might very well begin to endorse greater government aid if its attribution for poverty became more structural instead of individual. Public education campaigns that call attention to the lack of opportunity and other structural problems that account for poverty thus might further poverty policy by beginning to change public perceptions of the poor.

Most sociologists favor the structural explanation. As our earlier Monopoly example illustrates, poverty greatly blocks opportunities for success. Later chapters document racial and ethnic discrimination, lack of adequate schooling and health care, and other problems that make it difficult to rise out of poverty. On the other hand, some ethnographic research supports the individual explanation by showing that the poor do have certain values and follow certain practices that augment their plight (Small, Harding, & Lamont, 2010). For example, the poor have higher rates of cigarette smoking (34% of people with annual incomes between $6,000 and $11,999 smoke, compared to only 13% of those with incomes $90,000 or greater (Goszkowski, 2008), which helps lead them to have more serious health problems. Adopting an integrated perspective, some researchers say these values and practices are in many ways the result of poverty itself (Small, Harding, & Lamont, 2010). These scholars concede a culture of poverty does exist, but they also say it exists because it helps the poor cope daily with the structural effects of being poor. If these effects lead to a culture of poverty, they add, then poverty becomes self-perpetuating. If poverty is both cultural and structural in origin, these scholars say, a comprehensive national effort must be launched to improve the lives of the people in the "other America."

The Effects of Poverty

However poverty is explained, it has important and enduring effects, which later chapters will continue to discuss. For now, we can list some of the major consequences of poverty (and near-poverty) in the United States. As we do so, recall the sociological perspective's emphasis on how our social backgrounds influence our attitudes, behaviors, and life chances. This influence on life chances is quite evident when we look at some of the effects of poverty (Moore, Redd, Burkhauser, Mbawa, & Collins, 2009; Iceland, 2006; D. Lindsey, 2009):

Poor children are more likely to have inadequate nutrition and to experience health, behavioral, and cognitive problems.

Kelly Short – Poverty: "Damaged Child," Oklahoma City, OK, USA, 1936. (Colorized). – CC BY-SA 2.0.

- The poor are at greater risk for family problems, including divorce and domestic violence. The stress of being poor is thought to be a major reason for these problems.
- The poor are also at greater risk for health problems, including infant mortality, earlier mortality during adulthood, mental illness, and inadequate medical care. Many poor people lack health insurance. Poor children are more likely to have inadequate nutrition and to suffer health, behavioral, and cognitive problems. These problems in turn impair their ability to do well in school and land stable employment as adults, helping to ensure that poverty will persist across generations.
- Poor children typically go to rundown schools with inadequate facilities where they receive inadequate schooling. They are much less likely than nonpoor children to graduate from high school or to go to college. Their lack of education in turn restricts them and their own children to poverty, once again helping to ensure a vicious cycle of continuing poverty across generations.
- The poor are, not surprisingly, more likely to be homeless than the nonpoor but also more likely to live in dilapidated housing and unable to buy their own homes. Many poor families spend more than half their income on rent. The lack of adequate housing for the poor remains a major national problem.

Key Takeaways

- Inequality refers to the gap between the rich and the poor. The United States has a high degree of inequality.
- Although the official poverty line measure has been criticized for several reasons, in 2007 about 12.5% of the U.S. population, or more than 37 million people, were living in official poverty.
- About 18% of U.S. children live in official poverty; this rate is the highest in the Western world.
- Explanations of poverty focus on problems either within the poor themselves or in the society in which they live. These two types of explanations reflect the functionalist and conflict views, respectively.
- Poverty has several important and enduring consequences, including many kinds of health problems.

For Your Review

1. Do you agree with the criticism of the official measure of poverty in the United States, or do you think it is probably accurate enough because it has been used since the 1960s? Explain your answer.
2. Which explanation of poverty makes the most sense to you? Why?

Reducing U.S. Poverty: What Sociology Suggests

It is easy to understand why the families in Wichita, Kansas, discussed in the news story that began this chapter might be poor in the middle of a deep economic recession. Yet a sociological understanding of poverty emphasizes its structural basis in bad times and good times alike. Poverty is rooted in social and economic problems of the larger society rather than in the lack of willpower, laziness, or other moral failings of poor individuals themselves. Individuals born into poverty suffer from a lack of opportunity from their first months up through adulthood, and poverty becomes a self-perpetuating, vicious cycle. To the extent a culture of poverty might exist, it is best seen as a logical and perhaps even inevitable outcome of, and adaptation to, the problem of being poor and not the primary force driving poverty itself.

This sort of understanding suggests that efforts to reduce poverty must address first and foremost the structural basis for poverty while not ignoring certain beliefs and practices of the poor that also make a difference. An extensive literature on poverty policy outlines many types of policies and strategies that follow this dual approach (Moore, Redd, Burkhauser, Mbawa, & Collins, 2009; Iceland, 2006; D. Lindsey, 2009; Cancian & Danziger, 2009; Turner & Rawlings, 2005). If these were fully adopted, funded, and implemented, they would offer great promise for reducing poverty. As two poverty experts recently wrote, "We are optimistic that poverty can be reduced significantly in the long term if the public and policymakers can muster the political will to pursue a range of promising antipoverty policies" (Cancian & Danziger, 2009, p. 32). Although a full discussion of these policies is beyond the scope of this chapter, the following measures are commonly cited as holding strong potential for reducing poverty:

1. Adopt a national "full employment" policy for the poor, involving federally funded job training and public works programs.
2. Increase federal aid for the working poor, including earned income credits and child care subsidies for those with children.
3. Establish well-funded early childhood intervention programs, including home visitations by trained professionals, for poor families.

4. Improve the schools that poor children attend and the schooling they receive and expand early childhood education programs for poor children.
5. Provide better nutrition and health services for poor families with young children.
6. Strengthen efforts to reduce teenage pregnancies.

References

Banfield, E. C. (1974). *The unheavenly city revisited.* Boston, MA: Little, Brown; Lewis, O. (1966). The culture of poverty. *Scientific American, 113,* 19–25.

Barlett, D. L., & Steele, J. B. (2002). *The great American tax dodge: How spiraling fraud and avoidance are killing fairness, destroying the income tax, and costing you.* Berkeley: University of California Press.

Bradley, C., & Cole, D. J. (2002). Causal attributions and the significance of self-efficacy in predicting solutions to poverty. *Sociological Focus, 35,* 381–396.

Cancian, M., & Danziger, S. (2009). *Changing poverty and changing antipoverty policies.* Ann Arbor: National Poverty Center, University of Michigan.

Davidson, T. C. (2009). Attributions for poverty among college students: The impact of service-learning and religiosity. *College Student Journal, 43,* 136–144.

DeNavas-Walt, C., Proctor, B. D., & Smith, J. C. (2010). *Income, poverty, and health insurance coverage in the United States: 2009* (Current Population Report P60-238). Washington, DC: U.S. Census Bureau.

Goszkowski, R. (2008). Among Americans, smoking decreases as income increases. Retrieved from http://www.gallup.com/poll/105550/among-americans-smoking-decreases-income-increases.aspx.

Harrington, M. (1962). *The other America: Poverty in the United States.* New York, NY: Macmillan.

Iceland, J. (2003). *Dynamics of economic well-being, 1996–1999* (Current Population Report P70–91). Washington, DC: U.S. Census Bureau.

Iceland, J. (2006). *Poverty in America: A handbook.* Berkeley: University of California Press.

Lindsey, D. (2009). *Child poverty and inequality: Securing a better future for America's children.* New York, NY: Oxford University Press.

Mishel, L., Bernstein, J., & Shierholz, H. (2009). *The state of working America 2008/2009.* Ithaca, NY: ILR Press [An imprint of Cornell University Press].

Moore, K. A., Redd, Z., Burkhauser, M., Mbawa, K., & Collins, A. (2009). *Children in poverty: Trends, consequences, and policy options*. Washington, DC: Child Trends. Retrieved from http://www.childtrends.org/Files//Child_Trends-2009_04_07_RB_ChildreninPoverty.pdf.

Schwartz, J. E. (1984, June 18). The war we won: How the great society defeated poverty. *The New Republic*, 18–19.

Small, M. L., Harding, D. J., & Lamont, M. (2010, May). Reconsidering culture and poverty. *The Annals of the American Academy of Political and Social Science, 629*, 6–27.

Turner, M. A., & Rawlings, L. A. (2005). *Overcoming concentrated poverty and isolation: Ten lessons for policy and practice*. Washington, DC: The Urban Institute.

Wilson, W. J. (2009). The economic plight of inner-city black males. In E. Anderson (Ed.), *Against the wall: Poor, young, black, and male* (pp. 55–70). Philadelphia: University of Pennsylvania Press.

8.5 End-of-Chapter Material

Summary

1. Almost all societies are stratified according to wealth, power, prestige, and other resources the societies value. Societies are often categorized into systems of stratification according to the degrees of inequality and vertical social mobility that characterize them.
2. Systems of stratification include slave societies, caste societies, and class societies, with class societies the most open in terms of vertical social mobility. Classless societies exist in theory, according to Karl Marx and other thinkers, but have never been achieved in reality. Certain social democracies in Western Europe have succeeded in limiting their degree of inequality while preserving political freedom.
3. The two major explanations of stratification are the functionalist and conflict views. Functionalist theory says that stratification is necessary and inevitable because of the need to induce people with the needed knowledge and skills to decide to pursue the careers that are most important to society. Conflict theory says stratification exists because of discrimination against, and blocked opportunities for, the have-nots of society. A set of ideological beliefs supports the existence and perpetuation of systems of stratification and domination. In the United States, these beliefs include the ideas surrounding the American Dream ethos that even poor people can succeed by working hard and pulling themselves up by their bootstraps.
4. Social class in the United States is usually measured in terms of socioeconomic status, but some conflict theory scholars prefer measures more related to Marx's concept of the ownership of the means of production. Many typologies of the American class structure exist, but four commonly delineated classes include the upper class, middle class, working class, and lower class or the poor. Within the upper class and middle class are subclasses distinguished by their incomes and lifestyles.
5. Many studies examine the degree of vertical social mobility in the United States. Some vertical mobility does exist, but overall it's fairly small. Your family's socioeconomic status (SES) greatly affects your own chances for success in life; people on the bottom of society usually can move up only a little bit, if at all.
6. The United States has the highest degree of economic inequality in the industrial world, and its degree of inequality has increased in the last two decades. Although our poverty rate declined in the late 1990s, it was as high as in the middle 1960s, before the war on poverty began reducing the poverty rate.
7. Poverty rates are strongly related to factors such as race and ethnicity, age, and gender. Although most poor people are white, people of color have higher poverty rates than whites. About 40% of all poor people are children under the age of 18. Single-parent households headed by women have especially high poverty rates.
8. In explaining poverty, observers attribute it either to personal deficiencies of the poor themselves or instead to structural problems in American society such as racial discrimination and rundown schools that block the ability and opportunity of the poor to improve their lot. Poverty has dire effects for the poor in many areas of life, including illness and health care, schooling, and housing.

Using Sociology

It is Thanksgiving dinner, and your family and other relatives are gathered around a very large table. Having taken a few sociology courses, you subscribe to the structural explanation for poverty presented in this chapter. One of your cousins asks if you have any career plans after college, and you reply that you're thinking of becoming a community activist in your home state to help the poor deal with the many problems they have. Your cousin is surprised to hear this and says that poor people are just lazy and don't like to work. A silence sets over the table, and everyone is staring at you, wondering what you will say in response to your cousin. What do you say?

Chapter 9: Global Stratification

Social Issues in the News

"Hunger Staring Country in the Face," the headline said. Although India has been experiencing economic growth and is far from the poorest nation in the world, hunger remains a serious problem throughout the country. According to the news report, India's economic numbers "could be masking the reality that growth has not translated into better lives for Indians." More than 40% of Indians live below the international poverty line, defined by the World Bank as income under $1.25 per day. More than 200 million Indians, about one-fifth of the nation's population, experience food insecurity, even though India is a leading producer of grains, fruits, and vegetables. More than 80 million Indian children are malnourished. According to the news report, India's high hunger rate stems from its poverty, inadequate distribution of food, and political corruption. To help reduce hunger, the report said it was important to develop programs focused on women and children, who are especially likely to live in hunger. (Golikeri, 2010, p. MM28)

We learn several things from this news story about India: (a) poverty and hunger are rampant; (b) although India apparently has enough food to help feed its people, inadequate distribution and political corruption help keep food from the mouths of the hungry; (c) women and children bear the brunt of poverty and hunger; and, finally, (d) if India is far from the poorest nation and so many Indians are going hungry, conditions in poorer nations must be almost unimaginable. In all these respects, India's situation tells us much about global stratification, the subject of this chapter. We first discuss the dimensions and extent of global stratification before turning to its impact and possible reasons for it. We will see that many nations around the world are in, and have long been in, a dire situation, but we will also examine possible strategies for improving their situation.

References

Golikeri, P. (2010, March 26). Hunger staring country in the face. *Daily News and Analysis* (Mumbai). Retrieved from http://findarticles.com/p/news-articles/dna-daily-news-analysis-mumbai/mi_8111/is_20100326/hunger-staring-eye/ai_n52925597/?tag=content;col1.

9.1 The Nature and Extent of Global Stratification

Learning Objectives

1. Explain why the terms First World, Second World, and Third World have fallen out of use.
2. Describe the most important characteristics of wealthy nations, middle-income nations, and poor nations.
3. Explain why it is important to measure global poverty.
4. Describe which world regions have higher or lower inequality and why.

Stratification within the United States was discussed in Chapter 8 "Social Stratification". As we saw then, there is a vast difference between the richest and poorest segments of American society. Stratification also exists across the world. **Global stratification** refers to the unequal distribution of wealth, power, prestige, resources, and influence among the world's nations. Put more simply, there is an extreme difference between the richest and poorest nations. A few nations, such as the United States, are very, very wealthy, while many more nations are very, very poor. Reflecting this latter fact, 40% of the world's population, or about 2 billion people, lives on less than $2 per day (United Nations Development Programme, 2005).

If the world were one nation, its median annual income (at which half of the world's population is below this income and half is above it) would be only $1,700 (data from 2000). The richest fifth of the world's population would have three-fourths of the world's entire income, while the poorest fifth of the world's population would have only 1.5% of the world's income, and the poorest two-fifths would have only 5.0% of the world's income (Dikhanov, 2005). As Figure 9.1 "Global Income Distribution (Percentage of World Income Held by Each Fifth of World Population)" illustrates, this distribution of income resembles a champagne glass.

Figure 9.1 Global Income Distribution (Percentage of World Income Held by Each Fifth of World Population)

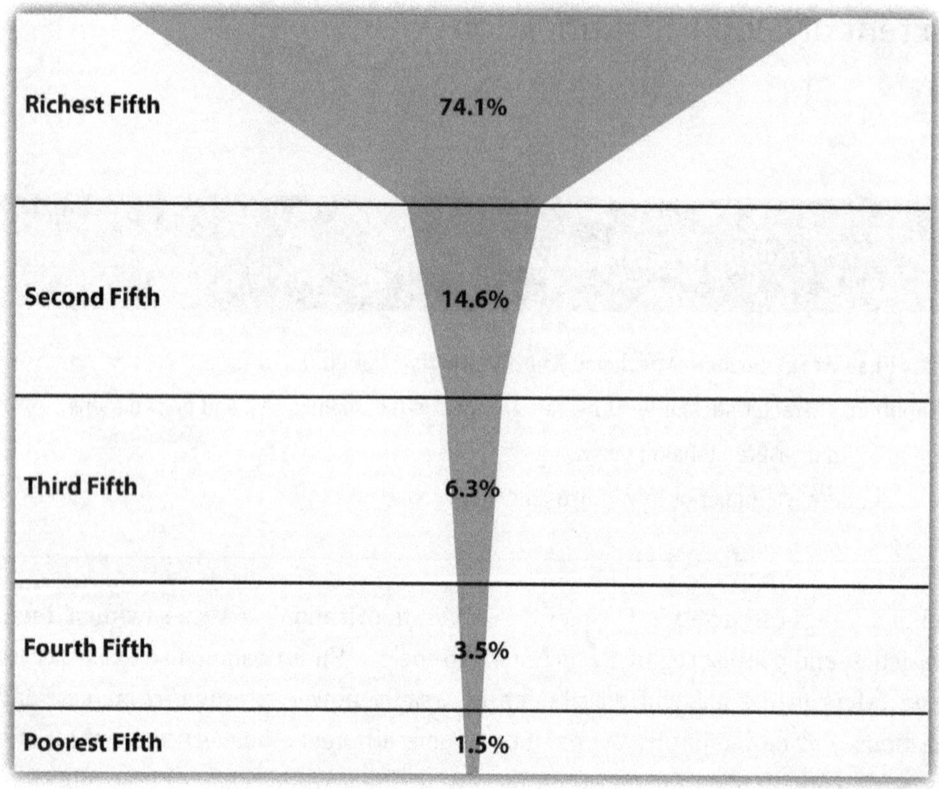

Source: Data from Dikhanov, Y. (2005). *Trends in global income distribution, 1970–2000, and scenarios for 2015*. New York, NY: United Nations Development Programme.

The game of Monopoly, used in Chapter 8 "Social Stratification" to illustrate U.S. stratification, again helps illustrate global stratification. Recall that if five people play Monopoly, each person would start out with $1,500. If each player represented one-fifth of the world's population, and we divided the $7,500 according to the global distribution of income, then the richest player would begin with $5,558 of the $7,500 distributed to the five players combined. The next richest player would have $1,095. The third player would start with $473, while the next would have $263. The fifth and poorest player would begin with only $113. Figure 9.2 "Distribution of Starting Cash if Monopoly Resembled the Global Distribution of Income" depicts this huge disparity in money at the beginning of the game. Who would win? Who would be first to lose?

Figure 9.2 Distribution of Starting Cash if Monopoly Resembled the Global Distribution of Income

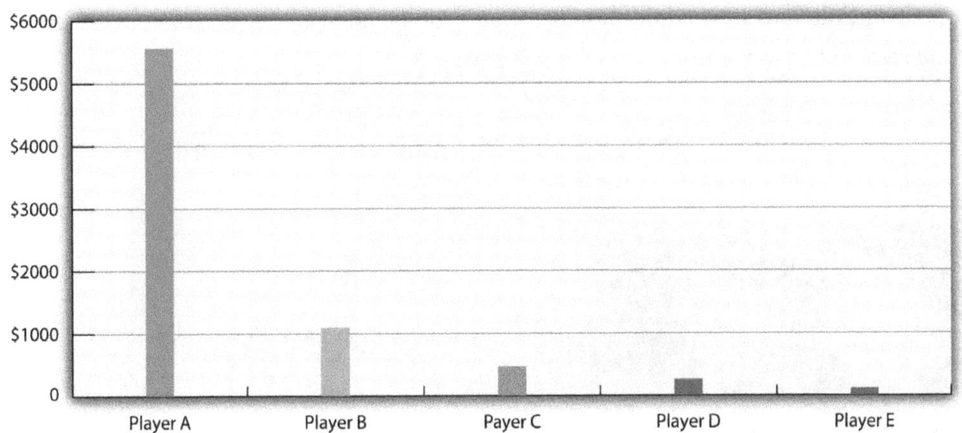

Source: Based on distribution of wealth data from Dikhanov, Y. (2005). *Trends in global income distribution, 1970–2000, and scenarios for 2015*. New York, NY: United Nations Development Programme.

Classifying Global Stratification

As these figures make clear, the world is indeed stratified. To understand global stratification, it is helpful to classify nations into three or four categories based on their degree of wealth or poverty, their level of industrialization and economic development, and related factors. Over the decades, scholars and international organizations such as the United Nations and the World Bank have used various classification systems, or *typologies*.

One of the first typologies came into use after World War II and classified nations as falling into the *First World, Second World,* and *Third World.* The First World was generally the Western capitalist democracies of North America and of Europe and certain other nations (e.g., Australia, New Zealand, and Japan). The Second World was the communist nations belonging to the Soviet Union, while the Third World was all the remaining nations, almost all of them from Central and South America, Africa, and Asia. This classification was useful in distinguishing capitalist and communist countries and in calling attention to the many nations composing the Third World. However, it was primarily a political classification rather than a stratification classification. This problem, along with the demise of the Soviet Union by the end of 1991, caused this typology to fall out of favor.

A replacement typology placed nations into *developed, developing,* and *undeveloped* categories, respectively. Although this typology was initially popular, critics said that calling nations "developed" made them sound superior, while calling nations "undeveloped" made them sound inferior. Although this classification scheme is still used, it, too, has begun to fall out of favor.

Today a popular typology simply ranks nations into groups called *wealthy* (or *high-income*) nations, *middle-income nations,* and *poor* (or *low-income*) nations, based on measures such as gross domestic product (GDP) per capita (the total value of a nation's goods and services divided by its population). This typology has the advantage of emphasizing the most important variable in global stratification: how much wealth a nation has. At the risk of being somewhat simplistic, the other important differences among the world's nations all stem from their degree of wealth or poverty. Figure 9.3 "Global Stratification Map" depicts these three categories of nations (with the middle category divided into upper-middle and lower-middle). As should be clear, whether a nation is wealthy, middle-income, or poor is heavily related to the continent on which it is found.

Figure 9.3 Global Stratification Map

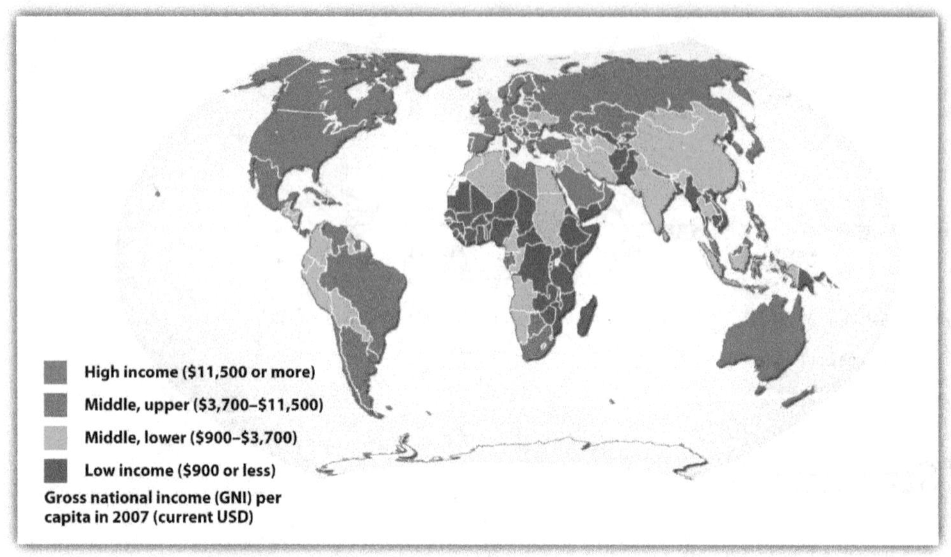

Source: Adapted from UNEP/GRID-Arendal Maps and Graphics Library. (2009). Country income groups (World Bank classification). Retrieved from http://maps.grida.no/go/graphic/country-income-groups-world-bank-classification.

Typologies based on GDP per capita or similar economic measures are very useful, but they also have a significant limitation. Nations can rank similarly on GDP per capita (or another economic measure) but still differ in other respects. One nation might have lower infant mortality, another might have higher life expectancy, and a third might have better sanitation. Recognizing this limitation, organizations such as the United Nations Development Programme (UNDP) use typologies based on a broader range of measures than GDP per capita. A very popular typology is the UNDP's Human Development Index (HDI), which is a composite measure of a nation's income, health, and education. This index is based on a formula that combines a nation's GDP per capita as a measure of income; life expectancy at birth as a measure of health; and the adult literacy rate and enrollment in primary, secondary, and higher education as measures of education. Figure 9.4 "International Human Development, 2008" shows how nations rank according to the HDI. As will be evident, this map looks fairly similar to the map in Figure 9.3 "Global Stratification Map" that was based only on GDP per capita; the nations that rank high on human development are the wealthiest nations, and those that rank lowest on human development, such as Ethiopia and Rwanda, are the poorest nations.

Figure 9.4 International Human Development, 2008

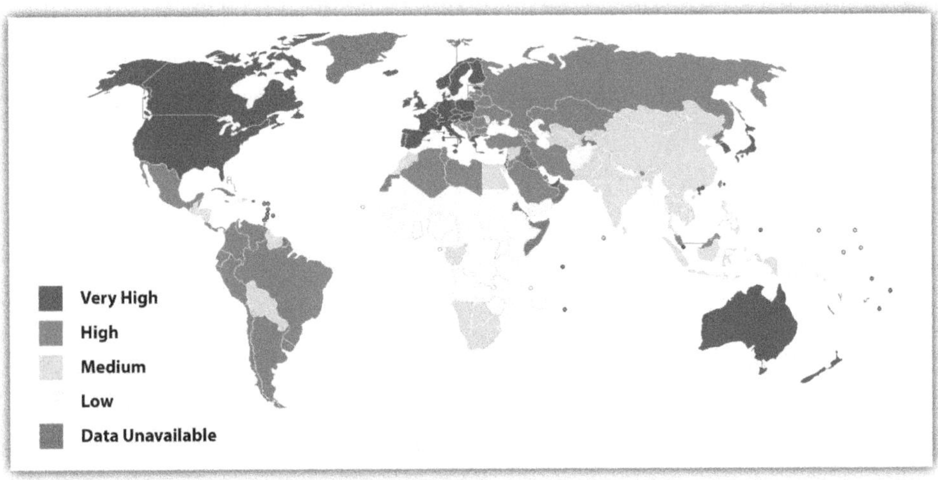

Source: Adapted from United Nations Development Programme. (2010). International human development indicators. Retrieved from http://hdr.undp.org/en/data/map.

This scene illustrates poverty in Ethiopia. Nations that rank lowest on human development, such as Ethiopia, also are the poorest nations.

David Stanley – Coffee Beans Drying – CC BY 2.0.

This similarity prompts some observers to say that the HDI is not really that much of an improvement over typologies based only on GDP per capita or similar economic measures. Still, the HDI has been widely used since the 1990s and reminds us that nations differ dramatically not only in their economic well-being but also in their social well-being. However, because health, education, and other social indicators do depend so heavily on wealth, our discussion of global stratification for the remainder of this chapter will use the familiar classification of wealthy, middle-income, and poor nations. We now highlight the basic differences among these three categories of nations.

Wealthy Nations

The wealthy nations are the most industrialized nations, and they consist primarily of the nations of North America and Western Europe; Australia, Japan, and New Zealand; and certain other nations in the Middle East and Asia (e.g., Japan and Singapore). Many of them were the first nations to become industrialized starting in the 19th century, when the Industrial Revolution began, and their early industrialization certainly contributed to the great wealth they enjoy today. Yet it is also true that many Western European nations were also wealthy before the Industrial Revolution, thanks in part to the fact that they had been colonial powers and acquired wealth from the resources of the lands they colonized.

Although there is much poverty in England, where this home is located, people in England and other wealthy nations live a much more comfortable existence than people in middle-income and poor nations.

Anguskirk – Avington Park mansion in Hampshire – CC BY-NC-ND 2.0.

Although wealthy nations constitute only about one-sixth of the world's population, they hold about four-fifths of the world's entire wealth. They are the leading nations in industry, high finance, and information technology and exercise political, economic, and cultural influence across the planet. As the global economic crisis that began in 2007 illustrates, when the economies of just a few wealthy nations suffer, the economies of other nations and indeed of the entire world can suffer. Although each of the world's wealthy nations is internally stratified to a greater or lesser degree, these nations as a group live a much more comfortable existence than middle-income nations and, especially, poor nations. People in wealthy nations are healthier and more educated, and they enjoy longer lives. At the same time, wealthy nations use up more than their fair share of the world's natural resources, and their high level of industrialization causes them to pollute and otherwise contribute to climate change to a far greater degree than is true of nations in the other two categories.

Middle-Income Nations

Middle-income nations are generally less industrialized than wealthy nations but more industrialized than poor nations. They consist primarily of nations in Central and South America, Eastern Europe, and parts of Africa and Asia and constitute about one-third of the world's population. Many of these nations have abundant natural resources but still have high levels of poverty, partly because political and economic leaders sell the resources to wealthy nations and keep much of the income from these sales for themselves.

Chile, depicted here, is one of the many middle-income nations found in South America. Several of these nations are rich in natural resources but still have high levels of poverty.

saf2285 – Coloured houses in Valparaiso – CC BY 2.0.

There is much variation in income and wealth within the middle-income category, even within the same continent. In South America, for example, the gross national income per capita in Chile, adjusted to U.S. dollars, is $13,270 (2008 figures), compared to only $4,140 in Bolivia (Population Reference Bureau, 2009). Many international organizations and scholars thus find it useful to further divide middle-income nations into upper-middle-income nations and lower-middle-income nations. Not surprisingly, many more people in the latter nations live in dire economic circumstances than those in the former nations. In Bolivia, for example, 30% of the population lives on less than $2 per day, compared to only 5% in Chile.

Poor Nations

Poor nations are certainly the least industrialized and most agricultural of all the world's countries. This category consists primarily of nations in Africa and parts of Asia and constitutes roughly half of the world's population. They have some natural resources that political leaders again sell to wealthier nations while keeping much of the income they gain from these sales. Many of these nations rely heavily on one or two crops, and if weather conditions render a crop unproductive in a particular season, the nations' hungry become even hungrier. By the same token, if economic conditions reduce the price of a crop or other natural resource, the income from exports of these commodities plummets, and these already poor nations become even poorer. An example of this latter problem occurred in Vietnam, a leading exporter of coffee. As coffee prices rose during the 1990s, Vietnam expanded its coffee production by greatly increasing the amount of acreage devoted to growing coffee beans. When the price of coffee plummeted in the early 2000s, Vietnam's coffee industry, including the farmers who grow coffee, suffered huge losses. Many farmers destroyed their coffee plants to be able to grow other crops they thought would be more profitable (Huy, 2010). Because farmers in poor nations often change their crops in this manner for economic reasons, it is difficult for these nations to sustain a stable agricultural industry.

People in poor nations live in the most miserable conditions possible.

United Nations Photo – Maslakh Camp for Displaced, Afghanistan – CC BY-NC-ND 2.0.

By any standard, people in these nations live a desperate existence in the most miserable conditions possible. They suffer from AIDS and other deadly diseases, live on the edge of starvation, and lack indoor plumbing, electricity, and other modern conveniences that most Americans take for granted. Most of us have seen unforgettable photos or video footage of African children with stick-thin limbs and distended stomachs reflecting severe malnutrition. We revisit their plight in Chapter 9 "Global Stratification", Section 9.2 "The Impact of Global Poverty".

Global Poverty

In addition to classifying nations according to their ranking on a stratification typology, scholars and international organizations also determine the level of poverty in each nation. This determination provides valuable information beyond a nation's GDP per capita or similar measure of wealth. Wealth and poverty are, of course, highly correlated: generally speaking, the wealthier a nation, the lower its level of poverty. However, this correlation is not perfect, and considering nations only in terms of their wealth may obscure important differences in their levels of poverty. For example, two nations, which we will call Nation A and Nation B, may have similar GDP per capita. In Nation A, wealth from its GDP is fairly evenly distributed, and relatively few people are poor. In Nation B, almost all wealth is held by a small number of incredibly rich people, and many people are poor. A nation's level of poverty thus tells us what proportion of the population is living in dire straits, regardless of the nation's level of wealth.

The measurement of global poverty is important for additional reasons (Haughton & Khandker, 2009). First, political and economic officials will not recognize the problem of poverty and try to do something about it unless they have reliable poverty data to motivate them to do so and to guide their decisions. As two experts on international poverty note, "It is easy to ignore the poor if they are statistically invisible" (Haughton & Khandker, 2009, p. 3). Second, valid measures of poverty reveal which regions of the world are poorest and which people in a given nation are poorest in terms of household characteristics (e.g., households headed by a single woman), location (e.g., region of country or urban vs. rural), and other factors. This type of knowledge enables antipoverty programs and strategies to be focused on the locations and people in those locations who are most in need of help. Third, valid measures of poverty enable officials and policymakers to know how well efforts to help the poor are working, as a poverty measure after some intervention can be compared to the poverty measure before the intervention.

Although it is important, then, to measure the poverty level of the nations of the world, it is rather difficult to do so. One problem is that the different nations have different standards of living. If an American woman who has a family to feed earns $10 per day, or about $3,650 per year, she and her family are very poor by American standards. However, a woman who earns the equivalent of $10 per day in many poor nations would be very wealthy by those nations' standards, and she would be able to afford many more goods and services (because they cost so much less in those nations than in the United States) than her American counterpart.

Another problem was first encountered in Chapter 8 "Social Stratification"'s discussion of poverty in the United States. No matter what income level might be used as an "official" poverty line for the nations of the world, this level is inevitably an arbitrary poverty line. An individual or family whose income is just a bit above the official poverty line is not counted as being officially poor, even though they are still poor for all practical purposes. Moreover, the most common measures of official global poverty ignore *episodic poverty*. As Chapter 8 "Social Stratification" explained, individuals and families may move into and out of poverty within a given year or two, often more than once. Measures of global poverty (as well as measures of U.S. poverty) determine the number of poor people at one point in time and thus provide an underestimate of the number of people who are poor at least once in a given year or two years.

A third problem concerns exactly what is meant by poverty. Although poverty is usually thought of in monetary terms, some analysts emphasize that poverty involves things in addition to money, including inadequate nutrition, illiteracy, and other correlates of poverty. These analysts favor using measures such as calorie consumption or degree of malnutrition as indicators of poverty. Although these and related measures are indeed often used, monetary measures are most common and will be emphasized here.

Despite these problems, measures of global poverty are still useful for the reasons stated earlier. How, then, is global poverty measured? A very common and popular measure is one used by the World Bank, an international institution, funded by wealthy nations, that provides loans, grants, and other aid to help poor and middle-income nations develop their infrastructure and thus reduce their poverty. Each year the World Bank publishes its *World Development Report,* which, as its name implies, provides statistics and other information on the economic and social well-being of the globe's almost 200 nations. The World Bank puts the official global poverty line (which is considered a measure of *extreme* poverty) at income under $1.25 per person per day, which amounts to about $456 yearly per person or $1,825 for a family of four. According to this measure, 1.4 billion people, making up more than one-fifth of the world's population and more than one-fourth of the population of developing (poor and middle-income) nations, are poor. This level of poverty rises to 40% of South Asia and 51% of sub-Saharan Africa (Haughton & Khandker, 2009).

In view of the measurement problems noted earlier, the actual number of poor people worldwide is certainly much higher than this figure. Note also that the official global poverty line is based on an exceedingly low income level. By this standard, most of the millions of Americans commonly considered to be poor (see Chapter 8 "Social Stratification") would not be considered poor. Moreover, despite the lower standard of living in developing nations, this income level is so low as to underestimate the actual number of poor people in some of these nations.

Returning to the issue of episodic poverty discussed earlier, the World Bank has begun to emphasize the concept of **vulnerability to poverty**, which refers to a significant probability that people who are not officially poor will become poor within the next year. Determining vulnerability to poverty is important because it enables antipoverty strategies to be aimed at those most at risk for sliding into poverty, with the hope of preventing them from doing so.

The World Bank has begun to emphasize vulnerability to poverty. Many people who are not officially poor have a good chance of becoming poor within a year. Strategies to prevent this from happening are a major focus of the World Bank.

Wikimedia Commons – CC BY-SA 2.0.

Vulnerability to poverty appears widespread; in several developing nations, about one-fourth of the population is always poor, while almost one-third is sometimes poor, or vulnerable to poverty, slipping into and out of poverty. In these nations, then, more than half the population is always or sometimes poor. Haughton and Khandker (2009, p. 246) summarize this situation: "As typically defined, vulnerability to poverty is more widespread than poverty itself. A wide swathe of society risks poverty at some point of time; put another way, in most societies, only a relatively modest portion of society may be considered as economically secure."

Poverty Indexes

The United Nations Development Programme (UNDP), which developed the Human Development Index, discussed earlier, to measure global stratification, also developed a similar measure, the Human Poverty Index (HPI), to measure global poverty, and it has reported this measure since the 1990s. This measure reflects UNDP's belief that poverty means more than a lack of money and that measures of poverty must include nonmonetary components of social well-being. Accordingly, the HPI incorporates measures of the following indicators for developing nations: (a) the probability of not surviving to age 40, (b) the percentage of adults who are illiterate, (c) the percentage of people without access to clean water, and (d) the percentage of underweight children. In UNDP's 2009 Human Development Report, the five poorest countries according to HPI were Afghanistan, Niger,

Mali, Chad, and Burkina Faso, with more than half the population in each of these countries classified as poor (United Nations Development Programme, 2009).

Although the HPI has been very useful, it was recently replaced by a more comprehensive measure, the Multidimensional Poverty Index (MPI). The MPI incorporates a range of deprivation measures applied to each nation's households that is fuller than that of the HPI. Households are considered poor according to their composite score on three categories of indicators of deprivation:

1. Health
    1. Child mortality (any child in the household has died)
    2. Nutrition (anyone in the family is malnourished)
2. Education
    1. Schooling (no household member has completed 5 years of schooling)
    2. Enrollment (any child in the family is not in school before grade 9)
3. Standard of living
    1. Electricity (the household does not have electricity)
    2. Drinking water (the household does not have access to clean drinking water)
    3. Sanitation (the household does not have adequate disposal of human waste)
    4. Flooring (the floor is made out of dirt, sand, or manure [dung])
    5. Cooking fuel (the household cooks with charcoal, dung, or wood)
    6. Assets (the household does not own more than one of the following: bicycle, motorbike, radio, telephone, or television)

A person is considered poor if he or she experiences deprivation in any of the following combinations of indicators:

- any two health and/or education indicators, **or**
- all six standard of living indicators, **or**
- one health/education indicator plus three standard of living indicators.

When the MPI is used to measure poverty in 104 developing nations, 1.7 billion people, amounting to one-third the population of these nations, live in poverty. Half of the poor people on the planet according to the MPI live in South Asia, and one-fourth live in Africa (Alkire & Santos, 2010). The five poorest nations according to the MPI are all African: Niger, Ethiopia, Mali, Burkina Faso, and Burundi. In these nations, at least 85% of the population is poor.

Although monetary and index measures of global poverty yield somewhat different results, the measures are still fairly highly correlated, and they all indicate that the poorest regions of the world are Africa and South Asia.

These measures have played an essential role in our understanding of global poverty and in international efforts to address it and its consequences.

Global Inequality

As first discussed in Chapter 8 “Social Stratification”, another dimension of stratification is *economic inequality*, which refers to the gap between the richest and poorest segments of society. We saw then that the United States has more economic inequality than other Western democracies, as the income and wealth difference between the richest and poorest people in the United States is greater than that in these other nations.

As this discussion suggested, to understand stratification it is important to understand economic inequality. Global economic inequality (hereafter *global inequality*) has two dimensions. The first dimension involves the extremely large economic gap between the wealthy and poor nations of the world (Neckerman & Torche, 2007). We saw evidence of this gap in our earlier Monopoly discussion: the richest one-fifth of nations have almost 75% of the world’s income, while the poorest fifth of nations have only 1.5% of the world’s income. Dividing the larger figure by the smaller figure (75 ÷ 1.5) yields a very high income-gap ratio of 50: the income of the richest fifth of nations is 50 times greater than the income of the poorest fifth of nations. By comparison, in the United States the income of the richest fifth of the population is 11.5 times higher than the income of the poorest fifth (see Chapter 8 “Social Stratification”). Although economic inequality within the United States is greater than its Western counterparts, economic inequality between the richest and poorest nations is much greater yet.

The second form of global inequality involves comparisons of the degree of economic inequality found within each nation. This type of information adds a valuable complement to measures of wealth (e.g., GDP per capita) and measures of poverty (e.g., the World Bank’s $1.25 per person per day). For example, Nation A and Nation B may have similar levels of poverty. In Nation A, however, poverty is evenly distributed throughout the population, and almost everyone is poor. In Nation B, a small segment of the population is very rich, while a much larger segment is very poor. Nation B would thus have more economic inequality than Nation A.

As our comparison of the United States with other Western democracies illustrated, some nations have higher levels of economic inequality, and some nations have lower levels. Around the world, inequality is generally higher in agricultural nations (or those that are poor or middle-income) and lower in industrial nations (or the wealthiest ones in the world). (See Chapter 5 “Social Structure and Social Interaction”.) In agricultural societies, a small elite usually owns most of the land and is very wealthy, and the masses of people either work for the elite or on their own small, poor farms. Many of these societies thus have a high level of economic inequality; however, the poorest of these societies are so poor that there is less wealth for an elite to control, and inequality in these societies thus tends to be somewhat lower. Industrial societies have lower inequality because they have higher literacy rates and more political rights and because they generally provide more opportunity for people to move up the socioeconomic ladder (Nolan & Lenski, 2009).

The most popular measure of economic inequality, and one used by the World Bank, is the *Gini coefficient*. Its calculation need not concern us, but it ranges from 0 to 1, where 0 means that income is the same for everyone (no economic inequality at all, or perfect equality), and 1 means that one person has all the income (perfect inequality). Thus the nearer the Gini coefficient is to 1, the higher the degree of a nation’s economic inequality.

Figure 9.5 "Gini Coefficients, 2007–2008" shows Gini coefficients around the world; economic inequality is indeed higher in the agricultural regions of Latin America and the Caribbean, Africa, South Asia, and elsewhere than in the industrial region of Western Europe. In the developing world, the region of Latin America and the Caribbean has a more advanced agricultural economy than other regions, and it also has the highest degree of inequality, with a small elite owning a great amount of land (Hoffman & Centeno, 2003).

Figure 9.5 Gini Coefficients, 2007–2008

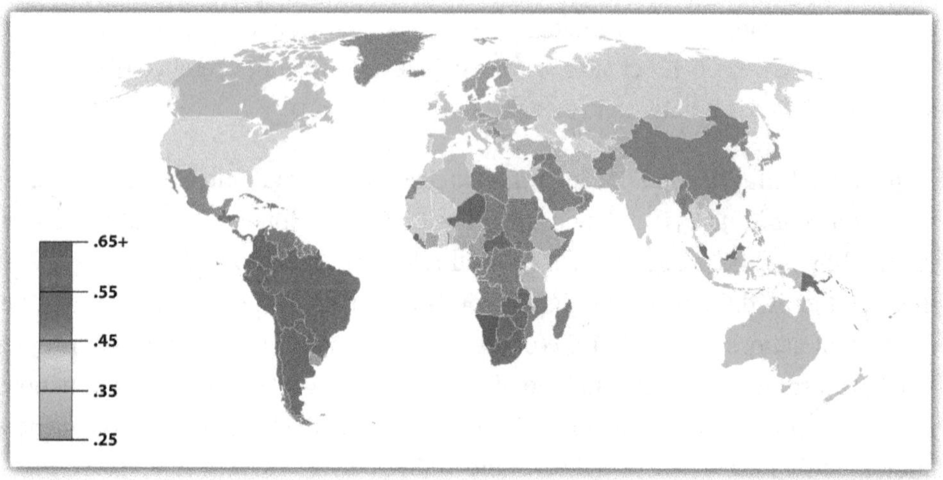

Source: http://commons.wikimedia.org/wiki/File:Gini_Coefficient_World_Human_Development_Report_2007-2008.png.

Another popular measure of economic inequality is the *decile dispersion ratio*. Here the average income or expenditure of people in the richest 10% of a nation is divided by the average income or expenditure of people in the poorest 10% of a nation; the higher the ratio, the greater the income inequality. This measure is cruder than the Gini coefficient because it does not consider the income distribution of the remaining 80% of a nation, but its ratio is more understandable by laypeople. For example, a ratio of 12 means that the average income or expenditure of the richest tenth of a nation's population is 12 times greater than the average income or expenditure of the poorest tenth of a nation's population.

Figure 9.6 "Global Income Inequality (Average Ratio of Income or Expenditure of Wealthiest Tenth of Population to Income or Expenditure of Poorest Tenth)" depicts the average decile dispersion ratio for four groups of nations as determined by the United Nations' HDI: very high development, high development, medium development, and low development. These four groups roughly correspond to wealthy nations (primarily industrial), high-middle-income nations (industrial and agricultural), low-middle-income nations (primarily agricultural), and poor nations (agricultural), respectively. As the figure indicates, overall inequality as measured by the decile dispersion ratio is once again lower for wealthy (industrial) nations than for less wealthy nations that are more agricultural.

Figure 9.6 Global Income Inequality (Average Ratio of Income or Expenditure of Wealthiest Tenth of Population to Income or Expenditure of Poorest Tenth)

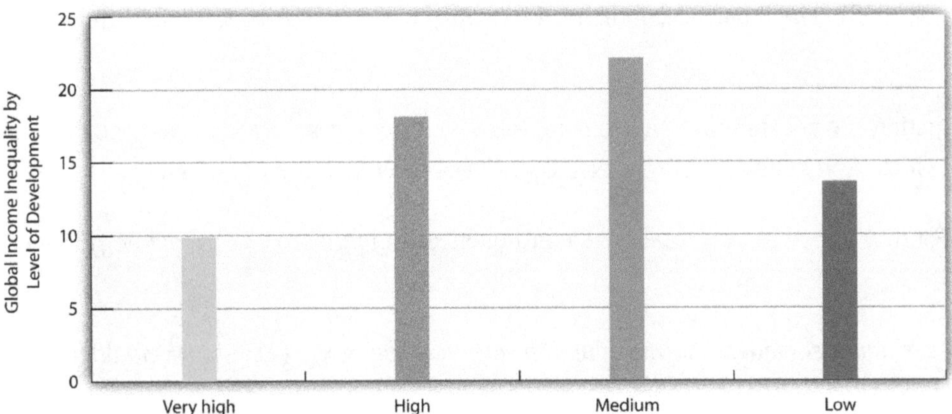

Source: Author's analysis of data from United Nations Development Programme. (2009). *Human development report 2009*. New York, NY: Author.

Key Takeaways

- The world is greatly stratified. A relatively small number of nations holds most of the world's wealth and income.
- It is useful to classify the world's nations as wealthy nations, middle-income nations, and poor nations. These three groups of nations differ dramatically in their standard of living and many other aspects of human existence.
- It is important for several reasons to measure global poverty and global inequality. These measures indicate which countries are most in need of help, and they help remind us of the problems they measure.

For Your Review

1. Write a brief essay that summarizes the various problems in measuring global poverty and the reasons for developing and using accurate measures of global poverty.
2. Why is it useful to know the extent of a nation's inequality in addition to the extent of its poverty?

References

Alkire, S., & Santos, M. E. (2010). *Acute multidimensional poverty: A new index for developing countries*. Oxford, England: Oxford Poverty & Human Development Initiative, University of Oxford.

Dikhanov, Y. (2005). *Trends in global income distribution, 1970–2000, and scenarios for 2015*. New York, NY: United Nations Development Programme.

Haughton, J., & Khandker, S. R. (2009). *Handbook on poverty and inequality*. Washington, DC: World Bank.

Hoffman, K., & Centeno, M. A. (2003). The lopsided continent: Inequality in Latin America. *Annual Review of Sociology, 29*(1), 363–390.

Huy, N. Q. (2010). Coffee production and consumption in Vietnam. Retrieved from http://www.docstoc.com/docs/27139628/COFFEE-PRODUCTION-AND-CONSUMPTION-IN-VIETNAM-Prepared-by-Nguyen-.

Neckerman, K. M., & Torche, F. (2007). Inequality: Causes and consequences. *Annual Review of Sociology, 33*(1), 335–357.

Nolan, P., & Lenski, G. (2009). *Human societies: An introduction to macrosociology* (11th ed.). Boulder, CO: Paradigm.

Population Reference Bureau. (2009). *2009 world population data sheet*. Washington, DC: Author.

United Nations Development Programme. (2005). *Human development report 2005*. New York, NY: Author.

9.2 The Impact of Global Poverty

Learning Objectives

1. List the major indicators of human development that reflect the impact of global poverty.
2. Describe how women in poor nations fare worse than men in those nations.
3. Provide two examples that illustrate the plight of children in poor nations.

Behind all the numbers for poverty and inequality presented in the preceding pages are the lives of more than 1.4 billion desperately poor people across the world who live in some of the worst conditions possible. AIDS, malaria, starvation, and other deadly diseases are common. Many children die before reaching adolescence, and many adults die before reaching what in the richest nations would be considered middle age. Many people in the poorest nations are illiterate, and a college education remains as foreign to them as their way of life would be to us. Occasionally, we see the world's poor in TV news reports or in film documentaries before they fade quickly from our minds. Meanwhile, millions of people on our planet die every year because they do not have enough to eat, because they lack access to clean water or adequate sanitation, or because they lack access to medicine that is found in every CVS, Rite Aid, and Walgreens in the United States.

As noted earlier, the United Nations Development Programme, the World Bank, and other international agencies issue annual reports on human development indicators that show the impact of living in a poor nation. This section begins with a look at some of the most important of these indicators.

Human Development

The status of a nation's health is commonly considered perhaps the most important indicator of human development. When we look around the world, we see that global poverty is literally a matter of life and death. The clearest evidence of this fact comes from data on **life expectancy**, the average number of years that a nation's citizens can be expected to live. Life expectancy certainly differs within each nation, with some people dying younger and others dying older, but poverty and related conditions affect a nation's overall life expectancy to a startling degree.

A map of global life expectancy appears in Figure 9.7 "Average Life Expectancy Across the Globe (Years)". Life expectancy is highest in North America, Western Europe, and certain other regions of the world and lowest in Africa and South Asia, where life expectancy in many nations is some 30 years shorter than in other regions. Another way of visualizing the relationship between global poverty and life expectancy appears in Figure 9.8 "Global Stratification and Life Expectancy, 2006", which depicts average life expectancy for wealthy nations, upper-middle-income nations, lower-middle-income nations, and poor nations. Men in wealthy nations can expect to live 76 years on average, compared to only 56 in poor nations; women in wealthy nations can expect to live 82 years, compared to only 58 in poor nations. Life expectancy in poor nations is thus 20 and 24 years lower, respectively, for the two sexes.

Figure 9.7 Average Life Expectancy Across the Globe (Years)

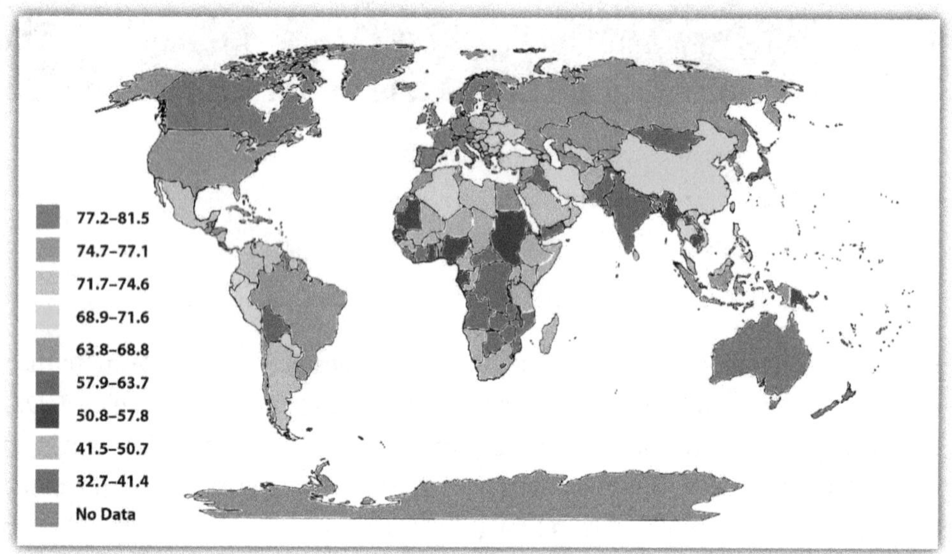

Source: Adapted from Global Education Project. (2004). Human conditions: World life expectancy map. Retrieved from http://www.theglobaleducationproject.org/earth/human-conditions.php.

Figure 9.8 Global Stratification and Life Expectancy, 2006

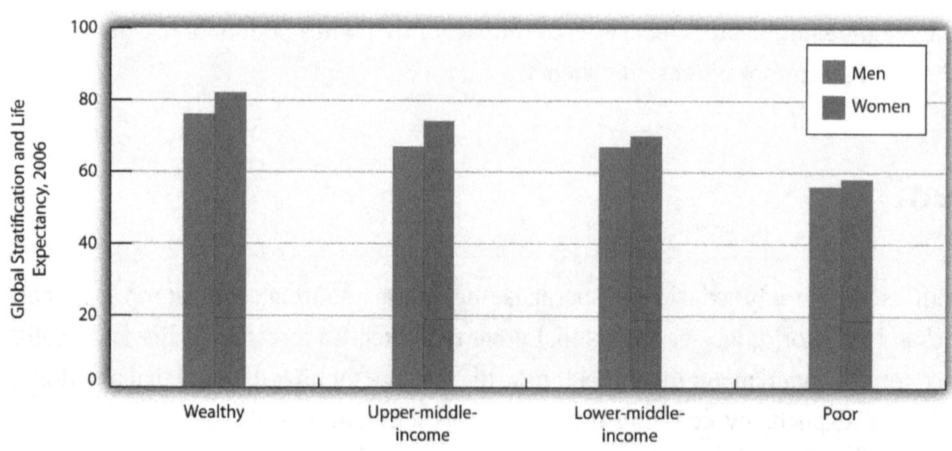

Source: Data from World Bank. (2009). *World development report 2009*. Washington, DC: Author.

Child Mortality

A key contributor to life expectancy and also a significant indicator of human development in its own right is **child mortality**, the number of children who die before age 5 per 1,000 children. As Figure 9.9 "Global Stratification and Child Mortality, 2006" shows, the rate of child mortality in poor nations is 135 per 1,000 children, meaning that 13.5% of all children in these nations die before age 5. In a few African nations, child mortality exceeds 200 per 1,000. In contrast, the rate in wealthy nations is only 7 per 1,000. Children in poor nations are thus about 19 times (13.5 ÷ 0.7) more likely to die before age 5 than children in wealthy nations.

Figure 9.9 Global Stratification and Child Mortality, 2006

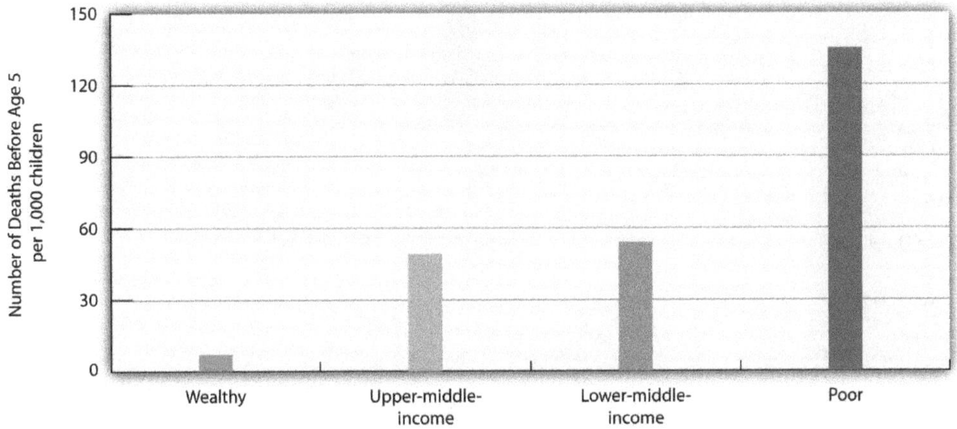

Source: Data from World Bank. (2009). *World development report 2009.* Washington, DC: Author.

Sanitation and Clean Water

Two other important indicators of a nation's health are access to adequate sanitation (disposal of human waste) and access to clean water. When people lack adequate sanitation and clean water, they are at much greater risk from life-threatening diarrhea, from serious infectious diseases such as cholera and typhoid, and from parasitic diseases such as schistosomiasis (World Health Organization, 2010). About 2.4 billion people around the world, almost all of them in poor and middle-income nations, do not have adequate sanitation, and more than 2 million, most of them children, die annually from diarrhea. More than 40 million people worldwide, almost all of them again in poor and middle-income nations, suffer from a parasitic infection caused by flatworms.

As Figure 9.10 "Global Stratification and Access to Adequate Sanitation, 2006" and Figure 9.11 "Global Stratification and Access to Clean Water, 2006" show, access to adequate sanitation and clean water is strongly related to national wealth. Poor nations are much less likely than wealthier nations to have adequate access to both sanitation and clean water. Adequate sanitation is virtually universal in wealthy nations but is available to only 38% of people in poor nations. Clean water is also nearly universal in wealthy nations but is available to only 67% of people in poor nations.

Figure 9.10 Global Stratification and Access to Adequate Sanitation, 2006

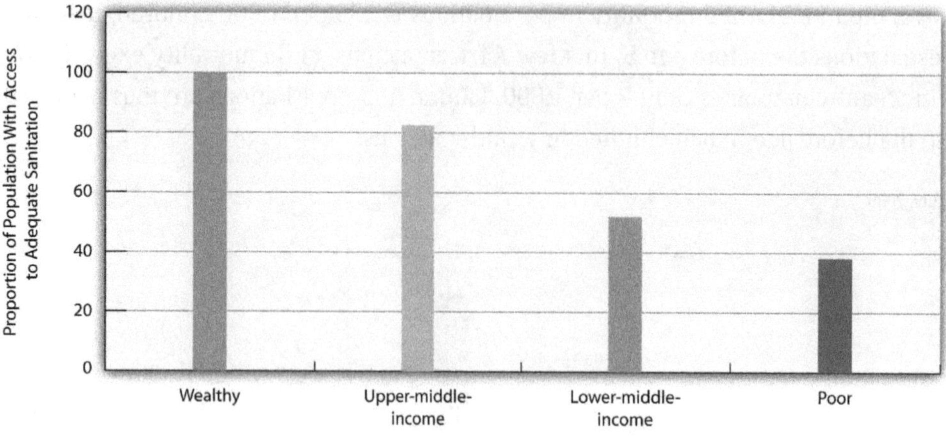

Source: Data from World Bank. (2010). Health nutrition and population statistics. Retrieved from http://databank.worldbank.org/ddp/home.do?Step=2&id=4.

Figure 9.11 Global Stratification and Access to Clean Water, 2006

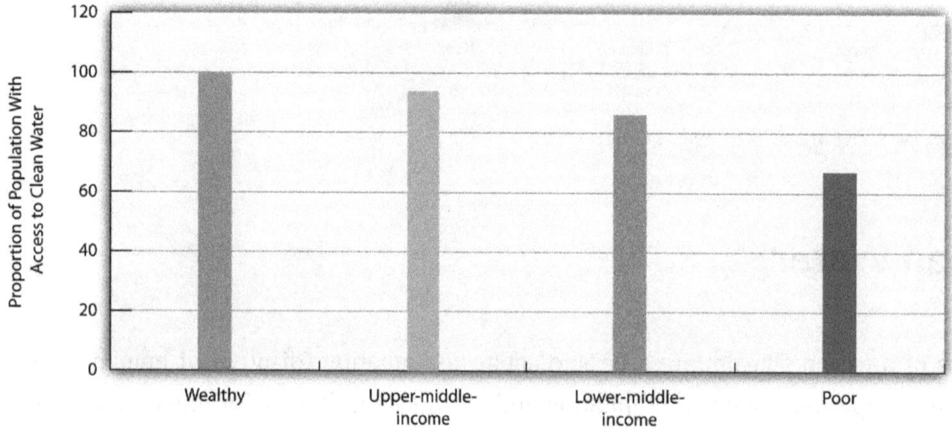

Source: Data from World Bank. (2010). Health nutrition and population statistics. Retrieved from http://databank.worldbank.org/ddp/home.do?Step=2&id=4.

Malnutrition

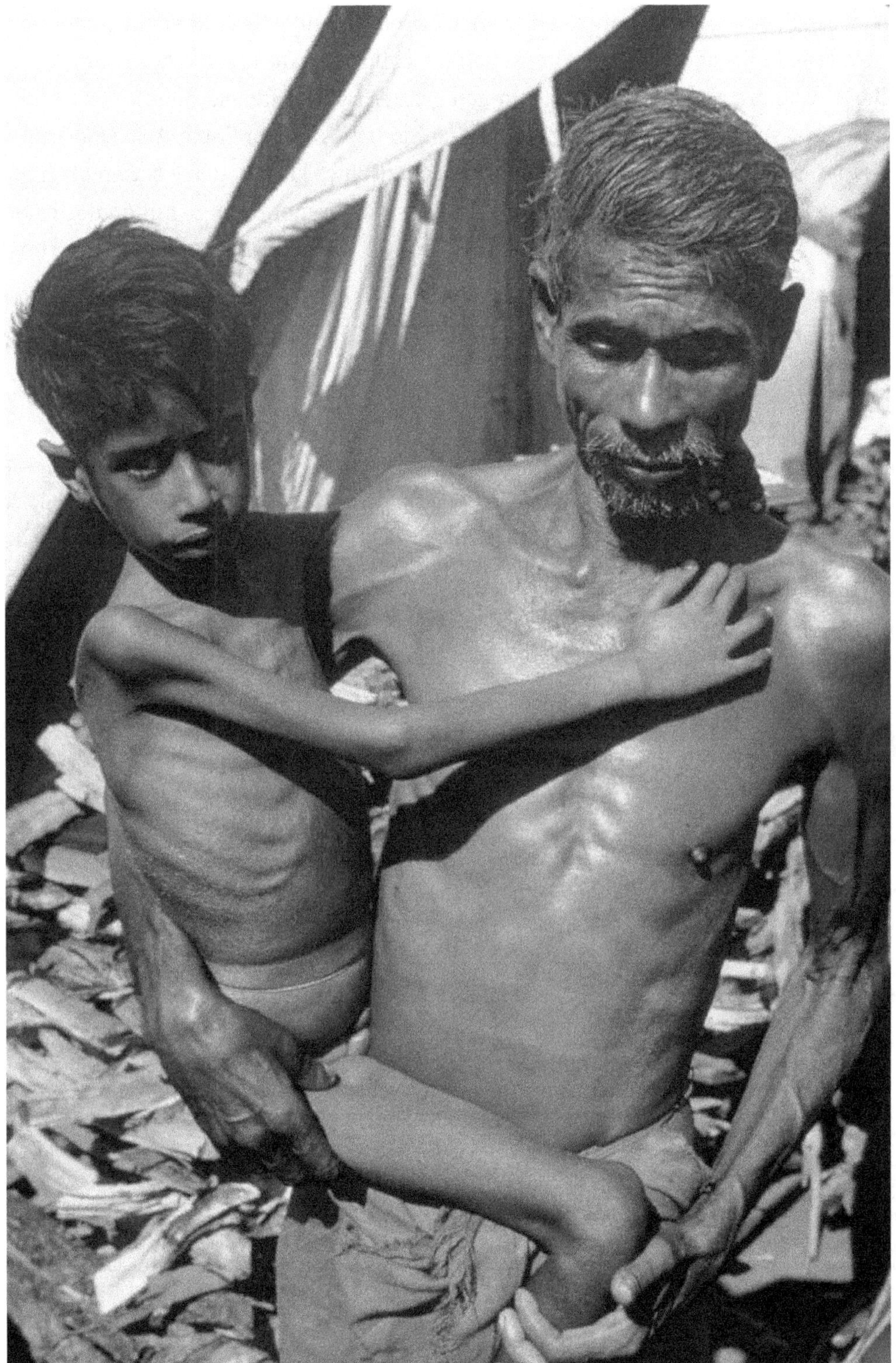

About one-fifth of the population of poor nations, some 800 million individuals altogether, are malnourished.

CDC – public domain.

Another health indicator is **malnutrition**. This problem is caused by a lack of good food combined with infections and diseases such as diarrhea that sap the body of essential nutrients. About one-fifth of the population of poor nations, or about 800 million individuals, are malnourished; looking just at children, in developing nations more than one-fourth of children under age 5, or about 150 million altogether, are underweight. Half of all these children live in only three nations: Bangladesh, India, and Pakistan; almost half the children in these and other South Asian nations are underweight. Children who are malnourished are at much greater risk for fat and muscle loss, brain damage, blindness, and death; perhaps you have seen video footage of children in Africa or South Asia who are so starved that they look like skeletons. Not surprisingly, child malnutrition contributes heavily to the extremely high rates of child mortality that we just examined and is estimated to be responsible for more than 5 million deaths of children annually (UNICEF, 2006; World Health Organization, 2010). The "Sociology Making a Difference" box further discusses the issue of world hunger.

Sociology Making a Difference

World Hunger and the Scarcity Fallacy

A popular belief is that world hunger exists because there is too little food to feed too many people in poor nations in Africa, Asia, and elsewhere. Sociologists Stephen J. Scanlan, J. Craig Jenkins, and Lindsey Peterson (2010) call this belief the "scarcity fallacy." According to these authors, "The conventional wisdom is that world hunger exists primarily because of natural disasters, population pressure, and shortfalls in food production" (p. 35). However, this conventional wisdom is mistaken, as world hunger stems not from a shortage of food but from the inability to deliver what is actually a sufficient amount of food to the world's poor. As Scanlan and colleagues note,

> A good deal of thinking and research in sociology suggests that world hunger has less to do with the shortage of food than with a shortage of *affordable* or *accessible* food. Sociologists have found that social inequalities, distribution systems, and other economic and political factors create barriers to food access. (p. 35)
>
> This sociological view has important implications for how the world should try to reduce global hunger, say these authors. International organizations such as the World Bank and several United Nations agencies have long believed that hunger is due to food scarcity, and this belief underlies the typical approaches to reducing world hunger that focus on increasing food supplies with new technologies and developing more efficient methods of delivering food. But if food scarcity is not a problem, then other approaches are necessary.
>
> Scanlan and colleagues argue that food scarcity is, in fact, not the problem that international agencies and most people believe it to be:
>
> > The bigger problem with emphasizing food supply as the problem, however, is that scarcity is largely a myth. On a per capita basis, food is more plentiful today than any other time in human history….[E]ven in times of localized production shortfalls or regional famines there has long been a global food surplus. (p. 35)
> >
> > If the problem is not a lack of food, then what is the problem? Scanlan and colleagues argue that the real problem is a lack of access to food and a lack of equitable distribution of food: "Rather than food scarcity, then, we should focus our attention on the persistent inequalities that often accompany the growth in food supply" (p. 36).
> >
> > What are these inequalities? Recognizing that hunger is especially concentrated in the poorest nations, the authors note that these nations lack the funds to import the abundant food that does exist. These nations' poverty, then, is one inequality that leads to world hunger, but gender and ethnic inequalities are also responsible. For example, women around the world are more likely than men to suffer from hunger, and hunger is more common in nations with greater rates of gender inequality (as measured by gender differences in education and income, among other criteria). Hunger is also more common among ethnic minorities not only in poor nations but also in wealthier nations. In findings from their own research, these sociologists add, hunger lessens when nations democratize, when political rights are protected, and when gender and ethnic inequality is reduced.
> >
> > If inequality underlies world hunger, they add, then efforts to reduce world hunger will succeed only to the extent that they recognize the importance of inequality in this regard: "To get at inequality, policy must give attention to democratic governance and human rights, fixing the politics of food aid, and tending to the challenges posed by the global economy" (p. 38). For this to happen, they say, food must be upheld as a "fundamental human right." More generally, world hunger cannot be effectively reduced unless and until ethnic and gender inequality is reduced. Scanlan and colleagues conclude,

> The challenge, in short, is to create a more equitable and just society in which food access is ensured for all. Food scarcity matters. However, it is rooted in social conditions and institutional dynamics that must be the focus of any policy innovations that might make a real difference. (p. 39)

In calling attention to the myth of food scarcity and the inequalities that contribute to world hunger, Scanlan and colleagues point to better strategies for addressing this significant international problem. Once again, sociology is making a difference.

Adult Literacy

Moving from the area of health, a final indicator of human development is **adult literacy**, the percentage of people 15 and older who can read and write a simple sentence. Once again we see that people in poor and middle-income nations are far worse off (see Figure 9.12 "Global Stratification and Adult Literacy, 2008"). In poor nations, only about 69% of adults 15 and older can read and write a simple sentence. The high rate of illiteracy in poor nations not only reflects their poverty but also contributes to it, as people who cannot read and write are obviously at a huge disadvantage in the labor market.

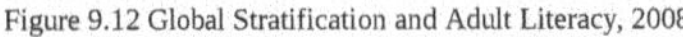

Figure 9.12 Global Stratification and Adult Literacy, 2008

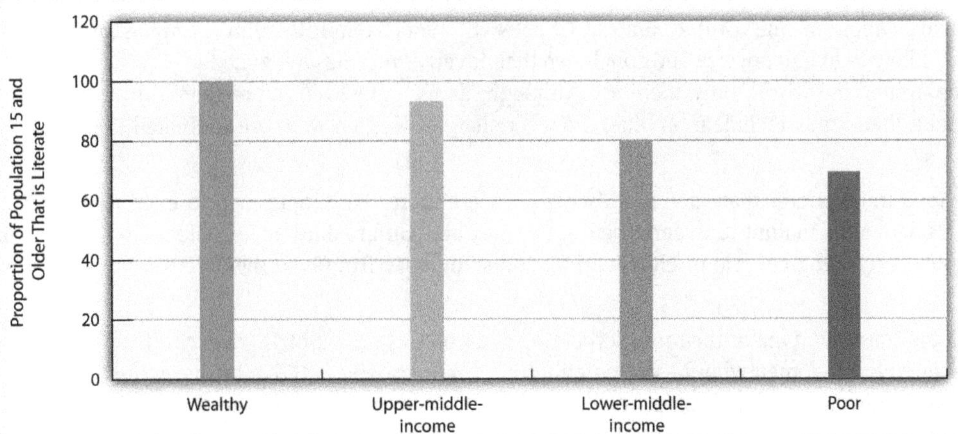

Source: Data from World Bank. (2010). Health nutrition and population statistics. Retrieved from http://databank.worldbank.org/ddp/home.do?Step=2&id=4.

United States and Uganda

Before we leave the issue of human development, it is instructive to compare the United States, an extremely wealthy nation, with one poor nation from Africa, Uganda, on some economic and human development indicators as presented in Table 9.1 "The United States and Uganda". As will be obvious, Americans and Ugandans live very different lives, notwithstanding the high degree of poverty found in the United States compared to other wealthy nations. The typical American lives a comfortable life that the typical Ugandan can only dream of, while the typical Ugandan lives a life that the typical American would find only in her or his worst nightmare.

Table 9.1 The United States and Uganda

	United States	Uganda
Gross national income per capita ($)	46,970	1,140
Population living below $2 per day (%)	—	76
Infant mortality rate (number of infant deaths per 1,000 live births)	6.6	76
Life expectancy at birth (years)	78	50
Lifetime births per woman	2.1	6.7
Underweight children, ages < 5 (%)	1	20
Motor vehicles per 1,000 population	787	6

Source: Population Reference Bureau. (2009). *2009 world population data sheet.* Washington, DC: Author.

The Status of Women

In discussing stratification in the United States, Chapter 8 "Social Stratification" emphasized that women are disproportionately likely to live in poverty and concluded that poverty "thus has a female face." What is true in the United States is also true around the world, only more so. Although, as we have seen, more than 1.4 billion people on earth are desperately poor, their ranks include more than their fair share of women, who are estimated to make up 70% of the world's poor.

Because women tend to be poorer than men worldwide, they are more likely than men to experience all the problems that poverty causes, including malnutrition and disease. But they also suffer additional problems. Some of these problems derive from women's physiological role of childbearing, and some arise from how they are treated simply because they are women.

Let's first look at childbearing. One of the most depressing examples of how global poverty affects women is **maternal mortality**, or the number of women who die during childbirth for every 100,000 live births. More than 500,000 women die worldwide from complications during pregnancy or childbirth. Maternal mortality usually results from one or more of the following: inadequate prenatal nutrition, disease and illness, and inferior obstetrical care, all of which are much more common in poor nations than in wealthy nations. Figure 9.13 "Global Stratification and Maternal Mortality, 2005" shows the difference that national poverty makes for maternal mortality. In wealthy nations, the rate of maternal mortality is a minuscule 10 per 100,000 births, but in poor nations the rate is a distressingly high 790 per 100,000 births, equivalent to almost 1 death for every 100 births. Women in poor nations are thus 79 times more likely than those in wealthy nations to die from complications during pregnancy or childbirth. Figure 9.14 "Global Stratification and Medically Assisted Births, 2000–2007" suggests a reason for this difference, as it shows that births in poor nations are less than half as likely as those in wealthy nations to be attended by skilled medical staff.

Figure 9.13 Global Stratification and Maternal Mortality, 2005

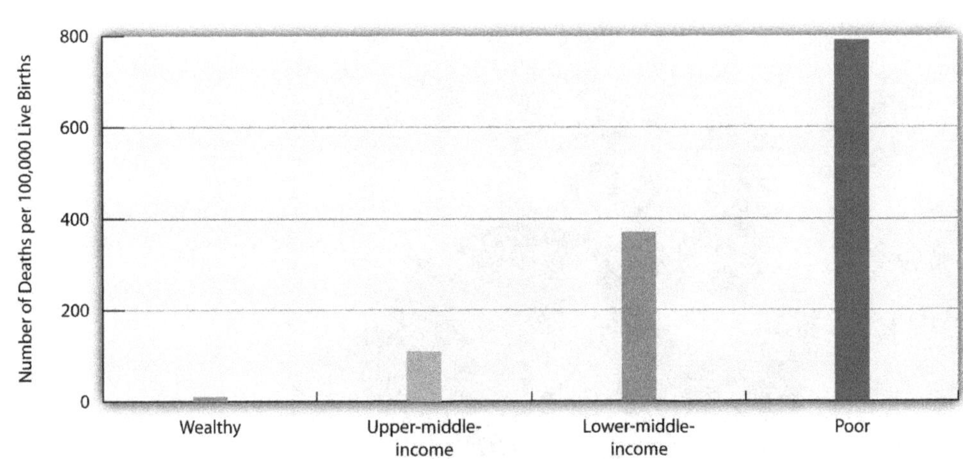

Source: Data from World Bank. (2010). Health nutrition and population statistics. Retrieved from http://databank.worldbank.org/ddp/home.do?Step=2&id=4.

Figure 9.14 Global Stratification and Medically Assisted Births, 2000–2007

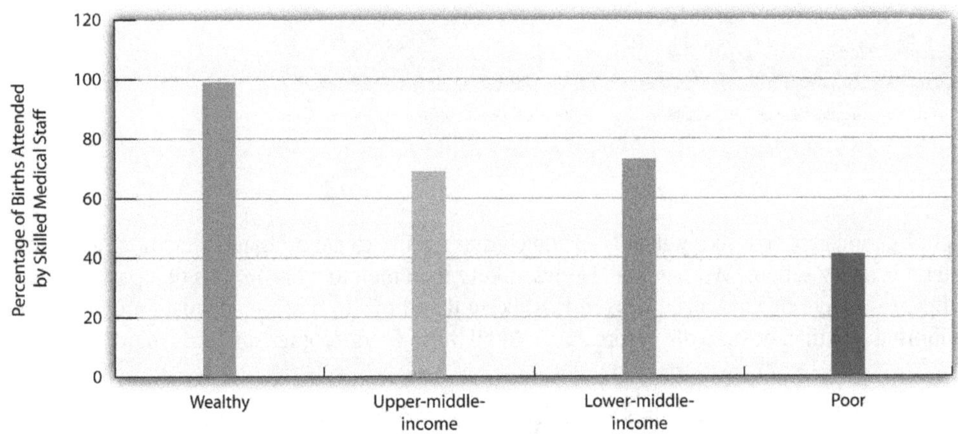

Source: Data from World Bank. (2010). Health nutrition and population statistics. Retrieved from http://databank.worldbank.org/ddp/home.do?Step=2&id=4.

In addition to these problems, women in poor nations fare worse than men in other ways because of how they are treated as women. One manifestation of this fact is the violence they experience. About one-third of women worldwide have been raped or beaten, and Amnesty International (2004) calls violence against women "the greatest human rights scandal of our times." Although violence against women certainly occurs in wealthy nations, it is more common and extreme in poor and middle-income nations. More than half of women in Uganda, for example, have been physically or sexually abused (Amnesty International, 2010). In India and Pakistan, thousands of women are killed every year in **dowry deaths**, in which a new wife is murdered by her husband and/or his relatives if she does not pay the groom money or goods (Kethineni & Srinivasan, 2009).

In India and Pakistan, thousands of new wives every year are murdered in dowry deaths because they have not provided their husbands a suitable amount of money and goods.

Wikimedia Commons – CC BY 2.0.

Beyond violence, women in poor nations are less likely than their male counterparts to get a higher education, and girls are less likely than boys to attend primary school. Women are also less likely than men to work in jobs that pay a decent wage and to hold political office. In many poor nations, girls are less likely than boys to receive adequate medical care when they become ill and are more likely than boys to die before age 5. In all these ways, women and girls in poor nations especially suffer.

The United Nations Development Programme (UNDP) uses a *gender empowerment measure* (GEM) to determine the status of women compared to men in about half the nations across the world. This measure is based on such things as the percentage of national legislative seats and professional and technical jobs held by women and the ratio of female-to-male earned income. In the UNDP's 2009 Human Development Report, the nations with the five highest GEM rankings were Sweden, Norway, Finland, Denmark, and the Netherlands (the United States ranked only 18th), all very wealthy nations; the nations with the five lowest GEM rankings were Yemen, Bangladesh, Egypt, Saudi Arabia, and Algeria.

All these latter nations are very poor with the exception of Saudi Arabia, which is fairly wealthy. Still, women in Saudi Arabia are not allowed to drive a car or to vote. Each woman must have a male relative who acts as her legal guardian; a woman cannot work outside the home or travel outside the country without her guardian's permission. The two sexes are segregated in public: women have women-only stores to shop in and women-only lines in fast-food restaurants to stand in. Law enforcement agents watch carefully to make sure that the sexes do not interact in public (Zoepf, 2010).

Two sets of international statistics cited by writers Nicholas D. Kristof and Sheryl WuDunn (2009) are especially troubling. Because women outlive men, ordinarily there should be more females than males in a country. Yet China has 107 males for every 100 females, and India has 108 males for every 100 females. In these nations, girls and women have died at far greater numbers than men because of abuse, murder, and lack of health care, only because they are female. It is estimated that the number of "missing women" in the world today because of these problems is between 60 million and 107 million.

A second set of statistics concerns sexual slavery. As Kristof and WuDunn (2009, p. MM28) summarize this problem,

> In the developing world,…millions of women and girls are actually enslaved. While a precise number is hard to pin down, the International Labor Organization, a U.N. agency, estimates that at any one time there are 12.3 million people engaged in forced labor of all kinds, including sexual servitude. In Asia alone about one million children working in the sex trade are held in conditions

indistinguishable from slavery, according to a U.N. report. Girls and women are locked in brothels and beaten if they resist, fed just enough to be kept alive and often sedated with drugs—to pacify them and often to cultivate addiction.

This situation is so horrid that Kristof and WuDunn (2009, p. MM28) call for a moral crusade to save women's lives. "In the 19th century," they write, "the paramount moral challenge was slavery. In the 20th century, it was totalitarianism. In this century, it is the brutality inflicted on so many women and girls around the globe: sex trafficking, acid attacks, bride burnings and mass rape." They add that an important reason for global poverty is that women in poor nations are uneducated, victimized by violence, and generally oppressed. For this reason, they say, international organizations are increasingly recognizing that "focusing on women and girls is the most effective way to fight global poverty."

The Status of Children

Because of their size, immaturity, and lack of resources, children are considered the weakest members of any society. When we look around world, we see that this fact of life is also true of the global society. In poor nations, children especially suffer. We have already seen evidence of this suffering in this chapter's earlier discussion of childhood disease, malnutrition, and mortality.

International agencies estimate that 8.8 million children under age 5 died in 2008 across the world, or an average of about 24,000 child deaths every day (You, Wardlaw, Salama, & Jones, 2010). In sub-Saharan Africa, 1 of every 7 children dies before age 5; in South Asia, 1 of every 13 children dies before age 5. Three-fourths of all child deaths occur in only 18 countries, and half of all child deaths occur in only 5 countries: China, the Democratic Republic of the Congo, India, Nigeria, and Pakistan. Diarrhea and pneumonia cause many of the child deaths, of which about 40% occur during the first month of life. The conditions discussed earlier, including inadequate sanitation and lack of access to clean water, account for the bulk of fatal disease that children suffer.

If almost 9 million children under age 5 die annually, other numbers also tell an unsettling tale (UNICEF, 2009):

- 148 million children under age 5 are underweight for their age;
- 101 million children, including more girls than boys, do not attend elementary school;
- 22 million children are not immunized against common diseases;
- 4 million infants die before reaching the age of 1 month;
- 500 million to 1.5 billion children have been exposed to violence or are victims of violence;
- 150 million children aged 5–14 are engaged in child labor;
- 145 million children have had one or both of their biological parents die;
- 70 million girls have experienced genital mutilation; and
- 1.2 million children are victims of trafficking, taken from their parents and subjected to child labor and sexual slavery.

As disturbing as these statistics might be, there is also good news, as much progress has been made during the past few decades in helping the world's children, thanks to agencies such as UNICEF. For example, child mortality worldwide declined from 142 per 1,000 live births in 1970 to 65 per 1,000 in 2008; the rate in Africa declined from 231 to 132. Reflecting this decline, the number of child deaths dropped from 16.7 million in 1970 to 8.8 million in 2008. International efforts have saved millions of children's lives during the past four decades.

Before we leave the issue of children's welfare, it is worth noting one additional problem they face in certain parts of the world. In some developing countries, children are taken by force to join the armed forces or armed groups, or they join out of economic necessity or to escape abuse. These "child soldiers" may bear arms and engage in combat, serve as cooks and messengers, or be sexual slaves. Approximately 300,000 children (under age 18) worldwide are thought to be child soldiers. Beyond the dangers of being involved in arm conflict, these children are not in school and are often sexually abused. Since the 1980s, UNICEF and other international agencies have worked for the release of child soldiers in many nations, including Angola, Burundi, the Democratic Republic of the Congo, Rwanda, Somalia, and Uganda.

Key Takeaways

- Global poverty has a devastating impact. Poor nations suffer tremendously on human development indicators such as health, education, and mortality.
- Women in poor nations fare much worse than men in these nations. They are victims of violence and other abuse because they are women, and they are less likely to attend school and more likely to be poor.
- Children in poor nations are much more likely than those in wealthy nations to die before age 5 and to suffer from malnutrition and disease.

For Your Review

1. Considering all the ways in which poor nations fare much worse than wealthy nations, which one seems to you to be the most important problem that poor nations experience? Explain your answer.
2. Some scholars attribute global violence against women to women's general inequality, and some scholars attribute it to men's biological nature. Why do you think global violence against women is so common?

References

Amnesty International. (2010). *"I can't afford justice": Violence against women in Uganda continues unpunished and unchecked.* London, England: Author.

Amnesty International. (2004). *It's in our hands: Stop violence against women. Summary.* London, England: Author.

Kethineni, S., & Srinivasan, M. (2009). Police handling of domestic violence cases in Tamil Nadu, India. *Journal of Contemporary Criminal Justice, 25,* 202–213.

Kristof, N. D., & WuDunn, S. (2009, August 23). The women's crusade. *The New York Times*, p. MM28.

Scanlan, S. J., Jenkins, J. C., & Peterson, L. (2010). The scarcity fallacy. *Contexts, 9*(1), 34–39.

UNICEF. (2006). *Progress for children: A report card on nutrition.* New York, NY: Author; World Health Organization. (2010). *Children's environmental health.* Retrieved from http://www.who.int/ceh/risks/cehwater2/en/index.html.

UNICEF. (2009). *The state of the world's children: Special edition.* New York, NY: Author.

World Health Organization. (2010). *Children's environmental health.* Retrieved from http://www.who.int/ceh/risks/cehwater2/en/index.html.

You, D., Wardlaw, T., Salama, P., & Jones, G. (2010). Levels and trends in under-5 mortality, 1990–2008. *Lancet, 375*(9709), 100–103.

Zoepf, K. (2010, June 12). Fighting for the right to have limited rights. *The New York Times*, p. A7.

9.3 Explaining Global Stratification

Learning Objectives

1. Describe the main arguments of modernization theory.
2. Describe the main arguments of dependency theory.

Explanations of global stratification parallel those of U.S. stratification (see Chapter 8 “Social Stratification”) in their focus on individual versus structural problems. One type of explanation takes an individual approach by in effect blaming the people in the poorest nations for their own poverty, while a second explanation takes a structural approach in blaming the plight of poor nations on their treatment by the richest ones. Again there is evidence to support both types of explanations, but many sociologists favor the structural explanation. Table 9.2 “Theory Snapshot” summarizes the two sets of explanations.

Table 9.2 Theory Snapshot

Theory	Major assumptions
Modernization theory	Wealthy nations became wealthy because early on they were able to develop the necessary beliefs, values, and practices for trade, industrialization, and rapid economic growth to occur. Poor nations remained poor because they failed to develop these beliefs, values, and practices; instead, they continued to follow traditional beliefs and practices that stymied industrial development and modernization.
Dependency theory	The poverty of poor nations stems from their colonization by European nations, which exploited the poor nations’ resources and either enslaved their populations or used them as cheap labor. The colonized nations were thus unable to develop a professional and business class that would have enabled them to enter the industrial age and to otherwise develop their economies.

Modernization Theory

The individual explanation is called **modernization theory** (McClelland, 1967; Rostow, 1990). According to this theory, rich nations became wealthy because early on they were able to develop the “correct” beliefs, values, and practices—in short, the correct culture—for trade, industrialization, and rapid economic growth to occur. These cultural traits include a willingness to work hard, to abandon tradition in favor of new ways of thinking and doing things, and to adopt a future orientation rather than one focused on maintaining present conditions.

Modernization theory has direct relevance for the experience of Western Europe. According to the theory, Western European nations began to emerge several centuries ago as economic powers because their populations adopted the kinds of values and practices just listed. Max Weber (1904/1958), one of the founders of sociology, wrote that Western Europe was able to do this because the Protestant Reformation diminished the traditional distrust of the Catholic Church for material success and social and economic change. The new Protestant ethic that Western Europeans adopted stressed the importance of hard work and material success in one's lifetime rather than the Church's traditional emphasis on rewards in an afterlife.

According to modernization theory, poor nations are poor because their people never developed values such as an emphasis on hard work.

United Nations Photo – OLS Brings Support to Strained Medical Services – CC BY-NC-ND 2.0.

According to modernization theory, nations in other parts of the world never became wealthy and remain poor today because they never developed the appropriate values and practices. Instead, they continued to follow traditional beliefs and practices that stymied industrial development and modernization.

Modernization theory has much in common with the culture of poverty theory discussed in Chapter 8 "Social Stratification". It attributes the poverty of poor nations to their failure to develop the "proper" beliefs, values, and practices necessary for economic success both at the beginning of industrialization during the 19th century and in the two centuries that have since transpired. Because modernization theory implies that people in poor nations do not have the talent and ability to improve their lot, it falls into the functionalist explanation of stratification.

As should be clear, modernization theory has direct implications for strategies to reduce global poverty. The theory implies that people in poor nations must learn the proper beliefs, values, and practices to succeed economically. If they do not do so, they will prevent themselves from profiting as fully as possible from the financial aid they get from wealthy nations, with much of this aid thereby being wasted.

Dependency Theory

The structural explanation for global stratification is called **dependency theory**. Not surprisingly, this theory's views sharply challenge modernization theory's assumptions (Packenham, 1992). Whereas modernization theory attributes global stratification to the "wrong" cultural values and practices in poor nations, dependency theory blames global stratification on the exploitation of these nations by wealthy nations. According to this view, poor nations never got the chance to pursue economic growth because early on they were conquered and colonized by European ones. The European nations stole the poor nations' resources and either enslaved their populations or used them as cheap labor. They installed their own governments and often prevented the local populace from getting a good education. As a result, the colonized nations were unable to develop a professional and business class that would have enabled them to enter the industrial age and to otherwise develop their economies. Along the way, wealthy nations sold their own goods to colonized nations and forced them to run up enormous debt that continues to amount today. Because dependency theory implies that poor nations remain poor because of lack of opportunity owing to exploitation by wealthy nations, it falls into the conflict perspective on stratification.

In today's world, huge multinational corporations continue to exploit the labor and resources of the poorest nations, say dependency theorists. These corporations run sweatshops in many nations, in which workers toil in inhumane conditions at extremely low wages (Sluiter, 2009). Often the corporations work hand-in-hand with corrupt officials in the poor nations to strengthen their economic stake in the countries. An example of this dynamic occurred during the 1990s in the poor western African country of Nigeria, where the Royal Dutch/Shell oil company at the time was pumping half of that nation's oil. Activists in southern Nigeria began to claim that Shell's oil drilling was destroying their land and that Shell was paying them too little for their oil. In response to their protests, the government sent in police at Shell's request, with Shell paying some of the police costs. The police put down the activists' dissent by destroying several villages and killing 2,000 people (Lewis, 1996).

Dependency theory also has direct implications for strategies to reduce global poverty. Very simply, the theory implies that wealthy nations and multinational corporations must stop exploiting the resources of poor nations. Until that happens, poor nations will be unable to develop their natural resources and to enter the industrial age. Some dependency theorists also say that poor nations should limit their importation of goods from wealthy nations, and that wealthy nations should even be forbidden from investing in poor nations.

Which makes more sense, modernization theory or dependency theory? As with many theories, both make sense to some degree (see the "Learning From Other Societies" box), but both have their faults. Modernization theory places too much blame on poor nations for their own poverty and ignores the long history of exploitation of poor nations by rich nations and multinational corporations alike. For its part, dependency theory cannot explain why some of the poorest countries are poor even though they were never European colonies; neither can it explain why some former colonies such as Hong Kong have been able to attain enough economic growth to leave the rank of the poorest nations. Together, both theories help us understand the reasons for global stratification, but most sociologists would probably favor dependency theory because of its emphasis on structural factors in the world's historic and current economy.

Learning From Other Societies

Why Haiti Is So Poor: Culture or Exploitation?

In January 2010, an earthquake with a magnitude of 7.0 devastated Haiti, one of the poorest countries in the world. The quake reportedly killed more than 200,000 people, about 2.5% of Haiti's population, injured 300,000, and left 1 million homeless. Because Haiti had ramshackle buildings, a weak infrastructure, and inadequate public services, many more people died or otherwise suffered from this earthquake than from earthquakes of similar magnitude in wealthier countries.

In the aftermath of this natural disaster, a flurry of news articles and op-ed columns discussed why Haiti had been so poor before the earthquake despite efforts by thousands of international agencies during the past few decades. The contrasting positions presented in these articles reflected the views of the modernization and dependency theories presented in the text, and they illustrate the complexity of understanding global poverty.

Reflecting the views of modernization theory, some observers attributed Haiti's situation to a culture of poverty. They noted that Haiti shares an island with the Dominican Republic, which is not nearly as poor as Haiti. Beyond sharing a general location and climate, the two nations also have similar histories of colonialism and governmental corruption. Given these similarities, why, then, was Haiti so desperately poorer than the Dominican Republic?

To answer this question, Jonah Goldberg, a *Los Angeles Times* columnist, reasoned, "Haiti's problems in large part boil down to a culture of poverty. Haitians do not lack the desire to make their lives better, nor do they reject hard work. But what they sorely lack is a legal, social and intellectual culture that favors economic growth and entrepreneurialism" (Goldberg, 2010, p. 9A). Western nations, he continued, must do more than provide aid to Haiti and other poor nations, as they must also teach them "how to stop being poor." People in these nations, he said, must learn the concept of *entrepreneurialism* (the development and practice of a business), and they must also learn how to be entrepreneurs.

Taking a similar stance, David Brooks, a *New York Times* columnist, wrote that several aspects of the Haitian culture contribute to the nation's poverty by inhibiting its ability to achieve economic growth. First, Haitians' voodoo religion prompts them to believe that life is unpredictable and that planning is futile. Second, Haitians have high levels of social mistrust and a low sense of personal responsibility. Third, parental neglect during early childhood is common. Brooks concluded, "We're all supposed to politely respect each other's cultures. But some cultures are more progress-resistant than others, and a horrible tragedy [the damage caused by Haiti's earthquake] was just exacerbated by one of them" (Brooks, 2010, p. A27).

Reflecting the views of dependency theory, other observers attributed Haiti's deep poverty to its history of colonialism, which puts it at a severe disadvantage even compared to other formerly colonized nations. Michele Wucker, executive director of the World Policy Institute, and Ben Macintyre, a columnist for *The Times* of London, both wrote that Haiti was a rich slave colony of France before a bloody revolution won Haitians their independence in 1804. The new nation's economy then suffered for two reasons. First, the revolution destroyed much of the country's agriculture and infrastructure. Second, France used ships to block Haitian trade and required Haiti to pay a huge indemnity, equal to about $13 billion in today's dollars, to restore normal trade and diplomatic relations. Haiti had to take out huge loans from Western nations' banks at very high interest rates to do so. The consequence for Haiti was devastating, wrote Macintyre (2010, p. 30):

> Weighed down by this financial burden, Haiti was born almost bankrupt. In 1900 some 80 per cent of the national budget was still being swallowed up by debt repayments. Money that might have been spent on building a stable economy went to foreign bankers....The debt was not finally paid off until 1947. By then, Haiti's economy was hopelessly distorted, its land deforested, mired in poverty, politically and economically unstable, prey equally to the caprice of nature and the depredations of autocrats.

Haiti's plight only worsened when U.S. Marines occupied Haiti from 1915 to 1934 and when a series of corrupt dictators afterward "left Haiti economically devastated," added Wucker (Smith, 2010). In short, as one headline put it, Haiti's dire poverty stems from a "crippling legacy of imperialism" (Macintyre, 2010).

Where does the truth lie? Is Haiti's poverty today due more to its culture or more to its history of colonialism and imperialism? People who favor modernization theory would answer culture, and those who favor dependency theory would answer colonialism and imperialism. In the end, both sets of factors probably matter. The debate over Haiti's poverty shows that the experience of other societies can illuminate theories of global poverty and, in turn, help us understand which types of strategies hold the most potential for helping poor nations.

Key Takeaways

- According to modernization theory, rich nations became rich because their peoples possessed certain values, beliefs, and practices conducive to the acquisition of wealth. Poor nations remained poor because their peoples did not possess these values, beliefs, and practices and never developed them.
- According to dependency theory, poor nations have remained poor because they have been exploited by rich nations and by multinational corporations.

For Your Review

1. Which theory makes more sense to you, modernization theory or dependency theory? Explain your answer.
2. What strategies does modernization theory suggest for helping poor nations? What strategies does dependency theory suggest for helping poor nations?

Reducing Global Stratification: What Sociology Suggests

Years of international aid to poor nations have helped them somewhat, but, as this chapter has shown, their situation remains dire. International aid experts acknowledge that efforts to achieve economic growth in poor nations have largely failed, but they disagree why this is so and what alternative strategies may prove more successful (Cohen & Easterly, 2009). One trend has been a switch from "macro" efforts focusing on infrastructure problems and on social institutions such as the schools to "micro" efforts, such as providing cash payments or small loans directly to poor people in poor nations (a practice called *microfinancing*) and giving them bed nets to prevent mosquito bites, but the evidence on the success of these efforts is mixed (Bennett, 2009; *The Economist*, 2010). Much more obviously needs to be done.

In this regard, sociology's structural approach is in line with dependency theory and suggests that global stratification results from the history of colonialism and by continuing exploitation today of poor nations' resources by wealthy nations and multinational corporations. To the extent such exploitation exists, global poverty will lessen if and only if this exploitation lessens. As the "Sociology Making a Difference" box indicated, a sociological approach also emphasizes the role that class, gender, and ethnic inequality play in perpetuating global poverty. For global poverty to be reduced, gender and ethnic inequality must be reduced.

Writers Kristof and WuDunn (2009) emphasize the need to focus efforts to reduce global poverty of women. We have already seen one reason why this emphasis makes sense: women are much worse off than men in poor nations in many ways, so helping them is crucial for both economic and humanitarian reasons. An additional reason is especially illuminating: when women in poor nations acquire extra money, they typically spend it on food, clothing, and medicine, essentials for their families. However, when men in poor nations acquire extra money, they often spend it on alcohol, tobacco, and gambling. This gender difference might sound like a stereotype, but it does indicate that aid to women will help in many ways, while aid to men might be less effective and often even wasted.

References

Bennett, D. (2009, September 20). Small change. *The Boston Globe*. Retrieved from http://www.boston.com/bostonglobe/ideas/articles/2009/2009/2020/small_change_does_microlending_actually_fight_poverty/#.

Brooks, D. (2010, January 14). The underlying tragedy. *The New York Times*, p. A27.

Cohen, J., & Easterly, W. (Eds.). (2009). *What works in development? Thinking big and thinking small.* Washington, DC: Brookings Institution Press.

Goldberg, J. (2010, August 3). End poverty: Export capitalism. *USA Today*, p. 9A.

Kristof, N. D., & WuDunn, S. (2009, August 23). The women's crusade. *The New York Times*, p. MM28.

Lewis, P. (1996, February 13). Nigeria's deadly war: Shell defends its record. *The New York Times*, p. 1.

Macintyre, B. (2010, January 21). The fault line in Haiti runs straight to France. *The Times* (London), p. 30.

McClelland, D. C. (1967). *The achieving society*. New York, NY: Free Press.

Packenham, R. A. (1992). *The dependency movement: Scholarship and politics in development studies.* Cambridge, MA: Harvard University Press.

Rostow, W. W. (1990). *The stages of economic growth: A non-communist manifesto*. New York, NY: Cambridge University Press.

Savings and the poor: A better mattress. (2010, March 11). *Economist, 394*(8673), 75–76.

Sluiter, L. (2009). *Clean clothes: A global movement to end sweatshops*. New York, NY: Pluto Press.

Smith, K. F. (2010, January 16). Haiti: A historical perspective. *Newsweek*. Retrieved from http://www.newsweek.com/2010/2001/2015/haiti-a-historical-perspective.html.

Weber, M. (1958). *The Protestant ethic and the spirit of capitalism* (T. Parsons, Trans.). New York, NY: Scribner. (Original work published 1904).

9.4 End-of-Chapter Material

Summary

1. The nations of the world differ dramatically in wealth and other resources, with the poorest nations being found in Africa and parts of Asia.
2. To understand global stratification, it is useful to classify the world's nations into three categories: wealthy nations, middle-income nations, and poor nations. The middle category is often subdivided into upper-middle-income nations and lower-middle-income nations.
3. Several measures of global poverty and global inequality help us to understand the nature and extent of global stratification and identify the nations most in need of help.
4. Global poverty has a devastating impact on the lives of hundreds of millions of people throughout the world. Poor nations have much higher rates of mortality and disease and lower rates of literacy.
5. Global poverty especially affects women and children, who suffer in many ways from the effects of poverty in poor nations.
6. Modernization theory attributes global poverty to the failure of poor nations to develop the necessary beliefs, values, and practices to achieve economic growth.
7. Dependency theory attributes global poverty to the colonization and exploitation by European nations of nations in other parts of the world.
8. A sociological perspective suggests that efforts to reduce global poverty need to address continuing exploitation of poor nations by wealthy nations and multinational corporations, and that these efforts will succeed to the extent that they also reduce ethnic and gender inequality.

Using Sociology

Three months ago, you began a job as a policy assistant to one of the two U.S. senators from your home state. The senator is helping to draft a bill for foreign aid assistance for poor countries and reasons that most of the aid should be aimed at helping men find jobs, since these countries are patriarchal and might resent aid that helps women find jobs. What do you tell your senator when your opinion is solicited?

Chapter 10: Race and Ethnicity

Social Issues in the News

"White Supremacist Held Without Bond in Tuesday's Attack," the headline said. James Privott, a 76-year-old African American, had just finished fishing in a Baltimore city park when he was attacked by several white men. They knocked him to the ground, punched him in the face, and hit him with a baseball bat. Privott lost two teeth and had an eye socket fractured in the assault. One of his assailants was arrested soon afterwards and told police the attack "wouldn't have happened if he was a white man." The suspect was a member of a white supremacist group, had a tattoo of Hitler on his stomach, and used "Hitler" as his nickname. At a press conference attended by civil rights and religious leaders, the Baltimore mayor denounced the hate crime. "We all have to speak out and speak up and say this is not acceptable in our communities," she said. "We must stand together in opposing this kind of act." (Fenton, 2009, p. 11)

In 1959, John Howard Griffin, a white writer, changed his race. Griffin decided that he could not begin to understand the discrimination and prejudice that African Americans face every day unless he experienced these problems himself. So he went to a dermatologist in New Orleans and obtained a prescription for an oral medication to darken his skin. The dermatologist also told him to lie under a sunlamp several hours a day and to use a skin-staining pigment to darken any light spots that remained.

Griffin stayed inside, followed the doctor's instructions, and shaved his head to remove his straight hair. About a week later he looked, for all intents and purposes, like an African American. Then he went out in public and passed as black.

New Orleans was a segregated city in those days, and Griffin immediately found he could no longer do the same things he did when he was white. He could no longer drink at the same water fountains, use the same public restrooms, or eat at the same restaurants. When he went to look at a menu displayed in the window of a fancy restaurant, he later wrote,

I read, realizing that a few days earlier I could have gone in and ordered anything on the menu. But now, though I was the same person with the same appetite, no power on earth could get me inside this place for a meal. (Griffin, 1961, p. 42)

Because of his new appearance, Griffin suffered other slights and indignities. Once when he went to sit on a bench in a public park, a white man told him to leave. Later a white bus driver refused to let Griffin get off at his stop and let him off only eight blocks later. A series of stores refused to cash his traveler's checks. As he traveled by bus from one state to another, he was not allowed to wait inside the bus stations. At times white men of various ages cursed and threatened him, and he became afraid for his life and safety. Months later, after he wrote about his experience, he was hanged in effigy, and his family was forced to move from their home.

Griffin's reports about how he was treated while posing as a black man, and about the way African Americans he met during that time were also treated, helped awaken white Americans across the United States to racial prejudice and discrimination. The Southern civil rights movement, which had begun a few years earlier and then exploded into the national consciousness with sit-ins at lunch counters in February 1960 by black college students in Greensboro, North Carolina, ended Southern segregation and changed life in the South and across the rest of the nation.

What has happened since then? Where do we stand more than 50 years after the beginning of the civil rights movement and Griffin's travels in the South? In answering this question, this chapter discusses the changing nature of racial and ethnic prejudice and inequality in the United States but also documents their continuing importance for American society, as the hate crime story that began this chapter signifies. We begin our discussion of the present with a brief look back to the past.

References

Fenton, J. (2009, August 20). Details emerge on suspect: White supremacist held without bail in Tuesday's attack at Fort Armistead Park. *The Baltimore Sun*. Retrieved from http://www.baltimoresun.com/news/maryland/baltimore-city/bal-md.ci.lockner20aug20,20,1843383.story.

Griffin, J. H. (1961). *Black like me*. Boston, MA: Houghton Mifflin.

10.1 Racial and Ethnic Relations: An American Dilemma

Learning Objectives

1. Describe the targets of 19th-century mob violence in U.S. cities.
2. Discuss why the familiar saying "The more things change, the more they stay the same" applies to the history of race and ethnicity in the United States.

Race and ethnicity have torn at the fabric of American society ever since the time of Christopher Columbus, when about 1 million Native Americans were thought to have populated the eventual United States. By 1900, their numbers had dwindled to about 240,000, as tens of thousands were killed by white settlers and U.S. troops and countless others died from disease contracted from people with European backgrounds. Scholars have said that this mass killing of Native Americans amounted to genocide (Wilson, 1999).

African Americans obviously also have a history of maltreatment that began during the colonial period, when Africans were forcibly transported from their homelands to be sold and abused as slaves in the Americas. During the 1830s, white mobs attacked African Americans in cities throughout the nation, including Philadelphia, Cincinnati, Buffalo, and Pittsburgh. This mob violence led Abraham Lincoln to lament "the worse than savage mobs" and "the increasing disregard for law which pervades the country" (Feldberg, 1980, p. 4). The mob violence stemmed from a "deep-seated racial prejudice…in which whites saw blacks as 'something less than human'" (Brown, 1975, p. 206) and continued well into the 20th century, when whites attacked African Americans in several cities, with at least seven antiblack riots occurring in 1919 alone that left dozens dead. Meanwhile, an era of Jim Crow racism in the South led to the lynchings of thousands of African Americans, segregation in all facets of life, and other kinds of abuses (Litwack, 2009).

During the era of Jim Crow racism in the South, several thousand African Americans were lynched.

U.S. Library of Congress – public domain.

Blacks were not the only targets of native-born white mobs back then (Dinnerstein & Reimers, 2009). As immigrants from Ireland, Italy, Eastern Europe, Mexico, and Asia flooded into the United States during the 19th and early 20th centuries, they, too, were beaten, denied jobs, and otherwise mistreated. During the 1850s, mobs beat and sometimes killed Catholics in cities such as Baltimore and New Orleans. During the 1870s, whites rioted against Chinese immigrants in cities in California and other states. Hundreds of Mexicans were attacked and/or lynched in California and Texas during this period.

Not surprisingly, scholars have written about U.S. racial and ethnic prejudice ever since the days of slavery. In 1835, the great social observer Alexis de Tocqueville (1835/1994) despaired that whites' prejudice would make it impossible for them to live in harmony with African Americans. Decades later, W. E. B. Du Bois (1903/1968, p. vii), one of the first sociologists to study race (see Chapter 1 "Sociology and the Sociological Perspective"), observed in 1903 that "the problem of the Twentieth Century is the problem of the color-line" and cited example after example of economic, social, and legal discrimination against African Americans.

Nazi racism in the 1930s and 1940s helped awaken Americans to the evils of prejudice in their own country. Against this backdrop, a monumental two-volume work by Swedish social scientist Gunnar Myrdal (1944) attracted much attention when it was published. The book, *An American Dilemma: The Negro Problem and Modern Democracy*, documented the various forms of discrimination facing blacks back then. The "dilemma" referred to by the book's title was the conflict between the American democratic ideals of egalitarianism and liberty and justice for all and the harsh reality of prejudice, discrimination, and lack of equal opportunity. Using the common term for African American of his time, Myrdal wrote optimistically,

> If America in actual practice could show the world a progressive trend by which the Negro finally became integrated into modern democracy, all mankind would be given faith again—it would have reason to believe that peace, progress, and order are feasible....America is free to choose whether the Negro shall remain her liability or become her opportunity. (Myrdal, 1944, pp. 1121–1122)

Unfortunately, Myrdal was too optimistic, as legal segregation did not end until the Southern civil rights movement won its major victories in the 1960s. Even after segregation ended, improvement in other areas was slow. Thus in 1968, the so-called Kerner Commission (1968, p. 1), appointed by President Lyndon Johnson in response to the 1960s urban riots, warned in a famous statement, "Our nation is moving toward two societies, one black, one white—separate and unequal." Despite this warning, and despite the civil rights movement's successes, 30 years later writer David K. Shipler (1997, p. 10) felt compelled to observe that there is "no more intractable, pervasive issue than race" and that when it comes to race, we are "a country of strangers." Sociologists and other social scientists have warned since then that the conditions of people of color have actually been worsening (Massey, 2007; W. J. Wilson, 2009). Despite the historic election of Barack Obama in 2008 as the first president of color, race and ethnicity remain an "intractable, pervasive issue." As the old French saying goes, *plus ça change, plus la meme chose* (the more things change, the more they stay the same). Indeed, it would be accurate to say, to paraphrase Du Bois, that "the problem of the 21st century is the problem of the color line." Evidence of this continuing problem appears in much of the remainder of this chapter.

Key Takeaways

- U.S. history is filled with violence and other maltreatment against Native Americans, blacks, and immigrants.
- The familiar saying "The more things change, the more they stay the same" applies to race and ethnic relations in the United States.

For Your Review

1. Describe why Myrdal said U.S. race relations were an "American dilemma."
2. How much did you learn in high school about the history of race and ethnicity in the United States? Do you think you should have learned more?

References

Brown, R. M. (1975). *Strain of violence: Historical studies of American violence and vigilantism*. New York, NY: Oxford University Press.

Dinnerstein, L., & Reimers, D. M. (2009). *Ethnic Americans: A history of immigration*. New York, NY: Columbia University Press.

Du Bois, W. E. B. (1968). *The souls of black folk*. New York, NY: Fawcett World Library. (Original work published 1903).

Feldberg, M. (1980). *The turbulent era: Riot and disorder in Jacksonian America*. New York, NY: Oxford University Press.

Kerner Commission. (1968). *Report of the National Advisory Commission on Civil Disorders*. New York, NY: Bantam Books.

Litwack, L. F. (2009). *How free is free? The long death of Jim Crow*. Cambridge, MA: Harvard University Press.

Massey, D. S. (2007). *Categorically unequal: The American stratification system*. New York, NY: Russell Sage Foundation.

Myrdal, G. (1944). *An American dilemma: The Negro problem and modern democracy*. New York, NY: Harper and Brothers.

Shipler, D. K. (1997). *A country of strangers: Blacks and whites in America*. New York, NY: Knopf.

Tocqueville, A. (1994). *Democracy in America*. New York, NY: Knopf. (Original work published 1835).

Wilson, J. (1999). *The earth shall weep: A history of Native America*. New York, NY: Atlantic Monthly Press.

Wilson, W. J. (2009). Toward a framework for understanding forces that contribute to or reinforce racial inequality. *Race and Social Problems, 1*, 3–11.

10.2 The Meaning of Race and Ethnicity

Learning Objectives

1. Critique the biological concept of race.
2. Discuss why race is a social construction.
3. Discuss the advantages and disadvantages of a sense of ethnic identity.

To understand this problem further, we need to take a critical look at the very meaning of race and ethnicity in today's society. These concepts may seem easy to define initially but are much more complex than their definitions suggest.

Race

Let's start first with **race**, which refers to a category of people who share certain inherited physical characteristics, such as skin color, facial features, and stature. A key question about race is whether it is more of a biological category or a social category. Most people think of race in biological terms, and for more than 300 years, or ever since white Europeans began colonizing populations of color elsewhere in the world, race has indeed served as the "premier source of human identity" (Smedley, 1998, p. 690).

It is certainly easy to see that people in the United States and around the world differ physically in some obvious ways. The most noticeable difference is skin tone: some groups of people have very dark skin, while others have very light skin. Other differences also exist. Some people have very curly hair, while others have very straight hair. Some have thin lips, while others have thick lips. Some groups of people tend to be relatively tall, while others tend to be relatively short. Using such physical differences as their criteria, scientists at one point identified as many as nine races: African, American Indian or Native American, Asian, Australian Aborigine, European (more commonly called "white"), Indian, Melanesian, Micronesian, and Polynesian (Smedley, 1998).

Although people certainly do differ in the many physical features that led to the development of such racial categories, anthropologists, sociologists, and many biologists question the value of these categories and thus the value of the biological concept of race (Smedley, 2007). For one thing, we often see more physical differences *within* a race than *between* races. For example, some people we call "white" (or European), such as those with Scandinavian backgrounds, have very light skins, while others, such as those from some Eastern European backgrounds, have much darker skins. In fact, some "whites" have darker skin than some "blacks," or African Americans. Some whites have very straight hair, while others have very curly hair; some have blonde hair and blue eyes, while others have dark hair and brown eyes. Because of interracial reproduction going back to the days of slavery, African Americans also differ in the darkness of their skin and in other physical characteristics. In fact it is estimated that about 80% of African Americans have some white (i.e., European) ancestry; 50% of Mexican Americans have European or Native American ancestry; and 20% of whites have African or Native American ancestry. If clear racial differences ever existed hundreds or thousands of years ago (and many scientists doubt such differences ever existed), in today's world these differences have become increasingly blurred.

Another reason to question the biological concept of race is that an individual or a group of individuals is often assigned to a race on arbitrary or even illogical grounds. A century ago, for example, Irish, Italians, and Eastern European Jews who left their homelands for a better life in the United States were not regarded as white once they reached the United States but rather as a different, inferior (if unnamed) race (Painter, 2010). The belief in their inferiority helped justify the harsh treatment they suffered in their new country. Today, of course, we call people from all three backgrounds white or European.

In this context, consider someone in the United States who has a white parent and a black parent. What race is this person? American society usually calls this person black or African American, and the person may adopt the same identity (as does Barack Obama, who had a white mother and African father). But where is the logic for doing so? This person, as well as President Obama, is as much white as black in terms of parental ancestry. Or consider someone with one white parent and another parent who is the child of one black parent and one white parent. This person thus has three white grandparents and one black grandparent. Even though this person's ancestry is thus 75% white and 25% black, she or he is likely to be considered black in the United States and may well adopt this racial identity. This practice reflects the traditional "one-drop rule" in the United States that defines someone as black if she or he has at least one drop of "black blood," and that was used in the antebellum South to keep the slave population as large as possible (Wright, 1993). Yet in many Latin American nations, this person would be considered white. In Brazil, the term *black* is reserved for someone with no European (white) ancestry at all. If we followed this practice in the United States, about 80% of the people we call "black" would now be called "white." With such arbitrary designations, race is more of a social category than a biological one.

President Barack Obama had an African father and a white mother. Although his ancestry is equally black and white, Obama considers himself an African American, as do most Americans. In several Latin American nations, however, Obama would be considered white because of his white ancestry.

Steve Jurvetson – Barack Obama on the Primary – CC BY 2.0.

A third reason to question the biological concept of race comes from the field of biology itself and more specifically from the studies of genetics and human evolution. Starting with genetics, people from different races are more than 99.9% the same in their DNA (Begley, 2008). To turn that around, less than 0.1% of all the DNA in our bodies accounts for the physical differences among people that we associate with racial differences. In terms of DNA, then, people with different racial backgrounds are much, much more similar than dissimilar.

Even if we acknowledge that people differ in the physical characteristics we associate with race, modern evolutionary evidence reminds us that we are all, really, of one human race. According to evolutionary theory, the human race began thousands and thousands of years ago in sub-Saharan Africa. As people migrated around the world over the millennia, natural selection took over. It favored dark skin for people living in hot, sunny climates (i.e., near the equator), because the heavy amounts of melanin that produce dark skin protect against severe sunburn, cancer, and other problems. By the same token, natural selection favored light skin for people who migrated farther from the equator to cooler, less sunny climates, because dark skins there would have interfered with the production of vitamin D (Stone & Lurquin, 2007). Evolutionary evidence thus reinforces the common humanity of people who differ in the rather superficial ways associated with their appearances: we are one human species composed of people who happen to look different.

Race as a Social Construction

The reasons for doubting the biological basis for racial categories suggest that race is more of a social category than a biological one. Another way to say this is that race is a **social construction**, a concept that has no objective reality but rather is what people decide it is (Berger & Luckmann, 1963). In this view race has no real existence other than what and how people think of it.

This understanding of race is reflected in the problems, outlined earlier, in placing people with multiracial backgrounds into any one racial category. We have already mentioned the example of President Obama. As another example, the famous (and now notorious) golfer Tiger Woods was typically called an African American by the news media when he burst onto the golfing scene in the late 1990s, but in fact his ancestry is one-half Asian (divided evenly between Chinese and Thai), one-quarter white, one-eighth Native American, and only one-eighth African American (Leland & Beals, 1997).

Historical examples of attempts to place people in racial categories further underscore the social constructionism of race. In the South during the time of slavery, the skin tone of slaves lightened over the years as babies were born from the union, often in the form of rape, of slave owners and other whites with slaves. As it became difficult to tell who was "black" and who was not, many court battles over people's racial identity occurred. People who were accused of having black ancestry would go to court to prove they were white in order to avoid enslavement or other problems (Staples, 1998). Litigation over race continued long past the days of slavery. In a relatively recent example, Susie Guillory Phipps sued the Louisiana Bureau of Vital Records in the early 1980s to change her official race to white. Phipps was descended from a slave owner and a slave and thereafter had only white ancestors. Despite this fact, she was called "black" on her birth certificate because of a state law, echoing the "one-drop rule," that designated people as black if their ancestry was at least 1/32 black (meaning one of their great-great-great grandparents was black). Phipps had always thought of herself as white and was surprised after seeing a copy of her birth certificate to discover she was officially black because she had one black ancestor about 150 years earlier. She lost her case, and the U.S. Supreme Court later refused to review it (Omi & Winant, 1994).

Although race is a social construction, it is also true, as noted in an earlier chapter, that things perceived as real are real in their consequences. Because people *do* perceive race as something real, it has real consequences. Even though so little of DNA accounts for the physical differences we associate with racial differences, that low amount leads us not only to classify people into different races but to treat them differently—and, more to the point, unequally—based on their classification. Yet modern evidence shows there is little, if any, scientific basis for the racial classification that is the source of so much inequality.

Ethnicity

Because of the problems in the meaning of *race*, many social scientists prefer the term *ethnicity* in speaking of people of color and others with distinctive cultural heritages. In this context, **ethnicity** refers to the shared social, cultural, and historical experiences, stemming from common national or regional backgrounds, that make subgroups of a population different from one another. Similarly, an **ethnic group** is a subgroup of a population with a set of shared social, cultural, and historical experiences; with relatively distinctive beliefs, values, and behaviors; and with some sense of identity of belonging to the subgroup. So conceived, the terms *ethnicity* and *ethnic group* avoid the biological connotations of the terms *race* and *racial group* and the biological differences these terms imply. At the same time, the importance we attach to ethnicity illustrates that it, too, is in many ways a social construction, and our ethnic membership thus has important consequences for how we are treated.

The sense of identity many people gain from belonging to an ethnic group is important for reasons both good and bad. Because, as we learned in Chapter 6 "Groups and Organizations", one of the most important functions of groups is the identity they give us, ethnic identities can give individuals a sense of belonging and a recognition of the importance of their cultural backgrounds. This sense of belonging is illustrated in Figure 10.1 "Responses to "How Close Do You Feel to Your Ethnic or Racial Group?"", which depicts the answers of General Social Survey respondents to the question, "How close do you feel to your ethnic or racial group?" More than three-fourths said they feel close or very close. The term **ethnic pride** captures the sense of self-worth that many people derive from their ethnic backgrounds. More generally, if group membership is important for many ways in which members of the group are socialized, ethnicity certainly plays an important role in the socialization of millions of people in the United States and elsewhere in the world today.

Figure 10.1 Responses to "How Close Do You Feel to Your Ethnic or Racial Group?"

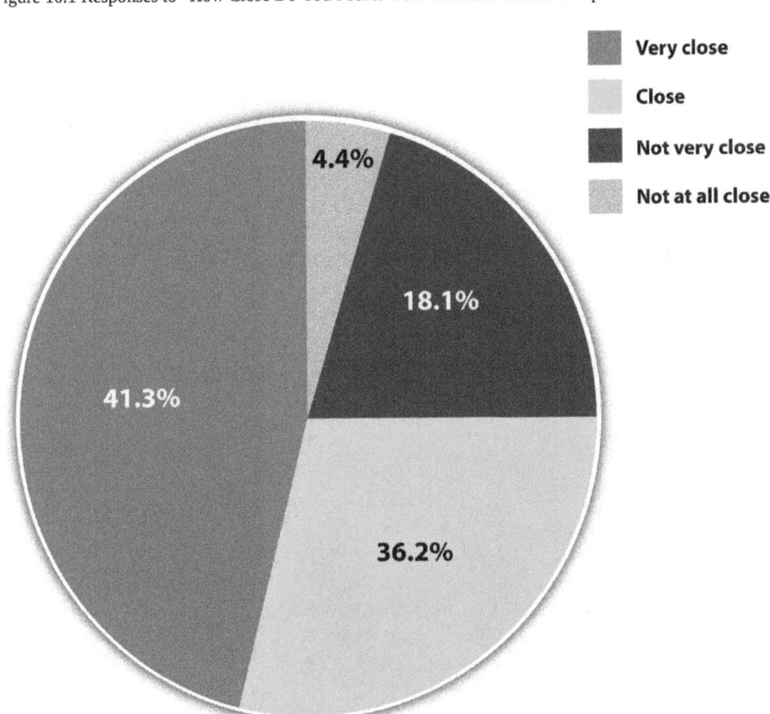

Source: Data from General Social Survey, 2004.

A downside of ethnicity and ethnic group membership is the conflict they create among people of different ethnic groups. History and current practice indicate that it is easy to become prejudiced against people with different ethnicities from our own. Much of the rest of this chapter looks at the prejudice and discrimination operating today in the United States against people whose ethnicity is not white and European. Around the world today, ethnic conflict continues to rear its ugly head. The 1990s and 2000s were filled with "ethnic cleansing" and pitched battles among ethnic groups in Eastern Europe, Africa, and elsewhere. Our ethnic heritages shape us in many ways and fill many of us with pride, but they also are the source of much conflict, prejudice, and even hatred, as the hate crime story that began this chapter so sadly reminds us.

Key Takeaways

- Sociologists think race is best considered a social construction rather than a biological category.
- "Ethnicity" and "ethnic" avoid the biological connotations of "race" and "racial."

For Your Review

1. List everyone you might know whose ancestry is biracial or multiracial. What do these individuals consider themselves to be?
2. List two or three examples that indicate race is a social construction rather than a biological category.

References

Begley, S. (2008, February 29). Race and DNA. *Newsweek.* Retrieved from http://www.newsweek.com/blogs/lab-notes/2008/02/29/race-and-dna.html.

Berger, P., & Luckmann, T. (1963). *The social construction of reality.* New York, NY: Doubleday.

Leland, J., & Beals, G. (1997, May 5). In living colors: Tiger Woods is the exception that rules. *Newsweek* 58–60.

Omi, M., & Winant, H. (1994). *Racial formation in the United States: From the 1960s to the 1990s* (2nd ed.). New York, NY: Routledge.

Painter, N. I. (2010). *The history of white people.* New York, NY: W. W. Norton.

Smedley, A. (1998). "Race" and the construction of human identity. *American Anthropologist, 100,* 690–702.

Staples, B. (1998, November 13). The shifting meanings of "black" and "white," *The New York Times,* p. WK14.

Stone, L., & Lurquin, P. F. (2007). *Genes, culture, and human evolution: A synthesis.* Malden, MA: Blackwell.

Wright, L. (1993, July 12). One drop of blood. *The New Yorker,* pp. 46–54.

10.3 Prejudice

Learning Objectives

1. Define *prejudice, racism,* and *stereotypes.*
2. Discuss the major social-psychological and sociological theories of prejudice.
3. Describe how the nature of prejudice has changed.

Let's examine racial and ethnic prejudice further and then turn to discrimination in Chapter 10 "Race and Ethnicity", Section 10.4 "Discrimination". Prejudice and discrimination are often confused, but the basic difference between them is this: prejudice is the attitude, while discrimination is the behavior. More specifically, racial and ethnic **prejudice** refers to a set of negative attitudes, beliefs, and judgments about whole categories of people, and about individual members of those categories, because of their perceived race and/or ethnicity. A closely related concept is **racism**, or the belief that certain racial or ethnic groups are inferior to one's own. Prejudice and racism are often based on racial and ethnic **stereotypes**, or simplified, mistaken generalizations about people because of their race and/or ethnicity. While cultural and other differences do exist among the various American racial and ethnic groups, many of the views we have of such groups are unfounded and hence are stereotypes. An example of the stereotypes that white people have of other groups appears in Figure 10.2 "Perceptions by Non-Latino White Respondents of the Intelligence of White and Black Americans", in which white respondents in the General Social Survey (GSS) are less likely to think blacks are intelligent than they are to think whites are intelligent.

Figure 10.2 Perceptions by Non-Latino White Respondents of the Intelligence of White and Black Americans

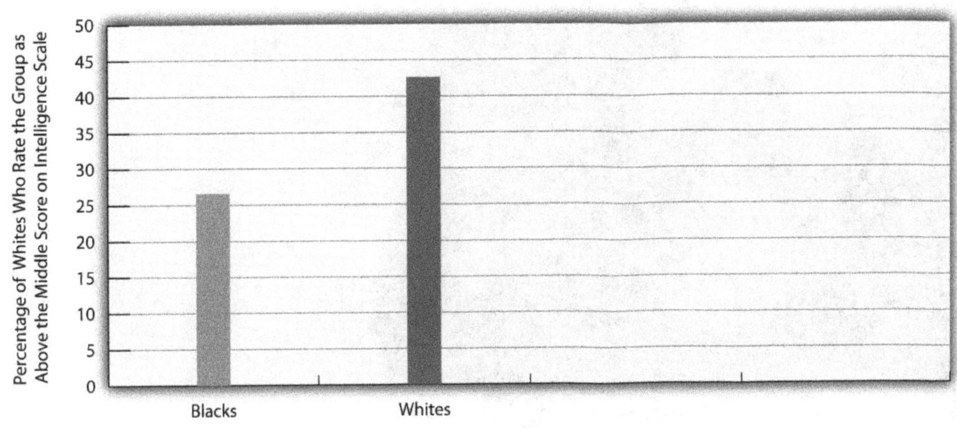

Source: Data from General Social Survey, 2008.

Explaining Prejudice

Where do racial and ethnic prejudices come from? Why are some people more prejudiced than others? Scholars have tried to answer these questions at least since the 1940s, when the horrors of Nazism were still fresh in people's minds. Theories of prejudice fall into two camps, social-psychological and sociological. We will look at social-psychological explanations first and then turn to sociological explanations. We will also discuss distorted mass media treatment of various racial and ethnic groups.

Social-Psychological Explanations

One of the first social-psychological explanations of prejudice centered on the **authoritarian personality** (Adorno, Frenkel-Brunswick, Levinson, & Sanford, 1950). According to this view, authoritarian personalities develop in childhood in response to parents who practice harsh discipline. Individuals with authoritarian personalities emphasize such things as obedience to authority, a rigid adherence to rules, and low acceptance of people (out-groups) not like oneself. Many studies find strong racial and ethnic prejudice among such individuals (Sibley & Duckitt, 2008). But whether their prejudice stems from their authoritarian personalities or instead from the fact that their parents were probably prejudiced themselves remains an important question.

Authoritarian personalities are said to develop in childhood from harsh parental discipline and to be linked to racial and ethnic prejudice. Although many people with authoritarian personalities are prejudiced, it remains unclear whether their prejudice stems from their personalities or from their parents' own prejudice.

Flickr – CC BY-NC-ND 2.0.

Another early and still popular social-psychological explanation is called **frustration or scapegoat theory** (Dollard, Doob, Miller, Mowrer, & Sears, 1939). In this view individuals who experience various kinds of problems become frustrated and tend to blame their troubles on groups that are often disliked in the real world (e.g., racial, ethnic, and religious minorities). These minorities are thus scapegoats for the real sources of people's misfortunes. Several psychology experiments find that when people are frustrated, they indeed become more prejudiced. In one early experiment, college students who were purposely not given enough time to solve a puzzle were more prejudiced after the experiment than before it (Cowen, Landes, & Schaet, 1959).

In the real world, scapegoating at a mass level has been quite common. In medieval Europe, Jews were commonly blamed and persecuted when economic conditions were bad or when war efforts were failing. After the bubonic plague broke out in 1348 and eventually killed more than one-third of all Europeans, Jews were blamed either for deliberately spreading the plague or for angering God because they were not Christian. When Germany suffered economic hardship after World War I, Jews again proved a convenient scapegoat, and anti-Semitism helped fuel the rise of Hitler and Nazism (Litvinoff, 1988).

Sociological Explanations

Sociological explanations of prejudice incorporate some of the principles and processes discussed in previous chapters. One popular explanation emphasizes *conformity and socialization* (also called *social learning theory*). In this view, people who are prejudiced are merely conforming to the culture in which they grow up, and prejudice is the result of socialization from parents, peers, the news media, and other various aspects of their culture. Supporting this view, studies have found that people tend to become more prejudiced when they move to areas where people are very prejudiced and less prejudiced when they move to locations where people are less prejudiced (Aronson, 2008). If people in the South today continue to be more prejudiced than those outside the South, as we discuss later, even though legal segregation ended more than four decades ago, the influence of their culture on their socialization may help explain these beliefs.

A second sociological explanation emphasizes *economic and political competition* and is commonly called *group threat theory* (Quillian, 2006; Hughes & Tuch, 2003). In this view prejudice arises from competition over jobs and other resources and from disagreement over various political issues. When groups vie with each other over these matters, they often become hostile toward each other. Amid such hostility, it is easy to become prejudiced toward the group that threatens your economic or political standing. A popular version of this basic explanation is Susan Olzak's (1992) *ethnic competition theory*, which holds that ethnic prejudice and conflict increase when two or more ethnic groups find themselves competing for jobs, housing, and other goals.

During the 1870s, whites feared that Chinese immigrants would take away their jobs. This fear led to white mob violence against the Chinese and to an act of Congress that prohibited Chinese immigration.

Wikimedia Commons – public domain.

As might be clear, the competition explanation is the macro or structural equivalent of the frustration/scapegoat theory already discussed. Much of the white mob violence discussed earlier stemmed from whites' concern that the groups they attacked threatened their jobs and other aspects of their lives. Thus lynchings of African Americans in the South increased when the Southern economy worsened and decreased when the economy improved (Tolnay & Beck, 1995). Similarly, white mob violence against Chinese immigrants in the 1870s began after the railroad construction that employed so many Chinese immigrants slowed and the Chinese began looking for work in other industries. Whites feared that the Chinese would take jobs away from white workers and that their large supply of labor would drive down wages. Their assaults on the Chinese killed several people and prompted the passage by Congress of the Chinese Exclusion Act in 1882 that prohibited Chinese immigration (Dinnerstein & Reimers, 2009). Several nations today, including the United States, have experienced increased anti-immigrant prejudice because of the growing numbers of immigrants onto their shores (Bauer, 2009). We return to anti-immigrant prejudice later in this chapter.

The Role of the Mass Media

Growing evidence suggests that news media coverage of people of color helps fuel racial prejudice and stereotypes. By presenting people of color in a negative light, the media may unwittingly reinforce the prejudice that individuals already have or even increase their prejudice (Larson, 2005).

Examples of distorted media coverage abound. Even though poor people are more likely to be white than any other race or ethnicity (see Chapter 6 "Groups and Organizations"), the news media use pictures of African Americans far more often than those of whites in stories about poverty. In one study, national news magazines such as *Time* and *Newsweek* and television news shows portrayed African Americans in almost two-thirds of their stories on poverty, even though only about one-fourth of poor people are African Americans. In the magazine stories, only 12% of the African Americans had a job, even though in the real world more than 40% of poor African Americans were working at the time the stories were written (Gilens, 1996). In another study of Chicago television stations, African Americans arrested for violent crime were twice as likely as whites arrested for violent crime to be shown being handcuffed or held by police. Even though whites and African Americans live in Chicago in roughly equal numbers, the television news shows there depicted whites 14 times more often in stories of "good Samaritans" (Entman & Rojecki, 2001). Many other studies find that newspaper and television stories about crime and drugs feature higher proportions of African Americans as offenders than is true in arrest statistics (Lundman, 2003; Surette, 2011). Studies like these show that the news media "convey the message that black people are violent, lazy, and less civic minded" (Jackson, 1997, p. A27).

Nor are African Americans the only group receiving biased media coverage. A study of television business stories in San Francisco found that no Asian Americans were shown in these stories, even though Asian Americans constituted 29% of San Francisco's population at the time of the study (Jackson, 1997). Similarly, a study of the 12,000 stories on the national television evening news shows in 1997 found that less than 1% featured Latinos, even though Latinos made up about 10% of the U.S. population at that time. About two-thirds of the Latinos' stories focused on their crime, immigration, and employment problems rather than on their achievements in politics, business, and popular culture (Alvear, 1998).

Does this stereotypical media coverage actually affect public views about racial and ethnic groups? The answer appears to be yes, as research finds a link between the proportion of African American offenders in television news stories and crime shows and fear of crime experienced by white viewers of these programs: the higher the proportion of African American offenders, the greater the fear of crime the viewers expressed (Eschholz, 2002). An interesting experiment also indicated that stereotypical media coverage does indeed make a difference. The experiment involved white students in an introduction to psychology class at the University of Michigan. The researcher, Tali Mendelberg (1997), randomly assigned subjects to one of two groups. The experimental group viewed news coverage of a young black man, Willie Horton, who, while away on a weekend pass from prison where he was serving a life term for first-degree murder, kidnapped a white couple and then raped the woman and stabbed the man; his story was the feature of a key campaign commercial on behalf of the 1988 presidential campaign of then vice president George H. W. Bush. The control group viewed a video about pollution in Boston Harbor. After watching the videos, subjects in both groups were asked their views on several racial issues, including government efforts to help African Americans. The experimental group that watched the Horton video was more likely than the control group to oppose these efforts and in other respects to have negative views about African Americans. Mendelberg concluded that prejudicial media depictions of racial matters do indeed have prejudicial effects.

Correlates of Prejudice

Since the 1940s, social scientists have investigated the individual correlates of racial and ethnic prejudice (Stangor, 2009). These correlates help test the theories of prejudice just presented. For example, if authoritarian personalities do produce prejudice, then people with these personalities should be more prejudiced. If frustration also produces prejudice, then people who are frustrated with aspects of their lives should also be more prejudiced. Other correlates that have been studied include age, education, gender, region of country, race, residence in integrated neighborhoods, and religiosity. We can take time here to focus on gender, education, and region of country and discuss the evidence for the racial attitudes of whites, as most studies do in view of the historic dominance of whites in the United States.

The findings on gender are rather surprising. Although women are usually thought to be more empathetic than men and thus to be less likely to be racially prejudiced, recent research indicates that the racial views of (white) women and men are in fact very similar and that the two genders are about equally prejudiced (Hughes & Tuch, 2003). This similarity supports group threat theory, outlined earlier, in that it indicates that white women and men are responding more as whites than as women or men, respectively, in formulating their racial views.

Findings on education and region of country are not surprising. Focusing again just on whites, less educated people are usually more racially prejudiced than better educated people, and Southerners are usually more prejudiced than non-Southerners (Krysan, 2000; Schuman, Steeh, Bobo, & Krysan, 1997). Evidence of these differences appears in Figure 10.3 "Education, Region, and Opposition by Non-Latino Whites to a Close Relative Marrying an African American", which depicts educational and regional differences in a type of racial prejudice that social scientists call *social distance*, or feelings about interacting with members of other races and ethnicities. The General Social Survey asks respondents how they feel about a "close relative" marrying an African American. Figure 10.3 "Education, Region, and Opposition by Non-Latino Whites to a Close Relative Marrying an African American" shows how responses by white (non-Latino) respondents to this question vary by education and by Southern residence. Whites without a high school degree are much more likely than those with more education to oppose these marriages, and whites in the South are also much more likely than their non-Southern counterparts to oppose them. To recall the sociological perspective, our social backgrounds certainly do seem to affect our attitudes.

Figure 10.3 Education, Region, and Opposition by Non-Latino Whites to a Close Relative Marrying an African American

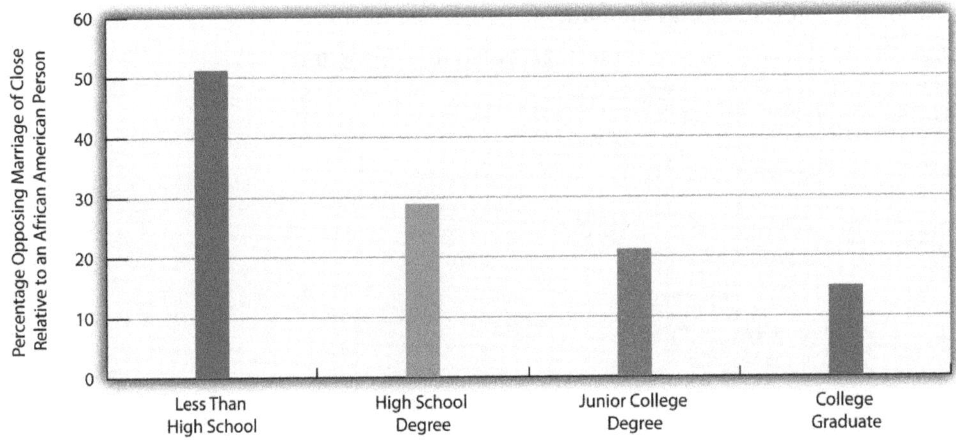

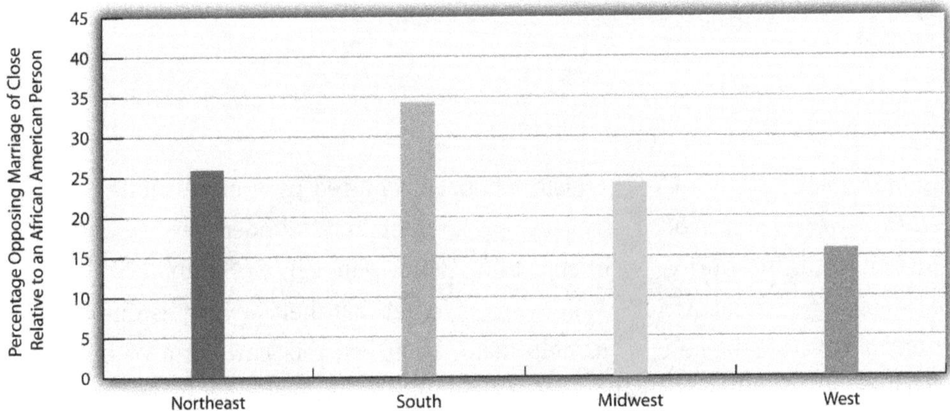

Source: Data from General Social Survey, 2008.

The Changing Nature of Prejudice

Although racial and ethnic prejudice still exists in the United States, its nature has changed during the past half-century. Studies of these changes focus on whites' perceptions of African Americans. Back in the 1940s and before, an era of overt, *Jim Crow* racism (also called *traditional* or *old-fashioned* racism) prevailed, not just in the South but in the entire nation. This racism involved blatant bigotry, firm beliefs in the need for segregation, and the view that blacks were biologically inferior to whites. In the early 1940s, for example, more than half of all whites thought that blacks were less intelligent than whites, more than half favored segregation in public transportation, more than two-thirds favored segregated schools, and more than half thought whites should receive preference over blacks in employment hiring (Schuman, Steeh, Bobo, & Krysan, 1997).

The Nazi experience and then the civil rights movement led whites to reassess their views, and Jim Crow racism gradually waned. Few whites believe today that African Americans are biologically inferior, and few favor segregation. As just one example, Figure 10.4 "Changes in Support by Whites for Segregated Housing, 1972–1996" shows with General Social Survey data that whites' support for segregated housing declined dramatically from about 40% in the early 1970s to about 13% in 1996. So few whites now support segregation and other Jim Crow views that national surveys no longer include many of the questions that were asked some 50 years ago, and the General Social Survey stopped asking about segregated housing after 1996.

Figure 10.4 Changes in Support by Whites for Segregated Housing, 1972–1996

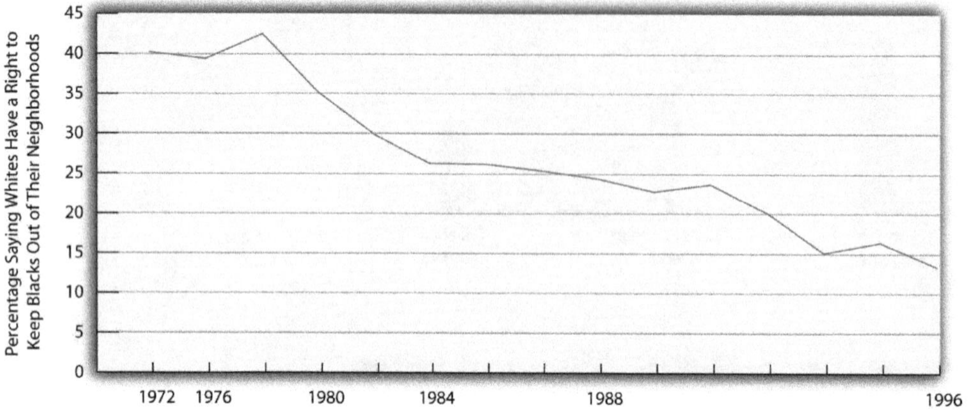

Source: Data from General Social Survey, 2008.

Despite these changes, several scholars say that Jim Crow racism has been replaced by a more subtle form of racial prejudice, termed *laissez-faire*, *symbolic*, or *modern* racism, that amounts to a "kinder, gentler, antiblack ideology" that avoids notions of biological inferiority (Quillian, 2006; Bobo, Kluegel, & Smith, 1997, p. 15; Sears, 1988). Instead, it involves stereotypes about African Americans, a belief that their poverty is due to their cultural inferiority, and opposition to government policies to help them. In effect, this new form of prejudice blames African Americans themselves for their low socioeconomic standing and involves such beliefs that they simply do not want to work hard. As Lawrence Bobo and colleagues (Bobo, Kluegel, & Smith, 1997, p. 31) put it, "Blacks are still stereotyped and blamed as the architects of their own disadvantaged status." They note that these views lead whites to oppose government efforts to help African Americans.

Evidence for this modern form of prejudice is seen in Figure 10.5 "Attribution by Non-Latino Whites of Blacks' Low Socioeconomic Status to Blacks' Low Innate Intelligence and to Their Lack of Motivation to Improve", which presents whites' responses to two General Social Survey questions that asked, respectively, whether African Americans' low socioeconomic status is due to their lower "in-born ability to learn" or to their lack of "motivation and will power to pull themselves up out of poverty." While only 9.2% of whites attributed blacks' status to lower innate intelligence (reflecting the decline of Jim Crow racism), almost 52% attributed it to their lack of motivation and willpower. Although this reason sounds "kinder" and "gentler" than a belief in blacks' biological inferiority, it is still one that blames African Americans for their low socioeconomic status.

Figure 10.5 Attribution by Non-Latino Whites of Blacks' Low Socioeconomic Status to Blacks' Low Innate Intelligence and to Their Lack of Motivation to Improve

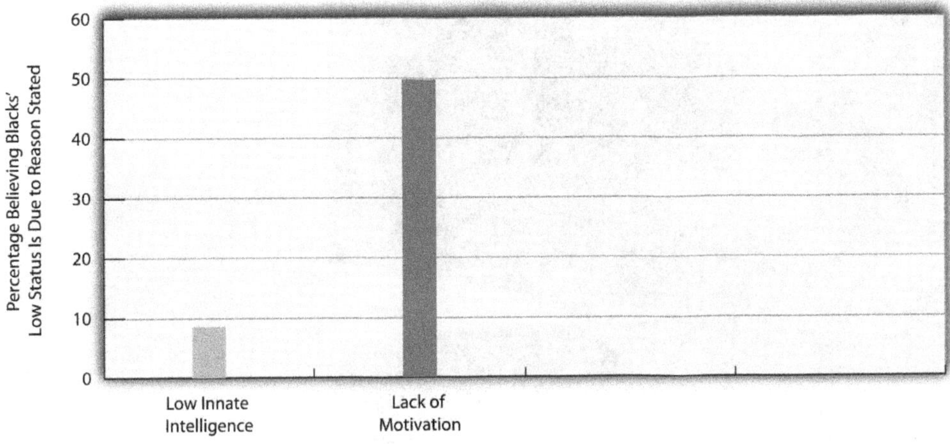

Source: Data from General Social Survey, 2008.

Prejudice and Public Policy Preferences

If whites do continue to believe in racial stereotypes, say the scholars who study modern prejudice, they are that much more likely to oppose government efforts to help people of color. For example, whites who hold racial stereotypes are more likely to oppose government programs for African Americans (Quillian, 2006; Krysan, 2000; Sears, Laar, Carrillo, & Kosterman, 1997). We can see an example of this type of effect in Figure 10.6 "Racial Stereotyping by Non-Latino Whites and Their Opposition to Government Spending to Help African Americans", which shows that whites who attribute blacks' poverty to lack of motivation are more likely than whites who cite discrimination to believe the government is spending too much to improve the conditions of blacks.

Figure 10.6 Racial Stereotyping by Non-Latino Whites and Their Opposition to Government Spending to Help African Americans

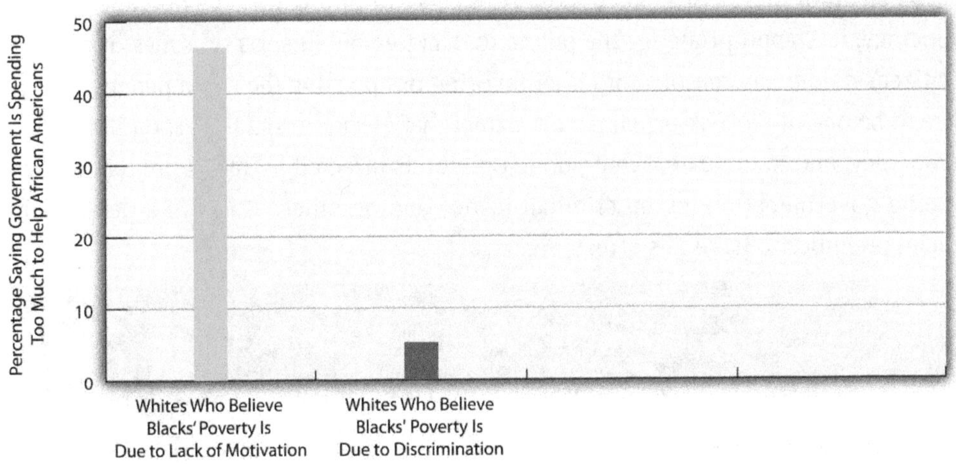

Source: Data from General Social Survey, 2008.

Racial prejudice influences other public policy preferences as well. In the area of criminal justice, whites who hold racial stereotypes or hostile feelings toward African Americans are more likely to be afraid of crime, to think that the courts are not harsh enough, to support the death penalty, to want more money spent to fight crime, and to favor excessive use of force by police (Barkan & Cohn, 1998, 2005; Unnever & Cullen, 2010).

Whites who are racially prejudiced are more likely to favor harsher treatment of criminals and in particular are more likely to support the death penalty.

Wikimedia Commons – CC BY-SA 3.0.

If racial prejudice influences views on all of these issues, then these results are troubling for a democratic society like the United States. In a democracy, it is appropriate for the public to disagree on all sorts of issues, including criminal justice. For example, citizens hold many reasons for either favoring or opposing the death penalty. But is it appropriate for racial prejudice to be one of these reasons? To the extent that elected officials respond to public opinion, as they should in a democracy, and to the extent that public opinion is affected by racial prejudice, then racial prejudice may be influencing government policy on criminal justice and on other issues. In a democratic society, it is unacceptable for racial prejudice to have this effect.

Key Takeaways

- Social-psychological explanations of prejudice emphasize authoritarian personalities and frustration, while sociological explanations emphasize social learning and group threat.
- Education and region of residence are related to racial prejudice among whites; prejudice is higher among whites with lower levels of formal education and among whites living in the South.
- Jim Crow racism has been replaced by symbolic or modern racism that emphasizes the cultural inferiority of people of color.

- Racial prejudice among whites is linked to certain views they hold about public policy. Prejudice is associated with lower support among whites for governmental efforts to help people of color and with greater support for a more punitive criminal justice system.

For Your Review

1. Think about the last time you heard someone say a remark that was racially prejudiced. What was said? What was your reaction?
2. The text argues that it is inappropriate in a democratic society for racial prejudice to influence public policy. Do you agree with this argument? Why or why not?

References

Adorno, T. W., Frenkel-Brunswick, E., Levinson, D. J., & Sanford, R. N. (1950). *The authoritarian personality.* New York, NY: Harper.

Alvear, C. (1998). No Chicanos on TV. *Nieman Reports, 52,* 49–50.

Aronson, E. (2008). *The social animal* (10th ed.). New York, NY: Worth.

Barkan, S. E., & Cohn, S. F. (2005). On reducing white support for the death penalty: A pessimistic appraisal. *Criminology & Public Policy, 4,* 39–44.

Barkan, S. E., & Cohn, S. F. (1998). Racial prejudice and support by whites for police use of force: A research note. *Justice Quarterly, 15,* 743–753.

Bauer, M. (2009). *Under siege: Life for low-income Latinos in the South.* Montgomery, AL: Southern Poverty Law Center.

Bobo, L., Kluegel, J. R., & Smith, R. A. (1997). Laissez-faire racism: The crystallization of a kinder, gentler, antiblack ideology. In S. A. Tuch & J. K. Martin (Eds.), *Racial attitudes in the 1990s: Continuity and change* (pp. 15–44). Westport, CT: Praeger.

Cowen, E. L., Landes, J., & Schaet, D. E. (1959). The effects of mild frustration on the expression of prejudiced attitudes. *Journal of Abnormal and Social Psychology, 64,* 33–38.

Dinnerstein, L., & Reimers, D. M. (2009). *Ethnic Americans: A history of immigration.* New York, NY: Columbia University Press.

Dollard, J., Doob, L. W., Miller, N. E., Mowrer, O. H., & Sears, R. R. (1939). *Frustration and aggression.* New Haven, CT: Yale University Press.

Entman, R. M., & Rojecki, A. (2001). *The black image in the white mind.* Chicago, IL: University of Chicago Press.

Eschholz, S. (2002). Racial composition of television offenders and viewers' fear of crime. *Critical Criminology, 11,* 41–60.

Gilens, M. (1996). Race and poverty in America: Public misperceptions and the American news media. *Public Opinion Quarterly, 60,* 515–541.

Hughes, M., & Tuch, S. A. (2003). Gender differences in whites' racial attitudes: Are women's attitudes really more favorable? *Social Psychology Quarterly, 66,* 384–401.

Jackson, D. Z. (1997, December 5). Unspoken during race talk. *The Boston Globe,* p. A27.

Krysan, M. (2000). Prejudice, politics, and public opinion: Understanding the sources of racial policy attitudes. *Annual Review of Sociology, 26,* 135–168.

Larson, S. G. (2005). *Media & minorities: The politics of race in news and entertainment*. Lanham, MD: Rowman & Littlefield.

Litvinoff, B. (1988). *The burning bush: Anti-Semitism and world history*. New York, NY: E. P. Dutton.

Lundman, R. J. (2003). The newsworthiness and selection bias in news about murder: Comparative and relative effects of novelty and race and gender typifications on newspaper coverage of homicide. *Sociological Forum, 18,* 357–386.

Mendelberg, T. (1997). Executing Hortons: Racial crime in the 1988 presidential campaign. *Public Opinion Quarterly, 61,* 34–57.

Olzak, S. (1992). *The dynamics of ethnic competition and conflict*. Stanford, CA: Stanford University Press.

Quillian, L. (2006). New approaches to understanding racial prejudice and discrimination. *Annual Review of Sociology, 32,* 299–328.

Schuman, H., Steeh, C., Bobo, L., & Krysan, M. (1997). *Racial attitudes in America: Trends and interpretations* (Rev. ed.). Cambridge, MA: Harvard University Press.

Sears, D. O. (1988). Symbolic racism. In P. A. Katz & D. A. Taylor (Eds.), *Eliminating racism: Profiles in controversy* (pp. 53–84). New York, NY: Plenum.

Sears, D. O., Laar, C. V., Carrillo, M., & Kosterman, R. (1997). Is it really racism? The origins of white Americans' opposition to race-targeted policies. *Public Opinion Quarterly, 61,* 16–57.

Sibley, C. G., & Duckitt, J. (2008). Personality and prejudice: A meta-analysis and theoretical review. *Personality and Social Psychology Review, 12,* 248–279.

Stangor, C. (2009). The study of stereotyping, prejudice, and discrimination within social psychology: A quick history of theory and research. In T. D. Nelson (Ed.), *Handbook of prejudice, stereotyping, and discrimination* (pp. 1–22). New York, NY: Psychology Press.

Surette, R. (2011). *Media, crime, and criminal justice: Images, realities, and policies* (4th ed.). Belmont, CA: Wadsworth.

Tolnay, S. E., & Beck, E. M. (1995). *A festival of violence: An analysis of Southern lynchings, 1882–1930.* Urbana, IL: University of Illinois Press.

Unnever, J. D., & Cullen, F. T. (2010). The social sources of Americans' punitiveness: A test of three competing models. *Criminology, 48*, 99–129.

10.4 Discrimination

Learning Objectives

1. Discuss Merton's views on whether prejudice and discrimination always coincide.
2. Distinguish between individual discrimination and institutional discrimination.
3. Provide two examples of institutional discrimination.

Often racial and ethnic prejudice lead to discrimination against the subordinate racial and ethnic groups in a given society. **Discrimination** in this context refers to the arbitrary denial of rights, privileges, and opportunities to members of these groups. The use of the word *arbitrary* emphasizes that these groups are being treated unequally not because of their lack of merit but because of their race and ethnicity.

Usually prejudice and discrimination go hand-in-hand, but Robert Merton (1949) stressed that this is not always the case. Sometimes we can be prejudiced and not discriminate, and sometimes we might not be prejudiced and still discriminate. Table 10.1 "The Relationship Between Prejudice and Discrimination" illustrates his perspective. The top-left cell and bottom-right cells consist of people who behave in ways we would normally expect. The top-left one consists of "active bigots," in Merton's terminology, people who are both prejudiced and discriminatory. An example of such a person is the white owner of an apartment building who dislikes people of color and refuses to rent to them. The bottom-right cell consists of "all-weather liberals," as Merton called them, people who are neither prejudiced nor discriminatory. An example would be someone who holds no stereotypes about the various racial and ethnic groups and treats everyone the same regardless of her/his background.

Table 10.1 The Relationship Between Prejudice and Discrimination

	Prejudiced?	
Discriminates?	*Yes*	*No*
Yes	Active bigots	Fair-weather liberals
No	Timid bigots	All-weather liberals

Source: Adapted from Merton, R. K. (1949). Discrimination and the American creed. In R. M. MacIver (Ed.), *Discrimination and national welfare* (pp. 99–126). New York, NY: Institute for Religious Studies.

The remaining two cells of the table in Table 10.1 "The Relationship Between Prejudice and Discrimination" are the more unexpected ones. On the bottom left, we see people who are prejudiced but who nonetheless do not discriminate; Merton called them "timid bigots." An example would be white restaurant owners who do not like people of color but still serve them anyway because they want their business or are afraid of being sued if they do not serve them. At the top right, we see "fair-weather liberals": people who are not prejudiced but who still discriminate. An example would be white store owners in the South during the segregation era who thought it was wrong to treat blacks worse than whites but who still refused to sell to them because they were afraid of losing white customers.

Individual Discrimination

Sociologist Joe Feagin's study of middle-class African Americans found that many had been harassed by police and otherwise had experienced various kinds of racial slights.

USAG- Humphreys – USAG-Humphreys teens participate in a focus group – CC BY 2.0.

The discussion so far has centered on **individual discrimination**, or discrimination that individuals practice in their daily lives, usually because they are prejudiced but sometimes even if they are not prejudiced. Examples of individual discrimination abound in today's world. The slights and indignities John Howard Griffin suffered in his experiment some 40 years ago ended when he went back to being white, but people of color do not have the luxury of switching their race or ethnicity. For them, individual discrimination by whites is a routine occurrence.

Joe Feagin (1991), a former president of the American Sociological Association, documented such discrimination when he interviewed middle-class African Americans about their experiences. Many of the people he interviewed said they had been refused service, or at least received poor service, in stores or restaurants. Others said they had been harassed by the police, and even put in fear of their lives, just for being black. Feagin concluded that these examples are not just isolated incidents but rather reflect the larger racism that characterizes U.S. society. To many observers, the arrest of Henry Louis Gates Jr., a renowned African American scholar at Harvard University, at his home in July 2009 was another example of individual discrimination. Gates had returned home after a trip and was trying to open his jammed front door. Fearing a burglary, a passerby called the police. A white officer responded and confirmed that Gates owned the house. Tempers evidently flared, and Gates was arrested. The incident aroused a national controversy and led President Obama to invite Gates and the officer, James Crowley, to the White House for a beer (Wallsten, 2009).

Harvard University scholar Henry Louis Gates Jr. was arrested in July 2009 in front of his house by police officer James Crowley, who was investigating a report of a possible burglary. This incident aroused a national controversy and led President Obama to invite both men to the White House for a beer.

The White House – public domain.

Sociologist Denise Segura found that more than 40% of the Mexican American women she interviewed at a public university had encountered workplace discrimination based on their ethnicity and/or gender.

Jodi Womack – DSC05104 – CC BY 2.0.

Much individual discrimination occurs in the workplace, as sociologist Denise Segura (1992) documented when she interviewed 152 Mexican American women working in white-collar jobs at a public university in California. More than 40% of the women said they had encountered workplace discrimination based on their ethnicity and/ or gender, and they attributed their treatment to stereotypes held by their employers and coworkers. Along with discrimination, they were the targets of condescending comments like "I didn't know that there were any educated people in Mexico that have a graduate degree."

Institutional Discrimination

Individual discrimination is important to address, but at least as consequential in today's world is **institutional discrimination**, or discrimination that pervades the practices of whole institutions, such as housing, medical care, law enforcement, employment, and education. This type of discrimination does not just affect a few isolated people of color. Instead, it affects large numbers of individuals simply because of their race or ethnicity. Sometimes institutional discrimination is also based on gender, disability, and other characteristics.

In the area of race and ethnicity, institutional discrimination often stems from prejudice, as was certainly true in the South during segregation. However, just as individuals can discriminate without being prejudiced, so can institutions when they engage in practices that seem to be racially neutral but in fact have a discriminatory effect. Individuals in institutions can also discriminate without realizing it. They make decisions that turn out upon close inspection to discriminate against people of color even if they did not mean to do so.

The bottom line is this: institutions can discriminate even if they do not intend to do so. Consider height requirements for police. Before the 1970s, police forces around the United States commonly had height requirements, say 5 feet 10 inches. As women began to want to join police forces in the 1970s, many found they were too short. The same was true for people from some racial/ethnic backgrounds, such as Latinos, whose stature is smaller on the average than that of non-Latino whites. Of course, even many white males were too short be become police officers, but the point is that even more women, and even more men of certain ethnicities, were too short.

This gender and ethnic difference is not, in and of itself, discriminatory as the law defines the term. The law allows for *bona fide* (good faith) physical qualifications for a job. As an example, we would all agree that someone has to be able to see to be a school bus driver; sight therefore is a *bona fide* requirement for this line of work. Thus, even though people who are blind cannot become school bus drivers, the law does not consider such a physical requirement to be discriminatory.

But were the height restrictions for police work in the early 1970s *bona fide* requirements? Women and members of certain ethnic groups challenged these restrictions in court and won their cases, as it was decided that there was no logical basis for the height restrictions then in effect. In short (pun intended), the courts concluded that a person did not have to be 5 feet 10 inches to be an effective police officer. In response to these court challenges, police forces lowered their height requirements, opening the door for many more women, Latino men, and some other men to join police forces (Appier, 1998). Whether police forces back then intended their height requirements to discriminate, or whether they honestly thought their height requirements made sense, remains in dispute. Regardless of the reason, their requirements did discriminate.

Institutional discrimination can occur even if this type of discrimination is not intended. Police forces used to have height requirements, but these were deemed by courts to discriminate against women, Latinos, and other individuals. In response, police forces lowered their height requirements.

Thomas Hawk – Oakland Police Memorial – CC BY-NC 2.0.

Institutional discrimination affects the life chances of people of color in many aspects of life today. To illustrate this, we turn to some examples of institutional discrimination that have been the subject of government investigation and scholarly research. (We have discussed gender-based institutional discrimination in Chapter 11 "Gender and Gender Inequality".)

Health Care

People of color have higher rates of disease and illness than whites, a fact we explore further in Chapter 13 "Work and the Economy"'s treatment of health and medicine. One question that arises is why their health is worse. Do they have poorer diets, less healthy lifestyles, and the like, or do they receive worse medical care because of their higher poverty and, perhaps, because of institutional discrimination in the health-care industry? We examine these possible answers in Chapter 13 "Work and the Economy", but for now focus on evidence of institutional discrimination based on race and ethnicity.

Several studies use hospital records to investigate whether people of color receive optimal medical care, including coronary bypass surgery, angioplasty, and catheterization. After taking the patients' medical symptoms and needs into account, these studies find that African Americans are much less likely than whites to receive the procedures just listed. This is true when poor blacks are compared to poor whites and also when middle-class blacks are compared to middle-class whites (Smedley, Stith, & Nelson, 2003). In a novel way of studying race and cardiac care, one study performed an experiment in which several hundred doctors viewed videos of African American and white patients, all of whom, unknown to the doctors, were actors. In the videos, each "patient" complained of identical chest pain and other symptoms. The doctors were then asked to indicate whether they thought the patient needed cardiac catheterization. The African American patients were less likely than the white patients to be recommended for this procedure (Schulman et al., 1999).

Why does discrimination like this occur? It is possible, of course, that some doctors are racists and decide that the lives of African Americans just are not worth saving, but it is far more likely that they have *unconscious* racial biases that somehow affect their medical judgments. Regardless of the reason, the result is the same: African Americans are less likely to receive potentially life-saving cardiac procedures simply because they are black. Institutional discrimination in health care, then, is literally a matter of life and death.

Mortgages, Redlining, and Residential Segregation

When loan officers review mortgage applications, they consider many factors, including the person's income, employment, and credit history. The law forbids them to consider race and ethnicity. Yet many studies find that African Americans and Latinos are more likely than whites to have their mortgage applications declined (Blank, Venkatachalam, McNeil, & Green, 2005). Because members of these groups tend to be poorer than whites and to have less desirable employment and credit histories, the higher rate of mortgage rejections may be appropriate, albeit unfortunate.

To control for this possibility, researchers take these factors into account and in effect compare whites, African Americans, and Latinos with similar incomes, employment, and credit histories. Some studies are purely statistical, and some involve white, African American, and Latino individuals who independently visit the same mortgage-lending institutions and report similar employment and credit histories. Both types of studies find that African Americans and Latinos are still more likely than whites with similar qualifications to have their mortgage applications rejected (Turner et al., 2002). We will probably never know whether loan officers are consciously basing their decisions on racial prejudice, but their practices still amount to racial and ethnic discrimination whether the loan officers are consciously prejudiced or not.

There is also evidence of banks rejecting mortgage applications for people who wish to live in certain urban, supposedly high-risk neighborhoods, and of insurance companies denying homeowner's insurance or else charging higher rates for homes in these same neighborhoods. Practices like these that discriminate against houses in certain neighborhoods are called *redlining*, and they also violate the law (Ezeala-Harrison, Glover, & Shaw-

Jackson, 2008). Because the people affected by redlining tend to be people of color, redlining, too, is an example of institutional discrimination.

Banks have rejected mortgage applications from people who wish to live in certain urban, high-risk neighborhoods. This practice, called redlining, violates the law. Because many of the loan applicants who experience redlining are people of color, redlining is an example of institutional discrimination.

Source: Photo courtesy of Taber Andrew Bain, http://www.flickr.com/photos/88442983@N00/2943913721.

The denial of mortgages and homeowner's insurance contributes to an ongoing pattern of residential segregation, which was once enforced by law but now is reinforced by a pattern of illegal institutional discrimination. Residential segregation involving African Americans in Northern cities intensified during the early 20th century, when tens of thousands of African Americans began migrating from the South to the North to look for jobs (Massey & Denton, 1993). Their arrival alarmed whites, who feared the job competition from the migration and considered African Americans their biological inferiors. Mob violence against African Americans and bombings of their houses escalated, and newspapers used racial slurs routinely and carried many stories linking African Americans to crime. Fear of white violence made African Americans afraid to move into white neighborhoods, and "improvement associations" in white neighborhoods sprung up in an effort to keep African Americans from moving in. These associations and real estate agencies worked together to implement *restrictive covenants* among property owners that stipulated they would not sell or rent their properties to African Americans. These covenants were common after 1910 and were not banned by the U.S. Supreme Court until 1948. Still, residential segregation worsened over the next few decades, as whites used various kinds of harassment, including violence, to keep African Americans out of their neighborhoods, and real estate agencies simply refused to sell property in white neighborhoods to them.

Because of continuing institutional discrimination in housing, African Americans remain highly segregated by residence in many cities, much more so than is true for other people of color. Sociologists Douglas S. Massey and Nancy A. Denton (1993) term this problem *hypersegregation* and say it is reinforced by a pattern of subtle discrimination by realtors and homeowners that makes it difficult for African Americans to find out about homes in white neighborhoods and to buy them. Realtors, for example, may tell African American clients that no homes are available in white neighborhoods. Housing "audits," in which white and African American couples of similar economic standing each inquire at a real estate agency about housing in white neighborhoods, confirm this practice: the white couples are told about houses for sale or apartments for rent, and the African American couples are told that none exist. Today, the routine posting of housing listings on the Internet might be reducing this form of housing discrimination, but not all houses and apartments are posted, and some are simply sold by word of mouth to avoid certain people finding out about them.

The hypersegregation that African Americans experience, say Massey and Denton, cuts them off from the larger society, as many rarely leave their immediate neighborhoods, and results in "concentrated poverty," where joblessness, crime, and other problems reign. Calling residential segregation "American apartheid," they urge vigorous federal, state, and local action to end this ongoing problem.

Employment Discrimination

Title VII of the federal Civil Rights Act of 1964 banned racial discrimination in employment, including hiring, wages, and firing. Table 10.2 "Median Weekly Earnings of Full-Time Workers, 2009" presents weekly earnings data by race and ethnicity and shows that African Americans and Latinos have much lower earnings than whites. Several factors explain this disparity, including the various structural obstacles discussed in Chapter 6 "Groups and Organizations"'s examination of poverty. Despite Title VII, however, an additional reason is that African Americans and Latinos continue to face discrimination in hiring and promotion (Hirsh & Cha, 2008). It is again difficult to determine whether such discrimination stems from conscious prejudice or from unconscious prejudice on the part of potential employers, but it is racial discrimination nonetheless.

A now-classic field experiment documented such discrimination. Sociologist Devah Pager (2007) had young white and African American men apply independently in person for entry-level jobs. They dressed the same and reported similar levels of education and other qualifications. Some applicants also admitted having a criminal record, while other applicants reported no such record. As might be expected, applicants with a criminal record were hired at lower rates than those without a record. However, in striking evidence of racial discrimination in hiring, African American applicants *without* a criminal record were hired at the same low rate as the white applicants *with* a criminal record. Other evidence of racial discrimination in employment abounds. As just one example, in 1996 a major oil company, Texaco, agreed to a $176 million settlement after it was sued by African American employees for rampant discrimination in its promotion practices. Texaco executives had also been caught on tape uttering racial slurs at a meeting where they were discussing the lawsuit (Hammonds, 1996).

Table 10.2 Median Weekly Earnings of Full-Time Workers, 2009

	Median weekly earnings ($)
African American	601
Asian	880
Latino	541
White	757

Source: Data from U.S. Bureau of Labor Statistics. (2010). Annual average data: Weekly earnings. *Labor Force Statistics from the Current Population Survey*. Retrieved from http://www.bls.gov/cps/tables.htm#weekearn.

Key Takeaways

- People who practice racial or ethnic discrimination are usually also prejudiced, but not always. Some people practice discrimination without being prejudiced, and some may not practice discrimination even though they are prejudiced.
- Individual discrimination is common and can involve various kinds of racial slights. Much individual discrimination occurs in the workplace.
- Institutional discrimination often stems from prejudice, but institutions can also practice racial and ethnic discrimination when they engage in practices that seem to be racially neutral but in fact have a discriminatory effect.

For Your Review

1. If you have ever experienced individual discrimination, either as the person committing it or as the person affected by it, briefly describe what happened. How do you now feel when you reflect on this incident?
2. Do you think institutional discrimination occurs because people are purposely acting in a racially discriminatory manner? Why or why not?

References

Appier, J. (1998). *Policing women: The sexual politics of law enforcement and the LAPD.* Philadelphia, PA: Temple University Press.

Blank, E. C., Venkatachalam, P., McNeil, L., & Green, R. D. (2005). Racial discrimination in mortgage lending in Washington, D.C.: A mixed methods approach. *The Review of Black Political Economy, 33*(2), 9–30.

Ezeala-Harrison, F., Glover, G. B., & Shaw-Jackson, J. (2008). Housing loan patterns toward minority borrowers in Mississippi: Analysis of some micro data evidence of redlining. *The Review of Black Political Economy, 35*(1), 43–54.

Feagin, J. R. (1991). The continuing significance of race: Antiblack discrimination in public places. *American Sociological Review, 56*, 101–116.

Hammonds, K. H. (1996, December 16). Texaco was just the beginning: Expect more civil rights tangles with corporate America. *BusinessWeek*, pp. 34–35.

Hirsh, C. E., & Cha, Y. (2008). Understanding employment discrimination: A multilevel approach. *Sociology Compass, 2*(6), 1989–2007.

Massey, D. S., & Denton, N. A. (1993). *American apartheid: Segregation and the making of the underclass.* Cambridge, MA: Harvard University Press.

Merton, R. K. (1949). Discrimination and the American creed. In R. M. MacIver (Ed.), *Discrimination and national welfare* (pp. 99–126). New York, NY: Institute for Religious Studies.

Pager, D. (2007). *Marked: Race, crime, and finding work in an era of mass incarceration.* Chicago, IL: University of Chicago Press.

Schulman, K. A., Berlin, J. A., Harless, W., Kerner, J. F., Sistrunk, S., Gersh, B. J.,...Escarce, J. J. (1999). The effect of race and sex on physicians' recommendations for cardiac catheterization. *The New England Journal of Medicine, 340*, 618–626.

Segura, D. A. (1992). Chicanas in white-collar jobs: "You have to prove yourself more." In C. G. Ellison & W. A. Martin (Eds.), *Race and ethnic relations in the United States: Readings for the 21st century* (pp. 79–88). Los Angeles, CA: Roxbury.

Smedley, B. D., Stith, A. Y., & Nelson, A. R. (Eds.). (2003). *Unequal treatment: Confronting racial and ethnic disparities in health care.* Washington, DC: National Academies Press.

Turner, M. A., Freiberg, F., Godfrey, E., Herbig, C., Levy, D. K., & Smith, R. R. (2002). *All other things being equal: A paired testing study of mortgage lending institutions*. Washington, DC: The Urban Institute.

Wallsten, P. (2009, August 17). Speech follows beer summit; at a Long Beach convention, the man who arrested a black professor will thank police for support. *Los Angeles Times*, p. A10.

10.5 Racial and Ethnic Inequality in the United States

Learning Objectives

1. Describe three explanations for why racial and ethnic inequality exist in the United States.
2. Provide two examples of white privilege.

Probably the best way to begin to understand racial and ethnic inequality in the United States is to read first-hand accounts by such great writers of color as Maya Angelou, Toni Morrison, Piri Thomas, Richard Wright, and Malcolm X, all of whom wrote moving, autobiographical accounts of the bigotry and discrimination they faced while growing up. Sociologists and urban ethnographers have written their own accounts of the daily lives of people of color, and these, too, are well worth reading. One of the classics here is Elliot Liebow's (1967) *Tally's Corner*, a study of black men and their families in Washington, DC.

Statistics also give a picture of racial and ethnic inequality in the United States. We can begin to get a picture of this inequality by examining racial and ethnic differences in such life chances as income, education, and health. Table 10.3 "Selected Indicators of Racial and Ethnic Inequality in the United States" presents data on some of these differences.

Table 10.3 Selected Indicators of Racial and Ethnic Inequality in the United States

	White	African American	Latino	Asian	Native American
Median family income, 2009 ($)	67,341	38,409	39,730	75,027	39,740 (2007)
Persons who are college educated, 2008 (%)	32.6	19.6	13.3	52.6	12.9 (2007)
Persons in poverty, 2009 (%)	9.4	25.8	25.3	12.5	24.2 (2008)
Infant mortality (number of infant deaths per 1,000 births), 2005	5.8	13.6	5.6	4.9	8.1

Sources: Data from U.S. Census Bureau. (2010). *Statistical abstract of the United States: 2010.* Washington, DC: U.S. Government Printing Office. Retrieved from http://www.census.gov/compendia/statab; MacDorman, M., & Mathews, T. J. (2008). Recent trends in infant mortality in the United States. *NCHS Data Brief, Number 9 (October).* Retrieved from http://www.cdc.gov/nchs/data/databriefs/db09.htm#arethere; Ogunwole, S. U. (2006). *We the people: American Indians and Alaska natives in the United States.* Washington, DC: U.S. Census Bureau; U.S. Census Bureau. (2010). Historical income tables: Families. Retrieved from http://www.census.gov/hhes/www/income/data/historical/families/index.html.

The data are clear: U.S. racial and ethnic groups differ dramatically in their life chances. Compared to whites, for example, African Americans, Latinos, and Native Americans have much lower family incomes and much higher rates of poverty; they are also much less likely to have college degrees. In addition, African Americans and Native Americans have much higher infant mortality rates than whites: black infants, for example, are more than twice as likely as white infants to die. These comparisons obscure some differences *within* some of the groups just mentioned. Among Latinos, for example, Cuban Americans have fared better than Latinos overall, and Puerto Ricans worse. Similarly, among Asians, people with Chinese and Japanese backgrounds have fared better than those from Cambodia, Korea, and Vietnam.

Asian Americans have higher family incomes than whites on the average. Although Asian Americans are often viewed as a "model minority," some Asians have been less able than others to achieve economic success, and stereotypes of Asians and discrimination against them remain serious problems.

LindaDee2006 – CC BY-NC-ND 2.0.

Although Table 10.3 "Selected Indicators of Racial and Ethnic Inequality in the United States" shows that African Americans, Latinos, and Native Americans fare much worse than whites, it presents a more complex pattern for Asian Americans. Compared to whites, Asian Americans have higher family incomes and are more likely to hold college degrees, but they also have a higher poverty rate. Thus many Asian Americans do relatively well, while others fare relatively worse, as just noted. Although Asian Americans are often viewed as a "model minority," meaning that they have achieved economic success despite not being white, some Asians have been less able than others to climb the economic ladder. Moreover, stereotypes of Asian Americans and discrimination against them remain serious problems (Chou & Feagin, 2008; Fong, 2007). Even the overall success rate of Asian Americans obscures the fact that their occupations and incomes are often lower than would be expected from their educational attainment. They thus have to work harder for their success than whites do (Hurh & Kim, 1999).

Explaining Racial and Ethnic Inequality

Why do racial and ethnic inequality exist? Why do African Americans, Latinos, Native Americans, and some Asian Americans fare worse than whites? In answering these questions, many people have some very strong opinions.

One long-standing explanation is that blacks and other people of color are *biologically inferior*: they are naturally less intelligent and have other innate flaws that keep them from getting a good education and otherwise doing what needs to be done to achieve the American Dream. As discussed earlier, this racist view is no longer common today. However, whites historically used this belief to justify slavery, lynchings, the harsh treatment of Native Americans in the 1800s, and lesser forms of discrimination. In 1994, Richard J. Herrnstein and Charles Murray revived this view in their controversial book, *The Bell Curve* (Herrnstein & Murray, 1994), in which they argued that the low IQ scores of African Americans, and of poor people more generally, reflect their genetic inferiority in the area of intelligence. African Americans' low innate intelligence, they said, accounts for their poverty and other problems. Although the news media gave much attention to their book, few scholars agreed with its views, and many condemned the book's argument as a racist way of "blaming the victim" (Gould, 1994).

Another explanation of racial and ethnic inequality focuses on supposed *cultural deficiencies* of African Americans and other people of color (Murray, 1984). These deficiencies include a failure to value hard work and, for African Americans, a lack of strong family ties, and are said to account for the poverty and other problems facing these minorities. This view echoes the "culture of poverty" argument presented in Chapter 6 "Groups and Organizations" and is certainly popular today: as we saw earlier, more than half of non-Latino whites think that blacks' poverty is due to their lack of motivation and willpower. Ironically some scholars find support for this "cultural deficiency" view in the experience of many Asian Americans, whose success is often attributed to their culture's emphasis on hard work, educational attainment, and strong family ties (Min, 2005). If that is true, these scholars say, then the lack of success of other people of color stems from the failure of their own cultures to value these attributes.

How accurate is the cultural deficiency argument? Whether people of color have "deficient" cultures remains hotly debated (Bonilla-Silva, 2006; Steele, 2006). Many social scientists find little or no evidence of cultural problems in minority communities and say that the belief in cultural deficiencies is an example of symbolic racism that blames the victim. Yet other social scientists, including those sympathetic to the structural problems facing people of color, believe that certain cultural problems do exist, but they are careful to say that these cultural problems arise out of the structural problems. For example, Elijah Anderson (1999) wrote that a "street culture" or "oppositional culture" exists among African Americans in urban areas that contributes to high levels of violent behavior, but he emphasized that this type of culture stems from the segregation, extreme poverty, and other difficulties these citizens face in their daily lives and helps them deal with these difficulties. Thus even if cultural problems do exist, they should not obscure the fact that structural problems are responsible for the cultural ones.

A third explanation for U.S. racial and ethnic inequality is based in conflict theory and falls into the blaming-the-system approach outlined in Chapter 1 "Sociology and the Sociological Perspective". This view attributes racial and ethnic inequality to institutional and individual discrimination and a lack of opportunity in education and other spheres of life (Feagin, 2006). Segregated housing, for example, prevents African Americans from escaping the inner city and from moving to areas with greater employment opportunities. Employment discrimination keeps the salaries of people of color much lower than they would be otherwise. The schools that many children of color attend every day are typically overcrowded and underfunded. As these problems continue from one generation to the next, it becomes very difficult for people already at the bottom of the socioeconomic ladder to climb up it because of their race and ethnicity.

The Benefits of Being White

American whites enjoy certain privileges merely because they are white. For example, they usually do not have to fear that a police officer will stop them simply because they are white, and they can count on being able to move into any neighborhood they desire as long as they can afford the rent or mortgage. They also generally do not have to worry about being the victims of hate crimes based on their race and to be mistaken for a bellhop, parking valet, or maid.

Loren Kerns – Day 73 – CC BY 2.0.

Before we leave this section on racial and ethnic inequality, it is important to discuss the advantages that U.S. whites enjoy in their daily lives *simply because they are white*. Social scientists term these advantages **white privilege** and say that whites benefit from being white whether or not they are aware of their advantages (McIntosh, 2007). This chapter's discussion of the problems facing people of color points to some of these advantages. For example, whites can usually drive a car at night or walk down a street without having to fear that a police officer will stop them simply because they are white. They can count on being able to move into any neighborhood they desire to as long as they can afford the rent or mortgage. They generally do not have to fear being passed up for promotion simply because of their race. College students who are white can live in dorms without having to worry that racial slurs will be directed their way. White people in general do not have to worry about being the victims of hate crimes based on their race. They can be seated in a restaurant without having to worry that they will be served more slowly or not at all because of their skin color. If they are in a hotel, they do not have to think that someone will mistake them for a bellhop, parking valet, or maid. If they are trying to hail a taxi, they do not have to worry about the taxi driver ignoring them because the driver fears he or she will be robbed.

Social scientist Robert W. Terry (1981, p. 120) once summarized white privilege as follows: "*To be white in America is not to have to think about it.* Except for hard-core racial supremacists, the meaning of being white is having the choice of attending to or ignoring one's own whiteness" (emphasis in original). For people of color in the United States, it is not an exaggeration to say that race and ethnicity is a daily fact of their existence. Yet whites do not generally have to think about being white. As all of us go about our daily lives, this basic difference is one of the most important manifestations of racial and ethnic inequality in the United States.

Key Takeaways

- Three explanations for racial and ethnic inequality in the United States are that (a) people of color are biologically inferior, now considered a racist explanation; (b) people of color have cultural deficiencies; and (c) people of color face many structural obstacles, lack of opportunity, and discriminatory practices.
- Whites benefit from being white, whether or not they realize it. This benefit is called white privilege.

For Your Review

1. Which of the three explanations of racial and ethnic inequality makes the most sense to you? Why?
2. If you are white, describe a time when you benefited from white privilege, whether or not you realized it at the time. If you are a person of color, describe an experience when you would have benefited if you had been white.

References

Anderson, E. (1999). *Code of the street: Decency, violence, and the moral life of the inner city*. New York, NY: W. W. Norton.

Bonilla-Silva, E. (2006). *Racism without racists: Color-blind racism and the persistence of racial inequality in the United States* (2nd ed.). Lanham, MD: Rowman & Littlefield.

Chou, R. S., & Feagin, J. R. (2008). *The myth of the model minority: Asian Americans facing racism*. Boulder, CO: Paradigm.

Feagin, J. R. (2006). *Systematic racism: A theory of oppression*. New York, NY: Routledge.

Fong, T. P. (2007). *The contemporary Asian American experience: Beyond the model minority* (3rd ed.). Upper Saddle River, NJ: Prentice Hall.

Gould, S. J. (1994, November 28). Curveball. *The New Yorker* 139–149.

Herrnstein, R. J., & Murray, C. (1994). *The bell curve: Intelligence and class structure in American life*. New York, NY: Free Press.

Hurh, W. M., & Kim, K. C. (1999). The "success" image of Asian Americans: Its validity, and its practical and theoretical implications. In C. G. Ellison & W. A. Martin (Eds.), *Race and ethnic relations in the United States* (pp. 115–122). Los Angeles, CA: Roxbury.

Liebow, E. (1967). *Tally's corner*. Boston, MA: Little, Brown.

McIntosh, P. (2007). White privilege and male privilege: A personal account of coming to see correspondence through work in women's studies. In M. L. Andersen & P. H. Collins (Eds.), *Race, class, and gender: An anthology* (6th ed.). Belmont, CA: Wadsworth.

Min, P. G. (Ed.). (2005). *Asian Americans: Contemporary trends and issues* (2nd ed.). Thousand Oaks, CA: Sage.

Murray, C. (1984). *Losing ground: American social policy, 1950–1980*. New York, NY: Basic Books.

Steele, S. (2006). *White guilt*. New York, NY: HarperCollins.

Terry, R. W. (1981). The negative impact on white values. In B. P. Bowser & R. G. Hunt (Eds.), *Impacts of racism on white Americans* (pp. 119–151). Beverly Hills, CA: Sage.

10.6 Race and Ethnicity in the 21st Century

Learning Objectives

1. Discuss why there is cause for hope and despair in regard to race and ethnic relations in the United States.
2. Summarize the debate over affirmative action.
3. Summarize recent reaction to growing immigration into the United States.

At the beginning of this chapter we noted that the more things change, the more they stay the same. We saw evidence of this in proclamations over the years about the status of people of color in the United States. As a reminder, in 1903 sociologist W. E. B. Du Bois wrote in his classic book *The Souls of Black Folk* that "the problem of the Twentieth Century is the problem of the color line." Some six decades later, social scientists and government commissions during the 1960s continued to warn us about the race problem in the United States and placed the blame for this problem squarely in the hands of whites and of the social and economic institutions that discriminate against people of color (Kerner Commission, 1968). Three to four decades after these warnings, social scientists during the 1990s and 2000s wrote that conditions had actually worsened for people of color since the 1960s (Massey & Denton, 1993; Wilson, 1996; Hacker, 2003).

Now that we have examined race and ethnicity in the United States, what have we found? Where do we stand a decade into the new century and just more than 100 years after Du Bois wrote about the problem of the color line? Did the historic election of Barack Obama as president in 2008 signify a new era of equality between the races, as many observers wrote, or did his election occur despite the continued existence of pervasive racial and ethnic inequality?

On the one hand, there is cause for hope. Legal segregation is gone. The vicious, "old-fashioned" racism that was so rampant in this country into the 1960s has declined dramatically since that tumultuous time. People of color have made important gains in several spheres of life, and African Americans and other people of color occupy some important elected positions in and outside the South, a feat that would have been unimaginable a generation ago. Perhaps most notably, Barack Obama has African ancestry and identifies as an African American, and on his election night people across the country wept with joy at the symbolism of his victory. Certainly progress has been made in U.S. racial and ethnic relations.

On the other hand, there is also cause for despair. The old-fashioned racism has been replaced by a modern, symbolic racism that still blames people of color for their problems and reduces public support for government policies to deal with their problems. Institutional discrimination remains pervasive, and hate crimes, such as the beating of the elderly African American that began this chapter, remain all too common. Americans of different racial and ethnic backgrounds remain sharply divided on many issues, reminding us that the United States as a nation remains divided by race and ethnicity. Two issues that continue to arouse controversy are affirmative action and immigration, to which we now turn.

Affirmative Action

Affirmative action refers to the preferential treatment of minorities and women in employment and education. Affirmative action programs were begun in the 1960s to provide African Americans and then other people of color and women access to jobs and education to make up for past discrimination. President John F. Kennedy was the first known official to use the term, when he signed an executive order in 1961 ordering federal contractors to "take affirmative action" in ensuring that applicants are hired and treated without regard to their race and national origin. Six years later, President Lyndon B. Johnson added sex to race and national origin as demographic categories for which affirmative action should be used.

Although many affirmative action programs remain in effect today, court rulings, state legislation, and other efforts have limited their number and scope. Despite this curtailment, affirmative action continues to spark much controversy, with scholars, members of the public, and elected officials all holding strong views on the issue (Karr, 2008; Wise, 2005; Cohen & Sterba, 2003).

One of the major court rulings just mentioned was the U.S. Supreme Court's decision in *Regents of the University of California v. Bakke*, 438 U.S. 265 (1978). Allan Bakke was a 35-year-old white man who had twice been rejected for admission into the medical school at the University of California, Davis. At the time he applied, UC–Davis had a policy of reserving 16 seats in its entering class of 100 for qualified people of color to make up for their underrepresentation in the medical profession. Bakke's college grades and scores on the Medical College Admission Test were higher than those of the people of color admitted to UC–Davis either time Bakke applied. He sued for admission on the grounds that his rejection amounted to reverse racial discrimination on the basis of his being white (Stefoff, 2005).

The case eventually reached the Supreme Court, which ruled 5–4 that Bakke must be admitted into the UC–Davis medical school because he had been unfairly denied admission on the basis of his race. As part of its historic but complex decision, the Court thus rejected the use of strict racial quotas in admission as it declared that no applicant could be excluded based solely on the applicant's race. At the same time, however, the Court also declared that race may be used as one of the several criteria that admissions committees consider when making their decisions. For example, if an institution desires racial diversity among its students, it may use race as an admissions criterion along with other factors such as grades and test scores.

Two more recent Supreme Court cases both involved the University of Michigan: *Gratz v. Bollinger*, 539 U.S. 244 (2003), which involved the university's undergraduate admissions, and *Grutter v. Bollinger*, 539 U.S. 306 (2003), which involved the university's law school admissions. In *Grutter* the Court reaffirmed the right of institutions of higher education to take race into account in the admissions process. In *Gratz*, however, the Court invalidated the university's policy of awarding additional points to high school students of color as part of its use of a point system to evaluate applicants; the Court said that consideration of applicants needed to be more individualized than a point system allowed.

Drawing on these Supreme Court rulings, then, affirmative action in higher education admissions on the basis of race/ethnicity is permissible as long as it does not involve a rigid quota system and as long as it does involve an individualized way of evaluating candidates. Race may be used as one of several criteria in such an individualized evaluation process, but it must not be used as the only criterion.

The Debate Over Affirmative Action

Opponents of affirmative action cite several reasons for opposing it. Affirmative action, they say, is reverse discrimination and, as such, is both illegal and immoral. The people benefiting from affirmative action are less qualified than many of the whites with whom they compete for employment and college admissions. In addition, opponents say, affirmative action implies that the people benefiting from it need extra help and thus are indeed less qualified. This implication stigmatizes the groups benefiting from affirmative action.

In response proponents of affirmative action give several reasons for favoring it. Many say it is needed to make up not just for past discrimination and a lack of opportunities for people of color but also for ongoing discrimination and a lack of opportunity. For example, because of their social networks, whites are much better able than people of color to find out about and to get jobs (Reskin, 1998). If this is true, people of color are automatically at a disadvantage in the job market, and some form of affirmative action is needed to give them an equal chance at employment. Proponents also say that affirmative action helps add diversity to the workplace and to the campus. Many colleges, they note, give some preference to high school students who live in a distant state in order to add needed diversity to the student body; to "legacy" students—those with a parent who went to the same institution—to reinforce alumni loyalty and to motivate alumni to donate to the institution; and to athletes, musicians, and other applicants with certain specialized talents and skills. If all of these forms of preferential admission make sense, proponents say, it also makes sense to take students' racial and ethnic backgrounds into account as admissions officers strive to have a diverse student body.

Proponents add that affirmative action has indeed succeeded in expanding employment and educational opportunities for people of color, and that individuals benefiting from affirmative action have generally fared well in the workplace or on the campus. In this regard research finds that African American students graduating from selective U.S. colleges and universities after being admitted under affirmative action guidelines are slightly *more* likely than their white counterparts to obtain professional degrees and to become involved in civic affairs (Bowen & Bok, 1998).

As this brief discussion indicates, several reasons exist for and against affirmative action. A cautious view is that affirmative action may not be perfect but that some form of it is needed to make up for past and ongoing discrimination and lack of opportunity in the workplace and on the campus. Without the extra help that affirmative action programs give disadvantaged people of color, the discrimination and other difficulties they face are certain to continue.

Immigration

Since the 1980s, large numbers of immigrants have entered the United States from countries in Asia, Latin America, and elsewhere. This new wave of immigration has had important consequences for American social, economic, and political life (Dinnerstein & Reimers, 2009; Waters & Ueda, 2007).

One of the most important consequences is competition over jobs. The newcomers have tended to move into the large cities on the East and West Coasts and in the southwestern region of the country. At the same time, eastern and western cities were losing jobs as manufacturing and other industries moved south or overseas. The new immigrants thus began competing with native-born Americans for increasingly scarce jobs. Their increasing numbers also prompted native-born whites to move out of these cities in a search for all-white neighborhoods. As they did so, they left behind them neighborhoods that were increasingly segregated along ethnic lines.

Sociology Making a Difference

Immigration and the Crime Rate

Many Americans take a dim view of immigration. In a 2009 Gallup Poll, 50% of Americans thought that immigration should be decreased, 32% thought it should stay at its present level, and only 14% thought it should be increased (Morales, 2009). As the text notes, fear of job competition is a primary reason for the concern that Americans show about immigration. Yet another reason might be their fear that immigration raises the crime rate. A 2007 Gallup Poll asked whether immigrants are making "the situation in the country better or worse, or not having much effect" for the following dimensions of our national life: food, music and the arts; the economy; social and moral values; job opportunities; taxes; and the crime situation. The percentage of respondents saying "worse" was higher for the crime situation (58%) than for any other dimension. Only 4% of respondents said that immigration has made the crime situation better (Newport, 2007).

However, research conducted by sociologists and criminologists finds that these 4% are in fact correct: immigrants have lower crime rates than native-born Americans, and immigration has apparently helped lower the U.S. crime rate (Immigration Policy Center, 2008; Vélez, 2006; Sampson, 2008). What accounts for this surprising consequence? One reason is that immigrant neighborhoods tend to have many small businesses, churches, and other social institutions that help ensure neighborhood stability and, in turn, lower crime rates. A second reason is that the bulk of recent immigrants are Latinos, who tend to have high marriage rates and strong family ties, both of which again help ensure lower crime rates (Vélez, 2006). A final reason may be that undocumented immigrants hardly want to be deported and thus take extra care to obey the law by not committing street crime (Immigration Policy Center, 2008).

Reinforcing the immigration-lower crime conclusion, other research also finds that immigrants' crime rates rise as they stay in the United States longer. Apparently, as the children of immigrants become more "Americanized," their criminality increases. As one report concluded, "The children and grandchildren of many immigrants—as well as many immigrants themselves the longer they live in the United States—become subject to economic and social forces that increase the likelihood of criminal behavior" (Rumbaut & Ewing, 2007, p. 11).

As the United States continues to address immigration policy, it is important that the public and elected officials have the best information possible about the effects of immigration. The findings by sociologists and other social scientists that immigrants have lower crime rates and that immigration has apparently helped lower the U.S. crime rate add an important dimension to the ongoing debate over immigration policy.

One other impact of the new wave of immigration has been increased prejudice and discrimination against the new immigrants. As noted earlier, the history of the United States is filled with examples of prejudice and discrimination against immigrants. Such problems seem to escalate as the number of immigrants increases. The past two decades have been no exception to this pattern. As the large numbers of immigrants moved into the United States, blogs and other media became filled with anti-immigrant comments, and hate crimes against immigrants increased. As one report summarized this trend,

> There's no doubt that the tone of the raging national debate over immigration is growing uglier by the day. Once limited to hard-core white supremacists and a handful of border-state extremists, vicious public denunciations of undocumented brown-skinned immigrants are increasingly common among supposedly mainstream anti-immigration activists, radio hosts, and politicians. While their dehumanizing rhetoric typically stops short of openly sanctioning bloodshed, much of it implicitly encourages or even endorses violence by characterizing immigrants from Mexico and Central America as "invaders,"

"criminal aliens," and "cockroaches."

The results are no less tragic for being predictable: although hate crime statistics are highly unreliable, numbers that are available strongly suggest a marked upswing in racially motivated violence against all Latinos, regardless of immigration status. (Mock, 2007)

As just one recent example of one of these hate crimes, a New York City resident from Ecuador who owned a real estate company died in December 2008 after being beaten with a baseball bat by three men who shouted anti-Hispanic slurs. His murder was preceded by the death a month earlier of another Ecuadorean immigrant, who was attacked on Long Island by a group of males who beat him with lead pipes, chair legs, and other objects (Fahim & Zraick, 2008).

Meanwhile, the new immigrants have included thousands who came to the United States illegally. When they are caught, many are detained by U.S. Immigration and Customs Enforcement (ICE) in local jails, federal prisons, and other detention facilities. Immigrants who are in the United States legally but then get arrested for minor infractions are often also detained in these facilities to await deportation. It is estimated that ICE detains about 300,000 immigrants of both kinds every year. Human rights organizations say that all of these immigrants suffer from lack of food, inadequate medical care, and beatings; that many are being detained indefinitely; and that their detention proceedings lack due process.

Learning From Other Societies

Immigration and Ill Will in the Netherlands

Sometimes we can learn from other countries' positive examples, but sometimes we can also learn from their negative examples. In thinking about immigration and immigrants in the United States, the experience of the Netherlands provides a negative example from which there is much to learn.

Normally considered a very tolerant nation, and one whose crime policy was featured in the "Learning From Other Societies" box in Chapter 5 "Social Structure and Social Interaction", the Netherlands in recent years has exhibited marked intolerance for the immigrants in its midst. More than 4% of the Netherlands' 16.7 million population are of Moroccan or Turkish descent, and many of these are Muslim. After the terrorist attacks of September 11, 2001, hostility toward Muslim immigrants increased not only in the United States but also in the Netherlands and other European nations. In the Netherlands, the political climate worsened in 2002 when a politician named Pim Fortuyn campaigned on an explicit anti-immigrant, anti-Muslim platform. He termed Islam "a backward culture," wrote a book entitled *Against the Islamization of Our Culture,* and called for the repeal of an antidiscrimination amendment of the Netherlands' constitution. He also said that immigration to the Netherlands should be sharply curtailed and even eliminated, explaining, "This is a full country. I think 16 million Dutchmen are about enough." Just as Fortuyn's popularity was reaching a peak, he was assassinated by a native white Dutch citizen who was angered by Fortuyn's views. The assassination only served to win sympathy for Fortuyn's beliefs. Sympathy for anti-immigration views strengthened in 2004, when a Dutch filmmaker, the great-grandson of a brother of painter Vincent van Gogh, was murdered by a Moroccan immigrant angered by the filmmaker's production of a short movie that condemned the treatment of women in Islamic nations.

In the ensuing years, relations between native Dutch and Muslim immigrants have worsened. In March 2006 the Dutch government established what were called "some of Europe's most stringent requirements for would-be immigrants." Among other stipulations, the new rules required anyone seeking a residency visa to pass both a Dutch language test and a "civic-integration examination" before arriving in the Netherlands. They also had to take an exam to prove their values were not at odds with Dutch values. Because the exam included a movie depicting a nude beach and gay people kissing, critics said the exam was explicitly designed to exclude Muslim immigrants, whose values would likely differ.

As 2009 began, the Netherlands' anti-immigrant stance had spread across the political spectrum. In late 2008 the nation's

Labor Party, its largest left-wing political group, issued a position paper in which it called for an end to the Netherlands' acceptance of people with non-Dutch backgrounds and urged that immigrants accommodate themselves to Dutch society rather than the reverse. "We have to stop the existence of parallel societies within our country," the chair of the Labor Party said. In mid-2009 the anti-Islam Dutch Freedom Party, headed by Geert Wilders, made electoral advances. Wilders had once written, "I've had enough of Islam in the Netherlands; let not one more Muslim immigrate. I've had enough of the Koran in the Netherlands: Forbid that fascist book."

The Netherlands' experience indicates that ethnic prejudice can arise even in nations normally known for their tolerance and generosity. In view of the growing anti-immigrant prejudice in the United States discussed in the text, Americans who believe prejudice is wrong must maintain vigilance lest the Netherlands' extreme experience replicate itself in the United States. (BBC News, 2002; Vinocur, 2008; Bransten, 2006; Smyth, 2009)

Key Takeaways

- There is reason to be both hopeful and less hopeful in regard to the future of racial and ethnic relations and inequality in the United States.
- Affirmative action continues to be a very controversial issue. Proponents think it is necessary to compensate for past and continuing racial and ethnic discrimination and lack of opportunity, while opponents think it discriminates against qualified whites.
- Recent waves of immigration have increased anti-immigration prejudice, including hate crimes, in the United States. This result mimics earlier periods of American history.

For Your Review

1. How hopeful are you in regard to race and ethnicity in the United States? Explain your answer.
2. Do you favor or oppose affirmative action? Why?
3. Do you think the United States should try to increase immigration, reduce immigration, or let its level stay about the same? Explain your answer.

Reducing Racial and Ethnic Inequality: What Sociology Suggests

The American racial and ethnic landscape is expected to change dramatically during the next few decades. Figure 10.7 "Racial and Ethnic Composition of the United States, 2008 and 2050 (Projected)" shows the current racial and ethnic distribution in the United States and the projected one for the year 2050. Whereas about two-thirds of the country now consists of whites of European backgrounds, in 2050 only about 46% of the country is expected to be white, with Latinos making the greatest gains of all the other racial and ethnic groups. On the other side of the coin, people of color now constitute about one-third of the country but their numbers will increase to about 54% of the country in 2050 (Roberts, 2008).

Figure 10.7 Racial and Ethnic Composition of the United States, 2008 and 2050 (Projected)

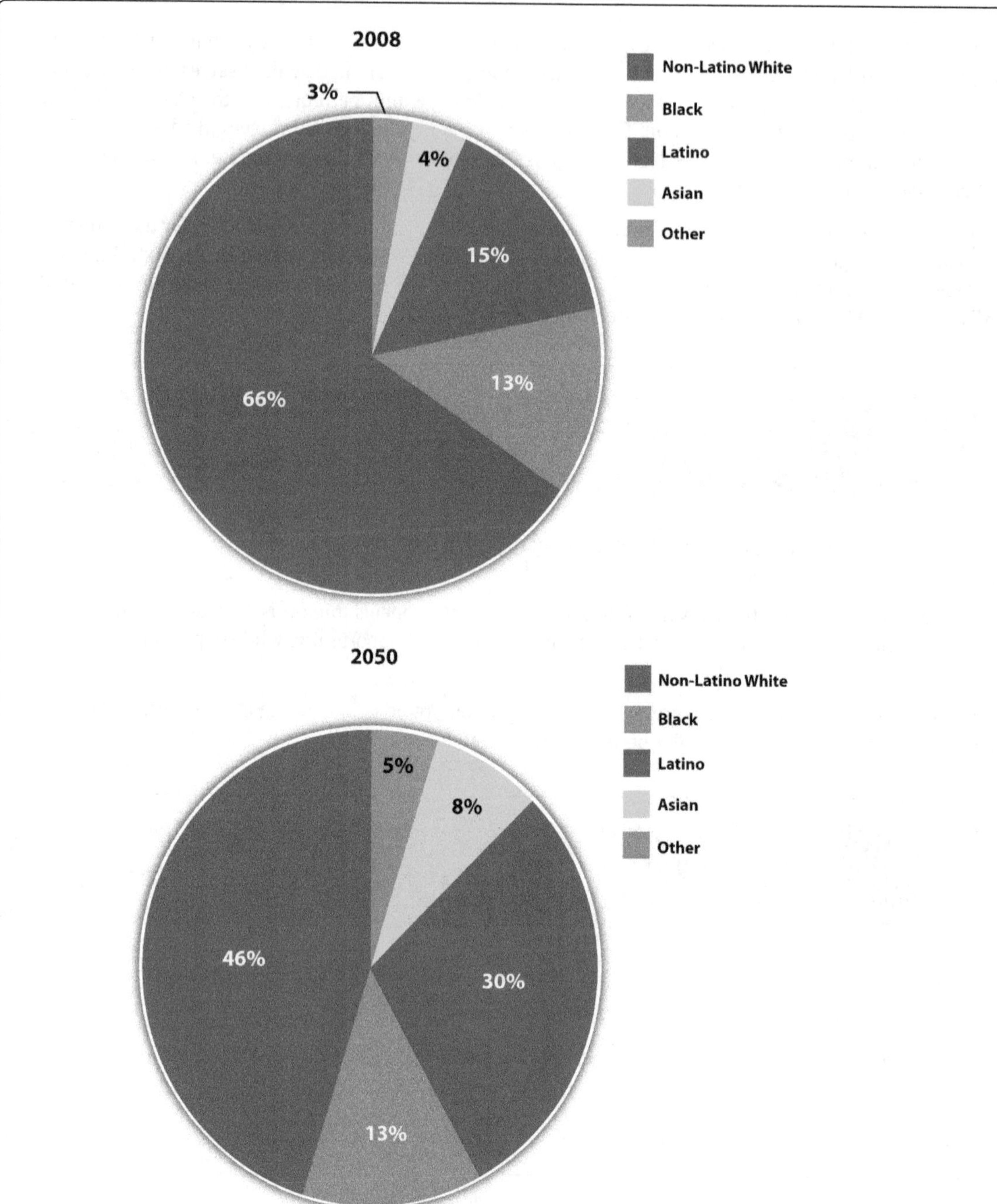

Source: Data from Roberts, S. (2008, August 14). In a generation, minorities may be the U.S. majority. *The New York Times*, p. A1.

Four decades from now, then, whites, the dominant racial group today in terms of power and privilege, will constitute less than half the country. It is difficult at this early date to predict what difference this demographic shift will mean for racial and ethnic relations in the United States. As the number of Latinos and other people of color increases, whites may fear and resent the competition they will provide for jobs and other resources and respond with racial violence and legal efforts to control the growing population of color. As we saw earlier, this was the pattern of the white response in the late 1800s and early 1900s to the great waves of immigration and to black migration from the South. If whites repeat this pattern during the next few decades, we may well be in for even more racial and ethnic strife than we have been seeing in the recent past.

This possibility makes it even more urgent that individuals in their daily lives and the local, state, and federal governments in their policies do everything possible to foster mutual understanding and to eliminate individual and institutional discrimination. As mentioned at the beginning of this chapter, one message of both evolution and of religion is that we are all part of one human race, and if we fail to recognize this lesson we are doomed to repeat the experiences of the past, when racial and ethnic hostility overtook good reason and subjected people who happened to look different from the white majority to legal, social, and violent oppression. In the democracy that is America, we must try to do better so that there will truly be "liberty and justice for all."

As the United States attempts, however haltingly, to reduce racial and ethnic inequality, sociology has much insight to offer in its emphasis on the structural basis for this inequality. This emphasis strongly indicates that racial and ethnic inequality has much less to do with any personal faults of people of color than with the structural obstacles they face, including ongoing discrimination and lack of opportunity. Efforts aimed at such obstacles, then, are in the long run essential to reducing racial and ethnic inequality (Danziger, Reed, & Brown, 2004; Loury, 2003; Syme, 2008). Some of these efforts resemble those for reducing poverty, given the greater poverty of many people of color, and include the following:

1. Adopt a national "full employment" policy involving federally funded job-training and public-works programs.
2. Increase federal aid for the working poor, including earned income credits and child-care subsidies for those with children.
3. Establish well-funded early childhood intervention programs, including home visitation by trained professionals, for poor families.
4. Improve the schools that poor children attend and the schooling they receive, and expand early childhood education programs for poor children.
5. Provide better nutrition and health services for poor families with young children.
6. Strengthen efforts to reduce teenage pregnancies.
7. Strengthen affirmative action programs within the limits imposed by court rulings.
8. Strengthen legal enforcement of existing law forbidding racial and ethnic discrimination in hiring and promotion.
9. Strengthen efforts to reduce residential segregation.

References

BBC News. (2002, May 6). Obituary: Pim Fortuyn. Retrieved from http://news.bbc.co.uk/2/hi/europe/1971462.stm.

Bowen, W. G., & Bok, D. C. (1998). *The shape of the river: Long-term consequences of considering race in college and university admissions*. Princeton, NJ: Princeton University Press.

Bransten, J. (2006, August 30). EU: Netherlands leading trend to more stringent immigration rules. *Radio Free Europe/Radio Liberty*. Retrieved from http://www.rferl.org/content/Article/1067418.html.

Cohen, C., & Sterba, J. P. (2003). *Affirmative action and racial preference: A debate*. New York, NY: Oxford University Press.

Danziger, S., Reed, D., & Brown, T. N. (2004). *Poverty and prosperity: Prospects for reducing racial/ethnic economic disparities in the United States*. Geneva, Switzerland: United Nations Research Institute for Social Development.

Dinnerstein, L., & Reimers, D. M. (2009). *Ethnic Americans: A history of immigration*. New York, NY: Columbia University Press.

Fahim, K., & Zraick, K. (2008, December 15). Killing haunts Ecuadoreans' rise in New York. *The New York Times*, p. A28.

Hacker, A. (2003). *Two nations: Black and white, separate, hostile, unequal* (Rev. ed.). New York, NY: Scribner.

Immigration Policy Center. (2008, September 10). From anecdotes to evidence: Setting the record straight on immigrants and crime. Retrieved from http://immigrationpolicy.org/just-facts/anecdotes-evidence-setting-record-straight-immigrants-and-crime.

Karr, J. (Ed.). (2008). *Affirmative action*. Detroit, MI: Greenhaven Press.

Kerner Commission. (1968). *Report of the National Advisory Commission on Civil Disorders*. New York, NY: Bantam Books.

Loury, G. C. (2003). *The anatomy of racial inequality*. Cambridge, MA: Harvard University Press.

Massey, D. S., & Denton, N. A. (1993). *American apartheid: Segregation and the making of the underclass*. Cambridge, MA: Harvard University Press.

Mock, B. (2007). Immigration backlash: Hate crimes against Latinos flourish. Retrieved from http://www.splcenter.org/intel/intelreport/article.jsp?aid=845.

Morales, L. (2009, August 5). Americans return to tougher immigration stance. Retrieved from http://www.gallup.com/poll/122057/Americans-Return-Tougher-Immigration-Stance.aspx.

Newport, F. (2007, July 13). Americans have become more negative on impact of immigrants. Retrieved from http://www.gallup.com/poll/28132/Americans-Become-More-Negative-Impact-Immigrants.aspx.

Rumbaut, R. G., & Ewing, W. A. (2007). *The myth of immigrant criminality and the paradox of assimilation: Incarceration rates among native and foreign-born men*. Washington, DC: American Immigration Law Foundation.

Reskin, B. F. (1998). *Realities of affirmative action in employment*. Washington, DC: American Sociological Association.

Roberts, S. (2008, August 14). In a generation, minorities may be the U.S. majority. *The New York Times*, p. A1.

Sampson, R. J. (2008). Rethinking crime and immigration. *Contexts, 7*(2), 28–33.

Smyth, J. (2009, June 1). EU critic's anti-Islam stance wins controversy and votes. *The Irish Times*, p. 8.

Stefoff, R. (2005). *The Bakke case: Challenging affirmative action*. New York, NY: Marshall Cavendish Benchmark.

Syme, S. L. (2008). Reducing racial and social-class inequalities in health: The need for a new approach. *Health Affairs, 27,* 456–459.

Vélez, M. B. (2006). Toward an understanding of the lower rates of homicide in Latino versus black neighborhoods: A look at Chicago. In R. D. Peterson, L. J. Krivo, & J. Hagan (Eds.), *The many colors of crime: Inequalities of race, ethnicity, and crime in America* (pp. 91–107). New York, NY: New York University Press.

Vinocur, J. (2008, November 29). From the left, a call to end the current Dutch notion of tolerance. *The New York Times.* Retrieved from http://www.nytimes.com/2008/12/29/world/europe/29iht-politicus.3.18978881.html?scp=1&sq=From%20the%20Left,%20a%20call%20to%20end%20the%20current%20Dutch%20notion%20of%20tolerance&st=cse.

Waters, M. C., & Ueda, R. (Eds.). (2007). *The new Americans: A guide to immigration since 1965.* Cambridge, MA: Harvard University Press.

Wilson, W. J. (1996). *When work disappears: The world of the new urban poor.* New York, NY: Knopf.

Wise, T. J. (2005). *Affirmative action: Racial preference in black and white.* New York, NY: Routledge.

10.7 End-of-Chapter Material

Summary

1. Racial and ethnic prejudice and discrimination have been an "American dilemma" in the United States ever since the colonial period. Slavery was only the ugliest manifestation of this dilemma. In the 19th century, white mobs routinely attacked blacks and immigrants, and these attacks continued well into the 20th century. The urban riots of the 1960s led to warnings about the racial hostility and discrimination confronting African Americans and other groups, and these warnings continue down to the present.
2. Social scientists today tend to consider race more of a social category than a biological one for several reasons. People within a given race often look more different from each other than people do across races. Over the decades, so much interracial reproduction has occurred that many people have mixed racial ancestry. DNA evidence indicates that only a small proportion of our DNA accounts for the physical differences that lead us to put people into racial categories. Given all of these reasons, race is best considered a social construction and not a fixed biological category.
3. Ethnicity refers to a shared cultural heritage and is a term increasingly favored by social scientists over race. Membership in ethnic groups gives many people an important sense of identity and pride but can also lead to hostility toward people in other ethnic groups.
4. Prejudice, racism, and stereotypes all refer to negative attitudes about people based on their membership in racial or ethnic categories. Social-psychological explanations of prejudice focus on scapegoating and authoritarian personalities, while sociological explanations focus on conformity and socialization or on economic and political competition. Before the 1970s old-fashioned or Jim Crow racism, which considered African Americans and some other groups biologically inferior, prevailed. This form of racism has since given way to modern or "symbolic" racism that considers these groups to be culturally inferior and that affects the public's preferences for government policy touching on racial issues. Stereotypes in the mass media fuel racial and ethnic prejudice.
5. Discrimination and prejudice often go hand in hand, but not always. People can discriminate without being prejudiced, and they can be prejudiced without discriminating. Individual and institutional discrimination both continue to exist in the United States, but institutional discrimination in such areas as employment, housing, and medical care is especially pervasive.
6. Racial and ethnic inequality in the United States is reflected in income, employment, education, and health statistics. In all of these areas, African Americans, Native Americans, and Latinos lag far behind whites. As a "model minority," many Asian Americans have fared better than whites, but some Asian groups also lag behind whites. In their daily lives, whites enjoy many privileges denied their counterparts in other racial and ethnic groups. They don't have to think about being white, and they can enjoy freedom of movement and other advantages simply because of their race.
7. On many issues Americans remain sharply divided along racial and ethnic lines. One of the most divisive issues is affirmative action. Its opponents view it among other things as reverse discrimination, while its proponents cite many reasons for its importance, including the need to correct past and present discrimination against racial and ethnic minorities.
8. By the year 2050, whites of European backgrounds will constitute only about half of the American population, whereas now they make up about three-fourths of the population. This demographic change may exacerbate racial tensions if whites fear the extra competition for jobs and other resources that their dwindling numbers may engender. Given this possibility, intense individual and collective efforts are needed to help people of all races and ethnicities realize the American Dream.

Using Sociology

Kim Smith is the vice president of a multicultural group on her campus named Students Operating Against Racism (SOAR). Recently two black students at her school said that they were walking across campus at night and were stopped by campus police for no good reason. SOAR has a table at the campus dining commons with flyers protesting the incident and literature about racial profiling. Kim is sitting at the table, when suddenly two white students come by, knock the literature off the table, and walk away laughing. What, if anything, should Kim do next?

Chapter 11: Gender and Gender Inequality

Social Issues in the News

September 2009 was Rape Awareness Month at the University of Missouri–Columbia. The coordinator of the Relationship & Sexual Violence Prevention Center (RSVP), the group sponsoring the month-long series of events, said they chose September because of the high rates of sexual violence committed against new women students during the first few weeks of the semester. As on many campuses around the country since the late 1970s, a Take Back the Night march and rally was the highlight of RSVP's effort to call attention to violence against women. An RSVP staff member explained that Take Back the Night marches began when women decided, "No, we're not going to live in fear, we're not going to stay inside, these are our streets. This is our community; we're not going to be frightened." At her own campus, she said, "It's women getting together and saying, 'You know what, these are our lives. We own these streets just like anyone else, we walk these streets just like anyone else.' It's a very empowering kind of event and evening." (Silverman, 2009)

It was the early 1970s. Susan (a pseudonym), a sophomore college student, wanted to become a physician, so she went to talk to her biology professor about the pre-med program at her school. The professor belittled her interest in medicine and refused to discuss the program. Women, he advised her, should just become wives and mothers and leave the doctoring to men.

At the same college and about the same time, John (also a pseudonym) went to talk to a draft counselor for advice as he considered his options, including military service in Vietnam. John said he had something very embarrassing to say and hesitated a long time before speaking. Finally John explained, as if revealing a deep secret, that he had never liked to fight, not even as a young boy, and wondered aloud if there was something wrong with him. It was not that he was scared to fight, he assured the draft counselor, it was that he thought fighting was wrong, even though his friends had sometimes called him a "sissy" and other words for refusing to fight. John was advised that he might qualify as a conscientious objector and was informed about that and his other alternatives to being drafted. He left the room, and the draft counselor never saw him again.

Much has changed during the almost four decades since these two real-life stories occurred and since Take Back the Night marches began. Women have entered medicine, engineering, and other professions and careers in unprecedented numbers, no doubt dismaying the biology professor who thought them best suited as wives and mothers. Many men have begun to realize that "real men" do not necessarily have to enjoy fighting and other traditionally male behaviors and attitudes. Our society now has an awareness of rape and other violence against women that would astonish students of the 1970s. Still, gender roles and gender inequality persist and violence against women continues, with important consequences for both women and men and for society as a whole. To begin our discussion of gender and gender inequality, this chapter begins with a critical look at the concepts of sex and gender.

References

Silverman, J. (2009, September 1). RSVP educates students for Rape Awareness Month. *The Maneater* [Official student newspaper of the University of Missouri–Columbia]. Retrieved from http://www.themaneater.com/stories/2009/9/1/rsvp-educates-students-rape-awareness-month.

11.1 Understanding Sex and Gender

Learning Objectives

1. Define sex and gender and femininity and masculinity.
2. Critically assess the evidence on biology, culture and socialization, and gender.
3. Discuss agents of gender socialization.

Although the terms *sex* and *gender* are sometimes used interchangeably and do in fact complement each other, they nonetheless refer to different aspects of what it means to be a woman or man in any society.

Sex refers to the anatomical and other biological differences between females and males that are determined at the moment of conception and develop in the womb and throughout childhood and adolescence. Females, of course, have two X chromosomes, while males have one X chromosome and one Y chromosome. From this basic genetic difference spring other biological differences. The first to appear are the different genitals that boys and girls develop in the womb and that the doctor (or midwife) and parents look for when a baby is born (assuming the baby's sex is not already known from ultrasound or other techniques) so that the momentous announcement, "It's a boy!" or "It's a girl!" can be made. The genitalia are called **primary sex characteristics**, while the other differences that develop during puberty are called **secondary sex characteristics** and stem from hormonal differences between the two sexes. In this difficult period of adolescents' lives, boys generally acquire deeper voices, more body hair, and more muscles from their flowing testosterone. Girls develop breasts and wider hips and begin menstruating as nature prepares them for possible pregnancy and childbirth. For better or worse, these basic biological differences between the sexes affect many people's perceptions of what it means to be female or male, as we shall soon discuss.

Gender as a Social Construction

If sex is a biological concept, then **gender** is a social concept. It refers to the social and cultural differences a society assigns to people based on their (biological) sex. A related concept, **gender roles**, refers to a society's expectations of people's behavior and attitudes based on whether they are females or males. Understood in this way, gender, like race as discussed in Chapter 7 "Deviance, Crime, and Social Control", is a *social construction*. How we think and behave as females and males is not etched in stone by our biology but rather is a result of how society expects us to think and behave based on what sex we are. As we grow up, we learn these expectations as we develop our **gender identity**, or our beliefs about ourselves as females or males.

These expectations are called *femininity* and *masculinity*. **Femininity** refers to the cultural expectations we have of girls and women, while **masculinity** refers to the expectations we have of boys and men. A familiar nursery rhyme nicely summarizes these two sets of traits:

What are little boys made of?

Snips and snails,

And puppy dog tails,

That's what little boys are made of.

What are little girls made of?

Sugar and spice,

And everything nice,

That's what little girls are made of.

As this nursery rhyme suggests, our traditional notions of femininity and masculinity indicate that we think females and males are fundamentally different from each other. In effect, we think of them as two sides of the same coin of being human. What we traditionally mean by femininity is captured in the adjectives, both positive and negative, we traditionally ascribe to women: gentle, sensitive, nurturing, delicate, graceful, cooperative, decorative, dependent, emotional, passive, and weak. Thus when we say that a girl or woman is very feminine, we have some combination of these traits, usually the positive ones, in mind: she is soft, dainty, pretty, even a bit flighty. What we traditionally mean by masculinity is captured in the adjectives, again both positive and negative, our society traditionally ascribes to men: strong, assertive, brave, active, independent, intelligent, competitive, insensitive, unemotional, and aggressive. When we say that a boy or man is very masculine, we have some combination of these traits in mind: he is tough, strong, and assertive.

Infant girls traditionally wear pink, while infant boys wear blue. This color difference reflects the different cultural expectations we have for babies based on their (biological) sex.

Abby Bischoff – CC BY-NC-ND 2.0.

These traits might sound like stereotypes of females and males in today's society, and to some extent they are, but differences between men and women in attitudes and behavior do in fact exist (Aulette, Wittner, & Blakeley, 2009). For example, women cry more often than men do. Men are more physically violent than women. Women take care of children more than men do. Women smile more often than men. Men curse more often than women. When women talk with each other, they are more likely to talk about their personal lives than men are when they talk with each other (Tannen, 2001). The two sexes even differ when they hold a cigarette (not that anyone should smoke). When a woman holds a cigarette, she usually has the palm of her cigarette-holding hand facing upward. When a man holds a cigarette, he usually has his palm facing downward.

Sexual Orientation

Sexual orientation refers to a person's preference for sexual relationships with individuals of the other sex (*heterosexuality*), one's own sex (*homosexuality*), or both sexes (*bisexuality*). The term also increasingly refers to *transgendered* individuals, those whose behavior, appearance, and/or gender identity fails to conform to conventional norms. Transgendered individuals include *transvestites* (those who dress in the clothing of the opposite sex) and *transsexuals* (those whose gender identity differs from the physiological sex and who sometimes undergo a sex change).

It is difficult to know precisely how many people are gay, lesbian, bisexual, or transgendered. One problem is conceptual. For example, what does it mean to be gay or lesbian? Does one need to actually have sexual relations with a same-sex partner to be considered gay? What if someone is attracted to same-sex partners but does not actually engage in sex with such persons? What if someone identifies as heterosexual but engages in homosexual sex for money (as in certain forms of prostitution) or for power and influence (as in much prison sex)? These conceptual problems make it difficult to determine the extent of homosexuality.

A second problem is empirical. Even if we can settle on a definition of homosexuality, how do we then determine how many people fit this definition? For better or worse, our best evidence of the number of gays and lesbians in the United States comes from surveys of national samples of Americans in which they are asked various questions about their sexuality. Although these are anonymous surveys, obviously at least some individuals may be reluctant to disclose their sexual activity and thoughts to an interviewer. Still, scholars think the estimates from these surveys are fairly accurate but that they probably underestimate by at least a small amount the number of gays and lesbians.

A widely cited survey carried out by researchers at the University of Chicago found that 2.8% of men and 1.4% of women identified themselves as gay/lesbian or bisexual, with greater percentages reporting having had sexual relations with same-sex partners or being attracted to same-sex persons (see Table 11.1 "Prevalence of Homosexuality in the United States"). In the 2008 General Social Survey, 2.2% of men and 3.5% of women identified themselves as gay/lesbian or bisexual. Among individuals having had any sexual partners since turning 18, 2.2% of men reported having had at least some male partners, while 4.6% of women reported having had at least some female partners. Although precise numbers must remain unknown, it seems fair to say that between about 2% and 5% of Americans are gay/lesbian or bisexual.

Table 11.1 Prevalence of Homosexuality in the United States

Activity, attraction, or identity	**Men (%)**	**Women (%)**
Find same-sex sexual relations appealing	4.5	5.6
Attracted to people of same sex	6.2	4.4
Identify as gay or bisexual	2.8	1.4
At least one sex partner of same sex during past year among those sexually active	2.7	1.3
At least one sex partner of same sex since turning 18	4.9	4.1

Source: Data from Laumann, E. O., Gagnon, J. H., Michael, R. T., & Michaels, S. (1994). *The social organization of sexuality*. Chicago, IL: University of Chicago Press.

If it is difficult to determine the number of people who are gay/lesbian or bisexual, it is even more difficult to determine why some people have this sexual orientation while most do not have it. Scholars disagree on the "causes" of sexual orientation (Engle, McFalls, Gallagher, & Curtis, 2006; Sheldon, Pfeffer, Jayaratne, Feldbaum, & Petty, 2007). Some scholars attribute it to unknown biological factor(s) over which individuals have no control, just as individuals do not decide whether they are left-handed or right-handed. Supporting this view, many gays say they realized they were gay during adolescence, just as straights would say they realized they were straight during their own adolescence. Other scholars say that sexual orientation is at least partly influenced by cultural norms, so that individuals are more likely to identify as gay or straight depending on the cultural views of sexual orientation into which they are socialized as they grow up. At best, perhaps all we can say is that sexual orientation stems from a complex mix of biological and cultural factors that remain to be determined.

The Development of Gender Differences

What accounts for differences in female and male behavior and attitudes? Do the biological differences between the sexes account for other differences? Or do these latter differences stem, as most sociologists think, from cultural expectations and from differences in the ways in which the sexes are socialized? These are critical questions, for they ask whether the differences between boys and girls and women and men stem more from biology or from society. As Chapter 2 "Eye on Society: Doing Sociological Research" pointed out, biological explanations for human behavior implicitly support the status quo. If we think behavioral and other differences between the sexes are due primarily to their respective biological makeups, we are saying that these differences are inevitable or nearly so and that any attempt to change them goes against biology and will likely fail.

As an example, consider the obvious biological fact that women bear and nurse children and men do not. Couple this with the common view that women are also more gentle and nurturing than men, and we end up with a "biological recipe" for women to be the primary caretakers of children. Many people think this means women are therefore much better suited than men to take care of children once they are born, and that the family might be harmed if mothers work outside the home or if fathers are the primary caretakers. Figure 11.1 "Belief That Women Should Stay at Home" shows that more than one-third of the public agrees that "it is much better for everyone involved if the man is the achiever outside the home and the woman takes care of the home and family." To the extent this belief exists, women may not want to work outside the home or, if they choose to do so, they face difficulties from employers, family, and friends. Conversely, men may not even think about wanting to stay at home and may themselves face difficulties from employees, family, and friends if they want to do so. A belief in a strong biological basis for differences between women and men implies, then, that there is little we can or should do to change these differences. It implies that "anatomy is destiny," and destiny is, of course, by definition inevitable.

Figure 11.1 Belief That Women Should Stay at Home

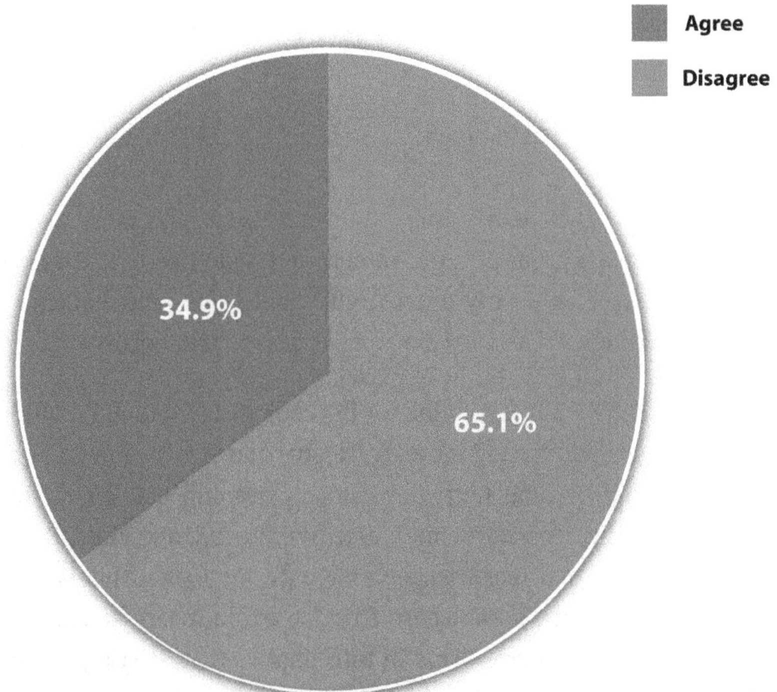

Agreement or disagreement with statement that "it is much better for everyone involved if the man is the achiever outside the home and the woman takes care of the home and family."

Source: Data from General Social Survey, 2008.

This implication makes it essential to understand the extent to which gender differences do, in fact, stem from biological differences between the sexes or, instead, stem from cultural and social influences. If biology is paramount, then gender differences are perhaps inevitable and the status quo will remain. If culture and social influences matter much more than biology, then gender differences can change and the status quo may give way. With this backdrop in mind, let's turn to the biological evidence for behavioral and other differences between the sexes and then examine the evidence for their social and cultural roots.

Biology and Gender

Several biological explanations for gender roles exist, and we discuss two of the most important ones here. One explanation is from the related fields of sociobiology (see Chapter 2 "Eye on Society: Doing Sociological Research") and evolutionary psychology (Workman & Reader, 2009) and argues an evolutionary basis for traditional gender roles.

Scholars advocating this view reason as follows (Barash, 2007; Thornhill & Palmer, 2000). In prehistoric societies, few social roles existed. A major role centered on relieving hunger by hunting or gathering food. The other major role centered on bearing and nursing children. Because only women could perform this role, they were also the primary caretakers for children for several years after birth. And because women were frequently pregnant, their roles as mothers confined them to the home for most of their adulthood. Meanwhile, men were better suited than women for hunting because they were stronger and quicker than women. In prehistoric societies, then, biology was indeed destiny: for biological reasons, men in effect worked outside the home (hunted), while women stayed at home with their children.

Evolutionary reasons also explain why men are more violent than women. In prehistoric times, men who were more willing to commit violence against and even kill other men would "win out" in the competition for female mates. They thus were more likely than less violent men to produce offspring, who would then carry these males' genetic violent tendencies. By the same token, men who were prone to rape women were more likely to produce offspring, who would then carry these males' "rape genes." This early process guaranteed that rape tendencies would be biologically transmitted and thus provided a biological basis for the amount of rape that occurs today.

If the human race evolved along these lines, sociobiologists and evolutionary psychologists continue, natural selection favored those societies where men were stronger, braver, and more aggressive and where women were more fertile and nurturing. Such traits over the millennia became fairly instinctual, meaning that men's and women's biological natures evolved differently. Men became, by nature, more assertive, daring, and violent than women, and women are, by nature, more gentle, nurturing, and maternal than men. To the extent this is true, these scholars add, traditional gender roles for women and men make sense from an evolutionary standpoint, and attempts to change them go against the sexes' biological natures. This in turn implies that existing gender inequality must continue because it is rooted in biology. As the title of a book presenting the evolutionary psychology argument summarizes this implication, "biology at work: rethinking sexual equality" (Browne, 2002).

According to some sociobiologists and evolutionary psychologists, today's gender differences in strength and physical aggression are ultimately rooted in certain evolutionary processes that spanned millennia.

Vladimir Pustovit – Couple – CC BY 2.0.

Critics challenge the evolutionary explanation on several grounds (Hurley, 2007; Buller, 2006; Begley, 2009). First, much greater gender variation in behavior and attitudes existed in prehistoric times than the evolutionary explanation assumes. Second, even if biological differences did influence gender roles in prehistoric times, these differences are largely irrelevant in today's world, in which, for example, physical strength is not necessary for survival. Third, human environments throughout the millennia have simply been too diverse to permit the simple, straightforward biological development that the evolutionary explanation assumes. Fourth, evolutionary arguments implicitly justify existing gender inequality by implying the need to confine women and men to their traditional roles.

Recent anthropological evidence also challenges the evolutionary argument that men's tendency to commit violence, including rape, was biologically transmitted. This evidence instead finds that violent men have trouble finding female mates who would want them and that the female mates they find and the children they produce are often killed by rivals to the men. The recent evidence also finds those rapists' children are often abandoned and then die. As one anthropologist summarizes the rape evidence, "The likelihood that rape is an evolved adaptation [is] extremely low. It just wouldn't have made sense for men in the [prehistoric epoch] to use rape as a reproductive strategy, so the argument that it's preprogrammed into us doesn't hold up" (Begley, 2009, p. 54).

A second biological explanation for traditional gender roles centers on hormones and specifically on testosterone, the so-called male hormone. One of the most important differences between boys and girls and men and women in the United States and many other societies is their level of aggression. Simply put, males are much more physically aggressive than females and in the United States commit about 85%–90% of all violent crimes (see Chapter 7 "Deviance, Crime, and Social Control"). Why is this so? As Chapter 7 "Deviance, Crime, and Social Control" pointed out, this gender difference is often attributed to males' higher levels of testosterone (Mazur, 2009).

To see whether testosterone does indeed raise aggression, researchers typically assess whether males with higher testosterone levels are more aggressive than those with lower testosterone levels. Several studies find that this is indeed the case. For example, a widely cited study of Vietnam-era male veterans found that those with higher levels of testosterone had engaged in more violent behavior (Booth & Osgood, 1993). However, this correlation does not necessarily mean that their testosterone increased their violence: as has been found in various animal species, it is also possible that their violence increased their testosterone. Because studies of human males can't for ethical and practical reasons manipulate their testosterone levels, the exact meaning of the results from these testosterone-aggression studies must remain unclear, according to a review sponsored by the National Academy of Sciences (Miczek, Mirsky, Carey, DeBold, & Raine, 1994).

Another line of research on the biological basis for sex differences in aggression involves children, including some as young as ages 1 or 2, in various situations (Card, Stucky, Sawalani, & Little, 2008). They might be playing with each other, interacting with adults, or writing down solutions to hypothetical scenarios given to them by a researcher. In most of these studies, boys are more physically aggressive in thought or deed than girls, even at a very young age. Other studies are more experimental in nature. In one type of study, a toddler will be playing with a toy, only to have it removed by an adult. Boys typically tend to look angry and try to grab the toy back, while girls tend to just sit there and whimper. Because these gender differences in aggression are found at very young ages, researchers often say they must have some biological basis. However, critics of this line of research counter that even young children have already been socialized along gender lines (Begley, 2009; Eliot, 2009), a point to which we return later. To the extent this is true, gender differences in children's aggression may simply reflect socialization and not biology.

In sum, biological evidence for gender differences certainly exists, but its interpretation remains very controversial. It must be weighed against the evidence, to which we next turn, of cultural variations in the experience of gender and of socialization differences by gender. One thing is clear: to the extent we accept biological explanations for gender, we imply that existing gender differences and gender inequality must continue to exist. This implication prompts many social scientists to be quite critical of the biological viewpoint. As Linda L. Lindsey (2011, p. 52) notes, "Biological arguments are consistently drawn upon to justify gender inequality and the continued oppression of women." In contrast, cultural and social explanations of gender differences and gender inequality promise some hope for change. Let's examine the evidence for these explanations.

Culture and Gender

Some of the most compelling evidence against a strong biological determination of gender roles comes from anthropologists, whose work on preindustrial societies demonstrates some striking gender variation from one culture to another. This variation underscores the impact of culture on how females and males think and behave.

Margaret Mead (1935) was one of the first anthropologists to study cultural differences in gender. In New Guinea she found three tribes—the Arapesh, the Mundugumor, and the Tchambuli—whose gender roles differed dramatically. In the Arapesh both sexes were gentle and nurturing. Both women and men spent much time with their children in a loving way and exhibited what we would normally call maternal behavior. In the Arapesh, then, different gender roles did not exist, and in fact, both sexes conformed to what Americans would normally call the female gender role.

Margaret Mead made important contributions to the anthropological study of gender. Her work suggested that culture dramatically influences how females and males behave and that gender is rooted much more in culture than in biology.

U.S. Library of Congress – public domain.

The situation was the reverse among the Mundugumor. Here both men and women were fierce, competitive, and violent. Both sexes seemed to almost dislike children and often physically punished them. In the Mundugumor society, then, different gender roles also did not exist, as both sexes conformed to what we Americans would normally call the male gender role.

In the Tchambuli, Mead finally found a tribe where different gender roles did exist. One sex was the dominant, efficient, assertive one and showed leadership in tribal affairs, while the other sex liked to dress up in frilly clothes, wear makeup, and even giggle a lot. Here, then, Mead found a society with gender roles similar to those found in the United States, but with a surprising twist. In the Tchambuli, women were the dominant, assertive sex that showed leadership in tribal affairs, while men were the ones wearing frilly clothes and makeup.

Mead's research caused a firestorm in scholarly circles, as it challenged the biological view on gender that was still very popular when she went to New Guinea. In recent years, Mead's findings have been challenged by other anthropologists. Among other things, they argue that she probably painted an overly simplistic picture of gender roles in her three societies (Scheper-Hughes, 1987). Other anthropologists defend Mead's work and note that much subsequent research has found that gender-linked attitudes and behavior do differ widely from one culture to another (Morgan, 1989). If so, they say, the impact of culture on what it means to be a female or male cannot be ignored.

Extensive evidence of this impact comes from anthropologist George Murdock, who created the Standard Cross-Cultural Sample of almost 200 preindustrial societies studied by anthropologists. Murdock (1937) found that some tasks in these societies, such as hunting and trapping, are almost always done by men, while other tasks, such as cooking and fetching water, are almost always done by women. These patterns provide evidence for the evolutionary argument presented earlier, as they probably stem from the biological differences between the sexes. Even so there were at least some societies in which women hunted and in which men cooked and fetched water.

More importantly, Murdock found much greater gender variation in several of the other tasks he studied, including planting crops, milking, and generating fires. Men primarily performed these tasks in some societies, women primarily performed them in other societies, and in still other societies both sexes performed them equally. Figure 11.2 "Gender Responsibility for Weaving" shows the gender responsibility for yet another task, weaving. Women are the primary weavers in about 61% of the societies that do weaving, men are the primary weavers in 32%, and both sexes do the weaving in 7% of the societies. Murdock's findings illustrate how gender roles differ from one culture to another and imply they are not biologically determined.

Figure 11.2 Gender Responsibility for Weaving

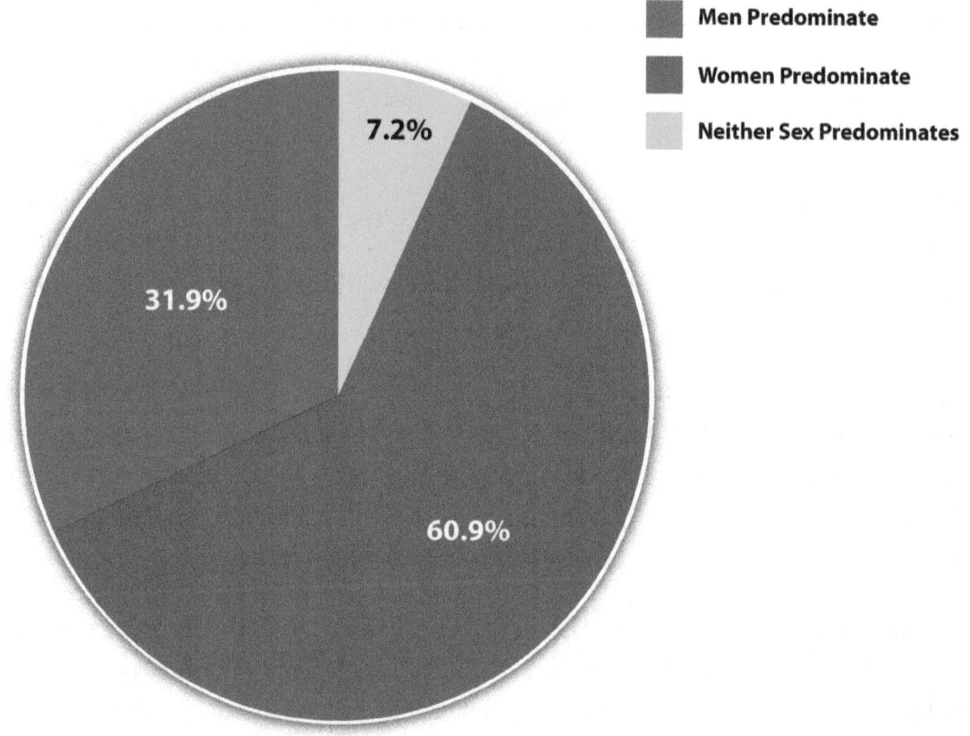

Source: Data from Standard Cross-Cultural Sample.

Anthropologists since Mead and Murdock have continued to investigate cultural differences in gender. Some of their most interesting findings concern gender and sexuality (Morgan, 1989; Brettell & Sargent, 2009). Although all societies distinguish "femaleness" and "maleness," additional gender categories exist in some societies. The Native Americans known as the Mohave, for example, recognize four genders: a woman, a woman who acts like a man, a man, and a man who acts like a woman. In some societies, a third, intermediary gender category is recognized. Anthropologists call this category the *berdache*, who is usually a man who takes on a woman's role. This intermediary category combines aspects of both femininity and masculinity of the society in which it is found and is thus considered an **androgynous** gender. Although some people in this category are born as *intersexed* individuals (formerly known as *hermaphrodites*), meaning they have genitalia of both sexes, many are born biologically as one sex or the other but adopt an androgynous identity.

An example of this intermediary gender category may be found in India, where the *hirja* role involves males who wear women's clothing and identify as women (Reddy, 2006). The *hirja* role is an important part of Hindu mythology, in which androgynous figures play key roles both as humans and as gods. Today people identified by themselves and others as *hirjas* continue to play an important role in Hindu practices and in Indian cultural life in general. Serena Nanda (1997, pp. 200–201) calls *hirjas* "human beings who are neither man nor woman" and says they are thought of as "special, sacred beings" even though they are sometimes ridiculed and abused.

Anthropologists have found another androgynous gender composed of women warriors in 33 Native American groups in North America. Walter L. Williams (1997) calls these women "amazons" and notes that they dress like men and sometimes even marry women. In some tribes girls exhibit such "masculine" characteristics from childhood, while in others they may be recruited into "amazonhood." In the Kaska Indians, for example, a married couple with too many daughters would select one to "be like a man." When she was about 5 years of age, her parents would begin to dress her like a boy and have her do male tasks. Eventually she would grow up to become a hunter.

The androgynous genders found by anthropologists remind us that gender is a social construction and not just a biological fact. If culture does affect gender roles, socialization is the process through which culture has this effect. What we experience as girls and boys strongly influences how we develop as women and men in terms of behavior and attitudes. To illustrate this important dimension of gender, let's turn to the evidence on socialization.

Socialization and Gender

Chapter 3 "Culture" identified several agents of socialization, including the family, peers, schools, the mass media, and religion. While that chapter's discussion focused on these agents' impact on socialization in general, ample evidence of their impact on gender-role socialization also exists. Such socialization helps boys and girls develop their gender identity (Andersen & Hysock, 2009).

The Family

Parents play with their daughters and sons differently. For example, fathers generally roughhouse more with their sons than with their daughters.

Jagrap – Roughhousing – CC BY-NC 2.0.

Socialization into gender roles begins in infancy, as almost from the moment of birth parents begin to socialize their children as boys or girls without even knowing it (Begley, 2009; Eliot, 2009). Many studies document this process (Lindsey, 2011). Parents commonly describe their infant daughters as pretty, soft, and delicate and their infant sons as strong, active, and alert, even though neutral observers find no such gender differences among infants when they do not know the infants' sex. From infancy on, parents play with and otherwise interact with their daughters and sons differently. They play more roughly with their sons—for example, by throwing them up in the air or by gently wrestling with them—and more quietly with their daughters. When their infant or toddler daughters cry, they warmly comfort them, but they tend to let their sons cry longer and to comfort them less. They give their girls dolls to play with and their boys "action figures" and toy guns. While these gender differences in socialization are probably smaller now than a generation ago, they certainly continue to exist. Go into a large toy store and you will see pink aisles of dolls and cooking sets and blue aisles of action figures, toy guns, and related items.

Peers

Peer influences also encourage gender socialization. As they reach school age, children begin to play different games based on their gender (see the "Sociology Making a Difference" box). Boys tend to play sports and other competitive team games governed by inflexible rules and relatively large numbers of roles, while girls tend to play smaller, cooperative games such as hopscotch and jumping rope with fewer and more flexible rules. Although girls are much more involved in sports now than a generation ago, these gender differences in their play as youngsters persist and continue to reinforce gender roles. For example, they encourage competitiveness in boys and cooperation and trust among girls. Boys who are not competitive risk being called "sissy" or other words by their peers. The patterns we see in adult males and females thus have their roots in their play as young children (King, Miles, & Kniska, 1991).

Sociology Making a Difference

Gender Differences in Children's Play and Games

In considering the debate, discussed in the text, between biology and sociology over the origins of gender roles, some widely cited studies by sociologists over gender differences in children's play and games provide important evidence for the importance of socialization.

Janet Lever (1978) studied fifth-grade children in three different communities in Connecticut. She watched them play and otherwise interact in school and also had the children keep diaries of their play and games outside school. One of her central aims was to determine how complex the two sexes' play and games were in terms of such factors as number of rules, specialization of roles, and size of the group playing. In all of these respects, Lever found that boys' play and games were typically more complex than girls' play and games. She attributed these differences to socialization by parents, teachers, and other adults and argued that the complexity of boys' play and games helped them to be better able than girls to learn important social skills such as dealing with rules and coordinating actions to achieve goals.

Meanwhile, Barrie Thorne (1993) spent many months in two different working-class communities in California and Michigan observing fourth and fifth graders sit in class and lunchrooms and play on the school playgrounds. Most children were white, but several were African American or Latino. As you might expect, the girls and boys she observed usually played separately from each other, and the one-sex groups in which they played were very important for the development of their gender identity, with boys tending to play team sports and other competitive games and girls tending to play cooperative games such as jump rope. These differences led Thorne to conclude that gender-role socialization stems not only from practices by adults but also from the children's own activities without adult involvement. When boys and girls did interact, it was often "girls against the boys" or vice versa in classroom spelling contests and in games such as tag. Thorne concluded that these "us against them" contests helped the children learn that boys and girls are two different and antagonistic sexes and that gender itself is antagonistic, even if there were also moments when both sexes interacted on the playground in more relaxed, noncompetitive situations. Boys also tended to disrupt girls' games more than the reverse and in this manner both exerted and learned dominance over females. In all of these ways, children were not just the passive recipients of gender-role socialization from adults (their teachers), but they also played an active role in ensuring that such socialization occurred.

The studies by Lever and Thorne were among the first to emphasize the importance of children's play and peer relationships for gender socialization. They also called attention to the importance of the traits and values learned through such socialization for outcomes later in life. The rise in team sports opportunities for girls in the years since Lever and Thorne did their research is a welcome development that addresses the concerns expressed in their studies, but young children continue to play in the ways that Lever and Thorne found. To the extent children's play has the consequences just listed, and to the extent these consequences impede full gender inequality, these sociological studies suggest the need for teachers, parents, and other adults to help organize children's play that is more egalitarian along the lines discussed by Lever, Thorne, and other scholars. In this way, their sociological work has helped to make a difference and promises to continue to do so.

Schools

School is yet another agent of gender socialization (Klein, 2007). First of all, school playgrounds provide a location for the gender-linked play activities just described to occur. Second, and perhaps more important, teachers at all levels treat their female and male students differently in subtle ways of which they are probably not aware. They tend to call on boys more often to answer questions in class and to praise them more when they give the right answer. They also give boys more feedback about their assignments and other school work (Sadker & Sadker, 1994). At all grade levels, many textbooks and other books still portray people in gender-stereotyped ways. It is true that the newer books do less of this than older ones, but the newer books still contain some stereotypes, and the older books are still used in many schools, especially those that cannot afford to buy newer volumes.

Mass Media

Women's magazines reinforce the view that women need to be slender and wear many cosmetics in order to be considered beautiful.

Photo Editing Services Tucia.com – Glamour /Fashion Retouching by Tucia – CC BY 2.0.

Gender socialization also occurs through the mass media (Dow & Wood, 2006). On children's television shows, the major characters are male. On Nickelodeon, for example, the very popular SpongeBob SquarePants is a male, as are his pet snail, Gary; his best friend, Patrick Star; their neighbor, Squidward Tentacles; and SpongeBob's employer, Eugene Crabs. Of the major characters in Bikini Bottom, only Sandy Cheeks is a female. For all its virtues, *Sesame Street* features Bert, Ernie, Cookie Monster, and other male characters. Most of the Muppets are males, and the main female character, Miss Piggy, depicted as vain and jealous, is hardly an admirable female role model. As for adults' prime-time television, more men than women continue to fill more major roles in weekly shows, despite notable women's roles in shows such as *The Good Wife* and *Grey's Anatomy*. Women are also often portrayed as unintelligent or frivolous individuals who are there more for their looks than for anything else. Television commercials reinforce this image (Yoder, Christopher, & Holmes, 2008). Cosmetics ads abound, suggesting not only that a major task for women is to look good but also that their sense of self-worth stems from looking good. Other commercials show women becoming ecstatic over achieving a clean floor or sparkling laundry. Judging from the world of television commercials, then, women's chief goals in life are to look good and to have a clean house. At the same time, men's chief goals, judging from many commercials, are to drink beer and drive cars.

Women's and men's magazines reinforce these gender images (Milillo, 2008). Most of the magazines intended for teenaged girls and adult women are filled with pictures of thin, beautiful models, advice on dieting, cosmetics ads, and articles on how to win and please your man. Conversely, the magazines intended for teenaged boys and men are filled with ads and articles on cars and sports, advice on how to succeed in careers and other endeavors, and pictures of thin, beautiful (and sometimes nude) women. These magazine images again suggest that women's chief goals are to look good and to please men and that men's chief goals are to succeed, win over women, and live life in the fast lane.

Religion

Another agent of socialization, religion, also contributes to traditional gender stereotypes. Many traditional interpretations of the Bible yield the message that women are subservient to men (Tanenbaum, 2009). This message begins in Genesis, where the first human is Adam, and Eve was made from one of his ribs. The major figures in the rest of the Bible are men, and women are for the most part depicted as wives, mothers, temptresses, and prostitutes; they are praised for their roles as wives and mothers and condemned for their other roles. More generally, women are constantly depicted as the property of men. The Ten Commandments includes a neighbor's wife with his house, ox, and other objects as things not to be coveted (Exodus 20:17), and many biblical passages say explicitly that women belong to men, such as this one from the New Testament:

> Wives be subject to your husbands, as to the Lord. For the husband is the head of the wife as Christ is the head of the Church. As the Church is subject to Christ, so let wives also be subject in everything to their husbands. (Ephesians 5:22–24)

Several passages in the Old Testament justify the rape and murder of women and girls. The Koran, the sacred book of Islam, also contains passages asserting the subordinate role of women (Mayer, 2009).

This discussion suggests that religious people should believe in traditional gender views more than less religious people, and research confirms this relationship (Morgan, 1988). To illustrate this, Figure 11.3 "Frequency of Prayer and Acceptance of Traditional Gender Roles in the Family" shows the relationship in the General Social Survey between frequency of prayer and the view (seen first in Figure 11.1 "Belief That Women Should Stay at Home") that "it is much better for everyone involved if the man is the achiever outside the home and the woman takes care of the home and family." People who pray more often are more likely to accept this traditional view of gender roles.

Figure 11.3 Frequency of Prayer and Acceptance of Traditional Gender Roles in the Family

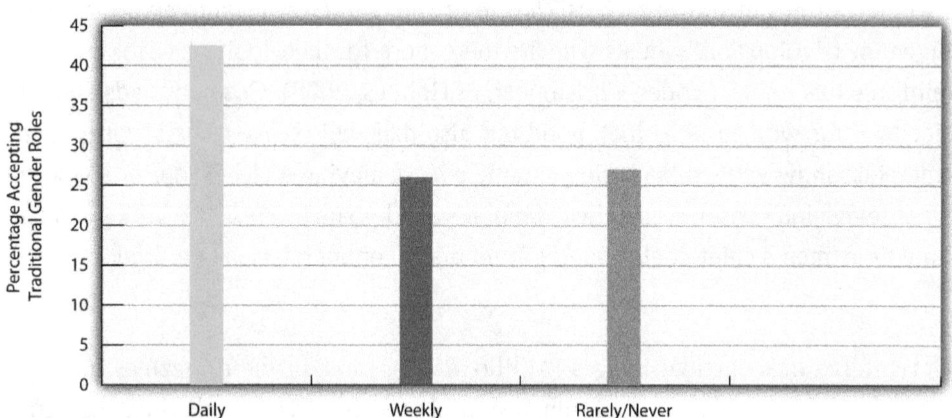

Percentage agreeing that "it is much better for everyone involved if the man is the achiever outside the home and the woman takes care of the home and family."

Source: Data from General Social Survey, 2008.

A Final Word on the Sources of Gender

Scholars in many fields continue to debate the relative importance of biology and of culture and socialization for how we behave and think as girls and boys and as women and men. The biological differences between females and males lead many scholars and no doubt much of the public to assume that masculinity and femininity are to a large degree biologically determined or at least influenced. In contrast, anthropologists, sociologists, and other social scientists tend to view gender as a social construction. Even if biology does matter for gender, they say, the significance of culture and socialization should not be underestimated. To the extent that gender is indeed shaped by society and culture, it is possible to change gender and to help bring about a society where both men and women have more opportunity to achieve their full potential.

Key Takeaways

- Sex is a biological concept, while gender is a social concept and refers to the social and cultural differences a society assigns to people based on their sex.
- Several biological explanations for gender roles exist, but sociologists think culture and socialization are

more important sources of gender roles than biology.

- Families, schools, peers, the mass media, and religion are agents of socialization for the development of gender identity and gender roles.

For Your Review

1. Write a short essay about one or two events you recall from your childhood that reflected or reinforced your gender socialization.
2. Do you think gender roles are due more to biology or to culture and socialization? Explain your answer.

References

Andersen, M., & Hysock, D. (2009). *Thinking about women: Sociological perspectives on sex and gender* (8th ed.). Boston, MA: Allyn & Bacon.

Aulette, J. R., Wittner, J., & Blakeley, K. (2009). *Gendered worlds*. New York, NY: Oxford University Press.

Barash, D. P. (2007). *Natural selections: Selfish altruists, honest liars, and other realities of evolution*. New York, NY: Bellevue Literary Press.

Begley, S. (2009, June 29). Don't blame the caveman. *Newsweek* 52–62.

Begley, S. (2009, September 14). Pink brain, blue brain: Claims of sex differences fall apart. *Newsweek* 28.

Booth, A., & Osgood, D. W. (1993). The influence of testosterone on deviance in adulthood: Assessing and explaining the relationship. *Criminology, 31*(1), 93–117.

Brettell, C. B., & Sargent, C. F. (Eds.). (2009). *Gender in cross-cultural perspective* (5th ed.). Upper Saddle River, NJ: Prentice Hall.

Browne, K. (2002). *Biology at work: Rethinking sexual equality*. New Brunswick, NJ: Rutgers University Press.

Buller, D. J. (2006). *Adapting minds: Evolutionary psychology and the persistent quest for human nature*. Cambridge, MA: MIT Press.

Card, N. A., Stucky, B. D., Sawalani, G. M., & Little, T. D. (2008). Direct and indirect aggression during childhood and adolescence: A meta-analytic review of gender differences, intercorrelations, and relations to maladjustment. *Child Development, 79*(5), 1185–1229. doi:10.1111/j.1467-8624.2008.01184.x.

Dow, B. J., & Wood, J. T. (Eds.). (2006). *The SAGE handbook of gender and communication*. Thousand Oaks, CA: Sage.

Eliot, L. (2009). *Pink brain, blue brain: How small differences grow into troublesome gaps—and what we can do about it*. Boston, MA: Houghton Mifflin Harcourt.

Engle, M. J., McFalls, J. A., Jr., Gallagher, B. J., III, & Curtis, K. (2006). The attitudes of American sociologists toward causal theories of male homosexuality. *The American Sociologist, 37*(1), 68–67.

Hurley, S. (2007). Sex and the social construction of gender: Can feminism and evolutionary psychology be reconciled? In J. Browne (Ed.), *The future of gender* (pp. 98–115). New York, NY: Cambridge University Press.

King, W. C., Jr., Miles, E. W., & Kniska, J. (1991). Boys will be boys (and girls will be girls): The attribution of gender role stereotypes in a gaming situation. *Sex Roles, 25*, 607–623.

Klein, S. S. (Ed.). (2007). *Handbook for achieving gender equity through education* (2nd ed.). Mahwah, NJ: Lawrence Erlbaum Associates.

Lever, J. (1978). Sex differences in the complexity of children's play and games. *American Sociological Review, 43*, 471–483.

Lindsey, L. L. (2011). *Gender roles: A sociological perspective* (5th ed.). Upper Saddle River, NJ: Prentice Hall.

Mayer, A. E. (2009). Review of "Women, the Koran and international human rights law: The experience of Pakistan" [Book review]. *Human Rights Quarterly, 31*(4), 1155–1158.

Mazur, A. (2009). Testosterone and violence among young men. In A. Walsh & K. M. Beaver (Eds.), *Biosocial criminology: New directions in theory and research* (pp. 190–204). New York, NY: Routledge.

Mead, M. (1935). *Sex and temperament in three primitive societies*. New York, NY: William Morrow.

Miczek, K. A., Mirsky, A. F., Carey, G., DeBold, J., & Raine, A. (1994). An overview of biological influences on violent behavior. In J. Albert, J. Reiss, K. A. Miczek, & J. A. Roth (Eds.), *Understanding and preventing violence: Biobehavioral influences* (Vol. 2, pp. 1–20). Washington, DC: National Academy Press.

Milillo, D. (2008). Sexuality sells: A content analysis of lesbian and heterosexual women's bodies in magazine advertisements. *Journal of Lesbian Studies, 12*(4), 381–392.

Morgan, M. (1988). The impact of religion on gender-role attitudes. *Psychology of Women Quarterly, 11*, 301–310.

Morgan, S. (Ed.). (1989). *Gender and anthropology: Critical reviews for research and teaching*. Washington, DC: American Anthropological Association.

Murdock, G. (1937). Comparative data on the division of labor by sex. *Social Forces, 15*, 551–553.

Nanda, S. (1997). Neither man nor woman: The Hirjas of India. In C. B. Brettell & C. F. Sargent (Eds.), *Gender in cross-cultural perspective* (2nd ed., pp. 198–201). Upper Saddle River, NJ: Prentice Hall.

Reddy, G. (2006). *With respect to sex: Negotiating Hirja identity in South India*. New Delhi, India: Yoda.

Sadker, M., & Sadker, D. (1994). *Failing at fairness: How America's schools cheat girls.* New York, NY: Charles Scribner's.

Scheper-Hughes, N. (1987). The Margaret Mead controversy: Culture, biology and anthropological inquiry. In H. Applebaum (Ed.), *Perspectives in cultural anthropology* (pp. 443–454). Albany, NY: State University of New York Press.

Sheldon, J. P., Pfeffer, C. A., Jayaratne, T. E., Feldbaum, M., & Petty, E. M. (2007). Beliefs about the etiology of homosexuality and about the ramifications of discovering its possible genetic origin. *Journal of Homosexuality, 52*(3/4), 111–150.

Tanenbaum, L. (2009). *Taking back God: American women rising up for religious equality.* New York, NY: Farrar, Straus and Giroux.

Tannen, D. (2001). *You just don't understand: Women and men in conversation.* New York, NY: Quill.

Thorne, B. (1993). *Gender play: Girls and boys in school.* New Brunswick, NJ: Rutgers University Press.

Thornhill, R., & Palmer, C. T. (2000). *A natural history of rape: Biological bases of sexual coercion.* Cambridge, MA: MIT Press.

Williams, W. L. (1997). Amazons of America: Female gender variance. In C. B. Brettell & C. F. Sargent (Eds.), *Gender in cross-cultural perspective* (2nd ed., pp. 202–213). Upper Saddle River, NJ: Prentice Hall.

Workman, L., & Reader, W. (2009). *Evolutionary psychology* (2nd ed.). New York, NY: Cambridge University Press.

Yoder, J. D., Christopher, J., & Holmes, J. D. (2008). Are television commercials still achievement scripts for women? *Psychology of Women Quarterly, 32*(3), 303–311. doi:10.1111/j.1471-6402.2008.00438.x.

11.2 Feminism and Sexism

Learning Objectives

1. Define feminism, sexism, and patriarchy.
2. Discuss evidence for a decline in sexism.
3. Understand some correlates of feminism.

Recall that more than one-third of the public (as measured in the General Social Survey) agrees with the statement, "It is much better for everyone involved if the man is the achiever outside the home and the woman takes care of the home and family." Do you agree or disagree with this statement? If you are like the majority of college students, you disagree.

Today a lot of women, and some men, will say, "I'm not a feminist, but…," and then go on to add that they hold certain beliefs about women's equality and traditional gender roles that actually fall into a feminist framework. Their reluctance to self-identify as feminists underscores the negative image that feminists and feminism hold but also suggests that the actual meaning of feminism may be unclear.

Feminism and sexism are generally two sides of the same coin. **Feminism** refers to the belief that women and men should have equal opportunities in economic, political, and social life, while **sexism** refers to a belief in traditional gender role stereotypes and in the inherent inequality between men and women. Sexism thus parallels the concept of racial and ethnic prejudice discussed in Chapter 7 "Deviance, Crime, and Social Control". Both women and people of color are said, for biological and/or cultural reasons, to lack certain qualities for success in today's world.

Feminism as a social movement began in the United States during the abolitionist period before the Civil War. Elizabeth Cady Stanton and Lucretia Mott were outspoken abolitionists who made connections between slavery and the oppression of women.

The US Library of Congress – public domain; The US Library of Congress – public domain.

In the United States, feminism as a social movement began during the abolitionist period preceding the Civil War, as such women as Elizabeth Cady Stanton and Lucretia Mott, both active abolitionists, began to see similarities between slavery and the oppression of women. This new women's movement focused on many issues but especially on the right to vote. As it quickly grew, critics charged that it would ruin the family and wreak havoc on society in other ways. They added that women were not smart enough to vote and should just concentrate on being good wives and mothers (Behling, 2001).

One of the most dramatic events in the women's suffrage movement occurred in 1872, when Susan B. Anthony was arrested because she voted. At her trial a year later in Canandaigua, New York, the judge refused to let her say anything in her defense and ordered the jury to convict her. Anthony's statement at sentencing won wide acclaim and ended with words that ring to this day: "I shall earnestly and persistently continue to urge all women to the practical recognition of the old revolutionary maxim, 'Resistance to tyranny is obedience to God'" (Barry, 1988).

After women won the right to vote in 1920, the women's movement became less active but began anew in the late 1960s and early 1970s, as women active in the Southern civil rights movement turned their attention to women's rights, and it is still active today. To a profound degree, it has changed public thinking and social and economic institutions, but, as we will see coming up, much gender inequality remains. Because the women's movement challenged strongly held traditional views about gender, it has prompted the same kind of controversy that its 19th-century predecessor did. Feminists quickly acquired a bra-burning image, even though there is no documented instance of a bra being burned in a public protest, and the movement led to a backlash as conservative elements echoed the concerns heard a century earlier (Faludi, 1991).

Several varieties of feminism exist. Although they all share the basic idea that women and men should be equal in their opportunities in all spheres of life, they differ in other ways (Lindsey, 2011). *Liberal feminism* believes that the equality of women can be achieved within our existing society by passing laws and reforming social, economic, and political institutions. In contrast, *socialist feminism* blames capitalism for women's inequality and says that true gender equality can result only if fundamental changes in social institutions, and even a socialist revolution, are achieved. *Radical feminism,* on the other hand, says that **patriarchy** (male domination) lies at the root of women's oppression and that women are oppressed even in noncapitalist societies. Patriarchy itself must be abolished, they say, if women are to become equal to men. Finally, an emerging *multicultural feminism* emphasizes that women of color are oppressed not only because of their gender but also because of their race and class (Andersen & Collins, 2010). They thus face a triple burden that goes beyond their gender. By focusing their attention on women of color in the United States and other nations, multicultural feminists remind us that the lives of these women differ in many ways from those of the middle-class women who historically have led U.S. feminist movements.

The Growth of Feminism and the Decline of Sexism

What evidence is there for the impact of the women's movement on public thinking? The General Social Survey, the Gallup Poll, and other national surveys show that the public has moved away from traditional views of gender toward more modern ones. Another way of saying this is that the public has moved toward feminism.

To illustrate this, let's return to the General Social Survey statement that it is much better for the man to achieve outside the home and for the woman to take care of home and family. Figure 11.4 "Change in Acceptance of Traditional Gender Roles in the Family, 1977–2008" shows that agreement with this statement dropped sharply during the 1970s and 1980s before leveling off afterward to slightly more than one-third of the public.

Figure 11.4 Change in Acceptance of Traditional Gender Roles in the Family, 1977–2008

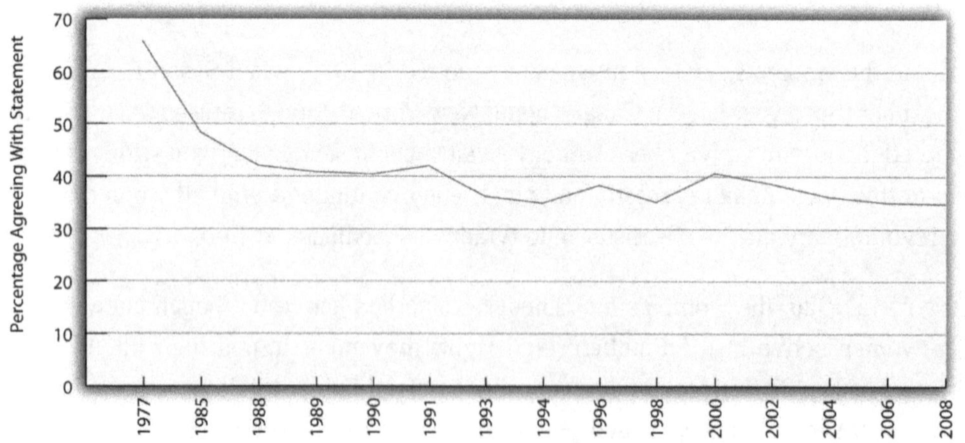

Percentage agreeing that "it is much better for everyone involved if the man is the achiever outside the home and the woman takes care of the home and family."

Source: Data from General Social Survey.

Another General Social Survey question over the years has asked whether respondents would be willing to vote for a qualified woman for president of the United States. As Figure 11.5 "Change in Willingness to Vote for a Qualified Woman for President" illustrates, this percentage rose from 74% in the early 1970s to a high of 94.1% in 2008. Although we have not yet had a woman president, despite Hillary Rodham Clinton's historic presidential primary campaign in 2007 and 2008 and Sarah Palin's presence on the Republican ticket in 2008, the survey evidence indicates the public is willing to vote for one. As demonstrated by the responses to the survey questions on women's home roles and on a woman president, traditional gender views have indeed declined.

Figure 11.5 Change in Willingness to Vote for a Qualified Woman for President

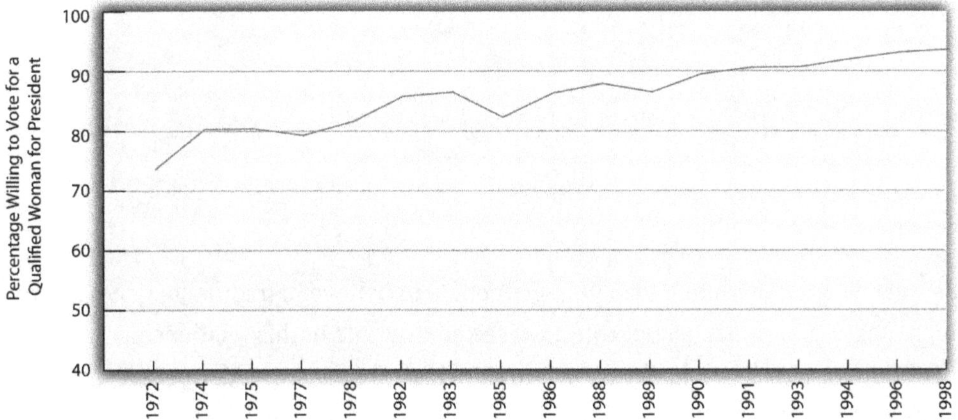

Source: Data from General Social Survey.

Correlates of Feminism

Because of the feminist movement's importance, scholars have investigated why some people are more likely than others to support feminist beliefs. Their research uncovers several correlates of feminism (Dauphinais, Barkan, & Cohn, 1992). We have already seen one of these when we noted that religiosity is associated with support for traditional gender roles. To turn that around, lower levels of religiosity are associated with feminist beliefs and are thus a correlate of feminism.

Several other such correlates exist. One of the strongest is education: the lower the education, the lower the support for feminist beliefs. Figure 11.6 "Education and Acceptance of Traditional Gender Roles in the Family" shows the strength of this correlation by using our familiar General Social Survey statement that men should achieve outside the home and women should take care of home and family. People without a high school degree are almost 5 times as likely as those with a graduate degree to agree with this statement.

Figure 11.6 Education and Acceptance of Traditional Gender Roles in the Family

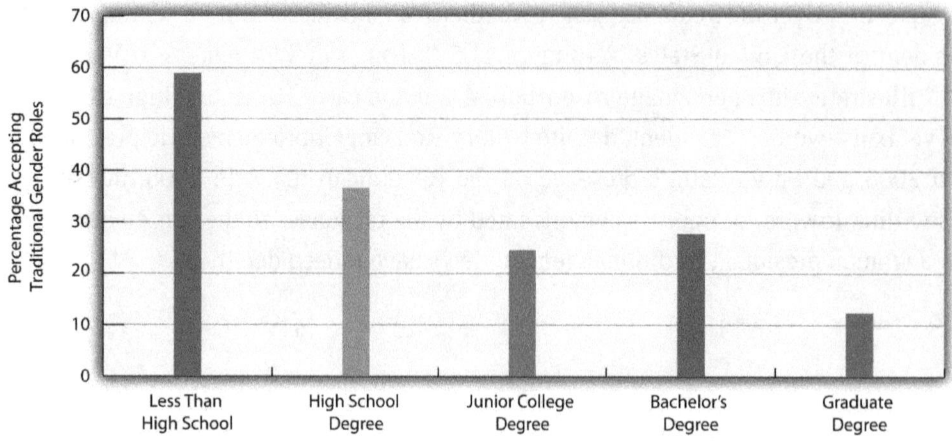

Percentage agreeing that "it is much better for everyone involved if the man is the achiever outside the home and the woman takes care of the home and family."

Source: Data from General Social Survey, 2008.

Age is another correlate, as older people are more likely than younger people to believe in traditional gender roles. Again using our familiar statement about traditional gender roles, we see an example of this relationship in Figure 11.7 "Age and Acceptance of Traditional Gender Roles in the Family", which shows that older people are more likely than younger people to accept traditional gender roles as measured by this statement.

Figure 11.7 Age and Acceptance of Traditional Gender Roles in the Family

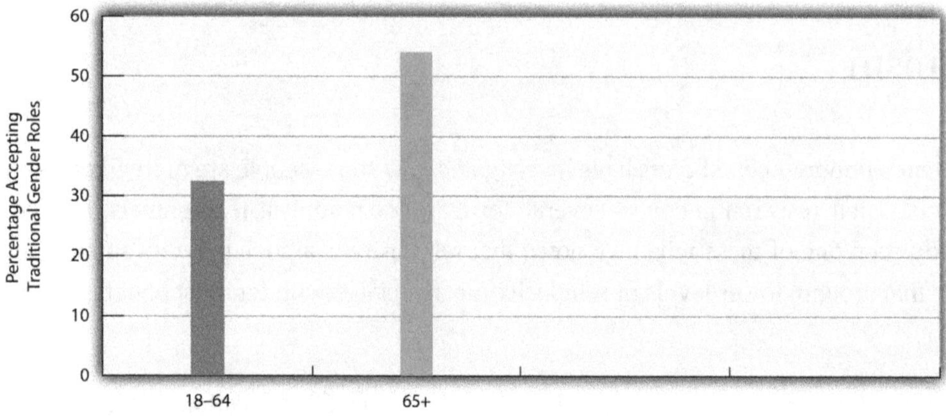

Percentage agreeing that "it is much better for everyone involved if the man is the achiever outside the home and the woman takes care of the home and family."

Source: Data from General Social Survey, 2008.

Key Takeaways

- Feminism refers to the belief that women and men should have equal opportunities in economic, political, and social life, while sexism refers to a belief in traditional gender role stereotypes and in the inherent

inequality between men and women.
- Sexist beliefs have declined in the United States since the early 1970s.
- Several correlates of feminist beliefs exist. In particular, people with higher levels of education are more likely to hold beliefs consistent with feminism.

For Your Review

1. Do you consider yourself a feminist? Why or why not?
2. Think about one of your parents or of another adult much older than you. Does this person hold more traditional views about gender than you do? Explain your answer.

References

Andersen, M. L., & Collins, P. H. (Eds.). (2010). *Race, class, and gender: An anthology* (7th ed.). Belmont, CA: Wadsworth.

Barry, K. L. (1988). *Susan B. Anthony: Biography of a singular feminist*. New York, NY: New York University Press.

Behling, L. L. (2001). *The masculine woman in America, 1890–1935*. Urbana: University of Illinois Press.

Dauphinais, P. D., Barkan, S. E., & Cohn, S. F. (1992). Predictors of rank-and-file feminist activism: Evidence from the 1983 General Social Survey. *Social Problems, 39*, 332–344.

Faludi, S. (1991). *Backlash: The undeclared war against American women*. New York, NY: Crown.

Lindsey, L. L. (2011). *Gender roles: A sociological perspective* (5th ed.). Upper Saddle River, NJ: Prentice Hall.

11.3 Gender Inequality

Learning Objectives

1. Understand the extent of and reasons for gender inequality in income and the workplace.
2. Understand the extent of and reasons for sexual harassment.
3. Explain how and why women of color experience a triple burden.
4. Describe how and why sexual orientation is a source of inequality.

We have said that the women's movement changed American life in many ways but that gender inequality persists. Let's look at examples of such inequality, much of it taking the form of institutional discrimination, which, as we saw in Chapter 7 "Deviance, Crime, and Social Control", can occur even if it is not intended to happen. We start with gender inequality in income and the workplace and then move on to a few other spheres of life.

Income and Workplace Inequality

In the last few decades, women have entered the workplace in increasing numbers, partly, and for many women mostly, out of economic necessity and partly out of desire for the sense of self-worth and other fulfillment that comes with work. This is true not only in the United States but also in other nations, including Japan, where views of women are more traditional than those in the United States (see the "Learning From Other Societies" box). In February 2010, 58.9% of U.S. women aged 16 or older were in the labor force, compared to only 43.3% in 1970; comparable figures for men were 71.0% in 2010 and 79.7% in 1970 (Bureau of Labor Statistics, 2010). Thus while women's labor force participation continues to lag behind men's, they have narrowed the gap. The figures just cited include women of retirement age. When we just look at younger women, labor force participation is even higher. For example, 76.1% of women aged 35–44 were in the labor force in 2008, compared to only 46.8% in 1970.

Learning From Other Societies

Women in Japan and Norway

The United Nations Development Programme ranks nations on a "gender empowerment measure" of women's involvement in their nation's economy and political life. Of the 93 nations included in the measure, Norway ranks 1st, while Japan ranks 54th, the lowest among the world's industrial nations (Watkins, 2007). This contrast provides some lessons for the status of women in the United States, which ranked only 15th.

Japan has historically been a nation with very traditional gender expectations. As the image of the woman's *geisha* role in

Japan illustrates, Japanese women have long been thought to be men's helpmates and subordinates. As Linda Schneider and Arnold Silverman (2010, p. 39) put it,

> The subordination of women is built into Japanese institutions, shaping family life, education, and the economy. Women are seen as fundamentally different from men and inferior to men. Almost everyone assumes that the purpose of a woman's life is to serve others: her children, her husband, perhaps her in-laws, the men at work.
> Many more Japanese women work outside the home now than just a few decades ago and now make up almost half the labor force. However, the percentage of all management jobs held by women was just 10.1% in 2005, up only slightly from its 6.6% level in 1985. Japan's work culture that demands 15-hour days is partly responsible for this low percentage, as it is difficult for women to meet this expectation and still bear and raise children. Another reason is outright employment discrimination. Although Japan enacted an equal opportunity law for women's employment in 1985, the law is more symbolic than real because the only penalty it provides for violations is the publication of the names of the violators (Fackler, 2007).
>
> In sharp contrast, Norway has made a concerted effort to boost women's involvement in the business and political worlds (Sumer, Smithson, Guerreiro, & Granlund, 2008). Like other Nordic countries (Denmark, Finland, Sweden) that also rank at the top of the UN's gender empowerment measure, Norway is a social democratic welfare state characterized by extensive government programs and other efforts to promote full economic and gender equality. Its government provides day care for children and adult care for older or disabled individuals, and it also provides 44 weeks of paid parental leave after the birth of a child. Parents can also work fewer hours without losing income until their child is 2 years of age. All of these provisions mean that women are much more likely than their American counterparts to have the freedom and economic means to work outside the home, and they have taken advantage of this opportunity. As a recent analysis concluded,
>
> > It has been extremely important for women that social rights have been extended to cover such things as the caring of young children and elderly, sick and disabled members of society. In the Nordic countries, women have been more successful than elsewhere in combining their dual role as mothers and workers, and social policy arrangements are an integral part of the gender equality policy. (Kangas & Palme, 2009, p. S65)
> > While the United States ranks much higher than Japan on the UN's gender empowerment measure, it ranks substantially lower than Norway and the other Nordic nations. An important reason for these nations' higher ranking is government policy that enables women to work outside the home if they want to do so. The experience of these nations indicates that greater gender equality might be achieved in the United States if it adopted policies similar to those found in these nations that make it easier for women to join and stay in the labor force.

The Gender Gap in Income

Women have earned less money than men ever since records started being kept. Women now earn about 80% of what men earn.

John Jacobi – receptionist answering phone at suburban eye care – CC BY 2.0.

Despite the gains women have made, problems persist. Perhaps the major problem is a gender gap in income. Women have earned less money than men ever since records started being kept (Reskin & Padavic, 2002). In the United States in the early 1800s, full-time women workers in agriculture and manufacturing earned less than 38% of what men earned. By 1885, they were earning about 50% of what men earned in manufacturing jobs. As the 1980s began, full-time women workers' median weekly earnings were about 65% of men's. Women have narrowed the gender gap in earnings since then: their weekly earnings now (2009) are 80.2% of men's among full-time workers (U.S. Census Bureau, 2010). Still, this means that for every $10,000 men earn, women earn only about $8,002. To turn that around, for every $10,000 women earn, men earn $12,469. This gap amounts to hundreds of thousands of dollars over a lifetime of working.

As Table 11.2 "Median Annual Earnings of Full-Time, Year-Round Workers Aged 25–64 by Educational Attainment, 2009" shows, this gender gap exists for all levels of education and even increases with higher levels of education. On the average, women with a bachelor's degree or higher and working full time earn almost $20,000 less per year than their male counterparts.

Table 11.2 Median Annual Earnings of Full-Time, Year-Round Workers Aged 25–64 by Educational Attainment, 2009

	Less than ninth grade	High school dropout	High school degree	Some college but no degree	Associate's degree	Bachelor's degree or higher
Men	24,133	27,958	39,516	47,238	50,313	71,471
Women	18,322	21,132	29,002	34,097	37,240	51,834
Difference	5,811	6,826	10,514	13,141	13,073	19,637
Gender gap (%; women ÷ men)	75.9	75.6	73.4	72.2	74.0	72.5

Source: Data from U.S. Census Bureau. (2010). Current population survey: Annual social and economic supplement. Retrieved from http://www.census.gov/hhes/www/cpstables/032010/perinc/new03_127.htm.

What accounts for the gender gap in earnings? A major reason is **sex segregation** in the workplace, which accounts for up to 45% of the gender gap (Reskin & Padavic 2002). Although women have increased their labor force participation, the workplace remains segregated by gender. Almost half of all women work in a few low-paying clerical and service (e.g., waitressing) jobs, while men work in a much greater variety of jobs, including high-paying ones. Table 11.3 "Gender Segregation in the Workplace for Selected Occupations, 2007" shows that many jobs are composed primarily of women or of men. Part of the reason for this segregation is that socialization affects what jobs young men and women choose to pursue, and part of the reason is that women and men do not want to encounter difficulties they may experience if they took a job traditionally assigned to the other sex. A third reason is that sex-segregated jobs discriminate against applicants who are not the "right" sex for that job. Employers may either consciously refuse to hire someone who is the "wrong" sex for the job or have job requirements (e.g., height requirements) and workplace rules (e.g., working at night) that unintentionally make it more difficult for women to qualify for certain jobs. Although such practices and requirements are now illegal, they still continue. The sex segregation they help create contributes to the continuing gender gap between female and male workers. Occupations dominated by women tend to have lower wages and salaries. Because women are concentrated in low-paying jobs, their earnings are much lower than men's (Reskin & Padavic, 2002).

Table 11.3 Gender Segregation in the Workplace for Selected Occupations, 2007

Occupation	Female workers (%)	Male workers (%)
Dental hygienists	99.2	0.8
Speech-language pathologists	98.0	2.0
Preschool and kindergarten teachers	97.3	2.7
Secretaries and administrative assistants	96.7	3.3
Registered nurses	91.7	9.3
Food servers (waiters/waitresses)	74.0	26.0
Lawyers	32.6	67.4
Physicians	30.0	70.0
Dentists	28.2	71.8
Computer software engineers	20.8	79.2
Carpenters	1.9	98.1
Electricians	1.7	98.3

Source: Data from U.S. Census Bureau. (2010). *Statistical abstract of the United States: 2010*. Washington, DC: U.S. Government Printing Office. Retrieved from http://www.census.gov/compendia/statab.

This fact raises an important question: why do women's jobs pay less than men's jobs? Is it because their jobs are not important and require few skills (recalling the functional theory of stratification discussed in Chapter 6 "Groups and Organizations")? The evidence indicates otherwise: women's work is devalued precisely because it is women's work, and women's jobs thus pay less than men's jobs because they are women's jobs (Magnusson, 2009).

Studies of **comparable worth** support this argument (Stone & Kuperberg, 2005; Wolford, 2005). Researchers rate various jobs in terms of their requirements and attributes that logically should affect the salaries they offer: the importance of the job, the degree of skill it requires, the level of responsibility it requires, the degree to which the employee must exercise independent judgment, and so forth. They then use these dimensions to determine what salary a job should offer. Some jobs might be "better" on some dimensions and "worse" on others but still end up with the same predicted salary if everything evens out.

Some women's jobs pay less than men's jobs even though their comparable worth is equal to or even higher than the men's jobs. For example, a social worker may earn less money than a probation officer, even though calculations based on comparable worth would predict that a social worker should earn at least as much.

Wikimedia Commons – CC BY 2.0.

When researchers make their calculations, they find that certain women's jobs pay less than men's even though their comparable worth is equal to or even higher than the men's jobs. For example, a social worker may earn less money than a probation officer, even though calculations based on comparable worth would predict that a social worker should earn at least as much. The comparable worth research demonstrates that women's jobs pay less than men's jobs of comparable worth and that the average working family would earn several thousand dollars more annually if pay scales were reevaluated based on comparable worth and women were paid more for their work.

Even when women and men work in the same jobs, women often earn less than men (Sherrill, 2009), and men are more likely than women to hold leadership positions in these occupations. Census data provide ready evidence of the lower incomes women receive even in the same occupations. For example, female marketing and sales managers earn only 68% of what their male counterparts earn; female human resource managers earn only 68% of what their male counterparts earn; female claims adjusters earn only 83%; female accountants earn only 72%; female elementary and middle school teachers earn only 90%; and even female secretaries and clerical workers earn only 86% (U.S. Department of Labor, 2008). When variables like number of years on the job, number of hours worked per week, and size of firm are taken into account, these disparities diminish but do not disappear altogether, and it is very likely that sex discrimination (conscious or unconscious) by employers accounts for much of the remaining disparity.

Litigation has suggested or revealed specific instances of sex discrimination in earnings and employment. In July 2009, the Dell computer company, without admitting any wrongdoing, agreed to pay $9.1 million to settle a class action lawsuit, brought by former executives, that alleged sex discrimination in salaries and promotions (Walsh, 2009). Earlier in the decade, a Florida jury found Outback Steakhouse liable for paying a woman site development assistant only half what it paid a man with the same title. After she trained him, Outback assigned him most of her duties, and when she complained, Outback transferred her to a clerical position. The jury awarded her $2.2 million in compensatory and punitive damages (U.S. Equal Employment Opportunity Commission, 2001).

Some of the sex discrimination in employment reflects the existence of two related phenomena, the **glass ceiling** and the **glass escalator**. Women may be promoted in a job only to find they reach an invisible "glass ceiling" beyond which they cannot get promoted, or they may not get promoted in the first place. In the largest U.S. corporations, women constitute only about 16% of the top executives, and women executives are paid much less than their male counterparts (Jenner & Ferguson, 2009). Although these disparities stem partly from the fact that women joined the corporate ranks much more recently than men, they also reflect a glass ceiling in the corporate world that prevents qualified women from rising up above a certain level (Hymowitz, 2009). Men, on the other hand, can often ride a "glass escalator" to the top, even in female occupations. An example is seen in elementary school teaching, where principals typically rise from the ranks of teachers. Although men constitute only about 20% of all public elementary school teachers, they account for about 44% of all elementary school principals (National Center for Education Statistics, 2009).

Women constitute only about 16% of the top executives in the largest U.S. corporations, and women executives are paid much less than their male counterparts. These disparities reflect a "glass ceiling" that limits women's opportunities for promotion.

Baltic Development Forum – Kristovskis meeting – CC BY 2.0.

Whatever the reasons for the gender gap in income, the fact that women make so much less than men means that female-headed families are especially likely to be poor. In 2009, about 30% of these families lived in poverty, compared to only 6% of married-couple families (DeNavas-Walt, Proctor, & Smith, 2010). The term *feminization of poverty* refers to the fact that female-headed households are especially likely to be poor. The gendering of poverty in this manner is one of the most significant manifestations of gender inequality in the United States.

Sexual Harassment

Another workplace problem (including schools) is **sexual harassment**, which, as defined by federal guidelines and legal rulings and statutes, consists of unwelcome sexual advances, requests for sexual favors, or physical conduct of a sexual nature used as a condition of employment or promotion or that interferes with an individual's job performance and creates an intimidating or hostile environment.

Although men can be, and are, sexually harassed, women are more often the targets of sexual harassment, which is often considered a form of violence against women (discussed in Chapter 11 "Gender and Gender Inequality", Section 11.4 "Violence Against Women: Rape and Pornography"). This gender difference exists for at least two reasons, one cultural and one structural. The cultural reason centers on the depiction of women and the socialization of men. As our discussion of the mass media and gender socialization indicated, women are still depicted in our culture as sexual objects that exist for men's pleasure. At the same time, our culture socializes men to be sexually assertive. These two cultural beliefs combine to make men believe that they have the right to make verbal and physical advances to women in the workplace. When these advances fall into the guidelines listed here, they become sexual harassment.

The second reason that most targets of sexual harassment are women is more structural. Reflecting the gendered nature of the workplace and of the educational system, typically the men doing the harassment are in a position of power over the women they harass. A male boss harasses a female employee, or a male professor harasses a female student or employee. These men realize that subordinate women may find it difficult to resist their advances for fear of reprisals: a female employee may be fired or not promoted, and a female student may receive a bad grade.

How common is sexual harassment? This is difficult to determine, as the men who do the sexual harassment are not about to shout it from the rooftops, and the women who suffer it often keep quiet because of the repercussions just listed. But anonymous surveys of women employees in corporate and other settings commonly find that 40%–65% of the respondents report being sexually harassed (Rospenda, Richman, & Shannon, 2009). In a survey of 4,501 women physicians, 36.9% reported being sexually harassed either in medical school or in their practice as physicians (Frank, Brogan, & Schiffman, 1998).

Sexual harassment in the workplace is a common experience. In surveys of women employees, up to two-thirds of respondents report being sexually harassed.

Wikimedia Commons – CC BY-SA 4.0.

Sexual harassment cases continue to make headlines. In one recent example, the University of Southern Mississippi paid $112,500 in September 2009 to settle a case brought by a women's tennis graduate assistant against the school's women's tennis coach; the coach then resigned for personal reasons (Magee, 2009). That same month, the CEO of a hospital in the state of Washington was reprimanded after a claim of sexual harassment was brought against him, and he was also fired for unspecified reasons (Mehaffey, 2009).

Women of Color: A Triple Burden

Earlier we mentioned multicultural feminism, which stresses that women of color face difficulties for three reasons: their gender, their race, and, often, their social class, which is frequently near the bottom of the socioeconomic ladder. They thus face a triple burden that manifests itself in many ways.

For example, women of color experience "extra" income inequality. Earlier we discussed the gender gap in earnings, with women earning 79.4% of what men earn, but women of color face both a gender gap *and* a racial/ethnic gap. Table 11.4 "The Race/Ethnicity and Gender Gap in Annual Earnings for Full-Time, Year-Round Workers, 2009" depicts this double gap for full-time workers. We see a racial/ethnic gap among both women and men, as African Americans and Latinos of either gender earn less than whites, and we also see a gender gap between men and women, as women earn less than men within any race/ethnicity. These two gaps combine to produce an especially high gap between African American and Latina women and white men: African American women earn only 63.0% of what white men earn, and Latina women earn only 54.6% of what white men earn.

Table 11.4 The Race/Ethnicity and Gender Gap in Annual Earnings for Full-Time, Year-Round Workers, 2009

	Annual earnings ($)	Percentage of white male earnings
Men		
White (non-Latino)	52,350	—
Black	40,133	76.7
Latino	32,372	61.8
Women		
White (non-Latina)	37,948	72.5
Black	32,993	63.0
Latina	28,567	54.6

Source: Data from U.S. Census Bureau. (2010). Current population survey: Annual social and economic supplement. Retrieved from http://www.census.gov/hhes/www/cpstables/032010/perinc/new03_127.htm.

These differences in income mean that African American and Latina women are poorer than white women. We noted earlier that about 31% of all female-headed families are poor. This figure masks race/ethnic differences among such families: 21.5% of families headed by non-Latina white women are poor, compared to 40.5% of families headed by African American women and also 40.5% of families headed by Latina women (Denavas-Walt, Proctor, & Smith, 2010). While white women are poorer than white men, African American and Latina women are clearly poorer than white women.

Sexual Orientation and Inequality

A recent report by a task force of the American Psychological Association stated that "same-sex sexual and romantic attractions, feelings, and behaviors are normal and positive variations of human sexuality" (Glassgold et al., 2009, p. v). A majority of Americans do not share this opinion. In the 2008 General Social Survey, 52% of respondents said that "sexual relations between two adults of the same sex" is "always wrong." Although this figure represents a substantial decline from the survey's 1973 finding of 74%, it is clear that many Americans remain sharply opposed to homosexuality. Not surprisingly, then, sexual orientation continues to be the source of much controversy and no small amount of abuse and discrimination directed toward members of the gay, lesbian, bisexual, and transgendered community.

These individuals experience various forms of abuse, mistreatment, and discrimination that their heterosexual counterparts do not experience. In this respect, their sexuality is the source of a good deal of inequality. For example, gay teenagers are very often the targets of taunting, bullying, physical assault, and other abuse in schools and elsewhere that sometimes drives them to suicide or at least to experience severe emotional distress (Denizet-Lewis, 2009). In 38 states, individuals can be denied employment or fired from a job because of their sexual orientation, even though federal and state laws prohibit employment discrimination for reasons related to race and ethnicity, gender, age, religious belief, and national origin. And in 45 states as of April 2010, same-sex couples are legally prohibited from marrying. In most of these states, this prohibition means that same-sex couples lack hundreds of rights, responsibilities, and benefits that spouses enjoy, including certain income tax and inheritance benefits, spousal insurance coverage, and the right to make medical decisions for a partner who can no longer communicate because of disease or traumatic injury (Gerstmann, 2008).

Household Inequality

We will talk more about the family in Chapter 11 "Gender and Gender Inequality", but for now the discussion will center on housework. Someone has to do housework, and that someone is usually a woman. It takes many hours a week to clean the bathrooms, cook, shop in the grocery store, vacuum, and do everything else that needs to be done. The best evidence indicates that women married to or living with men spend two to three times as many hours per work on housework as men spend (Gupta & Ash, 2008). This disparity holds true even when women work outside the home, leading sociologist Arlie Hochschild (1989) to observe in a widely cited book that women engage in a "second shift" of unpaid work when they come home from their paying job.

The good news is that gender differences in housework time are smaller than a generation ago. The bad news is that a large gender difference remains. As one study summarized the evidence on this issue, "women invest significantly more hours in household labor than do men despite the narrowing of gender differences in recent years" (Bianchi, Milkie, Sayer, & Robinson, 2000, p. 196). In the realm of household work, then, gender inequality persists.

Key Takeaways

- Among full-time workers, women earn about 79.4% of men's earnings. This gender gap in earnings stems from several factors, including sex segregation in the workplace and the lower wages and salaries found in occupations that involve mostly women.
- Sexual harassment results partly from women's subordinate status in the workplace and may involve up to two-thirds of women employees.
- Women of color may face a "triple burden" of difficulties based on their gender, their race/ethnicity, and their social class.
- Sexual orientation continues to be another source of inequality in today's world. Among other examples of this inequality, gays and lesbians are prohibited from marrying in most states in the nation.

For Your Review

1. Do you think it is fair for occupations dominated by women to have lower wages and salaries than those dominated by men? Explain your answer.
2. If you know a woman who works in a male-dominated occupation, interview her about any difficulties she might be experiencing as a result of being in this sort of situation.
3. Write a short essay in which you indicate whether you think same-sex marriage should be legal, and provide the reasoning for the position you hold on this issue.

References

Bianchi, S. M., Milkie, M. A., Sayer, L. C., & Robinson, J. P. (2000). Is anyone doing the Housework? Trends in the gender division of household labor. *Social Forces, 79*(1), 191–228.

Bureau of Labor Statistics. (2010). Employment & earnings online. Retrieved from http://www.bls.gov/opub/ee/home.htm.

DeNavas-Walt, C., Proctor, B. D., & Smith, J. C. (2010). *Income, poverty, and health insurance coverage in the United States: 2009* (Current Population Report P60-238). Washington, DC: U.S. Census Bureau.

Denizet-Lewis, B. (2009, September 27). Coming out in middle school. *The New York Times Magazine* MM36.

Fackler, M. (2007, August 6). Career women in Japan find a blocked path. *The New York Times*, p. A1.

Frank, E., Brogan, D., & Schiffman, M. (1998). Prevalence and correlates of harassment among U.S. women physicians. *Archives of Internal Medicine, 158*(4), 352–358.

Gerstmann, E. (2008). *Same-sex marriage and the Constitution* (2nd ed.). New York, NY: Cambridge University Press.

Glassgold, J. M., Beckstead, L., Drescher, J., Greene, B., Miller, R. L., & Worthington, R. L. (2009). Report of the American Psychological Association task force on appropriate therapeutic responses to sexual orientation. Washington, DC: American Psychological Association.

Gupta, S., & Ash, M. (2008). Whose money, whose time? A nonparametric approach to modeling time spent on housework in the United States. *Feminist Economics, 14*(1), 93–120.

Hochschild, A. (1989). *The second shift: Working parents and the revolution at home*. New York, NY: Viking.

Hymowitz, C. (2009, May 1). For executive women, it can be lonely at the top. *Forbes*. Retrieved from http://www.forbes.com/2009/05/01/executives-c-suite-leadership-forbes-woman-power-careers.html.

Jenner, L., & Ferguson, R. (2009). *2008 catalyst census of women corporate officers and top earners of the FP500*. New York, NY: Catalyst.

Kangas, O., & Palme, J. (2009). Making social policy work for economic development: The Nordic experience [Supplement]. *International Journal of Social Welfare, 18*(s1), S62–S72.

Magee, P. (2009, September 22). USM settles with ex-student. *Hattiesburg American*. Retrieved from http://pqasb.pqarchiver.com/hattiesburgamerican/access/1866160481.html?FMT=ABS&date=Sep+22%2C+2009.

Magnusson, C. (2009). Gender, occupational prestige, and wages: A test of devaluation theory. *European Sociological Review, 25*(1), 87–101.

Mehaffey, K. C. (2009, September 15). Chelan hospital board fires CEO. *The Wenatchee World*. Retrieved from http://www.wenatcheeworld.com/news/2009/sep/15/chelan-hospital-board-fires-ceo.

National Center for Education Statistics. (2009). *The condition of education*. Retrieved from http://nces.ed.gov/programs/coe/2007/section4/indicator34.asp.

Reskin, B., & Padavic, I. (2002). *Women and men at work* (2nd ed.). Thousand Oaks, CA: Pine Forge Press.

Rospenda, K. M., Richman, J. A., & Shannon, C. A. (2009). Prevalence and mental health correlates of harassment and discrimination in the workplace: Results from a national study. *Journal of Interpersonal Violence, 24*(5), 819–843.

Schneider, L., & Silverman, A. (2010). *Global sociology: Introducing five contemporary societies* (5th ed.). New York, NY: McGraw-Hill.

Sherrill, A. (2009). *Women's pay: Converging characteristics of men and women in the federal workforce help explain the narrowing pay gap*. Washington, DC: United States Government Accountability Office.

Stone, P., & Kuperberg, A. (2005). Anti-discrimination vs. anti-poverty? A comparison of pay equity and living wage reforms. *Journal of Women, Politics & Policy, 27*(5), 23–39. doi:10.1300/J501v27n03_3.

Sumer, S., Smithson, J., Guerreiro, M. d. D., & Granlund, L. (2008). Becoming working mothers: Reconciling work and family at three particular workplaces in Norway, the UK, and Portugal. *Community, Work & Family, 11*(4), 365–384.

U.S. Census Bureau. (2010). *Statistical abstract of the United States: 2010*. Washington, DC: U.S. Government Printing Office. Retrieved from http://www.census.gov/compendia/statab.

U.S. Department of Labor. (2008). *Highlights of women's earnings in 2007*. Washington, DC: U.S. Department of Labor.

U.S. Equal Employment Opportunity Commission. (2001). Jury finds Outback Steakhouse guilty of sex discrimination and illegal retaliation. Retrieved from http://www.eeoc.gov/press/9-19-01.html.

Walsh, S. (2009). Dell settles sex discrimination suit for $9 million. Retrieved from http://www.gadgetell.com/tech/comment/dell-settles-sex-discrimination-suit-for-9-million.

Watkins, K. (2007). *Human development report 2007/2008*. New York, NY: United Nations Development Programme.

Wolford, K. M. (2005). Gender discrimination in employment: Wage inequity for professional and doctoral degree holders in the United States and possible remedies. *Journal of Education Finance, 31*(1), 82–100. Retrieved from http://www.press.uillinois.edu/journals/jef.html.

11.4 Violence Against Women: Rape and Pornography

Learning Objectives

1. Describe the extent of rape and the reasons for it.
2. Discuss the debate over pornography.

When we consider interpersonal violence of all kinds—homicide, assault, robbery, and rape and sexual assault—men are more likely than women to be victims of violence. While true, this fact obscures another fact: women are far more likely than men to be raped and sexually assaulted. They are also much more likely to be portrayed as victims of pornographic violence on the Internet and in videos, magazines, and other outlets. Finally, women are more likely than men to be victims of *domestic violence*, or violence between spouses and others with intimate relationships. The gendered nature of these acts against women distinguishes them from the violence men suffer. Violence is directed against men not because they are men per se, but because of anger, jealousy, and the sociological reasons discussed in Chapter 5 "Social Structure and Social Interaction"'s treatment of deviance and crime. But rape and sexual assault, domestic violence, and pornographic portrayals of violence are directed against women precisely because they are women. These acts are thus an extreme extension of the gender inequality women face in other areas of life. We discuss rape and pornography here but will leave domestic violence for Chapter 11 "Gender and Gender Inequality".

Rape

Susan Griffin (1971, p. 26) began a classic essay on rape in 1971 with this startling statement:

> I have never been free of the fear of rape. From a very early age I, like most women, have thought of rape as a part of my natural environment—something to be feared and prayed against like fire or lightning. I never asked why men raped; I simply thought it one of the many mysteries of human nature.

What do we know about rape? Why do men rape? Our knowledge about the extent and nature of rape and reasons for it comes from three sources: the FBI Uniform Crime Reports and the National Crime Victimization Survey (NCVS), both discussed in Chapter 5 "Social Structure and Social Interaction", and surveys of and interviews with women and men conducted by academic researchers. From these sources we have a fairly good if not perfect idea of how much rape occurs, the context in which it occurs, and the reasons for it. What do we know?

The Extent and Context of Rape

According to the Uniform Crime Reports, about 88,100 reported rapes (including attempts) occurred in the United States in 2009 (Federal Bureau of Investigation, 2010). Because women often do not tell police they were raped, the NCVS probably yields a better estimate of rape. According to the NCVS, almost 126,000 rapes and sexual assaults occurred in 2009 (Truman & Rand, 2010). Other research indicates that up to one-third of U.S. women will experience a rape or sexual assault, including attempts, at least once in their lives (Barkan, 2012). A study of a random sample of 420 Toronto women involving intensive interviews yielded even higher figures: 56% said they had experienced at least one rape or attempted rape, and two-thirds said they had experienced at least one rape or sexual assault, including attempts. The researchers, Melanie Randall and Lori Haskell (1995, p. 22), concluded that "it is more common than not for a woman to have an experience of sexual assault during their lifetime."

Up to one-third of U.S. women experience a rape or sexual assault, including attempts, at least once in their lives.

Wikimedia Commons – public domain.

These figures apply not just to the general public but also to college students. About 20%–30% of women students in anonymous surveys report being raped or sexually assaulted (including attempts), usually by a male student they knew beforehand (Fisher, Cullen, & Turner, 2000; Gross, Winslett, Roberts, & Gohm, 2006). Thus at a campus of 10,000 students of whom 5,000 are women, about 1,000–1,500 will be raped or sexually assaulted over a period of 4 years, or about 10 per week in a 4-year academic calendar.

The public image of rape is of the proverbial stranger attacking a woman in an alleyway. While such rapes do occur, most rapes actually happen between people who know each other. A wide body of research finds that 60%–80% of all rapes and sexual assaults are committed by someone the woman knows, including husbands, ex-husbands, boyfriends, and ex-boyfriends, and only 20%–35% by strangers (Barkan, 2012). A woman is thus 2 to 4 times more likely to be raped by someone she knows than by a stranger.

Explaining Rape

Sociological explanations of rape fall into cultural and structural categories similar to those presented earlier for sexual harassment. Various "rape myths" in our culture support the absurd notion that women somehow enjoy being raped, want to be raped, or are "asking for it" (Franiuk, Seefelt, & Vandello, 2008). One of the most famous scenes in movie history occurs in the classic film *Gone with the Wind,* when Rhett Butler carries a struggling Scarlett O'Hara up the stairs. She is struggling because she does not want to have sex with him. The next scene shows Scarlett waking up the next morning with a satisfied, loving look on her face. The not-so-subtle message is that she enjoyed being raped (or, to be more charitable to the film, was just playing hard to get).

A related cultural belief is that women somehow ask or deserve to be raped by the way they dress or behave. If she dresses attractively or walks into a bar by herself, she wants to have sex, and if a rape occurs, well, then, what did she expect? In the award-winning film *The Accused*, based on a true story, actress Jodie Foster plays a woman who was raped by several men on top of a pool table in a bar. The film recounts how members of the public questioned why she was in the bar by herself if she did not want to have sex and blamed her for being raped.

A third cultural belief is that a man who is sexually active with a lot of women is a stud. Although this belief is less common in this day of AIDS and other STDs, it is still with us. A man with multiple sex partners continues to be the source of envy among many of his peers. At a minimum, men are still the ones who have to "make the first move" and then continue making more moves. There is a thin line between being sexually assertive and sexually aggressive (Kassing, Beesley, & Frey, 2005).

These three cultural beliefs—that women enjoy being forced to have sex, that they ask or deserve to be raped, and that men should be sexually assertive or even aggressive—combine to produce a cultural recipe for rape. Although most men do not rape, the cultural beliefs and myths just described help account for the rapes that do occur. Recognizing this, the contemporary women's movement began attacking these myths back in the 1970s, and the public is much more conscious of the true nature of rape than a generation ago. That said, much of the public still accepts these cultural beliefs and myths, and prosecutors continue to find it difficult to win jury convictions in rape trials unless the woman who was raped had suffered visible injuries, had not known the man who raped her, and/or was not dressed attractively (Levine, 2006).

Structural explanations for rape emphasize the power differences between women and men similar to those outlined earlier for sexual harassment. In societies that are male dominated, rape and other violence against women is a likely outcome, as they allow men to demonstrate and maintain their power over women. Supporting this view, studies of preindustrial societies and of the 50 states of the United States find that rape is more common in societies where women have less economic and political power (Baron & Straus, 1989; Sanday, 1981). Poverty is also a predictor of rape: although rape in the United States transcends social class boundaries, it does seem more common among poorer segments of the population than among wealthier segments, as is true for other types of violence (Rand, 2009). Scholars think the higher rape rates among the poor stem from poor men trying to prove their "masculinity" by taking out their economic frustration on women (Martin, Vieraitis, & Britto, 2006).

Reducing Rape

In sum, a sociological perspective tells us that cultural myths and economic and gender inequality help lead to rape, and that the rape problem goes far beyond a few psychopathic men who rape women. A sociological perspective thus tells us that our society cannot just stop at doing something about these men. Instead it must make more far-reaching changes by changing people's beliefs about rape and by making every effort to reduce poverty and to empower women. This last task is especially important, for, as Randall and Haskell (1995, p. 22), the authors of the Toronto study cited earlier, observed, a sociological perspective on rape "means calling into question the organization of sexual inequality in our society."

Aside from this fundamental change, other remedies, such as additional and better funded rape-crisis centers, would help women who experience rape and sexual assault. Yet even here women of color face an additional barrier. Because the anti-rape movement was begun by white, middle-class feminists, the rape-crisis centers they founded tended to be near where they live, such as college campuses, and not in the areas where women of color live, such as inner cities and Native American reservations. This meant that women of color who experienced sexual violence lacked the kinds of help available to their white, middle-class counterparts (Matthews, 1989), and, despite some progress, this is still true today.

Pornography

Back in the 1950s, young boys in the United States would page through *National Geographic* magazine to peek at photos of native women who were partially nude. Those photos, of course, were not put there to excite boys across the country; instead they were there simply to depict native people in their natural habitat. Another magazine began about the same time that also contained photos of nude women. Its name was *Playboy*, and its photos obviously had a much different purpose: to excite teenage boys and older men alike. Other, more graphic magazines grew in its wake, and today television shows and PG-13 and R-rated movies show more nudity and sex than were ever imaginable in the days when *National Geographic* was a boy's secret pleasure. Beyond these movies and television shows, a powerful pornography industry now exists on the Internet, in porn stores, and elsewhere. Although *Playboy* quickly became very controversial, it is now considered tame compared to what else is available.

If things as different as *National Geographic*, *Playboy*, R-rated movies, and hard-core pornography show nudity and can be sexually arousing, what, then, should be considered pornography? Are at least some of the tamer pictures in *Playboy* really that different from the great paintings in art history that depict nude women? This question is not necessarily meant to defend *Playboy*; rather it is meant to stimulate your thinking over what exactly is and is not pornography and over what, if anything, our society can and should do about it.

Many people obviously oppose pornography, but two very different groups have been especially outspoken over the years. One of these groups, religious moralists, condemns pornography as a violation of religious values and as an offense to society's moral order. The other group, feminists, condemns pornography for its sexual objectification of women and especially condemns the hard-core pornography that glorifies horrible sexual violence against women. Many feminists also charge that pornography promotes rape by reinforcing the cultural myths discussed earlier. As one writer put it in a famous phrase some 30 years ago, "Pornography is the theory, and rape the practice" (Morgan, 1980, p. 139).

This charge raises an important question: to what extent does pornography cause rape or other violence against women? The fairest answer might be that we do not really know. Many studies do conclude that pornography indeed causes rape. For example, male students who watch violent pornography in experiments later exhibit more hostile attitudes toward women than those watching consensual sex or nonsexual interaction. However, it remains unclear whether viewing pornography has a longer-term effect that lasts beyond the laboratory setting, and scholars and other observers continue to disagree over pornography's effects on the rape rate (Ferguson & Hartley, 2009). Even if pornography does cause rape, efforts to stop it run smack into the issue of censorship. In a free society, civil liberties advocates say, we must proceed very cautiously. Once we ban some forms of pornography, they ask, where do we stop (Strossen, 2000)?

This issue aside, much of what we call pornography still degrades women by depicting them as objects that exist for men's sexual pleasure and by portraying them as legitimate targets of men's sexual violence. These images should be troubling for any society that values gender equality. The extent of pornography in the United States may, for better or worse, reflect our historical commitment to freedom of speech, but it may also reflect our lack of commitment to full equality between women and men. Even if, as we have seen, the survey evidence shows growing disapproval of traditional gender roles, the persistence of pornography shows that our society has a long way to go toward viewing women as equally human as men.

Key Takeaways

- Rape and sexual assault result from a combination of structural and cultural factors. Up to one-third of U.S. women experience a rape or sexual assault, including attempts, in their lifetime.
- Pornography is another form of violence against women. Important questions remain regarding whether pornography leads to further violence against women and whether freedom of speech standards protect the production and distribution of pornography.

For Your Review

1. What evidence and reasoning indicate that rape and sexual assault are not just the result of psychological problems affecting the men who engage in these crimes?
2. Is pornography protected by freedom of speech? Write an essay in which you answer this question and explain the reasoning behind your answer.

References

Barkan, S. E. (2012). *Criminology: A sociological understanding* (5th ed.). Upper Saddle River, NJ: Prentice Hall.

Baron, L., & Straus, M. A. (1989). *Four theories of rape in American society: A state-level analysis*. New Haven, CT: Yale University Press.

Federal Bureau of Investigation. (2010). *Crime in the United States, 2009*. Washington, DC: Author.

Ferguson, C. J., & Hartley, R. D. (2009). The pleasure is momentary…the expense damnable? The influence of pornography on rape and sexual assault. *Aggression & Violent Behavior, 14*(5), 323–329. doi:10.1016/j.avb.2009.04.008.

Fisher, B. S., Cullen, F. T., & Turner, M. G. (2000). *The sexual victimization of college women*. Washington, DC: National Institute of Justice and Bureau of Justice Statistics, U.S. Department of Justice.

Franiuk, R., Seefelt, J., & Vandello, J. (2008). Prevalence of rape myths in headlines and their effects on attitudes toward rape. *Sex Roles, 58*(11/12), 790–801. doi:10.1007/s11199-007-9372-4.

Griffin, S. (1971, September). Rape: The all-American crime. *Ramparts, 10*, 26–35.

Gross, A. M., Winslett, A., Roberts, M., & Gohm, C. L. (2006). An examination of sexual violence against college women. *Violence Against Women, 12*, 288–300.

Kassing, L. R., Beesley, D., & Frey, L. L. (2005). Gender-role conflict, homophobia, age, and education as predictors of male rape myth acceptance. *Journal of Mental Health Counseling, 27*(4), 311–328.

Levine, K. L. (2006). The intimacy discount: Prosecutorial discretion, privacy, and equality in the statutory rape caseload. *Emory Law Journal, 55*(4), 691–749.

Martin, K., Vieraitis, L. M., & Britto, S. (2006). Gender equality and women's absolute status: A test of the feminist models of rape. *Violence Against Women, 12*(4), 321–339.

Matthews, N. A. (1989). Surmounting a legacy: The expansion of racial diversity in a local anti-rape movement. *Gender & Society, 3*, 518–532.

Morgan, R. (1980). Theory and practice: Pornography and rape. In L. Lederer (Ed.), *Take back the night* (pp. 134–140). New York, NY: William Morrow.

Rand, M. R. (2009). *Criminal victimization, 2008*. Washington, DC: Bureau of Justice Statistics, U.S. Department of Justice.

Randall, M., & Haskell, L. (1995). Sexual violence in women's lives: Findings from the Women's Safety Project, a community-based survey. *Violence Against Women*, 1, 6–31.

Sanday, P. R. (1981). The socio-cultural context of rape: A cross-cultural study. *Journal of Social Issues, 37*, 5–27.

Strossen, N. (2000). *Defending pornography: Free speech, sex, and the fight for women's rights*. New York, NY: New York University Press.

Truman, J. L., & Rand, M. R. (2010). *Criminal victimization, 2009*. Washington, DC: Bureau of Justice Statistics, U.S. Department of Justice.

11.5 The Benefits and Costs of Being Male

Learning Objectives

1. List some of the benefits of being male.
2. List some of the costs of being male.

Most of the discussion so far has been about women, and with good reason: in a sexist society such as our own, women are the subordinate, unequal sex. But *gender* means more than *female,* and a few comments about men are in order.

Benefits

In Chapter 7 "Deviance, Crime, and Social Control", we talked about "white privilege," the advantages that whites automatically have in a racist society whether or not they realize they have these advantages. Many scholars also talk about **male privilege**, or the advantages that males automatically have in a patriarchal society whether or not they realize they have these advantages (McIntosh, 2007).

A few examples illustrate male privilege. Men can usually walk anywhere they want or go into any bar they want without having to worry about being raped or sexually harassed. Susan Griffin was able to write "I have never been free of the fear of rape" because she was a woman: it is no exaggeration to say that few men could write the same thing and mean it. Although some men are sexually harassed, most men can work at any job they want without having to worry about sexual harassment. Men can walk down the street without having strangers make crude remarks about their looks, dress, and sexual behavior. Men can apply for most jobs without worrying about being rejected or, if hired, not being promoted because of their gender. We could go on with many other examples, but the fact remains that in a patriarchal society, men automatically have advantages just because they are men, even if race, social class, and sexual orientation affect the degree to which they are able to enjoy these advantages.

Costs

Yet it is also true that men pay a price for living in a patriarchy. Without trying to claim that men have it as bad as women, scholars are increasingly pointing to the problems men face in a society that promotes male domination and traditional standards of masculinity such as assertiveness, competitiveness, and toughness (Kimmel & Messner, 2010). Socialization into masculinity is thought to underlie many of the emotional problems men experience, which stem from a combination of their emotional inexpressiveness and reluctance to admit to, and seek help for, various personal problems (Wong & Rochlen, 2005). Sometimes these emotional problems build up and explode, as mass shootings by males at schools and elsewhere indicate, or express themselves in other ways. Compared to girls, for example, boys are much more likely to be diagnosed with emotional disorders, learning disabilities, and attention deficit disorder, and they are also more likely to commit suicide and to drop out of high school.

Men experience other problems that put themselves at a disadvantage compared to women. They commit much more violence than women do and, apart from rape, also suffer a much higher rate of violent victimization. They die earlier than women and are injured more often. Because men are less involved than women in child-rearing, they also miss out on the joy of parenting that women are much more likely to experience.

Growing recognition of the problems males experience because of their socialization into masculinity has led to increased concern over what is happening to American boys. Citing the strong linkage between masculinity and violence, some writers urge parents to raise their sons differently in order to help our society reduce its violent behavior (Miedzian, 2002). In all of these respects, boys and men—and our nation as a whole—are paying a very real price for being male in a patriarchal society.

Key Takeaways

- In a patriarchal society, males automatically have certain advantages, including a general freedom from fear of being raped and sexually assaulted and from experiencing job discrimination on the basis of their gender.
- Men also suffer certain disadvantages from being male, including higher rates of injury, violence, and death and a lower likelihood of experiencing the joy that parenting often brings.

For Your Review

1. What do you think is the most important advantage, privilege, or benefit that men enjoy in the United States? Explain your answer.
2. What do you think is the most significant cost or disadvantage that men experience? Again, explain your answer.

Reducing Gender Inequality: What Sociology Suggests

Gender inequality is found in varying degrees in most societies around the world, and the United States is no exception. Just as racial/ethnic stereotyping and prejudice underlie racial/ethnic inequality (see Chapter 7 "Deviance, Crime, and Social Control"), so do stereotypes and false beliefs underlie gender inequality. Although these stereotypes and beliefs have weakened considerably since the 1970s thanks in large part to the contemporary women's movement and the gay and lesbian rights movements, they obviously persist and hamper efforts to achieve full gender equality.

A sociological perspective reminds us that gender inequality stems from a complex mixture of cultural and structural factors that must be addressed if gender inequality is to be reduced further than it already has been since the 1970s. Despite changes during this period, children are still socialized from birth into traditional notions of femininity and masculinity, and gender-based stereotyping incorporating these notions still continues. Although people should generally be free to pursue whatever family and career responsibilities they desire, socialization and stereotyping still combine to limit the ability of girls and boys and women and men alike to imagine less traditional possibilities. Meanwhile, structural obstacles in the workplace and elsewhere continue to keep women in a subordinate social and economic status relative to men. Cultural and structural factors also continue to produce inequality based on sexual orientation, an inequality that is reinforced both by the presence of certain laws directed at gays and lesbians (such as laws in many states that prohibit same-sex marriage) and by the absence of other laws prohibiting discrimination based on sexual orientation (such as laws prohibiting employment discrimination).

To reduce gender inequality, then, a sociological perspective suggests various policies and measures to address the cultural and structural factors that help produce gender inequality. These might include, but are not limited to, the following:

1. Reduce socialization by parents and other adults of girls and boys into traditional gender roles.
2. Confront gender stereotyping and sexual orientation stereotyping by the popular and news media.
3. Increase public consciousness of the reasons for, extent of, and consequences of rape and sexual assault, sexual harassment, and pornography.
4. Increase enforcement of existing laws against gender-based employment discrimination and against sexual harassment.
5. Increase funding of rape-crisis centers and other services for girls and women who have been raped and/or sexually assaulted.
6. Increase government funding of high-quality day-care options to enable parents, and especially mothers, to work outside the home if they so desire, and to do so without fear that their finances or their children's well-being will be compromised.
7. Pass federal and state legislation banning employment discrimination based on sexual orientation and allowing same-sex couples to marry and enjoy all the rights, responsibilities, and benefits of heterosexual married couples.
8. Increase mentorship and other efforts to boost the number of women in traditionally male occupations and in positions of political leadership.

References

Kimmel, M. S., & Messner, M. A. (Eds.). (2010). *Men's lives* (8th ed.). Boston, MA: Allyn & Bacon.

McIntosh, P. (2007). White privilege and male privilege: A personal account of coming to see correspondence through work in women's studies. In M. L. Andersen & P. H. Collins (Eds.), *Race, class, and gender: An anthology* (6th ed.). Belmont, CA: Wadsworth.

Miedzian, M. (2002). *Boys will be boys: Breaking the link between masculinity and violence.* New York, NY: Lantern Books.

Wong, Y. J., & Rochlen, A. B. (2005). Demystifying men's emotional behavior: New directions and implications for counseling and research. *Psychology of Men & Masculinity, 6,* 62–72.

11.6 End-of-Chapter Material

Summary

1. *Sex* is a concept that refers to biological differences between females and males, while *gender* is a concept that refers to a society's expectations of how females and males should think and behave. To the extent that women and men and girls and boys are different, it's essential to determine how much of these differences stems from the biological differences between the sexes.
2. In understanding gender differences, scholars continue to debate the value of biological explanations. Biological explanations centering on evolution, natural selection, and hormonal differences are provocative but ultimately imply that gender differences are inevitable and that the status quo must be maintained. In contrast, cultural and socialization explanations imply some hope for changing gender roles and for reducing gender inequality. Anthropologists find gender similarities across cultures that probably reflect the biological differences between the sexes, but they also find much cultural variation in gender roles that underscores the importance of culture and socialization for understanding gender.
3. Many studies emphasize that socialization leads children in the United States to adopt the gender roles associated with femininity and masculinity. Parents view and interact with their daughters and sons differently, and children continue to learn their gender roles from their peers, schools, the mass media, and religion.
4. Feminism refers to the belief that women should be equal to men. With feminism defined in this way, many more people hold feminist beliefs than might be willing to admit to it. The feminist movement began during the pre–Civil War abolitionist period and eventually won women the right to vote. Its reemergence in the late 1960s has changed many aspects of American life. Since then support for traditional gender roles has declined dramatically in national surveys. Several variables, including education, are associated with a feminist outlook, but, surprisingly, women are not consistently more likely than men to support feminist beliefs.
5. Gender inequality in the workplace is manifested through the gender gap in earnings and through sexual harassment. Women earn less than 75% of what men earn. Several reasons account for this gap, including sex segregation in the workplace, the devaluing of women's work, and outright sex discrimination by employers. Sexual harassment against women is quite common and stems from cultural beliefs about women's and men's roles and structural differences in the workplace in power between women and men.
6. Gender inequality also exists in the household in the extent to which women and men perform housework. Women perform much more housework than men, even when they also work outside the home. Although some studies show that men perform more housework than they used to, recent evidence suggests that men are merely exaggerating the amount of housework they now perform by giving socially desirable responses to questions about their housework.
7. Although women have made great gains in the world of politics in the United States, they still lag behind men in the extent to which they occupy legislative seats. This extent is higher in the United States than in many other countries, but lower than in many nations in Europe and elsewhere.
8. Women of color experience a triple burden based on their gender, race/ethnicity, and social class. Even though white women earn less money and are poorer than white men, women of color earn less money and are poorer than white women.
9. Violence against women is another manifestation of gender inequality. Research shows that up to one-third of U.S. women will be raped or sexually assaulted and that about 70%–80% of their assailants will be men they know. Cultural beliefs and structural differences in power explain why rape occurs. Pornography is

often considered another type of violence against women, but questions continue over the definition of pornography and over whether it does indeed promote rape and other forms of antiwoman violence. Efforts to combat pornography may run afoul of First Amendment protections for freedom of speech.

10. In a patriarchal society men enjoy privileges just for being male, whether or not they recognize these privileges. At the same time, men also experience disadvantages, including violent behavior and victimization and higher rates of certain emotional problems than those experienced by women.

Using Sociology

You are helping to organize a Take Back the Night march similar to the one mentioned in the news story about the University of Missouri-Columbia that began this chapter. Naturally you tell all your friends about it and urge them to participate in the march. But two of them, one woman and one man, say they don't really think there is a need for the march. When you ask them why, they say that many women who claim to have been raped were dressed too provocatively or really wanted to have sex but then changed their minds. How do you respond to your friends?

Chapter 12: Aging and the Elderly

Social Issues in the News

"Wisdom of the Elders," the headline said. The story was about older Americans who have used insights gained from their many years of experience to accomplish great things. John Ammon, 66, founded and runs an after-school tutoring and mentoring center for Native American children in San Jose, California. "We don't twist their arms," he says. "The kids know we want them to do well." Natalie Casey, 82, is a nurse in Pittsburgh, Pennsylvania, who is very patient-oriented. "I found out that if I took a genuine interest in my patients, it took their minds off what they were in the hospital for," she told a reporter. "Nursing isn't just delivering medicine and changing bandages. If you listen to somebody, it's surprising how much their outlook can change."

John Freutel, 56, assistant fire chief in Minneapolis, Minnesota, helped coordinate rescue operations when a busy bridge collapsed over the Mississippi River in August 2007. He almost certainly saved several lives. "There isn't a manual on how to deal with a bridge collapse," Freutel recalled. "I was juggling 10 million things, but 30 years of experience helped me stay calm. When you're in command, I've learned, the most important lesson is: take a deep breath."

And in an interview with *CBS News* anchor Katie Couric, Chesley "Sully" Sullenberger III, 58, remembered the day, January 15, 2009, when he saved more than 150 lives by piloting a US Air jet safely on emergency landing into the Hudson River. "One way of looking at this might be that, for 42 years, I've been making small, regular deposits in this bank of experience: education and training," he said. "And on January 15 the balance was sufficient so that I could make a very large withdrawal." (Newcott, 2009)

As this news story makes so clear, older individuals have much to contribute to our society in many ways. Yet our society does not value them nearly as much as some other societies value their elders. At the same time, as these societies have changed, so have their views of their older members changed to some degree.

Consider the San (also known as the !Kung Bushmen, now considered a derogatory term), a hunting-and-gathering tribe in the Kalahari Desert in southern Africa. Although their land has been taken from them and most now are forced to live on farms and ranches, they struggle to maintain their traditional values even as they must abandon their hunting-and-gathering ways.

One of these values is respect for people in their old age. *Old* here is a relative term, as most San die before they reach 60. Although the San live a healthy lifestyle, they lack modern medicine and fall prey to various diseases that industrial nations have largely conquered. Only about 20% of the San live past 60, and those who do are revered because of the wisdom they have acquired over the years: they know the history of the San, they know various San quite well, and they know how and where to find food regardless of the weather (Schneider & Silverman, 2010; Thomas, 2006).

As the San have been forced to change from hunting and gathering to farming and herding, many aspects of their culture and social structure have changed as well (Yellen, 1990). Inequality has increased, and selfishness has slowly replaced their emphasis on sharing. Elderly San have lost status and respect, perhaps because the knowledge they possess of the old ways is no longer needed as these ways fade away.

The San society is very different from the United States and other industrial societies, yet it has much to tell us about the social process of aging and about the cultural and structural forces affecting older people. When the San were still hunters and gatherers, their elderly were respected and enjoyed living with their relatives. At the same time, some became a burden on their kin, and especially on people with whom they had to live if their own children had already died. After the San were forced to relocate, changes that affected their culture and social structure began affecting their elderly as well. If knowing about a society's culture and structure helps us to understand its elderly, it is also true that knowing about a society's elderly helps us understand the society itself, as this chapter will illustrate.

References

Newcott, B. (2009, May and June). Wisdom of the elders. *AARP The Magazine*. Retrieved from http://www.aarpmagazine.org/people/wisdom_of_the_elders.html.

Schneider, L., & Silverman, A. (2010). *Global sociology: Introducing five contemporary societies* (5th ed.). New York, NY: McGraw-Hill.

Thomas, E. M. (2006). *The old way: A story of the first people* (Rev. ed.). New York, NY: Farrar, Straus and Giroux.

Yellen, J. E. (1990, April). The transformation of the Kalahari !Kung. *Scientific American*, 96–105.

12.1 Gerontology and the Concept of Aging

Learning Objectives

1. Describe why it is important to understand age and aging.
2. Distinguish biological aging, psychological aging, and social aging.

The United States is far removed from the world of the San, but changes that have been occurring in this nation are also affecting its older citizens. For example, the numbers of older Americans are growing rapidly, with important repercussions for economic and social life. Somewhat like the San, we appreciate our elderly but also consider them something of a burden. We also hold some unfortunate stereotypes of them and seemingly view old age as something to be shunned. Television commercials and other advertisements extol the virtues of staying young by "washing away the gray" and by removing all facial wrinkles. In our youth-obsessed culture, older people seem to be second-class citizens.

Why study the elderly and the process of growing old? As just noted, understanding the elderly and the experience of aging will help us understand a society. An additional reason might be even more convincing: *you will be old someday*. At least you will be old if you do not die prematurely from an accident, cancer, a heart attack, some other medical problem, murder, or suicide. Although we do not often think about aging when we are in our late teens and early 20s, one of our major goals in life is to become old. That is partly why many people wear seat belts, watch their diets, and exercise. By studying age and aging and becoming familiar with some of the problems facing the elderly now and in the future, we are really studying something about ourselves and a stage in the life course we all hope to reach.

Because we all want to live into old age, the study of age and aging helps us understand something about ourselves and a stage in the life course we all hope to reach.

Carl Nenzén Lovén – Grandpa – CC BY 2.0.

The study of aging is so important and popular that it has its own name, **gerontology**. *Social gerontology* is the study of the social aspects of aging (Hooyman & Kiyak, 2011).The scholars who study aging are called *gerontologists*. The people they study go by several names, most commonly "older people," "elders," and "the elderly." The latter term is usually reserved for those 65 or older, while "older people" and "elders" (as the headline of the opening news story illustrates) often include people in their 50s as well as those 60 or older.

Gerontologists say that age and aging have at least four dimensions. The dimension most of us think of is **chronological age**, defined as the number of years since someone was born. A second dimension is **biological aging**, which refers to the physical changes that "slow us down" as we get into our middle and older years. For example, our arteries might clog up, or problems with our lungs might make it more difficult for us to breathe. A third dimension, **psychological aging**, refers to the psychological changes, including those involving mental functioning and personality, that occur as we age. Gerontologists emphasize that chronological age is not always the same thing as biological or psychological age. Some people who are 65, for example, can look and act much younger than some who are 50.

The fourth dimension of aging is social. **Social aging** refers to changes in a person's roles and relationships, both within their networks of relatives and friends and in formal organizations such as the workplace and houses of worship. Although social aging can differ from one individual to another, it is also profoundly influenced by the *perception* of aging that is part of a society's culture. If a society views aging positively, the social aging experienced by individuals in that society will be more positive and enjoyable than in a society that views aging negatively. Let's look at the perception of aging in more detail.

Key Takeaways

- The study of elderly and the aging helps us understand the society in which we live, and it also alerts us to certain processes and problems that we may experience as we grow into old age.
- Biological aging refers to the physical changes that accompany the aging process, while psychological aging refers to the psychological changes that occur.
- Social aging refers to the changes in a person's roles and relationships as the person ages.

For Your Review

1. Think about an older person whom you know. To what extent has this person experienced psychological aging? To what extent has this person experienced social aging?

References

Hooyman, N. R., & Kiyak, H. A. (2011). *Social gerontology: A multidisciplinary perspective* (9th ed.). Upper Saddle River, NJ: Pearson.

12.2 The Perception and Experience of Aging

Learning Objectives

1. Discuss any two factors that influence how the elderly are viewed in preindustrial societies.
2. Describe the view of aging in ancient Greece and Rome and how this view changed during the Middle Ages.

The perception of aging can vary from one society to another, and it can also change over time within any given society. Gerontologists have investigated these cross-cultural and historical differences. By understanding aging in other societies and also in our past, they say, we can better understand aging in our own society. To acquaint you with "other ways of growing old" (Amoss & Harrell, 1981), we discuss briefly some of the cross-cultural and historical evidence on the perception and experience of aging.

Aging in Preindustrial Societies

Gerontologists think that few people reached the age of 35 in the prehistoric societies that existed thousands of years ago. Those who did were considered "old" and treated as such. It is obviously difficult to know much about aging back then, and much of what we think we know is based on our knowledge about the preindustrial societies that anthropologists have been studying for many decades (Sokolovsky, 2009).

In such societies, older people are often respected, as in the San, for their knowledge and wisdom. But the extent of this respect, and whether a society scorns its elderly instead, depends on at least two factors. The first is the health and mental abilities of older people. Generally speaking, elders in good health are viewed with respect, while those in poor health are viewed with disdain. In this regard, many societies distinguish between the "young-old" and the "old-old." Usually in good health, the young-old are respected and sometimes even venerated as priests because they are thought to hold special insight into the world awaiting after death. In contrast, the old-old, who are often in bad health, are viewed more as a burden because of their physical frailties. Sometimes they are abused, left to die, killed via ritualistic sacrifice, or expected to kill themselves (Barker, 2009).

When older people are wealthy, they have more social influence among their relatives and other members of a society. When they are poorer, they have less influence.

Wikimedia Commons – CC BY 2.0.

A second factor affecting how the elderly are viewed is a society's economy. When older people are wealthy (which, depending on the society, might mean they own land, livestock, or real estate or have much money), they have more social influence among their kin and other members of a society. The stronger a society's economy, the more resources people can acquire by the time they reach old age and the greater their power and status in that time of life. Conversely, the weaker a society's economy, the fewer resources people can acquire by old age and the lower their power and status as they age.

If a society's economy makes a difference, then changes in the economy can affect how the elderly are viewed and treated. All other things equal, an improving economy should enhance respect for the elderly and improve how they are treated. Conversely, a worsening economy should decrease respect for the elderly and worsen their treatment.

Other sorts of changes in a society can also affect how the elderly are viewed. We saw earlier that the status of the San elderly declined after they had to move from their natural habitat to farms and ranches. The elderly in other preindustrial societies have also had their status change as their land has been taken from them and as modern ways have impinged on their traditional habits. In such situations, their knowledge is less useful and important than before. If "knowledge is power," as the saying goes, the decline in the importance of their knowledge has led to a decline in their status (Hooyman & Kiyak, 2011).

The elderly in traditional societies do not always pay a price for modernization. In many societies, the respect for the elderly has been strong enough to resist modernization. In others, people have fought to retain their old ways and, in doing so, have looked to their elders for guidance and knowledge.

Aging in Western Cultures

The ancient civilizations in Greece and Rome left art and writings that provide a good portrait of their experience and perception of aging (Thane, 2005; Minois, 1989). Few people back then reached what we would now call old age, as 80% died before what we would consider the middle age. That said, the older citizens of ancient Greece and Rome were highly respected for their wisdom, and councils of elders helped rule Greek and Roman society.

However, respect for the elderly in Greece declined during the fifth century B.C., as old age came to be depicted as a period of declining mental and physical ability and youth extolled as the ideal time of life. Reflecting this new view, Greek mythology from that time painted a negative portrait of the elderly and contrasted the youthfulness of the gods with the frailties of aging humans. In one myth Eos, the goddess of dawn, fell in love with a human named Tithonus. When he became old and weak, she left him and turned him into a grasshopper! This change in the view of the elderly was reversed about two centuries later, when old age in ancient Greece reacquired its respect and influence, and ancient Rome followed suit (Hooyman & Kiyak, 2011).

During the Middle Ages, many people died from the plague and other diseases, and few reached what we would now consider to be old age. Because so many people died and food was so scarce, the elderly were considered a burden and held in disrespect. When the Renaissance began, artists and writers drew on classical Greece for much of their inspiration and continued to depict old age negatively.

Their negative view had turned around by the American colonial period, as the Puritans thought that old age was a gift from God and gave their elderly (especially men) much respect and power (Cole, 1992). The fact that older Puritans owned a lot of land in an agricultural society reinforced their power. During the 19th century, however, land-owning by older Americans became less important as the United States shifted from an agricultural to an industrial economy. Regard for the elderly's authority weakened, and power transferred to younger men who were making large sums of money in the industrial world. As factory work became the dominant mode of production, older people were further seen as less and less useful. They could not keep up with younger workers in the factories and became seen as less useful to the needs of a manufacturing economy.

As the "information technology" revolution has taken hold since the 1980s, older people have again largely been left out of a fundamental economic shift. The people at the center of the information age have been in their 20s or 30s, not in their 60s and 70s. The impact of the information age on the status of older people will be an important topic for investigation in the years ahead.

Key Takeaways

- Two factors affected the view of older people in prehistoric societies: the physical and mental health of older people and the society's economy.
- During the Middle Ages, older people were considered a burden and held in disrespect because so many people died young and food was so scarce.
- As the United States industrialized during the 19th century, the view of the elderly became more negative.

For Your Review

1. The text notes that respect for older people changed from the American colonial period into the 19th century. Write a short essay in which you describe how and why this change occurred.

References

Amoss, P. T., & Harrell, S. (Eds.). (1981). *Other ways of growing old: Anthropological perspectives*. Stanford, CA: Stanford University Press.

Barker, J. C. (2009). Between humans and hosts: The decrepit elderly in a Polynesian society. In J. Sokolovsky (Ed.), *The cultural context of aging*. Westport, CT: Praeger.

Cole, T. R. (1992). *The journey of life: A cultural history of aging in America*. New York, NY: Cambridge University Press.

Hooyman, N. R., & Kiyak, H. A. (2011). *Social gerontology: A multidisciplinary perspective* (9th ed.). Upper Saddle River, NJ: Pearson.

Minois, G. (1989). *History of old age: From antiquity to the renaissance*. Chicago, IL: University of Chicago Press.

Sokolovsky, J. (Ed.). (2009). *The cultural context of aging: Worldwide perspectives*. Westport, CT: Praeger.

Thane, P. (Ed.). (2005). *A history of old age*. Los Angeles, CA: J. Paul Getty Museum.

12.3 Sociological Perspectives on Aging

Learning Objectives

1. State the assumptions of disengagement, activity, and conflict theories of aging.
2. Critically assess these three theories.

Recall that social aging refers to changes in people's roles and relationships in a society as they age. We have seen that social aging and views of the aging process both differ cross-culturally and over time. A few decades ago, social gerontologists began to explain how and why the aging process in the United States and other societies occurs. These explanations, summarized in Table 12.1 "Theory Snapshot", have their merits and shortcomings, but together they help us understand patterns of social aging. They fall roughly into either the functionalist, social interactionist, or conflict approaches discussed in Chapter 1 "Sociology and the Sociological Perspective".

Table 12.1 Theory Snapshot

Theoretical perspective	Major assumptions
Disengagement theory	To enable younger people to assume important roles, a society must encourage its older people to disengage from their previous roles and to take on roles more appropriate to their physical and mental decline. This theory is considered a functionalist explanation of the aging process.
Activity theory	Older people benefit themselves and their society if they continue to be active. Their positive perceptions of the aging process are crucial for their ability to remain active. This theory is considered an interactionist explanation of the aging process.
Conflict theory	Older people experience age-based prejudice and discrimination. Inequalities among the aged exist along the lines of gender, race/ethnicity, and social class. This theory falls into the more general conflict theory of society.

One of the first explanations was called **disengagement theory** (Cumming & Henry, 1961). This approach assumed that all societies must find ways for older people's authority to give way to younger people. A society thus encourages its elderly to disengage from their previous roles and to take on roles more appropriate to their physical and mental decline. In this way, a society effects a smooth transition of its elderly into a new, more sedentary lifestyle and ensures that their previous roles will be undertaken by a younger generation that is presumably more able to carry out these roles. Because disengagement theory assumes that social aging preserves a society's stability and that a society needs to ensure that disengagement occurs, it is often considered a functionalist explanation of the aging process.

A critical problem with this theory was that it assumed that older people are no longer capable of adequately performing their previous roles. As we have seen, however, older people in many societies continue to perform their previous roles quite well. In fact, society may suffer if its elderly do disengage, as it loses their insight and wisdom. It is also true that many elders cannot afford to disengage from their previous roles: if they leave their jobs, they are also leaving needed sources of income, and if they leave their jobs and other roles, they also reduce their social interaction and the benefits it brings (Hochschild, 1975).

Today most social gerontologists prefer **activity theory**, which assumes that older people benefit both themselves and their society if they remain active and try to continue to perform the roles they had before they aged (Joung & Miller, 2007). As they perform their roles, their perception of the situations they are in is crucial to their perception of their aging and thus to their self-esteem and other aspects of their psychological well-being. Because activity theory focuses on the individual and her/his perception of the aging process, it is often considered a social interactionist explanation of social aging.

One criticism of activity theory is that its appraisal of the ability of the elderly to maintain their level of activity is too optimistic: although some elders can remain active, others cannot. Another criticism is that activity theory is too much of an individualistic approach, as it overlooks the barriers many societies place to successful aging. Some elders are less able to remain active because of their poverty, gender, and social class, as these and other structural conditions may adversely affect their physical and mental health. Activity theory overlooks these conditions.

Explanations of aging grounded in conflict theory put these conditions at the forefront of their analyses. A **conflict theory** of aging, then, emphasizes the impact of **ageism**, or negative views about old age and prejudice and discrimination against the elderly (Hooyman & Kiyak, 2011). According to this view, older workers are devalued because they are no longer economically productive and because their higher salaries (because of their job seniority), health benefits, and other costs drive down capitalist profits. Conflict theory also emphasizes inequality among the aged along gender, race/ethnicity, and social class lines. Reflecting these inequalities in the larger society, some elders are quite wealthy, but others are very poor.

One criticism of conflict theory is that it blames ageism on modern, capitalist economies. As we have seen, negative views of the elderly also exist in preindustrial societies, even if the views there overall are often more positive than in their modern counterparts.

Key Takeaways

- Disengagement theory assumes that all societies must find ways for older people's authority to give way to younger people. A society thus encourages its elderly to disengage from their previous roles and to take on roles more appropriate to their physical and mental decline.
- Activity theory assumes that older people will benefit both themselves and their society if they remain active and try to continue to perform the roles they had before they aged.

For Your Review

1. Which theory of aging—disengagement theory, activity theory, or conflict theory—makes the most sense to

you? Why?

References

Cumming, E., & Henry, W. E. (1961). *Growing old: The process of disengagement*. New York, NY: Basic Books.

Hochschild, A. (1975). Disengagement theory: A critique and proposal. *American Sociological Review, 40,* 553–569.

Hooyman, N. R., & Kiyak, H. A. (2011). *Social gerontology: A multidisciplinary perspective* (9th ed.). Upper Saddle River, NJ: Pearson.

Joung, H.-M., & Miller, N. J. (2007). Examining the effects of fashion activities on life satisfaction of older females: Activity theory revisited. *Family and Consumer Sciences Research Journal, 35*(4), 338–356.

12.4 Life Expectancy, Aging, and the Graying of Society

Learning Objectives

1. Describe the differences in life expectancy around the world.
2. List the potential problems associated with the growing proportion of older individuals in poor nations.
3. Explain the evidence for inequality in U.S. life expectancy.

When we look historically and cross-culturally, we see that *old age* is a relative term, since few people in many of the societies we have discussed reach what most Americans would consider to be old, say 65 or older (or perhaps 50 or older, which entitles someone to membership in AARP, formerly called the American Association of Retired Persons). When we compare societies, we find that **life expectancy**, or the average age to which people can be expected to live, varies dramatically across the world. As Figure 12.1 "Average Life Expectancy Across the Globe (Years)" illustrates, life expectancy in North America, most of Europe, and Australia averages almost 75 years or more, while life expectancy in most of Africa, where the San live, averages less than 55 years. In some African nations, the average life expectancy is under 45 years (Population Reference Bureau, 2009).

Figure 12.1 Average Life Expectancy Across the Globe (Years)

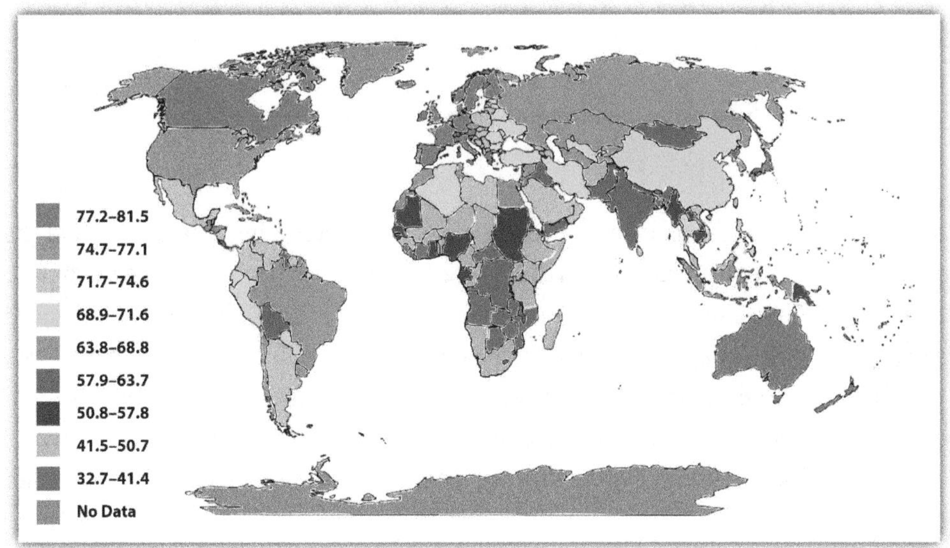

Source: Adapted from Global Education Project. (2004). Human conditions: World life expectancy map. Retrieved from http://www.theglobaleducationproject.org/earth/human-conditions.php.

What accounts for these large disparities? The major factor is the wealth or poverty of a nation, as the wealthiest nations have much longer life expectancies than the poorest ones. This is true because, as Chapter 6 "Groups and Organizations" noted, the poorest or least developed nations by definition have little money and few other resources. They suffer from hunger, AIDS, and other diseases, and they lack indoor plumbing and other modern conveniences found in almost every home in the wealthiest nations. As a result, they have high rates of infant and childhood mortality, and many people who make it past childhood die prematurely from disease, starvation, and other problems. We return to these problems in Chapter 13 "Work and the Economy".

These differences mean that few people in these societies reach the age of 65 that Western nations commonly mark as the beginning of old age. Figure 12.2 "Percentage of Population Aged 65 or Older, 2007" depicts the percentage of each nation's population that is 65 or older. Not surprisingly, the nations of Africa have very low numbers of people 65 or older. In Uganda, for example, only 3% of the population is at least 65, compared to 13% of Americans and 20% of Germans and Italians.

Figure 12.2 Percentage of Population Aged 65 or Older, 2007

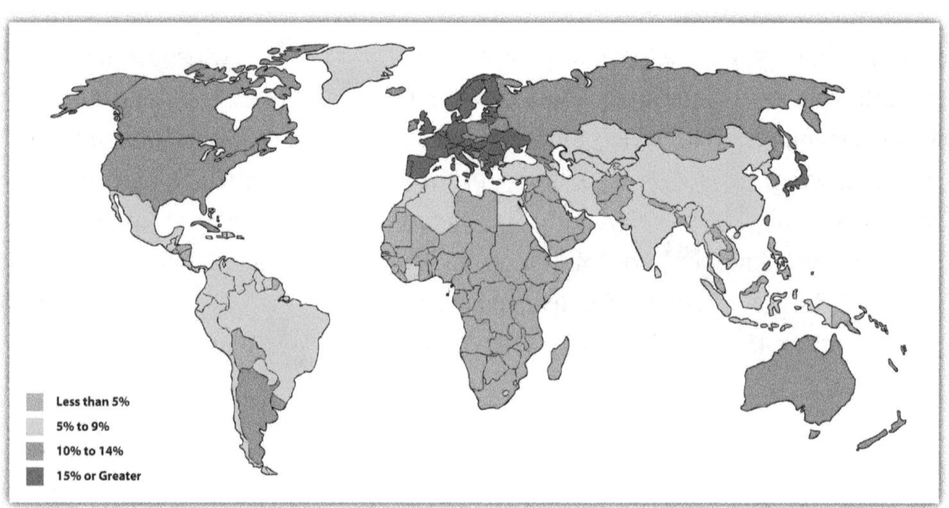

Source: Adapted from Population Reference Bureau. (2007). *2007 world population data sheet*. Retrieved from http://www.prb.org/pdf07/07WPDS_Eng.pdf.

Despite the international disparities we see in life expectancy, overall it has been increasing steadily around the world. It was only 46 years worldwide in the early 1950s but was 69 in 2009 and is expected to reach about 75 by 2050 (Population Reference Bureau, 2009; United Nations Population Division, 2009). This means that the number of people 65 or older is growing rapidly: they are expected to reach almost 1.5 billion worldwide by 2050, three times their number today and five times their number just 20 years ago (United Nations Population Division, 2009). Despite international differences in life expectancy and the elderly percentage of the population, the world as a whole is decidedly "graying," with important implications for the cost and quality of elder care and other issues (Hayutin, 2007).

In wealthy nations, older people (65 or older) now constitute 15% of the population but will account for 26% by 2050. Because so many people die so young, poor nations historically have had very low percentages of older people, but this percentage is expected to increase from about 6% now to 15% in 2050. Two factors will account for this growth. First, as in wealthy nations, life expectancy is increasing due to better health care and diets along with other factors, even if conditions in poor nations continue otherwise to be miserable overall. Second, poor nations are experiencing declining fertility; because fewer births means that a lower percentage of their populations will be young, a larger percentage of their populations will be older.

Older people now constitute 15% of the combined population of wealthy nations, but they will account for 26% by 2050.

Pedro Ribeiro Simões – Warming the bones – CC BY 2.0.

By 2050, the percentage of older people in poor nations will equal the percentage of older people in rich nations today. The graying of their populations promises to pose special problems. As Adele M. Hayutin (2007, p. 13) observes, "The rapid pace of aging in the less developed countries will require them to adjust much faster than has been necessary in more developed countries. Moreover, the sheer size of their populations will make their adjustments even more challenging."

A major problem will obviously involve paying for the increase in health care that the increase of older people in these nations will require. Because these nations are so poor, they will face even greater problems than the industrial world in paying for such care and for other programs and services their older citizens will need. Another problem stems from the fact that many poor nations are beginning or continuing to industrialize and urbanize. As they do so, traditional family patterns, including respect for the elderly and the continuation of their roles and influence, may weaken. One reason for this is that urban families have smaller dwelling units in which to accommodate their elderly relatives and lack any land onto which they can build new housing. As a result, families in poor nations will find it increasingly difficult to accommodate their elders. Moreover, elders in poor nations have not had a chance to acquire the financial assets enjoyed by many of their counterparts in the industrial world, making them more dependent on their children and grandchildren than the industrial world's elderly. Yet in sort of a Catch-22, their children and grandchildren typically have few assets of their own and thus have trouble affording to care for their elders.

Life Expectancy in the United States

Life expectancy has been increasing in the United States along with the rest of the world (see Figure 12.3 "Changes in U.S. Life Expectancy at Birth, 1900–2010"). It rose rapidly in the first half of the 20th century and has increased steadily since then. From a low of 47.3 years in 1900, it rose to about 71 years in 1970 and 77 years in 2000 and will rise to a projected 78.3 years in 2010. Americans born in 2010 will thus be expected to live about 31 years longer (a gain of almost 66%) than those born 110 years earlier.

Figure 12.3 Changes in U.S. Life Expectancy at Birth, 1900–2010

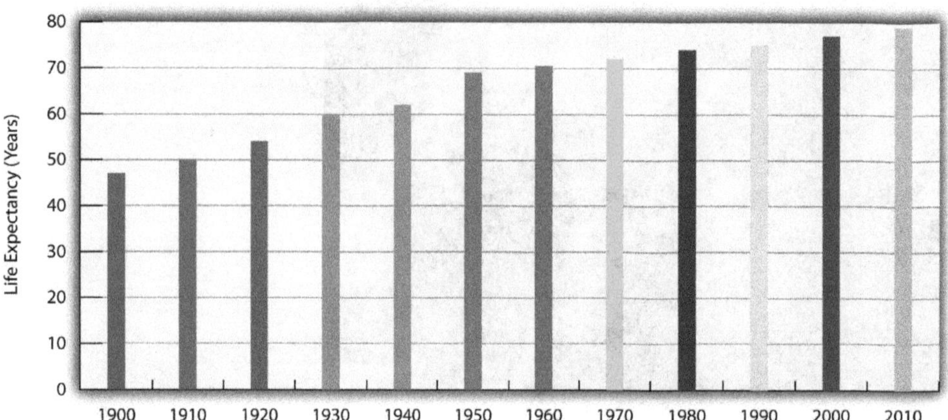

Sources: Data from Arias, E. (2010). United States life tables, 2006. *National Vital Statistics Reports, 58*(21), 1–40.

Note that the average U.S. life expectancy in 1900 was similar to that seen today in many poor nations. A century ago, many Americans lacked proper sanitation and good nutrition and lived before the advent of modern medicine, when many deadly diseases were rampant. Many infants died before age 1 and many children died before age 10, lowering overall life expectancy. Improved public sanitation and the development of new drugs such as antibiotics helped greatly to reduce infant and childhood mortality in the first half of the 20th century and, in turn, to increase life expectancy (Haines, 2008). Declining death rates among the elderly also help account for the increase in life expectancy shown in Figure 12.3 "Changes in U.S. Life Expectancy at Birth, 1900–2010". In 1900, a 65-year-old person could expect to live another 11.9 years; the comparable figure for a 65-year-old now is almost 19 years, an increase of almost 7 years.

During the next few decades, the numbers of the elderly will increase rapidly thanks to the large baby boom generation born after World War II (from 1946 to 1964) that is now entering its mid-60s. Figure 12.4 "Past and Projected Percentage of U.S. Population Aged 65 or Older, 1900–2050" shows the rapid rise of older Americans (65 or older) as a percentage of the population that is expected to occur. Elders numbered about 3.1 million in 1900 (4.1% of the population), number about 40 million today, and are expected to reach 89 million by 2050 (20.2% of the population). The large increase in older Americans overall has been called the *graying of America* and will have important repercussions for elderly care and other aspects of old age in the United States, as we discuss later.

Figure 12.4 Past and Projected Percentage of U.S. Population Aged 65 or Older, 1900–2050

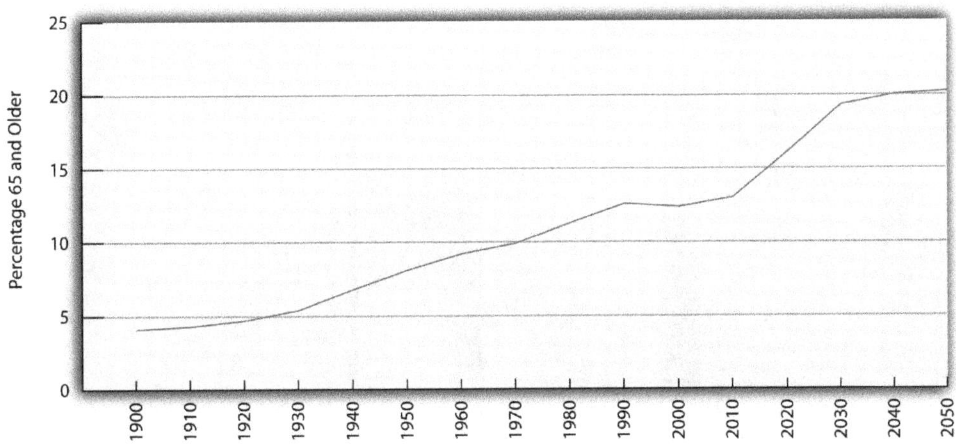

Source: Data from Administration on Aging. (n.d.). Projected future growth of the older population by age: 1900–2050. Retrieved from http://www.aoa.gov/AoARoot/Aging_Statistics/future_growth/docs/By_Age_65_and_over.xls.

Inequality in Life Expectancy

We have seen that worldwide differences in life expectancy reflect global stratification. Inequality in life expectancy also exists *within* a given society along gender, race/ethnicity, and social class lines.

For gender the inequality is in favor of women, who for both biological and social reasons (see Chapter 13 "Work and the Economy") outlive men across the globe. In the United States, for example, girls born in 2005 could expect to live 80.4 years on the average, but boys only 75.2 years.

In most countries, race and ethnicity combine with social class to produce longer life expectancies for the (wealthier) dominant race, which in the Western world is almost always white. The United States again reflects this international phenomenon: whites born in 2005 could expect to live 78.3 years on the average, but African Americans only 73.2 years. In fact, gender and race combine in the United States to put African American males at a particular disadvantage, as they can expect to live only 69.5 years (see Figure 12.5 "Sex, Race, and Life Expectancy for U.S. Residents Born in 2005"). The average African American male will die about 11.3 years earlier than the average white woman.

Figure 12.5 Sex, Race, and Life Expectancy for U.S. Residents Born in 2005

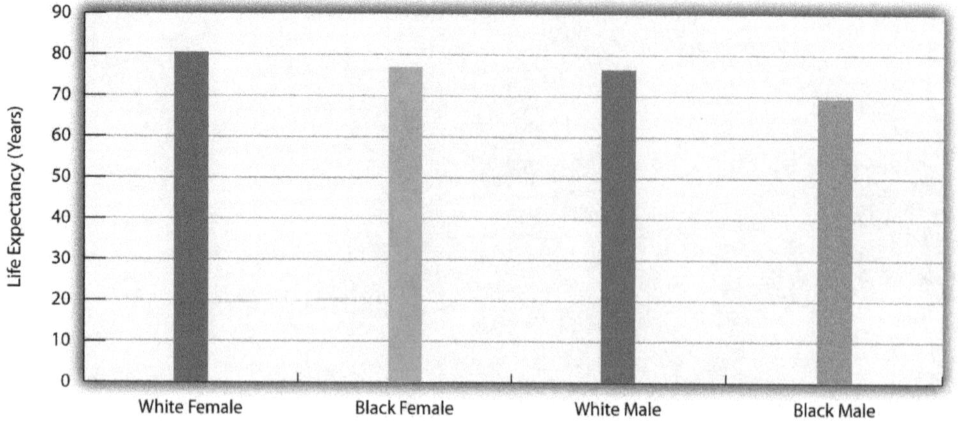

Source: Data from National Center for Health Statistics, U.S. Department of Health and Human Services. (2008). Health, United States, 2008, with special feature on the health of young adults. Retrieved from the Centers for Disease Control and Prevention Web site: http://www.cdc.gov/nchs/data/hus/hus08.pdf#026.

Key Takeaways

- Life expectancy differs widely around the world and is much higher in wealthy nations than in poor nations.
- Life expectancy has also been increasing around the world, including in the United States, and the increasing number of older people in the decades ahead will pose several serious challenges.
- Inequality in life expectancy exists within a given society along gender, race/ethnicity, and social class lines.

For Your Review

1. As our nation and the world both "gray," what do you think is the most important problem that will stem from the increasing number of older people?
2. Write a short essay in which you discuss the problems that an elderly person you know, perhaps a grandparent, has experienced related to being older.

References

Haines, M. (2008). Fertility and mortality in the United States. In R. Whaples (Ed.), *Eh.Net encyclopedia.* Retrieved from http://eh.net/encyclopedia/article/haines.demography.

Hayutin, A. M. (2007). Graying of the global population. *Public Policy & Aging Report, 17*(4), 12–17.

Population Reference Bureau. (2009). *2009 world population data sheet.* Washington, DC: Author.

United Nations Population Division. (2009). *World population prospects: The 2008 revision*. New York, NY: Author.

12.5 Biological and Psychological Aspects of Aging

Learning Objectives

1. Describe any four biological changes associated with aging.
2. List any three steps that individuals can try to undertake to achieve successful aging.

Our society, like many of the others discussed earlier, has a mixed view of aging and older people. While we generally appreciate our elderly, we have a culture oriented toward youth, as evidenced by the abundance of television characters in their 20s and lack of those in their older years. As individuals, we do our best not to look old, as the many ads for wrinkle creams and products to darken gray hair attest. Moreover, when we think of the elderly, negative images often come to mind. We often think of someone who has been slowed by age both physically and mentally. She or he may have trouble walking up steps, picking up heavy grocery bags, standing up straight, or remembering recent events. The term *senile* often comes to mind, and phrases like "doddering old fool," "geezer," and other disparaging remarks sprinkle our language when we talk about them. Meanwhile, despite some improvement, the elderly are often portrayed in stereotypical ways on television and in movies (Lee, Carpenter, & Meyers, 2007).

How true is this negative image? What do we know of physical and psychological changes among the elderly? How much of what we think we know about aging and the elderly is a myth, and how much is reality? Gerontologists have paid special attention to answering these questions (Craik & Salthouse, 2008; Binstock & George, 2006).

Biological changes certainly occur as we age. The first signs are probably in our appearance. Our hair begins to turn gray, our (male) hairlines recede, and a few wrinkles set in. The internal changes that often accompany aging are more consequential, among them being that (a) fat replaces lean body mass, and many people gain weight; (b) bone and muscle loss occurs; (c) lungs lose their ability to take in air, and our respiratory efficiency declines; (d) the functions of the cardiovascular and renal (kidney) systems decline; (e) the number of brain cells declines, as does brain mass overall; and (f) vision and hearing decline (Hooyman & Kiyak, 2011). Cognitive and psychological changes also occur. Learning and memory begin declining after people reach their 70s; depression and other mental/emotional disorders can set in; and dementia, including Alzheimer's disease, can occur. All of these conditions yield statistics such as follows: about half of people 65 or older have arthritis or high blood pressure; almost one-fifth have coronary heart disease; more than one-fifth have diabetes; and about 60% of women in their 70s have osteoporosis (Centers for Disease Control and Prevention & The Merck Company Foundation, 2007).

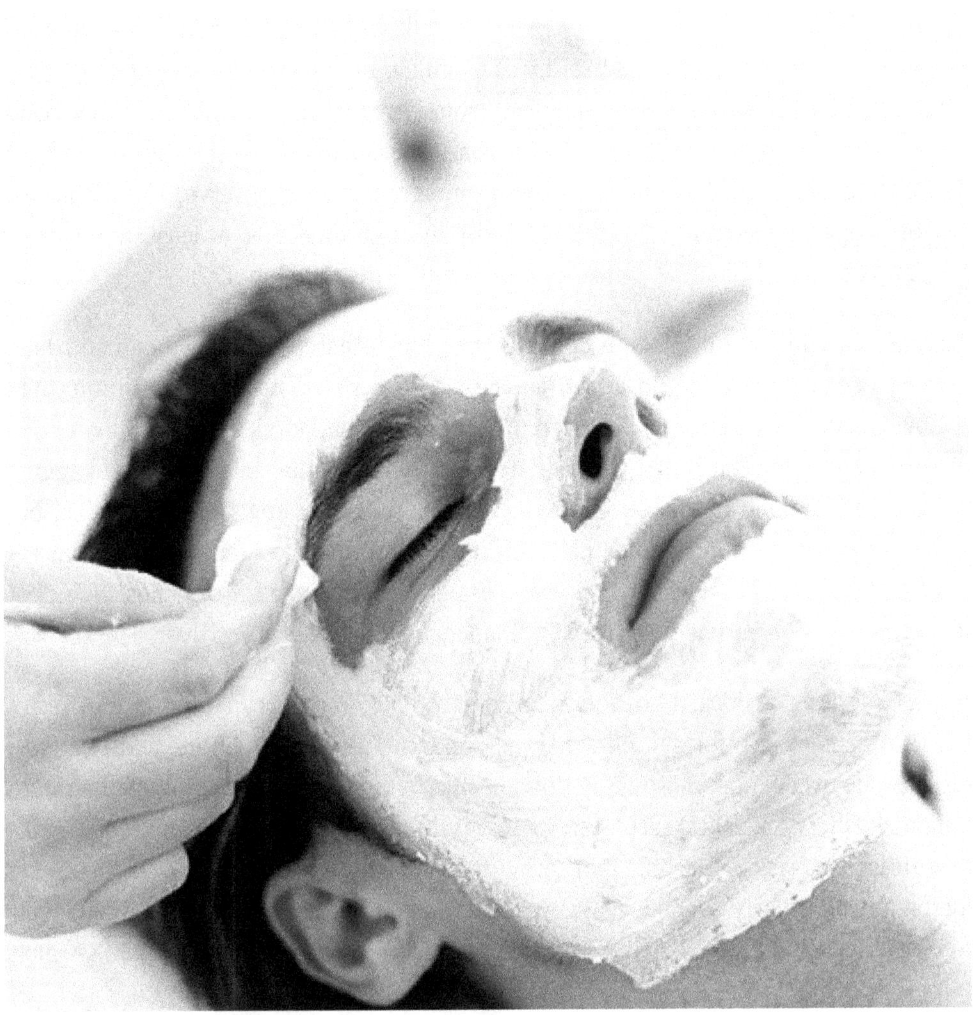

Because our society values youthfulness, many people try to do their best not to look old.

FoundryParkInn – Men's Facial – CC BY-NC-ND 2.0.

Still, the nature and extent of all of these changes vary widely among older people (Sawchuk, 2009). Some individuals are frail at 65, while others remain vigorous well into their 70s and beyond. People can be "old" at 60 or even 50, while others can be "young" at 80. Many elders are no longer able to work, but others remain in the labor force. All in all, then, most older people do not fit the doddering image myth and can still live a satisfying and productive life.

Enhancing Vitality for Successful Aging

To what extent are the effects of biological and psychological aging the inevitable results of chronological aging? Gerontologists are still trying to understand what causes these effects, and their explanations center on such things as a declining immune system, the slowing of cellular replication, and other processes that need not concern us here.

Some recent research has focused on centenarians—people at least 100 years of age—to try to find out what enables them to live so long. There are about 85,000 centenarians in the United States, and this number is expected to reach 580,000 by 2040 (Mozes, 2008). They tend to be as healthy as people in their early 80s, and their medical expenses are lower. Some eat red meat and some are vegetarians, and some exercise a lot while others exercise little. Scientists think they may have "supergenes" that protect them from cancer or Alzheimer's disease and are trying to find these genes. The relative health of the centenarians led one researcher to observe, "Now that we know that a substantial number of people can remain robust and healthy through their 90s, at least, that should change our attitude about old age. It is no longer a curse, but an opportunity" (Hilts, 1999, p. D7).

We do not all have supergenes and we will not all become centenarians, but research shows we can still take several steps to help us age better, because what we do as we enter our older years matters much more than genetics (Centers for Disease Control and Prevention & The Merck Company Foundation, 2007). To the extent this is true, the effects of biological and psychological aging are not necessarily inevitable, and "successful aging" is possible (Evans, 2009). The steps highlighted in the gerontological literature are by now almost a cliché, but regular exercise, good nutrition, and stress reduction stand at the top of most gerontologists' recommendations for continued vitality in later life. In fact, Americans live about 10 years less than an average set of genes should let them live because they do not exercise enough and because they eat inadequate diets (Perls & Silver, 1999).

Research by social gerontologists suggests at least two additional steps older people can take if they want "successful aging." The first is involvement in informal, personal networks of friends, neighbors, and relatives. The importance of such networks is one of the most thoroughly documented in the social gerontological literature (Binstock & George, 2006; Adams & Blieszner, 1995) (see the "Sociology Making a Difference" box). Networks enhance successful aging for at least two reasons. First, they provide practical support, such as help buying groceries and visiting the doctor, to the elderly who need it. Second, they help older people maintain their self-esteem, meet their desire for friendships, and satisfy other emotional needs and thereby enhance their psychological well-being.

A second step for successful aging suggested by scholarly research is religious involvement (Barkan & Greenwood, 2003; Moberg, 2008). Religious involvement enhances psychological well-being among older adults for at least two reasons. As people worship in a congregation, they interact with other congregants and, as just noted, enhance their social support networks. Moreover, as they practice their religious faith, they reduce their stress and can cope better with personal troubles. For both these reasons, attendance at religious services and the practice of prayer are thought to enhance psychological well-being among the elderly. Some elders cannot attend religious services regularly because they have health problems or are no longer able to drive a car. But prayer and other private devotional activities remain significant for many of them. To the extent that religion makes a difference for elders' well-being, health-care facilities and congregations should do what they can to enable older adults to attend religious services and to otherwise practice their religious faith.

Sociology Making a Difference

Friendships and Successful Aging

Building on the insights of Émile Durkheim, a founder of sociology discussed in Chapter 1 "Sociology and the Sociological Perspective", sociologists have long emphasized the importance of social networks for social stability and individual well-being.

As the text discusses, social networks improve the lives of older Americans by providing both practical and emotional support. Early research on social networks and aging focused more on relatives than on friends (Roscow, 1967). Rebecca G. Adams, former president of the Southern Sociological Society, was one of the first sociologists to emphasize the role that friends can also play in the lives of the elderly. She interviewed 70 older women who lived in a Chicago suburb and asked them many questions about the extent and quality of their friendships (Adams, 1986).

In one of her most important findings, Adams discovered that the women reported receiving more help from friends than other researchers had assumed was the case. The women were somewhat reluctant to ask friends for help but did so when family members were not available and when they would not overly inconvenience the friends whom they asked for help. Adams also found that "secondary" friendships—those involving friends that a woman spent time with but with whom she was not especially close—were more likely than "primary" friendships (very close friendships) to contribute to her interviewees' psychological well-being, as these friendships enabled the women to meet new people, to become involved in new activities, and thus to be engaged with the larger society. This finding led Adams (1986) to conclude that one should not underestimate how important friends are to older people, particularly to the elderly without family. Friends are an important source of companionship and possibly a more important source of service support than most of the current literature suggests.

Adams also asked the women about their friendships with men (Adams, 1985). The 70 women she interviewed reported 670 friendships, of which only 3.6% were with men. (About 91% were with other women, and 6% were with couples.) Although prior research had assumed that the number of these friendships is small because there are so few unmarried elderly men compared to the number of unmarried elderly women, Adams discovered from her interviews some additional reasons. Her respondents interpreted *any* friendship with a man as a courting or romantic friendship, which they thought would be viewed negatively by their children and by their peers. Adopting a traditional gender-role orientation, they also expected any man they might marry to be able to protect them physically and financially. Yet they also realized that any elderly man they might know would be very likely unable to do so. For all of these reasons, they shied away from friendships with men.

Work by Adams and other sociologists on the friendships and other aspects of the social support systems for older Americans has contributed greatly to our understanding of the components of successful aging. It points to the need for programs and other activities to make it easier for the elderly to develop and maintain friendships with both sexes to improve their ability to meet both their practical and emotional needs. In this manner, sociology is again making a difference.

Key Takeaways

- Certain biological, cognitive, and psychological changes occur as people age. These changes reinforce the negative view of the elderly, but this view nonetheless reflects stereotypes and myths about aging and the elderly.
- Regular exercise, good nutrition, stress reduction, involvement in personal networks, and religious involvement all enhance successful aging.

For Your Review

1. Do you think the negative view of older people that is often found in our society is an unfair stereotype, or do you think there is actually some truth to this stereotype? Explain your answer.
2. Referring back to Chapter 1 "Sociology and the Sociological Perspective"'s discussion of Émile Durkheim, how does research that documents the importance of personal networks for successful aging reflect

Durkheim's insights?

References

Adams, R. G. (1986). A look at friendship and aging. *Generations, 10*(4), 43.

Adams, R. G. (1985). People would talk: Normative barriers to cross-sex friendships for elderly women. *The Gerontologist, 25,* 605–611.

Adams, R. G. (1986). Secondary friendship networks and psychological well-being among elderly women. *Activities, Adaptation, and Aging, 8,* 59–72.

Adams, R. G., & Blieszner, R. (1995). Aging well with family and friends. *American Behavioral Scientist, 39,* 209–224.

Barkan, S. E., & Greenwood, S. F. (2003). Religious attendance and subjective well-being among older Americans: Evidence from the General Social Survey. *Review of Religious Research, 45*(2), 116–129.

Binstock, R. H., & George, L. K. (Eds.). (2006). *Handbook of aging and the social sciences* (6th ed.). Boston, MA: Academic Press.

Centers for Disease Control and Prevention & The Merck Company Foundation. (2007). *The state of aging and health in America 2007.* Whitehouse Station, NJ: The Merck Company Foundation.

Craik, F. I. M., & Salthouse, T. A. (Eds.). (2008). *Handbook of aging and cognition.* New York, NY: Psychology Press.

Evans, R. J. (2009). A comparison of rural and urban older adults in Iowa on specific markers of successful aging. *Journal of Gerontological Social Work, 52*(4), 423–438.

Hilts, P. J. (1999, June 1). Life at age 100 is surprisingly healthy, *The New York Times,* p. D7.

Hooyman, N. R., & Kiyak, H. A. (2011). *Social gerontology: A multidisciplinary perspective* (9th ed.). Upper Saddle River, NJ: Pearson.

Lee, M. M., Carpenter, B., & Meyers, L. S. (2007). Representations of older adults in television advertisements. *Journal of Aging Studies, 21*(1), 23–30.

Moberg, D. O. (2008). Spirituality and aging: Research and implications. *Journal of Religion, Spirituality & Aging, 20*(1–2), 95–134.

Mozes, A. (2008, October 13). Centenarians offer long-life secrets. *U.S. News & World Report.* Retrieved from http://health.usnews.com/articles/health/healthday/2008/2008/2001/centenarians-offer-long-life-secrets.html.

Perls, T. T., & Silver, M. H. (1999). *Living to 100: Lessons in living to your maximum potential at any age*. New York, NY: Basic Books.

Roscow, I. (1967). *Social integration of the aged*. New York, NY: Free Press.

Sawchuk, D. (2009). The raging grannies: Defying stereotypes and embracing aging through activism. *Journal of Women & Aging, 21*(3), 171–185. doi:10.1080/08952840903054898.

12.6 The U.S. Elderly

Learning Objectives

1. Present a brief sociodemographic profile of the U.S. elderly.
2. Discuss the several problems experienced by the U.S. elderly.
3. Describe how the social attitudes of older Americans generally differ from those of younger Americans.

We now turn our attention to older people in the United States. We first sketch a demographic profile of our elderly and then examine some of the problems they face because of their age.

Who Are the Elderly?

Table 12.2 "Demographic Composition of the Elderly, 2008" presents the demographic composition of Americans aged 65 or older. Slightly more than half the elderly are 65–74 years of age, and about 57% are female, reflecting males' shorter life spans as discussed earlier. About 76% of the elderly are non-Latino whites, compared to about 66% in the population as a whole; 8.5% are African American, compared to about 13% of the population; and 6.6% are Latino, compared to 15% of the population. The greater proportion of whites among the elderly and lower proportions of African Americans and Latinos reflects these groups' life expectancy differences discussed earlier and also their differences in birth rates.

Table 12.2 Demographic Composition of the Elderly, 2008

Age		**Marital status**	
65–74 years	51.8%	Married	57.0%
75–84 years	33.5%	Widowed	29.8%
85 years and over	14.7%	Divorced	9.1%
Gender		Never married	4.1%
Female	57.1%	**Years of school completed**	
Male	42.9%	0–8 years	11.2%
Labor force participation		1–3 years of high school	11.4%
Employed	16.1%	High school graduate	36.9%
Unemployed	0.7%	1–3 years of college	20.1%
Not in labor force	83.2%	College graduate	20.5%
Race and/or ethnicity		**Household income**[a]	
White, non-Latino	75.5%	Under $15,000	23.4%
African American	8.5%	$15,000–$24,999	20.6%
Latino	6.8%	$25,000–$34,999	15.0%
Asian/Pacific Islander	3.4%	$35,000–49,999	13.7%
Amer. Ind., Esk., Aleut.	0.6%	$50,000–$74,999	11.9%
Two or more races	0.7%	$75,000–$99,999	6.0%
Living in poverty	9.7%	$100,000 and over	9.3%
[a]2007 data			

Source: Data from U.S. Census Bureau. (2010). *Statistical abstract of the United States: 2010.* Washington, DC: U.S. Government Printing Office. Retrieved from http://www.census.gov/compendia/statab.

The lower proportions of African Americans and Latinos among the elderly partly reflect these groups' lower life expectancies.

Evgeni Zotov – Grandparents – CC BY-NC-ND 2.0.

The percentage of elders living in poverty is 9.7, compared to 13.2% of the entire population. Although most elders have fixed incomes, the fact that their family size is usually one or two means that they are less likely than younger people to live in poverty. In fact, today's elderly are financially much better off than their grandparents were, thanks to Social Security; Medicare, the federal health insurance program for older Americans; pensions; and their own assets. We will revisit the health and financial security of elders a little later.

Turning to education, about 21% of the elderly are college graduates, compared to about 29% of the population as a whole. This difference reflects the fact that few people went to college when today's elderly were in their late teens and early 20s. However, it is still true that today's elders are better educated than any previous generation of elders. Future generations of the elderly will be even better educated than those now.

While most elders are retired and no longer in the labor force, about 16% do continue to work (see Table 12.2 "Demographic Composition of the Elderly, 2008"). These seniors tend to be in good health and to find their jobs psychologically satisfying. Compared to younger workers, they miss fewer days of work for health or other reasons and are less likely to quit their jobs for other opportunities (Sears, 2009).

Problems Facing the Elderly

Although we emphasized earlier that many older Americans do not fit the negative image with which they are portrayed, it is still true that they face special problems because of their age and life circumstances. We discuss some of these here.

Physical and Mental Health

Perhaps the problem that comes most readily to mind is health, or, to be more precise, poor health. The biological and psychological effects of aging lead to greater physical and mental health problems among the elderly than in younger age groups. These problems are reflected in responses to the General Social Survey question, "Would you say your own health, in general, is excellent, good, fair, or poor?" Figure 12.6 "Age and Self-Reported Health" shows that the elderly are more likely than the nonelderly to report that their health is only fair or poor.

Figure 12.6 Age and Self-Reported Health

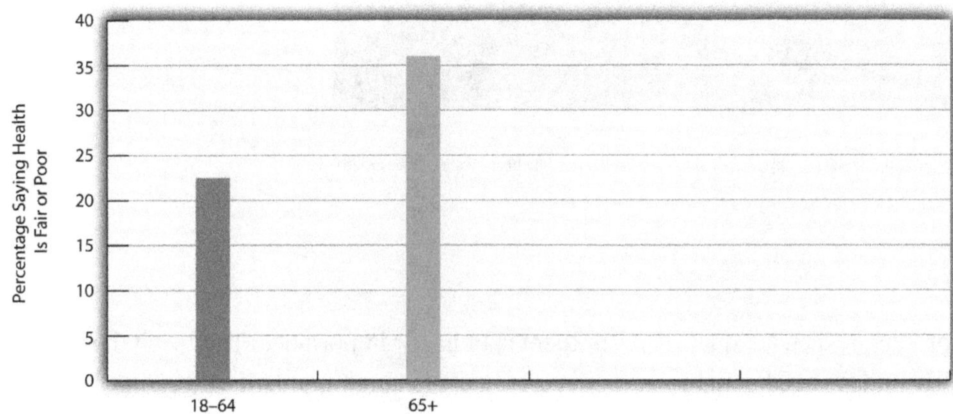

Source: Data from General Social Survey, 2008.

The elderly's perception of their own health is supported by government estimates of chronic health conditions for older Americans. For every 1,000 people aged 65 or older not living in a nursing home or other institution, 495 have arthritis, 533 have high blood pressure, 309 have heart disease, 405 have hearing loss, 174 have vision problems, and 180 have diabetes (these numbers add up to more than 1,000 as people may have several health conditions) (Federal Interagency Forum on Aging-Related Statistics, 2008). These rates are much higher than those for younger age groups.

The elderly also suffer from dementia, including Alzheimer's disease, which affects about 1 of every 8 people 65 or older (Alzheimer's Association, 2009). Another mental health problem is depression, which affects about 14% of people 65 or older. Because of mental or physical disability, 42% of all people 65 or older, or more than 16 million elders, need help with at least one "daily living" activity, such as preparing a meal (Federal Interagency Forum on Aging-Related Statistics, 2008).

Older people visit the doctor and hospital more often than younger people. Partly for this reason, adequate health care for the elderly is of major importance.

Ted Van Pelt – The Coopers – CC BY 2.0.

If the elderly have more health problems, then adequate care for them is of major importance. They visit the doctor and hospital more often than their middle-aged counterparts. Medicare covers about one-half of their health-care costs; this is a substantial amount of coverage but still forces many seniors to pay thousands of dollars annually themselves. Some physicians and other health-care providers do not accept Medicare "assignment," meaning that the patient must pay an even higher amount. Moreover, Medicare pays little or nothing for long-term care in nursing homes and other institutions and for mental health services. All of these factors mean that older Americans can still face high medical expenses or at least pay high premiums for private health insurance.

In addition, Medicare costs have risen rapidly along with other health-care costs. Medicare expenditures soared from about $37 billion in 1980 to more than $450 billion today (see Figure 12.7 "Medicare Expenditures, 1980–2007"). As the population continues to age and as health-care costs continue to rise, Medicare expenses will continue to rise as well, making it increasingly difficult to find the money to finance Medicare.

Figure 12.7 Medicare Expenditures, 1980–2007

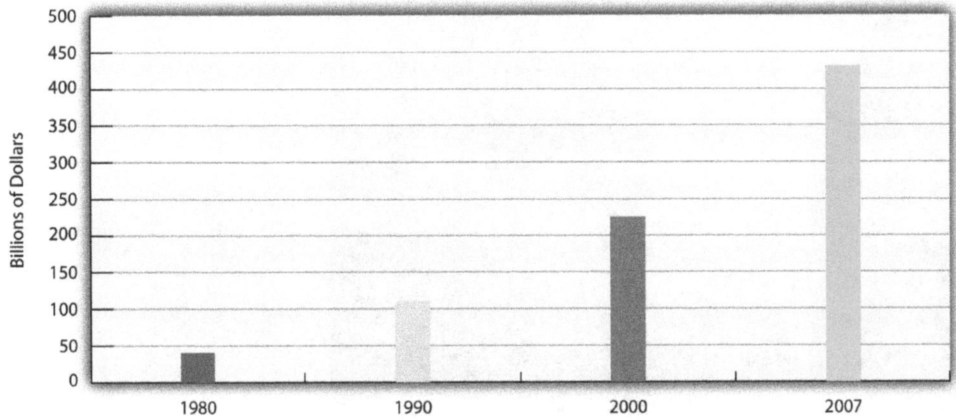

Source: Data from Centers for Medicare and Medicaid Services. (n.d.). National health expenditure data. Retrieved from http://www.cms.hhs.gov/NationalHealthExpendData/downloads/tables.pdf.

Nursing Home Care

While most older Americans live by themselves or with their families, a small minority live in group settings. A growing type of group setting is the *continuous care retirement community*, a setting of private rooms, apartments, and/or condominiums that offers medical and practical care to those who need it. In some such communities, residents eat their meals together, while in others they cook for themselves. Usually these communities offer above-average recreational facilities and can be very expensive, as some require a lifetime contract or at least monthly fees that can run into the thousands of dollars.

For elders who need high-level medical care or practical support, nursing homes are the primary option. About 16,100 nursing homes exist, and 3.5% of Americans 65 or older (or about 1.3 million individuals) live in them; this figure rises to 14% of people 85 or older (Federal Interagency Forum on Aging-Related Statistics, 2008). About three-fourths of all nursing home residents are women. Almost all residents (94%) receive assistance in bathing and showering, 80% receive help in using the bathroom, and one-third receive help in eating.

As noted earlier, Medicare does not pay for long-term institutional care for most older Americans. Because nursing home care costs at least $70,000 yearly, residents can quickly use up all their assets and then, ironically, become eligible for payments from *Medicaid*, the federal insurance program for people with low incomes.

Nursing homes are often understaffed to save costs and are also generally not subject to outside inspection. These conditions help contribute to the neglect of nursing home residents.

Sheila – Christian Nursing Home – CC BY-NC-ND 2.0.

If one problem of nursing homes is their expense, another problem is the quality of care they provide. Because their residents are typically in poor physical and/or mental health, their care must be the best possible, as they can do little to help themselves if their care is substandard. As more people enter nursing homes in the years ahead, the quality of nursing home care will become even more important. Yet there is much evidence that nursing home care is often substandard and is replete with neglect and abuse (DeHart, Webb, & Cornman, 2009).

Financial Security and Employment

Earlier we noted that the elderly are less likely than younger age groups to live in poverty and that their financial status is much better than that of previous generations of older people. However, this brief summary of their economic well-being obscures several underlying problems (Crawthorne, 2008; Treas, 1995).

First, recall Chapter 6 "Groups and Organizations"'s discussion of *episodic poverty*, which refers to the drifting of many people into and out of poverty as their jobs and other circumstances change. Once they become poor, older people are more likely than younger ones to *stay* poor, as younger people have more job and other opportunities to move out of poverty. Recall also that the official poverty rate obscures the fact that many people live just above it and are "near poor." This is especially true of the elderly, who, if hit by large medical bills or other expenses, can hardly afford to pay them. In another problem, older women are more likely than older men to live in poverty for at least two reasons: women earn less than men and thus have lower monthly benefits under Social Security than men, and women outlive men and thus use up their savings. Racial and ethnic disparities also exist among the elderly, reflecting poverty disparities in the entire population, as older people of color are much more likely than older whites to live in poverty (U.S. Census Bureau, 2010).

Older women are more likely than older men to live in poverty.

Christian Haugen – Old woman feeding the pigeon – CC BY 2.0.

Two final problems relate to Social Security, which is the largest income source for most elders. If Social Security did not exist, the poverty rate of the elderly would be 44%, or about five times higher than the actual rate (Crawthorne, 2008). Without Social Security, then, nearly half of all people 65 or older would be living in official poverty, and this rate would be even much higher for older women and older persons of color. Unfortunately, many observers think the Social Security system is facing a crisis as the large number of baby boomers now reaches retirement age (Sloan, 2009). Another problem is that, as noted earlier regarding women, monthly benefits are tied to people's earnings before retirement: the higher the earnings, the higher the monthly benefit. Thus a paradox occurs: people who earn low wages will get lower Social Security benefits after they retire, even though they need *higher* benefits to make up for their lower earnings. In this manner, the income inequality that exists before retirement continues to exist after it.

This paradox reflects a wider problem involving Social Security. However helpful it might be in aiding older Americans, the aid it provides lags far behind comparable programs in other wealthy Western nations (see the "Learning From Other Societies" box). Social Security payments are low enough that almost one-third of the elderly who receive no other income assistance live in official poverty. For all of these reasons, Social Security is certainly beneficial for many older Americans, but it remains inadequate compared to what other nations provide.

Learning From Other Societies

Elderly Policy and Programs in the Netherlands and Sweden

A few years ago, AARP assessed quality-of-life issues for older people and the larger society in 16 wealthy democracies (the nations of North America and Western Europe, along with Australia and Japan). Each nation was rated (on a scale of 1–5, with 5 being the highest score) on 17 criteria, including life expectancy, health care for the elderly, pension coverage, and age-discrimination laws. Of the 16 nations, the Netherlands ranked first, with a total score of 64, while Italy ranked last, with a score of 48; the United States was 13th, with a score of 50 (Edwards, 2004). Despite its immense wealth, then, the United States lagged behind most other democracies. Because a "perfect" score would have been 85 (17 × 5), even the Netherlands fell short of an ideal quality of life as measured by the AARP indicators.

Why did the United States not rank higher? The experience of the Netherlands and Sweden, both of which have longer life expectancies than the United States, points to some possible answers. In the Netherlands, everyone at age 65 receives a full pension that does not depend on how much money they earned while they were working. Everyone thus gets the same amount, and this amount is larger than the average American gets, since Social Security does depend on earnings and many people earned fairly low amounts during their working years. As a result Dutch elderly are much less likely than their American counterparts to be poor. The Dutch elderly (and also the nonelderly) have generous governed insurance for medical problems and for nursing home care; this financial help is much higher than older Americans obtain through Medicare.

As one example, the AARP article mentioned an elderly Dutch woman who had cancer surgery and 32 chemotherapy treatments, for which she paid nothing. In the United States, the chemotherapy treatments would have cost at least $30,000. Medicare would have covered only 80% of this amount, leaving a patient to pay $6,000.

The Netherlands also helps its elderly in other ways. One example is that about one-fourth of that nation's elderly receive regular government-subsidized home visits by health-care professionals and/or housekeepers; this practice enables the elderly to remain independent and avoid having to enter a nursing home. In another example, the elderly also receive 7 days of free riding on the nation's rail system.

Sweden has a home-care visitation program that is similar to the Netherlands' program. Many elderly are visited twice a day by a care assistant who helps them bathe and dress in the morning and go to bed at night. The care assistant also regularly cleans their residence and takes them out for exercise. The Swedish government pays about 80% of the costs of this assistance and subsidizes the remaining cost for elderly who cannot afford it. Like the Netherlands' program, Sweden's program helps the elderly to remain independent and live at home rather than enter a nursing institution.

Compared to the United States, then, other democracies generally provide their elderly less expensive or free health care, greater financial support during their retirement, and home visits by health-care professionals and other assistants. In these and other ways, these other governments encourage "active aging" (Hartlapp & Schmid, 2008; Ney, 2005). Adoption of similar policies in the United States would improve the lives of older Americans and perhaps prolong their life spans.

Older people who want to work may have trouble finding employment because of age discrimination and other factors.

Wikimedia Commons – CC BY 2.0.

Older Americans also face problems in employment. Recall that about 16% of seniors remain employed. Other elders are retired or unemployed because several obstacles make it difficult for them to find jobs. First, many workplaces do not permit part-time working arrangements that many seniors favor. Second, the rise in high-tech jobs means that older workers would need to be retrained for many of today's jobs, and few retraining programs exist. Third, although federal law prohibits age discrimination in employment, it exists anyway, as employers do not think older people are "up to" the job, even though the evidence indicates they are good, productive workers (E. D. Berger, 2009). Finally, earnings above a certain level reduce Social Security benefits before full retirement age (66), leading some older people to avoid working at all or to at least limit their hours. All of these obstacles lead seniors to drop out of the labor force or to remain unemployed (Gallo, Brand, Teng, Leo-Summers, & Byers, 2009).

Bereavement and Social Isolation

"We all need someone we can lean on," as a famous Rolling Stones song goes, and most older Americans do have adequate social support networks, which, as we saw earlier, are important for their well-being. However, a significant minority of elders live alone and do not see friends and relatives as often as they wish. Bereavement takes a toll, as elders who might have been married for many years suddenly find themselves living alone. Here a gender difference again exists. Because women outlive men and are generally younger than their husbands, they are three times more likely than men (42% compared to 13%) to be widowed and thus much more likely to live alone (see Table 12.3 "Living Arrangements of Noninstitutionalized Older Americans, 2008").

Table 12.3 Living Arrangements of Noninstitutionalized Older Americans, 2008

	Men	Women
Living alone	19%	42%
Living with spouse	72%	39%
Other arrangement	10%	19%

Source: Data from Administration on Aging. (2009). A profile of older Americans: 2009. Retrieved from http://www.aoa.gov/AoARoot/Aging_Statistics/Profile/2009/6.aspx.

Many elders have at least one adult child living within driving distance, and such children are an invaluable resource. At the same time, however, some elders have no children, because either they have outlived their children or they never had any. As baby boomers begin reaching their older years, more of them will have no children because they were more likely than previous generations to not marry and/or to not have children if they did marry. Thus baby boomers face not only the prospect of scarcer Social Security funds when they reach retirement age but also a relative lack of children to help them when they enter their "old-old" years (Leland, 2010).

Bereavement is always a difficult experience, but because so many elders lose a spouse, it is a particular problem in their lives (Hansson & Stroebe, 2007). Usually grief follows bereavement. It can last several years and, if it becomes extreme, can involve anxiety, depression, guilt, loneliness, and other problems. Of all of these problems, loneliness is perhaps the most common and the most difficult to overcome.

Elder Abuse

Some seniors fall prey to their own relatives who commit **elder abuse** against them. Such abuse involves one or more of the following: physical or sexual violence, psychological or emotional abuse, neglect of care, or financial exploitation (Killick & Taylor, 2009). Accurate data are hard to come by since few elders report their abuse, but estimates say that between 2% and 10% of older Americans have suffered at least one form of abuse, amounting to hundreds of thousands of cases annually. Fewer than 10% of these cases come to the attention of the police or other authorities (National Center on Elder Abuse, 2005).

Although we may never know the actual extent of elder abuse, it poses a serious health problem for the elders who are physically, sexually, and/or psychologically abused or neglected, and it may even raise their chances of dying. One study of more than 2,800 elders found that those who were abused or neglected were 3 times more likely than those who were not mistreated to die during the next 13 years. This difference was found even after injury and chronic illness were taken into account (Horn, 1998).

A major reason for elder abuse seems to be stress. The adult children and other relatives who care for elders often find it an exhausting, emotionally trying experience, especially if the person they are helping needs extensive help with daily activities. Faced with this stress, elders' caregivers can easily snap and take out their frustrations with physical violence, emotional abuse, or neglect of care.

Senior Power: Older Americans as a Political Force

Older Americans also hold strong views on issues that affect them directly, such as Medicare and Social Security. Although scholars continue to debate whether the many other differences (e.g., gender, race, social class) among the elderly prevent them from acting in their own interests as a unified political force (Walker, 2006), it is clear that politicians work to win the elderly vote and shape their political stances accordingly.

During the past few decades, older people have become more active politically on their own behalf.

Marc Nozell – Bernie Sanders – CC BY-NC 2.0.

Since the 1980s, organizations of older Americans have been established to act as interest groups in the political arena on the many issues affecting the elderly more than other age groups (Walker, 2006). One of the most influential such groups is AARP, which is open to people 50 or older. AARP provides travel and other discounts to its members and lobbies Congress and other groups extensively on elderly issues. Its membership numbers about 40 million, or 40% of the over-50 population. Some critics say AARP focuses too much on its largely middle-class membership's self-interests instead of working for more far-reaching economic changes that might benefit the elderly poor; others say its efforts on Medicare, Social Security, and other issues do benefit the elderly from all walks of life. This controversy aside, AARP is an influential force in the political arena because of its numbers and resources.

A very different type of political organization of the elderly was the Gray Panthers, founded by the late Maggie Kuhn in 1970 (Kuhn, Long, & Quinn, 1991). Although this group has been less newsworthy since Kuhn's death in 1995, at its height it had some 85 local chapters across the nation and 70,000 members and supporters. A more activist organization than AARP and other lobbying groups for the elderly, the Gray Panthers took more liberal stances. For example, it urged the establishment of a national health-care service and programs to increase affordable housing for the elderly.

As older Americans have engaged the political process on their own behalf, critics have charged that programs for the elderly are too costly to the nation, that the elderly are better off than groups like AARP claim, and that new programs for the elderly will take even more money from younger generations and leave them insufficient funds for their own retirement many years from now. Their criticism, which began during the 1980s, is termed the **generational equity** argument (Williamson, McNamara, & Howling, 2003).

Advocates for the elderly say that the generational equity critics exaggerate the financial well-being of older Americans and especially neglect the fact that many older Americans, especially women and those of color, are poor or near poor and thus need additional government aid. Anything we can do now to help the aged, they continue, will also help future generations of the elderly. As Lenard W. Kaye (1994, p. 346) observed in an early critique of the generational equity movement,

> In the long run, all of us can expect to live into extended old age, barring an unexpected fatal illness or accident. To do injustice to our current generation of elders, by means of policy change, can only come back to haunt us as each and every one of us—children, young families, and working people—move toward the latter stages of the life course.

Key Takeaways

- The U.S. elderly experience several health problems, including arthritis, high blood pressure, heart disease, hearing loss, vision problems, diabetes, and dementia.
- Nursing home care in the United States is very expensive and often substandard; neglect and abuse of nursing home residents is fairly common.
- Despite help from Social Security, many older Americans face problems of financial security.
- It is difficult to determine the actual extent of elder abuse, but elder abuse often has serious consequences for the health and lives of older Americans.
- During the last few decades, older Americans have been active in the political process on their own behalf and today are an important political force in the United States.

For Your Review

1. What do you think is the worst or most serious problem facing the U.S. elderly? Explain your answer.
2. The text suggests that the lives of the U.S. elderly would be improved if the United States were to adopt some of the policies and practices that other nations have for their elderly. Explain why you agree or disagree with this suggestion.

Aging and Ageism in the United States: What Sociology Suggests

We have seen some contradictory impulses that make it difficult to predict the status of older Americans in the decades ahead. On the one hand, the large number of baby boomers will combine with increasing longevity to swell the ranks of the elderly; this process has already begun and will accelerate during the coming years. The inevitable jump in the size of the aged population may well put unimaginable stress on Social Security, Medicare, and other programs for the aged, if the worst fears of some analysts come to pass. Even if these fears are exaggerated, the boost in the number of seniors will almost certainly strain elder programs. On the other hand, the baby boomer generation will reach its old age as a much better educated and more healthy and wealthy group than any previous generation. It will likely participate in the labor force, politics, and other arenas more than previous generations of elders and, as has been true for some time, exert a good deal of influence on national political and cultural affairs.

Although this sounds like a rosier picture, several concerns remain. Despite the relative affluence of the baby boomers, segments of the group, especially among women and people of color, remain mired in poverty, and these segments will continue to be once they reach their older years. Moreover, the relative health of the baby boomers means that they will outlive previous generations of the aged. Yet as more of them reach the ranks of the "old-old," they will become frailer and require care from health-care professionals and organizations and from social support networks. As noted earlier, some may not have children and will be in even more need of help.

Although older Americans fare much better than their counterparts in poor nations, they fare not nearly as well as their counterparts in other wealthy democracies, which generally provide many more extensive and better funded programs and services for their elderly. Older Americans also continue to confront stereotypes and prejudicial attitudes that add to the burden many of them already face from the biological process of aging.

A sociological understanding of aging and ageism reminds us that the problems that older Americans face are ultimately rooted not in their own failings but rather in the stereotypes about them and in the lack of adequate social programs like those found throughout other Western nations. A sociological understanding also reminds us that the older Americans who face the most severe problems of health, health care, and financial security are women and people of color and that their more severe problems reflect the many inequalities they have experienced throughout the life course, long before they reached their older years. These inequalities accumulate over the years to leave them especially vulnerable when they finally arrive into their 60s.

With this understanding, it becomes clear that efforts to improve the lives of older Americans must focus on providing them with more numerous and more extensive social services and programming of many kinds and on reducing the stereotypes and prejudicial attitudes that many Americans hold of older people. Possibilities involving improved social services and programming might be drawn from the example provided by other Western nations and include the following:

1. An expansion of Social Security to provide a much more comfortable life for all older Americans, regardless of their earnings history, and thus regardless of their gender and race/ethnicity
2. An expansion of Medicare and other health aid for older Americans to match the level of health-care assistance provided by many other Western nations. In one particular area that needs attention, Medicare pays for nursing home care only after nursing home patients use up most of their own assets, leaving a patient's spouse with severe financial problems. Other Western nations pay for nursing home care from the outset, and the United States should adopt this practice.
3. As with stereotypical and prejudicial views based on gender and on race/ethnicity, greater educational efforts should be launched to reduce stereotyping and prejudicial attitudes based on aging. Like sexism and racism, ageism has no place in a nation like the United States, which has historically promised equality and equal opportunity for all.

References

Alzheimer's Association. (2009). *2009 Alzheimer's disease facts and figures*. Chicago, IL: Author.

Berger, E. D. (2009). Managing age discrimination: An examination of the techniques used when seeking employment. *The Gerontologist, 49*(3), 317–332.

Crawthorne, A. (2008, July 30). Elderly poverty: The challenge before us. Retrieved from http://www.americanprogress.org/issues/2008/07/elderly_poverty.html.

DeHart, D., Webb, J., & Cornman, C. (2009). Prevention of elder mistreatment in nursing homes: Competencies for direct-care staff. *Journal of Elder Abuse & Neglect, 21*(4), 360–378. doi:10.1080/08946560903005174.

Edwards, M. (2004, November/December). As good as it gets: What country takes the best care of its older citizens? *AARP The Magazine*. Retrieved from http://www.aarpmagazine.org/lifestyle/Articles/a2004-2009-2022-mag-global.html.

Federal Interagency Forum on Aging-Related Statistics. (2008). *Older Americans 2008: Key indicators of well-being*. Washington, DC: U.S. Government Printing Office.

Gallo, W. T., Brand, J. E., Teng, H.-M., Leo-Summers, L., & Byers, A. L. (2009). Differential impact of involuntary job loss on physical disability among older workers: Does predisposition matter? *Research on Aging, 31*(3), 345–360.

Hansson, R. O., & Stroebe, M. S. (2007). Coping with bereavement. *Generations, 31*(3), 63–65.

Hartlapp, M., & Schmid, G. (2008). Labour market policy for "active ageing" in Europe: Expanding the options for retirement transitions. *Journal of Social Policy, 37*(3), 409–431.

Horn, D. (1998, August 17). Bad news on elder abuse. *Time* 82.

Kaye, L. W. (1994). Generational equity: Pitting young against old. In J. Robert B. Enright (Ed.), *Perspectives in social gerontology* (pp. 343–347). Boston, MA: Allyn & Bacon.

Killick, C., & Taylor, B. J. (2009). Professional decision making on elder abuse: Systematic narrative review. *Journal of Elder Abuse and Neglect, 21*(3), 211–238.

Kuhn, M., Long, C., & Quinn, L. (1991). *No stone unturned: The life and times of Maggie Kuhn*. New York, NY: Ballantine Books.

Leland, J. (2010, April 25). A graying population, a graying work force. *The New York Times*, p. A14.

National Center on Elder Abuse. (2005). *Elder abuse prevalence and incidence*. Washington, DC: National Center on Elder Abuse.

Ney, S. (2005). Active aging policy in Europe: Between path dependency and path departure. *Ageing International, 30*, 325–342.

Sears, D. (2009, September 6). Myths busted on older workers' job performance. Retrieved from http://www.career-line.com/job-search-news/myths-busted-on-older-workers-job-performance.

Sloan, A. (2009, August 2). A flimsy trust: Why Social Security needs some major repairs. *The Washington Post*, p. G01.

Treas, J. (1995). Older Americans in the 1990s and beyond. *Population Bulletin, 50*(2), 1–46.

U.S. Census Bureau. (2010). *Statistical abstract of the United States: 2010*. Washington, DC: U.S. Government Printing Office. Retrieved from http://www.census.gov/compendia/statab.

Walker, A. (2006). Aging and politics: An international perspective. In R. H. Binstock & L. K. George (Eds.), *Handbook of aging and the social sciences* (6th ed., pp. 338–358). New York, NY: Academic Press.

Williamson, J. B., McNamara, T. K., & Howling, S. A. (2003). Generational equity, generational interdependence, and the framing of the debate over Social Security reform. *Journal of Sociology and Social Welfare, 30*(3), 3–14.

12.7 End-of-Chapter Material

Summary

1. Gerontology is the study of aging. Gerontologists study the biological, psychological, and social dimensions of aging. Social gerontologists focus on social aging and distinguish several dimensions of aging, which refers to changes in people's roles and relationships as they age.
2. The perception and experience of aging vary from one society to another and within a given society over time. Studies of preindustrial societies indicate that at least two factors affect the perception of aging and the aged. The first is the physical and mental health of older people. When their health is better, the perception of them is more positive. The second is the status of a society's economy. The better the economy, the more wealth elders have and the less of a burden they are on relatives and others, and the more positive the view of aging and the elderly. Changes in a society's economy or in other aspects of its social structure can affect how it views its older population.
3. Ancient Greece and Rome respected their elders but at the same time extolled youthfulness and considered old age a declining period of life. The Middle Ages were a time of great disease, starvation, and other problems, and so the elderly were considered a burden. The Puritans of Massachusetts venerated their older members, who had considerable property, but this respect lessened as the new United States put more emphasis on equality and democracy and as industrialization in the 19th century put more money in the hands of young capitalists.
4. Sociological explanations of aging include disengagement theory, activity theory, and conflict theory. Disengagement theory emphasizes the need of society to disengage its elders from their previous roles to pave the way for a younger and presumably more able generation to take over those roles. In contrast, activity theory assumes that elders need to remain active to enhance their physical and mental health. Conflict theory emphasizes ageism, or discrimination and prejudice against the elderly, and the structural barriers society poses to elders' economic and other aspects of overall well-being.
5. Life expectancy differs dramatically around the world and within the United States, where it's lower for men and lower for people of color. Because life expectancy has increased, people are living longer, resulting in a "graying of society." In the United States, the imminent entrance of the baby boom generation into its older years will further fuel a large rise in the number of older Americans. This graying of society may strain traditional economic and medical programs for their care and affect views of aging and the elderly.
6. Although aging involves several physiological and psychological changes, negative stereotypes of aging and the elderly exaggerate the extent and impact of these changes. Proper exercise, nutrition, and stress reduction can minimize the effects of aging, as can religious involvement and informal social support networks.
7. As a diverse group, the U.S. elderly differ greatly in terms of wealth and poverty, education, health, and other dimensions. They face several problems because of their age, including illness and disability, financial security, employment obstacles, and elder abuse. For several reasons, older Americans generally hold more conservative views on social and moral issues. At the same time, groups working on behalf of older Americans in the political arena have succeeded in bringing elder issues to the attention of public officials and political parties.
8. As the ranks of older Americans swell in the years ahead, elders will be better educated and wealthier than their predecessors, but their sheer numbers may impose considerable strain on social institutions. Already there are signs of perceived conflict between the needs of the elderly and those of younger generations. However, advocates for older Americans believe that efforts to help elders now will in the long run help

younger Americans when they finally reach their old age.

Using Sociology

As a summer volunteer in a nursing home in your hometown, you generally enjoy your work and have begun thinking of a career in geriatric care. Yet you have begun to see some disturbing signs of possible neglect of several residents by nursing home staff. No one is apparently being abused, but it does seem that residents must wait far too long for assistance with various daily living activities, and some complain of certain medical problems but are ignored by staff. What do you do?

Chapter 13: Work and the Economy

Social Issues in the News

"99 Weeks Later, Jobless Have Only Desperation," the headline said. It was August 2010, and the unemployment rate in the United States had climbed to 9.5%. Around the country, millions of people were out of work, and many had lost their unemployment insurance benefits, which ordinarily last 26 weeks but, thanks to Congressional action, were extended to 60 or 99 weeks based on a state's unemployment rate. An estimated 1.4 million had now exceeded the 99-week limit. For the many people in this group who had been getting benefits, dubbed the "99ers," according to a news report, their "modest payments were a lifeline that enabled them to maintain at least a veneer of normalcy, keeping a roof over their heads, putting gas in their cars, paying electric and phone bills." One 99er was a 49-year-old woman who used to work as director of client services for a small technology company but now expected to be living in her car after being unable to find a job, despite many applications, being unable to pay her rent, and facing eviction. As she drove away from her apartment for good, she sobbed and later recalled, "At one point, I thought, you know, what if I turned the wheel in my car and wrecked my car?" Ironically, she had also fallen behind on her loan payments on her car, which was about to be repossessed. (Luo, 2010)

One of the most momentous events of the 20th century was the Great Depression, which engulfed the United States in 1929 and spread to the rest of the world, lasting almost a decade. Millions were thrown out of work, and bread lines became common. In the United States, a socialist movement gained momentum for a time as many workers blamed U.S. industry and capitalism for their unemployment.

The Depression involved the failing of the economy. The economy also failed in the United States beginning in late 2007, when the country entered what is being called the Great Recession. The news article that began this chapter provides just a small illustration of the millions of lives that have been affected.

This chapter presents a sociological perspective on the economy as a social institution. It reviews the history of the economy, the major types of economic systems, and the nature of work in the United States today. It also examines one of the most important if controversial aspects of the U.S. economy, the defense industry. Along the way, we will explore several sociological themes, including the importance of the economy as a key social institution for so many aspects of lives, the ways in which it reflects and reinforces the social inequalities discussed in previous chapters, and the need for change to address these inequalities.

References

Luo, M. (2010, August 3). 99 weeks later, jobless have only desperation. *The New York Times*, p. A1.

13.1 Economic Development in Historical Perspective

Learning Objectives

1. Describe the three sectors of the economy.
2. Outline the economic development of societies.

When we hear the term *economy*, it is usually in the context of how the economy "is doing": Is inflation soaring or under control? Is the economy growing or shrinking? Is unemployment rising, declining, or remaining stable? Are new college graduates finding jobs easily or not? All these questions concern the economy, but sociologists define **economy** more broadly as the social institution that organizes the production, distribution, and consumption of a society's goods and services. Defined in this way, the economy touches us all.

The economy is composed of three sectors. The **primary sector** is the part of the economy that takes and uses raw materials directly from the natural environment. Its activities include agriculture, fishing, forestry, and mining. The **secondary sector** of the economy transforms raw materials into finished products and is essentially the manufacturing industry. Finally, the **tertiary sector** is the part of the economy that provides services rather than products; its activities include clerical work, health care, teaching, and information technology services.

Clerical work and other occupations that provide services rather than products constitute the tertiary sector in the economy.

Wikimedia Commons – CC BY 2.0.

Societies differ in many ways, but they all have to produce, distribute, and consume goods and services. How this happens depends on which sectors of the economy are most important. This latter variable in turn depends heavily on the level of a society's development. Generally speaking, the less developed a society's economy, the more important its primary sector; the more developed a society's economy, the more important its tertiary sector. As societies developed economically over the centuries, the primary sector became less important and the tertiary sector became more important. Let's see how this happened.

Preindustrial Societies

When we reviewed the development of societies in Chapter 5 "Social Structure and Social Interaction", we saw that the earliest were *hunting-and-gathering* societies in which people eked out a meager existence by hunting animals and gathering plants to feed themselves. Most of their waking hours were devoted to these two tasks, and no separate economic institution for the production and distribution of goods and services existed. The *horticultural and pastoral* societies that next developed also lacked a separate economy. Although people in these societies raised animals and/or grew crops and were better off than their hunting-and-gathering counterparts, these tasks, too, were done within the family unit and monopolized most of their time. No separate institution for the production and distribution of these sources of food was involved.

This separate institution—the economy—finally did appear with the advent of *agricultural* societies about 5,000 years ago. These societies were able to produce food surpluses thanks to the invention of the plow and the wheel and other technological advances. These surpluses led to extensive trade within the societies themselves and also with other societies. The rise of trade was the first appearance of a separate economy. People also had to make the plows and wheels and repair them when they broke, and new *crafts* jobs arose to perform these functions. These jobs, too, marked the development of a separate economy. Despite this development, most people's work still took place in or very near their homes. Craftspeople and merchants may have been part of the new economy, but most still worked out of their homes or very near them.

Industrialization and the Division of Labor

Work and home finally began to separate in the 1700s and 1800s as machines and factories became the primary means of production with the emergence of industrial societies. For the first time, massive numbers of people worked in locations separate from their families, and they worked not for themselves and their families but for an employer. Whole industries developed to make the machines and build the factories and to use the machines and factories to manufacture household goods, clothing, and many other products. As should be clear, the secondary sector of the economy quickly became dominant. Perhaps inevitably it led to a growth in the tertiary (service) sector to respond to the demands of an industrial economy. For example, enterprises such as banks emerged to handle the money that industrialization brought not only to people with names like Carnegie and Rockefeller but also to a growing middle class of factory managers and the businesspeople that bought and sold the products that factories were producing.

One important consequence of industrialization was the *specialization* of work, more commonly called the

division of labor. In agricultural societies, the craftspeople who made plows, wheels, and other objects would make the whole object, not just a part of it, and then sell it themselves to a buyer. With the advent of the division of labor under industrialization, this process became more specialized: some factory workers would make only one part of an object, other factory workers would make a second part, and so on; other workers would package and ship the item; and still other workers would sell it. This division of labor meant that workers became separated from the fruits of their labor, to paraphrase Karl Marx, who also worried that the type of work just described was much more repetitive and boring for workers than the craft work that characterized earlier societies. Because of these problems, Marx said, workers in industrial societies were alienated both from their work and by their work.

Postindustrial Societies

Information technology, such as the smartphones depicted here, are a hallmark of the postindustrial economy. This economy is leaving behind workers without college degrees.

Carissa Rogers – HTC Windows 8X Cell phone smart phone – CC BY 2.0.

As Chapter 5 "Social Structure and Social Interaction" pointed out, today much of the world has moved from an industrial economy to a postindustrial economy. This is the *information age*, in which smartphones, netbooks, tablets, and other high-tech equipment have begun to replace machines and factories as the major means of production and in which the tertiary sector has supplanted the secondary sector. Although the information age has brought with it jobs and careers unimaginable a generation ago, it has also meant that a college education has become increasingly important for stable and well-paid employment. Postindustrial economies, then, are leaving behind workers without college degrees, who used to fare well in the manufacturing industries.

With the information age has also come an increasing globalization of the economy. The Internet connects workers and industries across the world, and multinational corporations have plants in many countries that make products for consumers in other countries. What happens economically in one part of the world can greatly affect what happens economically in other parts of the world. If the economies of Asia sour, their demand for U.S. products may decline, forcing a souring of the U.S. economy. A financial crisis in Greece and other parts of Europe during the spring of 2010 caused the stock markets in the United States to plunge. The world is indeed getting smaller all the time. We will return later to the implications of the postindustrial economy for U.S. workers.

Key Takeaways

- The economy is the social institution that organizes the production, distribution, and consumption of a society's goods and services. It consists of three sectors: the primary sector, the secondary sector, and the tertiary sector.
- As a separate institution, the economy appeared with the advent of agricultural societies about 5,000 years ago. Work and family separated during the 1700s and 1800s with the advent of industrialization. The division of labor also developed during industrialization.
- In postindustrial societies, information technology has replaced factories and machines as major means of production, and the economy has become increasingly globalized.

For Your Review

1. Write a brief essay in which you discuss the benefits and costs of industrialization during the 19th century.
2. In what ways have postindustrial economies helped and hurt various kinds of workers?

13.2 Types of Economic Systems

Learning Objectives

1. Distinguish the types of economic systems.
2. Discuss the advantages and disadvantages of capitalism and socialism.
3. Outline the elements of democratic socialism.

The two major economic systems in modern societies are capitalism and socialism. In practice, no one society is purely capitalist or socialist, so it is helpful to think of capitalism and socialism as lying on opposite ends of a continuum. Societies' economies mix elements of both capitalism and socialism but do so in varying degrees, so that some societies lean toward the capitalist end of the continuum, while other societies lean toward the socialist end. For example, the United States is a capitalist nation, but the government still regulates many industries to varying degrees. The industries usually would prefer less regulation, while their critics usually prefer more regulation. The degree of such regulation was the point of controversy after the failure of banks and other financial institutions in 2008 and 2009 and after the BP oil spill in 2010. Let's see how capitalism and socialism differ.

Capitalism

Capitalism is an economic system in which the means of production are privately owned. By *means of production*, we mean everything—land, tools, technology, and so forth—that is needed to produce goods and services. As outlined by famed Scottish philosopher Adam Smith (1723–1790), widely considered the founder of modern economics, the most important goal of capitalism is the pursuit of personal profit (Smith, 1776/1910). As individuals seek to maximize their own wealth, society as a whole is said to benefit. Goods get produced, services are rendered, people pay for the goods and services they need and desire, and the economy and society as a whole prosper.

One important hallmark of capitalism is competition for profit. This competition is thought to help ensure the best products at the lowest prices, as companies will ordinarily try to keep their prices as low as possible to attract buyers and maximize their sales.

Consumerist Dot Com – sale window – CC BY 2.0.

As people pursue personal profit under capitalism, they compete with each other for the greatest profits. Businesses try to attract more demand for their products in many ways, including lowering prices, creating better products, and advertising how wonderful their products are. In capitalist theory, such competition helps ensure the best products at the lowest prices, again benefiting society as a whole. Such competition also helps ensure that no single party controls an entire market. According to Smith, the competition that characterizes capitalism should be left to operate on its own, free of government intervention or control. For this reason, capitalism is often referred to as *laissez-faire* (French for "leave alone") capitalism, and terms to describe capitalism include the *free-enterprise system* and the *free market*.

The hallmarks of capitalism, then, are private ownership of the means of production, the pursuit of profit, competition for profit, and the lack of government intervention in this competition.

Socialism

The features of socialism are the opposite of those just listed for capitalism and were spelled out most famously by Karl Marx. **Socialism** is an economic system in which the means of production are collectively owned, usually by the government. Whereas the United States has several airlines that are owned by airline corporations, a socialist society might have one government-owned airline.

The most important goal of socialism is not the pursuit of personal profit but rather work for the collective good: the needs of society are considered more important than the needs of the individual. Because of this view, individuals do not compete with each other for profit; instead they work together for the good of everyone. If under capitalism the government is supposed to let the economy alone, under socialism the government controls the economy.

The ideal outcome of socialism, said Marx, would be a truly classless or *communist* society. In such a society all members are equal, and stratification does not exist. Obviously Marx's vision of a communist society was never fulfilled, and nations that called themselves communist departed drastically from his vision of communism.

Recall that societies can be ranked on a continuum ranging from mostly capitalist to mostly socialist. At one end of the continuum, we have societies characterized by a relatively free market, and at the other end we have those characterized by strict government regulation of the economy. Figure 13.1 "Capitalism and Socialism Across the Globe" depicts the nations of the world along this continuum. Capitalist nations are found primarily in North America and Western Europe but also exist in other parts of the world.

Figure 13.1 Capitalism and Socialism Across the Globe

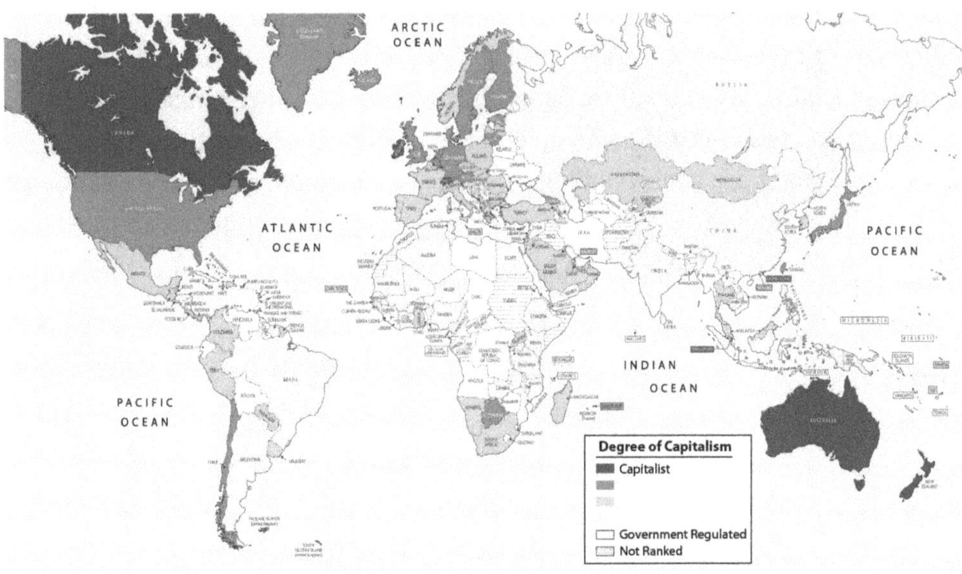

Source: Adapted from The Heritage Foundation. (2010). Distribution of economic freedom. Retrieved from http://www.heritage.org/index/pdf/2010/Index2010_map.pdf.

Comparing Capitalism and Socialism

People have debated the relative merits of capitalism and socialism at least since the time of Marx (Bowles, 2007; Cohen, 2009). Compared to socialism, capitalism seems to have several advantages. It produces greater economic growth and productivity, at least in part because it provides more incentives (i.e., profit) for economic innovation. It also is often characterized by greater political freedom in the form of civil rights and liberties. As an economic system, capitalism seems to lend itself to personal freedom: because its hallmarks include the private ownership of the means of production and the individual pursuit of profit, there is much more emphasis in capitalist societies on the needs and desires of the individual and less emphasis on the need for government intervention in economic and social affairs.

Yet capitalism also has its drawbacks. There is much more economic inequality in capitalism than in socialism. Although capitalism produces economic growth, not all segments of capitalism share this growth equally, and there is a much greater difference between the rich and poor than under socialism. People can become very rich in capitalist nations, but they can also remain quite poor. As we saw in Chapter 9 "Global Stratification", several Western European nations that are more socialist than the United States have fewer extremes of wealth and poverty and take better care of their poor.

Another possible drawback depends on whether you prefer competition or cooperation. As we saw in Chapter 3 "Culture", important values in the United States include competition and individualism, both of which arguably reflect this nation's capitalist system. Children in the United States are raised with more of an individual orientation than children in socialist societies, who learn that the needs of their society are more important than the needs of the individual. Whereas U.S. children learn to compete with each other for good grades, success in sports, and other goals, children in socialist societies learn to cooperate to achieve tasks.

More generally, capitalism is said by its critics to encourage selfish and even greedy behavior: if individuals try to maximize their profit, they do so at the expense of others. In competition, someone has to lose. A company's ultimate aim, and one that is generally lauded, is to maximize its profits by driving another company out of the market altogether. If so, that company succeeds even if some other party is hurting. The small Mom-and-Pop grocery stores, drugstores, and hardware stores are almost a thing of the past, as big-box stores open their doors and drive their competition out of business. To its critics, then, capitalism encourages harmful behavior. Yet it is precisely this type of behavior that is taught in business schools.

Democratic Socialism

The economies of Denmark, pictured here, and several other Western European nations feature a combination of capitalism and socialism that is called democratic socialism. In these economies, the government owns important industries, but private property and political freedom remain widespread.

bobthemagicdragon – Majestic – CC BY-NC-ND 2.0.

Some nations combine elements of both capitalism and socialism and are called *social democracies*, while their combination of capitalism and socialism is called **democratic socialism**. In these nations, which include Denmark, Sweden, and several other Western European nations, the government owns several important industries, but much property remains in private hands, and political freedom is widespread. The government in these nations has extensive programs to help the poor and other people in need. Although these nations have high tax rates to help finance their social programs, their experience indicates it is very possible to combine the best features of capitalism and socialism while avoiding their faults (see the "Learning From Other Societies" box).

Learning From Other Societies

Social Democracy in Scandinavia

The five Scandinavian nations, also called the Nordic nations, are Denmark, Finland, Iceland, Norway, and Sweden. These nations differ in many ways, but they also share many similarities. In particular, they are all social democracies, as their governments own important industries while their citizens enjoy much political freedom. Each nation has the three branches of government with which most people are familiar—executive, judicial, and legislative—and each nation has a national parliament to which people are elected by proportional representation.

Social democracies like the Scandinavian nations are often called controlled capitalist market economies. The word *controlled* here conveys the idea that their governments either own industries or heavily regulate industries they do not own. According to social scientist Tapio Lappi-Seppälä of Finland, a key feature of these social democracies' economies is that inequality in wealth and income is not generally tolerated. Employers, employees, and political officials are accustomed to working closely to ensure that poverty and its related problems are addressed as much as possible and in as cooperative a manner as possible.

Underlying this so-called *social welfare model* is a commitment to *universalism*. All citizens, regardless of their socioeconomic status or family situation, receive various services, such as child care and universal health care, that are free or heavily subsidized. To support this massive provision of benefits, the Scandinavian nations have very high taxes that their citizens generally accept as normal and necessary.

This model has been praised by political scientist Torben Iversen, who lauds its goal of achieving full employment and equality. This attempt has not been entirely free of difficulties but overall has been very successful, as the Scandinavian nations rank at or near the top in international comparisons of health, education, economic well-being, and other measures of quality of life. The Scandinavian experience of social democracy teaches us that it is very possible to have a political and economic model that combines the best features of capitalism and socialism while retaining the political freedom that citizens expect in a democracy. (Berman, 2006; Iversen, 1998; Lappi-Seppälä, 2007)

Key Takeaways

- The two major economic systems in modern societies are capitalism and socialism. In practice most societies have economies that mix elements of both systems but that lean toward one end of the capitalism–socialism continuum.
- Social democracies combine elements of both capitalism and socialism. They have achieved high economic

growth while maintaining political freedom and personal liberty.

For Your Review

1. In what ways might capitalism be a better economic system than socialism? In what ways might socialism be a better economic system than capitalism?
2. The text discusses the experience of Scandinavian economies. Do you agree with the positive view that the text presents? Why or why not?

References

Berman, S. (2006). *The primacy of politics: Social democracy and the making of Europe's twentieth century*. New York, NY: Cambridge University Press.

Bowles, P. (2007). *Capitalism*. New York, NY: Pearson/Longman.

Cohen, G. A. (2009). *Why not socialism?* Princeton, NJ: Princeton University Press.

Iversen, T. (1998). The choices for Scandinavian social democracy in comparative perspective. *Oxford Review of Economic Policy, 14*, 59–75.

Lappi-Seppälä, T. (2007). Penal policy in Scandinavia. *Crime and Justice, 36*, 217–296.

Smith, A. (1910). *The wealth of nations*. London, England: J. M. Dent & Sons; New York, NY: E. P. Dutton. (Original work published 1776).

13.3 Corporations

Learning Objective

1. Discuss two controversies involving corporations.

One of the most important but controversial features of modern capitalism is the **corporation**, a formal organization that has a legal existence, including the right to sign contracts, that is separate from that of its members. We have referred to corporations several times already and now discuss them in a bit more detail.

Corporations such as Exxon dominate the U.S. economy. They employ thousands of workers, and their assets total many trillions of dollars.

Wikimedia Commons – CC BY-SA 2.5.

Adam Smith, the founder of capitalism, envisioned that individuals would own the means of production and compete for profit, and this is the model the United States followed in its early stage of industrialization. After the Civil War, however, corporations quickly replaced individuals and their families as the owners of the means of production and as the competitors for profit. As corporations grew following the Civil War, they quickly tried to control their markets by, for example, buying up competitors and driving others out of business. To do so, they engaged in bribery, kickbacks, and complex financial schemes of dubious ethics. They also established factories and other workplaces with squalid conditions. Their shady financial practices won their chief executives the name "robber barons" and led the federal government to pass the Sherman Antitrust Act of 1890 designed to prohibit restraint of trade that raised prices (Hillstrom & Hillstrom, 2005).

More than a century later, corporations have increased in both number and size. Although several million U.S. corporations exist, most are fairly small. Each of the largest 500, however, has an annual revenue exceeding $4.6 billion (2008 data) and employs thousands of workers. Their total assets run into the trillions of dollars (Wiley, 2009). It is no exaggeration to say they control the nation's economy, as together they produce most of the U.S. private sector output, employ millions of people, and have revenues equal to most of the U.S. gross domestic product. In many ways, the size and influence of corporations stifle the competition that is one of the hallmarks of capitalism. For example, several markets, including that for breakfast cereals, are controlled by four or fewer corporations. This control reduces competition because it reduces the number of products and competitors, and it thus raises prices to the public (Parenti, 2007).

The last few decades have seen the proliferation and rise of the **multinational corporation**, a corporation with headquarters in one nation but with factories and other operations in many other nations (Wettstein, 2009). Multinational corporations centered in the United States and their foreign affiliates have more than $18 trillion in assets and employ more than 32 million people (U.S. Census Bureau, 2010). The assets of the largest multinational corporations exceed those of many of the world's nations. Often their foreign operations are in poor nations, whose low wages make them attractive sites for multinational corporation expansion. Many multinational employees in these nations work in sweatshops at very low pay and amid substandard living conditions. Dependency theorists, discussed in Chapter 9 "Global Stratification", say that multinationals not only mistreat workers in poor nations but also exploit these nations' natural resources. In contrast, modernization theorists, also discussed in Chapter 9 "Global Stratification", say that multinationals are bringing jobs to developing nations and helping them achieve economic growth. As this debate illustrates, the dominance of multinational corporations will certainly continue to spark controversy.

Another controversial aspect of corporations is the white-collar crime in which they engage (Rosoff, Pontell, & Tillman, 2010). As we saw in Chapter 7 "Deviance, Crime, and Social Control", price fixing by corporations costs the U.S. public some $60 billion annually (Simon, 2008). Workplace-related illnesses and injuries that could have been prevented if companies obeyed federal regulations kill about 50,000 workers each year (AFL-CIO, 2007). An estimated 10,000 U.S. residents die annually from dangerous products. All in all, corporate lawbreaking and neglect probably result in more than 100,000 deaths annually and cost the public more than $400 billion (Barkan, 2012).

In sum, corporations are the dominant actors in today's economy. They provide most of our products and many of our services and employ millions of people. It is impossible to imagine a modern industrial system without corporations. Yet they often stifle competition, break the law, and, according to their critics, exploit people and natural resources in developing nations. The BP oil spill in 2010 reminds us of the damage corporations can cause. BP's disaster was the possible result, according to news reports, of many violations of federal safety standards for oil drilling (Uhlmann, 2010).

Key Takeaways

- Corporations grew quickly after the Civil War, but many corporations tried to control their markets through illegal means and activities that were ethically questionable.
- Many multinational corporations operate in poor nations, where they often pay substandard wages and run sweatshops.
- Corporations often engage in white-collar crime that costs hundreds of billions of dollars annually and results in tens of thousands of deaths.

For Your Review

1. Write a brief essay in which you discuss the benefits and disadvantages of corporations in modern society.

References

AFL-CIO. (2007). *Death on the job: The toll of neglect*. Washington, DC: Author.

Barkan, S. E. (2012). *Criminology: A sociological understanding* (5th ed.). Upper Saddle River, NJ: Prentice Hall.

Hillstrom, K., & Hillstrom, L. C. (Eds.). (2005). *The Industrial Revolution in America*. Santa Barbara, CA: ABC-CLIO.

Parenti, M. (2007). *Democracy for the few* (6th ed.). Belmont, CA: Wadsworth.

Rosoff, S. M., Pontell, H. N., & Tillman, R. (2010). *Profit without honor: White collar crime and the looting of America* (5th ed.). Upper Saddle River, NJ: Prentice Hall.

Simon, D. R. (2008). *Elite deviance* (9th ed.). Boston, MA: Allyn & Bacon.

U.S. Census Bureau. (2010). *Statistical abstract of the United States: 2010*. Washington, DC: U.S. Government Printing Office. Retrieved from http://www.census.gov/compendia/statab.

Uhlmann, D. M. (2010, June 4). Prosecuting crimes against the earth. *The New York Times*, p. A27.

Wettstein, F. (2009). *Multinational corporations and global justice: Human rights obligations of a quasi-governmental institution*. Stanford, CA: Stanford Business Books.

Wiley, H. (2009). Welcome to the 2009 *Fortune* 500. *Fortune, 159*(9), 14.

13.4 Work and Labor in the United States

Learning Objectives

1. Discuss the changes industrialization brought in the relationship between workers and management.
2. Outline recent trends in jobs and wages.
3. Assess Marx's prediction regarding the alienation of work in a capitalist society like the United States.

The history of work and labor in the United States reflects the change, discussed earlier, in economies from agricultural to industrial to postindustrial. From the time the colonies began in the 1600s until well into the 19th century, the United States was primarily an agricultural society, as people worked on their own farms, and the family was the major unit of economic production. With the advent of industrialization came machines and factories, and the secondary, manufacturing sector became dominant. In the decades after the Civil War, the Industrial Revolution transformed the nation.

Workers and Management After Industrialization

One of the most important developments accompanying industrialization was the rise of labor unions and their conflict with management over wages and working conditions (Dubofsky & Dulles, 2010). The pay that workers received was quite low, and the conditions in which they worked were often miserable. The typical employee worked at least 10 hours a day for 6 or 7 days a week, with almost no overtime pay and no paid vacations or holidays. To improve wages and working conditions, many labor unions were founded after the Civil War, only to meet determined opposition from companies, the government, and the courts. Companies told each other which workers were suspected of being union members, and these workers were then prevented from getting jobs. Strikers were often arrested for violating laws prohibiting strikes. When juries began finding them not guilty, employers turned to asking judges for injunctions that prohibited strikes. Workers who then went on strike were held in contempt of court by the judge as juries were kept out of the process.

From the 1870s through the 1930s, labor unions fought companies over issues such as low wages and substandard working conditions.

DonkeyHotey – Together We Bargain – CC BY 2.0.

Many strikes became violent, as companies brought in armed guards, state troopers, and strikebreakers to put down the strikes. Workers themselves rioted to protest their low wages and abject working conditions. Summarizing this period, two labor historians note that the United States "has had the bloodiest and most violent labor history of any industrial nation in the world" (Taft & Ross, 1990, p. 174). During an 1897 coal-mining strike in Pennsylvania, for example, 18 miners were killed and 40 wounded after being shot in the back by a sheriff's deputies. Several years later, company guards and state troops in Ludlow, Colorado, opened fire on mining families as they fled from a tent city that the guards and troops had set on fire. Their bullets killed more than two dozen people, including 13 children (McGovern & Guttridge, 1972).

Labor strife reached a peak during the Great Depression, as masses of people blamed business leaders for their economic plight. Huge sit-ins and other labor protests occurred in Detroit at auto plants. In response the Congress passed several laws that gave workers a minimum wage, the right to join unions, a maximum-hour workweek, and other rights that Americans now take for granted.

Today labor unions have lost some of their influence, especially as postindustrialization has supplanted the industrial economy and as the United States has lost much of its manufacturing base. Four decades ago, about one-fourth of all private-sector nonagricultural workers belonged to labor unions. By 1985 this figure had dropped to 14.6%, and today it stands at less than 8% (Hirsch & Macpherson, 2009). In response, labor unions have ramped up their efforts to increase their membership, only to find that U.S. labor laws are filled with loopholes that allow companies to prevent their workers from forming a union. For example, after a company's workers vote to join a union, companies can appeal the vote, and it can take several years for courts to order the company to recognize the union. In the meantime, the low wages, the working conditions, and other factors that motivated workers to want to join a union are allowed to continue.

Recent Trends in Jobs and Wages

Recall that the United States has joined other industrial nations in moving into postindustrial economies. If physical prowess and skill with one's hands were prerequisites for many industrial jobs, mental prowess and communication skills are prerequisites for postindustrial jobs.

This move to a postindustrial economy has been a mixed blessing for many Americans. The information age has obvious benefits too numerous to mention, but there has also been a cost to the many workers whom postindustrialization and the globalization of the economy have left behind. Since the 1980s many manufacturing companies moved their plants from U.S. cities to sites in the developing world in Asia and elsewhere, a problem called **capital flight**. This shift has helped fuel a loss of more than 1.5 million manufacturing jobs in the United States (Mishel, Bernstein, & Shierholz, 2009).

A related problem is **outsourcing**, in which U.S. companies hire workers overseas for customer care, billing services, and other jobs that Americans used to do. China, India, and the Philippines, which have skilled workforces relatively fluent in English, are the primary nations to which U.S. companies outsource their work. At least 4 million jobs are estimated to have been transferred to these nations from the United States and other Western countries (Thomas, 2009). Many call centers employ workers in India, and when you call up a computer company or some other business for technical help, you might very well talk with an Indian. Because these call centers have cost Americans jobs and also because Americans and Indians often have trouble understanding each other's accents, outsourcing has been very controversial in the decade since it became popular.

All these problems reflect a more general shift in the United States from goods-producing jobs to service jobs. Although some of these service jobs, such as many in the financial and computer industries, are high paying, many are in low-wage occupations, such as restaurant and clerical work, that pay less than the goods-producing jobs they replaced. Partly as a result, the average hourly wage (in 2007 dollars) in the United States for workers (excluding managers and supervisors) rose only from $16.88 in 1979 to $17.42 in 2007. This change represented an increase of just 0.1% per year during that three-decade span (Mishel, Bernstein, & Shierholz, 2009).

These wage figures mask an important gender difference. Men's median hourly wages dropped (in 2007 dollars) by 4.4% from 1979 to 2007, while women's wages rose by 24.4% (while still remaining $3.11 less per hour than men's wages in 2007) (Mishel, Bernstein, & Shierholz, 2009). Although, as we saw in Chapter 11 "Gender and Gender Inequality", women have been catching up to men in wages, some of this catching up is due to the decline in male wages.

Wage changes in recent years also depend on what social class someone is in. While the average compensation of chief executive officers (CEOs) of large corporations grew by 167% from 1989 to 2007, the average compensation of the typical worker grew by only 10%. Another way of understanding this disparity is perhaps more striking. In 1965, CEOs earned 24 times more than the typical worker; in 2007 they earned 275 times more than the typical worker (Mishel, Bernstein, & Shierholz, 2009).

The U.S. Labor Force

The **civilian labor force** consists of all noninstitutionalized civilians 16 years of age or older who work for pay or are looking for work. The civilian labor force (hereafter *labor force*) consists of about 154 million people, or almost two-thirds of the population, including about 72% of men and 59% of women (Bureau of Labor Statistics, 2009). Chapter 11 "Gender and Gender Inequality" noted that women's labor force participation soared during the last few decades. This general increase is even steeper for married women with children under 6 years of age: in 2007 almost 62% of such women were in the labor force, compared to less than 19% in 1960 (U.S. Census Bureau, 2010), a threefold difference (see Figure 13.2 "Labor Force Participation Rate, Percentage of Married Women with Children Younger Than 6 Years of Age, 1960–2007").

Figure 13.2 Labor Force Participation Rate, Percentage of Married Women with Children Younger Than 6 Years of Age, 1960–2007

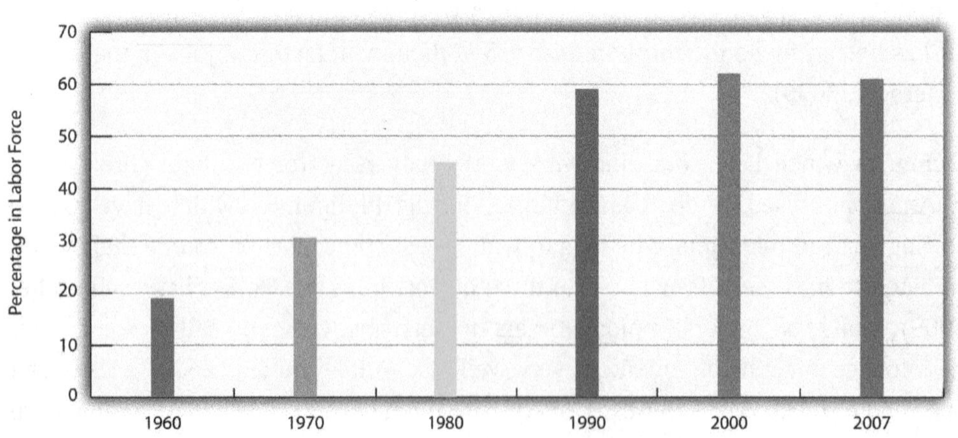

Source: Data from U.S. Census Bureau. (2010). *Statistical abstract of the United States: 2010*. Washington, DC: U.S. Government Printing Office. Retrieved from http://www.census.gov/compendia/statab.

Unemployment

Unemployment is a fact of life. There will always be people laid off or fired, who voluntarily quit their jobs, or who just graduated school and are still looking for work. But most unemployed people are involuntarily unemployed, and for them the financial and psychological consequences can be devastating, as we saw at the beginning of this chapter.

Unemployment rates rise and fall with the economy, and the national unemployment rate was as high as 10.2% in October 2009 amid the Great Recession that began almost two years earlier; it was still 9.8% in November 2010, amounting to some 15.1 million people. But whether unemployment is high or low, it always varies by race and ethnicity, with African American and Latino unemployment rates higher than the white rate (see Figure 13.3 "Race, Ethnicity, and Unemployment Rate, June 2010"). Unemployment is also higher for younger people than for older people. In June 2010, 25.7% of all teenagers in the labor force (aged 16–19) were unemployed, a figure almost three times higher than that for adults. The unemployment rate for African Americans in this age group was a very high 39.9%, considerably greater than the 23.2% figure for whites in this age group (Bureau of Labor Statistics, 2010).

Figure 13.3 Race, Ethnicity, and Unemployment Rate, June 2010

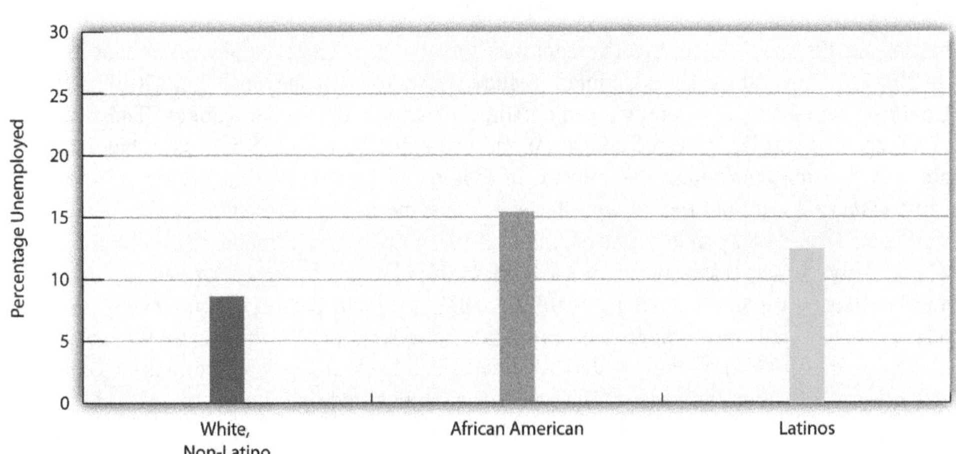

Source: Bureau of Labor Statistics (2010). Employment & earnings online. Retrieved from http://www.bls.gov/opub/ee/home.htm.

Unemployment figures are misleading in an important respect, as they do not include people who are *underemployed*. Underemployment includes unemployed and also two other types of people: (a) those who are working part time but who want to work full time and (b) those who have stopped looking for work because they have not been able to find a job. Many economists think that underemployment provides a more accurate measure than unemployment of the number of people with employment problems. For example, in June 2010, when the unemployment rate was 9.5% and 14.6 million people were officially unemployed, the underemployment rate was 16.5%, equal to more than 25 million people. Reflecting the racial/ethnic disparity in unemployment, 23.2% of Latino workers and 23.5% of African American workers were underemployed, compared to only 13.8% of white workers (Economic Policy Institute, 2010). Reflecting on the great amount of underemployment during the Great Recession, one economist commented, "When you combine the long-term unemployed with those who are dropping out and those who are working part time because they can't find anything else, it is just far beyond anything we've seen in the job market since the 1930s" (Herbert 2010, p. A25).

We have just seen that unemployment rises when the economy falters and that race and ethnicity affect the probability of being unemployed. These two facts provide evidence supporting the *sociological imagination*. As C. Wright Mills (1959) emphasized in his original discussion of this concept, unemployment is best viewed more as a public issue than as a personal trouble. When so many people are unemployed during an economic recession and when there is such striking evidence of higher unemployment rates among the persons of color who have the least opportunity for the education and training needed to obtain and keep a job, it is evident that high unemployment rates reflect a public issue rather than just a collection of public troubles.

Several kinds of problems make it difficult for people of color to be hired into jobs and thus contribute to the racial/ethnic disparity in unemployment. The "Sociology Making a Difference" box discusses these problems.

Sociology Making a Difference

Race, Ethnicity, and Employment

Sociological research has documented that people of color face several kinds of problems in securing employment. While their relative lack of education is an obvious factor, other kinds of problems are also apparent.

One problem is racial discrimination on the part of employers, regardless of how conscious employers are of their discriminatory behavior. Chapter 10 "Race and Ethnicity" recounted a study by sociologist Devah Pager (2007), who had young white and African American men apply independently in person for various jobs in Milwaukee. These men wore the same type of clothing and reported similar levels of education and other qualifications. Some said they had a criminal record, while others said they had not committed any crimes. In striking evidence of racial discrimination in hiring, African American applicants *without* a criminal record were hired at the same low rate as white applicants *with* a criminal record. Pager and sociologists Bruce Western and Bart Bonikowski also investigated racial discrimination in another field experiment in New York City (Pager, Bonikowski, & Western, 2009). They had white, African American, and Latino "testers," all of them "well-spoken, clean-cut young men" (p. 781), apply in person to low-level service jobs (e.g., retail sales and delivery drivers) requiring no more than a high school education; all the testers had similar (hypothetical) qualifications. Almost one-third (31%) of white testers received a call back or job offer, compared to only 25.2% of Latino testers and 15.2% of African American testers. The researchers concluded that their findings "add to a large research program demonstrating the continuing contribution of discrimination to racial inequality in the post-civil rights era" (p. 794).

Other kinds of evidence also reveal racial discrimination in hiring. Two scholars sent job applications in response to help-wanted ads in Boston and Chicago (Bertrand & Mullainathan, 2003). They randomly assigned the applications to feature either a "white-sounding" name (e.g., Emily or Greg) or an "African American–sounding" name (e.g., Jamal and Lakisha). White names received 50% more callbacks than African American names for job interviews.

Racial differences in access to the informal networks that are often so important in finding a job also contribute to the racial/ethnic disparity in employment. In a study using data from a nationwide survey of a random sample of Americans, sociologist Steve McDonald and colleagues found that people of color and women are less likely than white males to receive informal word of vacant, high-level supervisory positions (McDonald, Nan, & Ao, 2009).

As these studies indicate, research by sociologists and other social scientists reveals that race and ethnicity continue to make a difference in employment prospects for Americans. This body of research reveals clear evidence of discrimination, conscious or unconscious, in hiring and also of racial/ethnic differences in access to the informal networks that are often so important for hiring. By uncovering this evidence, these studies underscore the need to address discrimination, access to informal networks, and other factors that contribute to racial and ethnic disparities in employment. For this reason, sociology is again making a difference.

The Impact of Unemployment

Long-term unemployment often causes various social and psychological difficulties.

Rawle C. Jackman – The line of hope… – CC BY-NC-ND 2.0.

Although the news article that began this chapter gave us a heartrending account of a woman experiencing long-term unemployment, survey data also provide harsh evidence of the social and psychological effects of being unemployed. In July 2010, the Pew Research Center issued a report based on a survey of 810 adults who were currently unemployed or had been unemployed since the Great Recession began in December 2007 and 1,093 people who had never been unemployed during the recession (Morin & Kochhar, 2010). The report's title, *Lost Income, Lost Friends—and Loss of Self-Respect*, summarized its major findings. Of those who had been unemployed for at least 6 months (*long-term unemployment*), 44% said that the recession had caused "major changes" in their lives, versus only 20% of those who had never been unemployed. More than half of the long-term unemployed said their family income had declined, and more than 40% said that their family relations had been strained and that they had lost contact with close friends. In another finding, 38% said they had "lost some self-respect" from being unemployed. One-third said they were finding it difficult to pay their rent or mortage, compared to only 16% of those who had never been unemployed during the recession. Half had borrowed money from family or friends to pay bills, versus only 18% of the never unemployed. Of all the people who had been unemployed, almost half had experienced sleep difficulties, and 5% had experienced drug or alcohol problems. All these numbers paint a distressing picture of the social and psychological impact of unemployment during the Great Recession that began in late 2007.

Job Satisfaction and Alienation

Recall that Karl Marx thought that job alienation was a major problem in industrial societies. Following up on his concern, social scientists have tried to determine the extent of worker alienation and job satisfaction, as well as the correlates of these two attitudes (Bockerman & Ilmakunnas, 2009). They generally find that American workers like their jobs much more than Marx anticipated, but also that the extent to which they like their jobs depends on the income their jobs bring, the degree of autonomy they enjoy in their jobs, and other factors.

One way of measuring job satisfaction is simply to ask people, "On the whole, how satisfied are you with the work you do?" The General Social Survey uses precisely this question, and 85.8% of respondents (2008 data) say they are satisfied with their jobs, with only 14.1% saying they are dissatisfied. This latter figure is probably lower than Marx would have predicted for a capitalist society like the United States.

Friendships among employees are very common and may contribute to high levels of satisfaction with one's job in the United States.

Wonderlane – Co-workers laughing at Fat Smitty's – CC BY 2.0.

One possible reason for the low amount of job dissatisfaction, and one that Marx did not foresee, is that workers develop friendships in their workplace (McGuire, 2007). Coworkers discuss all kinds of topics with each other, including personal matters, sports, and political affairs, and they often will invite other coworkers over to their homes or go out with them to a movie or a restaurant. Such friendships can lead workers to like their jobs more than they otherwise would and help overcome the alienation they would feel without the friendships. Such coworker friendships are quite common, as research finds that about half of all workers have at least one close friend who is a coworker (Marks, 1994).

Crime in the Workplace

An unfortunate fact about work and labor in the United States is crime in the workplace. Two major types of such crime exist: employee theft and workplace violence.

Employee Theft

Chapter 7 "Deviance, Crime, and Social Control" briefly discussed **employee theft** as one of the many types of crime that occur in the United States and elsewhere. Employee theft takes two forms, pilferage and embezzlement. **Pilferage** involves the stealing of goods, while **embezzlement** involves the stealing of money in its various dimensions (cash, electronic transactions, etc.). Whichever form it takes, employee theft is so common that is has been called a "widespread, pervasive, and costly form of crime" (Langton, Piquero, & Hollinger, 2006, p. 539). It is estimated that about 75% of employees steal at least once from their employers and that the annual amount of employee theft is $19.5 billion (National Retail Federation, 2007).

Employee theft occurs for many reasons, but a common reason is worker dissatisfaction with various aspects of their job. They may think their wages or salaries are too low, they may feel they have been treated unfairly by their employer, and so forth. As the estimates of the amount of employee theft suggest, this form of theft is not condemned by many people, and, indeed, many workplaces have informal norms that approve of certain forms of theft—for example, it is okay to steal inexpensive objects such as (depending on the workplace) utensils, food, pencils and pens, or toilet paper. Not surprisingly, embezzlement is often more costly to an employer than pilferage; although it can involve just a few dollars from a cash register, it can also involve hundreds of thousands or millions of dollars acquired through more sophisticated means. In an example of a very costly embezzlement, the head cashier at the University of California, San Francisco, received a 7-year prison term for embezzling more than $4 million (Chiang, 2004).

Employee theft costs about $19.5 billion annually. Workers' dissatisfaction with various aspects of their jobs is a major reason for this form of theft.

A. Golden – the US$ 3 TRILLION HEIST – CC BY-NC-ND 2.0.

When we think of employee theft, we probably usually think of theft by blue-collar or lower white-collar employees. However, physicians, attorneys, and other professionals also steal from their patients/clients or from the government, even if their form of theft is often much more complex and sophisticated than what the term "employee theft" may usually imply. Attorneys may bill their clients for work that was never done, and physicians may bill Medicare or private insurance for patients they never saw or for procedures that were never performed. We call this form of "employee" theft **professional fraud**. Fraud by physicians and other health-care professionals (including nursing homes and medical testing laboratories) is thought to amount to $100 billion every year (Rosoff, Pontell, & Tillman, 2010), a figure that far exceeds the $19.5 billion in "conventional" employee theft and the similar figure lost to property crime (robbery, burglary, larceny, and motor vehicle theft).

Workplace Violence

In August 2010, a disgruntled employee went on a shooting rampage inside a beer distributor warehouse in Manchester, Connecticut, killing eight people before shooting himself. He had just been told he would be fired or forced to resign after being caught stealing beer and began the shootings at the end of a disciplinary hearing (Rivera & Haughney, 2010).

Many people die or are injured by acts of violence at their workplaces every year in the United States. In 2008, 517 people were slain at their workplaces, according to the U.S. Bureau of Labor Statistics. As disturbing as this number was, it represented a sharp drop from the numbers that prevailed a decade earlier, when 1,080 workplace homicides occurred in 1994. From 2003 through 2008, an average of 497 workplace homicides occurred every year (Needleman, 2010).

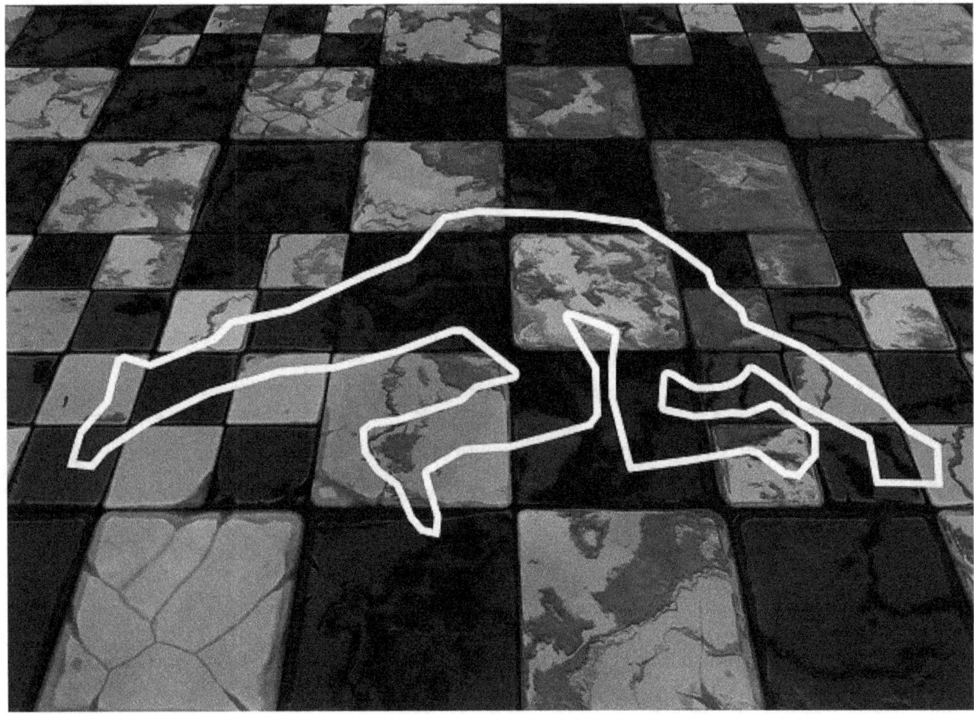

About 500 homicides occur at workplaces every year. The majority of these homicides result from robberies, not from the actions of disgruntled workers.

Pixabay – CC0 Public Domain.

In terms of who is involved and the reasons for their involvement, three kinds of workplace homicides are the most common. The first and by far the most common type is homicide as the result of robbery. This category includes the many store clerks, gas station attendants, taxi drivers, and other employees who are slain during a robbery, as well as police who are killed as they try to stop a robbery or apprehend the offender. The second category is homicide committed as an act of domestic violence; in this type, the offender, almost always a man, seeks out his wife or girlfriend (or ex-wife or ex-girlfriend) at her workplace and kills her. The third category involves disgruntled workers, such as the one at the Connecticut beer distributor just discussed, who kill one or more people at their workplace whom they blame for problems the killers have been having. Although this type of homicide is the type that the phrase "workplace violence" or "workplace killings" usually brings to mind, it is actually the least common of the three types listed here (Fox, 2010).

As noted, workplace violence was more common during the 1990s than today, reflecting a general drop in U.S. violence since that decade. National survey evidence indicates that an average of about 1.7 million acts of violence occurred every year in the workplace during the 1990s: 900 homicides, 70,000 robberies, 1.6 million aggravated and simple assaults, and more than 36,000 rapes and sexual assaults (Duhart, 2001).

Key Takeaways

- Conflict between labor and management was intense in the United States after the advent of industrialization. Strikes and labor-related violence were common after the Civil War.
- The move to a postindustrial economy has resulted in a loss of jobs in the United States, thanks in part to capital flight and outsourcing.
- Job satisfaction is higher and worker alienation lower than what Karl Marx would have predicted for the United States, thanks in part to workplace friendships.
- Unemployment has soared because of the Great Recession that began in late 2007. Joblessness has significant consequences for the financial and psychological well-being of the millions of people who are unemployed.
- Two significant problems in the workplace are employee theft and workplace violence. Both problems are common and together have serious repercussions for the financial health of businesses and the physical health of employees, respectively.

For Your Review

1. Fewer workers belong to labor unions now than just a few decades ago. Do you think this is a good development or a bad development? Explain your answer.
2. Think of a job you now have or your most recent job if you are currently not employed. On a scale of 1 = very dissatisfied to 10 = very satisfied, how satisfied are you (were you) with your job? Explain why you have (had) this level of satisfaction.

References

Bertrand, M., & Mullainathan, S. (2003). Are Emily and Greg more employable than Lakisha and Jamal? A field experiment on labor market discrimination. *National Bureau of Economic Research* (Working Paper No. 9873). Retrieved from http://papers.nber.org/papers/w9873.pdf.

Bockerman, P., & Ilmakunnas, P. (2009). Job disamenities, job satisfaction, quit intentions, and actual separations: Putting the pieces together. *Industrial Relations, 48*(1), 73–96.

Bureau of Labor Statistics. (2009). *Employment and earnings online*. Washington, DC: Bureau of Labor Statistics, U.S. Department of Labor. Retrieved from http://www.bls.gov/opub/ee/home.htm.

Chiang, H. (2004, July 2). Ex-UCSF employee gets 7-year sentence. *San Francisco Chronicle*. Retrieved from http://www.sfgate.com/cgi-bin/article.cgi?f=/chronicle/archive/2004/2007/2002/BAG2004S2007EU2921.DTL.

Dubofsky, M., & Dulles, F. R. (2010). *Labor in America: A history* (8th ed.). Wheeling, IL: Harlan Davidson.

Duhart, D. T. (2001). *Violence in the workplace, 1993–99*. Washington, DC: Bureau of Justice Statistics, U.S. Department of Justice.

Economic Policy Institute. (2010). Economy track. Retrieved from http://www.economytrack.org/underemployment.php.

Fox, J. A. (2010, August 5). Workplace homicide: What is the risk? [Web log post]. Retrieved from http://boston.com/community/blogs/crime_punishment/2010/08/workplace_homicide_the_risks.html.

Herbert, B. (2010, August 10). The horror show. *The New York Times*, p. A25.

Hirsch, B., & Macpherson, D. (2009). Union membership and coverage database from the CPS. Retrieved from http://unionstats.com.

Langton, L., Piquero, N. L., & Hollinger, R. (2006). An empirical test of the relationship between employee theft and low self-control. *Deviant Behavior 27*(5), 537–565.

Marks, S. R. (1994). Intimacy in the public realm: The case of co-workers. *Social Forces, 72*, 843–858.

McDonald, S., Nan, L., & Ao, D. (2009). Networks of opportunity: Gender, race, and job leads. *Social Problems, 56*(3), 385–402.

McGovern, G. S., & Guttridge, L. F. (1972). *The great coalfield war*. Boston, MA: Houghton Mifflin.

McGuire, G. M. (2007). Intimate work: A typology of the social support that workers provide to their network members. *Work and Occupations, 34*, 125–147.

Mills, C. W. (1959). *The sociological imagination*. London, England: Oxford University Press.

Mishel, L., Bernstein, J., & Shierholz, H. (2009). *The state of working America 2008/2009*. Ithaca, NY: ILR Press [An imprint of Cornell University Press].

Morin, R. and Kochhar, R. (2010). *Lost income, lost friends—and loss of self-respect: The impact of long-term unemployment*. Washington, DC: Pew Research Center.

Needleman, S. E. (2010, August 10). When violence strikes the workplace. *Wall Street Journal*. Retrieved from http://online.wsj.com/article/SB10001424052748704164904575421560153438240.html?mod=googlenews_wsj.

National Retail Federation. (2007, June 11). Retail losses hit $41.6 billion last year, according to National Retail Security Survey. [Press release]. Retrieved from http://www.nrf.com/modules.php?name=News&op=viewlive&sp_id=318.

Pager, D. (2007). *Marked: Race, crime, and finding work in an era of mass incarceration*. Chicago, IL: University of Chicago Press.

Pager, D., Bonikowski, B., & Western, B. (2009). Discrimination in a low-wage labor market: A field experiment. *American Sociological Review, 74*(5), 777–799.

Rivera, R. and Haughney, C. (2010, August 5). Amid mourning, eerie details emerge about Connecticut shootings. *The New York Times*, p. A19.

Rosoff, S. M., Pontell, H. N., & Tillman, R. (2010). *Profit without honor: White collar crime and the looting of America* (5th ed.). Upper Saddle River, NJ: Prentice Hall.

Taft, P., & Ross, P. (1990). American labor violence: Its causes, character, and outcome. In N. A. Weiner, M. A. Zahn, & R. J. Sagi (Eds.), *Violence: Patterns, causes, public policy* (pp. 174–186). San Diego, CA: Harcourt Brace Jovanovich.

Thomas, M. (2009, July 16). Outsourcing statistics: What figures will tell you. *EzineArticles*. Retrieved from http://ezinearticles.com/?Outsourcing-Statistics—What-Figures-Will-Tell-You&id=2621948.

U.S. Census Bureau. (2009). *Statistical abstract of the United States: 2009*. Washington, DC: U.S. Government Printing Office. Retrieved from http://www.census.gov/compendia/statab.

13.5 The Military-Industrial Complex

Learning Objectives

1. Summarize President Eisenhower's concerns over the military-industrial complex.
2. Discuss the controversy over the size of the military budget.

A key component of the U.S. economy is the defense industry. The military in the United States involves not just the armed forces but also some of the largest corporations that receive billions of dollars in defense contracts, as well as the government leaders who approve large military budgets to fund these contracts.

The military has played a fundamental role in some of the most significant events of the last 100 years and beyond. One of these, of course, was World War II. This war was what we now call "the good war." Millions died on the battlefield, in cities bombed by planes, and in concentration camps, and in the end Hitler and his allies were defeated. About 20 years after World War II ended, the United States began fighting another war meant to save the world for democracy, but this war was very different from the one against Hitler. This war was fought in Vietnam, and however a noble effort World War II might have been, the Vietnam War was just as ignoble to its critics. It was a war, some said, not to save the world for democracy but to help extend America's power where it did not belong. If the World War II generation grew up with a patriotic love for their nation, the Vietnam War generation grew up with much more cynicism about their government and about the military.

Ironically, that generation's concern about the military was shared by none other than President Dwight D. Eisenhower, who warned about the dangers of what he called the **military-industrial complex** in his farewell presidential address. Eisenhower himself had been a member of the military-industrial complex, having served as a five-star general and supreme commander of the Allied forces in Europe during World War II and head of Columbia University before becoming president. His military experience made him no fan of warfare, as he once observed, "I hate war as only a soldier who has lived it can, only as one who has seen its brutality, its futility, its stupidity." He also feared that the military-industrial complex was becoming too powerful and gaining "unwarranted influence" over American life as it acted for its own interests and not necessarily for those of the nation as a whole. He warned that the "potential for the disastrous rise of misplaced power exists and will persist" (Eisenhower, 1960, p. A1).

Eisenhower's fears about the military-industrial complex reflected his more general concern about **militarism**, or an overemphasis on military policy and spending, which he thought was costing the nation far too much money. In a remarkable and now famous statement made early in his presidency in April 1953, Eisenhower (1960) declared,

> Every gun that is made, every warship launched, every rocket fired, signifies in the final sense, a theft from those who hunger and are not fed, those who are cold and are not clothed. This world in arms is not spending money alone. It is spending the

sweat of its laborers, the genius of its scientists, the hopes of its children. This is not a way of life at all in any true sense. Under the clouds of war, it is humanity hanging on a cross of iron.

A half-century after Eisenhower made this statement, U.S. military spending continues unabated. In 2009 it was $767 billion (including $92 billion for veterans' benefits) and accounted for almost 22% of all federal spending (U.S. Census Bureau, 2010) but also for a much higher percentage of federal spending over which the government has any control. The federal budget includes both mandatory and discretionary spending. As the name implies, mandatory spending is required by various laws and includes such things as Social Security, Medicare and Medicaid, food stamps, and interest payments on the national debt; much of these mandatory expenses are funded by trust funds, such as Social Security taxes, which are raised and spent separately from income taxes. Discretionary spending involves the money the president and Congress must decide how to spend each year and includes income tax dollars only. Military spending accounts for about 43% of discretionary spending (Friends Committee on National Legislation, 2009).

The U.S. military budget is by far the highest in the world and dwarfs the military budgets for the nations ranking after the United States. In 2009, the U.S. military budget was $661 billion. The nations ranking after the United States were China, $100 billion; France, $64 billion; United Kingdom, $58 billion; Russia, $53 billion; Japan, $51 billion; and Germany, $46 billion. U.S. military spending accounted for 43% of the world's military spending in 2009 (Stockholm International Peace Research Institute, 2010).

Critics say that U.S. military spending is too high and takes needed dollars from domestic essentials like schooling and health care.

Jeremy Seitz – Swiss Jets – CC BY 2.0.

Another dimension of militarism involves arms exports by both the U.S. government and U.S. military contractors. Combining data on both types of exports, the United States sent $12.2 billion in arms deliveries to other nations in 2008. This figure ranked the highest in the world and constituted about 38% of all world arms exports. Russia ranked second with $5.4 billion in arms deliveries, while Germany ranked third with $2.9 billion

(Grimmett, 2009). Most arms exports from the United States and other exporters go to developing nations, and critics say that the exports help fuel the worldwide arms race and international discord and that they often go to nations ruled by dictators, who then use them to threaten their own people (Morgan, 2008; Stohl, Schroeder, & Smith, 2007).

Oscar Arias, a former president of Costa Rica and winner of the 1987 Nobel Peace Prize, echoed President Eisenhower when he wrote a decade ago that U.S. military spending took money away from important domestic needs. "Americans are hurt," he warned, "when the defense budget squanders money that could be used to repair schools or to guarantee universal health care" (Arias, 1999).

Cost equivalencies illustrate what is lost when so much money is spent on the military. An F-22 fighter aircraft, conceived and built to win fights with aircraft that the Soviet Union (and later, Russia) never built, costs about $350 million (Smith, 2009). This same sum could be used to pay the salaries of about 11,700 new teachers earning $30,000 per year or to build 23 elementary schools at a cost of $15 million each. A nuclear submarine can cost at least $2.5 billion. This sum could provide 500,000 scholarships worth $5,000 each to low- and middle-income high school students to help them pay for college.

A key question is whether U.S. military spending is higher than it needs to be. Experts disagree over this issue. Some think the United States needs to maintain and even increase its level of military spending, even with the Cold War long ended, to replace aging weapons systems, to meet the threat posed by terrorists and by "rogue" nations such as Iran, and to respond to various other trouble spots around the world. Military spending is good for workers, they add, because it creates jobs, and it also contributes to technological development (Ruttan, 2006).

Other experts think the military budget is much higher than it needs to be to defend the United States and to address its legitimate interests around the world. They say the military budget is bloated because the defense industry lobbies so successfully and because military spending provides jobs and income to the home districts of members of Congress. For these reasons, they say, military spending far exceeds the amount that needs to be spent to provide an adequate defense for the United States and its allies. They also argue that military spending actually produces fewer jobs than spending in other sectors. According to a recent estimate, $1 billion spent by the Pentagon creates 11,600 jobs, but the same $1 billion spent in other sectors would create 17,100 clean energy jobs, 19,600 health-care jobs, and 29,100 education jobs (Pollin & Garrett-Peltier, 2009).

As this overview of the debate over military spending indicates, the military remains a hot topic more than two decades after the Cold War ended following the demise of the Soviet Union. As we move further into the 21st century, the issue of military spending will present a major challenge for the U.S. political and economic institutions to address in a way that meets America's international and domestic interests.

Key Takeaways

- U.S. military spending amounted to almost $770 billion in 2009, reflecting the highest military budget in the world.
- Critics of the military budget say that the billions of dollars spent on weapons and other military needs would be better spent on domestic needs such as schools and day care.

For Your Review

1. Do you think the U.S. military budget should be increased, be reduced, or stay about the same? Explain your answer.

Improving Work and the Economy: What Sociology Suggests

Sociological theory and research are once again relevant for addressing certain issues raised by studies of the economy. One issue is racial and ethnic discrimination in hiring and employment. Several kinds of studies, but especially field experiments involving job applicants who are similar except for their race and ethnicity, provide powerful evidence of continuing discrimination despite federal and state laws banning it. This evidence certainly suggests the need for stronger enforcement of existing laws against racial and ethnic bias in employment and for public education campaigns to alert workers to signs of this type of discrimination.

A second issue concerns the satisfaction that American workers find in their jobs. Although the level of this satisfaction is fairly high, sociological research highlights the importance of coworker friendships for both job satisfaction and more general individual well-being. These research findings indicate that employers and employees alike should make special efforts to promote coworker friendships. Because work is such an important part of most people's lives, these efforts should prove beneficial for many reasons.

A third issue is unemployment. Sociologists, psychologists, and other scholars have documented the social and emotional consequences of unemployment. The effects of unemployment go far beyond the loss of money. Revealed by much research, these consequences sometimes seem forgotten in national debates over whether to extend unemployment insurance benefits. But unemployment does have a human face, and it is essential to provide monetary benefits and other kinds of help for the unemployed.

Because a sociological understanding of the economy emphasizes its structural problems rather than personal faults of the unemployed and underemployed, this sort of understanding points to the social democracies of Scandinavia as possible models for the United States to emulate. As the "Learning From Other Societies" box discussed, these nations have combined democratic freedom and economic prosperity. Although there are certainly no signs that the United States is about to follow their example, our nation has much to learn from these societies as it considers how best to rebuild its economy and to help the millions of people who are unemployed or underemployed.

References

Arias, O. (1999, June 23). Stopping America's most lethal export. *The New York Times*, p. A19.

Eisenhower, D. D. (1960). *Public papers of the presidents of the United States: Dwight D. Eisenhower*. Washington, DC: U.S. Government Printing Office.

Friends Committee on National Legislation. (2009). *How much of your 2008 income taxes pay for war?* Washington, DC: Friends Committee on National Legislation. Retrieved from http://www.fcnl.org/issues/item.php?item_id=3553&issue_id=19.

Grimmett, R. E. (2009). *Conventional arms transfers to developing nations, 2001–2008*. Washington, DC: Congressional Research Service.

Morgan, M. (2008). *The American military after 9/11: Society, state, and empire*. New York, NY: Palgrave Macmillan.

Pollin, R., & Garrett-Peltier, H. (2009). *The U.S. employment effects of military and domestic spending priorities: An updated analysis*. Washington, DC: Institute for Policy Studies.

Ruttan, V. (2006). *Is war necessary for economic growth? Military procurement and technology development*. New York, NY: Oxford University Press.

Smith, R. J. (2009, July 10). Premier U.S. fighter jet has major shortcomings. *The Washington Post*, p. A1.

Stockholm International Peace Research Institute. (2010). The 15 major spender countries in 2009. Retrieved from http://www.sipri.org/research/armaments/milex/resultoutput/15majorspenders.

Stohl, R., Schroeder, M., & Smith, D. (2007). *The small arms trade: A beginner's guide*. Oxford, England: Oneworld.

U.S. Census Bureau. (2010). *Statistical abstract of the United States: 2010*. Washington, DC: U.S. Government Printing Office. Retrieved from http://www.census.gov/compendia/statab.

13.6 End-of-Chapter Material

Summary

1. The type of economy characterizing societies has changed over the centuries. With the development of agricultural societies, economic functions began to be separated from family functions. Industrialization increased this separation further, and factories and machines became the primary means of production. The development of postindustrial societies in the last few decades has had important implications for the nature of work and other aspects of social and economic life in modern societies.
2. Capitalism and socialism are the two primary types of economic systems in the world today. Capitalism involves private ownership, the pursuit of profit, and competition for profit, while socialism involves the collective ownership of goods and resources and efforts for the common good. The relative merits of capitalism and socialism continue to be debated; several nations practice democratic socialism, which is meant to combine the best of capitalism and socialism.
3. Corporations are essential players in modern economic systems but remain quite controversial. They concentrate economic power in the hands of a few organizations and often act in a way that stifles competition and harms their own workers and much of the public.
4. The development of labor unions occurred amid a concerted effort by management to resist demands for wage increases and better working conditions. In the recent past, U.S. workers have faced declining wages in constant dollars, although this general trend obscures some important gender, race/ethnicity, and social class differences in wage trends. Postindustrialization has meant a loss of manufacturing jobs across the United States but especially in its large cities.
5. Unemployment, underemployment, and job alienation remain problems facing U.S. workers. Job alienation is probably less than what Karl Marx envisioned in a capitalist society, in part because workers develop workplace friendships.
6. Two significant problems in the workplace are employee theft and workplace violence. Employee theft involves pilferage and embezzlement. Most killings in workplaces result from robberies rather than from actions by disgruntled employees.
7. President Eisenhower warned of the dangers of a high military budget and the militarism of the United States. Even after the demise of the Soviet Union in 1991, the U.S. military budget remains quite large. Experts disagree over the proper size of the military budget, and militarism will remain a major challenge as we move further into the 21st century.

Using Sociology

You graduated from college a year ago and have begun working in the human relations department of a medium-sized company. You are very happy with your salary and prospects for promotion. However, part of your job involves processing application forms from prospective employees, and you have become concerned with one part of that process. Your supervisor has told you to put applications with “black-sounding” names like Jamal and Lakisha in a separate file to be examined only if a sufficient number of employees cannot be hired from the “regular” file. What, if anything, do you do? Explain your answer.

Chapter 14: Politics and Government

Social Issues in the News

"Student Leaders Vote to Oppose 21-Only," the headline said. In September 2010, the student government at the University of Iowa voted 16–9 to endorse the repeal of a bar ordinance in Iowa City. Adopted by the City Council the previous spring, the ordinance bans people younger than 21 from the city's bars after 10:00 p.m.; before the ordinance was adopted, 19- and 20-year-olds were allowed in the bars. Although the ordinance was meant to reduce underage drinking, student leaders argued that it instead made it more likely that students would end up at house parties where they would "engage in substantially heavier binge drinking and are left vulnerable to not only their own mistakes but the mistakes of others." A university sophomore agreed with this analysis: "I think if you are underage, there isn't much else for you to do. And there is the safety issue." Another sophomore applauded the student government vote. "I think it is very important students take a stand," he said. "This represents that the entire UI student body is against the ordinance." (Morelli, 2010)

The University of Iowa student government's vote on a bar ordinance is just one illustration, though perhaps not on the most momentous issue, of democracy in action. Voting and elections are certainly a defining feature of the United States and other democracies, but voting remains only a dream in much of the world. And although the United States is one of the world's leading democracies, many people fail to vote and otherwise participate in the political process. When the 20th century ended little more than a decade ago, Americans everywhere paused to reflect on its most significant events, including two World Wars, the Great Depression, the rise and fall of the Soviet Union, and the unleashing of the nuclear age. We thought about these and other events not only because they were historically important but also because they told us something about our society and the changes the last century brought. In all these events, our political system played a fundamental role.

This chapter discusses what sociologists and other social scientists say about politics and government. We will examine the dimensions of power and authority, the types of political systems, politics and political participation in the United States, and major aspects of war and terrorism, two violent phenomena in which governments are intricately involved whether or not they wish to be. The chapter ends with some sociological suggestions on how to achieve the Constitution's goal of "a more perfect union."

References

Morelli, B. A. (2010, September 15). Student leaders vote to oppose 21-only. *Iowa City Press-Citizen*. Retrieved from http://www.press-citizen.com/article/20100915/NEWS20100901/29150313/Student-leaders-vote-to-oppose-20100921-only.

14.1 Power and Authority

Learning Objectives

1. Define *power* and the three types of authority.
2. List Weber's three types of authority.
3. Explain why charismatic authority may be unstable in the long run.

Politics refers to the distribution and exercise of power within a society, and **polity** refers to the political institution through which power is distributed and exercised. In any society, decisions must be made regarding the allocation of resources and other matters. Except perhaps in the simplest societies, specific people and often specific organizations make these decisions. Depending on the society, they sometimes make these decisions solely to benefit themselves and other times make these decisions to benefit the society as a whole. Regardless of who benefits, a central point is this: some individuals and groups have more power than others. Because power is so essential to an understanding of politics, we begin our discussion of politics with a discussion of power.

Power refers to the ability to have one's will carried out despite the resistance of others. Most of us have seen a striking example of raw power when we are driving a car and see a police car in our rearview mirror. At that particular moment, the driver of that car has enormous power over us. We make sure we strictly obey the speed limit and all other driving rules. If, alas, the police car's lights are flashing, we stop the car, as otherwise we may be in for even bigger trouble. When the officer approaches our car, we ordinarily try to be as polite as possible and pray we do not get a ticket. When you were 16 and your parents told you to be home by midnight or else, your arrival home by this curfew again illustrated the use of power, in this case parental power. If a child in middle school gives her lunch to a bully who threatens her, that again is an example of the use of power, or, in this case, the misuse of power.

These are all vivid examples of power, but the power that social scientists study is both grander and, often, more invisible (Wrong, 1996). Much of it occurs behind the scenes, and scholars continue to debate who is wielding it and for whose benefit they wield it. Many years ago Max Weber (1921/1978), one of the founders of sociology discussed in earlier chapters, distinguished legitimate authority as a special type of power. **Legitimate authority** (sometimes just called *authority*), Weber said, is power whose use is considered just and appropriate by those over whom the power is exercised. In short, if a society approves of the exercise of power in a particular way, then that power is also legitimate authority. The example of the police car in our rearview mirrors is an example of legitimate authority.

Weber's keen insight lay in distinguishing different types of legitimate authority that characterize different types of societies, especially as they evolve from simple to more complex societies. He called these three types traditional authority, rational-legal authority, and charismatic authority. We turn to these now.

Traditional Authority

As the name implies, **traditional authority** is power that is rooted in traditional, or long-standing, beliefs and practices of a society. It exists and is assigned to particular individuals because of that society's customs and traditions. Individuals enjoy traditional authority for at least one of two reasons. The first is inheritance, as certain individuals are granted traditional authority because they are the children or other relatives of people who already exercise traditional authority. The second reason individuals enjoy traditional authority is more religious: their societies believe they are anointed by God or the gods, depending on the society's religious beliefs, to lead their society. Traditional authority is common in many preindustrial societies, where tradition and custom are so important, but also in more modern monarchies (discussed shortly), where a king, queen, or prince enjoys power because she or he comes from a royal family.

Traditional authority is granted to individuals regardless of their qualifications. They do not have to possess any special skills to receive and wield their authority, as their claim to it is based solely on their bloodline or supposed divine designation. An individual granted traditional authority can be intelligent or stupid, fair or arbitrary, and exciting or boring but receives the authority just the same because of custom and tradition. As not all individuals granted traditional authority are particularly well qualified to use it, societies governed by traditional authority sometimes find that individuals bestowed it are not always up to the job.

Rational-Legal Authority

If traditional authority derives from custom and tradition, **rational-legal authority** derives from law and is based on a belief in the legitimacy of a society's laws and rules and in the right of leaders to act under these rules to make decisions and set policy. This form of authority is a hallmark of modern democracies, where power is given to people elected by voters, and the rules for wielding that power are usually set forth in a constitution, a charter, or another written document. Whereas traditional authority resides in an individual because of inheritance or divine designation, rational-legal authority resides in the office that an individual fills, not in the individual per se. The authority of the president of the United States thus resides in the office of the presidency, not in the individual who happens to be president. When that individual leaves office, authority transfers to the next president. This transfer is usually smooth and stable, and one of the marvels of democracy is that officeholders are replaced in elections without revolutions having to be necessary. We might not have voted for the person who wins the presidency, but we accept that person's authority as our president when he (so far it has always been a "he") assumes office.

Rational-legal authority helps ensure an orderly transfer of power in a time of crisis. When John F. Kennedy was assassinated in 1963, Vice President Lyndon Johnson was immediately sworn in as the next president. When Richard Nixon resigned his office in disgrace in 1974 because of his involvement in the Watergate scandal, Vice President Gerald Ford (who himself had become vice president after Spiro Agnew resigned because of financial corruption) became president. Because the U.S. Constitution provided for the transfer of power when the presidency was vacant, and because U.S. leaders and members of the public accept the authority of the Constitution on these and so many other matters, the transfer of power in 1963 and 1974 was smooth and orderly.

Charismatic Authority

Charismatic authority stems from an individual's extraordinary personal qualities and from that individual's hold over followers because of these qualities. Such charismatic individuals may exercise authority over a whole society or only a specific group within a larger society. They can exercise authority for good and for bad, as this brief list of charismatic leaders indicates: Joan of Arc, Adolf Hitler, Mahatma Gandhi, Martin Luther King Jr., Jesus Christ, Muhammad, and Buddha. Each of these individuals had extraordinary personal qualities that led their followers to admire them and to follow their orders or requests for action.

Much of Dr. Martin Luther King Jr.'s appeal as a civil rights leader stemmed from his extraordinary speaking skills and other personal qualities that accounted for his charismatic authority.

U.S. Library of Congress – public domain.

Charismatic authority can reside in a person who came to a position of leadership because of traditional or rational-legal authority. Over the centuries, several kings and queens of England and other European nations were charismatic individuals as well (while some were far from charismatic). A few U.S. presidents—Washington, Lincoln, both Roosevelts, Kennedy, Reagan, and, for all his faults, even Clinton—also were charismatic, and much of their popularity stemmed from various personal qualities that attracted the public and sometimes even the press. Ronald Reagan, for example, was often called "the Teflon president," because he was so loved by much of the public that accusations of ineptitude or malfeasance did not stick to him (Lanoue, 1988).

Weber emphasized that charismatic authority in its pure form (i.e., when authority resides in someone solely because of the person's charisma and not because the person also has traditional or rational-legal authority) is less stable than traditional authority or rational-legal authority. The reason for this is simple: once charismatic leaders die, their authority dies as well. Although a charismatic leader's example may continue to inspire people long after the leader dies, it is difficult for another leader to come along and command people's devotion as intensely. After the deaths of all the charismatic leaders named in the preceding paragraph, no one came close to replacing them in the hearts and minds of their followers.

Because charismatic leaders recognize that their eventual death may well undermine the nation or cause they represent, they often designate a replacement leader, who they hope will also have charismatic qualities. This new leader may be a grown child of the charismatic leader or someone else the leader knows and trusts. The danger, of course, is that any new leaders will lack sufficient charisma to have their authority accepted by the followers of the original charismatic leader. For this reason, Weber recognized that charismatic authority ultimately becomes more stable when it is evolves into traditional or rational-legal authority. Transformation into traditional authority can happen when charismatic leaders' authority becomes accepted as residing in their bloodlines, so that their authority passes to their children and then to their grandchildren. Transformation into rational-legal authority occurs when a society ruled by a charismatic leader develops the rules and bureaucratic structures that we associate with a government. Weber used the term **routinization of charisma** to refer to the transformation of charismatic authority in either of these ways.

Key Takeaways

- Power refers to the ability to have one's will carried out despite the resistance of others.
- According to Max Weber, the three types of legitimate authority are traditional, rational-legal, and charismatic.
- Charismatic authority is relatively unstable because the authority held by a charismatic leader may not easily extend to anyone else after the leader dies.

For Your Review

1. Think of someone, either a person you have known or a national or historical figure, whom you regard as a charismatic leader. What is it about this person that makes her or him charismatic?
2. Why is rational-legal authority generally more stable than charismatic authority?

References

Lanoue, D. J. (1988). From Camelot to the teflon president: Economics and presidential popularaity since 1960. New York, NY: Greenwood Press.

Weber, M. (1978). *Economy and society: An outline of interpretive sociology* (G. Roth & C. Wittich, Eds.). Berkeley: University of California Press. (Original work published 1921).

Wrong, D. H. (1996). *Power: Its forms, bases, and uses*. New Brunswick, NJ: Transaction.

14.2 Types of Political Systems

Learning Objectives

1. Discuss the advantages and disadvantages of representative democracy.
2. Explain why authoritarian and totalitarian regimes are more unstable politically than democracies and monarchies.

Various states and governments obviously exist around the world. In this context, **state** means the political unit within which power and authority reside. This unit can be a whole nation or a subdivision within a nation. Thus the nations of the world are sometimes referred to as states (or nation-states), as are subdivisions within a nation, such as California, New York, and Texas in the United States. **Government** means the group of persons who direct the political affairs of a state, but it can also mean the type of rule by which a state is run. Another term for this second meaning of government is **political system**, which we will use here along with *government*. The type of government under which people live has fundamental implications for their freedom, their welfare, and even their lives. Accordingly we briefly review the major political systems in the world today.

Democracy

The type of government with which we are most familiar is **democracy**, or a political system in which citizens govern themselves either directly or indirectly. The term *democracy* comes from Greek and means "rule of the people." In Lincoln's stirring words from the Gettysburg Address, democracy is "government of the people, by the people, for the people." In *direct* (or *pure*) *democracies*, people make their own decisions about the policies and distribution of resources that affect them directly. An example of such a democracy in action is the New England town meeting, where the residents of a town meet once a year and vote on budgetary and other matters. However, such direct democracies are impractical when the number of people gets beyond a few hundred. *Representative democracies* are thus much more common. In these types of democracies, people elect officials to represent them in legislative votes on matters affecting the population.

Representative democracy is more practical than direct democracy in a society of any significant size, but political scientists cite another advantage of representative democracy. At least in theory, it ensures that the individuals who govern a society and in other ways help a society function are the individuals who have the appropriate talents, skills, and knowledge to do so. In this way of thinking, the masses of people are, overall, too uninformed, too uneducated, and too uninterested to run a society themselves. Representative democracy thus allows for "the cream to rise to the top" so that the people who actually govern a society are the most qualified to perform this essential task (Seward, 2010). Although this argument has much merit, it is also true that many of the individuals who do get elected to office turn out to be ineffective and/or corrupt. Regardless of our political orientations,

Americans can think of many politicians to whom these labels apply, from presidents down to local officials. As we discuss in Chapter 14 "Politics and Government", Section 14.4 "Politics in the United States" in relation to political lobbying, elected officials may also be unduly influenced by campaign contributions from corporations and other special-interest groups. To the extent this influence occurs, representative democracy falls short of the ideals proclaimed by political theorists.

The defining feature of representative democracy is voting in elections. When the United States was established more than 230 years ago, most of the world's governments were monarchies or other authoritarian regimes (discussed shortly). Like the colonists, people in these nations chafed under arbitrary power. The example of the American Revolution and the stirring words of its Declaration of Independence helped inspire the French Revolution of 1789 and other revolutions since, as people around the world have died in order to win the right to vote and to have political freedom.

Democracies are certainly not perfect. Their decision-making process can be quite slow and inefficient; as just mentioned, decisions may be made for special interests and not "for the people"; and, as we have seen in earlier chapters, pervasive inequalities of social class, race and ethnicity, gender, and age can exist. Moreover, in not all democracies have all people enjoyed the right to vote. In the United States, for example, African Americans could not vote until after the Civil War, with the passage of the 15th Amendment in 1870, and women did not win the right to vote until 1920, with the passage of the 19th Amendment.

In addition to generally enjoying the right to vote, people in democracies also have more freedom than those in other types of governments. Figure 14.1 "Freedom Around the World (Based on Extent of Political Rights and Civil Liberties)" depicts the nations of the world according to the extent of their political rights and civil liberties. The freest nations are found in North America, Western Europe, and certain other parts of the world, while the least free lie in Asia, the Middle East, and Africa.

Figure 14.1 Freedom Around the World (Based on Extent of Political Rights and Civil Liberties)

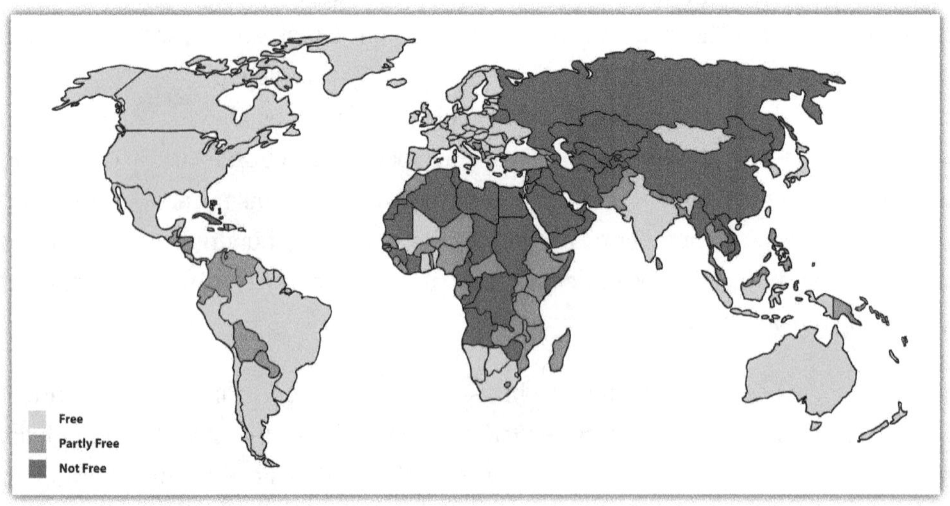

Source: Adapted from Freedom House. (2010). Map of freedom in the world. Retrieved from http://www.freedomhouse.org/template.cfm?page=363&year=2010.

Monarchy

Monarchy is a political system in which power resides in a single family that rules from one generation to the next generation. The power the family enjoys is *traditional authority*, and many monarchs command respect because their subjects bestow this type of authority on them. Other monarchs, however, have ensured respect through arbitrary power and even terror. Royal families still rule today, but their power has declined from centuries ago. Today the Queen of England holds a largely ceremonial position, but her predecessors on the throne wielded much more power.

Queen Elizabeth II of England holds a largely ceremonial position, but earlier English monarchs held much more power.

Wikimedia Commons – CC BY-SA 2.0.

This example reflects a historical change in types of monarchies from absolute monarchies to constitutional monarchies (Finer, 1997). In *absolute monarchies*, the royal family claims a divine right to rule and exercises considerable power over their kingdom. Absolute monarchies were common in both ancient (e.g., Egypt) and medieval (e.g., England and China) times. In reality, the power of many absolute monarchs was not totally absolute, as kings and queens had to keep in mind the needs and desires of other powerful parties, including the clergy and nobility. Over time, absolute monarchies gave way to *constitutional monarchies*. In these monarchies, the royal family serves a symbolic and ceremonial role and enjoys little, if any, real power. Instead the executive and legislative branches of government—the prime minister and parliament in several nations—run the government, even if the royal family continues to command admiration and respect. Constitutional monarchies exist today in several nations, including Denmark, Great Britain, Norway, Spain, and Sweden.

Authoritarianism and Totalitarianism

Authoritarianism and totalitarianism are general terms for nondemocratic political systems ruled by an individual or a group of individuals who are not freely elected by their populations and who often exercise arbitrary power. To be more specific, **authoritarianism** refers to political systems in which an individual or a group of individuals holds power, restricts or prohibits popular participation in governance, and represses dissent. **Totalitarianism** refers to political systems that include all the features of authoritarianism but are even more repressive as they try to regulate and control all aspects of citizens' lives and fortunes. People can be imprisoned for deviating from acceptable practices or may even be killed if they dissent in the mildest of ways. The purple nations in Figure 14.1 "Freedom Around the World (Based on Extent of Political Rights and Civil Liberties)" are mostly totalitarian regimes, and the orange ones are authoritarian regimes.

Compared to democracies and monarchies, authoritarian and totalitarian governments are more unstable politically. The major reason for this is that these governments enjoy no legitimate authority. Instead their power rests on fear and repression. The populations of these governments do not willingly lend their obedience to their leaders and realize that their leaders are treating them very poorly; for both these reasons, they are more likely than populations in democratic states to want to rebel. Sometimes they do rebel, and if the rebellion becomes sufficiently massive and widespread, a revolution occurs. In contrast, populations in democratic states usually perceive that they are treated more or less fairly and, further, that they can change things they do not like through the electoral process. Seeing no need for revolution, they do not revolt.

Since World War II, which helped make the United States an international power, the United States has opposed some authoritarian and totalitarian regimes while supporting others. The Cold War pitted the United States and its allies against Communist nations, primarily the Soviet Union, China, Cuba, and North Korea. But at the same time the United States opposed these authoritarian governments, it supported many others, including those in Chile, Guatemala, and South Vietnam, that repressed and even murdered their own citizens who dared to engage in the kind of dissent constitutionally protected in the United States (Sullivan, 2008). Earlier in U.S. history, the federal and state governments repressed dissent by passing legislation that prohibited criticism of World War I and then by imprisoning citizens who criticized that war (Goldstein, 2001). During the 1960s and 1970s, the FBI, the CIA, and other federal agencies spied on tens of thousands of citizens who engaged in dissent protected by the First Amendment (Cunningham, 2004). While the United States remains a beacon of freedom and hope to much of the world's peoples, its own support for repression in the recent and more distant past suggests that eternal vigilance is needed to ensure that "liberty and justice for all" is not just an empty slogan.

Key Takeaways

- The major types of political systems are democracies, monarchies, and authoritarian and totalitarian regimes.
- Authoritarian and totalitarian regimes are more unstable politically because their leaders do not enjoy legitimate authority and instead rule through fear.

For Your Review

1. Why are democracies generally more stable than authoritarian or totalitarian regimes?
2. Why is legitimate authority as Max Weber conceived it not a characteristic of authoritarian or totalitarian regimes?

References

Cunningham, D. (2004). *There's something happening here: The new left, the Klan, and FBI counterintelligence*. Berkeley: University of California Press.

Finer, S. E. (1997). *The history of government from the earliest times*. New York, NY: Oxford University Press.

Goldstein, R. J. (2001). *Political repression in modern America from 1870 to 1976* (Rev. ed.). Urbana: University of Illinois Press.

Seward, M. (2010). *The representative claim*. New York, NY: Oxford University Press.

Sullivan, M. (2008). *American adventurism abroad: Invasions, interventions, and regime changes since World War II* (Rev. and expanded ed.). Malden, MA: Blackwell.

14.3 Theories of Power and Society

Learning Objectives

1. Explain why veto-group competition is functional for society according to pluralist theory.
2. Outline the power-elite theory of C. Wright Mills.
3. Evaluate pluralist and elite theories.

These remarks raise some important questions: Just how democratic is the United States? Whose interests do our elected representatives serve? Is political power concentrated in the hands of a few or widely dispersed among all segments of the population? These and other related questions lie at the heart of theories of power and society. Let's take a brief look at some of these theories.

Pluralist Theory: A Functionalist Perspective

Recall (from Chapter 1 "Sociology and the Sociological Perspective") that the smooth running of society is a central concern of functionalist theory. When applied to the issue of political power, functionalist theory takes the form of **pluralist theory**, which says that political power in the United States and other democracies is dispersed among several "veto groups" that compete in the political process for resources and influence. Sometimes one particular veto group may win and other times another group may win, but in the long run they win and lose equally and no one group has any more influence than another (Dahl, 1956).

This photo of a labor strike depicts an example of the competition between two veto groups, labor and management, that characterizes American democracy. Pluralist theory assumes that veto groups win and lose equally in the long run and that no one group has more influence than another group.

peoplesworld – Chicago Teachers Strike 014 – CC BY-NC 2.0.

As this process unfolds, says pluralist theory, the government might be an active participant, but it is an impartial participant. Just as parents act as impartial arbiters when their children argue with each other, so does the government act as a neutral referee to ensure that the competition among veto groups is done fairly, that no group acquires undue influence, and that the needs and interests of the citizenry are kept in mind.

The process of veto-group competition and its supervision by the government is functional for society, according to pluralist theory, for three reasons. First, it ensures that conflict among the groups is channeled within the political process instead of turning into outright hostility. Second, the competition among the veto groups means that all of these groups achieve their goals to at least some degree. Third, the government's supervision helps ensure that the outcome of the group competition benefits society as a whole.

Elite Theories: Conflict Perspectives

Several **elite theories** dispute the pluralist model. According to these theories, power in democratic societies is concentrated in the hands of a few wealthy individuals and organizations—or *economic elites*—that exert inordinate influence on the government and can shape its decisions to benefit their own interests. Far from being a neutral referee over competition among veto groups, the government is said to be controlled by economic elites or at least to cater to their needs and interests. As should be clear, elite theories fall squarely within the conflict perspective as outlined in Chapter 1 "Sociology and the Sociological Perspective".

Perhaps the most famous elite theory is the *power-elite theory* of C. Wright Mills (1956). According to Mills, the **power elite** is composed of government, big business, and the military, which together constitute a *ruling class* that controls society and works for its own interests, not for the interests of the citizenry. Members of the power elite, Mills said, see each other socially and serve together on the boards of directors of corporations, charitable organizations, and other bodies. When cabinet members, senators, and top generals and other military officials retire, they often become corporate executives. Conversely, corporate executives often become cabinet members and other key political appointees. This circulation of the elites helps ensure their dominance over American life.

Mills's power-elite model remains popular, but other elite theories exist. They differ from Mills's model in several ways, including their view of the composition of the ruling class. Several theories see the ruling class as composed mostly of the large corporations and wealthiest individuals and see government and the military serving the needs of the ruling class rather than being part of it, as Mills implied. G. William Domhoff (2010) says that the ruling class is composed of the richest 0.5% to 1% of the population, who control more than half the nation's wealth, sit on the boards of directors just mentioned, and are members of the same social clubs and other voluntary organizations. Their control of corporations and other economic and political bodies helps maintain their inordinate influence over American life and politics.

Other elite theories say the government is more autonomous—not as controlled by the ruling class—than Mills thought. Sometimes the government takes the side of the ruling class and corporate interests, but sometimes it opposes them. Such *relative autonomy*, these theories say, helps ensure the legitimacy of the state, because if it always took the side of the rich it would look too biased and lose the support of the populace. In the long run, then, the relative autonomy of the state helps maintain ruling class control by making the masses feel the state is impartial when in fact it is not (Thompson, 1975).

Assessing Pluralist and Elite Theories

As a way of understanding power in the United States and other democracies, pluralist and elite theories have much to offer, but neither type of theory presents a complete picture. Pluralist theory errs in seeing all special-interest groups as equally powerful and influential. Certainly the success of lobbying groups such as the National Rifle Association and the American Medical Association in the political and economic systems is testimony to the fact that not all special-interest groups are created equal. Pluralist theory also errs in seeing the government as a neutral referee. Sometimes the government does take sides on behalf of corporations by acting, or failing to act, in a certain way.

For example, U.S. antipollution laws and regulations are notoriously weak because of the influence of major corporations on the political process. Through their campaign contributions, lobbying, and other types of influence, corporations help ensure that pollution controls are kept as weak as possible (Simon, 2008). This problem received worldwide attention in the spring of 2010 after the explosion of an oil rig owned by BP, a major oil and energy company, spilled tens of thousands of barrels of oil into the Gulf of Mexico in the biggest environmental disaster in U.S. history. As the oil was leaking, news reports emphasized that individuals or political action committees (PACs) associated with BP had contributed $500,000 to U.S. candidates in the 2008 elections, that BP had spent $16 million on lobbying in 2009, and that the oil and gas industry had spent tens of millions of dollars on lobbying that year (Montopoli, 2010).

Although these examples support the views of elite theories, the theories also paint too simple a picture. They err in implying that the ruling class acts as a unified force in protecting its interests. Corporations sometimes do oppose each other for profits and sometimes even steal secrets from each other, and governments do not always support the ruling class. For example, the U.S. government has tried to reduce tobacco smoking despite the wealth and influence of tobacco companies. While the United States, then, does not entirely fit the pluralist vision of power and society, neither does it entirely fit the elite vision. Yet the evidence that does exist of elite influence on the American political and economic systems reminds us that government is not always "of the people, by the people, for the people," however much we may wish it otherwise.

Key Takeaways

- Pluralist theory assumes that political power in democracies is dispersed among several veto groups that compete equally for resources and influence.
- Elite theories assume that power is instead concentrated in the hands of a few wealthy individuals and organizations that exert inordinate influence on the government and can shape its decisions to benefit their

own interests.

For Your Review

1. Do pluralist or elite theories better explain the exercise of power in the United States? Explain your answer.

References

Dahl, R. A. (1956). *A preface to democratic theory*. Chicago, IL: University of Chicago Press.

Domhoff, G. W. (2010). *Who rules America: Challenges to corporate and class dominance* (6th ed.). New York, NY: McGraw Hill.

Mills, C. W. (1956). *The power elite*. New York, NY: Oxford University Press.

Montopoli, B. (2010, May 5). BP spent millions on lobbying, campaign donations. *CBS News*. Retrieved from http://www.cbsnews.com/8301-503544_503162-20004240-20503544.html.

Simon, D. R. (2008). *Elite deviance* (9th ed.). Boston, MA: Allyn & Bacon.

Thompson, E. P. (1975). *Whigs and hunters: The origin of the Black Act*. London, England: Allen Lane.

14.4 Politics in the United States

Learning Objectives

1. Understand what political ideology is and how it is measured.
2. List the correlates of political participation.
3. Discuss the controversy over political lobbying.

The discussion of theories of power and society began to examine the U.S. political system. Let's continue this examination by looking at additional features of U.S. politics. We start with political ideology and political parties.

Political Ideology and Political Parties

Two central components of modern political systems are (a) the views that people hold of social, economic, and political issues and (b) the political organizations that try to elect candidates to represent those views. We call these components *political ideology* and *political parties*, respectively.

Political Ideology

Political ideology is a complex concept that is often summarized by asking people whether they are liberal or conservative. For example, the GSS asks, "I'm going to show you a seven-point scale on which the political views that people might hold are arranged from extremely liberal to extremely conservative. Where would you place yourself on this scale?" For convenience's sake, responses to this question in the 2008 GSS are grouped into three categories—liberal, moderate, and conservative—and displayed in Figure 14.2 "Political Ideology". We see that moderates slightly outnumber conservatives, who in turn outnumber liberals.

Figure 14.2 Political Ideology

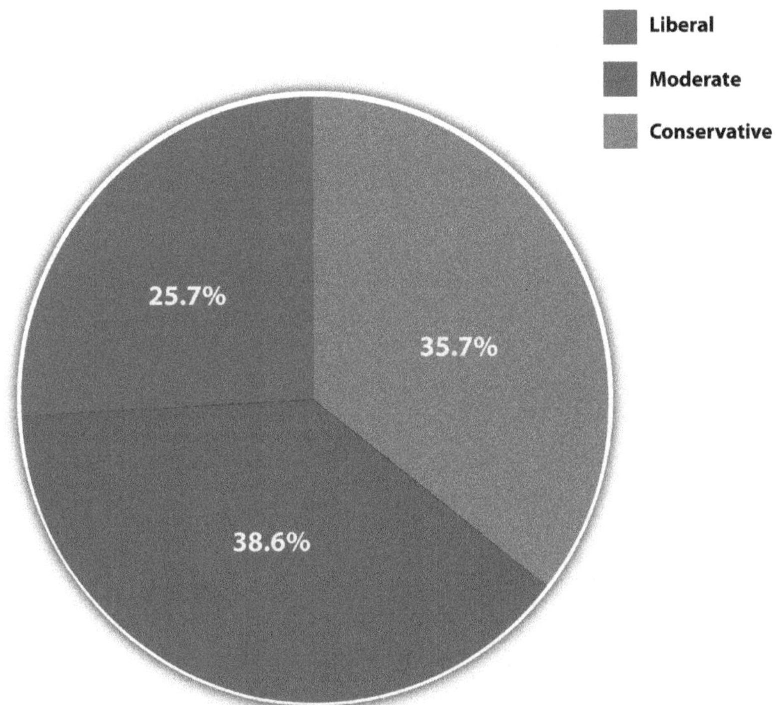

Source: Data from General Social Survey, 2008.

This is a common measure of political ideology, but social scientists often advise using a series of questions to measure political ideology, which consists of views on at least two sorts of issues, social and economic. *Social issues* concern attitudes on such things as abortion and other controversial behaviors and government spending on various social problems. *Economic issues,* on the other hand, concern such things as taxes and the distribution of income and wealth. People can hold either liberal or conservative attitudes on both types of issues, but they can also hold mixed attitudes: liberal on social issues and conservative on economic ones, or conservative on social issues and liberal on economic ones. Educated, wealthy people, for example, may want lower taxes (generally considered a conservative view) but also may favor abortion rights and oppose the death penalty (both considered liberal positions). In contrast, less educated, working-class people may favor higher taxes for the rich (a liberal view, perhaps) but oppose abortion rights and favor the death penalty.

We also see mixed political ideologies when we look at African Americans' and whites' views on social and economic issues. African Americans tend to be more conservative than whites on social issues but more liberal on economic concerns. This tendency is depicted in Figure 14.3 "Race and Attitudes on Social and Economic Issues", which shows responses to GSS questions on whether homosexual sex is wrong, a social issue, and on whether the government should reduce income differences between the rich and poor, an economic issue. African Americans are more likely than whites to take a conservative view on the social issue by thinking that homosexual sex is wrong but are more likely to take a liberal view on the economic issue by thinking that the government should reduce income inequality.

Figure 14.3 Race and Attitudes on Social and Economic Issues

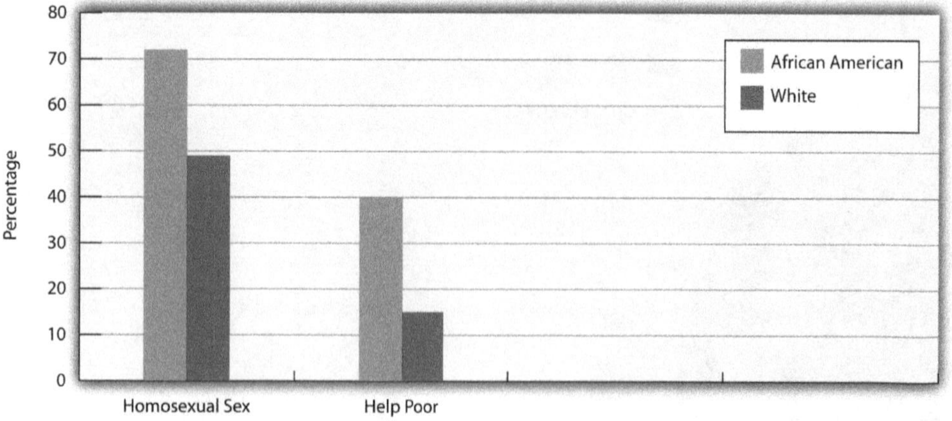

Percentage saying that homosexual sex is always wrong and percentage saying that government should help the poor.

Source: Data from General Social Survey, 2008.

Political Parties

People's political ideologies often lead them to align with a **political party**, or an organization that supports particular political positions and tries to elect candidates to office to represent those positions. The two major political parties in the United States are, of course, the Democratic and Republican parties. However, in a national poll in October 2009, 44% of Americans called themselves Independents, compared to 30% who called themselves Democrats and only 17% who called themselves Republicans. The number of Americans who consider themselves Independents, then, almost equals the number who consider themselves either Democrats or Republicans (Rich, 2009).

The number of Americans who call themselves political Independents almost equals the number who consider themselves either a Democrat or a Republican.

DonkeyHotey – Republican Elephant & Democratic Donkey – Icons – CC BY 2.0.

An important question for U.S. democracy is how much the Democratic and Republican parties differ on the major issues of the day. The Democratic Party is generally regarded as more liberal, while the Republican Party is regarded as more conservative, and voting records of their members in Congress generally reflect this difference. However, some critics of the U.S. political system think that in the long run there is not a "dime's worth of difference," to quote an old saying, between the two parties, as they both ultimately work to preserve corporate interests and capitalism itself (Alexander, 2008). In their view, the Democratic Party is part of the problem, as it tries only to reform the system instead of bringing about the far-reaching changes said to be needed to achieve true equality for all. These criticisms notwithstanding, it is true that neither of the major U.S. parties is as left-leaning as some of the major ones in Western Europe. The two-party system in the United States may encourage middle-of-the road positions, as each party is afraid that straying too far from the middle will cost it votes. In contrast, because several Western European nations have a greater number of political parties, a party may feel freer to advocate more polarized political views (Muddle, 2007).

Some scholars see this encouragement of middle-of-the-road positions (and thus political stability) as a benefit of the U.S. two-party system, while other scholars view it as a disadvantage because it limits the airing of views that might help a nation by challenging the status quo (Richard, 2010). One thing is clear: in the U.S. two-party model, it is very difficult for a third party to make significant inroads, because the United States lacks a *proportional representation system*, found in many other democracies, in which parties win seats proportional to their share of the vote (Disch, 2002). Instead, the United States has a winner-takes-all system in which seats go to the candidates with the most votes. Even though the Green Party has several million supporters across the country, for example, its influence on national policy has been minimal, although it has had more influence in a few local elections.

Whether or not the Democratic and Republican parties are that different, U.S. citizens certainly base their party preference in part on their own political ideology. Evidence of this is seen in Figure 14.4 "Political Ideology and Political Party Preference", which shows the political ideology of GSS respondents who call themselves Democrats or Republicans. People's political ideology is clearly linked to their party preference.

Figure 14.4 Political Ideology and Political Party Preference

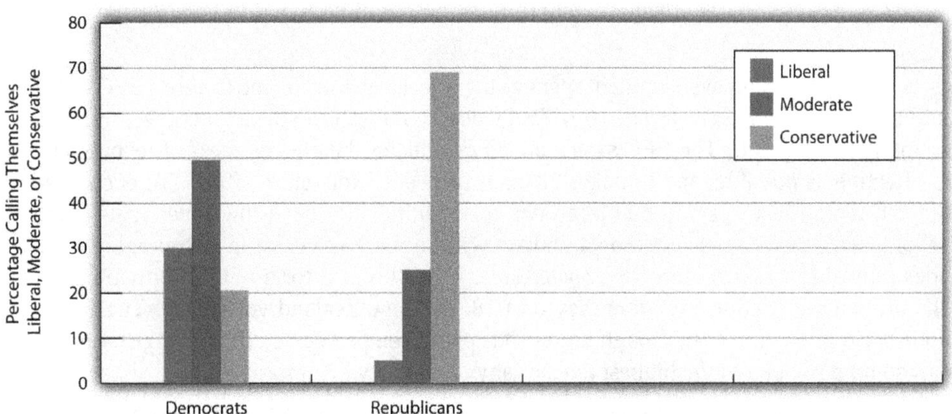

Source: Data from General Social Survey, 2008.

Political Participation

Perhaps the most important feature of representative democracies is that people vote for officials to represent their views, interests, and needs. For a democracy to flourish, political theorists say, it is essential that "regular" people participate in the political process. The most common type of political participation, of course, is voting; other political activities include campaigning for a candidate, giving money to a candidate or political party, and writing letters to political officials. Despite the importance of these activities in a democratic society, not very many people take part in them. Voting is also relatively uncommon among Americans, as the United States ranks lower than most of the world's democracies in voter turnout (International Institute for Democracy and Electoral Assistance, 2009).

Learning From Other Societies

Increasing Voter Turnout in the United States

As the text discusses, the United States ranks low internationally in voter turnout. In 2008, about 133 million Americans voted in the federal elections. Although this number sounds impressive, it represented only about 57% of the voting-age population. Thus, only slightly more than half of Americans voted in 2008 despite the excitement produced by having the first African American, Barack Obama, on the national ticket for one of the two major political parties.

Why does the United States not rank higher in voter turnout? Although the text discusses voter apathy among Americans, other factors also make a difference. In this regard, the experience of other democratic nations provides guidance for increasing voter turnout in the United States, which trails these nations by a substantial margin.

Why is voter turnout so much higher in other democracies? Voting scholars emphasize that certain practices that make it easier or more difficult to register and vote can greatly influence voter turnout (Ellis, Gratschew, Pammett, & Thiessen, 2006). These practices include (a) allowing same-day voter registration versus requiring registration a month or more before an election, (b) having multiple voting days versus a single voting day, (c) having the election on a weekend or rest day versus a weekday or workday, (d) having or not having alternative voting procedures (e.g., mail-in voting), and (e) having more or fewer polling places. Nations differ in the extent to which they adopt and use practices that promote registration and voting, and they also differ in the degree to which they use voter information and advertising campaigns and other efforts to encourage voting. In general, these practices and efforts are more often found in other democracies than in the United States.

For example, New Zealand has a well-staffed and well-funded agency, the Electoral Enrolment Centre (EEC), that regularly engages in intensive publicity campaigns to encourage New Zealanders to register to vote. (Voter registration in New Zealand is compulsory, but voting itself is not.) The EEC systematically evaluates the effectiveness of its publicity efforts to ensure that they are as effective as possible, and it makes changes as needed for future efforts. To encourage registration among young people and members of certain ethnic groups that traditionally have low voter registration rates, the EEC visits their households with the hope that personal contact will be more effective in encouraging them to register. The EEC also provides provisional registration for 17-year-olds, who fill out a form with information that is automatically transferred to the official registration list when they turn 18, the New Zealand voting age. The EEC's many efforts combine with compulsory registration, even though no one has ever been prosecuted for not registering, to produce a voter registration rate of about 95%, one of the highest rates of any democracy (Thiessen, 2006).

In Sweden, a national agency called the Election Authority (translated from its Swedish name, *Valmyndigheten*) produces information campaigns before each election to educate eligible voters about the candidates and issues at stake. Advertisements and other information are transmitted through television, radio, and Internet outlets and also sent via email. A special effort is made to distribute materials at locations where large groups of people routinely gather, such as businesses, shopping areas, and bus and train stations. Special effort is also made to reach groups with traditionally lower voting rates, including young people, immigrants, and people with disabilities (Lemón & Gratschew, 2006). Elections in

Sweden occur on the third Sunday of September; because fewer people work on Sunday, it is thought that Sunday voting increases voter turnout.

Although many factors explain why voter turnout varies among the democracies of the world, many scholars think that the practices and efforts just listed help raise voter turnout. If so, the United States may be able to increase its own turnout by adopting and/or increasing its use of these practices and efforts. In this regard, the United States has much to learn from other democracies.

Not only is U.S. voter turnout relatively low in the international sphere, but it has also declined since the 1960s (see Figure 14.5 "Trends in Voter Turnout in Nonpresidential Election Years"). One factor that explains these related trends is *voter apathy*, prompted by a lack of faith that voting makes any difference and that government can be helpful. This lack of faith is often called **political alienation**. As Figure 14.6 "Trust in U.S. Government" dramatically shows, lack of faith in the government has dropped drastically since the 1960s, thanks in part, no doubt, to the Vietnam War during the 1960s and 1970s and the Watergate scandal of 1970s.

Figure 14.5 Trends in Voter Turnout in Nonpresidential Election Years

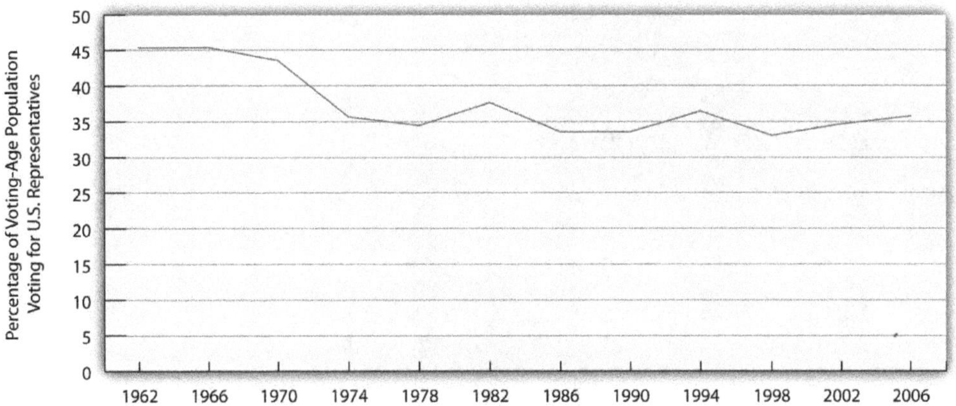

Source: Data from U.S. Census Bureau. (2009). *Statistical abstract of the United States: 2009*. Washington, DC: U.S. Government Printing Office. Retrieved from http://www.census.gov/compendia/statab.

Figure 14.6 Trust in U.S. Government

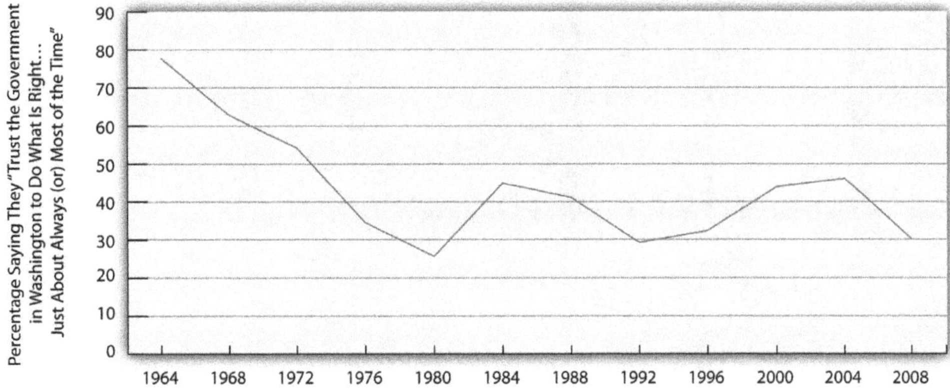

Source: Data from American National Election Study.

Yet it is also true that voter turnout varies greatly among Americans. In general, several sets of factors make citizens more likely to vote and otherwise participate in the political process (Burns, Schlozman, & Verba, 2001). These factors, or correlates of political participation, include (a) high levels of *resources*, including time, money, and communication skills; (b) *psychological engagement* in politics, including a strong interest in politics and a sense of trust in the political process; and (c) involvement in *interpersonal networks* of voluntary and other organizations that recruit individuals into political activity. Thus people who are, for example, wealthier, more interested in politics, and more involved in interpersonal networks are more likely to vote and take part in other political activities than those who are poorer, less interested in politics, and less involved in interpersonal networks. Reflecting these factors, age and high socioeconomic status are especially important predictors of voting and other forms of political participation, as citizens who are older, wealthier, and more educated tend to have more resources, to be more interested in politics and more trustful of the political process, and to be more involved in interpersonal networks. As a result, they are much more likely to vote than people who are younger and less educated (see Figure 14.7 "Age, Education, and Percentage Voting, 2008").

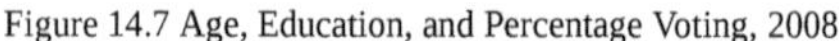

Figure 14.7 Age, Education, and Percentage Voting, 2008

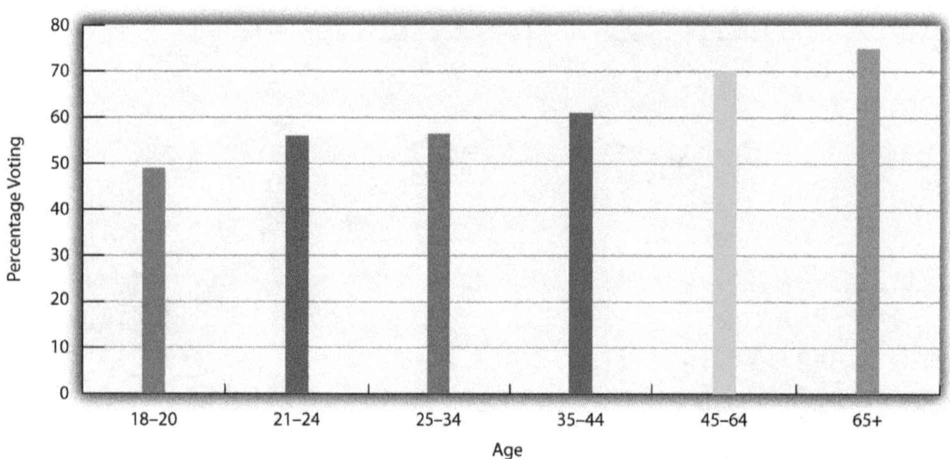

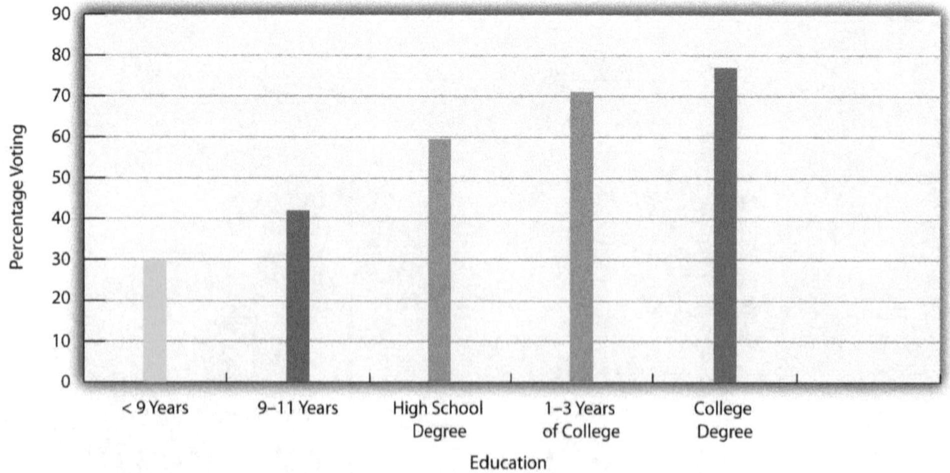

Source: Data from U.S. Census Bureau. (2009). *Statistical abstract of the United States: 2009*. Washington, DC: U.S. Government Printing Office. Retrieved from http://www.census.gov/compendia/statab.

The lower voting rates for young people might surprise many readers: because many college students are politically active, it seems obvious that they should vote at high levels. That might be true for some college students, but the bulk of college students are normally not politically active, because they are too busy with their studies, extracurricular activities, and/or work, and because they lack sufficient interest in politics to be active. It is also true that there are many more people aged 18 to 24 (about 30 million), the traditional ages for college attendance, than there are actual college students (11 million). In view of these facts, the lower voting rates for young people are not that surprising after all.

Sociology Making a Difference

Felony Disenfranchisement

As the text discusses, one of the fundamental principles of a democracy is a right to vote. Political scholars consider voting and other forms of political participation as important activities in their own right but also as effective means to help integrate people into a society and to give them a sense of civic responsibility. Some scholars thus mourn a decline they perceive in *civic engagement*, as they feel that this decline is undermining social integration and civic responsibility.

For these reasons, the *disenfranchisement* (deprival of voting rights) of convicted felons has attracted much attention in recent years, as most states have laws that take away the right to vote if someone has been convicted of a felony: 48 states prohibit felons from voting while they are incarcerated, with only Maine and Vermont permitting voting while someone is behind bars. Felony disenfranchisement often continues once someone is released from prison, as 35 states prohibit voting while an offender is still on parole; two states, Kentucky and Virginia, prohibit voting permanently for anyone with a felony conviction. According to The Sentencing Project, a nonprofit organization advocating for sentencing reform, about 5.3 million Americans cannot vote because they have felony convictions. Because felons are disproportionately likely to be poor and African American or Latino, felony disenfranchisement has a disproportionate impact on the African American and Latino communities. An estimated 13% of African American men cannot vote for this reason.

Two pioneering scholars on felony disenfranchisement are sociologists Jeff Manza and Christopher Uggen, who documented the impact of felony disenfranchisement on actual election outcomes. They found that felony disenfranchisement affected the results of seven U.S. Senate elections and led to a Republican majority in the U.S. Senate in the early 1980s and then again in the mid-1990s. They also found that felony disenfranchisement almost certainly affected the outcome of a presidential election. In 2000, George W. Bush was declared the winner of the presidential election in Florida, and thus of the whole nation, by only 537 votes. An estimated 600,000 felons were not allowed to vote in Florida in 2000. They were disproportionally African American and would thus have been very likely to vote for Bush's opponent, Al Gore, if they had been allowed to vote. Felony disenfranchisement thus affected the outcome of the 2000 presidential election and the course of U.S. domestic and foreign policy in the ensuing years.

In documenting the impact of felony disenfranchisement on actual elections, the research by sociologists Manza and Uggen helped underscore the need to reform felony disenfranchisement laws. Once again, sociology is helping make a difference. (Manza & Uggen, 2008; The Sentencing Project, 2010)

Race and ethnicity also influence voting. In particular, Asians and Latinos vote less often than African Americans and whites among the citizen population. In 2008, roughly 65% of African Americans and 66% of non-Latino whites voted, compared to only 48% of Asians and 50% of Latinos (File & Cressey, 2010). The voting percentage for African Americans and Latinos was the highest for these groups since the Census Bureau began measuring citizens' voting in 1996, possibly because of the presence of Barack Obama, who considers himself an African American, on the Democratic ticket.

Voting rates differ by race and ethnicity. In particular, Asians and Latinos are less likely than African Americans and non-Latino whites to vote.

Bread for the World – Latino family – CC BY-NC-ND 2.0.

The impact of age, race/ethnicity, education, and other variables on voting rates provides yet another example of the sociological perspective. As should be evident, they show that these aspects of our social backgrounds affect a very important political behavior, voting, even if we are not conscious of this effect.

Special-Interest Groups and Lobbying: The Influence Industry

From 2003 through 2008, **political action committees (PACs)**, organizations formed by special-interest groups to raise and spend money on behalf of political campaigns and various political issues, contributed more than $1 billion to the election campaigns of candidates for Congress (U.S. Census Bureau, 2010). In 2008 and 2009, special-interest groups spent more than $6.3 billion to lobby Congress, the White House, and various federal agencies. They employed some 14,000 lobbyists, who outnumbered members of Congress 27 to 1, on such issues as health care, military spending, and transportation (Center for Responsive Politics, 2009). The top lobbying group in 2009 was the U.S. Chamber of Commerce, which spent more than $65 million to lobby Congress, federal agencies, and other parties; in second place was Exxon Mobil, which spent more than $21 million. The pharmaceutical and health products industry as a whole spent more than $200 million in 2009, while the insurance industry spent $122 million, oil and gas companies $121 million, electric and gas utilities $108 million, and business associations $93 million.

The U.S. Chamber of Commerce and other lobbying groups spent more than $6.3 billion in 2008 and 2009 on their efforts to influence federal legislation and regulations.

NCinDC – U.S. Chamber of Commerce headquarters – CC BY-ND 2.0.

Dubbed the "influence industry," these lobbying efforts have long been criticized as having too much impact on federal policy and spending priorities. It is logical to think that the influence industry spends these large sums of money because it hopes to affect key legislation and other policies. This expenditure raises an important question: are PACs, special-interest groups, and lobbying good or bad for democracy? This question goes to the heart of the debate between pluralist and elite theories, discussed earlier. Representatives of PACs and lobbying groups say it is important that elected officials hear all possible views on complex issues and that these organizations merely give money to help candidates who already think a certain way. Supporting this notion, public officials say they listen to all sides before making up their minds and are not unduly influenced by the money they receive and by the lobbying they encounter. For their part, pluralist theorists say PACs and lobbying groups are examples of the competing veto groups favored by the pluralist model and that no one special-interest group wins out in the long run (James, 2004).

Critics of the influence industry say that its impact is both large and unwarranted and charge that PACs, lobbyists, and the special-interest groups that fund them are buying influence and subverting democracy. Ample evidence exists, they say, of the impact of the influence industry on which candidates get elected and on which legislation gets passed or not passed. While special-interest groups for various sides of an issue do compete with each other, they continue, corporations and their PACs are much better funded and much more influential than the groups that oppose them (Clawson, Neustadtl, & Weller, 1998; Cook & Chaddock, 2009). These concerns motivated sharp criticism of a U.S. Supreme Court decision in January 2010 regarding election advertisements by corporations and unions. The decision permitted corporations and unions to use money from their general funds to pay for ads urging the public to vote for or against a particular candidate. Because corporations have much more money than unions, the ruling was widely seen as being a procorporation one. The majority decision said that prohibitions of such advertising violated freedom of political speech by corporations and unions, while the minority decision said the ruling "threatens to undermine the integrity of elected institutions across the nation" (Vogel, 2010).

Key Takeaways

- Political ideology consists of views on social issues and on economic issues. An individual might be liberal or conservative on both kinds of issues, or liberal on one kind of issue and conservative on the other kind.
- Almost as many Americans consider themselves Independents as consider themselves either Democrats or Republicans. Although some scholars say that there is not very much difference between the Democratic and Republican parties, liberals are more likely to consider themselves Democrats, and conservatives are more likely to consider themselves Republicans.
- Voting is the most common form of political participation. Several factors influence the likelihood of voting, and socioeconomic status (education and income) is a very important factor in this regard.
- Political lobbying remains a very controversial issue, and critics continue to charge that the "influence industry" has too much sway over American social and economic policy.

For Your Review

1. Do you consider yourself to be politically conservative, moderate, or liberal? What are examples of some of your beliefs that lead you to define yourself in this manner?
2. Is political lobbying good or bad overall for the United States? Explain your answer.

References

Alexander, S. A. (2008, January 10). Socialists emerging as Democrats, Republicans lose voter confidence. *American Chronicle*. Retrieved from http://www.americanchronicle.com/articles/view/48507.

Burns, N., Schlozman, K. L., & Verba, S. (2001). *The private roots of public action: Gender, equality, and political participation*. Cambridge, MA: Harvard University Press.

Center for Responsive Politics. (2009). Lobbying database. Retrieved from http://www.opensecrets.org/lobbyists.

Clawson, D., Neustadtl, A., & Weller, M. (1998). *Dollars and votes: How business campaign contributions subvert democracy*. Philadelphia, PA: Temple University Press.

Cook, D. T., & Chaddock, G. R. (2009, September 28). How Washington lobbyists peddle power. *The Christian Science Monitor*. Retrieved from http://www.csmonitor.com/USA/Politics/2009/0928/how-washington-lobbyists-peddle-power.

Disch, L. J. (2002). *The tyranny of the two-party system*. New York, NY: Columbia University Press.

Ellis, A., Gratschew, M., Pammett, J. H., & Thiessen, E. (Eds.). (2006). *Engaging the electorate: Initiatives to promote voter turnout from around the world*. Stockholm, Sweden: International Institute for Democracy and Electoral Assistance.

File, T., & Cressey, S. (2010). *Voting and registration in the election of 2008* (Current Population Report P20-562). Washington, DC: U.S. Census Bureau.

International Institute for Democracy and Electoral Assistance. (2009). Voter turnout. Retrieved from http://www.idea.int/vt/index.cfm.

James, M. R. (2004). *Deliberative democracy and the plural polity*. Lawrence: University Press of Kansas.

Lemón, K., & Gratschew, M. (2006). Educating the voter about the electoral process: The Swedish election authority. In A. Ellis, M. Gratschew, J. H. Pammett, & E. Thiessen (Eds.), *Engaging the electorate: Initiatives to promote voter turnout from around the world* (pp. 32–34). Stockholm, Sweden: International Institute for Democracy and Electoral Assistance.

Manza, J., & Uggen, C. (2008). *Locked out: Felon disenfranchisement and American democracy*. New York, NY: Oxford University Press.

Muddle, C. (2007). *Populist radical right parties in Europe*. New York, NY: Cambridge University Press.

Rich, F. (2009, November 1). The G.O.P. Stalinists invade upstate New York. *The New York Times*, p. WK8.

Richard, J. (2010, May 29). One cheer for the two-party system. *OpEdNews*. Retrieved from http://www.opednews.com/articles/One-Cheer-for-the-Two-Part-by-Jerome-Richard-100527-100148.html.

Thiessen, E. (2006). Making the electoral process as easy as possible: Elections New Zealand. In A. Ellis, M. Gratschew, J. H. Pammett, & E. Thiessen (Eds.), *Engaging the electorate: Initiatives to promote voter turnout from around the world* (pp. 28–30). Stockholm, Sweden: International Institute for Democracy and Electoral Assistance.

The Sentencing Project. (2010). *Felony disenfranchisement laws in the United States*. Washington, DC: Author.

U.S. Census Bureau. (2010). *Statistical abstract of the United States: 2010*. Washington, DC: U.S. Government Printing Office. Retrieved from http://www.census.gov/compendia/statab.

Vogel, K. P. (2010, January 21). Court decision opens floodgates for corporate cash. *Politico*. Retrieved from http://www.politico.com/news/stories/0110/31786.html.

14.5 War and Terrorism

Learning Objectives

1. Distinguish international war and civil war.
2. List the major types of terrorism.
3. Evaluate the law enforcement and structural-reform approaches for dealing with terrorism.

War and terrorism are both forms of armed conflict that aim to defeat an opponent. Although war and terrorism have been part of the human experience for thousands of years, their manifestation in the contemporary era is particularly frightening, thanks to evermore powerful weapons, including nuclear arms, that threaten human existence. Because governments play a fundamental role in both war and terrorism, a full understanding of politics and government requires examination of key aspects of these two forms of armed conflict. We start with war and then turn to terrorism.

War

Wars occur both between nations and within nations, when two or more factions engage in armed conflict. War between nations is called **international war**, while war within nations is called **civil war**. The most famous civil war to Americans, of course, is the American Civil War, also called the War Between the States, that pitted the North against the South from 1861 through 1865. More than 600,000 soldiers on both sides died on the battlefield or from disease, a number that exceeds American deaths in all the other wars the United States has fought. More than 100 million soldiers and civilians are estimated to have died during the international and civil wars of the 20th century (Leitenberg, 2006). Many novels and films depict the heroism with which soldiers fight, while other novels and films show the horror that war entails. As Sydney H. Schanberg (2005), a former *New York Times* reporter who covered the wars in Vietnam and Cambodia, has bluntly observed, "'History,' Hegel said, 'is a slaughterhouse.' And war is how the slaughter is carried out."

Explaining War

Scholars have attempted to explain why human beings wage war. A popular explanation comes from the field of evolutionary biology and claims that a tendency toward warfare is hardwired into our genetic heritage because it conferred certain evolutionary advantages.

Wikimedia Commons – public domain.

The enormity of war has stimulated scholarly interest in why humans wage war. A popular explanation for war derives from evolutionary biology. According to this argument, war is part of our genetic heritage because the humans who survived tens of thousands of years ago were those who were most able, by virtue of their temperament and physicality, to take needed resources from other humans they attacked and to defend themselves from attackers. In this manner, a genetic tendency for physical aggression and warfare developed and thus still exists today. In support of this evolutionary argument, some scientists note that chimpanzees and other primates also engage in group aggression against others of their species (Wrangham, 2004).

However, other scientists dispute the evolutionary explanation for several reasons (Begley, 2009; Roscoe, 2007). First, the human brain is far more advanced than the brains of other primates, and genetic instincts that might drive their behavior do not necessarily drive human behavior. Second, many societies studied by anthropologists have been very peaceful, suggesting that a tendency to warfare is more cultural than biological. Third, most people are not violent, and most soldiers have to be resocialized (in boot camp or its equivalent) to overcome their deep moral convictions against killing; if warlike tendencies were part of human genetic heritage, these convictions would not exist.

If warfare is not biological in origin, then it is best understood as a social phenomenon, one that has its roots in the decisions of political and military officials. Sometimes, as with the U.S. entrance into World War II after Pearl Harbor, these decisions are sincere and based on a perceived necessity to defend a nation's people and resources, and sometimes these decisions are based on cynicism and deceit. A prime example of the latter dynamic is the Vietnam War. The 1964 Gulf of Tonkin Resolution, in which Congress authorized President Lyndon Johnson to wage an undeclared war in Vietnam, was passed after North Vietnamese torpedo boats allegedly attacked U.S. ships. However, later investigation revealed that the attack never occurred and that the White House lied to

Congress and the American people (Wells, 1994). Four decades later, questions of possible deceit were raised after the United States began the war against Iraq because of its alleged possession of weapons of mass destruction. These weapons were never found, and critics charged that the White House had fabricated and exaggerated evidence of the weapons in order to win public and congressional support for the war (Danner, 2006).

The Cost of War

Beyond its human cost, war also has a heavy financial cost. From 2003 through 2010, the war in Iraq cost the United States some $750 billion (O'Hanlon & Livingston, 2010); from 2001 through 2010, the war in Afghanistan cost the United States more than $300 billion (Mulrine, 2010). These two wars thus cost almost $1.1 trillion combined, for an average of $100 billion per year during this period. This same yearly amount could have paid for one year's worth (California figures) of **all** the following (National Priorities Project, 2010):

- 231,000 police officers,
- 11.4 million children receiving low-income health care (Medicaid),
- 2.6 million students receiving full tuition scholarships at state universities,
- 2.5 million Head Start slots for children, and
- 280,000 elementary school teachers.

These trade-offs bring to mind President Eisenhower's famous observation, quoted in Chapter 13 "Work and the Economy", that "every gun that is made, every warship launched, every rocket fired, signifies in the final sense, a theft from those who hunger and are not fed, those who are cold and are not clothed." War indeed has a heavy human cost, not only in the numbers of dead and wounded, but also in the diversion of funds from important social functions.

Terrorism

Terrorism is hardly a new phenomenon, but Americans became horrifyingly familiar with it on September 11, 2001, when about 3,000 people died after planes hijacked by Middle Eastern terrorists crashed into the World Trade Center, the Pentagon, and a field in Pennsylvania. The attacks on 9/11 remain in the nation's consciousness, and many readers may know someone who died on that terrible day. The attacks also spawned a vast national security network that now reaches into almost every aspect of American life. This network is so secretive, so huge, and so expensive that no one really knows precisely how large it is and how much it costs (Priest & Arkin, 2010). Questions of how best to deal with terrorism continue to be debated, and there are few, if any, easy answers to these questions.

Not surprisingly, sociologists and other scholars have written many articles and books about terrorism. This section draws on their work to discuss the definition of terrorism, the major types of terrorism, explanations for terrorism, and strategies for dealing with terrorism. An understanding of all these issues is essential to make sense of the concern and controversy about terrorism that exists throughout the world today.

Defining Terrorism

As the attacks on 9/11 remind us, terrorism involves the use of indiscriminate violence to instill fear in a population and thereby win certain political, economic, or social objectives.

Cliff – September 11th, 2001 – CC BY 2.0.

There is an old saying that "one person's freedom fighter is another person's terrorist." This saying indicates one of the defining features of terrorism but also some of the problems in coming up with a precise definition of it. Some years ago, the Irish Republican Army (IRA) waged a campaign of terrorism against the British government and its people as part of its effort to drive the British out of Northern Ireland. Many people in Northern Ireland and elsewhere hailed IRA members as freedom fighters, while many other people condemned them as cowardly terrorists. Although most of the world labeled the 9/11 attacks as terrorism, some individuals applauded them as acts of heroism. These examples indicate that there is only a thin line, if any, between terrorism on the one hand and freedom fighting and heroism on the other hand. Just as beauty is in the eyes of the beholder, so is terrorism. The same type of action is either terrorism or freedom fighting, depending on who is characterizing the action.

Although dozens of definitions of **terrorism** exist, most take into account what are widely regarded as the three defining features of terrorism: (a) the use of violence; (b) the goal of making people afraid; and (c) the desire for political, social, economic, and/or cultural change. A popular definition by political scientist Ted Robert Gurr (1989, p. 201) captures these features: "the use of unexpected violence to intimidate or coerce people in the pursuit of political or social objectives."

Types of Terrorism

When we think about this definition, 9/11 certainly comes to mind, but there are, in fact, several kinds of terrorism—based on the identity of the actors and targets of terrorism—to which this definition applies. A typology of terrorism again by Gurr (1989) is popular: (a) vigilante terrorism, (b) insurgent terrorism, (c) transnational (or international) terrorism, and (d) state terrorism.

Vigilante terrorism is committed by private citizens against other private citizens. Sometimes the motivation is racial, ethnic, religious, or other hatred, and sometimes the motivation is to resist social change. The violence of racist groups like the Ku Klux Klan was vigilante terrorism, as was the violence used for more than two centuries by white Europeans against Native Americans. What we now call "hate crime" is a contemporary example of vigilante terrorism.

Insurgent terrorism is committed by private citizens against their own government or against businesses and institutions seen as representing the "establishment." Insurgent terrorism is committed by both left-wing groups and right-wing groups and thus has no political connotation. U.S. history is filled with insurgent terrorism, starting with some of the actions the colonists waged against British forces before and during the American Revolution, when "the meanest and most squalid sort of violence was put to the service of revolutionary ideals and objectives" (Brown, 1989, p. 25). An example here is tarring and feathering: hot tar and then feathers were smeared over the unclothed bodies of Tories. Some of the labor violence committed after the Civil War also falls under the category of insurgent terrorism, as does some of the violence committed by left-wing groups during the 1960s and 1970s. A relatively recent example of right-wing insurgent terrorism is the infamous 1995 bombing of the federal building in Oklahoma City by Timothy McVeigh and Terry Nichols that killed 168 people.

Transnational terrorism is committed by the citizens of one nation against targets in another nation. This is the type that has most concerned Americans at least since 9/11, yet 9/11 was not the first time Americans had been killed by international terrorism. A decade earlier, a truck bombing at the World Trade Center killed six people and injured more than 1,000 others. In 1988, 189 Americans were among the 259 passengers and crew who died when a plane bound for New York exploded over Lockerbie, Scotland; agents from Libya were widely thought to have planted the bomb. Despite all these American deaths, transnational terrorism has actually been much more common in several other nations: London, Madrid, and various cities in the Middle East have frequently been the targets of international terrorists.

State terrorism involves violence by a government that is meant to frighten its own citizens and thereby stifle their dissent. State terrorism may involve mass murder, assassinations, and torture. Whatever its form, state terrorism has killed and injured more people than all the other kinds of terrorism combined (Wright, 2007). Genocide, of course is the most deadly type of state terrorism, but state terrorism also occurs on a smaller scale. As just one example, the violent response of Southern white law enforcement officers to the civil rights protests of the 1960s amounted to state terrorism, as officers murdered or beat hundreds of activists during this period. Although state terrorism is usually linked to authoritarian regimes, many observers say that the U.S. government also engaged in state terror during the 19th century, when U.S. troops killed thousands of Native Americans (Brown, 1971).

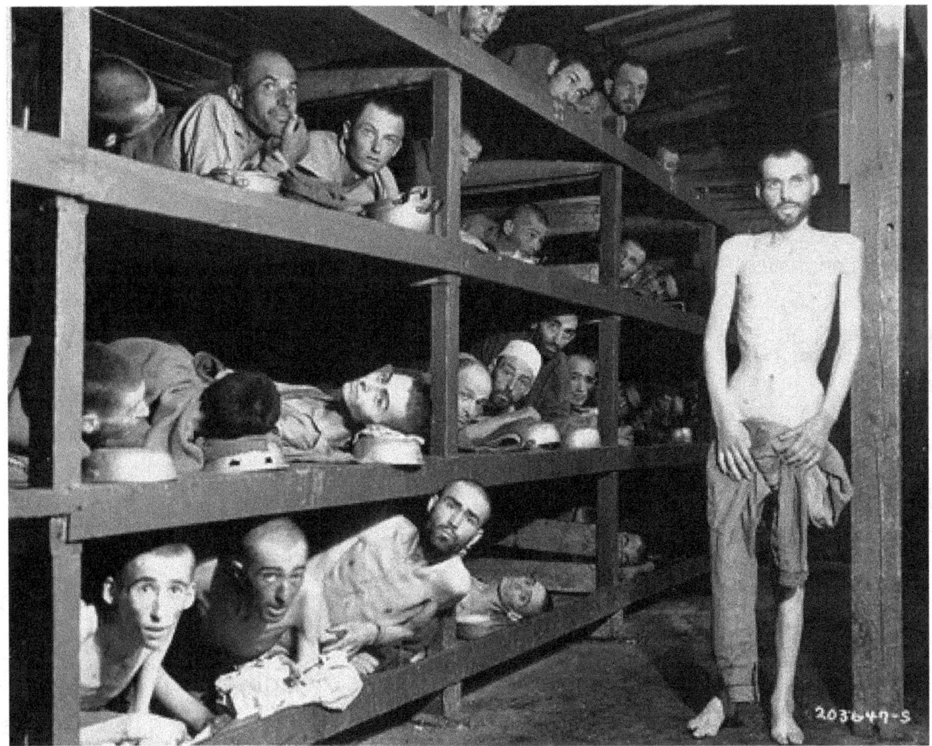

Genocide is the most deadly type of state terrorism. The Nazi holocaust killed some 6 million Jews and 6 million other people.

Wikimedia Commons – public domain.

Explaining Terrorism

Why does terrorism occur? It is easy to assume that terrorists must have psychological problems that lead them to have sadistic personalities, and that they are simply acting irrationally and impulsively. However, most scholars agree that terrorists are psychologically normal despite their murderous violence and, in fact, are little different from other types of individuals who use violence for political ends. As one scholar observed,

> Most terrorists are no more or less fanatical than the young men who charged into Union cannonfire at Gettysburg or those who parachuted behind German lines into France. They are no more or less cruel and coldblooded than the Resistance fighters who executed Nazi officials and collaborators in Europe, or the American GI's ordered to "pacify" Vietnamese villages. (Rubenstein, 1987, p. 5)

Contemporary terrorists tend to come from well-to-do families and to be well-educated themselves; ironically, their social backgrounds are much more advantaged in these respects than are those of common street criminals, despite the violence they commit.

If terrorism cannot be said to stem from individuals' psychological problems, then what are its roots? In answering this question, many scholars say that terrorism has structural roots. In this view, terrorism is a rational response, no matter horrible it may be, to perceived grievances regarding economic, social, and/or political conditions

(LaFree & Dugan, 2009). The heads of the U.S. 9/11 Commission, which examined the terrorist attacks of that day, reflected this view in the following assessment:

> We face a rising tide of radicalization and rage in the Muslim world—a trend to which our own actions have contributed. The enduring threat is not Osama bin Laden but young Muslims with no jobs and no hope, who are angry with their own governments and increasingly see the United States as an enemy of Islam. (Kean & Hamilton, 2007, p. B1)

As this assessment indicates, structural conditions do not justify terrorism, of course, but they do help explain why some individuals decide to commit it.

Stopping Terrorism

Efforts to stop terrorism take two forms (White, 2012). The first form involves attempts to capture known terrorists and to destroy their camps and facilities and is commonly called a *law enforcement* or *military* approach. The second form stems from the recognition of the structural roots of terrorism just described and is often called a *structural-reform* approach. Each approach has many advocates among terrorism experts, and each approach has many critics.

Law enforcement and military efforts have been known to weaken terrorist forces, but terrorist groups have persisted despite these measures. Worse yet, these measures may ironically inspire terrorists to commit further terrorism and increase public support for their cause. Critics also worry that the military approach endangers civil liberties, as the debate over the U.S. response to terrorism since 9/11 so vividly illustrates (Cole & Lobel, 2007). This debate took an interesting turn in late 2010 amid the increasing use of airport scanners that generate body images. Many people criticized the scanning as an invasion of privacy, and they also criticized the invasiveness of the "pat-down" searches that were used for people who chose not to be scanned (Reinberg, 2010).

In view of all these problems, many terrorism experts instead favor the structural-reform approach, which they say can reduce terrorism by improving or eliminating the conditions that give rise to the discontent that leads individuals to commit terrorism. Here again the assessment of the heads of the 9/11 Commission illustrates this view:

> We must use all the tools of U.S. power—including foreign aid, educational assistance and vigorous public diplomacy that emphasizes scholarship, libraries and exchange programs—to shape a Middle East and a Muslim world that are less hostile to our interests and values. America's long-term security relies on being viewed not as a threat but as a source of opportunity and hope. (Kean & Hamilton, 2007, p. B1)

Key Takeaways

- War takes an enormous human and financial toll. Many critics dispute the evolutionary argument that a tendency toward warfare is hardwired into human genetics.

- Terrorism involves the use of intimidating violence to achieve political ends. Whether a given act of violence is perceived as terrorism or as freedom fighting often depends on whether someone approves of the goal of the violence.
- The law enforcement/military approach to countering terrorism may weaken terrorist groups, but it also may increase their will to fight and popular support for their cause and endanger civil liberties.

For Your Review

1. Do you think the evolutionary explanation of warfare makes sense? Why or why not?
2. Which means of countering terrorism do you prefer more, the law enforcement/military approach or the structural-reform approach? Explain your answer.

Toward a More Perfect Union: What Sociology Suggests

Sociological theory and research are once again relevant for addressing certain issues raised by studies of politics and government. Several issues especially come to mind.

The first is the possible monopolization and misuse of power by a relatively small elite composed of the powerful or the "haves," as they are often called. If elite theories are correct, this small elite takes advantage of its place at the top of American society and its concomitant wealth, power, and influence to benefit its own interests. Sociological work that supports the assumptions of elite theories does not necessarily imply any specific measures to reduce the elite's influence, but it does suggest the need for consumer groups and other public-interest organizations to remain vigilant about elite misuse of power and to undertake efforts to minimize this misuse.

The second issue is the lack of political participation from the segments of American society that traditionally have very little power: the poor, the uneducated, and people of color. Because voting and other forms of political participation are much more common among the more educated and wealthy segments of society, the relative lack of participation by those without power helps ensure that they remain without power. Sociological research on political participation thus underscores the need to promote voting and other political participation by the poor and uneducated if American democratic and egalitarian ideals are to be achieved. This need also applies to reversing the disenfranchisement of felons, as discussed in the "Sociology Making a Difference" box that appeared earlier in this chapter.

A third issue is how best to counter terrorism. Sociology's emphasis on the need to address the structural roots of social issues has been a theme of this book and was first highlighted in the discussion of the sociological imagination in Chapter 1 "Sociology and the Sociological Perspective". This emphasis is reflected in the structural-reform strategy for countering terrorism discussed in Chapter 14 "Politics and Government", Section 14.5 "War and Terrorism". Efforts to counter terrorism that do not address the structural conditions underlying many acts of terrorism ultimately help ensure that new acts of terrorism will arise. To say this is not meant to excuse or justify any terrorism, but it is meant to recognize an important reality that must be kept in mind as the world continues to deal with the threat of terrorism.

References

Begley, S. (2009, June 29). Don't blame the caveman. *Newsweek* 52–62.

Brown, D. A. (1971). *Bury my heart at Wounded Knee: An Indian history of the American West.* New York, NY: Holt, Rinehart and Winston.

Brown, R. M. (1989). Historical patterns of violence. In T. R. Gurr (Ed.), *Violence in America: Protest, rebellion, reform* (Vol. 2, pp. 23–61). Newbury Park, CA: Sage.

Cole, D., & Lobel, J. (2007). *Less safe, less free: Why America is losing the war on terror.* New York, NY: New Press.

Danner, M. (2006). *The secret way to war: The Downing Street memo and the Iraq War's buried history.* New York, NY: New York Review of Books.

Gurr, T. R. (1989). Political terrorism: Historical antecedents and contemporary trends. In T. R. Gurr (Ed.), *Violence in America: Protest, rebellion, reform* (Vol. 2, pp. 201–230). Newbury Park, CA: Sage.

Kean, T. H., & Hamilton, L. H. (2007, September 9). Are we safer today? *The Washington Post,* p. B1.

LaFree, G., & Dugan, L. (2009). Research on terrorism and countering terrorism. *Crime and Justice: A Review of Research, 39,* 413–477.

Leitenberg, M. (2006). Deaths in wars and conflicts in the 20th century. Ithaca, NY: Cornell University Peace Studies Program.

Mulrine, A. (2010, June 11). Will cost of Afghanistan War become a 2010 campaign issue? *U.S.News & World Report.* Retrieved from http://politics.usnews.com/news/articles/2010/2006/2011/will-cost-of-afghanistan-war-become-a-2010-campaign-issue.html.

National Priorities Project. (2010). Federal budget trade-offs. Retrieved from http://www.nationalpriorities.org/tradeoffs?location_type=1&state=6&program=707&tradeoff_item_item=999&submit_tradeoffs=Get+Trade+Off.

O'Hanlon, M. E., & Livingston, I. (2010). *Iraq index: Tracking variables of reconstruction & security in post-Saddam Iraq.* Washington, DC: Brookings Institution.

Priest, D., & Arkin, W. M. (2010, July 20). A hidden world, growing beyond control. *The Washington Post,* p. A1.

Reinberg, S. (2010, November 23). Airport body scanners safe, experts say. *BusinessWeek.* Retrieved from http://www.businessweek.com/lifestyle/content/healthday/646395.html.

Roscoe, P. (2007). Intelligence, coalitional killing, and the antecedents of war. *American Anthropologist, 109*(3), 487–495.

Rubenstein, R. E. (1987). *Alchemists of revolution: Terrorism in the modern world.* New York, NY: Basic Books.

Schanberg, S. H. (2005, May 10). Not a pretty picture. *The Village Voice,* p. 1.

Wells, T. (1994). *The war within: America's battle over Vietnam.* Berkeley: University of California Press.

White, J. R. (2012). *Terrorism and homeland security: An introduction* (7th ed.). Belmont, CA: Wadsworth.

Wrangham, R. W. (2004). Killer species. *Daedalus, 133*(4), 25–35.

Wright, T. C. (2007). *State terrorism in Latin America: Chile, Argentina, and international human rights*. Lanham, MD: Rowman & Littlefield.

14.6 End-of-Chapter Material

Summary

1. Politics involves the distribution of power in a society. Three types of authority, or the legitimate use of power, exist. Traditional authority is based on a society's customs and traditions, while rational-legal authority stems from a society's rules. Charismatic authority derives from an individual's extraordinary personal qualities and is the most unstable of the three types of authority, because it ends with the death of the person who possesses this type of authority.
2. The major types of political systems in the world today are democracies, monarchies, and authoritarian and totalitarian regimes. Few pure democracies exist, and most take the form of representative democracies, in which people elect officials to represent their views and interests. Monarchies are much less common than they used to be, and today's monarchs primarily serve symbolic and ceremonial functions. Authoritarian and totalitarian regimes exist in different parts of the world and typically involve harsh repression of their citizenries.
3. Pluralist and elite theories both try to explain the distribution and exercise of power. Pluralist theory says that society is composed of special-interest groups whose competition ensures that the interests of all segments of society are represented. Elite theory says that power is concentrated in the hands of relatively few individuals and organizations. Mills's power-elite model attributes power to the nation's top government, business, and military leaders, while other elite theories say that power is concentrated in the hands of a relatively few families at the top of the socioeconomic system.
4. Political ideology is usually classified along a continuum from very liberal to very conservative. It consists of social and economic views on which some people may hold inconsistent positions; for example, they may hold liberal views on social issues but conservative views on economic issues. Political participation is the cornerstone of democracy, but in the United States relatively few people vote or otherwise take part in the political process. Voter apathy and alienation help account for the lack of voting, as do low levels of education and other variables.
5. Lobbying by various special-interest groups certainly influences the political process, but the different parties disagree on whether lobbying is good or bad. To the extent that lobbying by corporate interests unduly influences the political process, elite theories of the political system are supported.
6. War takes an enormous human and financial toll. Some scientists believe that a tendency toward warfare is hardwired into human genes because of the evolutionary advantages it once conferred, but other scientists question this explanation on several grounds.
7. Terrorism involves the use of violence to intimidate people to gain political, social, or economic advantages. Debate continues on whether a law enforcement/military approach or a structural-reform approach is the better method for countering terrorism.

Using Sociology

You are a key aide to a U.S. senator who has been asked to participate on a university forum on voter apathy. The senator asks you to write a memo for her that outlines important steps that would help reduce apathy and increase voter turnout. What actions and policies do you recommend in the memo?

Chapter 15: The Family

Social Issues in the News

"Stabbing Conviction Upheld," the headline said. In January 2010, the North Carolina Court of Appeals upheld the conviction of a man who had attempted to kill his wife in December 2007 by stabbing her repeatedly in the face and back with a butcher knife. The victim was on her way to deliver Christmas presents to her parents, but her husband attacked her because he thought she was having an affair. With a sentence of almost 21 years, the husband is due to be released from prison 3 days before Christmas in 2027. (Schulman, 2010)

Once upon a time, domestic violence did not exist, or so the popular television shows of the 1950s would have had us believe. Neither did single-parent households, gay couples, interracial couples, mothers working outside the home, heterosexual spouses deciding not to have children, or other family forms and situations that are increasingly common today. Domestic violence existed, of course, but it was not something that television shows and other popular media back then depicted. The other family forms and situations also existed to some degree but have become much more common today.

The 1950s gave us *Leave It to Beaver* and other television shows that depicted loving, happy, "traditional" families living in the suburbs. The father worked outside the home, the mother stayed at home to take care of the kids and do housework, and their children were wholesome youngsters who rarely got into trouble and certainly did not use drugs or have sex. Today we have ABC's *Modern Family*, which features one traditional family (two heterosexual parents and their three children) and two nontraditional families (one with an older white man and a younger Latina woman and her child, and another with two gay men and their adopted child). Many other television shows today and in recent decades have featured divorced couples or individuals, domestic violence, and teenagers doing drugs or committing crime.

In the real world, we hear that parents are too busy working at their jobs to raise their kids properly. We hear of domestic violence like the sad story from North Carolina described at the start of this chapter. We hear of kids living without fathers, because their parents either are divorced or never were married in the first place. We hear of young people having babies, using drugs, and committing violence. We hear that the breakdown of the nuclear family, the entrance of women into the labor force, and the growth of single-parent households are responsible for these problems. Some observers urge women to work only part time or not at all so they can spend more time with their children. Some yearn wistfully for a return to the 1950s, when everything seemed so much easier and better. Children had what they needed back then: one parent to earn the money, and another parent to take care of them full time until they started kindergarten, when this parent would be there for them when they came home from school.

Families have indeed changed, but this yearning for the 1950s falls into what historian Stephanie Coontz (2000) once called the "nostalgia trap." The 1950s television shows did depict what some families were like back then, but they failed to show what many other families were like. Moreover, the changes in families since that time have probably not had the harmful effects that many observers allege. Historical and cross-cultural evidence even suggests that the *Leave It to Beaver*–style family of the 1950s was a relatively recent and atypical phenomenon and that many other types of families can thrive just as well as the 1950s television families did.

This chapter expands on these points and looks at today's families and the changes they have undergone. It also examines some of the controversies now surrounding families and relationships. We start with a cross-cultural and historical look at the family.

References

Coontz, S. (2000). *The way we never were: American families and the nostalgia trap.* New York, NY: Basic Books.

Schulman, M. (2010, January 7). Stabbing conviction upheld. *Hendersonville [NC] Times-News*. Retrieved from http://www.blueridgenow.com/article/20100107/SERVICES03/1071032.

15.1 The Family in Cross-Cultural and Historical Perspectives

Learning Objectives

1. Describe the different family arrangements that have existed throughout history.
2. Understand how the family has changed in the United States since the colonial period.
3. Describe why the typical family in the United States during the 1950s was historically atypical.

A **family** is a group of two or more people who are related by blood, marriage, adoption, or a mutual commitment and who care for one another. Defined in this way, the family is universal or nearly universal: some form of the family has existed in every society, or nearly every society, that we know about (Starbuck, 2010). Yet it is also true that many types of families have existed, and the cross-cultural and historical record indicates that these different forms of the family can all "work": they provide practical and emotional support for their members and they socialize their children.

Types of Families and Family Arrangements

It is important to keep this last statement in mind, because Americans until recently thought of only one type of family when they thought of the family at all, and that is the **nuclear family**: a married heterosexual couple and their young children living by themselves under one roof. The nuclear family has existed in most societies with which scholars are familiar, and several of the other family types we will discuss stem from a nuclear family. **Extended families**, for example, which consist of parents, their children, and other relatives, have a nuclear family at their core and were quite common in the preindustrial societies studied by George Murdock (Murdock & White, 1969) that make up the Standard Cross-Cultural Sample (see Figure 15.1 "Types of Families in Preindustrial Societies").

Figure 15.1 Types of Families in Preindustrial Societies

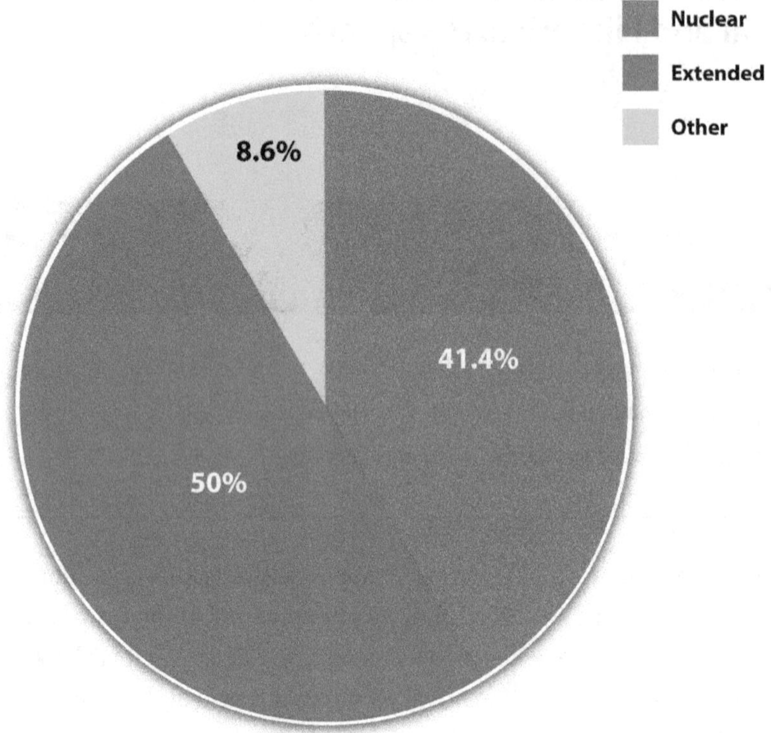

The nuclear family that was so popular on television shows during the 1950s remains common today but is certainly less common than during that decade.

Source: Data from Standard Cross-Cultural Sample.

Similarly, many *one-parent* families begin as (two-parent) nuclear families that dissolve upon divorce/separation or, more rarely, the death of one of the parents. In recent decades, one-parent families have become more common in the United States because of divorce and births out of wedlock, but they were actually very common throughout most of human history because many spouses died early in life and because many babies were born out of wedlock. We return to this theme shortly.

When Americans think of the family, they also think of a *monogamous* family. *Monogamy* refers to a marriage in which one man and one woman are married only to each other. That is certainly the most common type of marriage in the United States and other Western societies, but in some societies *polygamy*—the marriage of one person to two or more people at a time—is more common. In the societies where polygamy has prevailed, it has been much more common for one man to have many wives (*polygyny*) than for one woman to have many husbands (*polyandry*).

The selection of spouses also differs across societies but also to some degree within societies. The United States and many other societies primarily practice **endogamy**, in which marriage occurs within one's own social category or social group: people marry others of the same race, same religion, same social class, and so forth. Endogamy helps reinforce the social status of the two people marrying and to pass it on to any children they may have. Consciously or not, people tend to select spouses and mates (boyfriends or girlfriends) who resemble them not only in race, social class, and other aspects of their social backgrounds but also in appearance. As Chapter 1 "Sociology and the Sociological Perspective" pointed out, attractive people marry attractive people, ordinary-looking people marry ordinary-looking people, and those of us in between marry other in-betweeners. This tendency to choose and marry mates who resemble us in all of these ways is called *homogamy*.

Some societies and individuals within societies practice **exogamy**, in which marriage occurs across social categories or social groups. Historically exogamy has helped strengthen alliances among villages or even whole nations, when we think of the royalty of Europe, but it can also lead to difficulties. Sometimes these difficulties are humorous, and some of filmdom's best romantic comedies involve romances between people of very different backgrounds. As Shakespeare's great tragedy *Romeo and Juliet* reminds us, however, sometimes exogamous romances and marriages can provoke hostility among friends and relatives of the couple and even among complete strangers. Racial intermarriages, for example, are exogamous marriages, and in the United States they often continue to evoke strong feelings and were even illegal in some states until a 1967 Supreme Court decision (*Loving v. Virginia*, 388 U.S. 1) overturned laws prohibiting them.

Families also differ in how they trace their descent and in how children inherit wealth from their parents. *Bilateral descent* prevails in the United States and many other Western societies: we consider ourselves related to people on both parents' sides of the family, and our parents pass along their wealth, meager or ample, to their children. In some societies, though, descent and inheritance are **patrilineal** (children are thought to be related only to their father's relatives, and wealth is passed down only to sons), while in others they are **matrilineal** (children are thought to be related only to their mother's relatives, and wealth is passed down only to daughters).

Another way in which families differ is in their patterns of authority. In **patriarchal families**, fathers are the major authority figure in the family (just as in patriarchal societies men have power over women; see Chapter 11 "Gender and Gender Inequality"). Patriarchal families and societies have been very common. In **matriarchal families**, mothers are the family's major authority figure. Although this type of family exists on an individual basis, no known society has had matriarchal families as its primary family type. In **egalitarian families**, fathers and mothers share authority equally. Although this type of family has become more common in the United States and other Western societies, patriarchal families are still more common.

The Family Before Industrialization

Now that we are familiar with the basic types of family structures and patterns, let's take a quick look at the cross-cultural and historical development of the family. We will start with the family in preindustrial times, drawing on research by anthropologists and other scholars, and then move on to the development of the family in Western societies.

People in hunting-and-gathering societies probably lived in small groups composed of two or three nuclear families. These groupings helped ensure that enough food would be found for everyone to eat. While men tended to hunt and women tended to gather food and take care of the children, both sexes' activities were considered fairly equally important for a family's survival. In horticultural and pastoral societies, food was more abundant, and families' wealth depended on the size of their herds. Because men were more involved than women in herding, they acquired more authority in the family, and the family became more patriarchal than previously (Quale, 1992). Still, as Chapter 13 "Work and the Economy" indicated, the family continued to be the primary economic unit of society until industrialization.

Societies Without Nuclear Families

Although many preindustrial societies featured nuclear families, a few societies studied by anthropologists have not had them. One of these was the Nayar in southwestern India, who lacked marriage and the nuclear family. A woman would have several sexual partners during her lifetime, but any man with whom she had children had no responsibilities toward them. Despite the absence of a father, this type of family arrangement seems to have worked well for the Nayar (Fuller, 1976). Nuclear families are also mostly absent among many people in the West Indies. When a woman and man have a child, the mother takes care of the child almost entirely; the father provides for the household but usually lives elsewhere. As with the Nayar, this fatherless arrangement seems to have worked well in the parts of the West Indies where it is practiced (Smith, 1996).

A more contemporary setting in which the nuclear family is largely absent is the Israeli *kibbutz*, a cooperative agricultural community where all property is collectively owned. In the early years of the *kibbutzim* (plural of kibbutz), married couples worked for the whole kibbutz and not just for themselves. Kibbutz members would eat together and not as separate families. Children lived in dormitories from infancy on and were raised by nurses and teachers, although they were able to spend a fair amount of time with their birth parents. The children in a particular kibbutz grew up thinking of each other as siblings and thus tended to fall in love with people from outside the kibbutz (Garber-Talmon, 1972). Although the traditional family has assumed more importance in kibbutz life in recent years, extended families continue to be very important, with different generations of a particular family having daily contact (Lavee, Katz, & Ben-Dror, 2004).

These examples do not invalidate the fact that nuclear families are almost universal and important for several reasons we explore shortly. But they do indicate that the functions of the nuclear family can be achieved through other family arrangements. If that is true, perhaps the oft-cited concern over the "breakdown" of the 1950s-style nuclear family in modern America is at least somewhat undeserved. As indicated by the examples just given, children can and do thrive without two parents. To say this is meant neither to extol divorce, births out of wedlock, and fatherless families nor to minimize the problems they may involve. Rather, it is meant simply to indicate that the nuclear family is not the only viable form of family organization (Eshleman & Bulcroft, 2010).

In fact, although nuclear families remain the norm in most societies, in practice they are something of a historical rarity: many spouses used to die by their mid-40s, and many babies were born out of wedlock. In medieval Europe, for example, people died early from disease, malnutrition, and other problems. One consequence of early mortality was that many children could expect to outlive at least one of their parents and thus essentially were raised in one-parent families or in stepfamilies (Gottlieb, 1993).

The Family in the American Colonial Period

Moving quite a bit forward in history, different family types abounded in the colonial period in what later became the United States, and the nuclear family was by no means the only type. Nomadic Native American groups had relatively small nuclear families, while nonnomadic groups had larger extended families; in either type of society, though, "a much larger network of marital alliances and kin obligations [meant that]…no single family was forced to go it alone" (Coontz, 1995, p. 11). Nuclear families among African Americans slaves were very difficult to achieve, and slaves adapted by developing extended families, adopting orphans, and taking in other people not related by blood or marriage. Many European parents of colonial children died because average life expectancy was only 45 years. The one-third to one-half of children who outlived at least one of their parents lived in stepfamilies or with just their surviving parent. Mothers were so busy working the land and doing other tasks that they devoted relatively little time to child care, which instead was entrusted to older children or servants.

American Families During and After Industrialization

During industrialization, people began to move into cities to be near factories. A new division of labor emerged in many families: men worked in factories and elsewhere outside the home, while many women stayed at home to take care of children and do housework, including the production of clothing, bread, and other necessities, for which they were paid nothing (Gottlieb, 1993). For this reason, men's incomes increased their patriarchal hold over their families. In some families, however, women continued to work outside the home. Economic necessity dictated this: because families now had to buy much of their food and other products instead of producing them themselves, the standard of living actually declined for many families.

But even when women did work outside the home, men out-earned them because of discriminatory pay scales and brought more money into the family, again reinforcing their patriarchal hold. Over time, moreover, work outside the home came to be seen primarily as men's work, and keeping house and raising children came to be seen primarily as women's work. As Coontz (1997, pp. 55–56) summarizes this development,

> The resulting identification of masculinity with economic activities and femininity with nurturing care, now often seen as the "natural" way of organizing the nuclear family, was in fact a historical product of this 19th-century transition from an agricultural household economy to an industrial wage economy.

This marital division of labor began to change during the early 20th century. Many women entered the workforce in the 1920s because of a growing number of office jobs, and the Great Depression of the 1930s led even more women to work outside the home. During the 1940s, a shortage of men in shipyards, factories, and other workplaces because of World War II led to a national call for women to join the labor force to support the war effort and the national economy. They did so in large numbers, and many continued to work after the war ended. But as men came home from Europe and Japan, books, magazines, and newspapers exhorted women to have babies, and babies they did have: people got married at younger ages and the birth rate soared, resulting in the now famous *baby boom generation*. Meanwhile, divorce rates dropped. The national economy thrived as auto and other factory jobs multiplied, and many families for the first time could dream of owning their own homes. Suburbs sprang up, and many families moved to them. Many families during the 1950s did indeed fit the *Leave It to Beaver* model of the breadwinner-homemaker suburban nuclear family. Following the Depression of the 1930s and the war of the 1940s, the 1950s seemed an almost idyllic decade.

The Women in Military Service for America Memorial at the Arlington National Cemetery honors the service of women in the U.S. military. During World War II, many women served in the military, and many other women joined the labor force to support the war effort and the national economy.

Wally Gobetz – Virginia – CC BY-NC-ND 2.0.

Even so, less than 60% of American children during the 1950s lived in breadwinner-homemaker nuclear families. Moreover, many lived in poverty, as the poverty rate then was almost twice as high as it is today. Teenage pregnancy rates were about twice as high as today, even if most pregnant teens were already married or decided to get married because of the pregnancy. Although not publicized back then, alcoholism and violence in families were common. Historians have found that many women in this era were unhappy with their homemaker roles, Mrs. Cleaver (Beaver's mother) to the contrary, suffering from what Betty Friedan (1963) famously called the "feminine mystique."

In the 1970s, the economy finally worsened. Home prices and college tuition soared much faster than family incomes, and women began to enter the labor force as much out of economic necessity as out of simple desire for fulfillment. As Chapter 13 "Work and the Economy" noted, more than 60% of married women with children under 6 years of age are now in the labor force, compared to less than 19% in 1960. Working mothers are no longer a rarity.

In sum, the cross-cultural and historical record shows that many types of families and family arrangements have existed. Two themes relevant to contemporary life emerge from our review of this record. First, although nuclear families and extended families with a nuclear core have dominated social life, many children throughout history have not lived in nuclear families because of the death of a parent, divorce, or birth out of wedlock. The few societies that have not featured nuclear families seem to have succeeded in socializing their children and in accomplishing the other functions that nuclear families serve. In the United States, the nuclear family has historically been the norm, but, again, many children have been raised in stepfamilies or by one parent.

Second, the nuclear family model popularized in the 1950s, in which the male was the breadwinner and the female the homemaker, must be considered a blip in U.S. history rather than a long-term model. At least up to the beginning of industrialization and, for many families, after industrialization, women as well as men worked to sustain the family. Breadwinner-homemaker families did increase during the 1950s and have decreased since, but their appearance during that decade was more of a historical aberration than a historical norm. As Coontz (1995, p. 11) summarized the U.S. historical record, "American families always have been diverse, and the male breadwinner-female homemaker, nuclear ideal that most people associate with 'the' traditional family has predominated for only a small portion of our history." Commenting specifically on the 1950s, sociologist Arlene Skolnick (1991, pp. 51–52) similarly observed, "Far from being the last era of family normality from which current trends are a deviation, it is the family patterns of the 1950s that are deviant."

Key Takeaways

- Although the nuclear family has been very common, several types of family arrangements have existed throughout time and from culture to culture.
- Industrialization changed the family in several ways. In particular, it increased the power that men held within their families because of the earnings they brought home from their jobs.
- The male breadwinner–female homemaker family model popularized in the 1950s must be considered a temporary blip in U.S. history rather than a long-term model.

For Your Review

1. Write a brief essay in which you describe the advantages and disadvantages of the 1950s-type nuclear family in which the father works outside the home and the mother stays at home.
2. The text discusses changes in the family that accompanied economic development over the centuries. How do these changes reinforce the idea that the family is a social institution?

References

Coontz, S. (1997). *The way we really are: Coming to terms with America's changing families*. New York, NY: Basic Books.

Coontz, S. (1995, Summer). The way we weren't: The myth and reality of the "traditional" family. *National Forum: The Phi Kappa Phi Journal*, 11–14.

Eshleman, J. R., & Bulcroft, R. A. (2010). *The family* (12th ed.). Boston, MA: Allyn & Bacon.

Friedan, B. (1963). *The feminine mystique*. New York, NY: W. W. Norton.

Fuller, C. J. (1976). *The Nayars today*. Cambridge, England: Cambridge University Press.

Garber-Talmon, Y. (1972). *Family and community in the kibbutz*. Cambridge, MA: Harvard University Press.

Gottlieb, B. (1993). *The family in the Western world from the Black Death to the industrial age*. New York, NY: Oxford University Press.

Lavee, Y., Katz, R., & Ben-Dror, T. (2004). Parent-child relationships in childhood and adulthood and their effect on marital quality: A comparison of children who remained in close proximity to their parents and those who moved away. *Marriage & Family Review, 36*(3/4), 95–113.

Murdock, G. P., & White, D. R. (1969). Standard cross-cultural sample. *Ethnology, 8*, 329–369.

Quale, G. R. (1992). *Families in context: A world history of population*. New York, NY: Greenwood Press.

Skolnick, A. (1991). *Embattled paradise: The American family in an age of uncertainty*. New York, NY: Basic Books.

Smith, R. T. (1996). *The matrifocal family: Power, pluralism and politics*. New York, NY: Routledge.

Starbuck, G. H. (2010). *Families in context* (2nd ed.). Boulder, CO: Paradigm.

15.2 Sociological Perspectives on the Family

Learning Objective

1. Summarize understandings of the family as presented by functional, conflict, and social interactionist theories.

Sociological views on today's families generally fall into the functional, conflict, and social interactionist approaches introduced earlier in this book. Let's review these views, which are summarized in Table 15.1 "Theory Snapshot".

Table 15.1 Theory Snapshot

Theoretical perspective	Major assumptions
Functionalism	The family performs several essential functions for society. It socializes children, it provides emotional and practical support for its members, it helps regulate sexual activity and sexual reproduction, and it provides its members with a social identity. In addition, sudden or far-reaching changes in the family's structure or processes threaten its stability and weaken society.
Conflict	The family contributes to social inequality by reinforcing economic inequality and by reinforcing patriarchy. The family can also be a source of conflict, including physical violence and emotional cruelty, for its own members.
Symbolic interactionism	The interaction of family members and intimate couples involves shared understandings of their situations. Wives and husbands have different styles of communication, and social class affects the expectations that spouses have of their marriages and of each other. Romantic love is the common basis for American marriages and dating relationships, but it is much less common in several other contemporary nations.

Social Functions of the Family

Recall that the functional perspective emphasizes that social institutions perform several important functions to help preserve social stability and otherwise keep a society working. A functional understanding of the family thus stresses the ways in which the family as a social institution helps make society possible. As such, the family performs several important functions.

First, the family is the primary unit for *socializing children*. As previous chapters indicated, no society is possible without adequate socialization of its young. In most societies, the family is the major unit in which socialization happens. Parents, siblings, and, if the family is extended rather than nuclear, other relatives all help socialize children from the time they are born.

One of the most important functions of the family is the socialization of children. In most societies the family is the major unit through which socialization occurs.

Colleen Kelly – Kids Playing Monopoly Chicago – CC BY 2.0.

Second, the family is ideally a major source of *practical and emotional support* for its members. It provides them food, clothing, shelter, and other essentials, and it also provides them love, comfort, help in times of emotional distress, and other types of intangible support that we all need.

Third, the family helps *regulate sexual activity and sexual reproduction.* All societies have norms governing with whom and how often a person should have sex. The family is the major unit for teaching these norms and the major unit through which sexual reproduction occurs. One reason for this is to ensure that infants have adequate emotional and practical care when they are born. The *incest taboo* that most societies have, which prohibits sex between certain relatives, helps minimize conflict within the family if sex occurred among its members and to establish social ties among different families and thus among society as a whole.

Fourth, the family provides its members with a *social identity*. Children are born into their parents' social class, race and ethnicity, religion, and so forth. As we have seen in earlier chapters, social identity is important for our life chances. Some children have advantages throughout life because of the social identity they acquire from their parents, while others face many obstacles because the social class or race/ethnicity into which they are born is at the bottom of the social hierarchy.

Beyond discussing the family's functions, the functional perspective on the family maintains that sudden or far-reaching changes in conventional family structure and processes threaten the family's stability and thus that of society. For example, most sociology and marriage-and-family textbooks during the 1950s maintained that the male breadwinner–female homemaker nuclear family was the best arrangement for children, as it provided for a family's economic and child-rearing needs. Any shift in this arrangement, they warned, would harm children and by extension the family as a social institution and even society itself. Textbooks no longer contain this warning, but many conservative observers continue to worry about the impact on children of working mothers and one-parent families. We return to their concerns shortly.

The Family and Conflict

Conflict theorists agree that the family serves the important functions just listed, but they also point to problems within the family that the functional perspective minimizes or overlooks altogether.

First, the family as a social institution contributes to social inequality in several ways. The social identity it gives to its children does affect their life chances, but it also reinforces a society's system of stratification. Because families pass along their wealth to their children, and because families differ greatly in the amount of wealth they have, the family helps reinforce existing inequality. As it developed through the centuries, and especially during industrialization, the family also became more and more of a patriarchal unit (see earlier discussion), helping to ensure men's status at the top of the social hierarchy.

Second, the family can also be a source of conflict for its own members. Although the functional perspective assumes the family provides its members emotional comfort and support, many families do just the opposite and are far from the harmonious, happy groups depicted in the 1950s television shows. Instead, and as the news story that began this chapter tragically illustrated, they argue, shout, and use emotional cruelty and physical violence. We return to family violence later in this chapter.

Families and Social Interaction

Social interactionist perspectives on the family examine how family members and intimate couples interact on a daily basis and arrive at shared understandings of their situations. Studies grounded in social interactionism give us a keen understanding of how and why families operate the way they do.

Some studies, for example, focus on how husbands and wives communicate and the degree to which they communicate successfully (Tannen, 2001). A classic study by Mirra Komarovsky (1964) found that wives in blue-collar marriages liked to talk with their husbands about problems they were having, while husbands tended to be quiet when problems occurred. Such gender differences seem less common in middle-class families, where men are better educated and more emotionally expressive than their working-class counterparts. Another classic study by Lillian Rubin (1976) found that wives in middle-class families say that ideal husbands are ones who communicate well and share their feelings, while wives in working-class families are more apt to say that ideal husbands are ones who do not drink too much and who go to work every day.

Other studies explore the role played by romantic love in courtship and marriage. *Romantic love*, the feeling of deep emotional and sexual passion for someone, is the basis for many American marriages and dating relationships, but it is actually uncommon in many parts of the contemporary world today and in many of the societies anthropologists and historians have studied. In these societies, marriages are arranged by parents and other kin for economic reasons or to build alliances, and young people are simply expected to marry whoever is chosen for them. This is the situation today in parts of India, Pakistan, and other developing nations and was the norm for much of the Western world until the late 18th and early 19th centuries (Lystra, 1989).

Key Takeaways

- The family ideally serves several functions for society. It socializes children, provides practical and emotional support for its members, regulates sexual reproduction, and provides its members with a social identity.
- Reflecting conflict theory's emphases, the family may also produce several problems. In particular, it may contribute for several reasons to social inequality, and it may subject its members to violence, arguments, and other forms of conflict.
- Social interactionist understandings of the family emphasize how family members interact on a daily basis. In this regard, several studies find that husbands and wives communicate differently in certain ways that sometimes impede effective communication.

For Your Review

1. As you think how best to understand the family, do you favor the views and assumptions of functional theory, conflict theory, or social interactionist theory? Explain your answer.
2. Do you think the family continues to serve the function of regulating sexual behavior and sexual reproduction? Why or why not?

References

Komarovsky, M. (1964). *Blue-collar marriage*. New York, NY: Random House.

Lystra, K. (1989). *Searching the heart: Women, men, and romantic love in nineteenth-century America*. New York, NY: Oxford University Press.

Rubin, L. B. (1976). *Worlds of pain: Life in the working-class family*. New York, NY: Basic Books.

Tannen, D. (2001). *You just don't understand: Women and men in conversation*. New York, NY: Quill.

15.3 Family Patterns in the United States Today

Learning Objectives

1. Describe the major marriage and family arrangements in the United States today.
2. Discuss racial and ethnic differences in marriage and family arrangements.

It is time now to take a closer look at families in the United States today. Using U.S. census data (U.S. Census Bureau, 2010), we first sketch the major types of family arrangements that now exist.

Marriage

The census defines a household as being all the people who live together in a dwelling unit, whether or not they are related by blood, marriage, or adoption. About 117 million households exist in the United States. Of this number, about 67% are family households and 33% are nonfamily households. Most of the nonfamily households consist of only one person. About half of all households involve a married couple, and half do not involve a married couple.

This last figure should not suggest that marriage is unimportant. Only 26% of all adults (18 or older) have never been married, about 57% are currently married, 10% are divorced, and 6% are widowed (see Figure 15.2 "Marital Status of the U.S. Population, 2008, Persons 18 Years of Age or Older"). Because more than half of the never-married people are under 30, it is fair to say that many of them will be getting married sometime in the future. When we look just at people aged 45–54, about 88% are currently married or had been married at some point in their lives. These figures all indicate that marriage remains an important ideal in American life, even if not all marriages succeed.

Figure 15.2 Marital Status of the U.S. Population, 2008, Persons 18 Years of Age or Older

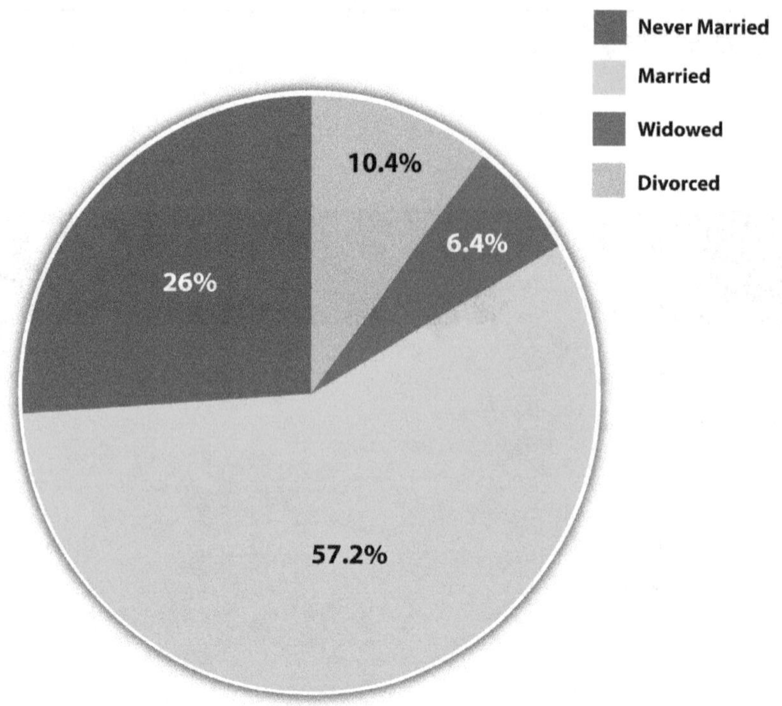

Source: Data from U.S. Census Bureau. (2010). *Statistical abstract of the United States: 2010*. Washington, DC: U.S. Government Printing Office. Retrieved from http://www.census.gov/compendia/statab.

Most marriages (96.1%) are *intraracial*, or between people of the same race, with only 3.9% of marriages between people of different races. As small as it is, this figure is 3 times greater than the 1.3% of marriages in 1980 that were *interracial*. Moreover, almost 15% of new marriages in 2008 were interracial. This increase (Chen, 2010) is reflected in dating patterns, as more than half of African American, Latino, and Asian adults have dated someone from a different racial/ethnic group (Qian, 2005). More than half of married Asians and Native Americans are in an interracial marriage, compared to about 40% of Latinos, 10% of African Americans, and 4% of whites. These percentages heavily reflect the numbers of people in these groups, because mathematically it is easiest to end up in an interracial relationship and marriage if there are relatively few people in one's own racial/ethnic group. Because there are so many whites compared to the other groups, more than 90% of all interracial marriages have a white spouse.

Although only 3.9% of marriages are between people of different races, this figure is 3 times greater than the proportion of marriages in 1980 that were interracial.

Jennifer Borget – CC BY-NC-ND 2.0.

It is interesting to see how the age at which people first get married has changed. Figure 15.3 "Median Age at First Marriage for Men and Women, 1890–2009" shows that age at first marriage declined gradually during the first half of the 20th century, before dropping more sharply between 1940 and 1950 because of World War II. It then rose after 1970 and today stands at almost 28 years for men and 26 years for women.

Figure 15.3 Median Age at First Marriage for Men and Women, 1890–2009

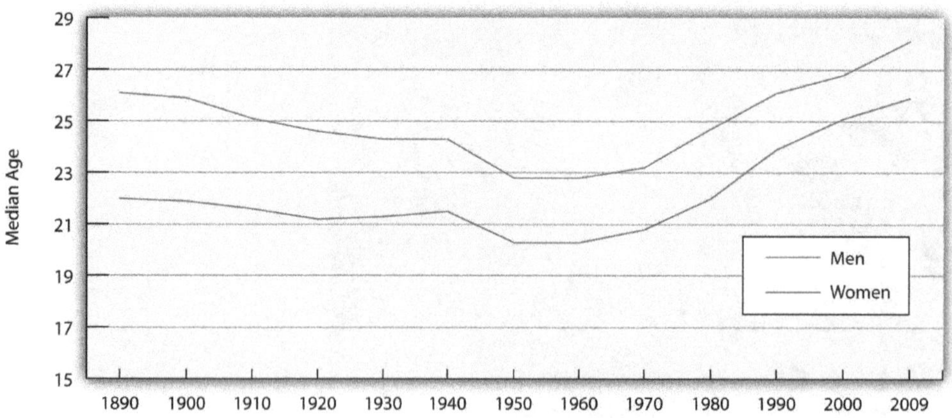

Source: Data from U.S. Census Bureau. (2010). Estimated median age at first marriage, by sex: 1890 to the present. Retrieved from http://www.census.gov/population/socdemo/hh-fam/ms2.xls.

The United States Compared With Other Western Nations

In many ways, the United States differs from other Western democracies in its view of marriage and in its behavior involving marriage and other intimate relationships (Cherlin, 2010; Hull, Meier, & Ortyl, 2010). First, Americans place more emphasis than their Western counterparts on the ideal of romantic love as a basis for marriage and other intimate relationships and on the cultural importance of marriage. Second, the United States has higher rates of marriage than other Western nations. Third, the United States also has higher rates of divorce than other Western nations; for example, 42% of American marriages end in divorce after 15 years, compared to only 8% in Italy and Spain. Fourth, Americans are much more likely than other Western citizens to remarry once they are divorced, to cohabit in short-term relationships, and, in general, to move from one intimate relationship to another, a practice called *serial monogamy*. This practice leads to instability that can have negative impacts on any children that may be involved and also on the adults involved.

The U.S. emphasis on romantic love helps account for its high rates of marriage, divorce, and serial monogamy. It leads people to want to be in an intimate relationship, marital or cohabiting. Then, when couples get married because they are in love, many quickly find that passionate romantic love can quickly fade; because their expectations of romantic love were so high, they become more disenchanted once this happens and unhappy in their marriage. The American emphasis on independence and individualism also makes divorce more likely than in other nations; if a marriage is not good for us, we do what is best for us as individuals and end the marriage. As Andrew J. Cherlin (2010, p. 4) observes, “Americans are conflicted about lifelong marriage: they value the stability and security of marriage, but they tend to believe that individuals who are unhappy with their marriages should be allowed to end them.” Still, the ideal of romantic love persists even after divorce, leading to remarriage and/or other intimate relationships.

Families and Children in the United States

The United States has about 36 million families with children under 18. About 70% of these are married-couple families, while 30% (up from about 14% in the 1950s) are one-parent families. Most of these latter families are headed by the mother (see Figure 15.4 "Family Households With Children Under 18 Years of Age, 2008").

Figure 15.4 Family Households With Children Under 18 Years of Age, 2008

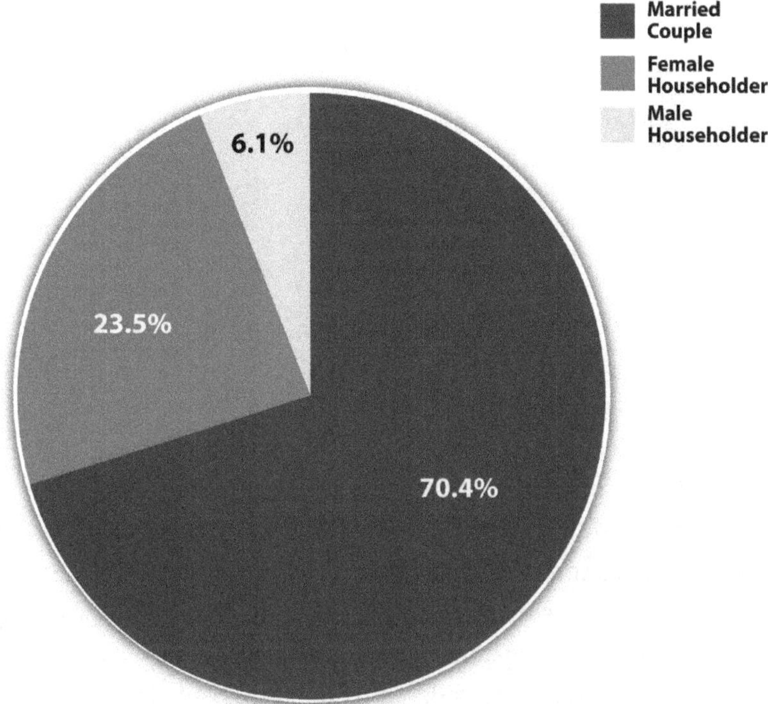

Source: Data from U.S. Census Bureau. (2010). *Statistical abstract of the United States: 2010.* Washington, DC: U.S. Government Printing Office. Retrieved from http://www.census.gov/compendia/statab.

The proportion of families with children under 18 that have only one parent varies significantly by race and ethnicity: Latino and African American families are more likely than white and Asian American households to have only one parent (see Figure 15.5 "Race, Ethnicity, and Percentage of Family Groups With Only One Parent, 2008"). Similarly, whereas 30% of all children do not live with both their biological parents, this figure, too, varies by race and ethnicity: 22% for non-Latino white children, compared to 15% of Asian children, 30% of Latino children, and 62.5% of African American children.

Figure 15.5 Race, Ethnicity, and Percentage of Family Groups With Only One Parent, 2008

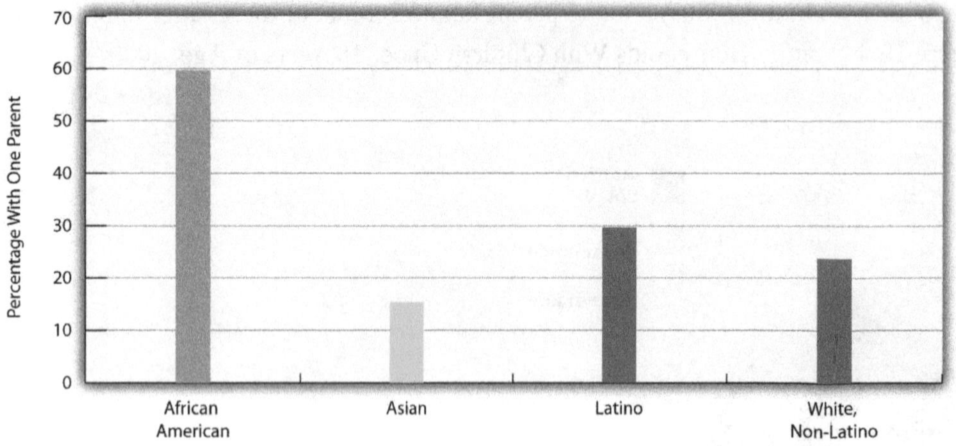

Source: Data from U.S. Census Bureau. (2010). *Statistical abstract of the United States: 2010*. Washington, DC: U.S. Government Printing Office. Retrieved from http://www.census.gov/compendia/statab.

We discuss single-parent families and racial and ethnic differences in family arrangements at greater length a little later, and we will also discuss several other issues affecting children. But before we leave the topic of children, it is worth noting that children, despite all the joy and fulfillment they so often bring to parents, also tend to reduce parents' emotional well-being. As a recent review summarized the evidence, "Parents in the United States experience depression and emotional distress more often than their childless adult counterparts. Parents of young children report far more depression, emotional distress and other negative emotions than non-parents, and parents of grown children have no better well-being than adults who never had children" (Simon, 2008, p. 41).

Children have these effects because raising them can be both stressful and expensive. Depending on household income, the average child costs parents between $134,000 and $270,000 from birth until age 18. College education obviously can cost tens of thousands of dollars beyond that. Robin W. Simon (2008) argues that American parents' stress would be reduced if the government provided better and more affordable day care and after-school options, flexible work schedules, and tax credits for various parenting costs. She also thinks that the expectations Americans have of the joy of parenthood are unrealistically positive and that parental stress would be reduced if expectations became more realistic.

Key Takeaways

- Most people eventually marry. This fact means that marriage remains an important ideal in American life, even if not all marriages succeed.
- About 30% of children live with only one parent, almost always their mother.

For Your Review

1. The text notes that most people eventually marry. In view of the fact that so many marriages end in divorce,

why do you think that so many people continue to marry?

2. Some of the children who live only with their mothers were born out of wedlock. Do you think the parents should have married for the sake of their child? Why or why not?

References

Chen, S. (2010, June 4). Interracial marriages at an all-time high, study says. *CNN*. Retrieved from http://articles.cnn.com/2010-06-04/living/pew.interracial.marriage_1_ interracial-marriages-millennial-generation-race-and-ethnicity-matter?_s=PM:LIVING.

Cherlin, A. J. (2010). *The marriage-go-round: The state of marriage and the family in America today*. New York, NY: Vintage.

Hull, K. E., Meier, A., & Ortyl, T. (2010). The changing landscape of love and marriage. *Contexts, 9*(2), 32–37.

Qian, Z. (2005). Breaking the last taboo: Interracial marriage in America. *Contexts, 4*(4), 33–37.

Simon, R. W. (2008). The joys of parenthood, reconsidered. *Contexts, 7*(2), 40–45.

U.S. Census Bureau. (2010). *Statistical abstract of the United States: 2010*. Washington, DC: U.S. Government Printing Office. Retrieved from http://www.census.gov/compendia/statab.

15.4 Changes and Issues Affecting American Families

Learning Objectives

1. Discuss why the U.S. divorce rate rose during the 1960s and 1970s and summarize the major individual-level factors accounting for divorce today.
2. Describe the effects of divorce for spouses and children.
3. Summarize the evidence on how children fare when their mothers work outside the home.
4. Discuss how children of same-sex couples fare compared to children of heterosexual couples.
5. Discuss evidence concerning the continuing debate over the absence of fathers in many African American families.

American families have undergone many changes since the 1950s. Scholars, politicians, and the public have strong and often conflicting views on the reasons for these changes and on their consequences. We now look at some of the most important changes and issues affecting U.S. families.

Cohabitation

Some people who are not currently married nonetheless *cohabit,* or live together with someone of the opposite sex in a romantic relationship. The census reports that almost 7 million opposite-sex couples are currently cohabiting; these couples constitute about 10% of all opposite-sex couples (married plus unmarried). The average cohabitation lasts less than 2 years and ends when the couple either splits up or gets married; about half of cohabiting couples do marry, and half split up. More than half of people in their 20s and 30s have cohabited, and roughly one-fourth of this age group is currently cohabiting (Brown, 2005). Roughly 55% of cohabiting couples have no biological children, about 45% live with a biological child of one of the partners, and 21% live with their own biological child. (These figures add to more than 100% because many couples live with their own child and a child of just one of the partners.) About 5% of children live with biological parents who are cohabiting.

Interestingly, married couples who have cohabited with each other before getting married are *more* likely to divorce than married couples who did not cohabit. As Susan I. Brown (2005, p. 34) notes, this apparent consequence is ironic: “The primary reason people cohabit is to test their relationship’s viability for marriage. Sorting out bad relationships through cohabitation is how many people think they can avoid divorce. Yet living together before marriage actually increases a couple’s risk of divorce.” Two possible reasons may account for this result. First, cohabitation may change the relationship between a couple and increase the chance they will divorce if they get married anyway. Second, individuals who are willing to live together without being married may not be very committed to the idea of marriage and thus may be more willing to divorce if they are unhappy in their eventual marriage.

Recent work has begun to compare the psychological well-being of cohabiting and married adults and also the behavior of children whose biological parent or parents are cohabiting rather than married (Apel & Kaukinen, 2008; Brown, 2005). On average, married adults are happier and otherwise have greater psychological well-being than cohabiting adults, while the latter, in turn, fare better psychologically than adults not living with anyone. Research has not yet clarified the reasons for these differences, but it seems that people with the greatest psychological and economic well-being are most likely to marry. If this is true, it is not the state of being married per se that accounts for the difference in well-being between married and cohabiting couples, but rather the extent of well-being that affects decisions to marry or not marry. Another difference between cohabitation and marriage concerns relationship violence. Among young adults (aged 18–28), this type of violence is more common among cohabiting couples than among married or dating couples. The reasons for this difference remain unknown but may again reflect differences in the types of people who choose to cohabit (Brown & Bulanda, 2008).

The children of cohabiting parents tend to exhibit lower well-being of various types than those of married parents: they are more likely to engage in delinquency and other antisocial behavior, and they have lower academic performance and worse emotional adjustment. The reasons for these differences remain to be clarified but may again stem from the types of people who choose to cohabit rather than marry.

Divorce and Single-Parent Households

The U.S. divorce rate has risen since the early 1900s, with several peaks and valleys, and is now the highest in the industrial world. It rose sharply during the Great Depression and World War II, probably because of the economic distress of the former and the family disruption caused by the latter, and fell sharply after the war as the economy thrived and as marriage and family were proclaimed as patriotic ideals. It dropped a bit more during the 1950s before rising sharply through the 1960s and 1970s (Cherlin, 2009). The divorce rate has since declined somewhat (see Figure 15.6 "Number of Divorces per 1,000 Married Women Aged 15 or Older, 1960–2008") and today is only slightly higher than its peak at the end of World War II. Still, the best estimates say that 40%–50% of all new marriages will one day end in divorce (Teachman, 2008). The surprising announcement in June 2010 of the separation of former vice president Al Gore and his wife, Tipper, was a poignant reminder that divorce is a common outcome of many marriages.

Figure 15.6 Number of Divorces per 1,000 Married Women Aged 15 or Older, 1960–2008

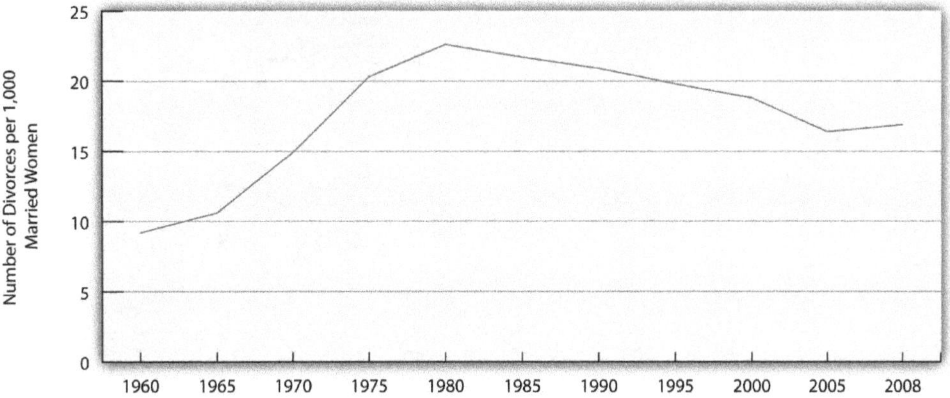

Source: Data from Wilcox, W. B. (Ed.). (2009). *The state of our unions, 2009: Marriage in America*. Charlottesville: The National Marriage Project, University of Virginia.

Reasons for Divorce

We cannot be certain about why the divorce rate rose so much during the 1960s and 1970s, but we can rule out two oft-cited causes. First, there is little reason to believe that marriages became any less happy during this period. We do not have good data to compare marriages then and now, but the best guess is that marital satisfaction did not decline after the 1950s ended. What did change was that people after the 1950s became more willing to seek divorces in marriages that were already unhappy.

Second, although the contemporary women's movement is sometimes blamed for the divorce rate by making women think marriage is an oppressive institution, the trends in Figure 15.6 "Number of Divorces per 1,000 Married Women Aged 15 or Older, 1960–2008" suggest this blame is misplaced. The women's movement emerged in the late 1960s and was capturing headlines by the early 1970s. Although the divorce rate obviously rose after that time, it also started rising several years *before* the women's movement emerged and capturing headlines. If the divorce rate began rising before the women's movement started, it is illogical to blame the women's movement. Instead, other structural and cultural forces must have been at work, just as they were at other times in the last century, as just noted, when the divorce rate rose and fell.

Why, then, did divorce increase during the 1960s and 1970s? One reason is the increasing economic independence of women. As women entered the labor force in the 1960s and 1970s, they became more economically independent of their husbands, even if their jobs typically paid less than their husbands' jobs. When women in unhappy marriages do become more economically independent, they are more able to afford to get divorced than when they have to rely entirely on their husbands' earnings (Hiedemann, Suhomlinova, & O'Rand, 1998). When both spouses work outside the home, moreover, it is more difficult to juggle the many demands of family life, especially child care, and family life can be more stressful. Such stress can reduce marital happiness and make divorce more likely. Spouses may also have less time for each other when both are working outside the home, making it more difficult to deal with problems they may be having.

Disapproval of divorce has declined since the 1950s, and divorce is now considered a normal if unfortunate part of life.

John C Bullas BSc MSc PhD MCIHT MIAT – Divorce Cakes a_005 – CC BY-NC-ND 2.0.

It is also true that disapproval of divorce has declined since the 1950s, even if negative views of it still remain (Cherlin, 2009). Not too long ago, divorce was considered a terrible thing; now it is considered a normal if unfortunate part of life. We no longer say a bad marriage should continue for the sake of the children. When New York Governor Nelson Rockefeller ran for president in the early 1960s, the fact that he had been divorced hurt his popularity, but when California Governor Ronald Reagan ran for president less than two decades later, the fact that he had been divorced was hardly noted. But is the growing acceptability of divorce a cause of the rising divorce rate, or is it the result of the rising divorce rate? Or is it both a cause and result? This important causal order question is difficult to resolve.

Another reason divorce rose during the 1960s and 1970s may be that divorces became easier to obtain legally. In the past, most states required couples to prove that one or both had committed actions such as mental cruelty, adultery, or other such behaviors in order to get divorced. Today almost all states have no-fault divorce laws that allow a couple to divorce if they say their marriage has failed from irreconcilable differences. Because divorce has become easier and less expensive to obtain, more divorces occur. But are no-fault divorce laws a cause or result of the post-1950s rise in the divorce rate? The divorce rate increase preceded the establishment of most states' no-fault laws, but it is probably also true that the laws helped make additional divorces more possible. Thus no-fault divorce laws are probably one reason for the rising divorce rate after the 1950s, but only one reason (Kneip & Bauer, 2009).

We have just looked at possible reasons for divorce rate trends, but we can also examine the reasons why certain marriages are more or less likely to end in divorce within a given time period. Although, as noted earlier, 40%–50% of all new marriages will probably end in divorce, it is also true that some marriages are more likely to end than others. Family scholars identify several correlates of divorce (Clarke-Stewart & Brentano, 2006; Wilcox, 2009). An important one is age at marriage: teenagers who get married are much more likely to get divorced than people who marry well into their 20s or beyond, partly because they have financial difficulties and are not yet emotionally mature. A second correlate of divorce is social class: people who are poor at the time of their marriage are more likely to get divorced than people who begin their marriages in economic comfort, as the stress of poverty causes stress in marriage. Divorce is thus another negative life chance of people at the bottom of the socioeconomic ladder.

Effects of Divorce and Single-Parent Households

Much research exists on the effects of divorce on spouses and their children, and scholars do not always agree on what these effects are. One thing is clear: divorce plunges many women into poverty or near-poverty (Gadalla, 2008). Many have been working only part time or not at all outside the home, and divorce takes away their husband's economic support. Even women working full time often have trouble making ends meet, because, as we saw in earlier chapters, so many are in low-paying jobs. One-parent families headed by a woman for any reason are much poorer ($30,296 in 2008 median annual income) than those headed by a man ($44,358). Meanwhile, the median income of married-couple families is much higher ($72,589). Almost 30% of all single-parent families headed by women are officially poor.

Although the economic consequences of divorce seem clear, what are the psychological consequences for husbands, wives, and their children? Are they better off if a divorce occurs, worse off, or about the same? The research evidence is very conflicting. Many studies find that divorced spouses are, on average, less happy and have poorer mental health after their divorce, but some studies find that happiness and mental health often improve after divorce (Williams, 2003; Waite, Luo, & Lewin, 2009). The postdivorce time period that is studied may affect what results are found: for some people psychological well-being may decline in the immediate aftermath of a divorce, given how difficult the divorce process often is, but rise over the next few years. The contentiousness of the marriage may also matter. Some marriages ending in divorce have been filled with hostility, conflict, and sometimes violence, while other marriages ending in divorce have not been very contentious at all, even if they have failed. Individuals seem to fare better psychologically after ending a very contentious marriage but fare worse after ending a less contentious marriage (Amato & Hohmann-Marriott, 2007).

What about the children? Parents used to stay together "for the sake of the children," thinking that divorce would cause their children more harm than good. Studies of this issue generally find that children in divorced families are indeed more likely, on average, to do worse in school, to use drugs and alcohol and suffer other behavioral problems, and to experience emotional distress and other psychological problems (Sun & Li, 2009; Amato & Cheadle, 2008).

However, it is sometimes difficult in these studies to determine whether the effects on children stem from the divorce itself or, instead, from the parental conflict that led to the divorce. This problem raises the possibility that children may fare better if their parents end a troubled marriage than if their parents stay married. The evidence on this issue generally mirrors the evidence for spouses just cited: children generally fare better if their parents end a highly contentious marriage, but they fare worse if their parents end a marriage that has not been highly contentious (Booth & Amato, 2001; Hull, Meier, & Ortyl, 2010).

Children in Poverty

The statistics on children and poverty are discouraging (DeNavas-Walt, Proctor, & Smith, 2009). Children under 18 represent 36% of all poor Americans even though they constitute only 25% of the population. About 19% of U.S. children live in poverty, a figure that rises to 44% for children living just with their mothers and to 53% for children under the age of 6 living just with their mothers. As with many things, race and ethnicity play an important role: African American and Latino children are more than three times as likely as non-Latino white children to live in poverty (see Figure 15.7 "Race, Ethnicity, and Percentage of Children Below Poverty Level, 2008").

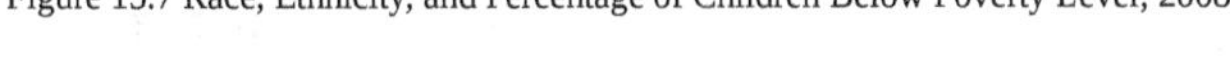
Figure 15.7 Race, Ethnicity, and Percentage of Children Below Poverty Level, 2008

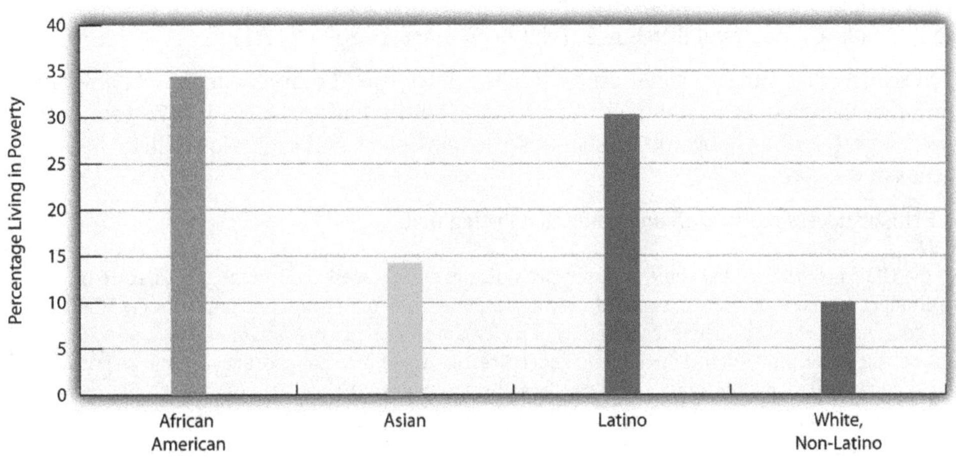

Source: Data from U.S. Census Bureau. (2010). Current population survey: Annual social and economic supplement. Retrieved from http://www.census.gov/hhes/www/cpstables/032009/pov/new03_100.htm.

Much research finds that poor children are at increased risk for behavioral, psychological, and health problems not only during childhood and adolescence but also well into their adult years (Wagmiller & Adelman, 2009). In a type of vicious cycle, children growing up in poor households are at greater risk of continuing to live in poverty after they reach adulthood.

Childhood poverty is higher in the United States than in any other Western democracy, and poor children in the United States fare worse than their counterparts in other Western democracies (Jäntti, 2009). A major reason for this is that the United States lacks the large, national programs other Western democracies have both for preventing poverty and for helping children and adults already living in poverty. These programs include housing allowances, free or subsidized day care and preschool programs, and some form of national health insurance. The experience of other Western democracies indicates that the number of U.S. poor children and the problems they face are much higher than they need to be (Waldfogel, 2009) (see the "Learning From Other Societies" box).

Learning From Other Societies

Reducing Child Poverty in Great Britain

When the Labour government under Prime Minister Tony Blair took power in the United Kingdom in the late 1990s, 26.1% of British children lived in poverty. The government announced an ambitious plan to eliminate child poverty entirely by 2020, and the success of the plan so far offers some important lessons for the United States.

The government devised an antipoverty strategy that included three components, borrowed generally from policies used in the United States but implemented with greater funding and carried out more extensively (Waldfogel, 2010): (a) a jobs program for poor parents, coupled with government-subsidized day care for their children; (b) substantial cash supports and tax credits for poor families; and (c) greatly increased programs and services for poor children and their families, including home visitation, parenting education, and early childhood education. In all of these respects, the British government viewed its antipoverty effort as more far-reaching than the U.S. effort. As one British official explained, "We have more public funding and we have more of a focused government view that we have to eliminate child poverty, not just ameliorate it. That's a big cultural difference" (Nelson & Whalen, 2006, p. A1).

The government's strategy helped reduce child poverty significantly in just a few years. From its rate of 26.1% when the Labour government took power in the later 1990s, the child poverty rate fell by half to 12.7% just 7 years later (2005–2006). Although it had risen slightly to 13.4% by 2007–2008, this rate remained significantly lower than the rate at the beginning of the government's new effort.

Some U.S. observers hailed this British success story, with one columnist noting that

> there's no denying that the Blair government has done a lot for Britain's have-nots. Modern Britain isn't paradise on earth, but the Blair government has ensured that substantially fewer people are living in economic hell….[T]he Blair years have shown that a government that seriously tries to reduce poverty can achieve a lot. (Krugman, 2006, p. A25)
> The British experience indicates that the United States could indeed reduce child poverty and the number of poor families significantly if it adopted policies, programs, and services similar to those Britain has used since the late 1990s. Ironically Britain's inspiration for many of these measures came from the United States, but Britain then funded and implemented them much more extensively. If the United States were to learn from Britain's example, it, too, could reduce child poverty and help poor families in other ways.

To help poor children, several U.S. states and communities have implemented prenatal and early childhood visitation programs, in which nurses, social workers, and other professionals make regular visits to the homes of low-income mothers whose children are at risk for the problems mentioned earlier (Olds, Sadler, & Kitzman, 2007). These programs have increased poor children's health and reduced their behavioral and psychological problems, not only during childhood but also into adolescence and young adulthood (Piquero, Farrington, Welsh, Tremblay, & Jennings, 2009). For this reason, the programs save much more money than they cost, and continued investment in such programs promises to provide a cost-effective means of helping the many U.S. children who live in poverty.

Working Mothers and Day Care

As noted earlier, women are now much more likely to be working outside the home than a few decades ago. This is true for both married and unmarried women and also for women with and without children. As women have entered the labor force, the question of who takes care of the children has prompted much debate and controversy. Many observers have said that young children suffer if they do not have a parent, implicitly their mother, taking care of them full time until they start school and being there every day when they get home from school (Morse, 2001). What does research say about how young children fare if their mothers work? (Notice that no one seems to worry that fathers work!)

Early studies compared the degree of attachment shown to their mothers by children in day care and that shown by children who stay at home with their mothers. In one type of study, children were put in a laboratory room with their mothers and observed as the mothers left and returned. The day-care kids usually treated their mothers' departure and returning casually and acted as if they did not care that their mothers were leaving or returning. In contrast the stay-at-home kids acted very upset when their mothers left and seemed much happier and even relieved when they returned. Several researchers concluded that these findings indicated that day-care children lacked sufficient emotional attachment to their mothers (Schwartz, 1983). However, other researchers reached a very different conclusion: the day-care children's apparent nonchalance when their mothers left and returned simply reflected the fact that they always saw her leave and return every day when they went to day care. The lack of concern over her behavior simply showed that they were more independent and self-confident than the stay-at-home children, who were fearful when their mothers left, and not that they were less attached to their mothers (Coontz, 1997).

More recent research has studied children, both those who stayed at home and those who entered day care, over time starting with infancy, with some of the most notable studies examining data from a large, $200 million study funded by the National Institute of Child Health and Human Development, a branch of the National Institutes of Health (Rabin, 2008). These studies have found that day-care children exhibit better cognitive skills (reading and arithmetic) than stay-at-home children but are also slightly more likely to engage in aggressive behavior that is well within the normal range of children's behavior. This research has also yielded two other conclusions. First, the quality of parenting and other factors such as parent's education and income matter much more for children's cognitive and social development than whether or not they are in day care. Second, to the extent that day care is beneficial for children, it is high-quality day care that is beneficial, as low-quality day care can be harmful.

Children in day care exhibit better cognitive skills than stay-at-home children but are also slightly more likely to engage in aggressive behavior that is within the normal range of children's behavior.

njxw – Daycare – CC BY-NC-ND 2.0.

This latter conclusion is an important finding, because many day-care settings in the United States are not high quality. Unfortunately, many parents who use day care cannot afford high-quality care, which can cost several hundred dollars per month. This problem reflects the fact that the United States lags far behind other Western democracies in providing subsidies for day care, as noted earlier. Because working women are certainly here to stay and because high-quality day care seems at least as good for children as full-time care by a parent, it is essential that the United States make good day care available and affordable.

Marriage and Well-Being

Is marriage good for people? This is the flip side of the question addressed earlier on whether divorce is bad for people. Are people better off if they get married in the first place? Or are they better off if they stay single?

In 1972, sociologist Jessie Bernard (1972) famously said that every marriage includes a "her marriage" and a "his marriage." By this she meant that husbands and wives view and define their marriages differently. When spouses from the same marriage are interviewed, they disagree on such things as how often they should have sex, how often they actually do have sex, and who does various household tasks. Women do most of the housework and child care, while men are freer to work and do other things outside the home. Citing various studies, she said that marriage is better for men than for women. Married women, she said, have poorer mental health and other aspects of psychological well-being than unmarried women, while married men have better psychological well-being than unmarried men. In short, marriage was good for men but bad for women.

Married people are generally happier than unmarried people and score higher on other measures of psychological well-being.

Silvia Sala – CC BY-NC-ND 2.0.

Critics later said that Bernard misinterpreted her data on women and that married women are also better off than unmarried women (Glenn, 1997). Contemporary research generally finds that marriage does benefit both sexes: married people, women and men alike, are generally happier than unmarried people (whether never married, divorced, or widowed), score better on other measures of psychological well-being, are physically healthier, have better sex lives, and have lower death rates (Williams, 2003; Waite, Luo, & Lewin, 2009). There is even evidence that marriage helps keep men from committing crime (Laub, 2004). Marriage has these benefits for several reasons, including the emotional and practical support spouses give each other, their greater financial resources compared to those of unmarried people, and the sense of obligation that spouses have toward each other.

Three issues qualify the general conclusion that marriage is beneficial. First, it would be more accurate to say that good marriages are beneficial, because bad marriages certainly are not (Frech & Williams, 2007). Second, although marriage is generally beneficial, its benefits seem greater for older adults than for younger adults, for whites than for African Americans, and for individuals who were psychologically depressed before marriage than for those who were not depressed (Frech & Williams, 2007). Third, psychologically happy and healthy people may be the ones who get married in the first place and are less apt to get divorced once they do marry. If so, then marriage does not promote psychological well-being; rather, psychological well-being promotes marriage. Research testing this *selectivity hypothesis* finds that both processes occur: psychologically healthy people are more apt to get and stay married, but marriage also promotes psychological well-being.

Sociology Making a Difference

Gender Ideology and Marital Happiness

As the text points out, marriage seems to promote personal happiness and other aspects of psychological well-being. One reason this happens is undoubtedly the happiness that many spouses find in the marriage itself. Not surprisingly, there is a large body of research on why some marriages are happier (or unhappier) than other marriages (Kaufman & Taniguchi, 2006). Also not surprisingly, some of the factors discussed elsewhere in the text that promote the likelihood of divorce, such as marrying at a young age and experiencing financial strain, also contribute to marital unhappiness. When spouses have health problems, marital happiness also tends to be lower.

An additional factor that may influence marital happiness is *gender ideology*. A spouse who holds *traditional* ideology believes that the man is the ruler of the household and that the woman's primary role is to be a homemaker and caretaker of children. A spouse who holds *egalitarian* (or *nontraditional*) ideology believes that a woman's place is not necessarily in the home and that both spouses should share housework, child care, and other responsibilities. Some scholars speculate that the rise in divorce during the 1960s and 1970s was partly due to a rise in egalitarian ideology among women, which conflicted with their husbands' traditional ideology. Supporting this speculation, some studies summarized by sociologists Gayle Kaufman and Hiromi Taniguchi (2006) find that wives with traditional attitudes are happier in their marriages than wives with egalitarian attitudes. At the same time, studies have also found that husbands with egalitarian attitudes are happier in their marriages than husbands with traditional attitudes.

Thus gender ideology may have opposite effects by gender on marital happiness: wives are happier in their marriages when they hold traditional attitudes, while husbands are happier when they hold egalitarian attitudes. This "dual" result is perhaps not very surprising. As wives moved increasingly into the labor force during the past few decades but still found themselves having the primary responsibility for housework and child care, it makes sense to think that those with traditional attitudes would be happier with this situation and those with egalitarian attitudes would be less happy. By the same token, it makes sense to think that husbands with egalitarian attitudes would be happier with this situation and husbands with traditional attitudes less happy.

This body of research has focused on relatively young couples and neglected those past their 40s. Addressing this neglect, Kaufman and Taniguchi examined the possible effects of gender ideology and other factors on marital happiness in a sample of married couples in Iowa whose ages were between 51 and 92. Wives' gender ideology did not affect their marital happiness, but men's gender ideology did affect their marital happiness, as men with egalitarian attitudes were happier.

By extending the research on gender ideology and marital happiness to couples past their 40s, Kaufman and Taniguchi's study reinforced the conclusion of prior research that egalitarian attitudes increase husbands' marital happiness. This finding has at least two practical implications. First, if we can assume that men's gender ideology will continue to become more egalitarian as traditional gender roles decline over time, it makes sense to think that their marital happiness will increase. Second, educational campaigns and other efforts that promote egalitarian attitudes among men should increase their marital happiness and thus reduce their desire to divorce. By pointing to the importance of expanding men's egalitarian attitudes for marital happiness, the work by sociologists Kaufman and Taniguchi has helped make a difference.

Gay and Lesbian Couples and Marriages

One of the most controversial issues concerning the family today is that of gay and lesbian marriages. According to census data, about 800,000 same-sex couples now live together in the United States, and about one-fifth of these couples are raising at least one child under age 18; the number of children being raised by same-sex couples is about 270,000 (Barkan, Marks, & Milardo, 2009). Five states permit same-sex marriage as of July 2010—Connecticut, Massachusetts, New Hampshire, Iowa, and Vermont—along with Washington, DC. Several other states recognize civil unions or provide some legal benefits to same-sex couples, but civil union status does not afford couples the full range of rights and privileges that married couples enjoy. Thirty-two states have laws or constitutional amendments that ban same-sex marriage. Internationally, same-sex marriage is permitted in Belgium, Canada, the Netherlands, Norway, Portugal, South Africa, Spain, and Sweden.

Same-sex marriage is one of the most controversial issues concerning the family today. Marriage between same-sex couples is currently permitted in only a handful of states and nations.

Elvert Barnes – 70a Marriage Equality US Capitol – CC BY-SA 2.0.

Among other arguments, opponents of same-sex marriages say that they threaten the stability of the institution of marriage and that children of same-sex couples fare worse in several respects than those raised by both their biological parents (Benne & McDermott, 2009). However, the social science evidence fails to support either of these two arguments. There is no evidence that heterosexual marriages have been undermined in the five states that have legalized same-sex marriage. For example, Massachusetts, which has allowed same-sex marriage since 2004, continues to have one of the lowest divorce rates in the nation. Regarding children of same-sex couples, studies find that their psychological well-being is as high as those of children of heterosexual couples. As a review of this body of research concluded, "Because every relevant study to date shows that parental sexual orientation per se has no measurable effect on the quality of parent-child relationships or on children's mental health or social adjustment, there is no evidentiary basis for considering parental sexual orientation in decisions about children's 'best interest'" (Stacey & Biblarz, 2001, p. 176).

Racial and Ethnic Diversity in Marriages and Families

Marriages and families in the United States exhibit a fair amount of racial and ethnic diversity, as we saw earlier in this chapter. Children are more likely to live with only one parent among Latino and especially African American families than among white and Asian American families. Moreover, African American, Latino, and Native American children and their families are especially likely to live in poverty. As a result, they are at much greater risk for the kinds of problems outlined earlier for children living in poverty.

Beyond these cold facts lie other racial and ethnic differences in family life (Taylor, 2002). Studies of Latino and Asian American families find they have especially strong family bonds and loyalty. Extended families in both groups and among Native Americans are common, and these extended families have proven a valuable shield against the problems all three groups face because of their race/ethnicity and poverty.

The status of the African American family has been the source of much controversy for several decades. This controversy stems from several related statistics. Two of these we noted earlier: the large number of single-parent households among African Americans and their large number of children in such households. A third statistic concerns the number of births out of wedlock. Whereas 40% of all births are to unmarried women, such births account for 72% of all births to African American women. Many scholars attribute the high number of fatherless families among African Americans to the forcible separation of families during slavery and to the fact that so many young black males today are unemployed, in prison or jail, or facing other problems (Patterson, 1998).

Many observers say this high number of fatherless families in turn contributes to African Americans' poverty, crime, and other problems (Haskins, 2009). But other observers argue that this blame is misplaced to at least some extent. Extended families and strong female-headed households in the African American community, they say, have compensated for the absence of fathers (Allen & James, 1998; Billingsley, 1994). The problems African Americans face, they add, stem to a large degree from their experience of racism, segregated neighborhoods, lack of job opportunities, and other structural difficulties (Sampson, 2009). Even if fatherless families contribute to these problems, these other factors play a larger role.

Key Takeaways

- The divorce rate rose for several reasons during the 1960s and 1970s but has generally leveled off since then.
- Divorce often lowers the psychological well-being of spouses and their children, but the consequences of divorce also depend on the level of contention in the marriage that has ended.
- Despite continuing controversy over the welfare of children whose mothers work outside the home, research indicates that children in high-quality day care fare better in cognitive development than those who stay at home.
- Children of same-sex couples have psychological well-being as high as those of heterosexual couples. There is no evidence that same-sex marriage has undermined the stability of heterosexual marriage in the states where same-sex marriages are legal.

For Your Review

1. Think of someone you know (either yourself, a relative, or a friend) whose parents are divorced. Write a brief essay in which you discuss how the divorce affected this person.
2. Did your mother work outside the home while you were growing up? If so, do you think you were better or worse off because of that? If she did not work outside the home, how do you think things would have gone for you if she had?
3. What are your views regarding same-sex marriage? Do you think same-sex couples should be allowed to marry? Why or why not?

References

Allen, W. R., & James, A. D. (1998). Comparative perspectives on black family life: Uncommon explorations of a common subject. *Journal of Comparative Family Studies, 29*, 1–11.

Amato, P. R., & Cheadle, J. E. (2008). Parental divorce, marital conflict and children's behavior problems: A comparison of adopted and biological children. *Social Forces, 86*(3), 1139–1161.

Amato, P. R., & Hohmann-Marriott, B. (2007). A comparison of high- and low-distress marriages that end in divorce. *Journal of Marriage & Family, 69*(3), 621–638.

Apel, R., & Kaukinen, C. (2008). On the relationship between family structure and antisocial behavior: Parental cohabitation and blended households. *Criminology, 46*(1), 35–70.

Barkan, S., Marks, S., & Milardo, R. (2009, September 22). Same-sex couples are families, too. *Bangor Daily News*. Retrieved from http://www.bangordailynews.com/detail/121751.html.

Benne, R., & McDermott, G. (2009). Gay marriage threatens families, children, and society. In R. Espejo (Ed.), *Gay and lesbian families* (pp. 11–15). Farmington Hills, MI: Greenhaven Press.

Bernard, J. (1972). *The future of marriage*. New York, NY: Bantam.

Billingsley, A. (1994). *Climbing Jacob's ladder: The enduring legacy of African American families*. New York, NY: Touchstone.

Booth, A., & Amato, P. R. (2001). Parental predivorce relations and offspring postdivorce well-being. *Journal of Marriage & Family, 63*(1), 197.

Brown, S. I. (2005). How cohabitation is reshaping American families. *Contexts, 4*(3), 33–37.

Brown, S. L., & Bulanda, J. R. (2008). Relationship violence in young adulthood: A comparison of daters, cohabitors, and marrieds. *Social Science Research, 37*(1), 73–87.

Cherlin, A. J. (2009). *The marriage-go-round: The state of marriage and the family in America today*. New York, NY: Knopf.

Cherlin, A. J. (2009). The origins of the ambivalent acceptance of divorce. *Journal of Marriage & Family, 71*(2), 226–229.

Clarke-Stewart, A., & Brentano, C. (2006). *Divorce: Causes and consequences*. New Haven, CT: Yale University Press.

Coontz, S. (1997). *The way we really are: Coming to terms with America's changing families*. New York, NY: Basic Books.

DeNavas-Walt, C., Proctor, B. D., & Smith, J. C. (2009). *Income, poverty, and health insurance coverage in the United States: 2008* (Current Population Report P60-236). Washington, DC: U.S. Government Printing Office.

Frech, A., & Williams, K. (2007). Depression and the psychological benefits of entering marriage. *Journal of Health and Social Behavior, 48*, 149–163.

Gadalla, T. M. (2008). Gender differences in poverty rates after marital dissolution: A longitudinal study. *Journal of Divorce & Remarriage, 49*(3/4), 225–238.

Glenn, N. D. (1997). A critique of twenty family and marriage and the family textbooks. *Family Relations, 46*, 197–208.

Haskins, R. (2009). Moynihan was right: Now what? *The ANNALS of the American Academy of Political and Social Science, 621*, 281–314.

Hiedemann, B., Suhomlinova, O., & O'Rand, A. M. (1998). Economic independence, economic status, and empty nest in midlife marital disruption. *Journal of Marriage and the Family, 60*, 219–231.

Hull, K. E., Meier, A., & Ortyl, T. (2010). The changing landscape of love and marriage. *Contexts, 9*(2), 32–37.

Jäntti, M. (2009). Mobility in the United States in comparative perspective. In M. Cancian & S. Danziger (Eds.), *Changing poverty, changing policies* (pp. 180–200). New York, NY: Russell Sage Foundation.

Kaufman, G., & Taniguchi, H. (2006). Gender and marital happiness in later life. *Journal of Family Issues, 27*(6), 735–757.

Kneip, T., & Bauer, G. (2009). Did unilateral divorce laws raise divorce rates in Western Europe? *Journal of Marriage & Family, 71*(3), 592–607.

Krugman, P. (2006, December 25). Helping the poor, the British way. *The New York Times*, p. A25.

Laub, J. H. (2004). The life course of criminology in the United States: The American Society of Criminology 2003 presidential address. *Criminology, 42*, 1–26.

Morse, J. R. (2001). *Love & economics: Why the laissez-faire family doesn't work.* Dallas, TX: Spence.

Nelson, E., & Whalen, J. (2006, December 22). With U.S. methods, Britain posts gains in fighting poverty. *The Wall Street Journal*, p. A1.

Olds, D. L., Sadler, L., & Kitzman, H. (2007). Programs for parents of infants and toddlers: Recent evidence from randomized trials. *Journal of Child Psychology and Psychiatry, 48*, 355–391.

Patterson, O. (1998). *Rituals of blood: Consequences of slavery in two American centuries*. Washington, DC: Civitas/CounterPoint.

Piquero, A. R., Farrington, D. P., Welsh, B. C., Tremblay, R., & Jennings, W. (2009). Effects of early family/parent training programs on antisocial behavior and delinquency. *Journal of Experimental Criminology 5*, 83–120.

Rabin, R. C. (2008, September 15). A consensus about day care: Quality counts. *The New York Times*, p. A1.

Sampson, R. J. (2009). Racial stratification and the durable tangle of neighborhood inequality. *The ANNALS of the American Academy of Political and Social Science, 621*, 260–280.

Schwartz, P. (1983). Length of day-care attendance and attachment behavior in eighteen-month-old infants. *Child Development, 54*, 1073–1078.

Stacey, J., & Biblarz, T. J. (2001). (How) does the sexual orientation of parents matter? *American Sociological Review, 66*(2), 159–183.

Sun, Y., & Li, Y. (2009). Parental divorce, sibship size, family resources, and children's academic performance. *Social Science Research, 38*(3), 622–634.

Taylor, R. L. (2002). *Minority families in the United States: A multicultural perspective* (3rd ed.). Upper Saddle River, NJ: Prentice Hall.

Teachman, J. (2008). Complex life course patterns and the risk of divorce in second marriages. *Journal of Marriage & Family, 70*(2), 294–305.

Wagmiller, R. L., & Adelman, R. M. (2009). *Childhood and intergenerational poverty: The long-term consequences of growing up poor*. New York, NY: National Center for Children in Poverty, Columbia University.

Waite, L. J., Luo, Y., & Lewin, A. C. (2009). Marital happiness and marital stability: Consequences for psychological well-being. *Social Science Research, 38*(1), 201–212.

Waldfogel, J. (2009). The role of family policies in antipoverty policy. In M. Cancian & S. Danziger (Eds.), *Changing poverty, changing policies* (pp. 242–265). New York, NY: Russell Sage Foundation.

Waldfogel, J. (2010). *Britain's war on poverty*. New York, NY: Russell Sage Foundation.

Wilcox, W. B. (Ed.). (2009). *The state of our unions, 2009: Marriage in America*. Charlottesville: The National Marriage Project, University of Virginia.

Williams, K. (2003). Has the future of marriage arrived? A contemporary examination of gender, marriage, and psychological well-being. *Journal of Health & Social Behavior, 44*, 470–487.

15.5 Children and Parental Discipline

Learning Objectives

1. Define the four major styles of parental discipline and summarize the differences among them.
2. Explain why spanking may ironically promote antisocial behavior by children.
3. Understand how parenting style may differ by social class.

How should parents raise their children? Given the critical importance of the first few years and even months of life for a child's intellectual, emotional, and behavioral development, it is essential to identify the best ways to raise kids. We can talk about how much time parents should spend with their children, how often they should read to them, what time they should put them to bed, and other topics. But for many people the question of raising children means how parents should *discipline* their children. While no one right answer to this question exists that will satisfy everyone, scholars identify at least four styles of discipline (Welch, 2010). We will look briefly at these types and at a related issue, spanking.

The first style of discipline, and the one that most childhood scholars favor, is called *authoritative* or *firm-but-fair* discipline. In this style of discipline, parents set clear rules for their children's behavior but at the same time let their kids exercise independent judgment. When their children do misbehave, the parents patiently explain to them why their behavior was wrong and, if necessary, discipline them with time-outs, groundings, and similar responses. They rarely, if ever, spank their children and in general provide them much emotional support. Most childhood experts think authoritative discipline aids children's moral development and helps produce children who are well behaved (Ginsburg, Durbin, Garcia-España, Kalicka, & Winston, 2009).

Many parents instead practice *authoritarian* discipline. These parents set firm but overly restrictive rules for their children's behavior and are generally not very warm toward them. When their children misbehave, the parents may yell at them and punish them with relatively frequent and even harsh spankings. Although these parents think such punishment is necessary to teach kids how to behave, many childhood experts think their authoritarian discipline ironically produces children who are more likely to misbehave (McKee et al., 2007).

Parents who practice authoritarian discipline may often spank their children, but spanking is thought to promote antisocial behavior among children overall rather than to inhibit it.

Lynae Zebest – Big Spank #1 – CC BY-NC-ND 2.0.

A third style of discipline is called *lax* or *permissive*. As these names imply, parents set few rules for their children's behavior and don't discipline them when they misbehave. These children, too, are more apt than children raised by authoritative parents to misbehave during childhood and adolescence.

Uninvolved discipline is the fourth and final type. Parents who practice this style generally provide their children little emotional support and fail to set rules for their behavior. This style of parenting is associated with antisocial behavior by children and other negative outcomes, especially when compared with authoritative parenting.

One reason that authoritative discipline is better than authoritarian discipline for children is that it avoids spanking in favor of other, more "reasoning" types of discipline and punishment. Many experts think spanking is bad for children and makes them more likely, not less likely, to misbehave. Spanking, they say, teaches children that they should behave to avoid being punished. This lesson makes children more likely to misbehave if they think they will not get caught, as they do not learn to behave for its own sake. Spanking also teaches children it is acceptable to hit someone to solve an interpersonal dispute and even to hit someone if you love her or him, because that is what spanking is all about. Children who are spanked may also resent their parents more than children raised authoritatively and thus be more likely to misbehave because their relationship with their parents is not as close. Thus even though parents who spank do so because they believe in the old saying "Spare the rod and spoil the child," spanking ironically can make children more likely, not less likely, to misbehave (Berlin et al., 2009).

Social Class Differences

Despite the modern evidence on spanking, most Americans continue to approve of it: almost three-quarters think that it's "sometimes necessary to discipline a child with a good, hard spanking" (see Figure 15.8 "Percentage Agreeing That "It Is Sometimes Necessary to Discipline a Child With a Good, Hard Spanking""). However, families do differ in the degree to which they use spanking and, more generally, the degree to which they practice authoritative versus authoritarian or the other styles of discipline. Several decades ago, Melvin Kohn (1969) found that working-class parents were more likely than middle-class parents to practice authoritarian discipline. In a related area, they were more likely than their middle-class counterparts to emphasize obedience rather than thinking for oneself as something their children should learn. To explain these social class differences, Kohn reasoned that working-class jobs tend to involve strict obedience to orders from a boss, while middle-class ones are more apt to involve autonomy and independent exercise of judgment. The values parents learn from their workplaces affect how they raise their children and the values they teach their children.

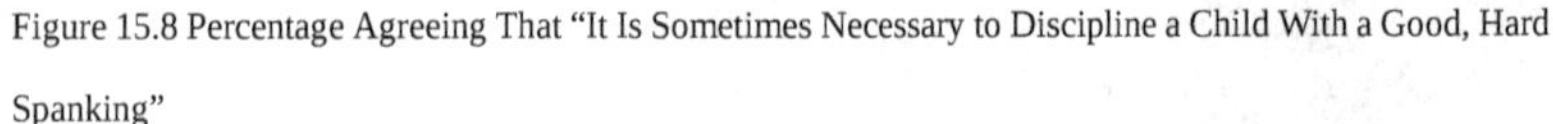

Figure 15.8 Percentage Agreeing That "It Is Sometimes Necessary to Discipline a Child With a Good, Hard Spanking"

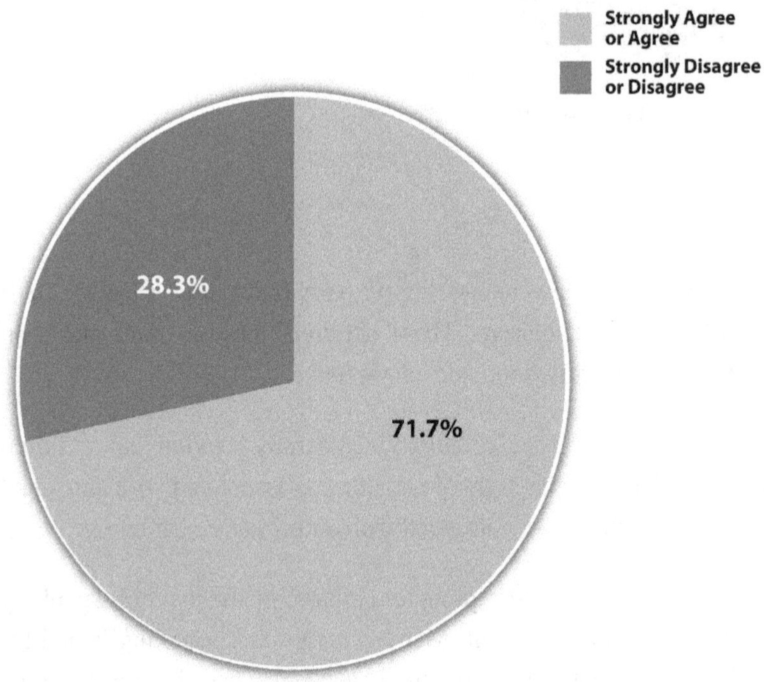

Source: Data from General Social Survey, 2006.

Key Takeaways

- Of the four styles of parental discipline, authoritative discipline is thought to be the best for children's development.
- Spanking may ironically promote antisocial behavior by children, in part because it conditions them to

behave only to avoid physical punishment.

- Classic research by Melvin Kohn found that working-class parents are more likely than middle-class parents to emphasize obedience in their children.

For Your Review

1. Thinking back to your childhood, which style of discipline did your parent(s) practice? Do you think this was a good style for them to use with you? Why or why not?
2. How often were you spanked when you were a child? Do you think spanking helped you behave better? Explain your answer.
3. Whether or not you plan to have children, imagine that you become a parent someday. Decide which style of discipline you would practice and write a brief essay in which you explain why you chose this style.

References

Berlin, L. J., Ispa, J. M., Fine, M. A., Malone, P. S., Brooks-Gunn, J., Brady-Smith, C.,…Bai, Y. (2009). Correlates and consequences of spanking and verbal punishment for low-income white, African American, and Mexican American toddlers. *Child Development, 80*(5), 1403–1420.

Ginsburg, K. R., Durbin, D. R., Garcia-España, J. F., Kalicka, E. A., & Winston, F. K. (2009). Associations between parenting styles and teen driving, safety-related behaviors and attitudes. *Pediatrics, 124*(4), 1040–1051.

Kohn, M. L. (1969). *Class and conformity: A study in values*. Homewood, IL: Dorsey Press.

McKee, L., Roland, E., Coffelt, N., Olson, A. L., Forehand, R., Massari, C.,…Zens, M. S. (2007). Harsh discipline and child problem behaviors: The roles of positive parenting and gender. *Journal of Family Violence, 22*(4), 187–196.

Welch, K. J. (2010). *Family life now* (2nd ed.). Upper Saddle River, NJ: Prentice Hall.

15.6 Family Violence

Learning Objectives

1. Describe the extent of violence against intimates and explain why it occurs.
2. Describe the extent of child abuse and explain why it occurs.

Although family violence has received much attention since the 1970s, families were violent long before scholars began studying family violence and the public began hearing about it. We can divide family violence into two types: violence against intimates (spouses, live-in partners, boyfriends, or girlfriends) and violence against children. (Violence against elders also occurs and was discussed in Chapter 12 "Aging and the Elderly".)

Violence Against Intimates

Intimates commit violence against each other in many ways: they can hit with their fists, slap with an open hand, throw an object, push or shove, or use or threaten to use a weapon. When all of these acts and others are combined, we find that much intimate violence occurs. While we can never be certain of the exact number of intimates who are attacked, the U.S. Department of Justice estimates from its National Crime Victimization Survey that almost 600,000 acts of violence (2008 data) are committed annually by one intimate against another intimate; 85% of these acts are committed by men against women (Rand, 2009). Another national survey about a decade ago found that 22% of U.S. women had been physically assaulted by a spouse or partner at some point in their lives (Tjaden & Thoennes, 1998). This figure, if still true, translates to more than 20 million women today. A national survey of Canadian women found that 29% had been attacked by a spouse or partner (Randall, 1995). Taken together, these different figures all indicate that intimate partner violence is very common and affects millions of people.

According to some estimates, about one-fifth of U.S. women have been assaulted by a spouse or partner at least once in their lives.

Neil Moralee – Not Defeated. – CC BY 2.0.

Some observers claim that husbands are just as likely as wives to be beaten by a spouse, and there is evidence that husbands experience an act of violence from their wives about as often as wives do from their husbands. Yet this "gender equivalence" argument has been roundly criticized. Although women do commit violence against husbands and boyfriends, their violence is less serious (e.g., a slap compared to using a fist) and usually in self-defense to their husbands' violence. And although some studies find an equal number of violent acts committed by husbands and wives, other studies find much more violence committed by husbands (Johnson, 2006).

Why do men hit their wives, partners, and girlfriends? As with rape (see Chapter 11 "Gender and Gender Inequality"), sociologists answer this question by citing both structural and cultural factors. Structurally, women are the subordinate gender in a patriarchal society and, as such, are more likely to be victims of violence, whether it is rape or intimate violence. Intimate violence is more common in poor families, and economic inequality thus may lead men to take out their frustration over their poverty on their wives and girlfriends (Martin, Vieraitis, & Britto, 2006).

Cultural myths also help explain why men hit their wives and girlfriends (Gosselin, 2010). Many men continue to believe that their wives should not only love and honor them but also obey them, as the traditional marriage vow says. If they view their wives in this way, it becomes that much easier to hit them. In another myth many people ask why women do not leave home if the hitting they suffer is really that bad. The implication is that the hitting cannot be that bad because they do not leave home. This reasoning ignores the fact that many women *do* try to leave home, which often angers their husbands and ironically puts the women more at risk for being hit, or they do not leave home because they have nowhere to go (Kim & Gray, 2008). Battered women's shelters are still few in number and can accommodate a woman and her children for only 2 or 3 weeks. Many battered women also have little money of their own and simply cannot afford to leave home. The belief that battering cannot be that bad if women hit by their husbands do not leave home ignores all of these factors and is thus a myth that reinforces spousal violence against women.

Dating Violence on Campus

Because intimate partner violence is so common, it is no surprise that much of it occurs among college students. Some studies suggest that one-fifth of intimate relationships on campus involve at least some violence. Young people (aged 16–24) report the highest rates of domestic and dating violence in government surveys. As one advocate of programs to end dating violence observes, "It's incredibly common both at the high school and college levels" (Kinzie, 2010, A9).

In May 2010, Yeardley Love, a University of Virginia senior, was allegedly killed by her ex-boyfriend on the campus (Yanda, Johnson, & Vise, 2010). Her death prompted many campuses to assess whether they had been doing enough to prevent dating violence and to deal adequately with the offenders who were committing it (Kinzie, 2010). Some officials said that stalking on campuses had been increasing because social media and technology like texting has made it easier to know someone's location. But some campuses were in states that made it more difficult to deal with dating violence. Virginia, for example, does not permit protective orders against someone a person is dating; instead, the offender must be a spouse, a live-in partner, or the parent of one's child. This restriction obviously prevents many Virginia students from obtaining protective orders.

Child Abuse

One of the hardest behaviors to understand is child abuse, which can be both physical and sexual in nature. Children can also suffer from emotional abuse and practical neglect.

It is especially difficult to know how much child abuse occurs. Infants obviously cannot talk, and toddlers and older children who are abused usually do not tell anyone about the abuse. They might not define it as abuse, they might be scared to tell on their parents, they might blame themselves for being abused, or they might not know whom they could talk to about their abuse. Whatever the reason, they usually remain silent, making it very difficult to know how much abuse takes place.

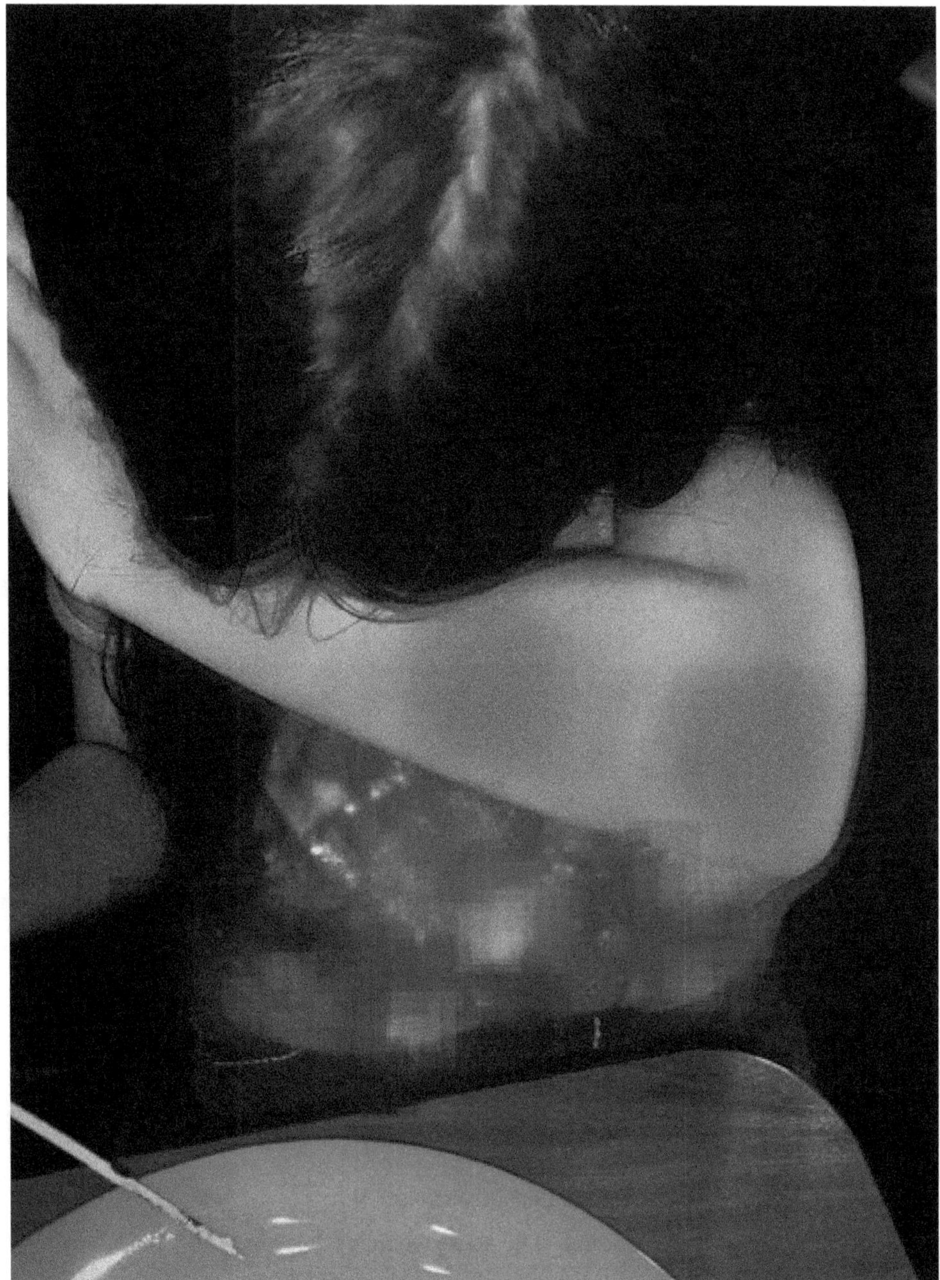

Government data estimate that about 800,000 children are abused or neglected each year. Because most children do not report their abuse or neglect, the actual number is probably much higher.

Jane Fox – Child Abuse mental – CC BY-ND 2.0.

Using information from child protective agencies throughout the country, the U.S. Department of Health and Human Services estimates that about 800,000 children (2007 data) are victims of child abuse and neglect annually (Administration on Children Youth and Families, 2009). This figure includes some 80,000 cases of physical abuse; 56,000 cases of sexual abuse; 437,000 cases of neglect; 31,000 cases of psychological maltreatment; and 7,000 cases of medical neglect. The total figure represents about 1.1% of all children under the age of 18. Obviously this is just the tip of the iceberg, as many cases of child abuse never become known. A 1994 Gallup Poll asked adult respondents about physical abuse they suffered as children. Twelve percent said they had been abused (punched, kicked, or choked), yielding an estimate of 23 million adults in the United States who were physically abused as children (Moore, 1994). Some studies estimate that about 25% of girls and 10% of boys are sexually abused at least once before turning 18 (Garbarino, 1989). In the study of Toronto women discussed earlier, 42% said they had been sexually abused before turning 16 (Randall & Haskell, 1995). Whatever the true figure is, most child abuse is committed by parents, step-parents, and other people the children know, not by strangers.

Why does child abuse occur? Structurally speaking, children are another powerless group and, as such, are easy targets of violence. Moreover, the best evidence indicates that child abuse is more common in poorer families. The stress these families suffer from their poverty is thought to be a major reason for the child abuse occurring within them (Gosselin, 2010). As with spousal violence, then, economic inequality is partly to blame for child abuse. Cultural values and practices also matter. In a nation where, as we saw, so many people think a good, hard spanking is sometimes necessary to discipline a child, it is inevitable that physical child abuse will occur, because there is a very thin line between a hard spanking and physical abuse: not everyone defines a good, hard spanking in the same way. As two family violence scholars once noted, "Although most physical punishment [of children] does not turn into physical abuse, most physical abuse begins as ordinary physical punishment" (Wauchope & Straus, 1990, p. 147).

Key Takeaways

- Violence between intimates is fairly common and stems from gender inequality, income inequality, and several cultural myths that minimize the harm that intimate violence causes.
- At least 800,000 children are abused or neglected each year in the United States. Because most abused children do not report the abuse, the number of cases of abuse and neglect is undoubtedly much higher.

For Your Review

1. Do you think it is ever acceptable for a spouse to slap or hit another spouse? Why or why not?
2. If spanking were somehow to end altogether, do you think child abuse would decline? Explain your answer.

Addressing Family Issues: What Sociology Suggests

As perhaps our most important and also most controversial social institution, the family seems to arouse strong passions from almost everyone. Sociological theory and research, along with research from the other social sciences, have important implications for how our society should address the various family issues discussed in this chapter.

One set of implications concerns the many children and families living in poverty. The households in which they live are mostly headed by women, and the majority of these households are the result of divorce. The programs and policies outlined in Chapter 6 "Groups and Organizations" are certainly relevant for any efforts to help these families. These efforts include, but are not limited to, increased government financial support, vocational training and financial aid for schooling for women who wish to return to the labor force or to increase their wages, early childhood visitation and intervention programs, and increases in programs providing nutrition and medical care to poor women and their children (Cherlin, 2009). In all of these efforts, the United States has much to learn from the nations of Western Europe (see the "Learning From Other Societies" box in Chapter 11 "Gender and Gender Inequality", Section 11.4 "Violence Against Women: Rape and Pornography").

Another issue and set of implications concern family violence. To the extent that much violence against intimates and children is rooted in the frustration and stress accompanying poverty, efforts that reduce poverty will also reduce family violence. And to the extent that gender inequality helps explain violence against women, continuing and strengthening efforts to reduce gender inequality should also reduce violence against intimates, as most of this violence is directed by men against women. Further, if, as many scholars believe, the violent nature of masculinity helps account for violence men commit against their wives and girlfriends, then efforts to change male gender-role socialization should also help. Turning to child abuse, because so much child abuse remains unknown to child protective authorities, it is difficult to reduce its seriousness and extent. However, certain steps might still help. Because child abuse seems more common among poorer families, then efforts that reduce poverty should also reduce child abuse. The home visitation programs mentioned earlier to help poor children also help reduce child abuse. Although, as noted earlier, approval of spanking is deeply rooted in our culture, a national educational campaign to warn about the dangers of spanking, including its promotion of children's misbehavior, may eventually reduce the use of spanking and thus the incidence of child physical abuse.

Same-sex marriage is another issue on which research by sociologists and other scholars is relevant. This research does not show that same-sex marriage threatens the stability of heterosexual marriage or the welfare of children, and opponents of same-sex marriage have no empirical grounds to claim otherwise. Because this evidence indicates that same-sex marriage does not have the dire consequences these opponents claim, the ongoing national and local debate on same-sex marriage should be informed by this evidence.

A final issue for which research by sociologists and other scholars is relevant is divorce. There is much evidence to suggest that divorce has very negative consequences for spouses and children, and there is also much evidence to suggest that these consequences arise not from the divorce itself but rather from the conflict preceding the divorce and the poverty into which many newly single-parent households are plunged. There is also evidence that spouses and children fare better after a divorce from a highly contentious marriage. Efforts to help preserve marriages should certainly continue, but these efforts should proceed cautiously or not proceed at all for the marriages that are highly contentious. To the extent that marital conflict partly arises from financial difficulties, once again government efforts that help reduce poverty should also help preserve marriages.

References

Administration on Children Youth and Families. (2009). *Child maltreatment 2007*. Washington, DC: U.S. Department of Health and Human Services, U.S. Government Printing Office.

Cherlin, A. J. (2009). *The marriage-go-round: The state of marriage and the family in America today*. New York, NY: Knopf.

Garbarino, J. (1989). The incidence and prevalence of child maltreatment. In L. Ohlin & M. Tonry (Eds.), *Family violence* (Vol. 11, pp. 219–261). Chicago, IL: University of Chicago Press.

Gosselin, D. K. (2010). *Heavy hands: An introduction to the crimes of family violence* (4th ed.). Upper Saddle River, NJ: Prentice Hall.

Johnson, M. P. (2006). Conflict and control: Gender symmetry and asymmetry in domestic violence. *Violence Against Women, 12*, 1003–1018.

Kim, J., & Gray, K. A. (2008). Leave or stay? Battered women's decision after intimate partner violence. *Journal of Interpersonal Violence, 23*(10), 1465–1482.

Kinzie, S. (2010, May 30). Efforts expand on campuses to end dating violence. *The Boston Globe*, p. A9.

Martin, K., Vieraitis, L. M., & Britto, S. (2006). Gender equality and women's absolute status: A test of the feminist models of rape. *Violence Against Women, 12*(4), 321–339.

Moore, D. W. (1994, May). One in seven Americans victim of child abuse. *The Gallup Poll Monthly*, 18–22.

Rand, M. R. (2009). *Criminal victimization, 2008*. Washington, DC: Bureau of Justice Statistics, U.S. Department of Justice.

Randall, D. (1995). The portrayal of business malfeasance in the elite and general media. In G. Geis, R. F. Meier & L. M. Salinger (Eds.), *White-collar crime: Classic and contemporary views* (3rd ed., pp. 105–115). New York, NY: Free Press.

Randall, M., & Haskell, L. (1995). Sexual violence in women's lives: Findings from the Women's Safety Project, a community-based survey. *Violence Against Women, 1*, 6–31.

Tjaden, P., & Thoennes, N. (1998). *Prevalence, incidence, and consequences of violence against women: Findings from the National Violence Against Women Survey*. Washington, DC: U.S. Department of Justice.

Wauchope, B., & Straus, M. A. (1990). Physical punishment and physical abuse of American children: Incidence rates by age, gender, and occupational class. In M. A. Straus & R. J. Gelles (Eds.), *Physical violence in American families: Risk factors and adaptations to violence in 8,145 families* (pp. 133–148). New Brunswick, NJ: Transaction.

Yanda, S., Johnson, J., & Vise, D. d. (2010, May 8). Mourners gather for funeral of U-Va. student Yeardley Love. *The Washington Post*. Retrieved from http://pqasb.pqarchiver.com/washingtonpost/access/2028459931.html?FMT= ABS&FMTS=ABS:FT&date=May+9%2C+2010&author=Jenna+Johnson+Steve+Yanda%3BDaniel+de+Vise&pub=The+Washington+Post&edition=&startpage=C.1&desc=Thousands+gather+to+mourn+U-Va.+student%3B+Tears+and+cheers++mingle+at+funeral+for+Yeardley+Love.

15.7 End-of-Chapter Material

Summary

1. As a social institution, the family is a universal or near-universal phenomenon. Yet the historical and cross-cultural record indicates that many types of families and family arrangements exist now and have existed in the past. Although the nuclear family has been the norm in many societies, in practice its use has been less common than many people think. Many societies have favored extended families, and in early times children could expect, because of the death of a parent or births out of wedlock, to live at least some part of their childhood with only one parent. A very few societies, including the Nayar of India, have not featured nuclear families, yet their children have apparently been raised successfully.
2. Industrialization took many families from their farms and put them into cities. For the first time a family's economic activity became separated from its home life. Men worked outside the home, primarily in factories and other sites of industrial labor, while many women stayed at home to take care of children, to bake and wash clothing, and to sew and perform other tasks that brought families some money. Middle-class women were more likely than working-class women to stay at home, as the latter worked in factories and other sites outside the home out of economic necessity. One consequence of the gender-based division of labor that developed during industrialization was that men's power within and over their families increased, as they were the ones providing the major part of their families' economic sustenance.
3. The male breadwinner–female homemaker family model depicted in 1950s television shows was more of a historical aberration than a historical norm. Both before and after the 1950s, women worked outside the home much more often than they did during that decade.
4. Contemporary sociological perspectives on the family fall into the more general functional, conflict, and social interactionist approaches guiding sociological thought. Functional theory emphasizes the several functions that families serve for society, including the socialization of children and the economic and practical support of family members. Conflict theory emphasizes the ways in which nuclear families contribute to ongoing gender, class, and race inequality, while social interactionist approaches examine family communication and interaction to make sense of family life.
5. Marriage rates and the proportion of two-parent households have declined in the last few decades, but marriage remains an important station in life for most people. Scholars continue to debate the consequences of divorce and single-parent households for women, men, and their children. Although children from divorced homes face several problems and difficulties, it remains unclear whether these problems were the result of their parents' divorce or instead of the conflict that preceded the divorce. Several studies find that divorce and single-parenting in and of themselves do not have the dire consequences for children that many observers assume. The low income of single-parent households, and not the absence of a second parent, seems to account for many of the problems that children in such households do experience.
6. The United States has the highest proportion of children in poverty of any industrial nation, thanks largely to its relative lack of social and economic support for poor children and their families. Almost one-fifth of American children live in poverty and face health, behavioral, and other problems as a result.
7. Despite ongoing concern over the effect on children of day care instead of full-time care by one parent, most contemporary studies find that children in high-quality day care are not worse off than their stay-at-home counterparts. Some studies find that day-care children are more independent and self-confident than children who stay at home and that they perform better on various tests of cognitive ability.
8. Controversy continues to exist over gay and lesbian couples and marriages. Although gay and lesbian couples sometimes seek legal marriages to ensure health and other benefits for both partners, no state has

yet legalized such marriages, although some communities do extend benefits to both partners.

9. Racial and ethnic diversity marks American family life. Controversy also continues to exist over the high number of fatherless families in the African American community. Many observers blame many of the problems African Americans face on their comparative lack of two-parent households, but other observers say this blame is misplaced.
10. Authoritative or firm-but-fair discipline is the type most childhood experts advocate. Although many people believe in spanking and practice authoritarian discipline, some studies suggest that this method of child-rearing is more apt to produce children with behavioral problems.
11. Family violence affects millions of spouses and children yearly. Structural and cultural factors help account for the high amount of intimate violence and child abuse. Despite claims to the contrary, the best evidence indicates that women are much more at risk than men for violence by spouses and partners.

Using Sociology

You're a second-grade teacher enjoying your second year of employment in an elementary school near Los Angeles. One day you notice that one of your students, Tommy Smith, has a large bruise on his arm. You ask Tommy what happened, and he hesitantly replies that he fell off a swing in the playground. You're no expert, but somehow his bruise doesn't look like something that would have resulted from a fall. But you have met his parents, and they seem like friendly people even if they did not seem very concerned about how well Tommy is doing in your class. Your school policy requires you to report any suspected cases of child abuse. What, if anything, do you do? Explain your answer.

Chapter 16: Education

Social Issues in the News

"Lewistown Voters Say No to Bond for School," the headline said. We usually associate crowded, decaying schools with urban areas, but they are also found in rural areas. In September 2010, voters in Lewistown, a small town in central Montana surrounded by prairies and mountains, defeated a bond issue for the construction of a new middle school. The new school would have replaced the town's only junior high school. Built in 1921, the school had a host of problems, according to the news article: it did not meet accessibility standards for people with physical disabilities; plaster was routinely falling off walls and ceilings, requiring six classrooms to add suspended ceilings to prevent injuries from falling plaster; and the school was so crowded that some classes met in the gym or hallways and some students had to take tests in closets. (Hall, 2010)

Education is one of our most important social institutions. Youngsters and adolescents spend most of their weekday waking hours in school, doing homework, or participating in extracurricular activities, and many then go on to college. People everywhere care deeply about what happens in our nation's schools, and issues about the schools ignite passions across the political spectrum. Yet, as this story about a very old school in Montana illustrates, many schools are ill equipped to prepare their students for the complex needs of today's world.

This chapter's discussion of education begins with the development of schooling in the United States and then turns to sociological perspectives on education. The remainder of the chapter discusses education in today's society. This discussion highlights education as a source and consequence of various social inequalities and examines several key issues affecting the nation's schools and the schooling of its children.

References

Hall, R. (2010, September 22). Lewistown voters say no to bond for school. *Great Falls [MT] Tribune*. Retrieved from http://www.greatfallstribune.com/article/20100922/NEWS20100901/29220302/Lewistown+voters+say+no+to+bond+for+school.

16.1 A Brief History of Education in the United States

Learning Objectives

1. Explain why compulsory education arose during the 19th century.
2. Outline some scholars' criticisms of the rise of compulsory education.

Education is the social institution through which a society teaches its members the skills, knowledge, norms, and values they need to learn to become good, productive members of their society. As this definition makes clear, education is an important part of socialization. Education is both *formal* and *informal*. **Formal education** is often referred to as *schooling*, and as this term implies, it occurs in schools under teachers, principals, and other specially trained professionals. **Informal education** may occur almost anywhere, but for young children it has traditionally occurred primarily in the home, with their parents as their instructors. Day care has become an increasingly popular venue in industrial societies for young children's instruction, and education from the early years of life is thus more formal than it used to be.

Education in early America was hardly formal. During the colonial period, the Puritans in what is now Massachusetts required parents to teach their children to read and also required larger towns to have an elementary school, where children learned reading, writing, and religion. In general, though, schooling was not required in the colonies, and only about 10% of colonial children, usually just the wealthiest, went to school, although others became apprentices (Urban, Jennings, & Wagoner, 2008).

To help unify the nation after the Revolutionary War, textbooks were written to standardize spelling and pronunciation and to instill patriotism and religious beliefs in students. At the same time, these textbooks included negative stereotypes of Native Americans and certain immigrant groups. The children going to school continued primarily to be those from wealthy families. By the mid-1800s, a call for free, compulsory education had begun, and compulsory education became widespread by the end of the century. This was an important development, as children from all social classes could now receive a free, formal education. Compulsory education was intended to further national unity and to teach immigrants "American" values. It also arose because of industrialization, as an industrial economy demanded reading, writing, and math skills much more than an agricultural economy had.

In colonial America, only about 10% of children went to school, and these children tended to come from wealthy families. After the Revolutionary War, new textbooks helped standardize spelling and pronunciation and promote patriotism and religious beliefs, but these textbooks also included negative stereotypes of Native Americans.

Wikimedia Commons – public domain.

Free, compulsory education, of course, applied only to primary and secondary schools. Until the mid-1900s, very few people went to college, and those who did typically came from the fairly wealthy families. After World War II, however, college enrollments soared, and today more people are attending college than ever before, even though college attendance is still related to social class, as we shall discuss shortly.

At least two themes emerge from this brief history. One is that until very recently in the record of history, formal schooling was restricted to wealthy males. This means that boys who were not white and rich were excluded from formal schooling, as were virtually all girls, whose education was supposed to take place informally at home. Today, as we will see, race, ethnicity, social class, and, to some extent, gender continue to affect both educational achievement and the amount of learning occurring in schools.

Second, although the rise of free, compulsory education was an important development, the reasons for this development trouble some critics (Bowles & Gintis, 1976; Cole, 2008). Because compulsory schooling began in part to prevent immigrants' values from corrupting "American" values, they see its origins as smacking of ethnocentrism. They also criticize its intention to teach workers the skills they needed for the new industrial economy. Because most workers were very poor in this economy, these critics say, compulsory education served the interests of the upper/capitalist class much more than it served the interests of workers. It was good that workers became educated, say the critics, but in the long run their education helped the owners of capital much more than it helped the workers themselves. Whose interests are served by education remains an important question addressed by sociological perspectives on education, to which we now turn.

Key Takeaways

- Until very recently in the record of history, formal schooling was restricted to wealthy males.
- The rise of free, compulsory education was an important development that nonetheless has been criticized for orienting workers in the 19th century to be disciplined and to obey authority.

For Your Review

1. Write a brief essay in which you summarize the benefits and disadvantages of the rise of compulsory education during the 19th century.

References

Bowles, S., & Gintis, H. (1976). *Schooling in capitalist America: Educational reforms and the contradictions of economic life*. New York, NY: Basic Books.

Cole, M. (2008). *Marxism and educational theory: Origins and issues*. New York, NY: Routledge.

Urban, W. J., Jennings L., & Wagoner, J. (2008). *American education: A history* (4th ed.). New York, NY: Routledge.

16.2 Sociological Perspectives on Education

Learning Objectives

1. List the major functions of education.
2. Explain the problems that conflict theory sees in education.
3. Describe how symbolic interactionism understands education.

The major sociological perspectives on education fall nicely into the functional, conflict, and symbolic interactionist approaches (Ballantine & Hammack, 2009). Table 16.1 "Theory Snapshot" summarizes what these approaches say.

Table 16.1 Theory Snapshot

Theoretical perspective	Major assumptions
Functionalism	Education serves several functions for society. These include (a) socialization, (b) social integration, (c) social placement, and (d) social and cultural innovation. Latent functions include child care, the establishment of peer relationships, and lowering unemployment by keeping high school students out of the full-time labor force.
Conflict theory	Education promotes social inequality through the use of tracking and standardized testing and the impact of its "hidden curriculum." Schools differ widely in their funding and learning conditions, and this type of inequality leads to learning disparities that reinforce social inequality.
Symbolic interactionism	This perspective focuses on social interaction in the classroom, on the playground, and in other school venues. Specific research finds that social interaction in schools affects the development of gender roles and that teachers' expectations of pupils' intellectual abilities affect how much pupils learn.

The Functions of Education

Functional theory stresses the functions that education serves in fulfilling a society's various needs. Perhaps the most important function of education is *socialization*. If children need to learn the norms, values, and skills they need to function in society, then education is a primary vehicle for such learning. Schools teach the three Rs, as we all know, but they also teach many of the society's norms and values. In the United States, these norms and values include respect for authority, patriotism (remember the Pledge of Allegiance?), punctuality, individualism, and competition. Regarding these last two values, American students from an early age compete as individuals over grades and other rewards. The situation is quite the opposite in Japan, where, as we saw in Chapter 4 "Socialization", children learn the traditional Japanese values of harmony and group belonging from their schooling (Schneider & Silverman, 2010). They learn to value their membership in their homeroom, or *kumi*, and are evaluated more on their *kumi*'s performance than on their own individual performance. How well a Japanese child's *kumi* does is more important than how well the child does as an individual.

A second function of education is *social integration*. For a society to work, functionalists say, people must subscribe to a common set of beliefs and values. As we saw, the development of such common views was a goal of the system of free, compulsory education that developed in the 19th century. Thousands of immigrant children in the United States today are learning English, U.S. history, and other subjects that help prepare them for the workforce and integrate them into American life. Such integration is a major goal of the English-only movement, whose advocates say that only English should be used to teach children whose native tongue is Spanish, Vietnamese, or whatever other language their parents speak at home. Critics of this movement say it slows down these children's education and weakens their ethnic identity (Schildkraut, 2005).

A third function of education is *social placement*. Beginning in grade school, students are identified by teachers and other school officials either as bright and motivated or as less bright and even educationally challenged. Depending on how they are identified, children are taught at the level that is thought to suit them best. In this way they are prepared in the most appropriate way possible for their later station in life. Whether this process works as well as it should is an important issue, and we explore it further when we discuss school tracking shortly.

Social and cultural innovation is a fourth function of education. Our scientists cannot make important scientific discoveries and our artists and thinkers cannot come up with great works of art, poetry, and prose unless they have first been educated in the many subjects they need to know for their chosen path.

Figure 16.1 The Functions of Education

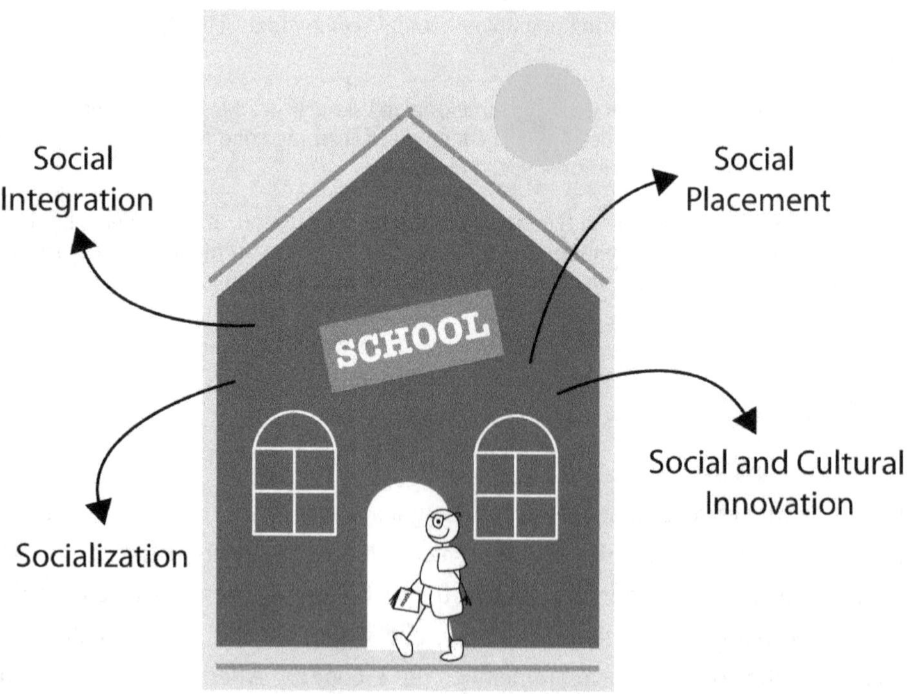

Schools ideally perform many important functions in modern society. These include socialization, social integration, social placement, and social and cultural innovation.

Education also involves several *latent* functions, functions that are by-products of going to school and receiving an education rather than a direct effect of the education itself. One of these is *child care*. Once a child starts kindergarten and then first grade, for several hours a day the child is taken care of for free. The *establishment of peer relationships* is another latent function of schooling. Most of us met many of our friends while we were in school at whatever grade level, and some of those friendships endure the rest of our lives. A final latent function of education is that it *keeps millions of high school students out of the full-time labor force*. This fact keeps the unemployment rate lower than it would be if they were in the labor force.

Education and Inequality

Conflict theory does not dispute most of the functions just described. However, it does give some of them a different slant and talks about various ways in which education perpetuates social inequality (Hill, Macrine, & Gabbard, 2010; Liston, 1990). One example involves the function of social placement. As most schools track their students starting in grade school, the students thought by their teachers to be bright are placed in the faster tracks (especially in reading and arithmetic), while the slower students are placed in the slower tracks; in high school, three common tracks are the college track, vocational track, and general track.

Such *tracking* does have its advantages; it helps ensure that bright students learn as much as their abilities allow them, and it helps ensure that slower students are not taught over their heads. But, conflict theorists say, tracking also helps perpetuate social inequality by *locking* students into faster and lower tracks. Worse yet, several studies show that students' social class and race and ethnicity affect the track into which they are placed, even though their intellectual abilities and potential should be the only things that matter: white, middle-class students are more likely to be tracked "up," while poorer students and students of color are more likely to be tracked "down." Once they are tracked, students learn more if they are tracked up and less if they are tracked down. The latter tend to lose self-esteem and begin to think they have little academic ability and thus do worse in school because they were tracked down. In this way, tracking is thought to be good for those tracked up and bad for those tracked down. Conflict theorists thus say that tracking perpetuates social inequality based on social class and race and ethnicity (Ansalone, 2006; Oakes, 2005).

Social inequality is also perpetuated through the widespread use of standardized tests. Critics say these tests continue to be culturally biased, as they include questions whose answers are most likely to be known by white, middle-class students, whose backgrounds have afforded them various experiences that help them answer the questions. They also say that scores on standardized tests reflect students' socioeconomic status and experiences in addition to their academic abilities. To the extent this critique is true, standardized tests perpetuate social inequality (Grodsky, Warren, & Felts, 2008).

As we will see, schools in the United States also differ mightily in their resources, learning conditions, and other aspects, all of which affect how much students can learn in them. Simply put, schools are unequal, and their very inequality helps perpetuate inequality in the larger society. Children going to the worst schools in urban areas face many more obstacles to their learning than those going to well-funded schools in suburban areas. Their lack of learning helps ensure they remain trapped in poverty and its related problems.

Conflict theorists also say that schooling teaches a **hidden curriculum**, by which they mean a set of values and beliefs that support the status quo, including the existing social hierarchy (Booher-Jennings, 2008) (see Chapter 4 "Socialization"). Although no one plots this behind closed doors, our schoolchildren learn patriotic values and respect for authority from the books they read and from various classroom activities.

Symbolic Interactionism and School Behavior

Symbolic interactionist studies of education examine social interaction in the classroom, on the playground, and in other school venues. These studies help us understand what happens in the schools themselves, but they also help us understand how what occurs in school is relevant for the larger society. Some studies, for example, show how children's playground activities reinforce gender-role socialization. Girls tend to play more cooperative games, while boys play more competitive sports (Thorne, 1993) (see Chapter 11 "Gender and Gender Inequality").

Another body of research shows that teachers' views about students can affect how much the students learn. When teachers think students are smart, they tend to spend more time with them, to call on them, and to praise them when they give the right answer. Not surprisingly these students learn more because of their teachers' behavior. But when teachers think students are less bright, they tend to spend less time with them and act in a way that leads the students to learn less. One of the first studies to find this example of a self-fulfilling prophecy was conducted by Robert Rosenthal and Lenore Jacobson (1968). They tested a group of students at the beginning of the school year and told their teachers which students were bright and which were not. They tested the students again at the end of the school year; not surprisingly the bright students had learned more during the year than the less bright ones. But it turned out that the researchers had randomly decided which students would be designated bright and less bright. Because the "bright" students learned more during the school year without actually being brighter at the beginning, their teachers' behavior must have been the reason. In fact, their teachers did spend more time with them and praised them more often than was true for the "less bright" students. To the extent this type of self-fulfilling prophecy occurs, it helps us understand why tracking is bad for the students tracked down.

Research guided by the symbolic interactionist perspective suggests that teachers' expectations may influence how much their students learn. When teachers expect little of their students, their students tend to learn less.

ijiwaru jimbo – Pre-school colour pack – CC BY-NC-ND 2.0.

Other research focuses on how teachers treat girls and boys. Several studies from the 1970s through the 1990s found that teachers call on boys more often and praise them more often (American Association of University Women Educational Foundation, 1998; Jones & Dindia, 2004). Teachers did not do this consciously, but their behavior nonetheless sent an implicit message to girls that math and science are not for girls and that they are not suited to do well in these subjects. This body of research stimulated efforts to educate teachers about the ways in which they may unwittingly send these messages and about strategies they could use to promote greater interest and achievement by girls in math and science (Battey, Kafai, Nixon, & Kao, 2007).

Key Takeaways

- According to the functional perspective, education helps socialize children and prepare them for their eventual entrance into the larger society as adults.
- The conflict perspective emphasizes that education reinforces inequality in the larger society.
- The symbolic interactionist perspective focuses on social interaction in the classroom, on school playgrounds, and at other school-related venues. Social interaction contributes to gender-role socialization, and teachers' expectations may affect their students' performance.

For Your Review

1. Review how the functionalist, conflict, and symbolic interactionist perspectives understand and explain education. Which of these three approaches do you most prefer? Why?

References

American Association of University Women Educational Foundation. (1998). *Gender gaps: Where schools still fail our children.* Washington, DC: American Association of University Women Educational Foundation.

Ansalone, G. (2006). Tracking: A return to Jim Crow. *Race, Gender & Class, 13,* 1–2.

Ballantine, J. H., & Hammack, F. M. (2009). *The sociology of education: A systematic analysis* (6th ed.). Upper Saddle River, NJ: Prentice Hall.

Battey, D., Kafai, Y., Nixon, A. S., & Kao, L. L. (2007). Professional development for teachers on gender equity in the sciences: Initiating the conversation. *Teachers College Record, 109*(1), 221–243.

Booher-Jennings, J. (2008). Learning to label: Socialisation, gender, and the hidden curriculum of high-stakes testing. *British Journal of Sociology of Education, 29,* 149–160.

Grodsky, E., Warren, J. R., & Felts, E. (2008). Testing and social stratification in American education. *Annual Review of Sociology, 34*(1), 385–404.

Hill, D., Macrine, S., & Gabbard, D. (Eds.). (2010). *Capitalist education: Globalisation and the politics of inequality.* New York, NY: Routledge; Liston, D. P. (1990). *Capitalist schools: Explanation and ethics in radical studies of schooling.* New York, NY: Routledge.

Jones, S. M., & Dindia, K. (2004). A meta-analytic perspective on sex equity in the classroom. *Review of Educational Research, 74,* 443–471.

Oakes, J. (2005). *Keeping track: How schools structure inequality* (2nd ed.). New Haven, CT: Yale University Press.

Rosenthal, R., & Jacobson, L. (1968). *Pygmalion in the classroom.* New York, NY: Holt.

Schildkraut, D. J. (2005). *Press "one" for English: Language policy, public opinion, and American identity.* Princeton, NJ: Princeton University Press.

Schneider, L., & Silverman, A. (2010). *Global sociology: Introducing five contemporary societies* (5th ed.). New York, NY: McGraw-Hill.

Thorne, B. (1993). *Gender play: Girls and boys in school.* New Brunswick, NJ: Rutgers University Press.

16.3 Education in the United States

Learning Objectives

1. Summarize social class, gender, and racial and ethnic differences in educational attainment.
2. Describe the impact that education has on income.
3. Discuss how education affects social and moral attitudes.

Education in the United States is a massive social institution involving millions of people and billions of dollars. About 75 million people, almost one-fourth of the U.S. population, attend school at all levels. This number includes 40 million in grades pre-K through 8, 16 million in high school, and 19 million in college (including graduate and professional school). They attend some 132,000 elementary and secondary schools and about 4,200 2-year and 4-year colleges and universities and are taught by about 4.8 million teachers and professors (U.S. Census Bureau, 2010). Education is a huge social institution.

Correlates of Educational Attainment

About 65% of U.S. high school graduates enroll in college the following fall. This is a very high figure by international standards, as college in many other industrial nations is reserved for the very small percentage of the population who pass rigorous entrance exams. They are the best of the brightest in their nations, whereas higher education in the United States is open to all who graduate high school. Even though that is true, our chances of achieving a college degree are greatly determined at birth, as social class and race/ethnicity have a significant effect on access to college. They affect whether students drop out of high school, in which case they do not go on to college; they affect the chances of getting good grades in school and good scores on college entrance exams; they affect whether a family can afford to send its children to college; and they affect the chances of staying in college and obtaining a degree versus dropping out. For these reasons, educational attainment depends heavily on family income and race and ethnicity.

Figure 16.2 "Race, Ethnicity, and High School Dropout Rate, 16–24-Year-Olds, 2007" shows how race and ethnicity affect dropping out of high school. The dropout rate is highest for Latinos and Native Americans and lowest for Asians and whites. One way of illustrating how income and race/ethnicity affect the chances of achieving a college degree is to examine the percentage of high school graduates who enroll in college immediately following graduation. As Figure 16.3 "Family Income and Percentage of High School Graduates Who Attend College Immediately After Graduation, 2007" shows, students from families in the highest income bracket are more likely than those in the lowest bracket to attend college. For race/ethnicity, it is useful to see the percentage of persons 25 or older who have at least a 4-year college degree. As Figure 16.4 "Race, Ethnicity, and Percentage of Persons 25 or Older With a 4-Year College Degree, 2008" shows, this percentage varies significantly, with African Americans and Latinos least likely to have a degree.

Figure 16.2 Race, Ethnicity, and High School Dropout Rate, 16–24-Year-Olds, 2007

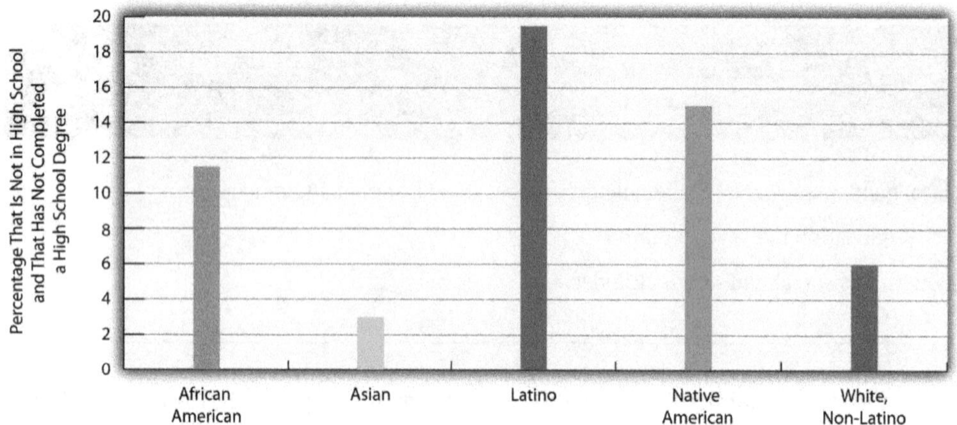

Source: Data from Planty, M., Hussar, W., Snyder, T., Kena, G., KewalRamani, A., Kemp, J.,...Nachazel, T. (2009). *The condition of education 2009* (NCES 2009-081). Washington, DC: National Center for Education Statistics, U.S. Department of Education.

Figure 16.3 Family Income and Percentage of High School Graduates Who Attend College Immediately After Graduation, 2007

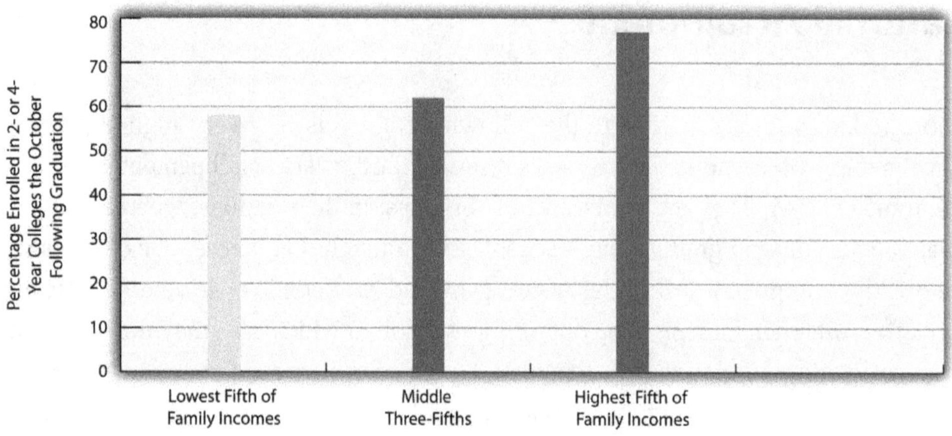

Source: Data from Planty, M., Hussar, W., Snyder, T., Kena, G., KewalRamani, A., Kemp, J.,...Nachazel, T. (2009). *The condition of education 2009* (NCES 2009-081). Washington, DC: National Center for Education Statistics, U.S. Department of Education.

Figure 16.4 Race, Ethnicity, and Percentage of Persons 25 or Older With a 4-Year College Degree, 2008

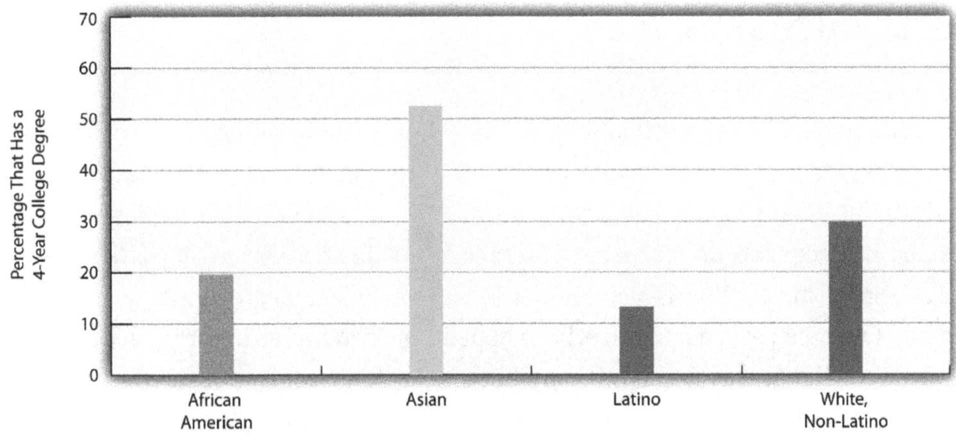

Source: Data from U.S. Census Bureau. (2010). *Statistical abstract of the United States: 2010*. Washington, DC: U.S. Government Printing Office. Retrieved from http://www.census.gov/compendia/statab.

Why do African Americans and Latinos have lower educational attainment? Two factors are commonly cited: (a) the underfunded and otherwise inadequate schools that children in both groups often attend and (b) the higher poverty of their families and lower education of their parents that often leave them ill-prepared for school even before they enter kindergarten (Ballantine & Hammack, 2009; Yeung & Pfeiffer, 2009).

Does gender affect educational attainment? The answer is yes, but perhaps not in the way you expect. If we do not take age into account, slightly more men than women have a college degree: 30.1% of men and 28.8% of women. This difference reflects the fact that women were less likely than men in earlier generations to go to college. But now there is a gender difference in the other direction: women now earn more than 57% of all bachelor's degrees, up from just 35% in 1960 (see Figure 16.5 "Percentage of All Bachelor's Degrees Received by Women, 1960–2007").

Figure 16.5 Percentage of All Bachelor's Degrees Received by Women, 1960–2007

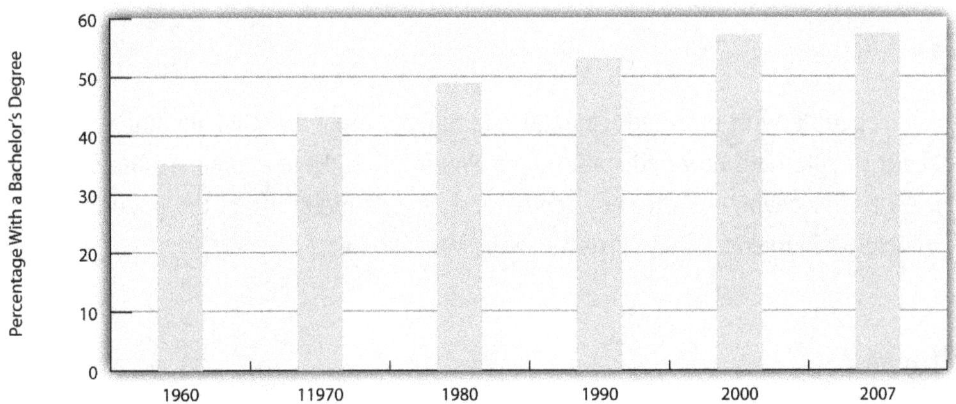

Source: Data from U.S. Census Bureau. (2010). *Statistical abstract of the United States: 2010*. Washington, DC: U.S. Government Printing Office. Retrieved from http://www.census.gov/compendia/statab.

The Difference Education Makes: Income

Have you ever applied for a job that required a high school degree? Are you going to college in part because you realize you will need a college degree for a higher-paying job? As these questions imply, the United States is a **credential society** (Collins, 1979). This means at least two things. First, a high school or college degree (or beyond) indicates that a person has acquired the needed knowledge and skills for various jobs. Second, a degree at some level is a requirement for most jobs. As you know full well, a college degree today is a virtual requirement for a decent-paying job. Over the years the ante has been upped considerably, as in earlier generations a high school degree, if even that, was all that was needed, if only because so few people graduated from high school to begin with (see Figure 16.6 "Percentage of Population 25 or Older With at Least a High School Degree, 1910–2008"). With so many people graduating from high school today, a high school degree is not worth as much. Then, too, today's technological and knowledge-based postindustrial society increasingly requires skills and knowledge that only a college education brings.

Figure 16.6 Percentage of Population 25 or Older With at Least a High School Degree, 1910–2008

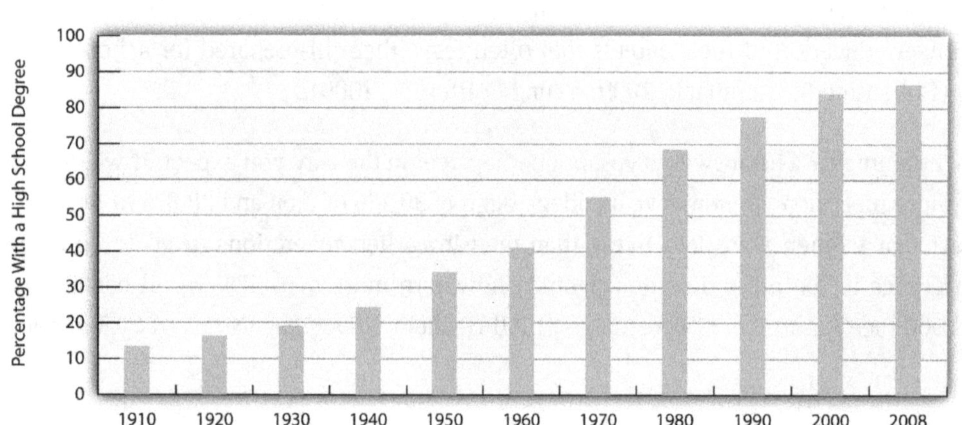

Source: Data from Snyder, T. D., Dillow, S. A., & Hoffman, C. M. (2009). *Digest of education statistics 2008*. Washington, DC: National Center for Education Statistics, U.S. Department of Education.

A credential society also means that people with more educational attainment achieve higher incomes. Annual earnings are indeed much higher for people with more education (see Figure 16.7 "Educational Attainment and Mean Annual Earnings, 2007"). As earlier chapters indicated, gender and race/ethnicity affect the payoff we get from our education, but education itself still makes a huge difference for our incomes.

On the average, college graduates have much higher annual earnings than high school graduates. How much does this consequence affect why you decided to go to college?

Merrimack College – Commencement 2012 – CC BY-NC-ND 2.0.

Figure 16.7 Educational Attainment and Mean Annual Earnings, 2007

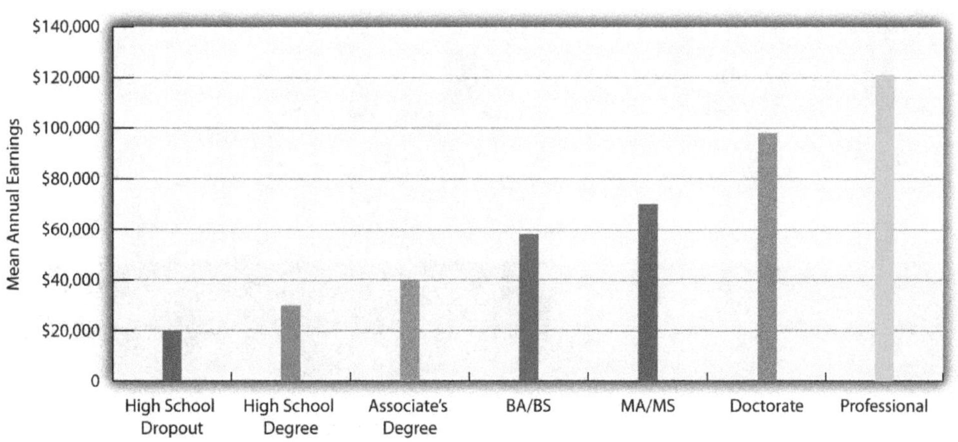

Source: Data from U.S. Census Bureau. (2010). *Statistical abstract of the United States: 2010*. Washington, DC: U.S. Government Printing Office. Retrieved from http://www.census.gov/compendia/statab.

The Difference Education Makes: Attitudes

Education also makes a difference for our attitudes. Researchers use different strategies to determine this effect.

They compare adults with different levels of education; they compare college seniors with first-year college students; and sometimes they even study a group of students when they begin college and again when they are about to graduate. However they do so, they typically find that education leads us to be more tolerant and even approving of nontraditional beliefs and behaviors and less likely to hold various kinds of prejudices (McClelland & Linnander, 2006; Moore & Ovadia, 2006). Racial prejudice and sexism, two types of belief explored in previous chapters, all reduce with education. Education has these effects because the material we learn in classes and the experiences we undergo with greater schooling all teach us new things and challenge traditional ways of thinking and acting.

We see evidence of education's effect in Figure 16.8 "Education and Agreement That "It Is Much Better for Everyone Involved If the Man Is the Achiever Outside the Home and the Woman Takes Care of the Home and Family"", which depicts the relationship in the General Social Survey between education and agreement with the statement that "it is much better for everyone involved if the man is the achiever outside the home and the woman takes care of the home and family." College-educated respondents are much less likely than those without a high school degree to agree with this statement.

Figure 16.8 Education and Agreement That "It Is Much Better for Everyone Involved If the Man Is the Achiever Outside the Home and the Woman Takes Care of the Home and Family"

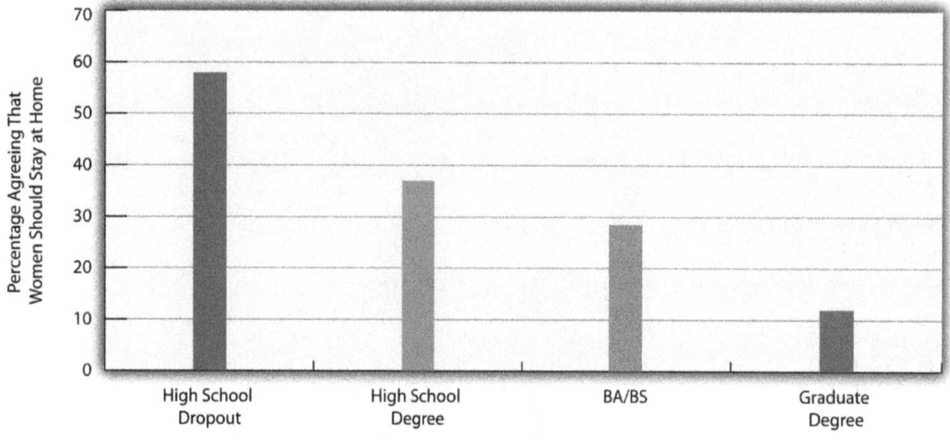

Source: Data from General Social Survey, 2008.

Key Takeaways

- Social class, race and ethnicity, and gender all influence the degree of educational attainment.
- Education has a significant impact both on income and on social and cultural attitudes. Higher levels of education are associated with higher incomes and with less conservative beliefs on social and cultural issues.

For Your Review

1. Do you think the government should take steps to try to reduce racial and ethnic differences in education, or do you think it should take a hands-off approach? Explain your answer.
2. Why do you think lower levels of education are associated with more conservative beliefs on social and cultural issues? What is it about education that often leads to less conservative beliefs on these issues?

References

Ballantine, J. H., & Hammack, F. M. (2009). *The sociology of education: A systematic analysis* (6th ed.). Upper Saddle River, NJ: Prentice Hall.

Collins, R. (1979). *The credential society: An historical sociology of education and stratification*. New York, NY: Academic Press.

McClelland, K., & Linnander, E. (2006). The role of contact and information in racial attitude change among white college students. *Sociological Inquiry, 76*(1), 81–115.

Moore, L. M., & Ovadia, S. (2006). Accounting for spatial variation in tolerance: The effects of education and religion. *Social Forces, 84*(4), 2205–2222.

U.S. Census Bureau. (2010). *Statistical abstract of the United States: 2010*. Washington, DC: U.S. Government Printing Office. Retrieved from http://www.census.gov/compendia/statab.

Yeung, W.-J. J., & Pfeiffer, K. M. (2009). The black-white test score gap and early home environment. *Social Science Research, 38*(2), 412–437.

16.4 Issues and Problems in Education

Learning Objectives

1. Describe how schooling in the United States helps perpetuate social inequality.
2. Explain the difference between de jure segregation and de facto segregation.
3. Summarize the evidence on the effectiveness of single-sex education.
4. Describe the extent of school violence and the controversy over zero-tolerance policies.
5. Discuss how and why social inequality in the larger society manifests itself in higher education.

The education system today faces many issues and problems of interest not just to educators and families but also to sociologists and other social scientists. We cannot discuss all of these issues here, but we will highlight some of the most interesting and important.

Schools and Inequality

Earlier we mentioned that schools differ greatly in their funding, their conditions, and other aspects. Noted author and education critic Jonathan Kozol refers to these differences as "savage inequalities," to quote the title of one of his books (Kozol, 1991). Kozol's concern over inequality in the schools stemmed from his experience as a young teacher in a public elementary school in a Boston inner-city neighborhood in the 1960s. Kozol was shocked to see that his school was literally falling apart. The physical plant was decrepit, with plaster falling off the walls and bathrooms and other facilities substandard. Classes were large, and the school was so overcrowded that Kozol's fourth-grade class had to meet in an auditorium, which it shared with another class, the school choir, and, for a time, a group of students practicing for the Christmas play. Kozol's observations led to the writing of his first award-winning book, *Death at an Early Age* (Kozol, 1967).

Jonathan Kozol has written movingly of "savage inequalities" in American schools arising from large differences in their funding and in the condition of their physical facilities.

Thomas Hawk – El Paso High School – CC BY-NC 2.0; Nitram242 – Detroit School – CC BY 2.0.

Kozol left this school after being fired for departing from the prescribed curriculum by teaching poems by Robert Frost and Langston Hughes to his fourth graders. He then taught in a wealthy school in one of Boston's suburbs, where his class had only 21 students. The conditions he saw there were far superior to those in his inner-city Boston school. "The shock of going from one of the poorest schools to one of the wealthiest cannot be overstated," he later wrote (Kozol, 1991, p. 2).

During the late 1980s, Kozol (1991) traveled around the country and systematically compared public schools in several cities' inner-city neighborhoods to those in the cities' suburbs. Everywhere he went, he found great discrepancies in school spending and in the quality of instruction. In schools in Camden, New Jersey, for example, spending per pupil was less than half the amount spent in the nearby, much wealthier town of Princeton. Chicago and New York City schools spent only about half the amount that some of the schools in nearby suburbs spent.

Learning From Other Societies

Successful Schooling in Denmark

Denmark's model for schooling from the earliest years up through high school offers several important lessons for U.S. education. The Danish model reflects that nation's strong belief that significant income inequality causes many problems and that it is the role of government to help the poorest members of society. This philosophy is seen in both the Danish approach to early childhood education and its approach to secondary schooling (Morrill, 2007).

In early childhood education, Denmark's policies also reflect its recognition of the importance of child cognitive and emotional development during the first few years of life, as well as its recognition to take special steps to help children of families living in poverty. Accordingly, along with several other Nordic and Western European nations, Denmark provides preschool and day care education for all children. According to one Danish scholar, "intervention in day-care/pre-school is considered the best way to give children a good beginning in life, particularly socially endangered children. [T]he dominant view is that the earlier children develop academic skills and knowledge the better, as these skills will enable them to participate in society on equal terms with children of the same age" (Jensen, 2009, p. 6).

Once students start elementary school, they join a class of about 20 students. Rather than being tracked (grouped by ability), students are simply assigned to a class with other children from their neighborhood. The class remains with the same "class teacher" from grades 1 through 9; this teacher instructs them in Danish language and literature. Other teachers teach them subjects such as arithmetic/mathematics, music, social studies, and science. Because the "class teacher" is with the students for so many years, they get to know each other very well, and the teacher and each child's parents also become very well acquainted. These rather close relationships help the teacher deal with any academic or behavioral problems that might occur. Because a class stays together for 9 years, the students develop close relationships with each other and a special sense of belonging to their class and to their school (Morrill, 2007).

The commitment to free or low-cost, high-quality early childhood education found in Denmark and many other Nordic and Western European nations is lacking in the United States, where parents who desire such education for their children usually must pay hundreds of dollars monthly. Many education scholars think the United States would do well to follow the example of these other nations in this regard. The interesting "class teacher" model in Denmark's lower grades seems to provide several advantages that the United States should also consider. In both these respects, the United States may have much to learn from Denmark's approach to how children should learn.

These numbers were reflected in other differences Kozol found when he visited city and suburban schools. In East St. Louis, Illinois, where most of the residents are poor and almost all are African American, schools had to shut down once because of sewage backups. The high school's science labs were 30 to 50 years out of date when Kozol visited them; the biology lab had no dissecting kits. A history teacher had 110 students but only 26 textbooks, some of which were missing their first 100 pages. At one of the city's junior high schools, many window frames lacked any glass, and the hallways were dark because light bulbs were missing or not working. Visitors could smell urinals 100 feet from the bathroom. When he visited an urban high school in New Jersey, Kozol found it had no showers for gym students, who had to wait 20 minutes to shoot one basketball because seven classes would use the school's gym at the same time.

Contrast these schools with those Kozol visited in suburbs. A high school in a Chicago suburb had seven gyms and an Olympic-sized swimming pool. Students there could take classes in seven foreign languages. A suburban New Jersey high school offered 14 AP courses, fencing, golf, ice hockey, and lacrosse, and the school district there had 10 music teachers and an extensive music program.

From his observations, Kozol concluded that the United States is shortchanging its children in poor rural and urban areas. As we saw in Chapter 8 "Social Stratification", poor children start out in life with many strikes against them. The schools they attend compound their problems and help ensure that the American ideal of equal opportunity for all remains just that—an ideal—rather than reality. As Kozol (1991, p. 233) observed, "All our children ought to be allowed a stake in the enormous richness of America. Whether they were born to poor white Appalachians or to wealthy Texans, to poor black people in the Bronx or to rich people in Manhasset or Winnetka, they are all quite wonderful and innocent when they are small. We soil them needlessly."

Although the book in which Kozol reported these conditions was published about 20 years ago, ample evidence indicates that little, if anything, has changed in the poor schools of the United States since then, with large funding differences continuing. In Philadelphia, for example, annual per-pupil expenditure is about $9,000; in nearby Lower Merion Township, it is more than twice as high, at about $19,000. Just a few years ago, a news report discussed public schools in Washington, DC. More than 75% of the schools in the city had a leaking roof at the time the report was published, and 87% had electrical problems, some of which involved shocks or sparks. Most of the schools' cafeterias, 85%, had health violations, including peeling paint near food and rodent and roach infestation. Thousands of requests for building repairs, including 1,100 labeled "urgent" or "dangerous," had been waiting more than a year to be addressed. More than one-third of the schools had a mouse infestation, and in one elementary school, there were so many mice that the students gave them names and drew their pictures. An official with the city's school system said, "I don't know if anybody knows the magnitude of problems at D.C. public schools. It's mind-boggling" (Keating & Haynes, 2007, p. A1).

Although it is widely assumed that school conditions like the ones in Washington, DC, and those depicted in Kozol's books impair student learning, there is surprisingly little research on this issue. Addressing this scholarly neglect, a recent study found that poor school conditions indeed impair learning, in part because they reduce students' attendance, which in turn impairs their learning (Durán-Narucki, 2008).

School Segregation

A related issue to inequality in the schools is school segregation. Before 1954, schools in the South were segregated by law (**de jure segregation**). Communities and states had laws that dictated which schools white children attended and which schools African American children attended. Schools were either all white or all African American, and, inevitably, white schools were much better funded than African American schools. Then in 1954, the U.S. Supreme Court outlawed de jure school segregation in its famous *Brown v. Board of Education* decision. In this decision the Court explicitly overturned its earlier, 1896 decision in *Plessy v. Ferguson*, which said that schools could be racially separate but equal. *Brown* rejected this conclusion as contrary to American egalitarian ideals and as also not supported by empirical evidence, which finds that segregated schools are indeed unequal. Southern school districts fought the *Brown* decision with legal machinations, and de jure school segregation did not really end in the South until the civil rights movement won its major victories a decade later.

Meanwhile, northern schools were also segregated and, in the years since the *Brown* decision, have become even more segregated. School segregation in the North stemmed, both then and now, not from the law but from neighborhood residential patterns. Because children usually go to schools near their homes, if adjacent neighborhoods are all white or all African American, then the schools children from these neighborhoods attend will also be all white or all African American, or mostly so. This type of segregation is called **de facto segregation**.

Many children today attend schools that are racially segregated because of neighborhood residential patterns.

halfrain – Swings – CC BY-SA 2.0.

Today many children continue to go to schools that are segregated because of neighborhood residential patterns, a situation that Kozol (2005) calls "apartheid schooling." About 40% of African American and Latino children attend schools that are very segregated (at least 90% of their students are of color); this level of segregation is higher than it was four decades ago. Although such segregation is legal, it still results in schools that are all African American and/or all Latino and that suffer severely from lack of funding, poor physical facilities, and inadequate teachers (Orfield, 2009).

During the 1960s and 1970s, states, municipalities, and federal courts tried to reduce de facto segregation by busing urban African American children to suburban white schools and, less often, by busing white suburban children to African American urban schools. Busing inflamed passions as perhaps few other issues during those decades (Lukas, 1985). White parents opposed it because they did not want their children bused to urban schools, where, they feared, the children would receive an inferior education and face risks to their safety. The racial prejudice that many white parents shared heightened their concerns over these issues. African American parents were more likely to see the need for busing, but they, too, wondered about its merits, especially because it was their children who were bused most often and faced racial hostility when they entered formerly all-white schools.

As one possible solution to reduce school segregation, some cities have established *magnet schools*, schools for high-achieving students of all races to which the students and their families apply for admission (Davis, 2007). Although these schools do help some students whose families are poor and of color, their impact on school segregation has been minimal because the number of magnet schools is low and because they are open only to the very best students who, by definition, are also few in number. Some critics also say that magnet schools siphon needed resources from public school systems and that their reliance on standardized tests makes it difficult for African American and Latino students to gain admission.

School Vouchers and School Choice

Another issue involving schools today is *school choice*. In a school choice program, the government gives parents certificates, or vouchers, that they can use as tuition at private or parochial (religious) schools.

Advocates of school choice programs say they give poor parents an option for high-quality education they otherwise would not be able to afford. These programs, the advocates add, also help improve the public schools by forcing them to compete for students with their private and parochial counterparts. In order to keep a large number of parents from using vouchers to send their children to the latter schools, public schools have to upgrade their facilities, improve their instruction, and undertake other steps to make their brand of education an attractive alternative. In this way, school choice advocates argue, vouchers have a "competitive impact" that forces public schools to make themselves more attractive to prospective students (Walberg, 2007).

Critics of school choice programs say they hurt the public schools by decreasing their enrollments and therefore their funding. Public schools do not have the money now to compete with private and parochial ones, and neither will they have the money to compete with them if vouchers become more widespread. Critics also worry that voucher programs will lead to a "brain drain" of the most academically motivated children and families from low-income schools (Caldas & Bankston, 2005).

Because school choice programs and school voucher systems are still relatively new, scholars have not yet had time to assess whether they improve the academic achievement of the students who attend them. Although some studies do find small improvements, methodological problems make it difficult to reach any firm conclusions at this point (DeLuca & Dayton, 2009). Although there is similarly little research on the impact of school choice programs on funding and other aspects of public school systems, some evidence does indicate a negative impact. In Milwaukee, for example, enrollment decline from the use of vouchers cost the school system $26 million in state aid during the 1990s, forcing a rise in property taxes to replace the lost funds. Because the students who left the Milwaukee school system came from most of its 157 public schools, only a few left any one school, diluting the voucher system's competitive impact. Another city, Cleveland, also lost state aid in the late 1990s because of the use of vouchers, and there, too, the competitive impact was small. Thus, although school choice programs may give some families alternatives to public schools, they might not have the competitive impact on public schools that their advocates claim, and they may cost public school systems state aid (Cooper, 1999; Lewin, 1999).

Single-Sex Schools and Classes

Before the late 1960s and early 1970s, many colleges and universities, including several highly selective campuses, were single-sex institutions. Since that time, almost all the male colleges and many of the female colleges have gone coed. A few women's colleges still remain, as their administrators and alumnae say that women can achieve much more in a women's college than in a coed institution. The issue of single-sex institutions has been more muted at the secondary school level, as most public schools have been coeducational since the advent of free, compulsory education during the 19th century. However, several private schools were single-sex ones from their outset, and many of these remain today. Still, the trend throughout the educational world was toward coeducation.

Single-sex schools and classes have become more popular for several reasons. The research so far indicates that single-sex education may be beneficial in certain respects for the students experiencing it.

Wikimedia Commons – CC BY 3.0.

Since the 1990s, however, some education specialists and other observers have considered whether single-sex secondary schools, or at least single-sex classes, might make sense for girls or for boys; in response, single-sex classes and single-sex schools have arisen in at least 17 U.S. cities. The argument for single-sex learning for girls rests on the same reasons advanced by advocates for women's colleges: girls can do better academically, and perhaps especially in math and science classes, when they are by themselves. The argument for boys rests on a different set of reasons (Sax, 2009). Boys in classes with girls are more likely to act "macho" and thus to engage in disruptive behavior; in single-sex classes, boys thus behave better and are more committed to their studies. They also feel freer to exhibit an interest in music, the arts, and other subjects not usually thought of as "macho" topics. Furthermore, because the best students in coed schools are often girls, many boys tend to devalue academic success in coed settings and are more likely to value it in single-sex settings. Finally, in a boys-only setting, teachers can use examples and certain teaching techniques that boys may find especially interesting, such as the use of snakes to teach biology. To the extent that single-sex education may benefit boys for any of these reasons, these benefits are often thought to be highest for boys from families living in poverty or near poverty.

What does the research evidence say about the benefits of single-sex schooling? A recent review of several dozen studies concluded that the results of single-sex schooling are mixed overall but that there are slightly more favorable outcomes for single-sex schools compared to coeducational schools: "There is some support for the premise that single-sex schooling can be helpful, especially for certain outcomes related to academic achievement and more positive academic aspirations. For many outcomes, there is no evidence of either benefit or harm" (U.S. Department of Education, 2005). None of the studies involved random assignment of students to single-sex or coeducational schooling, and the review cautioned that firmer conclusions must await higher-quality research of this nature (which may be ideal in terms of the research process but difficult and perhaps impossible to perform in real life). Also, because all the studies involved high school students and a majority involved students in Catholic schools, the review called for additional studies of younger students and those in public schools.

School Violence

The issue of school violence won major headlines during the 1990s, when many children, teachers, and other individuals died in the nation's schools. From 1992 until 1999, 248 students, teachers, and other people died from violent acts (including suicide) on school property, during travel to and from school, or at a school-related event, for an average of about 35 violent deaths per year (Zuckoff, 1999). Against this backdrop, the infamous April 1999 school shootings at Columbine High School in Littleton, Colorado, where two students murdered 12 other students and one teacher before killing themselves, led to national soul-searching over the causes of teen and school violence and on possible ways to reduce it.

The murders in Littleton were so numerous and cold-blooded that they would have aroused national concern under any circumstances, but they also followed a string of other mass shootings at schools. In just a few examples, in December 1997 a student in a Kentucky high school shot and killed three students in a before-school prayer group. In March 1998 two middle school students in Arkansas pulled a fire alarm to evacuate their school and then shot and killed four students and one teacher as they emerged. Two months later an Oregon high school student killed his parents and then went to his school cafeteria, where he killed two students and wounded 22 others. Against this backdrop, Littleton seemed like the last straw. Within days, school after school across the nation installed metal detectors, located police at building entrances and in hallways, and began questioning or suspending students joking about committing violence. People everywhere wondered why the schools were becoming so violent and what could be done about it (Zuckoff, 1999).

Violence can also happen on college and university campuses, although shootings are very rare. However, two recent examples illustrate that students and faculty are not immune from gun violence. In February 2010, Amy Bishop, a biology professor at the University of Alabama in Huntsville who had recently been denied tenure, allegedly shot and killed three faculty at a department meeting and wounded three others. Almost 3 years earlier, a student at Virginia Tech went on a shooting rampage and killed 32 students and faculty before killing himself.

Sociology Making a Difference

School Bonding and Delinquency

As discussed in Chapter 7 "Deviance, Crime, and Social Control", the social control theory of delinquency assumes that weak social bonds to family, schools, and other social institutions help promote juvenile delinquency. This theory was developed by sociologist Travis Hirschi (1969) about four decades ago. Hirschi's emphasis on social bonds was inspired by the work of sociology founder Émile Durkheim, who more broadly emphasized the importance of strong ties to society for social cohesion and individual well-being.

Since the development of social bonding theory, most studies testing it have focused on family and school bonds. They generally support Hirschi's view that weak bonds to family and school help promote delinquency. One issue that has received less study is whether *strong* bonds to school might help prevent delinquency by youths who otherwise might be at high risk for such behavior—for example, those who were born to a teenaged mother, who exhibited aggressive behavior during childhood, or who have delinquent friends.

A Canadian team of researchers examined this possibility with national data on youths studied from childhood to young adulthood (Sprott, Jenkins, & Doob, 2005). They identified children aged 10–11 with various risk factors for antisocial behavior and measured how strongly bonded they felt to their schools, based on their responses to several questions (including how much they liked their school and how often they finish their homework). They also determined the extent of their delinquency at ages 12–13 based on the youths' responses to a series of questions. Confirming their hypothesis, the researchers found that high-risk children were less likely to be delinquent at ages 12–13 if they had strong school bonds at ages 10–11 than if they had weak bonds. The researchers concluded that strong school bonds help prevent delinquency even by high-risk children, and they further speculated that zero-tolerance policies (as discussed in the text) that lead to suspension or expulsion may ironically promote delinquency because they weaken school bonding for the children who leave school.

As should be clear, the body of research on school bonding and delinquency inspired by social control theory suggests that schools play an important role in whether students misbehave both inside and outside school. It also suggests that efforts to improve the nation's schools will also reduce delinquency because these efforts will almost certainly strengthen the bonds children feel to their schools. As social control theory is ultimately rooted in the work of Émile Durkheim, sociology is again making a difference.

Fortunately, school violence has declined during the past decade, as fewer students and other people have died at the nation's schools than during 1990s. As this trend indicates, the risk of school violence should not be exaggerated: statistically speaking, schools are very safe. Less than 1% of homicides involving school-aged children take place in or near school. About 56 million students attend elementary and secondary schools. With about 17 student homicides a year, the chances are less than one in 3 million that a student will be killed at school. The annual rate of other serious violence (rape and sexual assault, aggravated assault, and robbery) is only 3 crimes per 100 students; although this is still three too many, it does indicate that 97% of students do not suffer these crimes. Bullying is a much more common problem, with about one-third of students reporting being bullied annually (National Center for Injury Prevention and Control, 2010).

To reduce school violence, many school districts have *zero-tolerance* policies involving weapons. These policies call for automatic suspension or expulsion of a student who has anything resembling a weapon for any reason. For better or worse, however, there have been many instances in which these policies have been applied too rigidly. In a recent example, a 6-year-old boy in Delaware excitedly took his new camping utensil—a combination of knife, fork, and spoon—from Cub Scouts to school to use at lunch. He was suspended for having a knife and ordered to spend 45 days in reform school. His mother said her son certainly posed no threat to anyone at school, but school officials replied that their policy had to be strictly enforced because it is difficult to determine who actually poses a threat from who does not (Urbina, 2009). In another case, a ninth grader took a knife and cigarette lighter away from a student who had used them to threaten a fellow classmate. The ninth grader was suspended for the rest of the school year for possessing a weapon, even though he had them only because he was protecting his classmate. According to a news story about this case, the school's reaction was "vigilance to a fault" (Walker, 2010, p. A12).

Ironically, one reason many school districts have very strict policies is to avoid the racial discrimination that was seen to occur in districts whose officials had more discretion in deciding which students needed to be suspended or expelled. In these districts, African American students with weapons or "near-weapons" were more likely than white students with the same objects to be punished in this manner. Regardless of the degree of discretion afforded officials in zero-tolerance policies, these policies have not been shown to be effective in reducing school violence and may actually raise rates of violence by the students who are suspended or expelled under these policies (Skiba & Rausch, 2006).

Focus on Higher Education

The issues and problems discussed so far in this chapter concern the nation's elementary and secondary schools in view of their critical importance for tens of millions of children and for the nation's social and economic well-being. However, issues also affect higher education, and we examine a few of them here.

Cost

Higher education can cost students and their parents tens of thousands of dollars per year. This expense prevents many students from going to college and puts many students and parents into considerable debt.

GotCredit – Student Loans – CC BY 2.0.

Perhaps the most important issue is that higher education, at least at 4-year institutions, is quite expensive and can cost tens of thousands of dollars per year. This figure varies by the type of college or university, as private institutions cost much more than public institutions (for in-state students). According to the College Board (2010), slightly more than half of all students attend a 4-year institution whose annual tuition and fees amount to less than $9,000; public schools charge an average of $7,000 for in-state students. That means that almost half of students attend an institution whose annual tuition and fees are $9,000 or more; this cost averages more than $26,000 at some private colleges and universities and exceeds $35,000 at many private institutions. Room and board expenses for on-campus students range from about $8,000 to $14,000, and books and supplies average at least an additional $1,000 for students who do not have the opportunity to read free or low-cost textbooks such as this one.

Combining these figures, students at the least expensive 4-year institutions might have bills that total $17,000 to $20,000 annually, and those at the most expensive private institutions might have bills that exceed $50,000. Scholarships and other financial aid reduce these costs for many students. Private institutions actually collect only about 67% of their published tuition and fees because of the aid they hand out, and public institutions collect only about 82% (Stripling, 2010). However, students who receive aid may still have bills totaling thousands of dollars annually and graduate with huge loans to repay. At 2-year institutions, annual tuition and fees average about $2,600; these colleges are more affordable but nonetheless can be very costly for their students and their families.

Floundering Students

Although college is often said to be the best time of one's life, many students have difficulties during their college years. These students are called *floundering students*. Homesickness during the first semester on campus is common, but a number of students have difficulties beyond homesickness. According to psychiatry professor David Leibow, who has studied troubled students, many floundering students mistakenly believe that they are the only ones who are floundering, and many fail to tell their parents or friends about their problems (Golden, 2010). The major cause of floundering, says Leibow, is academic difficulties; other causes include homesickness, relationship problems, family problems including family conflict and the serious illness or death of a family member, personal illness, and financial difficulties. It is estimated that every year 10% of students seek psychological counseling on their college campus, primarily for depression, anxiety, and relationship problems (Epstein, 2010). Many of these students are given medications to treat their symptoms. Leibow says these medications are often helpful but worries that they are overprescribed. Three reasons underlie his concern. First, although the students given these medications may have problems, often the problems are a normal part of growing into adulthood and not serious enough to justify medication. Second, some of these medications can have serious side effects. Third, students who take medications may be more likely to avoid dealing with the underlying reasons for their problems.

Social Class and Race in Admissions

We saw earlier in this chapter that African American, Latino, and low-income students are less likely to attend college. This fact raises important questions about the lack of diversity in college admissions and campus life. Chapter 10 "Race and Ethnicity" discussed the debate over racially based affirmative action in higher education. Partly because affirmative action is so controversial, attention has begun to focus on the low numbers of low-income students at many colleges and universities, especially the more selective institutions that rank highly in ratings issued by *U.S.News & World Report* and other sources. Many education scholars and policymakers feel that increasing the number of low-income students would not only help these students but also increase campus diversity along the lines of socioeconomic status and race/ethnicity (since students of color are more likely to be from low-income backgrounds). Efforts to increase the number of low-income students, these experts add, would avoid the controversy that has surrounded affirmative action.

In response to this new attention to social class, colleges and universities have begun to increase their efforts to attract and retain low-income students, which a recent news report called "one of the most underrepresented minority groups at many four-year colleges" (Schmidt, 2010). The dean of admissions and financial aid at Harvard University summarized these efforts as follows: "I honestly cannot think of any admissions person I know who is not looking—as sort of a major criteria of how well their year went—at how well they did in attracting people of different economic backgrounds" (Schmidt, 2010).

Although colleges and universities are making a greater effort to attract and retain low-income students, these students remain greatly underrepresented at institutions of higher education.

Bart Everson – Students – CC BY 2.0.

As part of their strategy to attract and retain low-income students, Harvard and other selective institutions are now providing financial aid to cover all or most of the students' expenses. Despite these efforts, however, the U.S. higher education system has become more stratified by social class in recent decades: the richest students now occupy a greater percentage of the enrollment at the most selective institutions than in the past, while the poorest students occupy a greater percentage of the enrollment at the least selective 4-year institutions and at community colleges (Schmidt, 2010).

Graduation Rates

For the sakes of students and their colleges and universities, it is important that as many students as possible go on to earn their diplomas. However, only 57% of students at 4-year institutitons graduate within 6 years. This figure varies by type of institution. At the highly selective private institutions, 80%–90% or more of students typically graduate within 6 years, while at many public institutions, the graduate rate is about 50%. Academic and financial difficulties and other problems explain why so many students fail to graduate.

The 57% overall rate masks a racial/ethnic difference in graduate rates: while 60% of white students graduate within 6 years, only 49% of Latino students and 40% of African American students graduate. At some institutions, the graduation rates of Latino and African American students match those of whites, thanks in large part to exceptional efforts by these institutions to help students of color. As one expert on this issue explains, "What colleges do for students of color powerfully impacts the futures of these young people and that of our nation" (Gonzalez, 2010). Another expert placed this issue into a larger context: "For both moral and economic reasons, colleges need to ensure that their institutions work better for all the students they serve" (Stephens, 2010).

In this regard, it is important to note that the graduation rate of low-income students from 4-year institutions is much lower than the graduation rate of wealthier students. Low-income students drop out at higher rates because of academic and financial difficulties and family problems (Berg, 2010). Their academic and financial difficulties are intertwined. Low-income students often have to work many hours per week during the academic year to be able to pay their bills. Because their work schedules reduce the time they have for studying, their grades may suffer. This general problem has been made worse by cutbacks in federal grants to low-income students that began during the 1980s. These cutbacks forced low-income students to rely increasingly on loans, which have to be repaid. This fact leads some to work more hours during the academic year to limit the loans they must take out, and their increased work schedule again may affect their grades.

Low-income students face additional difficulties beyond the financial (Berg, 2010). Their writing and comprehension skills upon entering college are often weaker than those of wealthier students. If they are first-generation college students (meaning that neither parent went to college), they often have problems adjusting to campus life and living amid students from much more advantaged backgrounds.

Key Takeaways

- Schools in America are unequal: they differ greatly in the extent in their funding, in the quality of their physical facilities, and in other respects. Jonathan Kozol calls these differences "savage inequalities."
- Single-sex education at the secondary level has become more popular. Preliminary evidence indicates that this form of education may be beneficial for several reasons, but more evidence on this issue is needed.
- Although school violence has declined since the 1990s, it continues to concern many Americans. Bullying at school is a common problem and can lead to more serious violence by the children who are bullied.
- The cost of higher education and other problems make it difficult for low-income students and students of color to enter college and to stay in college once admitted.

For Your Review

1. If you were the principal of a middle school, would you favor or oppose single-sex classes? Explain your answer.

2. If you were the director of admissions at a university, what steps would you take to increase the number of applications from low-income students?

Improving Education and Schools: What Sociology Suggests

Sociological theory and research have helped people to understand the reasons for various issues arising in formal education. Accordingly, this final section discusses strategies suggested by this body of work for addressing a few of these issues.

One issue is school inequality. The inequality that exists in American society finds its way into primary and secondary schools, and inequality in the schools in turn contributes to inequality in the larger society. Although scholars continue to debate the relative importance of family backgrounds and school funding and other school factors for academic achievement, it is clear that schools with decaying buildings and uncommitted teachers cannot be expected to produce students with high or even adequate academic achievement. At a minimum, schools need to be smaller and better funded, teachers need to be held accountable for their students' learning, and decaying buildings need to be repaired. On the national level, these steps will cost billions of dollars, but this expenditure promises to have a significant payoff (Smerdon & Borman, 2009).

School violence is another issue that needs to be addressed. The steps just outlined should reduce school violence, but other measures should also help. One example involves antibullying programs, which include regular parent meetings, strengthened playground supervision, and appropriate discipline when warranted. Research indicates that these programs reduce bullying by 20%–23% on the average (Farrington & Trofi, 2009). Any reduction in bullying should in turn help reduce the likelihood of school massacres like Columbine, as many of the students committing these massacres were humiliated and bullied by other students (Adler & Springen, 1999).

Experts also think that reducing the size of schools and the size of classes will reduce school violence, as having smaller classes and schools should help create a less alienating atmosphere, allow for more personal attention, and make students' attitudes toward their school more positive (Levin & Fox, 1999). More generally, because the roots of school violence are also similar to the roots of youth violence outside the schools, measures that reduce youth violence should also reduce school violence. As discussed in previous chapters, such measures include early childhood prevention programs for youths at risk for developmental and behavioral problems, and policies that provide income and jobs for families living in poverty (Welsh & Farrington, 2007).

At the level of higher education, our discussion highlighted the fact that social inequality in the larger society also plays out in colleges and universities. The higher dropout rates for low-income students and for students of color in turn contribute to more social inequality. Colleges and universities need to do everything possible to admit these students and then to help them once they are admitted, as they face many obstacles and difficulties that white students from more advantaged backgrounds are much less likely to encounter.

References

Adler, J., & Springen, K. (1999, May 3). How to fight back. *Newsweek* 36–38.

Berg, G. A. (2010). *Low-income students and the perpetuation of inequality: Higher education in America*. Burlington, VT: Ashgate.

Caldas, S. J., & Bankston, C. L., III. (2005). *Forced to fail: The paradox of school desegregation*. Westport, CT: Praeger.

College Board. (2010). What it costs to go to college. Retrieved from http://www.collegeboard.com/student/pay/add-it-up/4494.html.

Cooper, K. J. (1999, June 25). Under vouchers, status quo rules. *The Washington Post*, p. A3.

Davis, M. R. (2007). Magnet schools and diversity. *Education Week, 26*(18), 9.

DeLuca, S., & Dayton, E. (2009). Switching social contexts: The effects of housing mobility and school choice programs on youth outcomes. *Annual Review of Sociology, 35*(1), 457–491.

Durán-Narucki, V. (2008). School building condition, school attendance, and academic achievement in New York City public schools: A mediation model. *Journal of Environmental Psychology, 28*(3), 278–286.

Epstein, J. (2010, May 4). Stability in student mental health. *Inside Higher Ed*. Retrieved from http://www.insidehighered.com/news/2010/2005/2004/counseling.

Farrington, D. P., & Trofi, M. M. (2009). School-based programs to reduce bullying and victimization. *Campbell Systematic Reviews, 6*, 1–148. doi:10.4073/csr.2009.6.

Golden, S. (2010, September 15). When college is not the best time. *Inside Higher Ed*. Retrieved from http://www.insidehighered.com/news/2010/2009/2015/leibow.

Gonzalez, J. (2010, August 9). Reports highlight disparities in graduation rates among white and minority students. *The Chronicle of Higher Education*. Retrieved from http://chronicle.com/article/Reports-Highlight-Disparities/123857.

Hirschi, T. (1969). *Causes of delinquency*. Berkeley: University of California Press.

Jensen, B. (2009). A Nordic approach to early childhood education (ECE) and socially endangered children. *European Early Childhood Education Research Journal, 17*(1), 7–21.

Keating, D., & Haynes, V. D. (2007, June 10). Can D.C. schools be fixed? *The Washington Post*, p. A1.

Kozol, J. (1967). *Death at an early age: The destruction of the hearts and minds of Negro children in the Boston public schools*. Boston, MA: Houghton Mifflin.

Kozol, J. (1991). *Savage inequalities: Children in America's schools*. New York, NY: Crown.

Kozol, J. (2005). *The shame of the nation: The restoration of apartheid schooling in America*. New York, NY: Crown.

Levin, J., & Fox, J. A. (1999, April 25). Schools learning a grim lesson (but will society flunk?). *The Boston Globe*, p. C1.

Lewin, T. (1999, March 27). Few clear lessons from nation's first school-choice program. *The New York Times*, p. A10.

Lukas, J. A. (1985). *Common ground: A turbulent decade in the lives of three American families*. New York, NY: Knopf.

Morrill, R. (2007). Denmark: Lessons for American principals and teachers? In D. S. Eitzen (Ed.), *Solutions to social problems: Lessons from other societies* (pp. 125–130). Boston, MA: Allyn & Bacon.

National Center for Injury Prevention and Control. (2010). *Understanding school violence fact sheet.* Washington, DC: Centers for Disease Control and Prevention.

Orfield, G. (2009). *Reviving the goal of an integrated society: A 21st century challenge.* Los Angeles: The Civil Rights Project, University of California at Los Angeles.

Sax, L. (2009). *Boys adrift: The five factors driving the growing epidemic of unmotivated boys and underachieving young men*. New York, NY: Basic Books.

Schmidt, P. (2010, September 19). In push for diversity, colleges pay attention to socioeconomic class. *The Chronicle of Higher Education*. Retrieved from http://chronicle.com/article/Socioeconomic-Class-Gains/124446/?key= TjgnJ124441E124444aHZGM124443hiaT124448TZzgHPSRqZR124448jY124443AYPn124440pbl124449WFQ%124443D%124443D.

Skiba, R. J., & Rausch, M. K. (2006). Zero tolerance, suspension, and expulsion: Questions of equity and effectiveness. In C. M. Evertson & C. S. Weinstein (Eds.), *Handbook of classroom management: Research, practice, and contemporary issues* (pp. 1063–1089). Mahwah, NJ: Lawrence Erlbaum Associates.

Smerdon, B. A., & Borman, K. M. (Eds.). (2009). *Saving America's high schools.* Washington, DC: Urban Institute Press.

Sprott, J. B., Jenkins, J. M., & Doob, A. N. (2005). The importance of school: Protecting at-risk youth from early offending. *Youth Violence and Juvenile Justice, 3*(1), 59–77.

Stephens, L. (2010). *Reports reveal colleges with the biggest, smallest gaps in minority graduation rates in the U.S.* Washington, DC: The Education Trust.

Stripling, J. (2010, September 15). Refining aid choices. *Inside Higher Ed.* Retrieved from http://www.insidehighered.com/news/2010/2009/2015/discounting.

U.S. Department of Education. (2005). *Single-sex versus secondary schooling: A systematic review*. Washington, DC: Office of Planning, Evaluation and Policy Development, Policy and Program Studies Service, U.S. Department of Education.

Urbina, I. (2009, October 11). It's a fork, it's a spoon, it's a...weapon? *The New York Times*, p. A1.

Walberg, H. J. (2007). *School choice: The findings*. Washington, DC: Cato Institute.

Walker, A. (2010, January 23). Vigilance to a fault. *The Boston Globe*, p. A12.

Welsh, B. C., & Farrington, D. P. (Eds.). (2007). *Preventing crime: What works for children, offenders, victims and places*. New York, NY: Springer.

Zuckoff, M. (1999, May 21). Fear is spread around nation. *The Boston Globe*, p. A1.

16.5 End-of-Chapter Material

Summary

1. Education is both formal and informal. Formal education occurs in schools under specially trained teachers, while informal education takes place primarily in the home, with parents as instructors. For much of human history, education was informal, especially before the beginning of writing and numbers. As societies became more complex economically and socially, schools began to develop, but they were usually restricted to relatively wealthy boys.
2. In the early 19th century in the United States, a movement for free, compulsory education began. Reasons for interest in such education included the perceived needs to unify the country, to "Americanize" immigrants, and to give members of the working class the skills, knowledge, and discipline they needed to be productive workers.
3. Sociological perspectives on education fall into the functionalist, conflict, and symbolic interactionist approaches discussed in earlier chapters. Functional theory stresses the functions education serves for society, including socialization, social placement, social integration, and social and cultural innovation. Conflict theory stresses that education perpetuates and reinforces existing social inequality for several reasons, including the use of tracking and inequality in schooling between rich and poor communities. Symbolic interactionism emphasizes the social interaction that's part of schooling and calls attention to the ways in which the treatment of students as smart or dull can affect how much they end up learning.
4. In the United States, social class, race and ethnicity, and gender all affect educational attainment. Poor people end up with less schooling than middle- and upper-class people, and African Americans and Latinos have lower educational attainment than whites and Asian Americans. Although women had less schooling than men in the past, today they are more likely to graduate from high school and to attend college.
5. Education in the United States has a significant impact on two areas. One is income: the higher the education, the higher the income. The second is attitudes: the higher the education, the greater the tolerance for nontraditional behaviors and viewpoints.
6. Several issues and problems affect education in the United States today. Many schools are poor and rundown and lack sufficient books and equipment. Many schools are also segregated by race and ethnicity. These twin problems make it difficult for students in these schools to receive a good education. Increasing interest in school choice has led to controversy over whether the government should provide aid to parents to send their children to private and parochial schools. Additional controversy surrounds the issue of single-sex schools for girls, which their advocates say promotes girls' learning, especially in math, science, and technology. Finally, school violence is an issue of continuing concern and received even more attention after the massacre at a high school in Littleton, Colorado. Despite this concern, the best evidence indicates that the vast majority of schools are very safe for their students, teachers, and other personnel.
7. At the level of higher education, students of color and those from low-income backgrounds are less likely to attend college at all, and if they do attend, they are less likely to graduate.

Using Sociology

It is October, and you are now in your second year of teaching fifth graders in a poor urban neighborhood. You don't have enough textbooks for your 40 students, and the ones you do have are very much out of date. Worse yet, there is a leak in your classroom ceiling that seems to be getting worse every week, even though you asked that it be repaired, and a foul odor arose a few days ago from a nearby bathroom and also seems to be getting worse. You decide you have at least four choices: (a) quit your job immediately and look for another job; (b) stay through the end of the academic year and then quit, while keeping quiet about your concerns about the school; (c) complain to the principal and/or perhaps to school district officials; or (d) ask for an interview with the local newspaper to bring your school's problems to light. What do you decide to do? Explain your answer.

Chapter 17: Religion

Social Issues in the News

"America's First Muslim College to Open This Fall," the headline said. The United States has hundreds of colleges and universities run by or affiliated with the Catholic Church and several Protestant and Jewish denominations, and now it was about to have its first Muslim college. Zaytuna College in Berkeley, California, had just sent out acceptance letters to students who would make up its inaugural class in the fall of 2010. The school's founder said it would be a Muslim liberal arts college whose first degrees would be in Islamic law and theology and in the Arabic language. The chair of the college's academic affairs committee explained, "We are trying to graduate well-rounded students who will be skilled in a liberal arts education with the ability to engage in a wider framework of society and the variety of issues that confront them….We are thinking of how to set up students for success. We don't see any contradiction between religious and secular subjects."

The college planned to rent a building in Berkeley during its first several years and was doing fund-raising to pay for the eventual construction or purchase of its own campus. It hoped to obtain academic accreditation within a decade. Because the United States has approximately 6 million Muslims whose numbers have tripled since the 1970s, college officials were optimistic that their new institution would succeed. An official with the Islamic Society of North America, which aids Muslim communities and organizations and provides chaplains for the U.S. military, applauded the new college. "It tells me that Muslims are coming of age," he said. "This is one more thing that makes Muslims part of the mainstream of America. It is an important part of the development of our community." (Oguntoyinbo, 2010)

The opening of any college is normally cause for celebration, but the news about this particular college aroused a mixed reaction. Some people wrote positive comments on the Web page on which this news article appeared, but two anonymous writers left very negative comments. One asked, "What if they teach radical Islam?" while the second commented, "Dose [*sic*] anyone know how Rome fell all those years ago? We are heading down the same road."

As the reaction to this news story reminds us, religion and especially Islam have certainly been hot topics since 9/11, as America continues to worry about terrorist threats from people with Middle Eastern backgrounds. Many political and religious leaders urge Americans to practice religious tolerance, and advocacy groups have established programs and secondary school curricula to educate the public and students, respectively. Colleges and universities have responded with courses and workshops on Islamic culture, literature, and language. The controversy over Islam is just one example of the strong passions that religion and religious differences often arouse, in part because religion involves our dearest values.

This chapter presents a sociological understanding of religion. We begin by examining religion as a social institution and by sketching its history and practice throughout the world today. We then turn to the several types of religious organizations before concluding with a discussion of various aspects of religion in the United States.

References

Oguntoyinbo, L. (2010, May 20). America's first Muslim college to open this fall. *Diverse: Issues in Higher Education*. Retrieved from http://diverseeducation.com/article/13814/america-s-first-muslim-college-to-open-this-fall.html.

17.1 Religion as a Social Institution

Learning Objectives

1. Describe the difference between sacred beliefs and profane beliefs.
2. Explain what Émile Durkheim tried to understand about religion.

Religion clearly plays an important role in American life. Most Americans believe in a deity, three-fourths pray at least weekly, and more than half attend religious services at least monthly. We tend to think of religion in individual terms because religious beliefs and values are highly personal for many people. However, religion is also a social institution, as it involves patterns of beliefs and behavior that help a society meet its basic needs, to recall the definition of social institution in Chapter 5 "Social Structure and Social Interaction". More specifically, **religion** is the set of beliefs and practices regarding sacred things that help a society understand the meaning and purpose of life.

More than half of all Americans attend religious services at least once per week. This illustrates the important role that religion plays in American life.

Royal New Zealand Navy – CC BY-ND 2.0.

Because it is such an important social institution, religion has long been a key sociological topic. Émile Durkheim (1915/1947) observed long ago that every society has beliefs about things that are supernatural and awe-inspiring and beliefs about things that are more practical and down-to-earth. He called the former beliefs **sacred** beliefs and the latter beliefs **profane** beliefs. Religious beliefs and practices involve the sacred: they involve things our senses cannot readily observe, and they involve things that inspire in us awe, reverence, and even fear.

Durkheim did not try to prove or disprove religious beliefs. Religion, he acknowledged, is a matter of faith, and faith is not provable or disprovable through scientific inquiry. Rather, Durkheim tried to understand the role played by religion in social life and the impact on religion of social structure and social change. In short, he treated religion as a social institution.

Sociologists since his time have treated religion in the same way. Anthropologists, historians, and other scholars have also studied religion. Historical work on religion reminds us of the importance of religion since the earliest societies, while comparative work on contemporary religion reminds us of its importance throughout the world today. Accordingly, Chapter 17 "Religion", Section 17.2 "Religion in Historical and Cross-Cultural Perspective" examines key aspects of the history of religion and its practice across the globe.

Key Takeaways

- As a social institution, religion helps a society meet its basic needs.
- Émile Durkheim distinguished between sacred beliefs and profane beliefs and wrote about the role religion played in social life.

For Your Review

1. Explain why religion should be regarded as a social institution.

References

Durkheim, É. (1947). *The elementary forms of religious life* (J. Swain, Trans.). Glencoe, IL: Free Press. (Original work published 1915).

17.2 Religion in Historical and Cross-Cultural Perspective

Learning Objectives

1. Describe key developments in the history of religion since ancient times.
2. List the major religions in the world today.
3. Outline key beliefs of each of these religions.

Every known society has practiced religion, although the nature of religious belief and practice has differed from one society to the next. Prehistoric people turned to religion to help them understand birth, death, and natural events such as hurricanes. They also relied on religion for help in dealing with their daily needs for existence: good weather, a good crop, an abundance of animals to hunt (Noss & Grangaard, 2008).

Although the world's most popular religions today are **monotheistic** (believing in one god), many societies in ancient times, most notably Egypt, Greece, and Rome, were **polytheistic** (believing in more than one god). You have been familiar with their names since childhood: Aphrodite, Apollo, Athena, Mars, Zeus, and many others. Each god "specialized" in one area; Aphrodite, for example, was the Greek goddess of love, while Mars was the Roman god of war (Noss & Grangaard, 2008).

Ancient Greece and Rome were polytheistic, as they believed in many gods. This statue depicts Zeus, the king of gods in Greek mythology.

Alun Salt – Apollo of Centocelle – CC BY-SA 2.0.

During the Middle Ages, the Catholic Church dominated European life. The Church's control began to weaken with the Protestant Reformation, which began in 1517 when Martin Luther, a German monk, spoke out against Church practices. By the end of the century, Protestantism had taken hold in much of Europe. Another founder of sociology, Max Weber, argued a century ago that the rise of Protestantism in turn led to the rise of capitalism. In his great book *The Protestant Ethic and the Spirit of Capitalism*, Weber wrote that Protestant belief in the need for hard work and economic success as a sign of eternal salvation helped lead to the rise of capitalism and the Industrial Revolution (Weber, 1904/1958). Although some scholars challenge Weber's views for several reasons, including the fact that capitalism also developed among non-Protestants, his analysis remains a compelling treatment of the relationship between religion and society.

Moving from Europe to the United States, historians have documented the importance of religion since the colonial period. Many colonists came to the new land to escape religious persecution in their home countries. The colonists were generally very religious, and their beliefs guided their daily lives and, in many cases, the operation of their governments and other institutions. In essence, government and religion were virtually the same entity in many locations, and church and state were not separate. Church officials performed many of the duties that the government performs today, and the church was not only a place of worship but also a community center in most of the colonies (Gaustad & Schmidt, 2004). The Puritans of what came to be Massachusetts refused to accept religious beliefs and practices different from their own and persecuted people with different religious views. They expelled Anne Hutchinson in 1637 for disagreeing with the beliefs of the Puritans' Congregational Church and hanged Mary Dyer in 1660 for practicing her Quaker faith.

Key World Religions Today

Today the world's largest religion is *Christianity*, to which more than 2 billion people, or about one-third the world's population, subscribe. Christianity began 2,000 years ago in Palestine under the charismatic influence of Jesus of Nazareth and today is a Western religion, as most Christians live in the Americas and in Europe. Beginning as a cult, Christianity spread through the Mediterranean and later through Europe before becoming the official religion of the Roman Empire. Today, dozens of Christian denominations exist in the United States and other nations. Their views differ in many respects, but generally they all regard Jesus as the son of God, and many believe that salvation awaits them if they follow his example (Young, 2010).

The second largest religion is *Islam*, which includes about 1.6 billion Muslims, most of them in the Middle East, northern Africa, and parts of Asia. Muhammad founded Islam in the 600s A.D. and is regarded today as a prophet who was a descendant of Abraham. Whereas the sacred book of Christianity and Judaism is the Bible, the sacred book of Islam is the Koran. The Five Pillars of Islam guide Muslim life: (a) the acceptance of Allah as God and Muhammad as his messenger; (b) ritual worship, including daily prayers facing Mecca, the birthplace of Muhammad; (c) observing Ramadan, a month of prayer and fasting; (d) giving alms to the poor; and (e) making a holy pilgrimage to Mecca at least once before one dies.

These individuals are praying at a mosque, the place of worship for the religion of Islam. Islam is the world's second largest religion, with an estimated 1.6 billion adherents.

Omar Chatriwala – Praying late into the night – CC BY-NC-ND 2.0.

The third largest religion is *Hinduism*, which includes more than 800 million people, most of whom live in India and Pakistan. Hinduism began about 2000 B.C. and, unlike Christianity, Judaism, and Islam, has no historic linkage to any one person and no real belief in one omnipotent deity. Hindus live instead according to a set of religious precepts called *dharma*. For these reasons Hinduism is often called an *ethical religion*. Hindus believe in reincarnation, and their religious belief in general is closely related to India's caste system (see Chapter 9 "Global Stratification"), as an important aspect of Hindu belief is that one should live according to the rules of one's caste.

Buddhism is another key religion and claims almost 400 million followers, most of whom live in Asia. Buddhism developed out of Hinduism and was founded by Siddhartha Gautama more than 500 years before the birth of Jesus. Siddhartha is said to have given up a comfortable upper-caste Hindu existence for one of wandering and poverty. He eventually achieved enlightenment and acquired the name of Buddha, or "enlightened one." His teachings are now called the *dhamma*, and over the centuries they have influenced Buddhists to lead a moral life. Like Hindus, Buddhists generally believe in reincarnation, and they also believe that people experience suffering unless they give up material concerns and follow other Buddhist principles.

Another key religion is *Judaism*, which claims more than 13 million adherents throughout the world, most of them in Israel and the United States. Judaism began about 4,000 years ago when, according to tradition, Abraham was chosen by God to become the progenitor of his "chosen people," first called Hebrews or Israelites and now called Jews. The Jewish people have been persecuted throughout their history, with anti-Semitism having its ugliest manifestation during the Holocaust of the 1940s, when 6 million Jews died at the hands of the Nazis. One of the first monotheistic religions, Judaism relies heavily on the *Torah*, which is the first five books of the Bible, and the *Talmud* and the *Mishnah*, both collections of religious laws and ancient rabbinical interpretations of these laws. The three main Jewish dominations are the Orthodox, Conservative, and Reform branches, listed in order from the most traditional to the least traditional. Orthodox Jews take the Bible very literally and closely follow the teachings and rules of the Torah, Talmud, and Mishnah, while Reform Jews think the Bible is mainly a historical document and do not follow many traditional Jewish practices. Conservative Jews fall in between these two branches.

A final key religion in the world today is *Confucianism*, which reigned in China for centuries but was officially abolished in 1949 after the Chinese Revolution ended in Communist control. People who practice Confucianism in China today do so secretly, and its number of adherents is estimated at some 5 or 6 million. Confucianism was founded by K'ung Fu-tzu, from whom it gets its name, about 500 years before the birth of Jesus. His teachings, which were compiled in a book called the *Analects*, were essentially a code of moral conduct involving self-discipline, respect for authority and tradition, and the kind treatment of everyone. Despite the official abolition of Confucianism, its principles continue to be important for Chinese family and cultural life.

As this overview indicates, religion takes many forms in different societies. No matter what shape it takes, however, religion has important consequences. These consequences can be both good and bad for the society and the individuals in it. Sociological perspectives expand on these consequences, and we now turn to them.

Key Takeaways

- Although the Catholic Church dominated medieval Europe, Protestantism took hold by the end of the 16th century. According to Max Weber, Protestantism in turn helped lead to the rise of capitalism.
- The major religions in the world today are Christianity, Islam, Hinduism, Buddhism, Judaism, and Confucianism.

For Your Review

1. Although church and state were not separate in many of the American colonies, the new nation soon provided for the separation of church and state and the free exercise of religion in the First Amendment of the Bill of Rights. Why might the new government have taken this approach?
2. The second largest world religion today is Islam, which has aroused strong passions in the United States since 9/11. Write a short essay in which you summarize your thoughts about this religion.

References

Gaustad, E. S., & Schmidt, L. E. (2004). *The religious history of America.* San Francisco, CA: HarperSanFrancisco.

Noss, D. S., & Grangaard, B. R. (2008). *A history of the world's religions* (12th ed.). Upper Saddle River, NJ: Prentice Hall.

Weber, M. (1958). *The Protestant ethic and the spirit of capitalism* (T. Parsons, Trans.). New York, NY: Scribner. (Original work published 1904).

Young, W. A. (2010). *The world's religions: Worldviews and contemporary issues* (3rd ed.). Upper Saddle River, NJ: Prentice Hall.

17.3 Sociological Perspectives on Religion

Learning Objectives

1. Summarize the major functions of religion.
2. Explain the views of religion held by the conflict perspective.
3. Explain the views of religion held by the symbolic interactionist perspective.

Sociological perspectives on religion aim to understand the functions religion serves, the inequality and other problems it can reinforce and perpetuate, and the role it plays in our daily lives (Emerson, Monahan, & Mirola, 2011). Table 17.1 "Theory Snapshot" summarizes what these perspectives say.

Table 17.1 Theory Snapshot

Theoretical perspective	Major assumptions
Functionalism	Religion serves several functions for society. These include (a) giving meaning and purpose to life, (b) reinforcing social unity and stability, (c) serving as an agent of social control of behavior, (d) promoting physical and psychological well-being, and (e) motivating people to work for positive social change.
Conflict theory	Religion reinforces and promotes social inequality and social conflict. It helps convince the poor to accept their lot in life, and it leads to hostility and violence motivated by religious differences.
Symbolic interactionism	This perspective focuses on the ways in which individuals interpret their religious experiences. It emphasizes that beliefs and practices are not sacred unless people regard them as such. Once they are regarded as sacred, they take on special significance and give meaning to people's lives.

The Functions of Religion

Much of the work of Émile Durkheim stressed the functions that religion serves for society regardless of how it is practiced or of what specific religious beliefs a society favors. Durkheim's insights continue to influence sociological thinking today on the functions of religion.

First, religion *gives meaning and purpose to life*. Many things in life are difficult to understand. That was certainly true, as we have seen, in prehistoric times, but even in today's highly scientific age, much of life and death remains a mystery, and religious faith and belief help many people make sense of the things science cannot tell us.

Second, religion *reinforces social unity and stability*. This was one of Durkheim's most important insights. Religion strengthens social stability in at least two ways. First, it gives people a common set of beliefs and thus is an important agent of socialization (see Chapter 4 "Socialization"). Second, the communal practice of religion, as in houses of worship, brings people together physically, facilitates their communication and other social interaction, and thus strengthens their social bonds.

The communal practice of religion in a house of worship brings people together and allows them to interact and communicate. In this way religion helps reinforce social unity and stability. This function of religion was one of Émile Durkheim's most important insights.

Erin Rempel – Worship – CC BY-NC-ND 2.0.

A third function of religion is related to the one just discussed. Religion *is an agent of social control and thus strengthens social order*. Religion teaches people moral behavior and thus helps them learn how to be good members of society. In the Judeo-Christian tradition, the Ten Commandments are perhaps the most famous set of rules for moral behavior.

A fourth function of religion is *greater psychological and physical well-being*. Religious faith and practice can enhance psychological well-being by being a source of comfort to people in times of distress and by enhancing their social interaction with others in places of worship. Many studies find that people of all ages, not just the elderly, are happier and more satisfied with their lives if they are religious. Religiosity also apparently promotes better physical health, and some studies even find that religious people tend to live longer than those who are not religious (Moberg, 2008). We return to this function later.

A final function of religion is that it may *motivate people to work for positive social change*. Religion played a central role in the development of the Southern civil rights movement a few decades ago. Religious beliefs motivated Martin Luther King Jr. and other civil rights activists to risk their lives to desegregate the South. Black churches in the South also served as settings in which the civil rights movement held meetings, recruited new members, and raised money (Morris, 1984).

Religion, Inequality, and Conflict

Religion has all of these benefits, but, according to conflict theory, it can also reinforce and promote social inequality and social conflict. This view is partly inspired by the work of Karl Marx, who said that religion was the "opiate of the masses" (Marx, 1964). By this he meant that religion, like a drug, makes people happy with their existing conditions. Marx repeatedly stressed that workers needed to rise up and overthrow the bourgeoisie. To do so, he said, they needed first to recognize that their poverty stemmed from their oppression by the bourgeoisie. But people who are religious, he said, tend to view their poverty in religious terms. They think it is God's will that they are poor, either because he is testing their faith in him or because they have violated his rules. Many people believe that if they endure their suffering, they will be rewarded in the afterlife. Their religious views lead them not to blame the capitalist class for their poverty and thus not to revolt. For these reasons, said Marx, religion leads the poor to accept their fate and helps maintain the existing system of social inequality.

As Chapter 11 "Gender and Gender Inequality" discussed, religion also promotes gender inequality by presenting negative stereotypes about women and by reinforcing traditional views about their subordination to men (Klassen, 2009). A declaration a decade ago by the Southern Baptist Convention that a wife should "submit herself graciously" to her husband's leadership reflected traditional religious belief (Gundy-Volf, 1998).

As the Puritans' persecution of non-Puritans illustrates, religion can also promote social conflict, and the history of the world shows that individual people and whole communities and nations are quite ready to persecute, kill, and go to war over religious differences. We see this today and in the recent past in central Europe, the Middle East, and Northern Ireland. Jews and other religious groups have been persecuted and killed since ancient times. Religion can be the source of social unity and cohesion, but over the centuries it also has led to persecution, torture, and wanton bloodshed.

News reports going back since the 1990s indicate a final problem that religion can cause, and that is sexual abuse, at least in the Catholic Church. As you undoubtedly have heard, an unknown number of children were sexually abused by Catholic priests and deacons in the United States, Canada, and many other nations going back at least to the 1960s. There is much evidence that the Church hierarchy did little or nothing to stop the abuse or to sanction the offenders who were committing it, and that they did not report it to law enforcement agencies. Various divisions of the Church have paid tens of millions of dollars to settle lawsuits. The numbers of priests, deacons, and children involved will almost certainly never be known, but it is estimated that at least 4,400 priests and deacons in the United States, or about 4% of all such officials, have been accused of sexual abuse, although fewer than 2,000 had the allegations against them proven (Terry & Smith, 2006). Given these estimates, the number of children who were abused probably runs into the thousands.

Symbolic Interactionism and Religion

While functional and conflict theories look at the macro aspects of religion and society, symbolic interactionism looks at the micro aspects. It examines the role that religion plays in our daily lives and the ways in which we interpret religious experiences. For example, it emphasizes that beliefs and practices are not sacred unless people regard them as such. Once we regard them as sacred, they take on special significance and give meaning to our lives. Symbolic interactionists study the ways in which people practice their faith and interact in houses of worship and other religious settings, and they study how and why religious faith and practice have positive consequences for individual psychological and physical well-being.

The cross, Star of David, and the crescent and star are symbols of Islam, Christianity, and Judaism, respectively. The symbolic interactionist perspective emphasizes the ways in which individuals interpret their religious experiences and religious symbols.

zeevveez – Star of David Coexistence- 2 – CC BY 2.0.

Religious symbols indicate the value of the symbolic interactionist approach. A crescent moon and a star are just two shapes in the sky, but together they constitute the international symbol of Islam. A cross is merely two lines or bars in the shape of a "t," but to tens of millions of Christians it is a symbol with deeply religious significance. A Star of David consists of two superimposed triangles in the shape of a six-pointed star, but to Jews around the world it is a sign of their religious faith and a reminder of their history of persecution.

Religious rituals and ceremonies also illustrate the symbolic interactionist approach. They can be deeply intense and can involve crying, laughing, screaming, trancelike conditions, a feeling of oneness with those around you, and other emotional and psychological states. For many people they can be transformative experiences, while for others they are not transformative but are deeply moving nonetheless.

Key Takeaways

- Religion ideally serves several functions. It gives meaning and purpose to life, reinforces social unity and stability, serves as an agent of social control, promotes psychological and physical well-being, and may motivate people to work for positive social change.

- On the other hand, religion may help keep poor people happy with their lot in life, promote traditional views about gender roles, and engender intolerance toward people whose religious faith differs from one's own.
- The symbolic interactionist perspective emphasizes how religion affects the daily lives of individuals and how they interpret their religious experiences.

For Your Review

1. Of the several functions of religion that were discussed, which function do you think is the most important? Why?
2. Which of the three theoretical perspectives on religion makes the most sense to you? Explain your choice.

References

Emerson, M. O., Monahan, S. C., & Mirola, W. A. (2011). *Religion matters: What sociology teaches us about religion in our world*. Upper Saddle River, NJ: Prentice Hall.

Gundy-Volf, J. (1998, September–October). Neither biblical nor just: Southern Baptists and the subordination of women. *Sojourners*, 12–13.

Klassen, P. (Ed.). (2009). *Women and religion*. New York, NY: Routledge.

Marx, K. (1964). *Karl Marx: Selected writings in sociology and social philosophy* (T. B. Bottomore, Trans.). New York, NY: McGraw-Hill.

Moberg, D. O. (2008). Spirituality and aging: Research and implications. *Journal of Religion, Spirituality & Aging, 20*, 95–134.

Morris, A. (1984). *The origins of the civil rights movement: Black communities organizing for change*. New York, NY: Free Press.

Terry, K., & Smith, M. L. (2006). *The nature and scope of sexual abuse of minors by Catholic priests and deacons in the United States: Supplementary data analysis*. Washington, DC: United States Conference of Catholic Bishops.

17.4 Types of Religious Organizations

Learning Objectives

1. List the different types of religious organizations.
2. Describe the defining characteristics of each type of religious organization.

Many types of religious organizations exist in modern societies. Sociologists usually group them according to their size and influence. Categorized this way, three types of religious organizations exist: church, sect, and cult (Emerson, Monahan, & Mirola, 2011). A church further has two subtypes: the ecclesia and denomination. We first discuss the largest and most influential of the types of religious organization, the ecclesia, and work our way down to the smallest and least influential, the cult.

Church: The Ecclesia and Denomination

A **church** is a large, bureaucratically organized religious organization that is closely integrated into the larger society. Two types of church organizations exist. The first is the **ecclesia**, a large, bureaucratic religious organization that is a formal part of the state and has most or all of a state's citizens as its members. As such, the ecclesia is the national or state religion. People ordinarily do not join an ecclesia; instead they automatically become members when they are born. A few ecclesiae exist in the world today, including Islam in Saudi Arabia and some other Middle Eastern nations, the Catholic Church in Spain, the Lutheran Church in Sweden, and the Anglican Church in England.

As should be clear, in an ecclesiastic society there may be little separation of church and state, because the ecclesia and the state are so intertwined. In some ecclesiastic societies, such as those in the Middle East, religious leaders rule the state or have much influence over it, while in others, such as Sweden and England, they have little or no influence. In general the close ties that ecclesiae have to the state help ensure they will support state policies and practices. For this reason, ecclesiae often help the state solidify its control over the populace.

The second type of church organization is the **denomination**, a large, bureaucratic religious organization that is closely integrated into the larger society but is not a formal part of the state. In modern pluralistic nations, several denominations coexist. Most people are members of a specific denomination because their parents were members. They are born into a denomination and generally consider themselves members of it the rest of their lives, whether or not they actively practice their faith, unless they convert to another denomination or abandon religion altogether.

The Megachurch

A relatively recent development in religious organizations is the rise of the so-called *megachurch*, a church at which more than 2,000 people worship every weekend on the average. Several dozen have at least 10,000 worshippers (Priest, Wilson, & Johnson, 2010; Warf & Winsberg, 2010); the largest U.S. megachurch, in Houston, has more than 35,000 worshippers and is nicknamed a "gigachurch." There are more than 1,300 megachurches in the United States, a steep increase from the 50 that existed in 1970, and their total membership exceeds 4 million. About half of today's megachurches are in the South, and only 5% are in the Northeast. About one-third are nondenominational, and one-fifth are Southern Baptist, with the remainder primarily of other Protestant denominations. A third spend more than 10% of their budget on ministry in other nations. Some have a strong television presence, with Americans in the local area or sometimes around the country watching services and/or preaching by televangelists and providing financial contributions in response to information presented on the television screen.

Compared to traditional, smaller churches, megachurches are more concerned with meeting their members' practical needs in addition to helping them achieve religious fulfillment. Some even conduct market surveys to determine these needs and how best to address them. As might be expected, their buildings are huge by any standard, and they often feature bookstores, food courts, and sports and recreation facilities. They also provide day care, psychological counseling, and youth outreach programs. Their services often feature electronic music and light shows.

Although megachurches are popular, they have been criticized for being so big that members are unable to develop the close bonds with each other and with members of the clergy characteristic of smaller houses of worship. Their supporters say that megachurches involve many people in religion who would otherwise not be involved.

Sect

A sect is a relatively small religious organization that is not closely integrated into the larger society and that often conflicts with at least some of its norms and values. The Amish, who live in Pennsylvania, Ohio, and many other states, are perhaps the most well-known example of a sect in the United States today.

Ted Knudsen – Amish – CC BY-NC-ND 2.0.

A **sect** is a relatively small religious organization that is not closely integrated into the larger society and that often conflicts with at least some of its norms and values. Typically a sect has broken away from a larger denomination in an effort to restore what members of the sect regard as the original views of the denomination. Because sects are relatively small, they usually lack the bureaucracy of denominations and ecclesiae and often also lack clergy who have received official training. Their worship services can be intensely emotional experiences, often more so than those typical of many denominations, where worship tends to be more formal and restrained. Members of many sects typically proselytize and try to recruit new members into the sect. If a sect succeeds in attracting many new members, it gradually grows, becomes more bureaucratic, and, ironically, eventually evolves into a denomination. Many of today's Protestant denominations began as sects, as did the Mennonites, Quakers, and other groups. The Amish in the United States are perhaps the most well-known example of a current sect.

Cult

A **cult** is a small religious organization that is at great odds with the norms and values of the larger society. Cults are similar to sects but differ in at least three respects. First, they generally have not broken away from a larger denomination and instead originate outside the mainstream religious tradition. Second, they are often secretive and do not proselytize as much. Third, they are at least somewhat more likely than sects to rely on *charismatic leadership* based on the extraordinary personal qualities of the cult's leader.

Although the term *cult* today raises negative images of crazy, violent, small groups of people, it is important to keep in mind that major world religions, including Christianity, Islam, and Judaism, and denominations such as the Mormons all began as cults. Research challenges several popular beliefs about cults, including the ideas that they brainwash people into joining them and that their members are mentally ill. In a study of the Unification Church (Moonies), Eileen Barker (1984) found no more signs of mental illness among people who joined the Moonies than in those who did not. She also found no evidence that people who joined the Moonies had been brainwashed into doing so.

Another image of cults is that they are violent. In fact, most are not violent. However, some cults have committed violence in the recent past. In 1995 the *Aum Shinrikyo* (Supreme Truth) cult in Japan killed 10 people and injured thousands more when it released bombs of deadly nerve gas in several Tokyo subway lines (Strasser & Post, 1995). Two years earlier, the Branch Davidian cult engaged in an armed standoff with federal agents in Waco, Texas. When the agents attacked its compound, a fire broke out and killed 80 members of the cult, including 19 children; the origin of the fire remains unknown (Tabor & Gallagher, 1995). A few cults have also committed mass suicide. In another example from the 1990s, more than three dozen members of the Heaven's Gate cult killed themselves in California in March 1997 in an effort to communicate with aliens from outer space (Hoffman & Burke, 1997). Some two decades earlier, more than 900 members of the People's Temple cult killed themselves in Guyana under orders from the cult's leader, Jim Jones (Stoen, 1997).

Key Takeaways

- The major types of religious organization are the church, sect, and cult. Two types of church organizations include the ecclesia and denomination.
- Although the term *cult* brings to mind negative connotations, several world religions began as cults, and most of today's cults are not violent.

For Your Review

1. Write a brief essay in which you outline the differences among the church, sect, and cult.
2. When you hear the word *cult*, is your initial reaction positive, negative, or neutral? Explain your answer.

References

Barker, E. (1984). *The making of a Moonie: Choice or brainwashing*. New York, NY: Oxford University Press.

Emerson, M. O., Monahan, S. C., & Mirola, W. A. (2011). *Religion matters: What sociology teaches us about religion in our world*. Upper Saddle River, NJ: Prentice Hall.

Hoffman, B., & Burke, K. (1997). *Heaven's Gate: Cult suicide in San Diego*. New York, NY: Harper Paperbacks.

Priest, R. J., Wilson, D., & Johnson, A. (2010). U.S. megachurches and new patterns of global mission. *International Bulletin of Missionary Research, 34*(2), 97–104.

Stoen, T. (1997, April 7). The most horrible night of my life. *Newsweek* 44–45.

Strasser, S., & Post, T. (1995, April 3). A cloud of terror—and suspicion. *Newsweek* 36–41.

Tabor, J. D., & Gallagher, E. V. (1995). *Why Waco? Cults and the battle for religious freedom in America.* Berkeley: University of California Press.

Warf, B., & Winsberg, M. (2010). Geographies of megachurches in the United States. *Journal of Cultural Geography, 27*(1), 33–51.

17.5 Religion in the United States

Learning Objectives

1. Describe the extent and correlates of religious affiliation.
2. Explain the different dimensions of religiosity.
3. Describe the correlates and consequences of religiosity.

The United States is generally regarded as a fairly religious nation. In a 2009 survey administered by the Gallup Organization to 114 nations, 65% of Americans answered yes when asked, "Is religion an important part of your daily life?" (Crabtree, 2010). In a 2007 Pew Forum on Religion & Public Life survey, about 83% of Americans expressed a religious preference, 61% were official members of a local house of worship, and 39% attended religious services at least weekly (Pew Forum on Religion & Public Life, 2008). These figures show that religion plays a significant role in the lives of many Americans.

Moreover, Americans seem more religious than the citizens of almost all the other democratic, industrialized nations with which the United States is commonly compared. Evidence for this conclusion comes from the 2009 Gallup survey mentioned in the preceding paragraph. Whereas 65% of Americans said religion was an important part of their daily lives, comparable percentages from other democratic, industrialized nations included the following: Spain, 49%; Canada, 42%; France, 30%; United Kingdom, 27%; and Sweden, 17% (Crabtree, 2010). Among its peer nations, then, the United States stands out for being religious.

When we consider all the nations of the world, however, the U.S. ranking is much lower. In more than half the nations surveyed by Gallup in 2009, at least 84% of respondents said religion was an important part of their daily lives. The U.S. rate of 65% ranked 85th out of the 114 nations in this survey (Crabtree, 2010). However, because the United States ranks higher than most of the democratic, industrialized nations with which it is most aptly compared, it makes sense to regard the United States as fairly religious. The "Learning From Other Societies" box discusses what else can be learned from the international comparisons in the Gallup survey.

Learning From Other Societies

Poverty and the Importance of Religion

The 2009 Gallup international survey on religion discussed in the text revealed an interesting pattern that is relevant for understanding religious differences among the 50 states of the United States.

Of the 114 nations included in the Gallup survey, people in the poorest nations were most likely to say that religion was an important part of their daily lives, and people in the richest nations were least likely to feel this way. The 10 most religious nations according to this measure, with at least 98% of their populations saying that religion was an important part of their daily lives, all had a per-capita gross domestic product (GDP) below $5,000: Bangladesh, Niger, Yemen,

Indonesia, Malawi, Sri Lanka, Somaliland region, Djibouti, Mauritania, and Burundi. In contrast, among the 10 least religious nations, with 30% or fewer saying religion was important, were some of the world's wealthiest nations: Sweden, Denmark, Japan, Hong Kong, the United Kingdom, and France. In the world's poorest nations, those whose per-capita GDP is below $2,000, the median proportion whose citizens are religious according to the Gallup measure was 95%; in the richest nations, those whose per-capita GDP is above $25,000, the same median proportion was only 47%.

A Gallup report concluded that these results demonstrate "the strong relationship between a country's socioeconomic status and the religiosity of its residents" (Crabtree, 2010). Drawing on research by sociologists and other social scientists, the report explained that religion helps people in poorer nations cope with the many hardships that poverty creates.

Gallup's international findings and explanation for the poverty-religiosity relationship pattern they exhibited helps explain differences among the 50 states in the United States. In 2008, Gallup conducted surveys in each state in which respondents were asked whether religion was an important part of their daily lives. The 11 highest ranking states, with at least 74% of their populations saying that religion was an important part of their daily lives, were all Southern states. Mississippi ranked highest at 85%.

There are many reasons for the high degree of Southern religiosity, and a Gallup report noted that the states differ in their religious traditions, denominations, and racial and ethnic compositions (Newport, 2009). Although these and other factors might help explain Southern religiosity, it is notable that the Southern states are also generally the poorest in the nation. If the poorest nations of the world are more religious in part because of their poverty, then the Southern states may also be more religious partly because of their poverty. In understanding religious differences among the different regions of the country, the United States has much to learn from the other nations of the world.

Religious Affiliation and Religious Identification

Religious affiliation is a term that can mean actual membership in a church or synagogue, or just a stated *identification* with a particular religion whether or not someone actually belongs to a local house of worship. Another term for religious affiliation is **religious preference**. Recall from the Pew survey cited earlier that 83% of Americans express a religious preference, while 61% are official members of a local house of worship. As these figures indicate, more people identify with a religion than actually belong to it.

The Pew survey also included some excellent data on religious identification (see Figure 17.1 "Religious Preference in the United States"). Slightly more than half of Americans say their religious preference is Protestant, while about 24% call themselves Catholic. Almost 2% say they are Jewish, while 6% state another religious preference and 16% say they have no religious preference. Although Protestants are thus a majority of the country, the Protestant religion includes several denominations. About 34% of Protestants are Baptists; 12% are Methodists; 9% are Lutherans; 9% are Pentecostals; 5% are Presbyterians; and 3% are Episcopalians. The remainder identify with other Protestant denominations or say their faith is nondenominational. Based on their religious beliefs, Episcopalians, Presbyterians, and Congregationalists are typically grouped together as Liberal Protestants; Methodists, Lutherans, and a few other denominations as Moderate Protestants; and Baptists, Seventh-Day Adventists, and many other denominations as Conservative Protestants.

Figure 17.1 Religious Preference in the United States

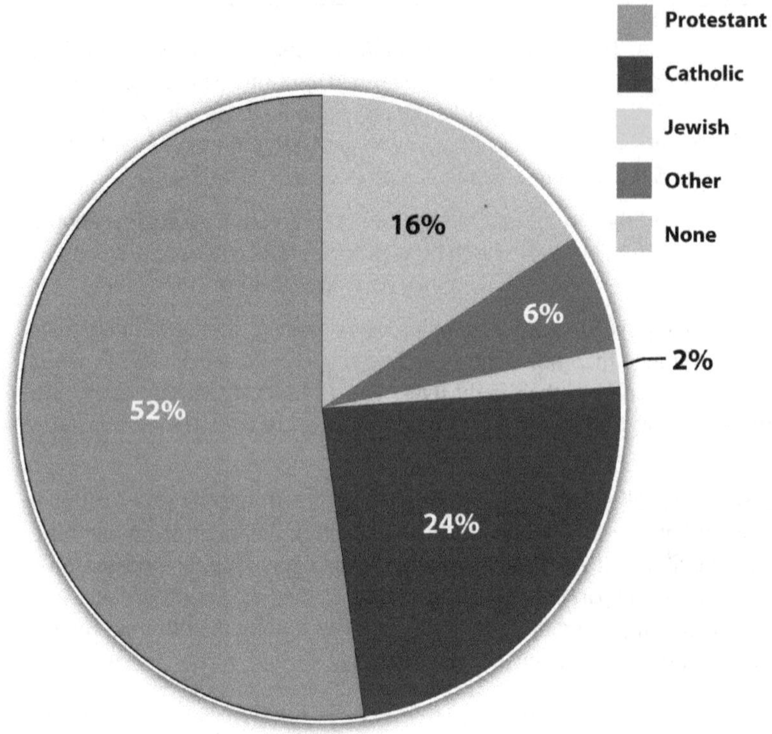

Source: Data from Pew Forum on Religion & Public Life. (2008). *U.S. religious landscape survey*. Washington, DC: Pew Research Center.

Correlates of Religious Affiliation

The religious affiliations just listed differ widely in the nature of their religious belief and practice, but they also differ in demographic variables of interest to sociologists (Finke & Stark, 2005). For example, Liberal Protestants tend to live in the Northeast and to be well educated and relatively wealthy, while Conservative Protestants tend to live in the South and to be less educated and working-class. In their education and incomes, Catholics and Moderate Protestants fall in between these two groups. Like Liberal Protestants, Jews also tend to be well educated and relatively wealthy.

Race and ethnicity are also related to religious affiliation. African Americans are overwhelmingly Protestant, usually Conservative Protestants (Baptists), while Latinos are primarily Catholic. Asian Americans and Native Americans tend to hold religious preferences other than Protestant, Catholic, or Jewish.

Race and ethnicity are related to religious affiliation. African Americans are overwhelmingly Protestant, for example, while Latinos are primarily Catholic.

Ian Britton – Trinity Choir from Trinity Baptist Church – CC BY-NC 2.0.

Older people are more likely than younger people to belong to a church or synagogue.

Asim Bharwani – Reading at the Wall – CC BY-NC-ND 2.0.

Age is yet another factor related to religious affiliation, as older people are more likely than younger people to belong to a church or synagogue. As young people marry and "put roots down," their religious affiliation increases, partly because many wish to expose their children to a religious education. In the Pew survey, 25% of people aged 18–29 expressed no religious preference, compared to only 8% of those 70 or older.

Religiosity

People can belong to a church, synagogue, or mosque or claim a religious preference, but that does not necessarily mean they are very religious. For this reason, sociologists consider **religiosity**, or the significance of religion in a person's life, an important topic of investigation.

Religiosity has a simple definition but actually is a very complex topic. What if someone prays every day but does not attend religious services? What if someone attends religious services but never prays at home and does not claim to be very religious? Someone can pray and read a book of scriptures daily, while someone else can read a book of scriptures daily but pray only sometimes. As these possibilities indicate, a person can be religious in some ways but not in other ways.

For this reason, religiosity is best conceived of as a concept involving several dimensions: experiential, ritualistic, ideological, intellectual, and consequential (Stark & Glock, 1968). *Experiential* religiosity refers to how important people consider religion to be in their lives and is the dimension used by the international Gallup Poll discussed earlier. *Ritualistic* religiosity refers to the extent of their involvement in prayer, reading a book of scriptures, and attendance at a house of worship. *Ideological* religiosity involves the degree to which people accept religious doctrine and includes the nature of their belief in a deity, while *intellectual* religiosity concerns the extent of their knowledge of their religion's history and teachings. Finally, *consequential* religiosity refers to the extent to which religion affects their daily behavior.

National data on prayer are perhaps especially interesting (see Figure 17.2 "Frequency of Prayer"), as prayer occurs both with others and by oneself. Almost 60% of Americans say they pray at least once daily outside religious services, and only 7% say they never pray (Pew Forum on Religion & Public Life, 2008). Women are more likely than men to pray daily: 66% of women say they pray daily, versus only 49% of men. Daily praying is also more common among older people than younger people, among African Americans than whites, and among people without a college degree than those with a college degree. As these demographic differences indicate, the social backgrounds of Americans affect this important dimension of their religiosity.

Figure 17.2 Frequency of Prayer

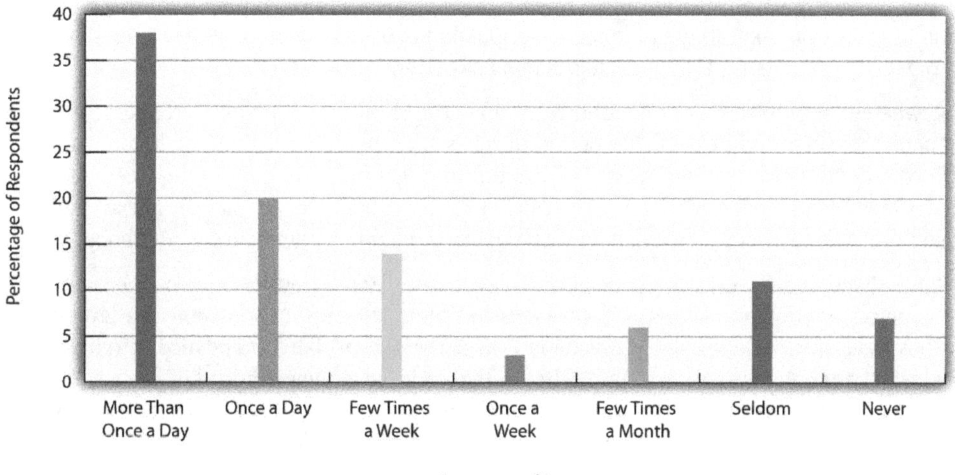

Source: Data from Pew Forum on Religion & Public Life. (2008). *U.S. religious landscape survey*. Washington, DC: Pew Research Center.

When we try to determine why some people are more religious than others, we are treating religiosity as a *dependent variable*. But religiosity itself can also be an *independent variable*, as it affects attitudes on a wide range of social, political, and moral issues. Generally speaking, the more religious people are, the more conservative their attitudes in these areas (Adamczyk & Pitt, 2009). An example of this relationship appears in Table 17.2 "Frequency of Prayer and Belief That Homosexual Sex Is "Always Wrong"", which shows that people who pray daily are *much* more opposed to homosexual sex. The relationship in the table once again provides clear evidence of the sociological perspective's emphasis on the importance of social backgrounds for attitudes.

Table 17.2 Frequency of Prayer and Belief That Homosexual Sex Is "Always Wrong"

	Several times a day	**Once a day**	**Several times a week**	**Once a week**	**Less than once a week**	**Never**
Percentage saying "always wrong"	74.3	57.4	44.9	44.0	29.1	26.4

Source: Data from General Social Survey, 2008.

While religiosity can affect attitudes on various issues, it can also affect behavior and health. The "Sociology Making a Difference" box discusses the effects that religiosity may have.

Sociology Making a Difference

The Benefits of Religiosity

As discussed earlier, Durkheim considered religion a moral force for socialization and social bonding. Building on this insight, sociologists and other scholars have thought that religiosity might reduce participation in "deviant" behaviors such as drinking, illegal drug use, delinquency, and certain forms of sexual behavior. A growing body of research, almost all of it on adolescents, finds that this is indeed the case. Holding other factors constant, more religious adolescents are less likely than other adolescents to drink and take drugs, to commit various kinds of delinquency, to have sex during early adolescence or at all, and to have sex frequently if they do start having sex (Regenerus, 2007).

There is much less research on whether this relationship continues to hold true during adulthood. If religion might have more of an impact during adolescence, an impressionable period of one's life, then the relationship found during adolescence may not persist into adulthood. However, two recent studies did find that more religious, unmarried adults were less likely than other unmarried adults to have premarital sex partners (Barkan, 2006; Uecker, 2008). These results suggest that religiosity may indeed continue to affect sexual behavior and perhaps other behaviors during adulthood.

Sociologists and other scholars have also built on Durkheim's insights to assess whether religious involvement promotes better physical health and psychological well-being. As the earlier discussion of religion's functions noted, a growing body of research finds that various measures of religious involvement, but perhaps especially attendance at religious services, are positively associated with better physical and mental health. Religious involvement is linked in many studies to lower rates of cardiovascular disease, hypertension (high blood pressure), and mortality (Ellison & Hummer, 2010; Green & Elliott, 2010). It is also linked to higher rates of happiness and lower rates of depression and anxiety.

These effects are thought to stem from several reasons. First, religious attendance increases social ties that provide emotional and practical support when someone has various problems and that also raise one's self-esteem. Second, personal religious belief can provide spiritual comfort in times of trouble. Third, and as noted in the preceding section, religious involvement promotes healthy lifestyles for at least some people, including lower use of tobacco, alcohol, and other drugs, and reduces the frequency of other risky behaviors such as gambling and unsafe sex. Lower participation in all of these activities helps in turn to increase one's physical and mental health.

In sum, research increasingly suggests that religiosity helps reduce risky, deviant behaviors and increase physical and psychological well-being. Although religion should not be forced on anyone, this body of research suggests that efforts that promote religiosity among both adolescents and adults may have the benefits just described. For example, older adults often have trouble traveling to a house of worship, whether they live at home or in an institutional setting such as a nursing home or assisted living center. Their well-being may be enhanced if they are provided free or low-cost transportation to attend a house of worship or if regular religious services are begun in the institutional settings that do not already have them. In helping demonstrate the benefits of religiosity in the areas discussed here, sociology has again made a difference.

Knowledge About Religion

Although the United States is a fairly religious nation, Americans "are also deeply ignorant about religion," according to a recent news report (Goodstein, 2010, p. A17). The report was based on a 2010 survey by the Pew Forum on Religion & Public Life of more than 3,400 U.S. residents. The survey respondents were asked 32 questions, mostly multiple-choice, about the Bible, the world's major religions, celebrated religious figures from various points in world history, and what U.S. Supreme Court rulings permit in the public practice of religion. Among other questions, respondents were asked what Ramadan is, where Jesus was born, who led the exodus out of Egypt in the Bible, and whose writings started the Protestant Reformation; they were also asked to identify the religious preference of the Dalai Lama, Joseph Smith, and Mother Teresa.

The average respondent provided correct answers to only half the questions. Researchers considered most of the questions to be fairly easy, but a few of the questions were fairly difficult.

For example, whereas 89% of respondents knew that teachers in public schools may not lead a class in prayer and 71% knew that Jesus was born in Bethlehem, only 54% knew that the Koran is the Islamic holy book, only 45% knew that the Jewish Sabbath begins on Friday, and only 23% knew that teachers in public schools are allowed to read from the Bible as an example of literature.

The respondents' level of education was strongly related to their percentage of correct answers. College graduates answered an average of 20.6 questions correctly, people who had taken only some college courses answered 17.5 questions correctly, and respondents with a high school degree or less answered 12.8 questions correctly. Higher scores were also achieved by respondents who were more religious, by men, by whites, and by non-Southerners (Pew Forum on Religion & Public Life, 2010).

Religiosity and College Students

During the last decade, the Higher Education Research Institute (HERI) at the University of California, Los Angeles, conducted a national longitudinal survey of college students' religiosity and religious beliefs (Astin, Astin, & Lindholm, 2010). They interviewed more than 112,000 entering students in 2004 and more than 14,000 of these students in spring 2007 toward the end of their junior year. This research design enabled the researchers to assess whether and how various aspects of religious belief and religiosity change during college. Several findings were notable.

First, *religious commitment* (measures of the students' assessment of how important religion is to them) stayed fairly stable during college. Students who drank alcohol and partied the most were more likely to experience a decline in religious commitment, although a cause-and-effect relationship here is difficult to determine.

The frequency of prayer and attendance at religious services tend to decline during a person's college years.

mer chau – Studying – CC BY 2.0.

Second, *religious engagement* (measures of religious services attendance, praying, religious singing, and reading sacred texts) declined during the college years. This decline was especially steep for religious attendance. Almost 40% of juniors reported less frequent attendance than during their high school years, while only 7% reported more frequent attendance.

Third, *religious skepticism* (measures of how well religion explains various phenomena compared to science) stayed fairly stable. Skepticism tended to rise among students who partied a lot, went on a study-abroad program, and attended a college with students who were very liberal politically.

Fourth, *religious/social conservatism* (views on such things as abortion, casual sex, and atheism) tended to decline during college, although the decline was not at all steep. This set of findings is in line with the research discussed earlier showing that students tend to become more liberal during their college years. To the extent students' views became more liberal, the beliefs of their friends among the student body mattered much more than the beliefs of their faculty.

Fifth, *religious struggle* (measures of questioning one's religious beliefs, disagreeing with parents about religion, feeling distant from God, and the like) tended to increase during college. This increase was especially high at campuses where a higher proportion of students were experiencing religious struggle when they entered college. Students who drank alcohol and watched television more often and who had a close friend or family member die were more likely to experience religious struggle, although a cause-and-effect relationship is again difficult to determine.

Key Takeaways

- The United States is a fairly religious nation, with most people expressing a religious preference. About half of Americans are Protestants, and one-fourth are Catholics.
- Religiosity is composed of several dimensions. Almost 60% of Americans say they pray at least once daily outside religious services.
- Generally speaking, higher levels of religiosity are associated with more conservative views on social, moral, and political issues; with lower rates of deviant behavior; and with greater psychological and physical well-being.

For Your Review

1. Do you consider yourself religious? Why or why not?
2. Why do you think religiosity is associated with more conservative views on social, moral, and political issues? What is it about religiosity that helps lead to such beliefs?

References

Adamczyk, A., & Pitt, C. (2009). Shaping attitudes about homosexuality: The role of religion and cultural context. *Social Science Research, 38*(2), 338–351.

Astin, A. W., Astin, H. S., & Lindholm, J. A. (2010). *Cultivating the spirit: How college can enhance students' inner lives*. Hoboken NJ: Jossey-Bass.

Barkan, S. E. (2006). Religiosity and premarital sex during adulthood. *Journal for the Scientific Study of Religion, 45*, 407–417.

Crabtree, S. (2010). Religiosity highest in world's poorest nations. Retrieved from http://www.gallup.com/poll/142727/religiosity-highest-world-poorest-nations.aspx.

Ellison, C. G., & Hummer, R. A. (Eds.). (2010). *Religion, families, and health: Population-based research in the United States*. New Brunswick, NJ: Rutgers University Press.

Finke, R., & Stark, R. (2005). *The churching of America: Winners and losers in our religious economy* (2nd ed.). New Brunswick, NJ: Rutgers University Press.

Goodstein, L. (2010, September 28). Basic religion test stumps many Americans. *The New York Times*, p. A17.

Green, M., & Elliott, M. (2010). Religion, health, and psychological well-being. *Journal of Religion & Health, 49*(2), 149–163. doi:10.1007/s10943-009-9242-1.

Newport, F. (2009). State of the states: Importance of religion. Retrieved from http://www.gallup.com/poll/114022/state-states-importance-religion.aspx.

Pew Forum on Religion & Public Life. (2010, September 28). U.S. religious knowledge survey. Retrieved from http://www.pewforum.org/Other-Beliefs-and-Practices/U-S-Religious-Knowledge-Survey.aspx.

Pew Forum on Religion & Public Life. (2008). *U.S. religious landscape survey*. Washington, DC: Pew Research Center.

Regenerus, M. D. (2007). *Forbidden fruit: Sex & religion in the lives of American teenagers*. New York, NY: Oxford Univeristy Press.

Stark, R., & Glock, C. Y. (1968). *Patterns of religious commitment*. Berkeley: University of California Press.

Uecker, J. E. (2008). Religion, pledging, and the premarital sexual behavior of married young adults. *Journal of Marriage and Family, 70*(3), 728–744.

17.6 Trends in Religious Belief and Activity

Learning Objectives

1. Summarize the evidence on the nature and extent of secularization.
2. Discuss trends in regard to religious conservatism in the United States.

Because religion is such an important part of our society, sociologists and other observers have examined how religious thought and practice have changed in the last few decades. Two trends have been studied in particular: (a) secularization and (b) the rise of religious conservatism.

Secularization

Secularization refers to the weakening importance of religion in a society. It plays less of a role in people's lives, as they are less guided in their daily behavior by religious beliefs. The influence of religious organizations in society also declines, and some individual houses of worship give more emphasis to worldly concerns such as soup kitchens than to spiritual issues. There is no doubt that religion is less important in modern society than it was before the rise of science in the 17th and 18th centuries. Scholars of religion have tried to determine the degree to which the United States has become more secularized during the last few decades (Finke & Stark, 2005; Fenn, 2001).

The best evidence shows that religion has declined in importance since the 1960s but still remains a potent force in American society as a whole and for the individual lives of Americans (Finke & Scheitle, 2005). Although membership in mainstream Protestant denominations has declined since the 1960s, membership in conservative denominations has risen. Most people (92% in the Pew survey) still believe in God, and, as already noted, more than half of all Americans pray daily.

Scholars also point to the continuing importance of **civil religion**, or the devotion of a nation's citizens to their society and government (Santiago, 2009). In the United States, love of country—patriotism—and admiration for many of its ideals are widespread. Citizens routinely engage in rituals, such as reciting the Pledge of Allegiance or singing the national anthem, that express their love of the United States. These beliefs and practices are the secular equivalent of traditional religious beliefs and practices and thus a functional equivalent of religion.

The Rise of Religious Conservatism

The rise of religious conservatism also challenges the notion that secularization is displacing religion in American life. **Religious conservatism** in the U.S. context is the belief that the Bible is the actual word of God. As noted earlier, religious conservatism includes the various Baptist denominations and any number of evangelical organizations, and its rapid rise was partly the result of fears that the United States was becoming too secularized. Many religious conservatives believe that a return to the teachings of the Bible and religious spirituality is necessary to combat the corrupting influences of modern life (Almond, Appleby, & Sivan, 2003).

The rise of religious conservatism in the United States was partly the result of fears that the nation was becoming too secularized.

Thomas Quine – Small brick church – CC BY 2.0.

Today about one-third of Americans state a religious preference for a conservative denomination (Pew Forum on Religion & Public Life, 2008). Because of their growing numbers, religious conservatives have been the subject of increasing research. They tend to hold politically conservative views on many issues, including abortion and the punishment of criminals, and are more likely than people with other religious beliefs to believe in such things as the corporal punishment of children (Burdette, Ellison, & Hill, 2005). They are also more likely to believe in traditional roles for women.

Closely related to the rise of religious conservatism has been the increasing influence of what has been termed the "new religious right" in American politics (Martin, 2005; Capps, 1990; Moen, 1992). Since the 1980s, the religious right has been a potent force in the political scene at both the national and local levels, with groups like the Moral Majority and the Christian Coalition effective in raising money, using the media, and lobbying elected officials. As its name implies, the religious right tries to advance a conservative political agenda consistent with conservative religious concerns. Among other issues, it opposes legal abortion, gay rights, and violence and sex in the media, and it also advocates an increased religious presence in public schools. Although the influence of the religious right has waned since the 1990s, its influence on American politics is bound to be controversial for many years to come.

Key Takeaways

- Despite concerns among many observers that secularization has been occurring, religion remains important in many Americans' lives and a potent force in American society.
- Membership in conservative denominations has increased in the United States in recent decades. Today about one-third of Americans state a religious preference for a conservative denomination.

For Your Review

1. What evidence that you have observed suggests to you that the United States has become a secular society? What evidence suggests to you that it remains a fairly religious society?
2. Why do you think religiosity is associated with lower levels of involvement in deviant behavior? What is it about religiosity that might reduce deviant behavior?

Addressing Religious Issues: What Sociology Suggests

Sociological theory and research are relevant for understanding and addressing certain religious issues. One major issue today is religious intolerance. Émile Durkheim did not stress the hatred and conflict that religion has promoted over the centuries, but this aspect of conflict theory's view of religion should not be forgotten. Certainly religious tolerance should be promoted among all peoples, and strategies for doing so include education efforts about the world's religions and interfaith activities for youth and adults. The Center for Religious Tolerance (http://www.c-r-t.org/index.php), headquartered in Sarasota, Florida, is one of the many local and national organizations in the United States that strive to promote interfaith understanding. In view of the hostility toward Muslims that increased in the United States after 9/11, it is perhaps particularly important for education efforts and other activities to promote understanding of Islam.

Religion may also help address other social issues. In this regard, we noted earlier that religious belief and practice seem to promote physical health and psychological well-being. To the extent this is true, efforts that promote the practice of faith may enhance one's physical and mental health.. In view of the health problems of older people and also their greater religiosity, some scholars urge that such efforts be especially undertaken for people in their older years (Moberg, 2008). We also noted that religiosity helps reduce drinking, drug use, and sexual behavior among adolescents and perhaps among adults. This does not mean that religion should be forced on anyone against his or her will, but this body of research does suggest that efforts by houses of worship to promote religious activities among their adolescents and younger children may help prevent or otherwise minimize risky behaviors during this important period of the life course.

References

Almond, G. A., Appleby, R. S., & Sivan, E. (2003). *Strong religion: The rise of fundamentalisms around the world.* Chicago, IL: University of Chicago Press.

Burdette, A. M., Ellison, C. G., & Hill, T. D. (2005). Conservative protestantism and tolerance toward homosexuals: An examination of potential mechanisms. *Sociological Inquiry, 75*(2), 177–196.

Capps, W. H. (1990). *The new religious Right: Piety, patriotism, and politics*. Columbia: University of South Carolina Press.

Fenn, R. K. (2001). *Beyond idols: The shape of a secular society*. New York, NY: Oxford University Press.

Finke, R., & Scheitle, C. (2005). Accounting for the uncounted: Computing correctives for the 2000 RCMS data. *Review of Religious Research, 47*, 5–22.

Finke, R., & Stark, R. (2005). *The churching of America: Winners and losers in our religious economy* (2nd ed.). New Brunswick, NJ: Rutgers University Press.

Martin, W. C. (2005). *With God on our side: The rise of the religious Right in America*. New York, NY: Broadway Books.

Moberg, D. O. (2008). Spirituality and aging: Research and implications. *Journal of Religion, Spirituality & Aging, 20*, 95–134.

Moen, M. (1992). *The transformation of the Christian Right*. Tuscaloosa: University of Alabama Press.

Pew Forum on Religion & Public Life. (2008). *U.S. religious landscape survey*. Washington, DC: Pew Research Center.

Santiago, J. (2009). From "civil religion" to nationalism as the religion of modern times: Rethinking a complex relationship. *Journal for the Scientific Study of Religion, 48*(2), 394–401.

17.7 End-of-Chapter Material

Summary

1. All societies have beliefs and practices that help them understand supernatural and spiritual phenomena. Religion takes different forms in the many types of societies that have existed, but ultimately it seeks to make sense out of life, death, and the other mysteries of human existence.
2. The world's major religions today include Christianity, Islam, Hinduism, Buddhism, Confucianism, and Judaism. They differ in many respects, including the nature of their belief in God, whether their religion began with the efforts of one particular individual, and whether a sacred text is involved.
3. Religion serves several functions for society. It gives meaning and purpose to life, reinforces social stability and social control, and promotes physical and psychological well-being. Yet religion can also perpetuate social inequality and promote social conflict among peoples with different religious faiths. Traditionally religion has also reinforced gender inequality. Symbolic interactionism explores the micro side of religion and focuses on the role religion plays in our daily lives and the ways in which we interpret religious experiences.
4. The primary types of religious organization include the church (either an ecclesia or a denomination), sect, and cult. These types differ in many ways, including their size and integration into society. Cults have a very negative image, but Christianity, Judaism, and various denominations all began as cults.
5. The United States is, according to many measures, one of the most religious societies in the industrial world. Most people believe in God, and a strong majority belong to a church or synagogue. Religious affiliation is related to several demographic variables in which sociologists are interested, including social class and race. Liberal Protestants and Jews tend to be relatively wealthy and well educated, while Conservative Protestants tend to be poorer and less educated. Catholics and Moderate Protestants tend to occupy a middle ground on these variables.
6. Religiosity is a multidimensional concept that gets beyond actual membership in a church or synagogue. The more religious people are, the more conservative they tend to be on various social and moral issues.
7. Two religious trends in recent decades in the United States include secularization and the rise of religious conservatism. Despite fears that the United States is becoming a less religious society, the best evidence indicates that religion continues to play an important role in the lives of individuals and their families. The rise of religious conservatism has an important and controversial impact on national political affairs.
8. Religion seems to have at least two important effects on the lives of individuals. Higher levels of religiosity are associated with reduced involvement in deviant behavior and with greater physical and psychological well-being.

Chapter 18: Health and Medicine

Social Issues in the News

"Children's Quality of Life Declining," the headline said. A study from the Foundation for Child Development noted that more than 21% of American children were living in poverty in 2010, up 5% from 2006 and the highest rate in two decades. Child experts warned that the increasing poverty could impair children's health. The sociologist who led the study worried that child obesity could increase as families were forced to move away from more expensive health food to processed and fast food. A child psychology professor said that people who grow up in poverty have higher rates of cancer, liver and respiratory disease, and other conditions. The president of the American Academy of Pediatrics agreed that family poverty is a health risk for children, who are more likely to be born prematurely and/or with low birth weight and to develop asthma and other health problems as they grow. She added that all these problems can have lifelong effects: "The consequences of poverty build on themselves, so that the outcomes can be felt for years to come." (Landau, 2010; Szabo, 2010)

This news story reminds us that social class is linked to health and illness, and it illustrates just one of the many ways in which health and medicine are an important part of the social fabric. Accordingly, this chapter examines the social aspects of health and medicine. It does not discuss the medical causes of various diseases and illnesses, and neither does it tell you how to become and stay healthy, as these are not, strictly speaking, sociological topics. But it will discuss the social bases for health and illnesses and some of today's most important issues and problems in health care.

References

Landau, E. (2010, June 8). Children's quality of life declining, says report. *CNN*. Retrieved from http://www.cnn.com/2010/HEALTH/06/08/children.wellbeing.

Szabo, L. (2010, June 8). More than 1 in 5 kids live in poverty. *USA Today*. Retrieved from http://www.usatoday.com/news/health/2010-06-08-1Achild08_ST_N.htm.

18.1 Understanding Health, Medicine, and Society

Learning Objectives

1. Understand the basic views of the sociological approach to health and medicine.
2. List the assumptions of the functionalist, conflict, and symbolic interactionist perspectives on health and medicine.

Health refers to the extent of a person's physical, mental, and social well-being. This definition, taken from the World Health Organization's treatment of health, emphasizes that health is a complex concept that involves not just the soundness of a person's body but also the state of a person's mind and the quality of the social environment in which she or he lives. The quality of the social environment in turn can affect a person's physical and mental health, underscoring the importance of social factors for these twin aspects of our overall well-being.

Medicine is the social institution that seeks both to prevent, diagnose, and treat illness and to promote health as just defined. Dissatisfaction with the medical establishment has been growing. Part of this dissatisfaction stems from soaring health-care costs and what many perceive as insensitive stinginess by the health insurance industry, as the 2009 battle over health-care reform illustrated. Some of the dissatisfaction also reflects a growing view that the social and even spiritual realms of human existence play a key role in health and illness. This view has fueled renewed interest in alternative medicine. We return later to these many issues for the social institution of medicine.

The Sociological Approach to Health and Medicine

We usually think of health, illness, and medicine in individual terms. When a person becomes ill, we view the illness as a medical problem with biological causes, and a physician treats the individual accordingly. A sociological approach takes a different view. Unlike physicians, sociologists and other public health scholars do not try to understand why any one person becomes ill. Instead, they typically examine rates of illness to explain why people from certain social backgrounds are more likely than those from others to become sick. Here, as we will see, our social location in society—our social class, race and ethnicity, and gender—makes a critical difference.

A sociological approach emphasizes that our social class, race and ethnicity, and gender, among other aspects of our social backgrounds, influence our levels of health and illness.

U.S. Army Garrison Japan – Arnn students celebrate diversity; weeklong recognition – CC BY-NC-ND 2.0.

The fact that our social backgrounds affect our health may be difficult for many of us to accept. We all know someone, and often someone we love, who has died from a serious illness or currently suffers from one. There is always a "medical" cause of this person's illness, and physicians do their best to try to cure it and prevent it from recurring. Sometimes they succeed; sometimes they fail. Whether someone suffers a serious illness is often simply a matter of bad luck or bad genes: we can do everything right and still become ill. In saying that our social backgrounds affect our health, sociologists do not deny any of these possibilities. They simply remind us that our social backgrounds also play an important role (Cockerham, 2009).

A sociological approach also emphasizes that a society's culture shapes its understanding of health and illness and practice of medicine. In particular, culture shapes a society's perceptions of what it means to be healthy or ill, the reasons to which it attributes illness, and the ways in which it tries to keep its members healthy and to cure those who are sick (Hahn & Inborn, 2009). Knowing about a society's culture, then, helps us to understand how it perceives health and healing. By the same token, knowing about a society's health and medicine helps us to understand important aspects of its culture.

An interesting example of culture in this regard is seen in Japan's aversion to organ transplants, which are much less common in that nation than in other wealthy nations. Japanese families dislike disfiguring the bodies of the dead, even for autopsies, which are also much less common in Japan than other nations. This cultural view often prompts them to refuse permission for organ transplants when a family member dies, and it leads many Japanese to refuse to designate themselves as potential organ donors (Sehata & Kimura, 2009; Shinzo, 2004).

As culture changes over time, it is also true that perceptions of health and medicine may also change. Recall from Chapter 2 "Eye on Society: Doing Sociological Research" that physicians in top medical schools a century ago advised women not to go to college because the stress of higher education would disrupt their menstrual cycles (Ehrenreich & English, 2005). This nonsensical advice reflected the sexism of the times, and we no longer accept it now, but it also shows that what it means to be healthy or ill can change as a society's culture changes.

A society's culture matters in these various ways, but so does its social structure, in particular its level of economic development and extent of government involvement in health-care delivery. As we will see, poor societies have much worse health than richer societies. At the same time, richer societies have certain health risks and health problems, such as pollution and liver disease (brought on by high alcohol use), that poor societies avoid. The degree of government involvement in health-care delivery also matters: as we will also see, the United States lags behind many Western European nations in several health indicators, in part because the latter nations provide much more national health care than does the United States. Although illness is often a matter of bad luck or bad genes, the society we live in can nonetheless affect our chances of becoming and staying ill.

Sociological Perspectives on Health and Medicine

The major sociological perspectives on health and medicine all recognize these points but offer different ways of understanding health and medicine that fall into the functional, conflict, and symbolic interactionist approaches. Together they provide us with a more comprehensive understanding of health, medicine, and society than any one approach can do by itself (Cockerham, 2009). Table 18.1 "Theory Snapshot" summarizes what they say.

Table 18.1 Theory Snapshot

Theoretical perspective	Major assumptions
Functionalism	Good health and effective medical care are essential for the smooth functioning of society. Patients must perform the "sick role" in order to be perceived as legitimately ill and to be exempt from their normal obligations. The physician-patient relationship is hierarchical: the physician provides instructions, and the patient needs to follow them.
Conflict theory	Social inequality characterizes the quality of health and the quality of health care. People from disadvantaged social backgrounds are more likely to become ill and to receive inadequate health care. Partly to increase their incomes, physicians have tried to control the practice of medicine and to define social problems as medical problems.
Symbolic interactionism	Health and illness are *social constructions*: Physical and mental conditions have little or no objective reality but instead are considered healthy or ill conditions only if they are defined as such by a society. Physicians "manage the situation" to display their authority and medical knowledge.

The Functionalist Approach

As conceived by Talcott Parsons (1951), the functionalist perspective on health and medicine emphasizes that good health and effective medical care are essential for a society's ability to function. Ill health impairs our ability to perform our roles in society, and if too many people are unhealthy, society's functioning and stability suffer. This was especially true for premature death, said Parsons, because it prevents individuals from fully carrying out all their social roles and thus represents a "poor return" to society for the various costs of pregnancy, birth, child care, and socialization of the individual who ends up dying early. Poor medical care is likewise dysfunctional for society, as people who are ill face greater difficulty in becoming healthy and people who are healthy are more likely to become ill.

For a person to be considered *legitimately* sick, said Parsons, several expectations must be met. He referred to these expectations as the **sick role**. First, sick people should not be perceived as having caused their own health problem. If we eat high-fat food, become obese, and have a heart attack, we evoke less sympathy than if we had practiced good nutrition and maintained a proper weight. If someone is driving drunk and smashes into a tree, there is much less sympathy than if the driver had been sober and skidded off the road in icy weather.

Second, sick people must want to get well. If they do not want to get well or, worse yet, are perceived as faking their illness or malingering after becoming healthier, they are no longer considered legitimately ill by the people who know them or, more generally, by society itself.

Third, sick people are expected to have their illness confirmed by a physician or other health-care professional and to follow the professional's advice and instructions in order to become well. If a sick person fails to do so, she or he again loses the right to perform the sick role.

Talcott Parsons wrote that for a person to be perceived as legitimately ill, several expectations, called the sick role, must be met. These expectations include the perception that the person did not cause her or his own health problem.

Nathalie Babineau-Griffith – grand-maman's blanket – CC BY-NC-ND 2.0.

If all of these expectations are met, said Parsons, sick people are treated as sick by their family, their friends, and other people they know, and they become exempt from their normal obligations to all these people. Sometimes they are even told to stay in bed when they want to remain active.

Physicians also have a role to perform, said Parsons. First and foremost, they have to diagnose the person's illness, decide how to treat it, and help the person become well. To do so, they need the cooperation of the patient, who must answer the physician's questions accurately and follow the physician's instructions. Parsons thus viewed the physician-patient relationship as hierarchical: the physician gives the orders (or, more accurately, provides advice and instructions), and the patient follows them.

Parsons was certainly right in emphasizing the importance of individuals' good health for society's health, but his perspective has been criticized for several reasons. First, his idea of the sick role applies more to acute (short-term) illness than to chronic (long-term) illness. Although much of his discussion implies a person temporarily enters a sick role and leaves it soon after following adequate medical care, people with chronic illnesses can be locked into a sick role for a very long time or even permanently. Second, Parsons's discussion ignores the fact, mentioned earlier, that our social location in society in the form of social class, race and ethnicity, and gender affects both the likelihood of becoming ill and the quality of medical care we receive. Third, Parsons wrote approvingly of the hierarchy implicit in the physician-patient relationship. Many experts say today that patients need to reduce this hierarchy by asking more questions of their physicians and by taking a more active role in maintaining their health. To the extent that physicians do not always provide the best medical care, the hierarchy that Parsons favored is at least partly to blame.

The Conflict Approach

The conflict approach emphasizes inequality in the quality of health and of health-care delivery (Conrad, 2009). As noted earlier, the quality of health and health care differ greatly around the world and within the United States. Society's inequities along social class, race and ethnicity, and gender lines are reproduced in our health and health care. People from disadvantaged social backgrounds are more likely to become ill, and once they do become ill, inadequate health care makes it more difficult for them to become well. As we will see, the evidence of inequities in health and health care is vast and dramatic.

The conflict approach also critiques the degree to which physicians over the decades have tried to control the practice of medicine and to define various social problems as medical ones. Their motivation for doing so has been both good and bad. On the good side, they have believed that they are the most qualified professionals to diagnose problems and treat people who have these problems. On the negative side, they have also recognized that their financial status will improve if they succeed in characterizing social problems as medical problems and in monopolizing the treatment of these problems. Once these problems become "medicalized," their possible social roots and thus potential solutions are neglected.

Several examples illustrate conflict theory's criticism. Alternative medicine is becoming increasingly popular (see Chapter 18 "Health and Medicine", Section 18.4 "Medicine and Health Care in the United States"), but so has criticism of it by the medical establishment. Physicians may honestly feel that medical alternatives are inadequate, ineffective, or even dangerous, but they also recognize that the use of these alternatives is financially harmful to their own practices. Eating disorders also illustrate conflict theory's criticism. Many of the women and girls who have eating disorders receive help from a physician, a psychiatrist, a psychologist, or another health-care professional. Although this care is often very helpful, the definition of eating disorders as a medical problem nonetheless provides a good source of income for the professionals who treat it and obscures its cultural roots in society's standard of beauty for women (Whitehead & Kurz, 2008).

Obstetrical care provides another example. In most of human history, midwives or their equivalent were the people who helped pregnant women deliver their babies. In the 19th century, physicians claimed they were better trained than midwives and won legislation giving them authority to deliver babies. They may have honestly felt that midwives were inadequately trained, but they also fully recognized that obstetrical care would be quite lucrative (Ehrenreich & English, 2005). In a final example, many hyperactive children are now diagnosed with ADHD, or attention deficit/hyperactivity disorder. A generation or more ago, they would have been considered merely as overly active. After Ritalin, a drug that reduces hyperactivity, was developed, their behavior came to be considered a medical problem and the ADHD diagnosis was increasingly applied, and tens of thousands of children went to physicians' offices and were given Ritalin or similar drugs. The definition of their behavior as a medical problem was very lucrative for physicians and for the company that developed Ritalin, and it also obscured the possible roots of their behavior in inadequate parenting, stultifying schools, or even gender socialization, as most hyperactive kids are boys (Conrad, 2008; Rao & Seaton, 2010).

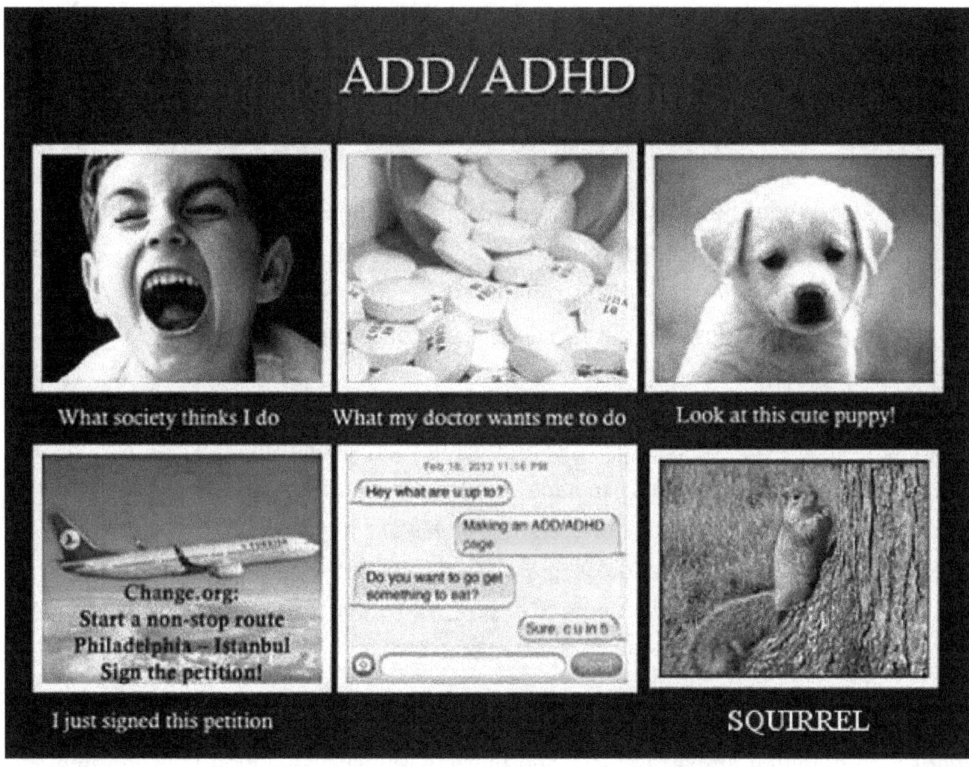

According to conflict theory, physicians have often sought to define various social problems as medical problems. An example is the development of the diagnosis of ADHD, or attention deficit/hyperactivity disorder.

birgerking – What I Really Do… ADD/ADHD – CC BY 2.0.

Critics of the conflict approach say that its assessment of health and medicine is overly harsh and its criticism of physicians' motivation far too cynical. Scientific medicine has greatly improved the health of people in the industrial world; even in the poorer nations, moreover, health has improved from a century ago, however inadequate it remains today. Although physicians are certainly motivated, as many people are, by economic considerations, their efforts to extend their scope into previously nonmedical areas also stem from honest beliefs that people's health and lives will improve if these efforts succeed. Certainly there is some truth in this criticism of the conflict approach, but the evidence of inequality in health and medicine and of the negative aspects of the medical establishment's motivation for extending its reach remains compelling.

The Interactionist Approach

The interactionist approach emphasizes that health and illness are *social constructions*. This means that various physical and mental conditions have little or no objective reality but instead are considered healthy or ill conditions only if they are defined as such by a society and its members (Buckser, 2009; Lorber & Moore, 2002). The ADHD example just discussed also illustrates interactionist theory's concerns, as a behavior that was not previously considered an illness came to be defined as one after the development of Ritalin. In another example, in the late 1800s opium use was quite common in the United States, as opium derivatives were included in all sorts of over-the-counter products. Opium use was considered neither a major health nor legal problem. That changed by the end of the century, as prejudice against Chinese Americans led to the banning of the opium dens (similar to today's bars) they frequented, and calls for the banning of opium led to federal legislation early in the 20th century that banned most opium products except by prescription (Musto, 2002).

In a more current example, an attempt to redefine obesity is now under way in the United States. Obesity is a known health risk, but a "fat pride" movement composed mainly of heavy individuals is arguing that obesity's health risks are exaggerated and calling attention to society's discrimination against overweight people. Although such discrimination is certainly unfortunate, critics say the movement is going too far in trying to minimize obesity's risks (Saulny, 2009).

The symbolic interactionist approach has also provided important studies of the interaction between patients and health-care professionals. Consciously or not, physicians "manage the situation" to display their authority and medical knowledge. Patients usually have to wait a long time for the physician to show up, and the physician is often in a white lab coat; the physician is also often addressed as "Doctor," while patients are often called by their first name. Physicians typically use complex medical terms to describe a patient's illness instead of the more simple terms used by laypeople and the patients themselves.

Management of the situation is perhaps especially important during a gynecological exam. When the physician is a man, this situation is fraught with potential embarrassment and uneasiness because a man is examining and touching a woman's genital area. Under these circumstances, the physician must act in a purely professional manner. He must indicate no personal interest in the woman's body and must instead treat the exam no differently from any other type of exam. To further "desex" the situation and reduce any potential uneasiness, a female nurse is often present during the exam (Cullum-Swan, 1992).

Critics fault the symbolic interactionist approach for implying that no illnesses have objective reality. Many serious health conditions do exist and put people at risk for their health regardless of what they or their society thinks. Critics also say the approach neglects the effects of social inequality for health and illness. Despite these possible faults, the symbolic interactionist approach reminds us that health and illness do have a subjective as well as an objective reality.

Key Takeaways

- A sociological understanding emphasizes the influence of people's social backgrounds on the quality of their health and health care. A society's culture and social structure also affect health and health care.
- The functionalist approach emphasizes that good health and effective health care are essential for a society's ability to function. The conflict approach emphasizes inequality in the quality of health and in the quality of health care.
- The interactionist approach emphasizes that health and illness are social constructions; physical and mental conditions have little or no objective reality but instead are considered healthy or ill conditions only if they are defined as such by a society and its members.

For Your Review

1. Which approach—functionalist, conflict, or symbolic interactionist—do you most favor regarding how you understand health and health care? Explain your answer.
2. Think of the last time you visited a physician or another health-care professional. In what ways did this person come across as an authority figure possessing medical knowledge? In formulating your answer, think about the person's clothing, body position and body language, and other aspects of nonverbal communication.

References

Buckser, A. (2009). Institutions, agency, and illness in the making of Tourette syndrome. *Human Organization, 68*(3), 293–306.

Cockerham, W. C. (2009). *Medical sociology* (11th ed.). Upper Saddle River, NJ: Prentice Hall.

Conrad, P. (2008). *The medicalization of society: On the transformation of human conditions into treatable disorders*. Baltimore, MD: Johns Hopkins University Press.

Conrad, P. (Ed.). (2009). *Sociology of health and illness: Critical perspectives* (8th ed.). New York, NY: Worth.

Cullum-Swan, B. (1992). *Behavior in public places: A frame analysis of gynecological exams*. Paper presented at the American Sociological Association, Pittsburgh, PA.

Ehrenreich, B., & English, D. (2005). *For her own good: Two centuries of the experts' advice to women* (2nd ed.). New York, NY: Anchor Books.

Hahn, R. A., & Inborn, M. (Eds.). (2009). *Anthropology and public health: Bridging differences in culture and society* (2nd ed.). New York, NY: Oxford University Press.

Lorber, J., & Moore, L. J. (2002). *Gender and the social construction of illness* (2nd ed.). Lanham, MD: Rowman & Littlefield.

Musto, D. F. (Ed.). (2002). *Drugs in America: A documentary history*. New York, NY: New York University Press.

Parsons, T. (1951). *The social system*. New York, NY: Free Press.

Rao, A., & Seaton, M. (2010). *The way of boys: Promoting the social and emotional development of young boys*. New York, NY: Harper Paperbacks.

Saulny, S. (2009, November 7). Heavier Americans push back on health debate. *The New York Times*, p. A23.

Sehata, G., & Kimura, T. (2009, February 28). A decade on, organ transplant law falls short. *The Daily Yomiuri* [Tokyo], p. 3.

Shinzo, K. (2004). Organ transplants and brain-dead donors: A Japanese doctor's perspective. *Mortality, 9*(1), 13–26.

Whitehead, K., & Kurz, T. (2008). Saints, sinners and standards of femininity: Discursive constructions of anorexia nervosa and obesity in women's magazines. *Journal of Gender Studies, 17*, 345–358.

18.2 Health and Medicine in International Perspective

Learning Objectives

1. Describe how the nations of the world differ in important indicators of health and illness.
2. Explain the health-care model found in industrial nations other than the United States.

As with many topics in sociology, understanding what happens in other societies and cultures helps us to understand what happens in our own society. This section's discussion of health and health care across the globe, then, helps shed some light on what is good and bad about U.S. health and medicine.

International Disparities in Health and Illness

Two-thirds of the 33 million people worldwide who have HIV/AIDS live in sub-Saharan Africa. This terrible fact illustrates just one of the many health problems that people in poor nations suffer.

khym54 – AIDS Orphans and their Guardians in Sophia Village – CC BY 2.0.

The nations of the world differ dramatically in the quality of their health and health care. The poorest nations suffer terribly. Their people suffer from poor nutrition, unsafe water, inadequate sanitation, a plethora of diseases, and inadequate health care. One disease they suffer from is AIDS. Some 33 million people worldwide have HIV/AIDS, and two-thirds of these live in sub-Saharan Africa. Two million people, most of them from this region, died in 2008 from HIV/AIDS (World Health Organization, 2010). All of these problems produce high rates of infant mortality and maternal mortality and high death rates. For all of these reasons, people in the poorest nations have shorter life spans than those in the richest nations.

A few health indicators should indicate the depth of the problem. Figure 18.1 "Infant Mortality for Low Income, Lower Middle Income, Higher Middle Income, and High Income Nations, 2008" compares an important indicator, infant mortality (number of deaths before age 1 per 1,000 live births) for nations grouped into four income categories. The striking contrast between the two groups provides dramatic evidence of the health problems poor nations face. When, as Figure 18.1 "Infant Mortality for Low Income, Lower Middle Income, Higher Middle Income, and High Income Nations, 2008" indicates, 80 children in the poorest nations die before their first birthday for every 1,000 live births (equivalent to 8 out of 100), the poor nations have serious problems indeed. Figure 18.2 "Percentage of Population With Access to Adequate Sanitation Facilities, 2008" shows how the world differs in access to adequate sanitation facilities (i.e., the removal of human waste from the physical environment, as by toilets). Whereas this percentage is at least 98% in the wealthy nations of North America, Western Europe, Australia, and New Zealand, it is less than 33% in many poor nations in Africa and Asia.

Figure 18.1 Infant Mortality for Low Income, Lower Middle Income, Higher Middle Income, and High Income Nations, 2008

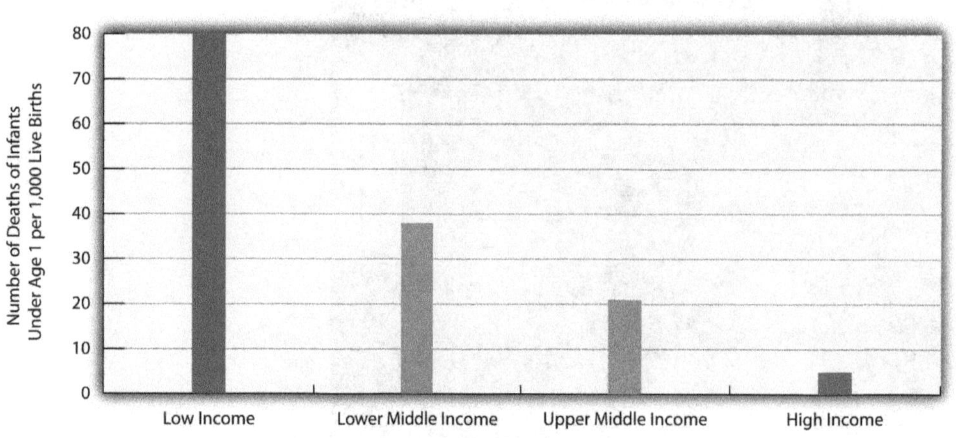

Source: Data from World Bank. (2010). Health nutrition and population statistics. Retrieved from http://databank.worldbank.org/ddp/home.do?Step=2&id=4.

Figure 18.2 Percentage of Population With Access to Adequate Sanitation Facilities, 2008

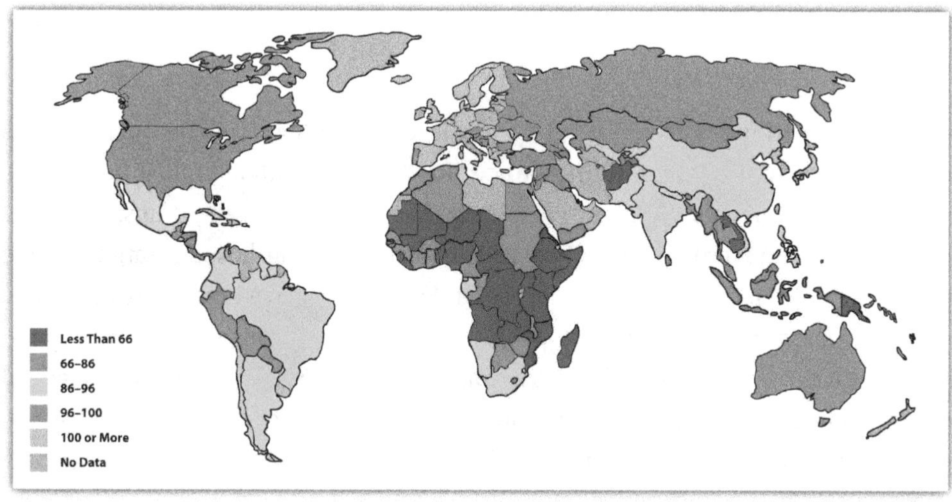

Source: Adapted from World Bank. (2010). Improved sanitation facilities (% of population with access). Retrieved from http://ddp-ext.worldbank.org/ext/ddpreports/ViewSharedReport?&CF=&REPORT_ID=5558&REQUEST_TYPE=VIEWADVANCEDMAP.

Chapter 9 "Global Stratification" presented an international map on life expectancy. That map was certainly relevant for understanding aging around the globe but is also relevant for understanding worldwide disparities in health and health care. We reproduce this map here (see Figure 18.3 "Average Life Expectancy Across the Globe (Years)"). Not surprisingly, the global differences in this map are similar to those for adequate sanitation in the map depicted in Figure 18.2 "Percentage of Population With Access to Adequate Sanitation Facilities, 2008". North America, Western Europe, Australia, and New Zealand have much longer life expectancies (75 years and higher) than Africa and Asia, where some nations have expectancies below 50 years. The society we live in can affect our life span by more than a quarter of a century.

Figure 18.3 Average Life Expectancy Across the Globe (Years)

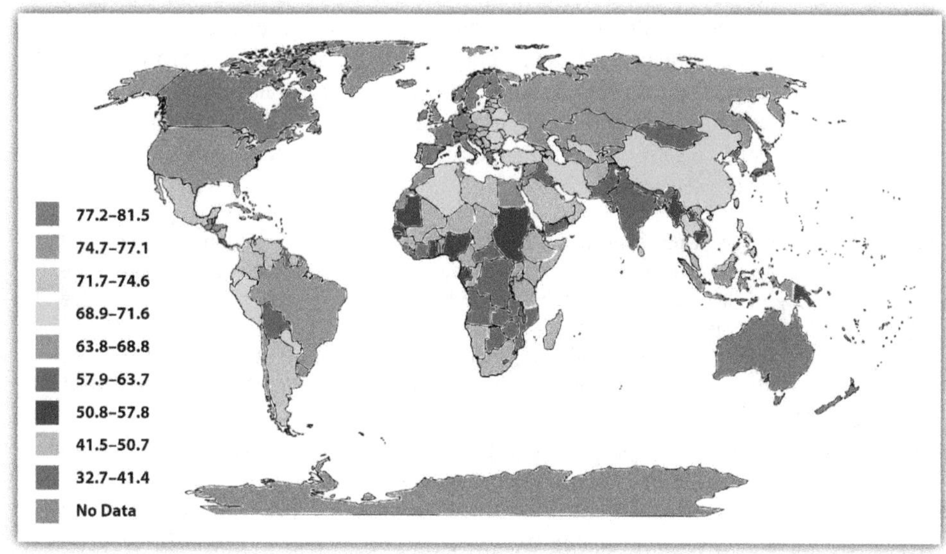

Source: Adapted from Global Education Project. (2004). Human conditions: World life expectancy map. Retrieved from http://www.theglobaleducationproject.org/earth/human-conditions.php.

Health Care in Industrial Nations

Industrial nations throughout the world, with the notable exception of the United States, provide their citizens with some form of national health care and **national health insurance** (Reid, 2009). Although their health-care systems differ in several respects, their governments pay all or most of the costs for health care, drugs, and other health needs. In Denmark, for example, the government provides free medical care and hospitalization for the entire population and pays for some medications and some dental care. In France, the government pays for some of the medical, hospitalization, and medication costs for most people and all of these expenses for the poor, unemployed, and children under the age of 10. In Great Britain, the National Health Service pays most medical costs for the population, including medical care, hospitalization, prescriptions, dental care, and eyeglasses. In Canada, the National Health Insurance system also pays for most medical costs. Patients do not even receive bills from their physicians, who instead are paid by the government.

Although these national health insurance programs are not perfect—for example, people sometimes must wait for elective surgery and some other procedures—they are commonly credited with reducing infant mortality, extending life expectancy, and more generally for enabling their citizenries to have relatively good health. In all of these respects, these systems offer several advantages over the health-care model found in the United States (Hacker, 2008) (see the "Learning From Other Societies" box).

Learning From Other Societies

National Health Care in Wealthy Nations

As the text discusses, industrial nations other than the United States provide free or low-cost health care to their citizens in what is known as national (or universal) health insurance and national health care. Although the United States spends more per capita than these nations on health care, it generally ranks much lower than they do on important health indicators. Of 23 wealthy nations from North America, Western Europe, and certain other parts of the world (Australia, Japan, New Zealand; the exact number of nations varies slightly by indicator), the United States has the lowest life expectancy and the highest infant mortality and rate of diabetes. It ranks only 21st in mortality from heart disease and stroke and only 15th in dental health among children. The United States also ranks lowest for annual doctor consultations per capita and among the highest for hospital admissions for various conditions, such as congestive heart failure, that are avoidable with adequate primary and outpatient care (Organisation for Economic Co-operation and Development, 2009). The conclusion from these international comparisons is inescapable:

> Although the United States spends more on health care than other countries with similar per capita income and populations, it has worse health outcomes, on average.…Compared to the United States, other countries are more committed to the health and well-being of their citizens through more-universal coverage and more-comprehensive health care systems. (Mishel, Bernstein, & Shierholz, 2009, pp. 349, 353)
> Because of Canada's proximity, many studies compare health and health-care indicators between the United States and Canada. A recent review summarized the evidence: "Although studies' findings go in both directions, the bulk of the research finds higher quality of care in Canada" (Docteur & Berenson, 2009, p. 7).
>
> Surveys of random samples of citizens in several nations provide additional evidence of the advantages of the type of health care found outside the United States and the disadvantages of the U.S. system. In surveys in 2007 of U.S. residents and those of six other nations (Australia, Canada, Germany, the Netherlands, New Zealand, and the United Kingdom), Americans ranked highest in the percentage uninsured (16% in the United States compared to 0%–2% elsewhere), highest in the percentage that did not receive needed medical care during the last year because of costs,

and highest by far in the percentage that had "serious problems" in paying medical bills in the past year (Schoen et al., 2007).

A fair conclusion from all the evidence is that U.S. health lags behind that found in other wealthy nations because the latter provide free or low-cost national health care to their citizens and the United States does not. If so, the United States has much to learn from their example. Because the health-care reform achieved in the United States in 2009 and 2010 did not include a national health-care model, the United States will likely continue to lag behind other democracies in the quality of health and health care. Even so, the cost of health care will certainly continue to be much higher in the United States than in other Western nations, in part because the United States uses a *fee-for-service* model in which physicians are paid for every procedure they do rather than the set salary that some other nations feature.

Key Takeaways

- The world's nations differ dramatically in the quality of their health and health care. People in poor nations suffer from many health problems, and poor nations have very high rates of infant mortality and maternal mortality.
- Except for the United States, industrial nations have national health-care systems and national health insurance. Their health-care models help their citizens to have relatively good health at affordable levels.

For Your Review

1. What do you think should be done to help improve the health of poor nations? What role should the United States play in any efforts in this regard?
2. Do you think the United States should move toward the national health insurance model found in other Western nations? Why or why not?

References

Docteur, E., & Berenson, R. A. (2009). *How does the quality of U.S. health care compare internationally?* Washington, DC: Urban Institute.

Hacker, J. S. (Ed.). (2008). *Health at risk: America's ailing health system—and how to heal it.* New York, NY: Columbia Univeristy Press.

Mishel, L., Bernstein, J., & Shierholz, H. (2009). *The state of working America 2008/2009.* Ithaca, NY: ILR Press [An imprint of Cornell University Press].

Organisation for Economic Co-operation and Development. (2009). *Health at a glance 2009: OECD indicators.* Paris, France: Author.

Reid, T. R. (2009). *The healing of America: A global quest for better, cheaper, and fairer health care.* New York, NY: Penguin Press.

Schoen, C., Osborn, R., Doty, M. M., Bishop, M., Peugh, J., & Murukutla, N. (2007). Toward higher-performance health systems: Adults' health care experiences in seven countries, 2007. *Health Affairs 26*(6), w717–w734.

World Health Organization. (2010). WHO and HIV/AIDS. Retrieved from http://www.who.int/hiv/en/index.html.

18.3 Health and Illness in the United States

Learning Objectives

1. Describe how and why social class, race and ethnicity, and gender affect health and health care in the United States.
2. Summarize how health and illness in the United States vary by sociodemographic characteristics.

When we examine health and illness in the United States, there is both good news and bad news. The good news is considerable. Health has improved steadily over the last century, thanks in large part to better public sanitation and the discovery of antibiotics. Illnesses and diseases such as pneumonia and polio that used to kill or debilitate people are either unknown today or treatable by modern drugs. Other medical discoveries and advances have also reduced the extent and seriousness of major illnesses, including many types of cancer, and have prolonged our lives. The mortality rate from heart disease is down 50% from the early 1980s, and the mortality rate from strokes is down about 51% (Centers for Disease Control and Prevention, 2010).

As a result of all of these factors, the U.S. average life expectancy climbed from about 47 years in 1900 to about 78 years in 2010 (recall Figure 9.7 "Average Life Expectancy Across the Globe (Years)"). Similarly, infant mortality dropped dramatically in the last half-century from 29.2 infant deaths per 1,000 live births in 1950 to only 6.7 in 2006 (see Figure 18.4 "Infant Deaths per 1,000 Live Births, United States, 1950–2006"). Public health campaigns have increased awareness of the sources and seriousness of some health problems and led to behavioral changes and, for some problems, legislation that has reduced these problems. For example, cigarette smoking declined from 51% for males and 34% for females in 1965 to 22% and 17.5%, respectively, in 2007 (National Center for Health Statistics, 2009). In another area, various policies during the past three decades have dramatically reduced levels of lead in young children's blood; 88% had unsafe levels in the mid-1970s, compared to less than 2% today (Centers for Disease Control and Prevention, 2007).

Figure 18.4 Infant Deaths per 1,000 Live Births, United States, 1950–2006

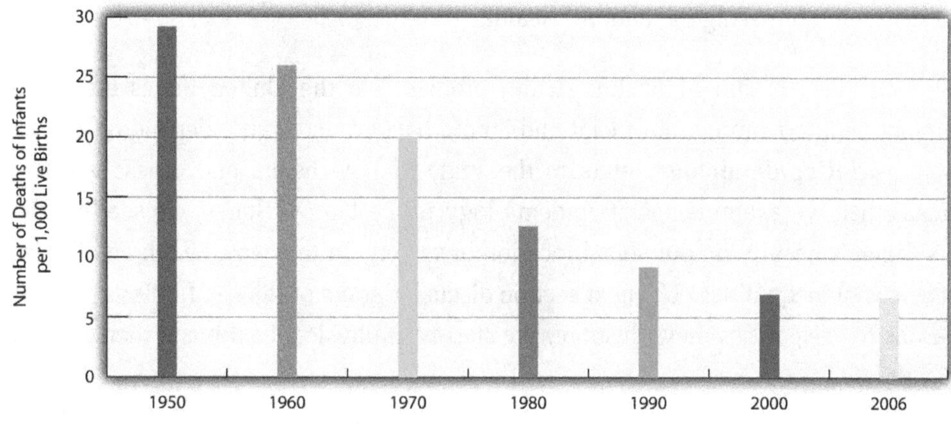

Source: Data from National Center for Health Statistics. (2009). *Health, United States, 2009.* Hyattsville, MD: Centers for Disease Control and Prevention.

Cigarette smoking in the United States has declined considerably since the 1960s.

Xava du – smoke souls – CC BY-NC-ND 2.0.

Unfortunately, the bad news is also considerable. While the United States has improved its health in many ways, it nonetheless lags behind most other wealthy nations in several health indicators, as we have seen, even though it is the wealthiest nation in the world. Moreover, about 15% of U.S. households and more than 32 million persons are "food-insecure" (lacking sufficient money for adequate food and nutrition) at least part of the year; more than one-fifth of all children live in such households (Nord, Andrews, & Carlson, 2009). More than 8% of all infants are born at low birth weight (under 5.5 pounds), putting them at risk for long-term health problems; this figure has risen steadily for a number of years and is higher than the 1970 rate (National Center for Health Statistics, 2009). In other areas, childhood rates of obesity, asthma, and some other chronic conditions are on the rise, with about one-third of children considered obese or overweight (Van Cleave, Gortmaker, & Perrin, 2010). Clearly the United States still has a long way to go in improving the nation's health.

There is also bad news in the social distribution of health. Health problems in the United States are more often found among the poor, among people from certain racial and ethnic backgrounds, and, depending on the problem, among women or men. **Social epidemiology** refers to the study of how health and illness vary by sociodemographic characteristics. When we examine social epidemiology in the United States, we see that the distribution of health and illness depends heavily on our social location in society. In this way, health and illness both reflect and reinforce society's social inequalities. The next section discusses some of the key findings on U.S. social epidemiology and the reasons for disparities they illustrate. We start with physical health and then discuss mental health.

The Social Epidemiology of Physical Health

Social Class

Not only do the poor have less money, but they also have much worse health. There is growing recognition in the government and in medical and academic communities that social class makes a huge difference when it comes to health and illness. A recent summary of the evidence concluded that social class inequalities in health are "pervasive" in the United States and other nations across the world (Elo, 2009, p. 553).

Many types of health indicators illustrate the social class–health link in the United States. In an annual survey conducted by the government, people are asked to indicate the quality of their health. As Figure 18.5 "Family Income and Self-Reported Health (Percentage of People 18 or Over Saying Health Is Only Fair or Poor)" shows, poor people are much more likely than those with higher incomes to say their health is only fair or poor. These *self-reports* of health are subjective indicators, and it is possible that not everyone interprets "fair" or "poor" health in the same way. But objective indicators of actual health also indicate a strong social class–health link, with some of the most unsettling evidence involving children. As a recent report concluded,

> The data illustrate a consistent and striking pattern of incremental improvements in health with increasing levels of family income and educational attainment: As family income and levels of education rise, health improves. In almost every state, shortfalls in health are greatest among children in the poorest or least educated households, but even middle-class children are less healthy than children with greater advantages. (Robert Wood Johnson Foundation, 2008, p. 2)

For example, infant mortality is 86% higher among infants born to mothers without a high school degree than those with a college degree, and low birth weight is 29% higher. According to their parents, one-third of children in poor families are in less than very good health, compared to only 7% of children in wealthy families (at least 4 times the poverty level). In many other health indicators, as the news story that began this chapter indicated, children in low-income families are more likely than children in wealthier families to have various kinds of health problems, many of which endure into adolescence and adulthood.

Figure 18.5 Family Income and Self-Reported Health (Percentage of People 18 or Over Saying Health Is Only Fair or Poor)

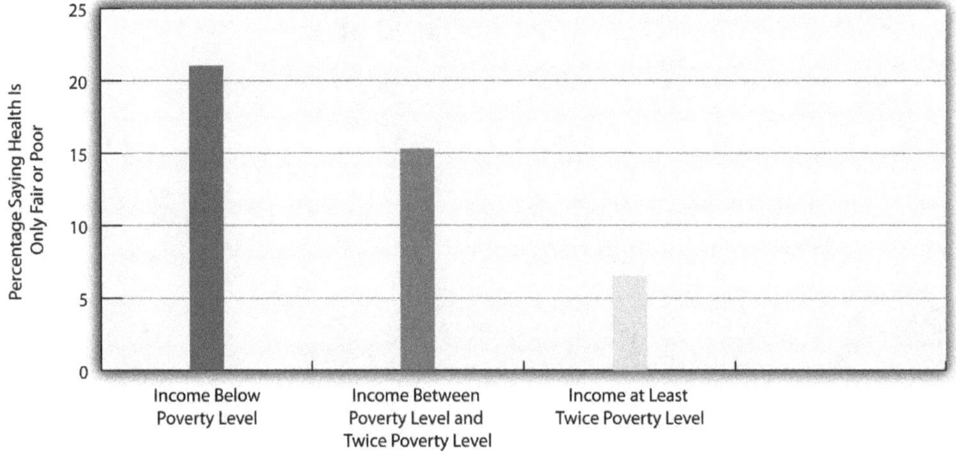

Source: Data from National Center for Health Statistics. (2009). *Health, United States, 2009*. Hyattsville, MD: Centers for Disease Control and Prevention.

Poor adults are also at much greater risk for many health problems, including heart disease, diabetes, arthritis, and some types of cancer (National Center for Health Statistics, 2009). Rates of high blood pressure, serious heart conditions, and diabetes are at least twice as high for middle-aged adults with family incomes below the poverty level than for those with incomes at least twice the poverty level. All of these social class differences in health contribute to a striking difference in life expectancy, with the wealthiest Americans expected to live four and a half years longer on average than the poorest Americans (Pear, 2008).

Several reasons account for the social class–health link (Elo, 2009; Pampel, Krueger, & Denney, 2010). One reason is stress, which is higher for people with low incomes because of unemployment, problems in paying for the necessities of life, and a sense of little control over what happens to them. Stress in turn damages health because it impairs the immune system and other bodily processes (Lantz, House, Mero, & Williams, 2005). A second reason is that poor people live in conditions, including crowded, dilapidated housing with poor sanitation, that are bad for their health and especially that of their children (Stewart & Rhoden, 2006). Although these conditions have improved markedly in the United States over the last few decades, they continue for many of the poor.

Another reason is the lack of access to adequate health care. As is well known, many poor people lack medical insurance and in other respects have inadequate health care. These problems make it more likely they will become ill in the first place and more difficult for them to become well because they cannot afford to visit a physician or to receive other health care. Still, social class disparities in health exist even in countries that provide free national health care, a fact that underscores the importance of the other reasons discussed here for the social class–health link (Elo, 2009).

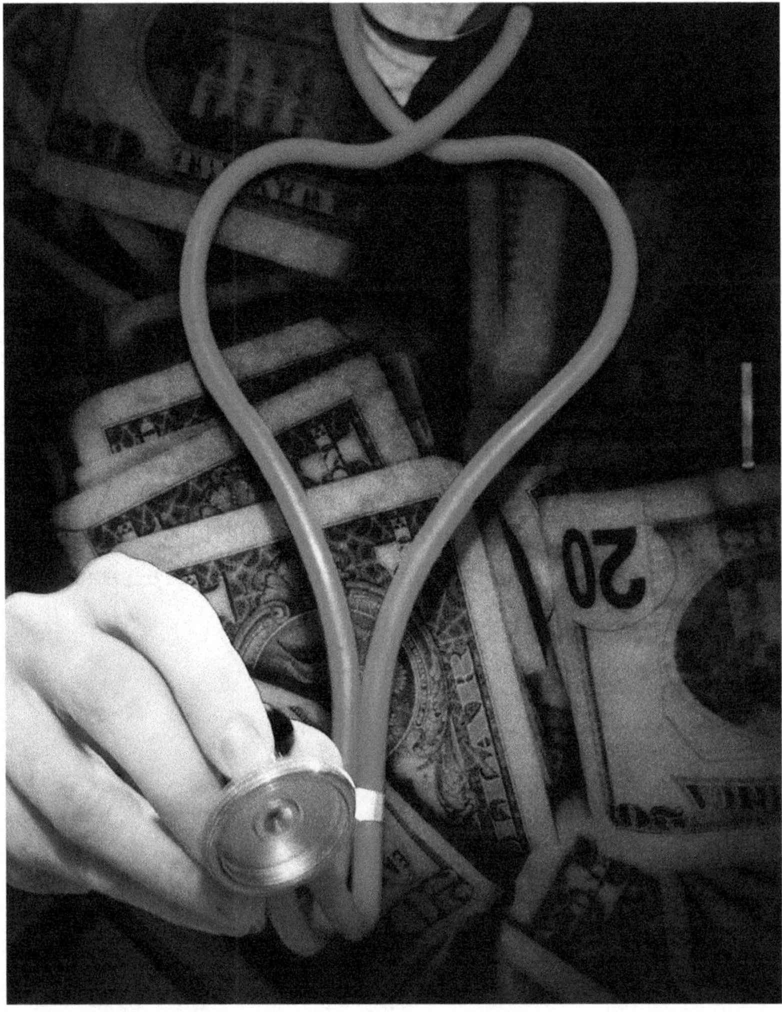

Many people who are poor or near-poor lack medical insurance and in other ways have inadequate health care. These problems make it more likely they will become ill and, once ill, less likely they will become well.

Truthout.org – Money Behind Health Care – CC BY-NC-SA 2.0.

A fourth reason is a lack of education, which, in ways not yet well understood, leads poor people to be unaware of risk factors for health and to have a fatalistic attitude that promotes unhealthy behaviors and reluctance to heed medical advice (Elo, 2009). In one study of whether smokers quit smoking after a heart attack, only 10% of heart attack patients without a high school degree quit smoking, compared to almost 90% of those with a college degree (Wray, Herzog, Willis, & Wallace, 1998).

A final and related reason for the poor health of poor people is unhealthy lifestyles, as just implied. Although it might sound like a stereotype, poor people are more likely to smoke, to eat high-fat food, to avoid exercise, to be overweight, and, more generally, not to do what they need to do (or to do what they should not be doing) to be healthy (Pampel, Krueger, & Denney, 2010; Cubbins & Buchanan, 2009). Scholars continue to debate whether unhealthy lifestyles are more important in explaining poor people's poor health than factors such as lack of access to health care, stress, and other negative aspects of the social and physical environments in which poor people live. Regardless of the proper mix of reasons, the fact remains that the poor have worse health.

In assessing the social class–health link, we have been assuming that poverty leads to poor health. Yet it is also possible that poor health leads to poverty or near-poverty because of high health-care expenses and decreased work hours. Recent evidence supports this causal linkage, as serious health problems in adulthood often do force people to reduce their work hours or even to retire altogether (J. P. Smith, 2005). Although this linkage accounts for some of the social class–health relationship that is so noticeable, evidence of the large impact of low income on poor health remains compelling.

Race and Ethnicity

Health differences also exist when we examine the effects of race and ethnicity (Barr, 2008), and they are literally a matter of life and death. We can see this when we compare life expectancies for whites and African Americans born in 2006 (Table 18.2 “U.S. Life Expectancy at Birth for People Born in 2006”). When we do not take gender into account, African Americans can expect to live 5 fewer years than whites. Among men, they can expect to live 6 fewer years, and among women, 4.1 fewer years.

Table 18.2 U.S. Life Expectancy at Birth for People Born in 2006

African American	Both sexes	73.2
	Men	69.7
	Women	76.5
White	Both sexes	78.2
	Men	75.7
	Women	80.6

Source: Data from National Center for Health Statistics. (2009). *Health, United States, 2009.* Hyattsville, MD: Centers for Disease Control and Prevention.

At the beginning of the life course, infant mortality also varies by race and ethnicity (Table 18.3 “Mother’s Race/Ethnicity and U.S. Infant Mortality, 2003–2005 (Average Annual Number of Infant Deaths per 1,000 Live Births)”), with African American infants more than twice as likely as white infants to die before their first birthday. Infant mortality among Native Americans is almost 1.5 times the white rate, while that for Latinos is about the same (although the Puerto Rican rate is also higher, at 8.1), and Asians a bit lower. In a related indicator, maternal mortality (from complications of pregnancy or childbirth) stands at 8.0 maternal deaths for every 100,000 live births for non-Latina white women, 8.8 for Latina women, and a troubling 28.7 for African American women. Maternal mortality for African American women is thus 3.5 times greater than that for non-Latina white women. In other indicators, African Americans are more likely than whites to die from heart disease, although the white rate of such deaths is higher than the rates of Asians, Latinos, and Native Americans. African Americans are also more likely than whites to be overweight and to suffer from asthma, diabetes, high blood pressure, and several types of cancer. Latinos and Native Americans have higher rates than whites of several illnesses and conditions, including diabetes.

Table 18.3 Mother's Race/Ethnicity and U.S. Infant Mortality, 2003–2005 (Average Annual Number of Infant Deaths per 1,000 Live Births)

African American	13.3
Asian	4.8
Latina	5.6
Central and South American	4.8
Cuban	4.5
Mexican	5.5
Puerto Rican	8.1
Native American	8.4
White	5.7

Source: Data from National Center for Health Statistics. (2009). *Health, United States, 2009*. Hyattsville, MD: Centers for Disease Control and Prevention.

Commenting on all of these disparities in health, a former head of the U.S. Department of Health and Human Services said a decade ago, "We have been—and remain—two nations: one majority, one minority—separated by the quality of our health" (Penn et al., 2000, p. 102). The examples just discussed certainly indicate that her statement is still true today.

Why do such large racial and ethnic disparities in health exist? To a large degree, they reflect the high poverty rates for African Americans, Latinos, and Native Americans compared to those for whites (Cubbins & Buchanan, 2009). In addition, inadequate medical care is perhaps a special problem for people of color, thanks to unconscious racial bias among health-care professionals that affects the quality of care that people of color receive (see discussion later in this chapter).

An additional reason for racial disparities in health is diet. Many of the foods that have long been part of African American culture are high in fat. Partly as a result, African Americans are much more likely than whites to have heart disease and high blood pressure and to die from these conditions (Lewis-Moss, Paschal, Redmond, Green, & Carmack, 2008). In contrast, first-generation Latinos tend to have diets consisting of beans, grains, and other low-fat foods, preventing health problems stemming from their poverty from being even worse. But as the years go by and they adopt the typical American's eating habits, their diets tend to worsen, and their health worsens as well (Pérez-Escamilla, 2009).

In a significant finding, African Americans have worse health than whites even among those with the same incomes. This racial gap is thought to stem from several reasons. One is the extra stress that African Americans of all incomes face because they live in a society that is still racially prejudiced and discriminatory (Williams, Neighbors, & Jackson, J., 2008). In this regard, a growing amount of research finds that African Americans and Latinos who have experienced the most racial discrimination in their daily lives tend to have worse physical health (Lee & Ferraro, 2009; Gee & Walsemann, 2009). Some middle-class African Americans may also have grown up in poor families and incurred health problems in childhood that still affect them. As a former U.S. surgeon general once explained, "You're never dealing with a person just today. You're dealing with everything they've been exposed to throughout their lives. Does it ever end? Our hypothesis is that it never ends" (Meckler, 1998, p. 4A).

To some degree, racial differences in health may also have a biological basis. For example, African American men appear to have higher levels of a certain growth protein that may promote prostate cancer; African American smokers may absorb more nicotine than white smokers; and differences in the ways African Americans' blood vessels react may render them more susceptible to hypertension and heart disease (Meckler, 1998). Because alleged biological differences have been used as the basis for racism, and because race is best thought of as a social construction rather than a biological concept (see Chapter 10 "Race and Ethnicity"), we have to be very careful in acknowledging such differences (Frank, 2007). However, if they do indeed exist, they may help explain at least some of the racial gap in health.

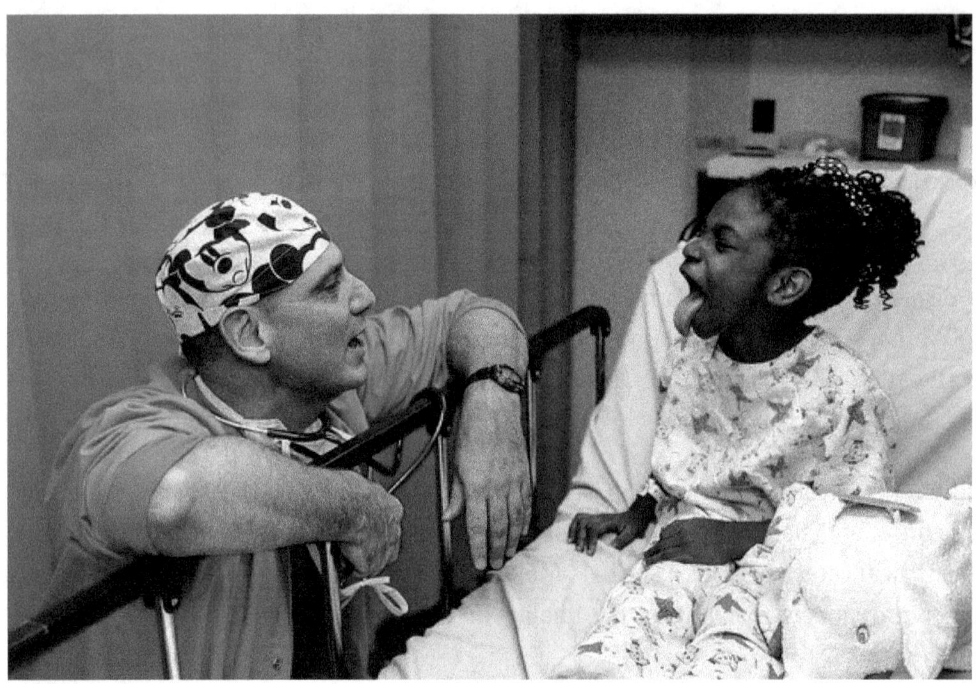

African Americans have worse health than whites, even when people with the same incomes are compared. One reason for this racial gap is the continuing racial discrimination that African Americans experience and the stress that accompanies this experience.

Pixabay – CC0 Public Domain.

A final factor contributing to racial differences in health is physical location: poor people of color tend to live in areas that are unhealthy places because of air and water pollution, hazardous waste, and other environmental problems. This problem is termed *environmental racism* (King & McCarthy, 2009). One example of this problem is found in the so-called Cancer Alley on a long stretch of the Mississippi River in Louisiana populated mostly by African Americans; 80% of these residents live within 3 miles of a polluting industrial facility.

Gender

The evidence on gender and health is both complex and fascinating. Women outlive men by more than 6 years, and, as Table 18.2 “U.S. Life Expectancy at Birth for People Born in 2006” showed, the gender difference in longevity persists across racial categories. At the same time, women have worse health than men in many areas. For example, they are much more likely to suffer from migraine headaches, osteoporosis, and immune diseases such as lupus and rheumatoid arthritis. Women thus have more health problems than men even though they outlive men, a situation commonly known as the *morbidity paradox* (Gorman & Read, 2006). Why, then, do women outlive men? Conversely, why do men die earlier than women? The obvious answer is that men have more life-threatening diseases, such as heart disease and emphysema, than women, but that raises the question of why this is so.

Several reasons explain the gender gap in longevity. One might be biological, as women’s estrogen and other sex-linked biological differences may make them less susceptible to heart disease and other life-threatening illnesses, even as they render them more vulnerable to some of the problems already listed (Kuller, 2010). A second reason is that men lead more unhealthy lifestyles than women because of differences in gender socialization. For example, men are more likely than women to smoke, to drink heavily, and to drive recklessly. All such behaviors make men more vulnerable than women to life-threatening illnesses and injuries (Gorman & Read, 2006). Men are also more likely than women to hold jobs in workplaces filled with environmental hazards and other problems that are thought to kill thousands of people—most of them men—annually (Simon, 2008).

A final reason is men’s reluctance to discuss medical problems they have and to seek help for them, owing to their masculine socialization into being “strong, silent types.” Just as men do not like to ask for directions, as the common wisdom goes, so do they not like to ask for medical help. As one physician put it, “I’ve often said men don’t come in for checkups because they have a big *S* tattooed on their chests; they think they’re Superman” (Guttman, 1999, p. 10). Studies find that men are less likely than women to tell anyone when they have a health problem and to seek help from a health-care professional (Emmers-Sommer et al., 2009). When both sexes do visit a physician, men ask fewer questions than women do. In one study, the average man asked no more than two questions, while the average woman asked at least six. Because patients who ask more questions get more information and recover their health more quickly, men’s silence in the exam room may contribute to their shorter longevity (Foreman, 1999). Interestingly, the development of erectile dysfunction drugs like Viagra may have helped improve men’s health, as men have had to visit physician’s offices to obtain prescriptions for these drugs when otherwise they would not have made an appointment (Guttman, 1999).

We have just discussed why men die sooner than women, which is one of the two gender differences that constitute the morbidity paradox. The other gender difference concerns why women have more nonfatal health problems than men. Several reasons seem to account for this difference (Read & Gorman, 2010).

One reason arises from the fact that women outlive men. Because women are thus more likely than men to be in their senior years, they are also more likely to develop the many health problems associated with old age. This suggests that studies that control for age (by comparing older women with older men, middle-aged women with middle-aged men, and so forth) should report fewer gender differences in health than those that do not control for age, and this is indeed true.

Women more than men tend to have more health problems that are not life threatening. Two reasons for this gender difference are gender inequality in the larger society and the stress accompanying women's traditional caregiving role in the family.

Francisco Osorio – CL Society 287: Waiting for a doctor – CC BY 2.0.

However, women still tend to have worse health than men even when age is taken into account. Medical sociologists attribute this gender difference to the gender inequality in the larger society (see the "Sociology Making a Difference" box). For example, women are poorer overall than men, as they are more likely to work only part time and in low-paying jobs even if they work full time. As discussed earlier in this chapter, poverty is a risk factor for health problems. Women's worse health, then, is partly due to their greater likelihood of living in poverty or near-poverty. Because of their gender, women also are more likely than men to experience stressful events in their everyday lives, such as caring for a child or an aging parent, and their increased stress is an important cause of their greater likelihood of depression and the various physical health problems (weakened immune systems, higher blood pressure, lack of exercise) that depression often causes. Finally, women experience discrimination in their everyday lives because of our society's sexism, and (as is also true for people of color) this discrimination is thought to produce stress and thus poorer physical health (Landry & Mercurio, 2009).

Sociology Making a Difference

Gender Inequality and Women's Health

Research during the past two decades has established that women are more likely than men to have health problems that are not life threatening. The text discusses that a major reason for this gender difference is gender inequality in the larger society and, in particular, the low incomes that many women have. As sociologists Bridget K. Gorman and Jen'nan

Ghazal Read (Gorman & Read, 2006, p. 96) explain, "Women are more likely than men to work part time, participate in unwaged labor, and receive lower wages, all of which drives down their chances for good health."

According to Gorman and Read, research on gender differences in health has failed to consider whether the size of this difference might vary by age. This research has also neglected measures of health beyond self-rated health, a common measure in many studies.

Gorman and Read addressed these research gaps with data on about 152,000 individuals from several years of the National Health Interview Survey, conducted annually by the federal government. Among other findings, women were much more likely than men overall to suffer from functional limitations (e.g., inability to walk steadily or to grasp small objects). When Gorman and Read controlled for age, this gender difference was greater for people in their middle and senior years than for those at younger ages. They also found that socioeconomic status was not related to functional limitations at younger ages but did predict these limitations at older ages (with poorer people more likely to have limitations). In an additional finding, socioeconomic status was strongly related to self-reported health at all ages.

The two sociologists drew a pair of policy conclusions from this set of findings. The first is the "need to understand and respond to women's greater burden of functional limitations at every age of adulthood, particularly in middle and late life" (p. 108). The second is the need for public policy to "continue to address the causes and consequences of women's disadvantaged social position relative to men," as their finding on the importance of socioeconomic status "highlights the health gains for women that would accompany improvement in their socioeconomic standing" (p. 108). In calling attention to the need for public policy on women's health to address women's functional limitations and lower economic resources, Gorman and Read's research was a fine example of sociology again making a difference.

Mental Health and Mental Illness

Health consists of mental well-being as well as physical well-being, and people can suffer mental health problems in addition to physical health problems. Scholars disagree over whether mental illness is real or, instead, a social construction. The predominant view in psychiatry, of course, is that people do have actual problems in their mental and emotional functioning and that these problems are best characterized as mental illnesses or mental disorders and should be treated by medical professionals (Kring & Sloan, 2010). But other scholars, adopting a labeling approach (see Chapter 7 "Deviance, Crime, and Social Control"), say that mental illness is a social construction or a "myth" (Szasz, 2008). In their view, all kinds of people sometimes act oddly, but only a few are labeled as mentally ill. If someone says she or he hears the voice of an angel, we attribute their perceptions to their religious views and consider them religious, not mentally ill. But if someone instead insists that men from Mars have been in touch, we are more apt to think there is something mentally wrong with that person. Mental illness thus is not real but rather is the reaction of others to problems they perceive in someone's behavior.

This intellectual debate notwithstanding, many people do suffer serious mental and emotional problems, such as severe mood swings and depression, that interfere with their everyday functioning and social interaction. Sociologists and other researchers have investigated the social epidemiology of these problems. Several generalizations seem warranted from their research (Cockerham, 2011).

First, social class affects the incidence of mental illness. To be more specific, poor people exhibit more mental health problems than richer people: they are more likely to suffer from schizophrenia, serious depression, and other problems (Mossakowski, 2008). A major reason for this link is the stress of living in poverty and the many living conditions associated with it. One interesting causal question here, analogous to that discussed earlier in assessing the social class–physical health link, is whether poverty leads to mental illness or mental illness leads to poverty. Although there is evidence of both causal paths, most scholars believe that poverty contributes to mental illness more than the reverse (Warren, 2009).

Women are more likely than men to be seriously depressed. Sociologists attribute this gender difference partly to gender socialization that leads women to keep problems inside themselves while encouraging men to express their problems outwardly.

Jessica B – Week Five – Face of depression… – CC BY-NC-ND 2.0.

Second, there is no clear connection between race/ethnicity and mental illness, as evidence on this issue is mixed: although many studies find higher rates of mental disorder among people of color, some studies find similar rates to whites' rates (Mossakowski, 2008). These mixed results are somewhat surprising because several racial/ethnic groups are poorer than whites and more likely to experience everyday discrimination, and for these reasons should exhibit more frequent symptoms of mental and emotional problems. Despite the mixed results, a fair conclusion from the most recent research is that African Americans and Latinos are more likely than whites to exhibit signs of mental distress (Mossakowski, 2008; Jang, Chiriboga, Kim, & Phillips, 2008; Araujo & Borrell, 2006).

Third, gender is related to mental illness but in complex ways, as the nature of this relationship depends on the type of mental disorder. Women have higher rates of manic-depressive disorders than men and are more likely to be seriously depressed, but men have higher rates of antisocial personality disorders that lead them to be a threat to others (Kort-Butler, 2009; Mirowsky & Ross, 1995). Although some medical researchers trace these differences to sex-linked biological differences, sociologists attribute them to differences in gender socialization that lead women to keep problems inside themselves while encouraging men to express their problems outwardly, as through violence. To the extent that women have higher levels of depression and other mental health problems, the factors that account for their poorer physical health, including their higher rates of poverty and stress and rates of everyday discrimination, are thought to also account for their poorer mental health (Read & Gorman, 2010).

Key Takeaways

- Social class, race and ethnicity, and gender all influence the quality of health in the United States. Health problems are more common among people from low-income backgrounds and among people of color. Women are more likely than men to have health problems that are not life threatening.
- Although debate continues over whether mental illness is a social construction, many people do suffer mental health problems. The social epidemiology for mental health and illness resembles that for physical health and illness, with social class, race/ethnicity, and gender disparities existing.

For Your Review

1. In thinking about the health problems of individuals from low-income backgrounds, some people blame lack of access to adequate health care for these problems, while other people blame unhealthy lifestyles practiced by low-income individuals. Where do you stand on this debate? Explain your answer.
2. Write a brief essay in which you present a sociological explanation of the higher rate of depression found among women than among men.

References

Araujo, B. Y., & Borrell, L. N. (2006). Understanding the link between discrimination, mental health outcomes, and life chances among Latinos. *Hispanic Journal of Behavioral Sciences, 28*(2), 245–266.

Barr, D. A. (2008). *Health disparities in the United States: Social class, race, and health.* Baltimore, MD: Johns Hopkins University Press.

Centers for Disease Control and Prevention. (2007). Interpreting and managing blood lead levels <10 μg/dL in children and reducing childhood exposures to lead: Recommendations of CDC's advisory committee on childhood lead poisoning prevention. *MMWR (Morbidity and Mortality Weekly Report), 56*(RR-8), 1–16.

Centers for Disease Control and Prevention. (2010). Mortality by underlying and multiple cause, ages 18+: US, 1981–2006. Retrieved from http://205.207.175.93/HDI/TableViewer/summary.aspx?ReportId=166.

Cockerham, W. C. (2011). *Sociology of mental disorder* (8th ed.). Upper Saddle River, NJ: Prentice Hall.

Cubbins, L. A., & Buchanan, T. (2009). Racial/ethnic disparities in health: The role of lifestyle, education, income, and wealth. *Sociological Focus, 42*(2), 172–191.

Elo, I. T. (2009). Social class differentials in health and mortality: Patterns and explanations in comparative perspective. *Annual Review of Sociology, 35*, 553–572.

Emmers-Sommer, T. M., Nebel, S., Allison, M.-L., Cannella, M. L., Cartmill, D., Ewing, S.,...Wojtaszek,

B. (2009). Patient-provider communication about sexual health: The relationship with gender, age, gender-stereotypical beliefs, and perceptions of communication inappropriateness. *Sex Roles: A Journal of Research, 60,* 9–10.

Foreman, J. (1999, June 14). A visit most men would rather not make. *The Boston Globe,* p. C1.

Frank, R. (2007). What to make of it? The (re)emergence of a biological conceptualization of race in health disparities research. *Social Science & Medicine, 64*(10), 1977–1983.

Gee, G., & Walsemann, K. (2009). Does health predict the reporting of racial discrimination or do reports of discrimination predict health? Findings from the National Longitudinal Study of Youth. *Social Science & Medicine, 68*(9), 1676–1684.

Gorman, B. K., & Read, J. G. (2006). Gender disparities in adult health: An examination of three measures of morbidity. *Journal of Health and Social Behavior, 47*(2), 95–110.

Guttman, M. (1999, June 11–13). Why more men are finally going to the doctor. *USA Weekend,* p. 10.

Jang, Y., Chiriboga, D. A., Kim, G., & Phillips, K. (2008). Depressive symptoms in four racial and ethnic groups: The Survey of Older Floridians (SOF). *Research on Aging, 30*(4), 488–502.

King, L., & McCarthy, D. (Eds.). (2009). *Environmental sociology: From analysis to action* (2nd ed.). Lanham, MD: Rowman & Littlefield.

Kort-Butler, L. A. (2009). Coping styles and sex differences in depressive symptoms and delinquent behavior. *Journal of Youth and Adolescence, 38*(1), 122–136.

Kring, A. M., & Sloan, D. M. (Eds.). (2010). *Emotion regulation and psychopathology: A transdiagnostic approach to etiology and treatment.* New York, NY: Guilford Press.

Kuller, L. H. (2010). Cardiovascular disease is preventable among women. *Expert Review of Cardiovascular Therapy, 8*(2), 175–187.

Landry, L. J., & Mercurio, A. E. (2009). Discrimination and women's mental health: The mediating role of control. *Sex Roles: A Journal of Research, 61,* 3–4.

Lantz, P. M., House, J. S., Mero, R. P., & Williams, D. R. (2005). Stress, life events, and socioeconomic disparities in health: Results from the Americans' Changing Lives Study. *Journal of Health and Social Behavior, 3,* 274–288.

Lee, M.-A., & Ferraro, K. F. (2009). Perceived discrimination and health among Puerto Rican and Mexican Americans: Buffering effect of the lazo matrimonial? *Social Science & Medicine, 68,* 1966–1974.

Lewis-Moss, R. K., Paschal, A., Redmond, M., Green, B. L., & Carmack, C. (2008). Health attitudes and behaviors of African American adolescents. *Journal of Community Health, 33*(5), 351–356.

Meckler, L. (1998, November 27). Health gap between races persists. *Ocala [FL] Star-Banner,* p. 4A.

Mirowsky, J., & Ross, C. E. (1995). Sex differences in distress: Real or artifact? *American Sociological Review, 60*, 449–468.

Mossakowski, K. N. (2008). Dissecting the influence of race, ethnicity, and socioeconomic status on mental health in young adulthood. *Research on Aging, 30*(6), 649–671.

National Center for Health Statistics. (2009). *Health, United States, 2009*. Hyattsville, MD: Centers for Disease Control and Prevention.

Nord, M., Andrews, M., & Carlson, S. (2009). *Household food security in the United States, 2008*. Washington, DC: U.S. Department of Agriculture.

Pampel, F. C., Krueger, P. M., & Denney, J. T. (2010, June). Socioeconomic disparities in health behaviors. *Annual Review of Sociology, 36*, 349–370. doi:10.1146/annurev.soc.012809.102529.

Pear, R. (2008, March 23). Gap in life expectancy widens for the nation. *The New York Times*. Retrieved from http://www.nytimes.com/2008/03/23/us/23health.html?scp=1&sq=Gap%20in%20life%20expectancy%20widens%20for%20the%20nation&st=cse.

Penn, N. E., Kramer, J., Skinner, J. F., Velasquez, R. J., Yee, B. W. K., Arellano, L. M., & Williams, J. P. (2000). Health practices and health-care systems among cultural groups. In R. M. Eisler & M. Hersen (Eds.), *Handbook of gender, culture, and health* (pp. 101–132). New York, NY: Routledge.

Pérez-Escamilla, R. (2009). Dietary quality among Latinos: Is acculturation making us sick? *Journal of the American Dietetic Association, 109*(6), 988–991.

Read, J. G., & Gorman, B. K. (2010, June). Gender and health inequality. *Annual Review of Sociology, 36*, 371–386. doi:10.1146/annurev.soc.012809.102535.

Robert Wood Johnson Foundation. (2008). *America's health starts with healthy children: How do states compare?* Princeton, NJ: Robert Wood Johnson Foundation.

Simon, D. R. (2008). *Elite deviance* (9th ed.). Boston, MA: Allyn & Bacon.

Smith, J. P. (2005). Unraveling the SES-health connection [Supplemental material]. *Population and Development Review, 30*, 108–132.

Stewart, J., & Rhoden, M. (2006). Children, housing and health. *International Journal of Sociology and Social Policy, 26*, 7–8.

Szasz, T. (2008). *Psychiatry: The science of lies*. Syracuse, NY: Syracuse University Press.

Van Cleave, J., Gortmaker, S. L., & Perrin, J. M. (2010). Dynamics of obesity and chronic health conditions among children and youth. *JAMA, 303*(7), 623–630.

Warren, J. R. (2009). Socioeconomic status and health across the life course: A test of the social causation and health selection hypotheses. *Social Forces, 87*(4), 2125–2153.

Williams, D. R., Neighbors, H. W., & James S. Jackson, P. (2008). Racial/ethnic discrimination and health: Findings from community studies [Supplemental material]. *American Journal of Public Health, 98,* S29–S37.

Wray, L. A., Herzog, A. R., Willis, R. J., & Wallace, R. B. (1998). The impact of education and heart attack on smoking cessation among middle-aged adults. *Journal of Health and Social Behavior, 39*, 271–294.

18.4 Medicine and Health Care in the United States

Learning Objectives

1. Summarize the major developments in the rise of scientific medicine.
2. Discuss several problems with the U.S. health-care model involving direct fees and private health insurance.
3. Describe any two issues in U.S. health care other than the lack of health insurance.

As the health-care debate in 2009 and 2010 illustrates, the practice of medicine in the United States raises many important issues about its cost and quality. Before we discuss some of these issues, a brief discussion of the history of medicine will sketch how we have reached our present situation (Louden, 1997; Porter, 2006).

The Rise of Scientific Medicine

The practice of medicine today in the United States and much of the rest of the globe follows a scientific approach. But scientific medicine is a relatively recent development in the history of the world. Prehistoric societies attributed illness to angry gods or to evil spirits that took over someone's body. The development of scientific medicine since then illustrates one of the sociological insights discussed at the beginning of this chapter: the type of society influences its beliefs about health and ways of healing.

The roots of today's scientific medicine go back to the ancient civilizations in the Middle East, Asia, and Greece and Rome, which began to view health and illness somewhat more scientifically. In ancient Egypt, for example, physicians developed some medications, such as laxatives, that are still used, and they also made advances in the treating of wounds and other injuries. The ancient Chinese developed several drugs, including arsenic, sulfur, and opium, that are also still used. Ancient India developed anesthesia, antidotes for poisonous snakebites, and several surgical techniques including amputation and the draining of abscesses (Porter, 2006). Ancient Greece built medical schools in which dissection of animals was used to help understand human anatomy. Later, a Greek physician named Galen, who lived in Rome during the 100s A.D., wrote influential treatises on inflammation, infectious disease, and the muscular and spinal cord systems. Medical advances continued in the Middle Ages and the Renaissance, as various physicians wrote about smallpox, measles, and other diseases, and several medical schools and hospitals were established. Leonardo da Vinci and other scientists performed many dissections and produced hundreds of drawings of human anatomy. Other major advances, including the development of surgical techniques and the treatment of burns, were also made during this period.

What is now called *modern medicine* began in the 1600s, as scientists learned how blood circulates through the body and used microscopes to discover various germs, including bacteria. By the end of the 1800s, the *germ theory* of disease had become widely accepted, thanks largely to the work of Louis Pasteur and other scientists.

Other key developments during this time included the discovery of ether gas as an effective anesthesia and the realization that surgery needed to be carried out under the strictest standards of cleanliness (Porter, 2006). During the 1800s, the American Medical Association and other professional associations of physicians were founded to advance medical knowledge and standards and to help give physicians a monopoly over the practice of medicine (Starr, 1982). In the early 1900s, scientists learned about the importance of vitamins, and penicillin was developed as the first antibiotic. Developments in immunology, physiology, and many other areas of medicine have advanced far beyond what we knew a century ago and remain too numerous and complex to discuss here.

Modern medicine began during the 17th century with the discovery by English physician William Harvey of how blood circulates through the body.

Wikimedia Commons – CC BY-SA 3.0.

Scientific medicine has saved countless lives: life spans used to average no more than the age of 40 or so, as we have seen, but in industrial nations now average well into the 70s. Still, as we have also seen, huge disparities remain across the world today in life spans and the quality of health. Disparities also exist in the quality of health care across the world. In the United States, questions about the cost and effectiveness of health care have dominated the news. We now turn to some of these issues.

U.S. Health Care and the Industrial World

Medicine in the United States is big business. Expenditures for health care, health research, and other health items and services have risen sharply in recent years, having increased tenfold since 1980, and now costs the nation more than $2.6 trillion annually (see Figure 18.6 "U.S. Health-Care Expenditure, 1980–2010 (in Billions of Dollars)"). This translates to the largest figure per capita in the industrial world. Despite this expenditure, the United States lags behind many other industrial nations in several important health indicators, as we have already seen. Why is this so?

Figure 18.6 U.S. Health-Care Expenditure, 1980–2010 (in Billions of Dollars)

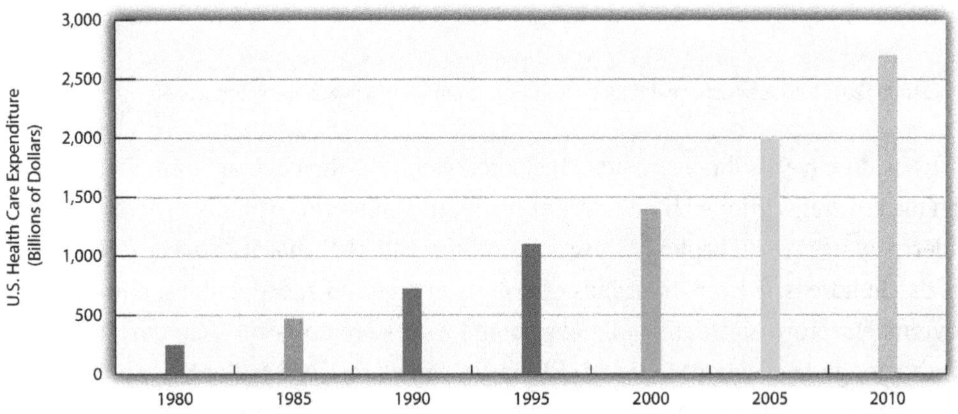

Source: Data from U.S. Census Bureau. (2010). *Statistical abstract of the United States: 2010.* Washington, DC: U.S. Government Printing Office. Retrieved from http://www.census.gov/compendia/statab.

The U.S. Health-Care Model

As discussed earlier, other Western nations have national systems of health care and health insurance. In stark contrast to these nations, the United States relies on a **direct-fee system**, in which patients are expected to pay for medical costs themselves, aided by *private health insurance*, usually through one's employer. Table 18.4 "Health Insurance Coverage in the United States, 2008" shows the percentages of Americans who have health insurance from different sources or who are not insured at all. (All figures are from the period before the major health-care reform package was passed by the federal government in early 2010.) Adding together the top two figures in the table, 57% of Americans have private insurance, either through their employers or from their own resources. Almost 28% have some form of public insurance (Medicaid, Medicare, other public), and 15.4% are uninsured. This final percentage amounts to about 46 million Americans, including 8 million children, who lack health insurance. Their lack of health insurance has deadly consequences because they are less likely to receive preventive health care and care for various conditions and illnesses. It is estimated that 45,000 people die each year because they do not have health insurance (Wilper et al., 2009).

Table 18.4 Health Insurance Coverage in the United States, 2008

Employer	52.3%
Individual	4.7%
Medicaid	14.1%
Medicare	12.4%
Other public	1.2%
Uninsured	15.4%

Source: Data from Kaiser Family Foundation. (2010). Kaiser state health facts. Retrieved from http://www.statehealthfacts.org.

Although almost 28% of Americans do have public insurance, this percentage and the coverage provided by this insurance do not begin to match the coverage enjoyed by the rest of the industrial world. Although Medicare pays some medical costs for the elderly, we saw in Chapter 12 “Aging and the Elderly” that its coverage is hardly adequate, as many people must pay hundreds or even thousands of dollars in premiums, deductibles, coinsurance, and copayments. The other government program, Medicaid, pays some health-care costs for the poor, but many low-income families are not poor enough to receive Medicaid. Eligibility standards for Medicaid vary from one state to another, and a family poor enough in one state to receive Medicaid might not be considered poor enough in another state. The State Children’s Health Insurance Program (SCHIP), begun in 1997 for children from low-income families, has helped somewhat, but it, too, fails to cover many low-income children. Largely for these reasons, about two-thirds of uninsured Americans come from low-income families.

Not surprisingly, the 15.4% uninsured rate varies by race and ethnicity (see Figure 18.7 “Race, Ethnicity, and Lack of Health Insurance, 2008 (Percentage With No Insurance)”). Among people under 65 and thus not eligible for Medicare, the uninsured rate rises to almost 21% of the African American population and 32% of the Latino population. Moreover, 45.3% of adults under 65 who live in official poverty lack health insurance, compared to only about 6% of high-income adults (those with incomes higher than 4 times the poverty level). Almost one-fifth of poor children have no health insurance, compared to only 3.5% of children in higher-income families (Kaiser Family Foundation, 2010). As discussed earlier, the lack of health insurance among the poor and people of color is a significant reason for their poorer health.

Figure 18.7 Race, Ethnicity, and Lack of Health Insurance, 2008 (Percentage With No Insurance)

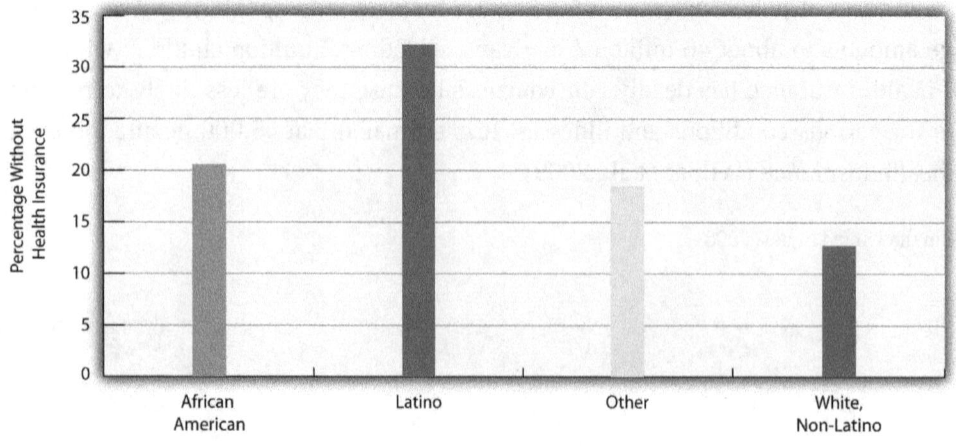

Source: Data from Statehealthfacts.org. (2010). Uninsured rates for the nonelderly by race/ethnicity, states (2007–2008), U.S. (2008).

Retrieved from http://www.statehealthfacts.org/comparetable.jsp?ind=143&cat=3.

Issues in U.S. Health Care

The lack of insurance of so many Americans is an important health-care issue, but other issues about health care also seem to make the news almost every day. We examine a few of these here.

Managed Care and HMOs

To many critics, a disturbing development in the U.S. health-care system has been the establishment of **health maintenance organizations**, or HMOs, which typically enroll their subscribers through their workplaces. HMOs are prepaid health plans with designated providers, meaning that patients must visit a physician employed by the HMO or included on the HMO's approved list of physicians. If their physician is not approved by the HMO, they either have to see an approved physician or see their own without insurance coverage. Popular with employers because they are less expensive than traditional private insurance, HMOs have grown rapidly in the last three decades and now enroll more than 70 million Americans (see Figure 18.8 "Growth of Health Maintenance Organizations (HMOs), 1980–2007 (Millions of Enrollees)").

Figure 18.8 Growth of Health Maintenance Organizations (HMOs), 1980–2007 (Millions of Enrollees)

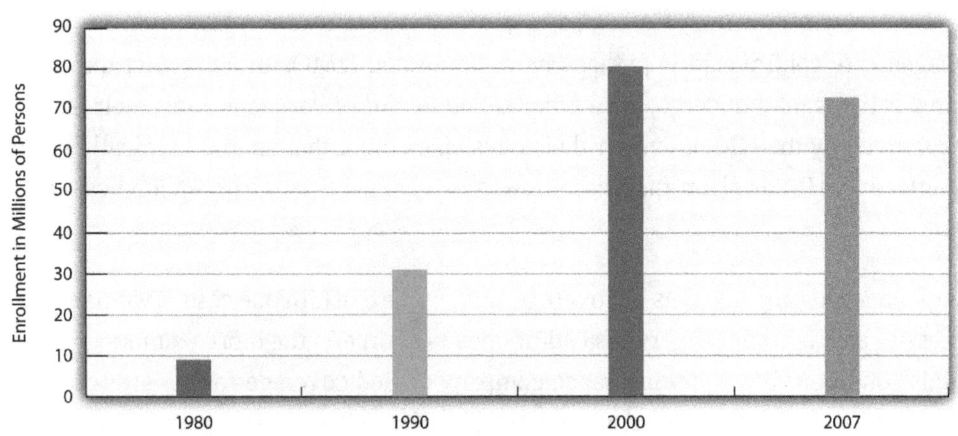

Source: Data from U.S. Census Bureau. (2010). *Statistical abstract of the United States: 2010.* Washington, DC: U.S. Government Printing Office. Retrieved from http://www.census.gov/compendia/statab.

Although HMOs have become popular, their *managed care* is also very controversial for at least two reasons (Kronick, 2009). The first is the HMOs' restrictions just noted on the choice of physicians and other health-care providers. Families who have long seen a family physician but whose employer now enrolls them in an HMO sometimes find they have to see another physician or risk going without coverage. In some HMOs, patients have no guarantee that they can see the same physician at every visit. Instead, they see whichever physician is assigned to them at each visit. Critics of HMOs argue that this practice prevents physicians and patients from getting to know each other, reduces patients' trust in their physician, and may for these reasons impair patient health.

The managed care that HMOs provide is controversial for several reasons. These reasons include restrictions on the choice of physicians and especially on the types of medical exams and procedures that patients may undergo.

Pixabay – CC0 Public Domain.

The second reason for the managed-care controversy is perhaps more important. HMOs often restrict the types of medical exams and procedures patients may undergo, a problem called *denial of care,* and limit their choice of prescription drugs to those approved by the HMO, even if their physicians think that another, typically more expensive drug would be more effective. HMOs claim that these restrictions are necessary to keep medical costs down and do not harm patients.

Several examples of the impact of managed care's denials of coverage and/or care exist. In one case, a woman with a bone spur on her hip had successful arthroscopic surgery instead of open hip surgery, the more common and far more expensive procedure for this condition. When her insurance company denied coverage for her arthroscopic surgery, the patient had to pay doctor and hospital fees of more than $21,000. After a lengthy appeal process, the insurance company finally agreed to pay for her procedure (Konrad, 2010). In a more serious case a decade ago, a 22-year-old woman died after going to a physician several times in the preceding week with chest pain and shortness of breath. She was diagnosed with a respiratory infection and "panic attacks" but in fact had pneumonia and a blood clot in her left lung. Her physician wanted her to have lab tests that would have diagnosed these problems, but her HMO's restrictions prevented her from getting the tests. A columnist who wrote about this case said that "an unconscionable obsession with the bottom line has resulted in widespread abuses in the managed-care industry. Simply stated, there is big money to be made by denying care" (Herbert, 1999, p. A25).

Racial and Gender Bias in Health Care

Another problem in the U.S. medical practice is apparent racial and gender bias in health care. Racial bias seems fairly common; as Chapter 10 "Race and Ethnicity" discussed, African Americans are less likely than whites with the same health problems to receive various medical procedures (Smedley, Stith, & Nelson, 2003). Gender bias also appears to affect the quality of health care (Read & Gorman, 2010). Research that examines either actual cases or hypothetical cases posed to physicians finds that women are less likely than men with similar health problems to be recommended for various procedures, medications, and diagnostic tests, including cardiac catheterization, lipid-lowering medication, kidney dialysis or transplant, and knee replacement for osteoarthritis (Borkhoff et al., 2008).

Other Problems in the Quality of Care

Other problems in the quality of medical care also put patients unnecessarily at risk. These include:

- **Sleep deprivation among health-care professionals.** As you might know, many physicians get very little sleep. Studies have found that the performance of surgeons and medical residents who go without sleep is seriously impaired (Institute of Medicine, 2008). One study found that surgeons who go without sleep for 24 hours have their performance impaired as much as a drunk driver. Surgeons who stayed awake all night made 20% more errors in simulated surgery than those who slept normally and took 14% longer to complete the surgery (Wen, 1998).
- **Shortage of physicians and nurses.** Another problem is a shortage of physicians and nurses (Shirey, McDaniel, Ebright, Fisher, & Doebbeling, 2010; Fuhrmans, 2009). This is a general problem around the country, but even more of a problem for two different settings. The first such setting is hospital emergency rooms, Because emergency room work is difficult and relatively low-paying, many specialist physicians do not volunteer for it. Many emergency rooms thus lack an adequate number of specialists, resulting in potentially inadequate emergency care for many patients.

  Rural areas are the second setting in which a shortage of physicians and nurses is a severe problem. The National Rural Health Association (2010) points out that although one-fourth of the U.S. population is rural, only one-tenth of physicians practice in rural areas. Compounding this shortage is the long distances that patients and emergency medical vehicles must travel and the general lack of high-quality care and equipment at small rural hospitals. Partly for these reasons, rural residents are more at risk than urban residents for health problems, including mortality. For example, only one-third of all motor vehicle accidents happen in rural areas, but two-thirds of all deaths from such accidents occur in rural areas. Rural areas are also much more likely than urban areas to lack mental health services.
- **Mistakes by hospitals.** Partly because of sleep deprivation and the shortage of health-care professionals, hundreds of thousands of hospital patients each year suffer from mistakes made by hospital personnel. They receive the wrong diagnosis, are given the wrong drug, have a procedure done on them that was really intended for someone else, or incur a bacterial infection. These and other mistakes are thought to kill almost 200,000 patients per year, or almost 2 million every decade

(Crowley & Nalder, 2009).

Complementary and Alternative Medicine (CAM)

As the medical establishment grew in the 19th and 20th centuries, it helped formulate many standards for medical care and training, including licensing restrictions that prevent anyone without a degree from a recognized medical school from practicing medicine. As noted earlier, some of its effort stemmed from well-intentioned beliefs in the soundness of a scientific approach to medical care, but some of it also stemmed from physicians' desire to "corner the market" on health care, and thus raise their profits, by keeping other health practitioners such as midwives out of the market.

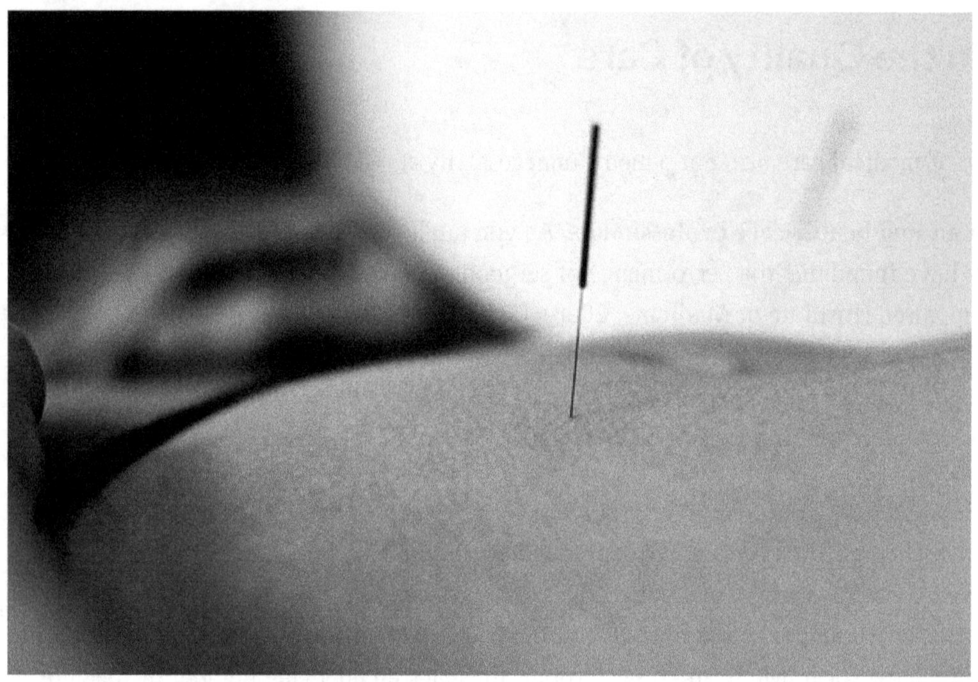

Acupuncture is one of the many forms of alternative medicine. It is used by about 40% of Americans annually.

Marnie Joyce – Alpha City Acupunks – CC BY 2.0.

There is increased recognition today that physical health depends at least partly on psychological well-being. As the old saying goes, your mind can play tricks on you, and a growing amount of evidence suggests the importance of a sound mind for a sound body. Many studies have found that stress reduction can improve many kinds of physical conditions and that high levels of stress can contribute to health problems (B. W. Smith et al., 2010).

Evidence of a mind-body connection has fueled the growing interest in complementary and alternative medicine (CAM) that takes into account a person's emotional health and can often involve alternative treatments such as acupuncture and hypnosis. In the last two decades, several major medical centers at the nation's top universities established alternative medicine clinics. Despite the growing popularity of alternative medicine, much of the medical establishment remains skeptical of its effectiveness. Even so, about 40% of Americans use an alternative medicine product or service each year, and they spend about $34 billion per year on the various kinds of products and services that constitute alternative medicine (Wilson, 2009) (see Figure 18.9 "Use of Selected Forms of Complementary and Alternative Medicine (CAM), 2007 (Percentage of U.S. Adults Using Each Form During Past Year)").

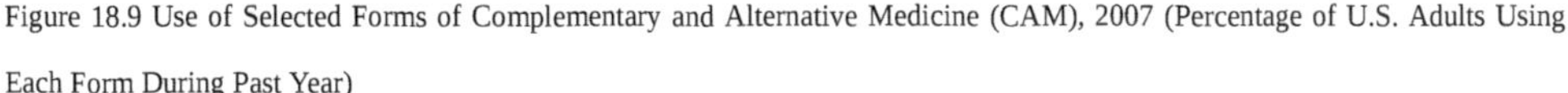

Figure 18.9 Use of Selected Forms of Complementary and Alternative Medicine (CAM), 2007 (Percentage of U.S. Adults Using Each Form During Past Year)

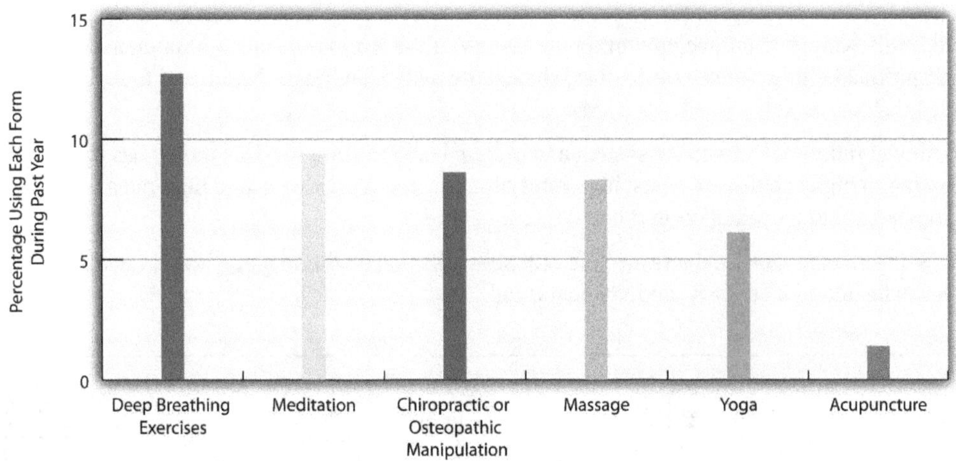

Source: Data from U.S. Census Bureau. (2010). *Statistical abstract of the United States: 2010.* Washington, DC: U.S. Government Printing Office. Retrieved from http://www.census.gov/compendia/statab.

Medical Ethics and Medical Fraud

A final set of issues in U.S. medicine concerns questions of medical ethics and outright medical fraud. Many types of health-care providers, including physicians, dentists, medical equipment companies, and nursing homes, engage in many types of health-care fraud. In a common type of fraud, they sometimes bill Medicare, Medicaid, and private insurance companies for exams or tests that were never done and even make up "ghost patients" who never existed or bill for patients who were dead by the time they were allegedly treated. In just one example, a group of New York physicians billed their state's Medicaid program for over $1.3 million for 50,000 psychotherapy sessions that never occurred. All types of health-care fraud combined are estimated to cost about $100 billion per year (Kavilanz, 2010).

Other practices are legal but ethically questionable. Sometimes physicians refer their patients for tests to a laboratory that they own or in which they have invested. They are more likely to refer patients for tests when they have a financial interest in the lab to which the patients are sent. This practice, called *self-referral,* is legal but does raise questions of whether the tests are in the patient's best interests or instead in the physician's best interests (Romano, 2009).

In another practice, physicians are asking hundreds of thousands of their patients to take part in drug trials. The physicians may receive more than $1,000 for each patient they sign up, but the patients are not told about these payments. Characterizing these trials, two reporters said that "patients have become commodities, bought and traded by testing companies and physicians" and said that it "injects the interests of a giant industry into the delicate physician-patient relationship, usually without the patient realizing it" (Galewitz, 2009; Eichenwald and Kolata, 1999). These trials raise obvious conflicts of interest for the physicians, who may recommend their patients do something that might not be good for them but would be good for the physicians' finances.

Key Takeaways

- Scientific medicine is a relatively recent development in the history of the world. For much of human history, religious and spiritual beliefs, not scientific ones, shaped the understanding of health and the practice of medicine
- The U.S. health-care model relies on a direct-fee system and private health insurance. This model has been criticized for contributing to high health-care costs, high rates of uninsured individuals, and high rates of health problems in comparison to the situation in other Western nations.
- Other problems in U.S. health care include the restrictive practices associated with managed care, racial/ethnic and gender bias in health-care delivery, and medical fraud.

For Your Review

1. Do you know anyone, including yourself or anyone in your family, who lacks health insurance? If so, do you think the lack of health insurance has contributed to any health problems? Write a brief essay in which you discuss the evidence for your conclusion.
2. Critics of managed care say that it overly restricts important tests and procedures that patients need to have, while proponents of managed care say that these restrictions are necessary to keep health-care costs in check. What is your view of managed care?

Improving Health and Health Care: What Sociology Suggests

A sociological perspective on health and health care emphasizes the profound role played by social class, race/ethnicity, and gender. As we have seen throughout this chapter, all three dimensions of social inequality in the larger society affect both the quality of health and the quality of health care. People from low-income backgrounds have higher rates of physical and mental illness because of the stress and other factors associated with living with little money and also because of their lack of access to adequate health care. Partly because they tend to be poorer and partly because of the discrimination they experience in their daily lives and in the health-care system, people of color also have higher rates of physical and mental illness. Findings on gender are more complex, but women have higher rates than men of nonfatal physical illness and of depression and other mental illness, and they experience lower quality of health care for certain conditions.

To improve health and health care in the United States, the importance of social class, race/ethnicity, and gender must be addressed. Efforts, as outlined in earlier chapters, that reduce poverty and racial/ethnic and gender inequality should also improve the physical and mental health of those currently at risk because of their low incomes, race or ethnicity, and/or gender. At the same time, special efforts must be made to ensure that these millions of individuals receive the best health care possible within the existing system of social inequality. In this regard, the national health-care and health insurance systems of Canada, the United Kingdom, and many other Western nations provide models for the United States. As discussed in this chapter, these nations provide better health care to their citizens in many ways and at a lower cost than that incurred under the U.S. model of private insurance. Their models are not perfect, but a government-funded and government-run single-payer system—or "Medicare for all," as it has been called—shows great promise for improving the health and health care of all Americans, especially for those now disadvantaged by their social class, race/ethnicity, and/or gender. The U.S. health-care system, despite the recent health-care reform legislation and medical advances that just a short time ago were only a dream, still has a long way to go before affordable and high-quality health care is available to all. With the health of so many people at stake, the United States needs to make every effort to achieve this essential goal.

This effort should certainly include an expansion of measures that fall broadly into what the field of public health calls *preventive care*. This approach recognizes that the best approach to health and health care is to prevent illness and disease before they begin. One facet of this approach focuses on the unhealthy behaviors and lifestyles, including lack of exercise, obesity, and smoking, characteristic of millions of Americans. Although the United States has public education campaigns and other initiatives on these risk factors, more could still be done. Another facet of this approach focuses on early childhood in general but especially on early childhood among low-income families. As this chapter has emphasized beginning with the "Social Issues in the News" story, many health problems begin very early in childhood and even in the womb. Home visitation and nutrition assistance programs must be expanded across the country to address these problems.

What can be done to improve world health? Because the poorest nations have the poorest health, it is essential that the wealthy nations provide them the money, equipment, and other resources they need to improve their health and health care. The residents of these nations also need to be given the resources they need to undertake proper sanitation and other good health practices. In this regard, organizations like the World Health Organization have been instrumental in documenting the dire status of health in the poor nations and in promoting efforts to help them, and groups like Doctors Without Borders have been instrumental in bringing health-care professionals and medical care to poor nations. Ultimately, however, these nations' poor health is just one of the consequences of the global stratification examined in Chapter 6 "Groups and Organizations". Until these nations' economic circumstances and high rates of illiteracy improve dramatically, their health status will remain a serious problem.

References

Borkhoff, C. M., Hawker, G. A., Kreder, H. J., Glazier, R. H., Mahomed, N. N., & Wright, J. G. (2008). The effect of patients' sex on physicians' recommendations for total knee arthroplasty. *Canadian Medical Association Journal, 178*(6), 681–687.

Crowley, C. F., & Nalder, E. (2009, August 9). Secrecy shields medical mishaps from public view. *San Francisco Chronicle*, p. A1.

Eichenwald, K., & Kolata, G. (1999, May 16). Drug trials hide conflicts for doctors. *The New York Times*, p. A1.

Fuhrmans, V. (2009, January 13). Surgeon shortage pushes hospitals to hire temps. *The Wall Street Journal*, p. A1.

Galewitz, P. (2009, February 22). Cutting-edge option: Doctors paid by drugmakers, but say trials not about money. *Palm Beach Post*. Retrieved from http://www.palmbeachpost.com/business/content/business/epaper/2009/02/22/a1f_drugtrials_0223.html.

Herbert, B. (1999, July 15). Money vs. reform. *The New York Times*, p. A25.

Institute of Medicine. (2008). *Resident duty hours: Enhancing sleep, supervision, and safety*. Washington, DC: National Academies Press.

Kaiser Family Foundation. (2010). Kaiser state health facts. Retrieved from http://www.statehealthfacts.org.

Kavilanz, P. (2010). Health care: A "goldmine" for fraudsters. *CNNMoney*. Retrieved from http://money.cnn.com/2010/01/13/news/economy/health_care_fraud/index.htm?postversion=2010011315.

Konrad, W. (2010, February 5). Fighting denied claims requires perseverance. *The New York Times*, p. B6.

Kronick, R. (2009). Medicare and HMOs—the search for accountability. *New England Journal of Medicine*, pp. 2048–2050. Retrieved from http://www.library.umaine.edu/auth/EZProxy/test/authej.asp?url=http://search.ebscohost.com/login.aspx?direct=true&db=aph&AN=39651608&site=ehost-live.

Louden, I. (1997). *Western medicine: An illustrated history*. Oxford, England: Oxford University Press.

National Rural Health Association. (2010). What's different about rural health care? Retrieved from http://www.ruralhealthweb.org/go/left/about-rural-health.

Porter, R. (Ed.). (2006). *The Cambridge history of medicine* (Rev. ed.). New York, NY: Cambridge University Press.

Read, J. G., & Gorman, B. K. (2010, June). Gender and health inequality. *Annual Review of Sociology, 36*, 371–386. doi:10.1146/annurev.soc.012809.102535.

Romano, D. H. (2009). Self-referral of imaging and increased utilization: Some practical perspectives on tackling the dilemma. *Journal of the American College of Radiology, 6*(11), 773–779.

Shirey, M. R., McDaniel, A. M., Ebright, P. R., Fisher, M. L., & Doebbeling, B. N. (2010). Understanding nurse manager stress and work complexity: Factors that make a difference. *The Journal of Nursing Administration, 40*(2), 82–91.

Smedley, B. D., Stith, A. Y., & Nelson, A. R. (Eds.). (2003). *Unequal treatment: Confronting racial and ethnic disparities in health care*. Washington, DC: National Academies Press.

Smith, B. W., Papp, Z. Z., Tooley, E. M., Montague, E. Q., Robinson, A. E., & Cosper, C. J. (2010). Traumatic events, perceived stress and health in women with fibromyalgia and healthy controls. *Stress & Health: Journal of the International Society for the Investigation of Stress, 26*(1), 83–93.

Starr, P. (1982). *The social transformation of American medicine*. New York, NY: Basic Books.

Wen, P. (1998, February 9). Tired surgeons perform as if drunk, study says. *The Boston Globe*, p. A9.

Wilper, A. P., Woolhandler, S., Lasser, K. E., McCormick, D., Bor, D. H., & Himmelstein, D. U. (2009). Health insurance and mortality in US adults. *American Journal of Public Health, 99*(12), 1–7.

Wilson, P. (2009). Americans spend $33.9 billion a year on alternative medicine. *Consumer Reports Health Blog*. Retrieved from http://blogs.consumerreports.org/health/2009/08/information-on-natural-medicine-money-spent-on-alternative- medicine-alternative-treatments-vitamins.html.

18.5 End-of-Chapter Material

Summary

1. A sociological approach emphasizes the relationship between health, medicine, and society. Our social backgrounds influence our health and access to health care, while the culture and social structure of a society influences its perceptions of health and illness and ways of healing.
2. Sociological perspectives on health and illness fall into the functional, conflict, and interactionist approaches encountered in previous chapters. The functional view emphasizes the importance of health for a society's stability and the roles that people play when they are sick. The conflict view stresses inequality in the quality of health and health-care delivery and efforts by physicians to monopolize the practice of medicine to increase their profits. According to the interactionist view, health and illness are social constructions subject to people's and society's interpretations. The interactionist view also studies how medical professionals and patients interact and the way professionals manage understandings of such interaction.
3. Health and the quality of health care differ widely around the world and reflect global stratification. The earth's poorest nations have extremely high rates of infant mortality and life-threatening diseases such as AIDS and very low life expectancy. Despite efforts of organizations like the World Health Organization, the poor health of the poor nations' residents remains a serious problem.
4. The United States ranks ahead of most of the world's nations in most health indicators, and health in the United States has greatly improved in the last century. At the same time, the United States lags behind most other industrial nations in important health indicators such as infant mortality and life expectancy. Moreover, serious disparities exist within the United States in the social distribution of health, as evidenced by the study of social epidemiology.
5. Social class, race and ethnicity, and gender all affect the quality of health. Poor people lack health insurance and access to health, face high amounts of stress, live in unhealthy social and physical environments, and are more apt to engage in unhealthy lifestyles. For all of these reasons, their health is worse than that of the nonpoor. African Americans, Hispanics, and Native Americans all fare worse than whites on many health indicators, in large part because of their poverty and history of discrimination. Women fare worse than men on several heath indicators, but men have lower life expectancies because of their higher rates of certain life-threatening illnesses. These rates are thought to be due to men's biology, unhealthy lifestyles brought on by their masculine socialization, and unwillingness to seek medical treatment.
6. Social factors also help explain different rates of mental illness. The poor have higher rates of mental disorders than the nonpoor because of the stress of poverty and other negative life conditions. Women are more likely than men to be depressed and to suffer from some other disorders, but men are more likely to have antisocial personality disorders with symptoms that make them a threat to others. Clear racial and ethnic differences in mental disorders have not been found, perhaps because the strong family bonds and religious faith of many minorities help protect them from disorders that would otherwise be expected from their poverty and discrimination. In looking at Mexican-Americans, there's some evidence that living in American society raises the risks of mental disorders.
7. The history of medicine reflects a move from religious and spiritual approaches to scientific approaches. In prehistoric societies priests tried to appease the angry gods or chase away the evil spirits who were thought to cause physical and mental illness. Ancient civilizations made great advances in our understanding of health and illness, and the rise of scientific medicine beginning in the 1600s helped pave the path for today's scientific approach.
8. Despite these medical advances, health care in the United States today faces several problems. The United

States is alone in not offering universal national health insurance; its absence is thought to help account for the country's low ranking in the industrial world on major health indicators, as significant numbers of our poor and minorities lack health insurance. Managed care has also come under criticism for restricting coverage of important medical procedures and prescription medicines. Racial and gender bias in health care is another problem that has adverse effects on the nation's health. Other quality-of-care problems include tired physicians, a lack of emergency room physicians, and numerous mistakes made in hospitals. Disagreement over alternative medicine reflects the historic battle between the medical establishment and other healers, while self-referral and other issues raise important questions for medical ethics. Meanwhile, health-care fraud costs the nation some $100 billion annually and remains an important problem for the nation to address.

Using Sociology

You have always had an interest in health care and 2 months ago received your license to work as a physician's assistant after taking 2 years of courses beyond your BA. Having had a course in medical sociology, you learned about health-care disparities related to social class. Within a few weeks of receiving your license, you started working at a health-care clinic in a low-income neighborhood of a medium-sized city. Since then you have enjoyed your work because you've enjoyed helping the patients and think you are making a difference, however small, to improve their health.

At the same time, you have become troubled by comments from two of the physicians on staff, who have scorned their patients for having so many health problems and for waiting too long to come in for medical help. You realize that you could jeopardize your job if you criticize the doctors' views to anyone in the office, but you also feel the need to say something. What, if anything, do you do? Explain your answer.

Chapter 19: Population and Urbanization

Social Issues in the News

"New Leaders Can't Shrink from Michigan Realities," the headline said. The realities stemmed from the fact that Michigan's population was shrinking. The state's birth rate was 21% lower than its 1990 rate, and it now had 22,500 fewer fifth graders than ninth graders. Another reason for the population decline was that for the past decade many more people had been moving out of Michigan than moving in. Because many of those moving out were young, college-educated adults, they were taking with them hundreds of millions of dollars in paychecks that would have bolstered Michigan's economy and tax revenue base. They were also leaving behind empty houses and apartments that were further depressing the state's real estate market. The population decline had already forced several schools to close, with additional closings likely, and it was also increasing the percentage of Michigan residents in their older years who would need additional state services. The population decline has been especially severe in Detroit but has also been occurring in smaller cities and towns. (French & Wilkinson, 2009; Dzwonkowski, 2010)

As this news story from Michigan reminds us, population change often has weighty consequences throughout a society. Among other consequences, Michigan's population decline has affected its economy, educational system, and services for its older residents. While Michigan and other states are shrinking, states in the southern and western regions of the nation are growing, with their large cities becoming even larger. This population growth also has consequences. For example, schools become more crowded, pressuring communities to hire more teachers and either enlarge existing schools or build new ones. It also puts strains on hospitals, social services, and many other sectors of society.

These considerations show that a change in one sector of society often affects other sectors of society. We cannot fully understand society without appreciating the sources, dynamics, and consequences of the changes societies undergo. This chapter's discussion of population and urbanization is the first of three chapters that examine various kinds of social change. Chapter 20 "Social Change and the Environment" looks more broadly at social change before examining sociological aspects of the environment, while Chapter 21 "Collective Behavior and Social Movements" discusses collective behavior and social movements—fads, riots, protests, and the like—which collectively are another significant source of social change.

References

Dzwonkowski, R. (2010, September 19). New leaders can't shrink from Michigan realities. *Detroit Free Press*, p. 2A.

French, R., & Wilkinson, M. (2009, April 2). Leaving Michigan behind: Eight-year population exodus staggers state. *The Detroit News*. Retrieved from http://detnews.com/article/20090402/METRO/904020403/Leaving-Michigan-Behind–Eight-year-population-exodus-staggers-state.

19.1 Population

Learning Objectives

1. Describe how demographers measure birth and death rates.
2. Explain how the net-migration rate is derived.

We have commented that population change is an important source of other changes in society. The study of population is so significant that it occupies a special subfield within sociology called **demography**. To be more precise, demography is the study of changes in the size and composition of population. It encompasses several concepts: fertility and birth rates, mortality and death rates, and migration (Weeks, 2012). Let's look at each of these briefly.

Fertility and Birth Rates

Fertility refers to the number of live births. Demographers use several measures of fertility. One measure is the **crude birth rate**, or the number of live births for every 1,000 people in a population in a given year. To determine the crude birth rate, the number of live births in a year is divided by the population size, and this result is then multiplied by 1,000. For example, in 2009 the United States had a population of about 307 million and roughly 4,136,000 births. Dividing the latter figure by the former figure gives us 0.0135 rounded off. We then multiply this quotient by 1,000 to yield a crude birth rate of 13.5 births per 1,000 population (U.S. Census Bureau, 2010). We call this a "crude" birth rate because the denominator, population size, consists of the total population, not just the number of women or even the number of women of childbearing age (commonly considered 15–44 years).

A second measure is the **general fertility rate** (also just called the *fertility rate* or *birth rate*), or the number of live births per 1,000 women aged 15–44 (i.e., of childbearing age). This is calculated in a manner similar to that for the crude fertility rate, but in this case the number of births is divided by the number of women aged 15–44 before multiplying by 1,000. The U.S. general fertility rate for 2009 was about 65.5 (i.e., 65.5 births per 1,000 women aged 15–44; Tejada-Vera & Sutton, 2010).

A third measure is the **total fertility rate**, or the number of children an average woman is expected to have in her lifetime. This measure often appears in the news media and is more easily understood by the public than either of the first two measures. In 2008, the U.S. total fertility rate was about 2.09. Sometimes the total fertility rate is expressed as the average number of births that an average group of 1,000 women would be expected to have. In this case, the average number of children that one woman is expected to have is simply multiplied by 1,000. Using this latter calculation, the U.S. total fertility rate in 2008 was about 2,090 (i.e., an average group of 1,000 women would be expected to have, in their lifetimes, 2,090 children; Hamilton, Martin, & Ventura, 2010).

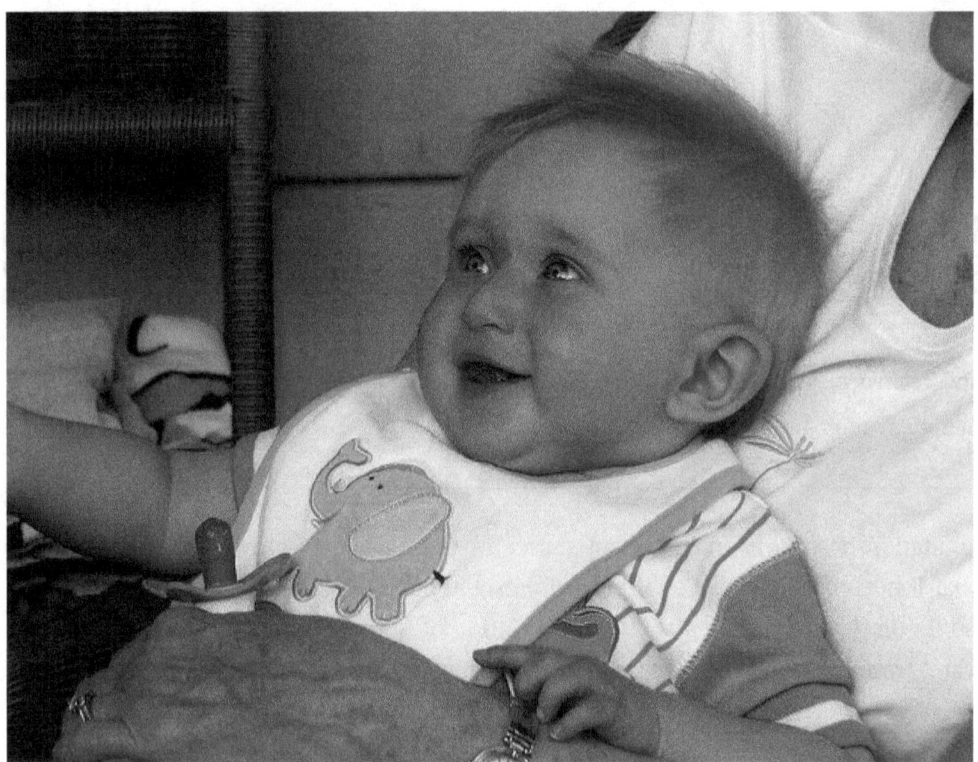

Demographers use several measures of fertility. The general fertility rate refers to the number of live births per 1,000 women aged 15–44. The U.S. general fertility rate is about 65.5.

Bev Sykes – Baby – CC BY 2.0.

As Figure 19.1 "U.S. General Fertility Rate, 1920–2007" indicates, the U.S. general fertility rate has changed a lot since 1920, dropping from 101 (per 1,000 women aged 15–44) in 1920 to 70 in 1935, during the Great Depression, before rising afterward until 1955. (Note the very sharp increase from 1945 to 1955, as the post–World War II baby boom began.) The fertility rate then fell steadily after 1960 until the 1970s but has remained rather steady since then, fluctuating only slightly between 65 and 70 per 1,000 women aged 15–44.

Figure 19.1 U.S. General Fertility Rate, 1920–2007

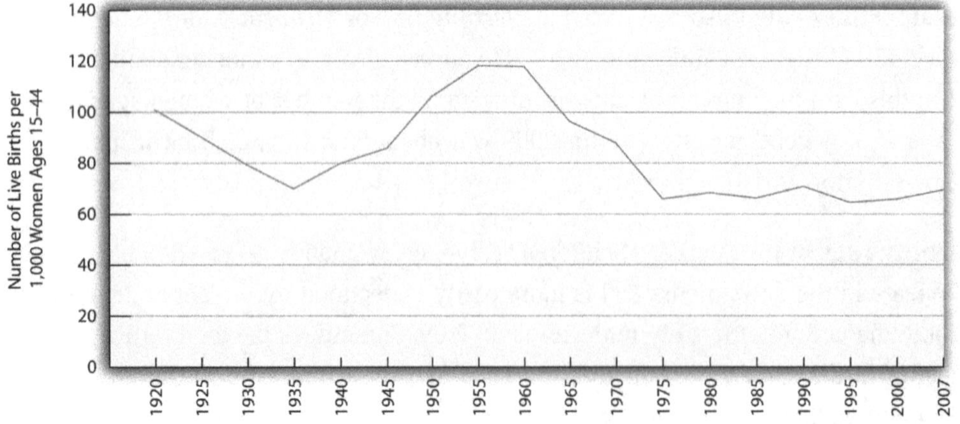

Sources: Data from Hamilton, B. E., Martin, J. A., & Ventura, S. J. (2010). Births: Preliminary data for 2008. *National vital statistics reports, 58*(16), 1–18; Martin, J. A., Hamilton, B. E., Sutton, P. D., Ventura, S. J., Menacker, F., Kirmeyer, S., & Mathews, T. J.

(2009). Births: Final data for 2006. *National vital statistics reports, 57*(7), 1–102; U.S. Census Bureau. (1951). *Statistical abstract of the United States: 1951.* Washington, DC: U.S. Government Printing Office.

The fertility rate varies by race and ethnicity. As Figure 19.2 "Race, Ethnicity, and U.S. Fertility Rates, 2006" shows, it is lowest for non-Latina white women and the highest for Latina women. Along with immigration, the high fertility rate of Latina women has fueled the large growth of the Latino population. Latinos now account for about 16% of the U.S. population, and their proportion is expected to reach more than 30% by 2050 (U.S. Census Bureau, 2010).

Figure 19.2 Race, Ethnicity, and U.S. Fertility Rates, 2006

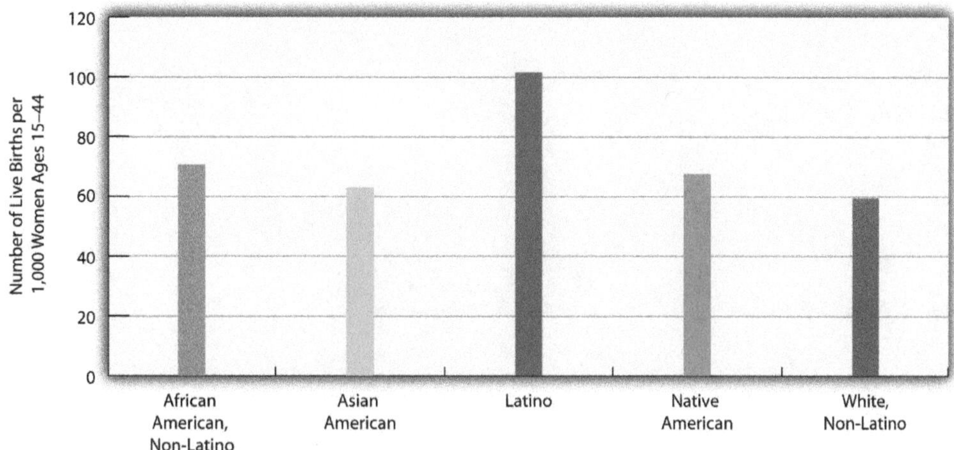

Source: Data from U.S. Census Bureau. (2010). *Statistical abstract of the United States: 2010.* Washington, DC: U.S. Government Printing Office. Retrieved from http://www.census.gov/compendia/statab.

The fertility rate of teenagers is a special concern because of their age. Although it is still a rate that most people wish were lower, it dropped steadily through the 1990s, before leveling off after 2002 and rising slightly afterward (see Figure 19.3 "U.S. Teenage Fertility Rate, 1990–2006"). Although most experts attribute this drop to public education campaigns and increased contraception, the United States still has the highest rate of teenage pregnancy and fertility of any industrial nation (Eckholm, 2009). Teenage fertility again varies by race and ethnicity, with Latina teenagers having the highest fertility rates and Asian American teenagers the lowest (see Figure 19.4 "Race, Ethnicity, and U.S. Teenage Fertility Rates, 2007").

Figure 19.3 U.S. Teenage Fertility Rate, 1990–2006

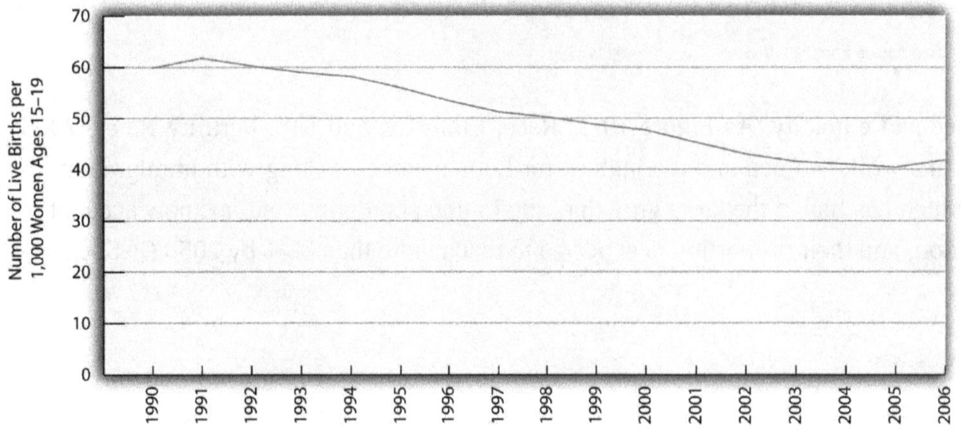

Source: Data from Martin, J. A., Hamilton, B. E., Sutton, P. D., Ventura, S. J., Menacker, F., Kirmeyer, S., & Mathews, T. J. (2009). Births: Final data for 2006. *National vital statistics reports, 57*(7), 1–102.

Figure 19.4 Race, Ethnicity, and U.S. Teenage Fertility Rates, 2007

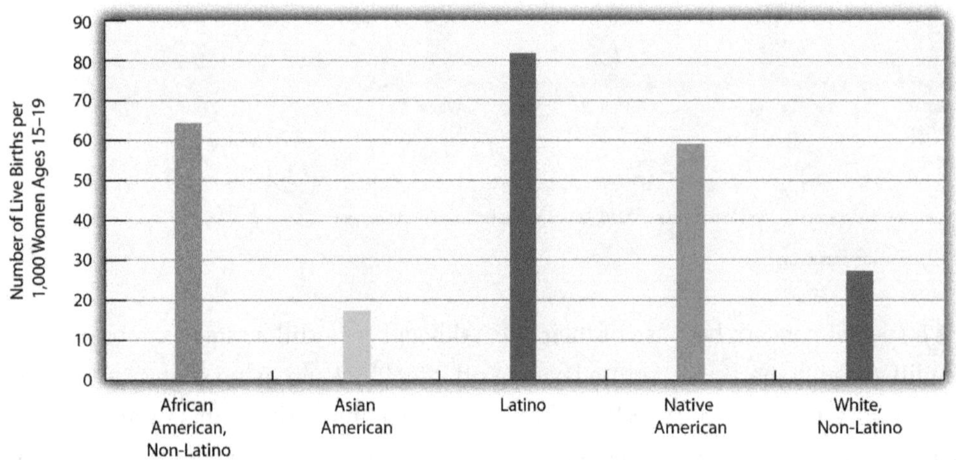

Source: Data from U.S. Census Bureau. (2010). *Statistical abstract of the United States: 2010*. Washington, DC: U.S. Government Printing Office. Retrieved from http://www.census.gov/compendia/statab.

Fertility rates also differ around the world and are especially high in poor nations (see Figure 19.5 "Crude Birth Rates Around the World, 2008 (Number of Births per 1,000 Population)"). Demographers identify several reasons for these high rates (Weeks, 2012).

Figure 19.5 Crude Birth Rates Around the World, 2008 (Number of Births per 1,000 Population)

Source: Adapted from http://en.wikipedia.org/wiki/File:Birth_rate_figures_for_countries.PNG.

Poor nations have higher birth rates for several reasons. One reason is the agricultural economies typical of these nations. In these economies, children are an important economic resource, and families will ordinarily try to have as many children as possible.

Wikimedia Commons – public domain.

First, poor nations are usually agricultural ones. In agricultural societies, children are an important economic resource, as a family will be more productive if it has more children. This means that families will ordinarily try to have as many children as possible. Second, infant and child mortality rates are high in these nations. Because parents realize that one or more of their children may die before adulthood, they have more children to "make up" for the anticipated deaths. A third reason is that many parents in low-income nations prefer sons to daughters, and, if a daughter is born, they "try again" for a son. Fourth, traditional gender roles are often very strong in poor nations, and these roles include the belief that women should be wives and mothers above all. With this ideology in place, it is not surprising that women will have several children. Finally, contraception is uncommon in poor nations. Without contraception, many more pregnancies and births certainly occur. For all of these reasons, then, fertility is much higher in poor nations than in rich nations.

Mortality and Death Rates

Mortality is the flip side of fertility and refers to the number of deaths. Demographers measure it with the **crude death rate**, the number of deaths for every 1,000 people in a population in a given year. To determine the crude death rate, the number of deaths is divided by the population size, and this result is then multiplied by 1,000. In 2006 the United States had slightly more than 2.4 million deaths for a crude death rate of 8.1 deaths for every 1,000 persons. We call this a "crude" death rate because the denominator, population size, consists of the total population and does not take its age distribution into account. All things equal, a society with a higher proportion of older people should have a higher crude death rate. Demographers often calculate *age–adjusted* death rates that adjust for a population's age distribution.

Migration

Another demographic concept is **migration**, the movement of people into and out of specific regions. Since the dawn of human history, people have migrated in search of a better life, and many have been forced to migrate by ethnic conflict or the slave trade.

Several classifications of migration exist. When people move into a region, we call it *in-migration*, or *immigration*; when they move out of a region, we call it *out-migration*, or *emigration*. The *in-migration rate* is the number of people moving into a region for every 1,000 people in the region, while the *out-migration rate* is the number of people moving from the region for every 1,000 people. The difference between the two is the *net migration rate* (in-migration minus out-migration). Recalling the news story about Michigan that began this chapter, Michigan has had a net migration of less than zero, as its out-migration has been greater than its in-migration.

Migration can also be either domestic or international in scope. *Domestic migration* happens within a country's national borders, as when retired people from the northeastern United States move to Florida or the Southwest. *International migration* happens across national borders. When international immigration is heavy, as it has been into the United States and Western Europe in the last few decades, the effect on population growth and other aspects of national life can be significant. Domestic migration can also have a large impact. The great migration of African Americans from the South into northern cities during the first half of the 20th century changed many aspects of those cities' lives (Berlin, 2010). Meanwhile, the movement during the past few decades of northerners into the South and Southwest also had quite an impact: the housing market initially exploded, for example, and traffic increased.

Key Takeaways

- To understand changes in the size and composition of population, demographers use several concepts, including fertility and birth rates, mortality and death rates, and migration.
- Net migration is the difference between the in-migration and out-migration rates. When a nation's in-migration exceeds its out-migration, its net migration is positive; when the reverse is true, its net migration is negative.

For Your Review

1. The text states that the average woman must have 2.1 children for a society to avoid population decline. Some women wish to have no children, some desire one or two children, and some prefer to have at least three children. What do you think is the ideal number of children for a woman to have? Explain your answer.

References

Berlin, I. (2010). *The making of African America: The four great migrations*. New York, NY: Viking.

Eckholm, E. (2009, March 18). '07 U.S. births break baby boom record. *The New York Times*, p. A14.

Hamilton, B. E., Martin, J. A., & Ventura, S. J. (2010). Births: Preliminary data for 2008. *National vital statistics reports, 58*(16), 1–18.

Tejada-Vera, B., & Sutton, P. D. (2010). Births, marriages, divorces, and deaths: Provisional data for 2009. *National vital statistics reports, 58*(25), 1–6.

U.S. Census Bureau. (2010). *Statistical abstract of the United States: 2010*. Washington, DC: U.S. Government Printing Office. Retrieved from http://www.census.gov/compendia/statab.

Weeks, J. R. (2012). *Population: An introduction to concepts and issues* (11th ed.). Belmont, CA: Wadsworth.

19.2 Population Growth and Decline

Learning Objectives

1. Understand demographic transition theory and how it compares with the views of Thomas Malthus.
2. Explain why there is less concern about population growth now than there was a generation ago.
3. Explain what pronatalism means.

Now that you are familiar with some basic demographic concepts, we can discuss population growth and decline in more detail. Three of the factors just discussed determine changes in population size: fertility (crude birth rate), mortality (crude death rate), and net migration. The **natural growth rate** is simply the difference between the crude birth rate and the crude death rate. The U.S. natural growth rate is about 0.6% (or 6 per 1,000 people) per year (Rosenberg, 2009). When immigration is also taken into account, the total population growth rate has been almost 1.0% per year (Jacobsen & Mather, 2010).

Figure 19.6 "International Annual Population Growth Rates (%), 2005–2010" depicts the annual population growth rate (including both natural growth and net migration) of all the nations in the world. Note that many African nations are growing by at least 3% per year or more, while most European nations are growing by much less than 1% or are even losing population, as discussed earlier. Overall, the world population is growing by about 80 million people annually.

Figure 19.6 International Annual Population Growth Rates (%), 2005–2010

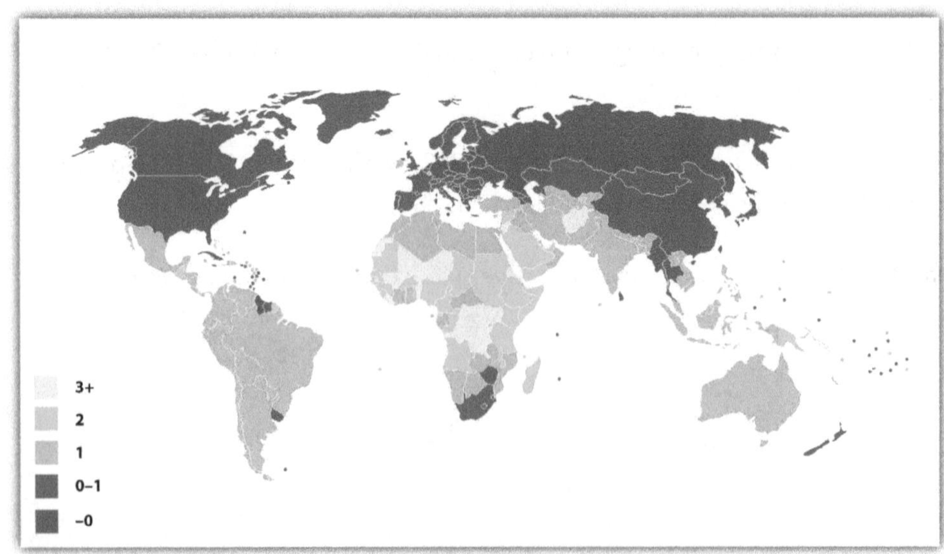

Source: Adapted from http://en.wikipedia.org/wiki/File:Population_growth_rate_world_2005-2010_UN.PNG.

To determine how long it takes for a nation to double its population size, divide the number 70 by its population growth rate. For example, if a nation has an annual growth rate of 3%, it takes about 23.3 years (70 ÷ 3) for that nation's population size to double. As you can see from the map in Figure 19.6 "International Annual Population Growth Rates (%), 2005–2010", several nations will see their population size double in this time span if their annual growth continues at its present rate. For these nations, population growth will be a serious problem if food and other resources are not adequately distributed.

Demographers use their knowledge of fertility, mortality, and migration trends to make *projections* about population growth and decline several decades into the future. Coupled with our knowledge of past population sizes, these projections allow us to understand population trends over many generations. One clear pattern emerges from the study of population growth. When a society is small, population growth is slow because there are relatively few adults to procreate. But as the number of people grows over time, so does the number of adults. More and more procreation thus occurs every single generation, and population growth then soars in a virtual explosion.

We saw evidence of this pattern when we looked at world population growth. When agricultural societies developed some 12,000 years ago, only about 8 million people occupied the planet. This number had reached about 300 million about 2,100 years ago, and by the 15th century it was still only about 500 million. It finally reached 1 billion by about 1850 and by 1950, only a century later, had doubled to 2 billion. Just 50 years later, it tripled to more than 6.8 billion, and it is projected to reach more than 9 billion by 2050 (U.S. Census Bureau, 2010) (see Figure 19.7 "Total World Population, 1950–2050").

Figure 19.7 Total World Population, 1950–2050

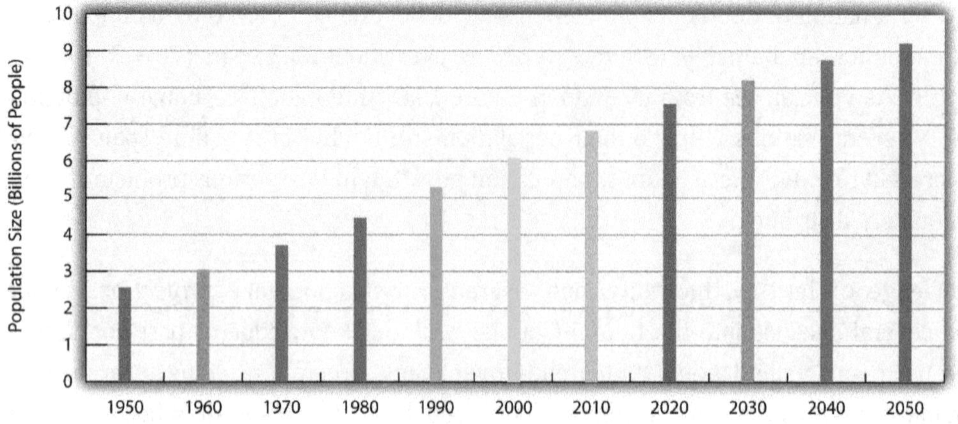

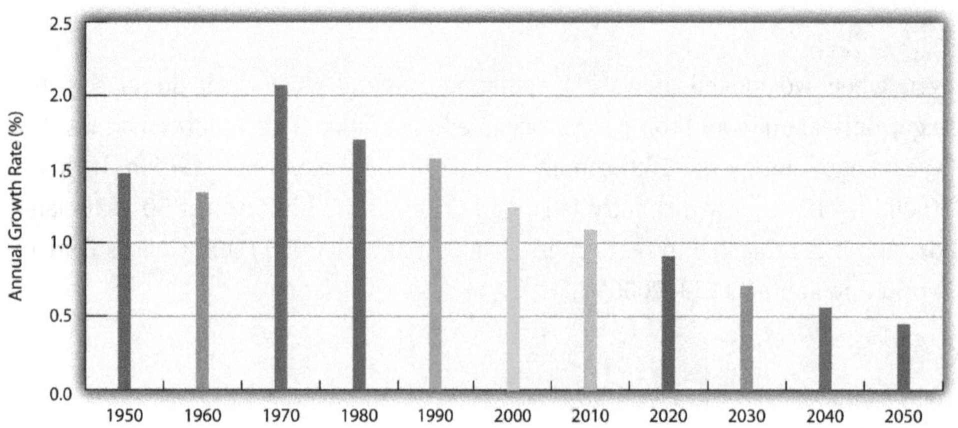

Source: Data from U.S. Census Bureau. (2010). *Statistical abstract of the United States: 2010*. Washington, DC: U.S. Government Printing Office. Retrieved from http://www.census.gov/compendia/statab.

Eventually, however, population growth begins to level off after exploding, as explained by *demographic transition theory*, discussed later. We see this in the bottom half of Figure 19.7 "Total World Population, 1950–2050", which shows the average annual growth rate for the world's population. This rate has declined over the last few decades and is projected to further decline over the next four decades. This means that while the world's population will continue to grow during the foreseeable future, it will grow by a smaller rate as time goes by. As Figure 19.6 "International Annual Population Growth Rates (%), 2005–2010" suggested, the growth that does occur will be concentrated in the poor nations in Africa and some other parts of the world. Still, even there the average number of children a woman has in her lifetime dropped from six a generation ago to about three today.

Past and projected sizes of the U.S. population appear in Figure 19.8 "Past and Projected Size of the U.S. Population, 1950–2050 (in Millions)". The U.S. population is expected to number about 440 million people by 2050.

Figure 19.8 Past and Projected Size of the U.S. Population, 1950–2050 (in Millions)

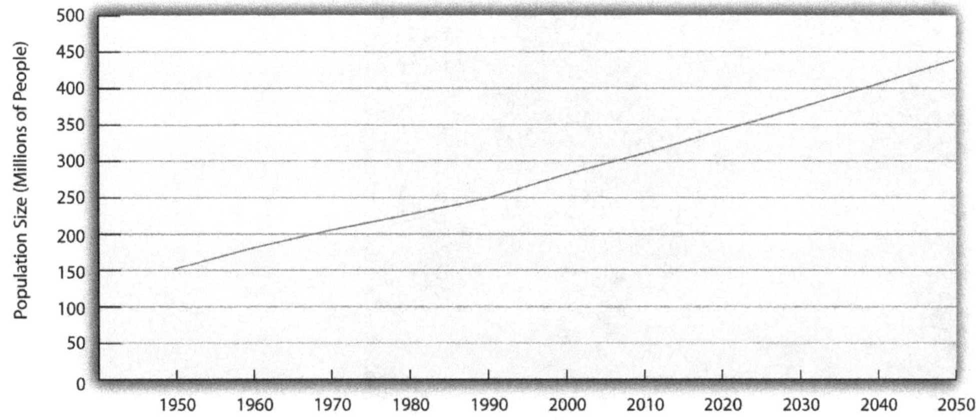

Source: Data from U.S. Census Bureau. (2010). *Statistical abstract of the United States: 2010*. Washington, DC: U.S. Government Printing Office. Retrieved from http://www.census.gov/compendia/statab.

Views of Population Growth

Thomas Malthus, an English economist who lived about 200 years ago, wrote that population increases geometrically while food production increases only arithmetically. These understandings led him to predict mass starvation.

Wikimedia Commons – public domain.

The numbers just discussed show that the size of the United States and world populations has increased tremendously in just a few centuries. Not surprisingly, people have worried about population growth and specifically overpopulation at least since the 18th century. One of the first to warn about population growth was Thomas Malthus (1766–1834), an English economist, who said that population increases *geometrically* (2, 4, 8, 16, 32, 64, 128, 256, 512, 1024…). If you expand this list of numbers, you will see that they soon become overwhelmingly large in just a few more "generations." Malthus (1798/1926) said that food production increases only *arithmetically* (1, 2, 3, 4, 5, 6…) and thus could not hope to keep up with the population increase, and he predicted that mass starvation would be the dire result.

During the 1970s, population growth became a major issue in the United States and some other nations. *Zero population growth,* or ZPG, was a slogan often heard. There was much concern over the rapidly growing population in the United States and, especially, around the world, and there was fear that our "small planet" could not support massive increases in the number of people (Ehrlich, 1969). Some of the most dire predictions of the time warned of serious food shortages by the end of the century.

Fortunately, Malthus and ZPG advocates were wrong to some degree. Although population levels have certainly soared, the projections in Figure 19.7 "Total World Population, 1950–2050" show that the rate of increase is slowing. Among other factors, the development of more effective contraception, especially the birth control pill, has limited population growth in the industrial world and, increasingly, in poorer nations. Food production has also increased by a much greater amount than Malthus and ZPG advocates predicted. Concern about overpopulation growth has weakened, as the world's resources seem to be standing up to population growth. Widespread hunger in Africa and other regions does exist, with hundreds of millions of people suffering from hunger and malnutrition, but many experts attribute this problem not to overpopulation and lack of food but rather to problems in distributing the sufficient amount of food that exists. The "Sociology Making a Difference" box discusses these problems.

Calls during the 1970s for zero population growth (ZPG) population control stemmed from concern that the planet was becoming overpopulated and that food and other resources would soon be too meager to support the world's population.

James Cridland – Crowd – CC BY 2.0.

Another factor might have played a role in weakening advocacy for ZPG: criticism by people of color that ZPG was directed largely at their ranks and smacked of racism. The call for population control, they said, was a disguised call for controlling the growth of their own populations and thus reducing their influence (Kuumba, 1993). Although the merits of this criticism have been debated, it may have still served to mute ZPG advocacy.

Sociology Making a Difference

World Hunger and the Scarcity Fallacy

A popular belief is that world hunger exists because there is too little food to feed too many people in poor nations in Africa, Asia, and elsewhere. Sociologists Stephen J. Scanlan, J. Craig Jenkins, and Lindsey Peterson (2010) call this belief the "scarcity fallacy." According to these authors, "The conventional wisdom is that world hunger exists primarily because of natural disasters, population pressure, and shortfalls in food production" (p. 35). However, this conventional wisdom is mistaken, as world hunger stems not from a shortage of food but from the inability to deliver what is actually a sufficient amount of food to the world's poor. As Scanlan and colleagues note,

> A good deal of thinking and research in sociology suggests that world hunger has less to do with the shortage of food than with a shortage of *affordable* or *accessible* food. Sociologists have found that social inequalities, distribution systems, and other economic and political factors create barriers to food access. (p. 35)
> This sociological view has important implications for how the world should try to reduce global hunger, say these authors. International organizations such as the World Bank and several United Nations agencies have long believed that hunger is due to food scarcity, and this belief underlies the typical approaches to reducing world hunger that focus on increasing food supplies with new technologies and developing more efficient methods of delivering food. But if food scarcity is not a problem, then other approaches are necessary.
>
> Scanlan and colleagues argue that food scarcity is, in fact, not the problem that international agencies and most people believe it to be:
>
> > The bigger problem with emphasizing food supply as the problem, however, is that scarcity is largely a myth. On a per capita basis, food is more plentiful today than any other time in human history.…[E]ven in times of localized production shortfalls or regional famines there has long been a global food surplus. (p. 35)
> > If the problem is not a lack of food, then what is the problem? Scanlan and colleagues argue that the real problem is a lack of access to food and a lack of equitable distribution of food: "Rather than food scarcity, then, we should focus our attention on the persistent inequalities that often accompany the growth in food supply" (p. 36).
> >
> > What are these inequalities? Recognizing that hunger is especially concentrated in the poorest nations, the authors note that these nations lack the funds to import the abundant food that does exist. These nations' poverty, then, is one inequality that leads to world hunger, but gender and ethnic inequalities are also responsible. For example, women around the world are more likely than men to suffer from hunger, and hunger is more common in nations with greater rates of gender inequality (as measured by gender differences in education and income, among other criteria). Hunger is also more common among ethnic minorities not only in poor nations but also in wealthier nations. In findings from their own research, these sociologists add, hunger lessens when nations democratize, when political rights are protected, and when gender and ethnic inequality is reduced.
> >
> > If inequality underlies world hunger, they add, then efforts to reduce world hunger will succeed only to the extent that they recognize the importance of inequality in this regard: "To get at inequality, policy must give attention to democratic governance and human rights, fixing the politics of food aid, and tending to the challenges posed by the global economy" (p. 38). For this to happen, they say, food must be upheld as a "fundamental human right." More generally, world hunger cannot be effectively reduced unless and until ethnic and gender inequality is reduced. Scanlan and colleagues conclude,
> >
> > > The challenge, in short, is to create a more equitable and just society in which food access is ensured for all. Food scarcity matters. However, it is rooted in social conditions and institutional dynamics that must be the focus of any policy innovations that might make a real difference. (p. 39)
> > > In calling attention to the myth of food scarcity and the inequalities that contribute to world hunger, Scanlan and colleagues point to better strategies for addressing this significant international problem. Once again, sociology is making a difference.

Demographic Transition Theory

Other dynamics also explain why population growth did not rise at the geometric rate that Malthus had predicted and is even slowing. The view explaining these dynamics is called **demographic transition theory** (Weeks, 2012), mentioned earlier. This theory links population growth to the level of technological development across three stages of social evolution. In the first stage, coinciding with preindustrial societies, the birth rate and death rate are both high. The birth rate is high because of the lack of contraception and the several other reasons cited earlier for high fertility rates, and the death rate is high because of disease, poor nutrition, lack of modern medicine, and other problems. These two high rates cancel each other out, and little population growth occurs.

In the second stage, coinciding with the development of industrial societies, the birth rate remains fairly high, owing to the lack of contraception and a continuing belief in the value of large families, but the death rate drops because of several factors, including increased food production, better sanitation, and improved medicine. Because the birth rate remains high but the death rate drops, population growth takes off dramatically.

In the third stage, the death rate remains low, but the birth rate finally drops as families begin to realize that large numbers of children in an industrial economy are more of a burden than an asset. Another reason for the drop is the availability of effective contraception. As a result, population growth slows, and, as we saw earlier, it has become quite low or even gone into a decline in several industrial nations.

Demographic transition theory, then, gives us more reason to be cautiously optimistic regarding the threat of overpopulation: as poor nations continue to modernize—much as industrial nations did 200 years ago—their population growth rates should start to decline. Still, population growth rates in poor nations continue to be high, and, as the "Sociology Making a Difference" box discussed, inequalities in food distribution allow rampant hunger to persist. Hundreds of thousands of women die in poor nations each year during pregnancy and childbirth. Reduced fertility would save their lives, in part because their bodies would be healthier if their pregnancies were spaced farther apart (Schultz, 2008). Although world population growth is slowing, then, it is still growing too rapidly in much of the developing and least developed worlds. To reduce it further, more extensive family-planning programs are needed, as is economic development in general.

Population Decline and Pronatalism

Still another reason for the reduced concern over population growth is that birth rates in many industrial nations have slowed considerably. Some nations are even experiencing population declines, while several more are projected to have population declines by 2050 (Goldstein, Sobotka, & Jasilioniene, 2009). For a country to maintain its population, the average woman needs to have 2.1 children, the *replacement level* for population stability. But several industrial nations, not including the United States, are far below this level. Increased birth control is one reason for their lower fertility rates but so are decisions by women to stay in school longer, to go to work right after their schooling ends, and to not have their first child until somewhat later.

Spain is one of several European nations that have been experiencing a population decline because of lower birth rates. Like some other nations, Spain has adopted pronatalist policies to encourage people to have more children; it provides 2,500 euros, about $3,400, for each child.

Wikimedia Commons – CC BY-SA 3.0.

Ironically, these nations' population declines have begun to concern demographers and policymakers (Shorto, 2008). Because people in many industrial nations are living longer while the birth rate drops, these nations are increasingly having a greater proportion of older people and a smaller proportion of younger people. In several European nations, there are more people 61 or older than 19 or younger. As this trend continues, it will become increasingly difficult to take care of the health and income needs of so many older persons, and there may be too few younger people to fill the many jobs and provide the many services that an industrial society demands. The smaller labor force may also mean that governments will have fewer income tax dollars to provide these services.

To deal with these problems, several governments have initiated **pronatalist** policies aimed at encouraging women to have more children. In particular, they provide generous child-care subsidies, tax incentives, and flexible work schedules designed to make it easier to bear and raise children, and some even provide couples outright cash payments when they have an additional child. Russia in some cases provides the equivalent of about $9,000 for each child beyond the first, while Spain provides 2,500 euros (equivalent to about $3,400) for each child (Haub, 2009).

Key Takeaways

- Concern over population growth has declined for at least three reasons. First, there is increasing recognition that the world has an adequate supply of food. Second, people of color have charged that attempts to limit population growth were aimed at their own populations. Third, several European countries have actually experienced population decline.
- Demographic transition theory links population growth to the level of technological development across three stages of social evolution. In preindustrial societies, there is little population growth; in industrial

societies, population growth is high; and in later stages of industrial societies, population growth slows.

For Your Review

1. Before you read this chapter, did you think that food scarcity was the major reason for world hunger today? Why do you think a belief in food scarcity is so common among Americans?
2. Do you think nations with low birth rates should provide incentives for women to have more babies? Why or why not?

References

Ehrlich, P. R. (1969). *The population bomb*. San Francisco, CA: Sierra Club.

Goldstein, J. R., Sobotka, T., & Jasilioniene, A. (2009). The end of "lowest-low" fertility? *Population & Development Review, 35*(4), 663–699. doi:10.1111/j.1728–4457.2009.00304.x.

Haub, C. (2009). *Birth rates rising in some low birth-rate countries*. Washington, DC: Population Reference Bureau. Retrieved from http://www.prb.org/Articles/2009/fallingbirthrates.aspx.

Jacobsen, L. A., & Mather, M. (2010). U.S. economic and social trends since 2000. *Population Bulletin, 65*(1), 1–20.

Kuumba, M. B. (1993). Perpetuating neo-colonialism through population control: South Africa and the United States. *Africa Today, 40*(3), 79–85.

Malthus, T. R. (1926). *First essay on population*. London, England: Macmillan. (Original work published 1798).

Rosenberg, M. (2009). Population growth rates. Retrieved from http://geography.about.com/od/populationgeography/a/populationgrow.htm.

Scanlan, S. J., Jenkins, J. C., & Peterson, L. (2010). The scarcity fallacy. *Contexts, 9*(1), 34–39.

Schultz, T. P. (2008). Population policies, fertility, women's human capital, and child quality. In T. P. Schultz & J. Strauss (Eds.), *Handbook of development economics* (Vol. 4, pp. 3249–3303). Amsterdam, Netherlands: North-Holland, Elsevier.

Shorto, R. (2008, June 2). No babies? *The New York Times Magazine*. Retrieved from http://www.nytimes.com/2008/06/29/magazine/29Birth-t.html?scp=1&sq=&st=nyt.

U.S. Census Bureau. (2010). *Statistical abstract of the United States: 2010*. Washington, DC: U.S. Government Printing Office. Retrieved from http://www.census.gov/compendia/statab.

Weeks, J. R. (2012). *Population: An introduction to concepts and issues* (11th ed.). Belmont, CA: Wadsworth.

19.3 Urbanization

Learning Objectives

1. Discuss the views and methodology of the human ecology school.
2. Describe the major types of urban residents.
3. List four major issues and/or problems affecting U.S. cities today.

An important aspect of social change and population growth over the centuries has been **urbanization**, or the rise and growth of cities. Urbanization has had important consequences for many aspects of social, political, and economic life (Kleniewski & Thomas, 2011).

The earliest cities developed in ancient times after the rise of horticultural and pastoral societies made it possible for people to stay in one place instead of having to move around to find food. Because ancient cities had no sanitation facilities, people typically left their garbage and human waste in the city streets or just outside the city wall (which most cities had for protection from possible enemies); this poor sanitation led to rampant disease and high death rates. Some cities eventually developed better sanitation procedures, including, in Rome, a sewer system (Smith, 2003).

Cities became more numerous and much larger during industrialization, as people moved to be near factories and other sites of industrial production. First in Europe and then in the United States, people crowded together as never before into living conditions that were often decrepit. Lack of sanitation continued to cause rampant disease, and death rates from cholera, typhoid, and other illnesses were high. In addition, crime rates soared, and mob violence became quite common (Feldberg, 1998).

Views of the City

During the early 20th century, social scientists at the University of Chicago began to study urban life in general and life in Chicago in particular. Although some of these scholars were very dismayed by the negative aspects of city life, other scholars emphasized several positive aspects of city life.

Wikimedia Commons – CC BY-SA 3.0.

Are cities good or bad? We asked a similar question—is modernization good or bad?—earlier in this chapter, and the answer here is similar as well: cities are both good and bad. They are sites of innovation, high culture, population diversity, and excitement, but they are also sites of high crime, impersonality, and other problems.

In the early 20th century, a group of social scientists at the University of Chicago established a research agenda on cities that is still influential today (Bulmer, 1984). Most notably, they began to study the effects of urbanization on various aspects of city residents' lives in what came to be called the **human ecology school** (Park, Burgess, & McKenzie, 1925). One of their innovations was to divide Chicago into geographical regions, or zones, and to analyze crime rates and other behavioral differences among the zones. They found that crime rates were higher in the inner zone, or central part of the city, where housing was crowded and poverty was common, and were lower in the outer zones, or the outer edges of the city, where houses were spread farther apart and poverty was much lower. Because they found these crime rate differences changed over time even as the ethnic backgrounds of people in these zones, they assumed that the social and physical features of the neighborhoods were affecting their crime rates (Shaw & McKay, 1942). Their work is still useful today, as it helps us realize that the social environment, broadly defined, can affect our attitudes and behavior. This theme, of course, lies at the heart of the sociological perspective.

Urbanism and Tolerance

One of the most notable Chicago sociologists was Louis Wirth (1897–1952), who, in a well-known essay entitled "Urbanism as a Way of Life" (Wirth, 1938), discussed several differences between urban and rural life. In one such difference, he said that urban residents are more tolerant than rural residents of nontraditional attitudes, behaviors, and lifestyles, in part because they are much more exposed than rural residents to these nontraditional ways. Supporting Wirth's hypothesis, contemporary research finds that urban residents indeed hold more tolerant views on several kinds of issues (Moore & Ovadia, 2006).

Life in U.S. Cities

Life in U.S. cities today reflects the dual view just outlined. On the one hand, many U.S. cities are vibrant places, filled with museums and other cultural attractions, nightclubs, theaters, and restaurants and populated by people from many walks of life and from varied racial and ethnic and national backgrounds. Many college graduates flock to cities, not only for their employment opportunities but also for their many activities and the sheer excitement of living in a metropolis. On the other hand, many U.S. cities are also filled with abject poverty, filthy and dilapidated housing, high crime rates, traffic gridlock, and dirty air. Many Americans would live nowhere but a city, and many would live anywhere but a city. Cities arouse strong opinions pro and con, and for good reason, because there are many things both to like and to dislike about cities.

Types of Urban Residents

The quality of city life depends on many factors, but one of the most important factors is a person's social background: social class, race/ethnicity, gender, age, and sexual orientation. As earlier chapters documented, these dimensions of our social backgrounds often yield many kinds of social inequalities, and the quality of life that city residents enjoy depends heavily on these dimensions. For example, residents who are white and wealthy have the money and access to enjoy the best that cities have to offer, while those who are poor and of color typically experience the worst aspects of city life. Because of fear of rape and sexual assault, women often feel more constrained than men from traveling freely throughout a city and being out late at night; older people also often feel more constrained because of physical limitations and fear of muggings; and gays and lesbians are still subject to physical assaults stemming from homophobia. The type of resident we are, then, in terms of our sociodemographic profile affects what we experience in the city and whether that experience is positive or negative.

This brief profile of city residents obscures other kinds of differences among residents regarding their lifestyles and experiences. A classic typology of urban dwellers by sociologist Herbert Gans (1962) is still useful today in helping to understand the variety of lives found in cities. Gans identified five types of city residents.

Herbert Gans identified several types of city residents. One of these types is the cosmopolites, who include students, writers, musicians, and intellectuals, all of whom live in a city because of its cultural attractions and other amenities.

Brian Evans – Street Musician – CC BY-ND 2.0.

The first type is *cosmopolites*. These are people who live in a city because of its cultural attractions, restaurants, and other features of the best that a city has to offer. Cosmopolites include students, writers, musicians, and intellectuals. *Unmarried and childless* individuals and couples are the second type; they live in a city to be near their jobs and to enjoy the various kinds of entertainment found in most cities. If and when they marry or have children, respectively, many migrate to the suburbs to raise their families. The third type is *ethnic villagers*, who are recent immigrants and members of various ethnic groups who live among each other in certain neighborhoods. These neighborhoods tend to have strong social bonds and more generally a strong sense of community. Gans wrote that all of these three types generally find the city inviting rather than alienating and have positive experiences far more often than negative ones.

In contrast, two final types of residents find the city alienating and experience a low quality of life. The first of these two types, and the fourth overall, is the *deprived*. These are people with low levels of formal education who live in poverty or near-poverty and are unemployed, are underemployed, or work at low wages. They live in neighborhoods filled with trash, broken windows, and other signs of disorder. They commit high rates of crime and also have high rates of victimization by crime. The final type is the *trapped*. These are residents who, as their name implies, might wish to leave their neighborhoods but are unable to do so for several reasons: they may be alcoholics or drug addicts, they may be elderly and disabled, or they may be jobless and cannot afford to move to a better area.

Problems of City Life

By definition, cities consist of very large numbers of people living in a relatively small amount of space. Some of these people have a good deal of money, but many people, and in some cities most people, have very little money. Cities must provide many kinds of services for all their residents, and certain additional services for their poorer residents. These basic facts of city life make for common sets of problems affecting cities throughout the nation, albeit to varying degrees, with some cities less able than others to address these problems.

Fiscal Problems

One evident problem is *fiscal*: cities typically have serious difficulties in paying for basic services such as policing, public education, trash removal, street maintenance, and, in cold climates, snow removal, and in providing certain services for their residents who are poor or disabled or who have other conditions. The fiscal difficulties that cities routinely face became even more serious with the onset of the nation's deep recession in 2009, as the term *fiscal crisis* became a more accurate description of the harsh financial realities that cities were now facing (McNichol, 2009).

Crowding

Cities experience many kinds of problems, and crowding is one of them. People who live amid crowding are more likely to experience stress and depression and to engage in aggressive behavior or be victimized by it.

Stròlic Furlàn – Davide Gambino – Lots of people – CC BY-ND 2.0.

Another problem is *crowding*. Cities are crowded in at least two ways. The first involves *residential crowding*: large numbers of people living in a small amount of space. City streets are filled with apartment buildings, condominiums, row houses, and other types of housing, and many people live on any one city block. The second type of crowding is *household crowding*: dwelling units in cities are typically small because of lack of space, and much smaller than houses in suburbs or rural areas. This forces many people to live in close quarters within a particular dwelling unit. Either type of crowding is associated with higher levels of stress, depression, and aggression (Regoeczi, 2008).

Housing

A third problem involves *housing*. Here there are several related issues. Much urban housing is *substandard* and characterized by such problems as broken windows, malfunctioning heating systems, peeling paint, and insect infestation. At the same time, adequate housing is *not affordable* for many city residents, as housing prices in cities can be very high, and the residents' incomes are typically very low. Cities thus have a great need for adequate, affordable housing.

Another housing issue concerns racial segregation. Although federal law prohibits segregated housing, cities across the country are nonetheless highly segregated by race, with many neighborhoods all or mostly African American. Sociologists Douglas S. Massey and Nancy A. Denton (1998) termed this situation "American apartheid." They said that these segregated neighborhoods result from a combination of several factors, including (a) "white flight" into suburbs, (b) informal—and often illegal—racially discriminatory actions that make it difficult for African Americans to move into white neighborhoods (such as real estate agents falsely telling black couples that no houses are available in a particular neighborhood), and (c) a general lack of income and other resources that makes it very difficult for African Americans to move from segregated neighborhoods.

Massey and Denton argued that residential segregation worsens the general circumstances in which many urban African Americans live. Several reasons account for this effect. As whites flee to the suburbs, the people left behind are much poorer. The tax base of cities suffers accordingly, and along with it the quality of city schools, human services, and other social functions. All these problems help keep the crime rate high and perhaps even raise it further. Because segregated neighborhoods are poor and crime-ridden, businesses do not want to invest in them, and employment opportunities are meager. This fact worsens conditions in segregated neighborhoods even further. Consequently, concluded Massey and Denton, racial segregation helps perpetuate the urban "underclass" of people who live jobless in deep poverty and decaying neighborhoods.

Other research supports this conclusion. As a recent review summarized the evidence,

> Whether voluntary or involuntary, living in racially segregated neighborhoods has serious implications for the present and future mobility opportunities of those who are excluded from desirable areas. Where we live affects our proximity to good job opportunities, educational quality, and safety from crime (both as victim and as perpetrator), as well as the quality of our social networks. (Charles, 2003, pp. 167–168)

To improve the socioeconomic status and living circumstances of African Americans, then, it is critical that residential segregation be reduced.

Traffic and Pollution

Traffic is a major problem in cities. The great number of motor vehicles in a relatively small space often leads to gridlock and contributes greatly to air pollution.

joiseyshowaa – World Class Traffic Jam 2 – CC BY-SA 2.0.

A fourth problem of city life is *traffic*. Gridlock occurs in urban areas, not rural ones, because of the sheer volume of traffic and the sheer number of intersections controlled by traffic lights or stop signs. Some cities have better public transportation than others, but traffic and commuting are problems that urban residents experience every day (see the "Learning From Other Societies" box).

Learning From Other Societies

Trains, Not Planes (or Cars): The Promise of High-Speed Rail

One of the costs of urbanization and modern life is traffic. Our streets and highways are clogged with motor vehicles, and two major consequences of so much traffic are air pollution and tens of thousands of deaths and injuries from vehicular accidents. One way that many other nations, including China, Germany, Japan, and Spain, have tried to lessen highway traffic in recent decades is through the construction of high-speed rail lines. According to one news report, the U.S. rail system "remains a caboose" compared to the high-speed system found in much of the rest of the world (Knowlton, 2009, p. A16). Japan has one line that averages 180 mph, while Europe's high-speed trains average 130 mph, with some exceeding 200 mph. These speeds are far faster than the 75 mph typical of Amtrak's speediest Acela line in the northeastern United States, which must usually go much more slowly than its top speed of 150 mph because of inferior tracking and interference by other trains. Although the first so-called bullet train appeared in Japan about 40 years ago, the United States does not yet have even one such train.

The introduction of high-speed rail in other nations was meant to reduce highway traffic and, in turn, air pollution and vehicular injuries and deaths. Another goal was to reduce air traffic between cities, as high-speed trains emit only one-fourth the carbon dioxide per passengers as planes do while transporting 8 times as many passengers in a given distance (Burnett, 2009). A final goal was to aid the national economies of the nations that introduced high-speed rail. The evidence indicates that these goals have been accomplished.

For example, Spain built its first high-speed line, between Madrid and Seville, in 1992 and now has rail reaching about 1,200 miles between its north and south coasts. The rail network has increased travel for work and leisure and thus helped Spain's economy. The high-speed trains are also being used instead of planes by the vast majority of people who travel between Madrid and either Barcelona or Seville.

China, the world's most populous nation but far from the richest, has recently opened, or plans to open during the next few years, several dozen high-speed rail lines. Its fastest train averages more than 200 mph and travels 664 miles between two cities, Guangzhou and Wuhan, in just over 3 hours. The Acela takes longer to travel between Boston and New York, a distance of only 215 miles. A news report summarized the economic benefits for China:

> Indeed, the web of superfast trains promises to make China even more economically competitive, connecting this vast country—roughly the same size as the United States—as never before, much as the building of the Interstate highway system increased productivity and reduced costs in America a half-century ago. (Bradsher, 2010, p. B1)
> In April 2009 President Barack Obama announced that $8 billion in federal stimulus funding would be made available for the construction of high-speed rail lines in certain parts of the United States to connect cities between 100 and 600 miles apart. The president said,
>
> > Imagine whisking through towns at speeds over 100 miles an hour, walking only a few steps to public transportation, and ending up just blocks from your destination. It is happening right now; it's been happening for decades. The problem is, it's been happening elsewhere, not here. (Knowlton, 2009)
> > As large as it is, the $8 billion figure announced by Obama pales in comparison with an estimated $140 billion that Spain plans to further spend on high-speed rail during the next decade, and a system of high-speed rail in the United States will cost more than even this expenditure. Despite the huge expense of high-speed rail, the positive experience of other nations that are using it suggests that the United States will benefit in many ways from following their example. If it does not do so, said one scholar, "the American preference for clogged-up highways and airports will make the country look so old, so 20th-century-ish. So behind the times" (Kennedy, 2010).
>
> A related problem is *pollution*. Traffic creates pollution from motor vehicles' exhaust systems, and some cities have factories and other enterprises that also pollute. As a result, air quality in cities is substandard, and the poor quality of air in cities has been linked to respiratory and heart disease and higher mortality rates (Stylianou & Nicolich, 2009).

Public Education

Yet another issue for cities is the state of their *public education*. Many city schools are housed in old buildings that, like much city housing, are falling apart. City schools are notoriously underfunded and lack current textbooks, adequate science equipment, and other instructional materials (see Chapter 16 "Education").

Crime

Although cities have many additional problems, *crime* is an appropriate issue with which to end this section because of its importance. Simply put, cities have much higher rates of violent and property crime than do small towns or rural areas. For example, the violent crime rate (number of crimes per 100,000 residents) in 2009 was 459 for the nation's largest cities, compared to only 202 for rural counties. The property crime rate in the largest cities was 3,160 crimes per 100,000, compared to only 1,570 in rural counties (Federal Bureau of Investigation, 2010). Crime rates in large cities are thus two to three times higher than those in rural counties.

Global Urbanization

Urbanization varies around the world. In general, wealthy nations are more urban than poor nations (see Figure 19.9 "Percentage of Population Living in Urban Areas, 2005"), thanks in large part to the latter's rural economies. This variation, however, obscures the fact that the world is becoming increasingly urban overall. In 1950, less than one-third of the world's population lived in cities or towns; in 2008, more than half the population lived in cities or towns, representing the first time in history that a majority of people were *not* living in rural areas (United Nations Population Fund, 2007). By 2030, almost two-thirds of the world's population is projected to live in urban areas.

The number of urban residents will increase rapidly in the years ahead, especially in Africa and Asia as people in these continents' nations move to urban areas and as their populations continue to grow through natural fertility. Fertility is a special problem in this regard for two reasons. First, and as we saw earlier, women in poor nations have higher fertility rates for several reasons. Second, poorer nations have very high proportions of young people, and these high rates mean that many births occur because of the large number of women in their childbearing years.

Figure 19.9 Percentage of Population Living in Urban Areas, 2005

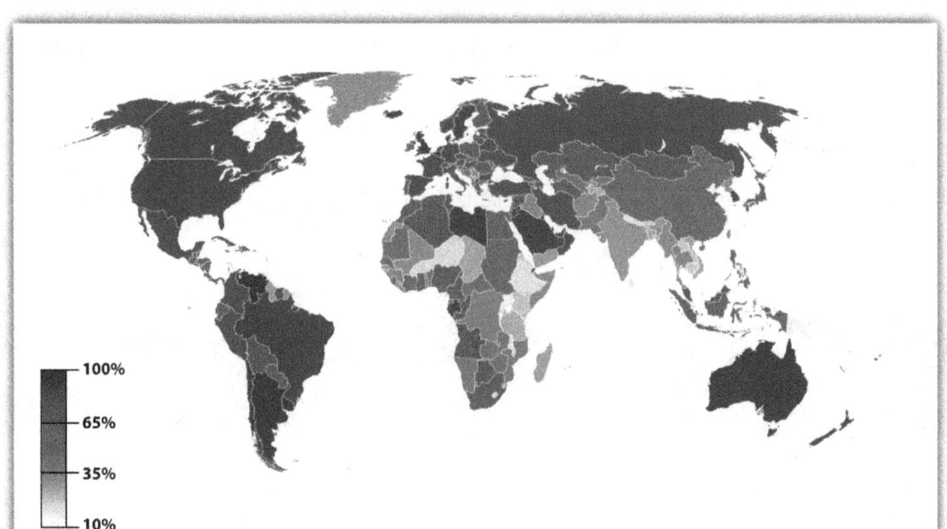

Source: Adapted from http://en.wikipedia.org/wiki/File:Urban_population_in_2005_world_map.PNG.

This trend poses both opportunities and challenges for poorer nations. The opportunities are many. Jobs are more plentiful in cities than in rural areas and incomes are higher, and services such as health care and schooling are easier to deliver because people are living more closely together. In another advantage, women in poorer nations generally fare better in cities than in rural areas in terms of education and employment possibilities (United Nations Population Fund, 2007).

But there are also many challenges. In the major cities of poor nations, homeless children live in the streets as beggars, and many people lack necessities and conveniences that urban dwellers in industrial nations take for granted. As the United Nations Population Fund (2007) warns, "One billion people live in urban slums, which are typically overcrowded, polluted and dangerous, and lack basic services such as clean water and sanitation." The rapid urbanization of poor nations will compound the many problems these nations already have, just as the rapid urbanization in the industrial world more than a century ago led to the disease and other problems discussed earlier. As cities grow rapidly in poor nations, moreover, these nations' poverty makes them ill equipped to meet the challenges of urbanization. Helping these nations meet the needs of their cities remains a major challenge for the world community in the years ahead. In this regard, the United Nations Population Fund (United Nations Population Fund, 2007) urges particular attention to housing:

Addressing the housing needs of the poor will be critical. A roof and an address in a habitable area are the first step to a better life. Improving access to basic social and health services, including reproductive health care, for poor people in urban slums is also critical to breaking the cycle of poverty.

Key Takeaways

- A double-edged view of cities has long existed in sociology. In the early 20th century, social scientists at the University of Chicago adopted Émile Durkheim's more positive view of urbanization.
- Social inequality based on social class, race/ethnicity, gender, age, and sexual orientation affects the quality of urban experiences. In addition to differences in their sociodemographic profiles, city residents differ in other ways. Herbert Gans identified several types of urban dwellers: cosmopolites, unmarried and childless, ethnic villagers, deprived, and trapped.
- Major issues and problems confronting U.S. cities today include those involving fiscal difficulties, crowding, housing, traffic, pollution, public education, and crime.
- Cities are rapidly growing in poor nations, and this type of urbanization poses many challenges that these nations are unable to meet because of their poverty and other difficulties.

For Your Review

1. If you had your preference, would you want to eventually live in a large city, medium-sized city, small town, or rural area? Explain your answer.
2. Americans often seem to blame city residents for many of the problems affecting U.S. cities today, including low academic achievement and rundown conditions in city schools and crime in the streets. Do you think it is fair to blame city residents for these problems, or are there other reasons for them? Explain your answer.

References

Bradsher, K. (2010, February 12). China sees growth engine in a web of fast trains. *The New York Times*, p. B1.

Bulmer, M. (1984). *The Chicago school of sociology: Institutionalization, diversity, and the rise of sociological research*. Chicago, IL: University of Chicago Press.

Burnett, V. (2009, May 29). Europe's travels with high-speed rail hold lessons for U.S. planners: The Spanish experience has been transformative but far from inexpensive. *International Herald Tribune*, p. 16.

Charles, C. Z. (2003). The dynamics of racial residential segregation. *Annual Review of Sociology, 29*, 167–207.

Federal Bureau of Investigation. (2010). *Crime in the United States, 2009*. Washington, DC: Author.

Feldberg, M. (1998). Urbanization as a cause of violence: Philadelphia as a test case. In A. F. Davis & M. H. Haller (Eds.), *The peoples of Philadelphia: A history of ethnic groups and lower-class life, 1790–1940* (pp. 53–69). Philadelphia: University of Pennsylvania Press.

Gans, H. J. (1962). *The urban villagers: Group and class in the life of Italian-Americans*. New York, NY: Free Press.

Kennedy, P. (2010, January 4). A trainspotter's guide to the future of the world. *The New York Times*. Retrieved from http://www.nytimes.com/2010/01/05/opinion/05iht-edkennedy.html?scp=1&sq=A%20trainspotter’s%20guide%20to %20the%20future%20of%20the%20world&st=cse.

Kleniewski, N., & Thomas, A. R. (2011). *Cities, change, and conflict* (4th ed.). Belmont, CA: Wadsworth.

Knowlton, B. (2009, April 16). Obama seeks high-speed rail system across U.S. *The New York Times*, p. A16.

Massey, D. S., & Denton, N. A. (1998). *American apartheid: Segregation and the making of the underclass*. Cambridge, MA: Harvard University Press.

McNichol, D. A. (2009, May 1). Revenue loss putting cities in fiscal vise. *The New York Times*, p. NJ1.

Moore, L. M., & Ovadia, S. (2006). Accounting for spatial variation in tolerance: The effects of education and religion. *Social Forces, 84*(4), 2205–2222.

Park, R. E., Burgess, E. W., & McKenzie, R. (1925). *The city*. Chicago, IL: University of Chicago Press.

Regoeczi, W. C. (2008). Crowding in context: An examination of the differential responses of men and women to high-density living environments. *Journal of Health and Social Behavior, 49*, 254–268.

Shaw, C. R., & McKay, H. D. (1942). *Juvenile delinquency and urban areas*. Chicago, IL: University of Chicago Press.

Smith, M. L. (Ed.). (2003). *The social construction of ancient cities*. Washington, DC: Smithsonian Institution Press.

Stylianou, M., & Nicolich, M. J. (2009). Cumulative effects and threshold levels in air pollution mortality: Data analysis of nine large US cities using the NMMAPS dataset. *Environmental Pollution, 157*, 2216–2223.

United Nations Population Fund. (2007). Linking population, poverty, and development. Urbanization: A majority in cities. Retrieved from http://www.unfpa.org/pds/urbanization.htm.

Wirth, L. (1938). Urbanism as a way of life. *American Journal of Sociology, 44*, 3–24.

19.4 Rural Life

Learning Objectives

1. List three positive aspects of rural life in the United States.
2. Describe two problems of rural life in the United States.

Before we leave the topic of cities and urbanization, it is important to note that one-fourth of the U.S. population and more than 40% of the world population continue to live in rural areas. The dual view of cities presented in Chapter 19 "Population and Urbanization", Section 19.3 "Urbanization" also applies to rural areas but does so in a sort of mirror image: the advantages of cities are often disadvantages for rural areas, and the disadvantages of cities are often advantages for rural areas.

Rural areas can be beautiful and relaxing, but they also must confront important challenges. These problems include a lack of public transportation, human services, and medical professionals and facilities.

Marina del Castell – Rural life – CC BY 2.0.

On the positive side, and focusing on the United States, rural areas feature much more open space and less crowding. Their violent and property crime rates are much lower than those in large cities, as we have seen. The air is cleaner because there is less traffic and fewer factories and other facilities that emit pollution. At least anecdotally, life in rural areas is thought to be slower-paced, resulting in lower levels of anxiety and a greater sense of relaxation.

On the negative side, rural areas are often poor and lack the services, employment opportunities, and leisure activities that cities have. Teens often complain of boredom, and drug and alcohol use can be high (Johnson et al., 2008). Public transportation is often lacking, making it difficult for people without motor vehicles, who tend to be low-income, to get to workplaces, stores, and other venues (Brown, 2008). Many rural areas in the United States lack high-speed broadband, a necessity in today's economy. As a result, their economic development is impaired (Whitacre, 2010). Rural areas also face several other challenges, which we now examine.

Rural Health and Rural Education

As Chapter 18 "Health and Medicine" noted, rural areas often lack sufficient numbers of health-care professionals and high-quality hospitals and medical clinics. The long distances that people must travel make it even more difficult for individuals with health problems to receive adequate medical care. Partly because of these problems, rural residents are less likely than urban residents to receive preventive services such as physical examinations; screenings for breast cancer, cervical cancer, and colorectal cancer; and vaccinations for various illnesses and diseases. These problems help explain why rural residents are more likely than urban residents to report being in only fair or poor health in government surveys (Bennett, Olatosi, & Probst, 2009). Compared to nonrural areas, rural areas also have an "aging population," or a greater percentage of adults aged 65 and older. This fact adds to the health-care problems that rural areas must address.

In the area of education, rural schools often face hurdles that urban and suburban schools do not encounter (Center for Rural Policy and Development, 2009). First, because rural areas have been losing population, they have been experiencing declining school enrollment and school closings. Second, rural populations are generally older than urban populations and have a greater percentage of retired adults. Therefore, rural areas' per-capita income and sales tax revenue is lower than that for urban and suburban areas, and this lower revenue makes the funding of public schools more challenging. Third, rural families live relatively far from the public schools, and the schools are relatively far from each other. As a result, rural school districts have considerable expenses for transporting children to and from school, after-school athletic events, and other activities. Finally, it is often difficult to recruit and retain quality teachers in rural areas, and this problem has forced some rural school districts to offer hiring bonuses or housing assistance to staff their schools.

Rural Poverty

Although, as we have seen, many U.S. cities have high poverty rates, more than 7 million rural residents are officially poor, and poverty in rural areas tends to be more severe and persistent than in nonrural areas. Rural poverty stems from several factors, including the out-migration of young, highly skilled workers; the lack of industrial jobs that typically have been higher paying than agricultural jobs; and limited opportunities for the high-paying jobs of the information age.

Compounding the general problem of poverty, rural areas are also more likely than nonrural areas to lack human service programs to help the poor, disabled, elderly, and other people in need of aid (National Advisory Committee on Rural Health and Human Services, 2008). Because rural towns are so small, they often cannot afford services such as soup kitchens, homeless shelters, and Meals on Wheels, and thus must rely on services located in other towns. Yet rural towns are often far from each other, making it difficult and expensive for rural residents to obtain the services they need. For example, a Meals on Wheels program in an urban area may travel just a few miles and serve dozens of people, while it may travel more than 100 miles in a rural area and serve only a few people. Adding to this problem is the strong sense in many rural areas that individuals should be strong enough to fend for themselves and not accept government help. Even when services are available, some people who need them decline to take advantage of them because of pride and shame.

Domestic Violence

In a problem that only recently has been recognized, rural women who experience domestic violence find it especially difficult to get help and/or to leave their abusers. Rural police may be unenlightened about domestic violence and may even know the abuser; for either reason, they may not consider his violence a crime. Battered women's shelters are also much less common in rural areas than in cities, and battered women in rural areas often lack neighbors and friends to whom they can turn for support. For all of these reasons, rural women who experience domestic violence face a problem that has been called "dangerous exits" (DeKeseredy & Schwartz, 2009).

Key Takeaways

- Like cities, rural areas also have their advantages and disadvantages. They can be beautiful, relaxing places in which to live, but they also lack many of the cultural advantages and other amenities that cities feature.
- Rural areas are characterized by sparse populations and long distances that people must travel. These conditions make it difficult to provide adequate public transportation and various kinds of human services. The poverty of many rural areas aggravates these problems.

For Your Review

1. If you had your choice, would you want to live in a large city, medium-sized city, small town, or rural area? Explain your answer.
2. Americans often seem to blame city residents for many of the problems affecting U.S. cities today, including low academic achievement, rundown conditions in city schools, and crime in the streets. Do you think it is fair to blame city residents for these problems, or are there other reasons for them? Explain your answer.

Addressing Population and Urbanization Issues: What Sociology Suggests

The topics of population and urbanization raise many issues within the United States and also across the globe for which a sociological perspective is very relevant. We address of few of these issues here.

Population Issues

Perhaps the most serious population issue is world hunger. Both across the globe and within the United States, children and adults go hungry every day, and millions starve in the poorest nations in Africa and Asia. As the "Sociology Making a Difference" box in this chapter discussed, sociological research indicates that it is mistaken to blame world hunger on a scarcity of food. Instead, this body of research attributes world hunger to various inequalities in access to, and in the distribution of, what is actually a sufficient amount of food to feed the world's people. To effectively reduce world hunger, inequalities across the globe and within the United States based on income, ethnicity, and gender must be addressed; some ways of doing so have been offered in previous chapters.

Population growth in poor nations has slowed but remains a significant problem. Their poverty, low educational levels, and rural settings all contribute to high birth rates. More effective contraception is needed to reduce their population growth, and the United Nations and other international bodies must bolster their efforts, with the aid of increased funding from rich nations, to provide contraception to poor nations. But contraceptive efforts will not be sufficient by themselves. Rather, it is also necessary to raise these nations' economic circumstances and educational levels, as birth rates are lower in nations that are wealthier and more educated. In particular, efforts that raise women's educational levels are especially important if contraceptive use is to increase. In all of these respects, we once again see the importance of a sociological perspective centering on the significance of socioeconomic inequality.

Urbanization Issues

Many urban issues are not, strictly speaking, sociological ones. For example, traffic congestion is arguably more of an engineering issue than a sociological issue, even if traffic congestion has many social consequences. Other urban issues are issues discussed in previous chapters that disproportionately affect urban areas. For example, crime is more common in urban areas than elsewhere, and racial and ethnic inequality is much more of an issue in urban areas than rural areas because of the concentration of people of color in our cities. Previous chapters have discussed such issues in some detail, and the strategies suggested by a sociological perspective for addressing these issues need not be repeated here.

Still other urban issues exist that this chapter was the first to present. Two of these involve crowding and housing. Cities are certainly crowded, and some parts of cities are especially crowded. Housing is expensive, and many urban residents live in dilapidated, substandard housing. Here again a sociological perspective offers some insight, as it reminds us that these problems are intimately related to inequalities of social class, race and ethnicity, and gender. Although it is critical to provide adequate, affordable housing to city residents, it is also important to remember that these various social inequalities affect who is in most need of such housing. Ultimately, strategies aimed at providing affordable housing will not succeed unless they recognize the importance of these social inequalities and unless other efforts reduce or eliminate these inequalities. Racial residential segregation also remains a serious problem in our nation's urban centers, and sociologists have repeatedly shown that residential segregation contributes to many of the problems that urban African Americans experience. Reducing such segregation must be a fundamental goal of any strategy to help American cities.

References

Bennett, K. J., Olatosi, B., & Probst, J. C. (2009). *Health disparities: A rural-urban chartbook*. Columbia: South Carolina Rural Health Research Center.

Brown, D. M. (2008). *Public transportation on the move in rural America*. Washington, DC: Economic Research Service, U.S. Department of Agriculture.

Center for Rural Policy and Development. (2009). *A region apart: A look at challenges and strategies for rural K–12 schools*. Saint Peter, MN: Author.

DeKeseredy, W. S., & Schwartz, M. D. (2009). *Dangerous exits: Escaping abusive relationships in rural America*. New Brunswick, NJ: Rutgers University Press.

Johnson, A. O., Mink, M. D., Harun, N., Moore, C. G., Martin, A. B., & Bennett, K. J. (2008). Violence and drug use in rural teens: National prevalence estimates from the 2003 youth risk behavior survey. *Journal of School Health, 78*(10), 554–561.

National Advisory Committee on Rural Health and Human Services. (2008). *The 2008 report to the secretary: Rural health and human services issues*. Washington, DC: U.S. Department of Health and Human Services.

Whitacre, B. E. (2010). The diffusion of internet technologies to rural communities: A portrait of broadband supply and demand. *American Behavioral Scientist, 53*, 1283–1303.

19.5 End-of-Chapter Material

Summary

1. Demography is the study of population. It encompasses three central concepts: fertility, morality, and migration, which together determine population growth. Fertility and mortality vary by race and ethnicity, and they also vary around the world, with low-income nations having both higher fertility and higher mortality than high-income nations.
2. The world's population is growing by about 80 million people annually. Population growth is greatest in the low-income nations of Africa and other regions, while in several industrial nations it's actually on the decline because birth rates have become so low. The world's population reached 6.8 billion by the beginning of the 21st century and is projected to grow to more than 9 billion by 2050, with most of this occurring in low-income nations. The annual rate of population growth will decline in the years ahead.
3. Thomas Malthus predicted that the earth's population would greatly exceed the world's food supply. Although his prediction did not come true, hunger remains a serious problem around the world. Although food supply is generally ample thanks to improved technology, the distribution of food is inadequate in low-income nations. Fresh water in these regions is also lacking. Demographic transition theory helps explain why population growth did not continue to rise as much as Malthus predicted. As societies become more technologically advanced, first death rates and then birth rates decline, leading eventually to little population growth.
4. Urbanization is a consequence of population growth. Cities first developed in ancient times after the rise of horticultural and pastoral societies and "took off" during the Industrial Revolution as people moved to be near factories. Urbanization led to many social changes then and continues today to affect society.
5. Sociologists have long been interested in the city and have both positive and negative views of urbanization and city life. Contemporary research supports Wirth's hypothesis that tolerance for nontraditional beliefs and behaviors will be higher in urban areas than in rural areas.
6. Cities continue to face many problems. Among the most serious of these problems are residential crowding, substandard and racially segregated housing, heavy traffic and great amounts of air pollution, and high crime rates.
7. Rural areas face many challenges that result from their sparse populations and the great distances that people must often travel. Among other problems, rural areas have a lack of economic opportunities in today's information age and a general lack of various kinds of human services.

Using Sociology

After graduating from college, you are now living in a working-class neighborhood in a fairly large city. You enjoy the excitement of the city, but you are also somewhat troubled by the conditions you have noticed in your neighborhood. One problem that has come to your attention is the existence of lead paint in some of the buildings on your street and adjoining streets. Despite being ordered some time ago to remove this paint and repaint their buildings, four landlords have not yet done so, and the issue is slowly making its way through the courts. Angered by the situation, a new group, Parents Concerned About Lead Paint (PCALP), has hung up flyers announcing a protest rally planned for Saturday of next week. Although your own building has no lead paint and you are not (yet) a parent, you sympathize with the goal of the protest, but you were also planning to visit a friend of yours out of town on the day of the protest. What do you decide to do? Why?

Chapter 20: Social Change and the Environment

Social Issues in the News

"Governor Signs Texting Law Inspired by Teen's Death," the headline said. In June 2010, the governor of Georgia signed the Caleb Sorohan Act, named for an 18-year-old student who died in a car accident caused by his texting while driving. The bill made it illegal for any drivers in Georgia to text unless they were parked. After Caleb died, his family started a campaign, along with dozens of his high school classmates, to enact a texting while driving ban. They signed petitions, started a Facebook page, and used phone banks to lobby members of their state legislature. Vermont enacted a similar ban about the same time. The new laws in Georgia and Vermont increased the number of states banning texting while driving to 28. (Downey, 2010)

"Amherst Sleeps Out to Protest Climate Change," another headline said. It was February 2010, and a student at the University of Massachusetts, Amherst, had been living in a tent for 121 days. His goal was to call attention to the importance of clean energy. The student was a member of a Massachusetts group, Students for a Just and Stable Future (SJSF), composed of college students across the state. To dramatize the problem of climate change, the group had engaged in sleep-outs in various parts of the state, including one on the Boston Common, a famed public park in that city, over a series of weekends in late 2009. About 200 students were arrested on trespassing charges for staying in the park after it was closed at 11:00 p.m. The UMass student in the tent thought he was making a difference; as he put it, "Hopefully people see me and realize that there are people out there who care about the Earth's future and civilization's stability enough to do something about it." Yet he knew that improvements to the environment would take some time: "It's not going to happen overnight." (Vincent, 2010, p. A16)

Societies change just as people do. The change we see in people is often very obvious, as when they have a growth spurt during adolescence, lose weight on a diet, buy new clothes, or get a new hairstyle. The change we see in society is usually more gradual. Unless it is from a natural disaster like an earthquake or from a political revolution, social change is usually noticeable only months or years after it began. This sort of social change arises from many sources, including changes in a society's technology, as the news story on texting and driving illustrates; in the size and composition of its population, as Chapter 19 "Population and Urbanization" discussed; and in its culture. But some social change stems from the concerted efforts of people acting in social movements to alter social policy, as the news story on the student in the tent illustrates, or even the very structure of their government.

This chapter continues this book's examination of social change that began with the discussion of population and urbanization in Chapter 19 "Population and Urbanization". The chapter begins with a conceptual look at social change and modernization before turning to sociological perspectives on social change and the sources of social change. It then presents a sociological understanding of the natural and physical environment. This focus on the environment is certainly timely in today's world but also appropriate for a chapter beginning with social change, as environmental changes have enormous implications for changes in societies around the globe.

References

Downey, M. (2010, June 4). Governor signs texting law inspired by teen's death. *The Atlanta Journal-Constitution*. Retrieved from http://blogs.ajc.com/get-schooled-blog/2010/06/04/governor-signs-texting-law-inspired-by-teens-death.

Vincent, L. (2010). Amherst sleeps out to protest climate change. *DailyCollegian.com*. Retrieved from http://dailycollegian.com/2010/2002/2021/amherst-sleeps-out-to-protest-climate-change.

20.1 Understanding Social Change

Learning Objectives

1. Understand the changes that accompany modernization.
2. Discuss the functionalist and conflict perspectives on social change.

Social change refers to the transformation of culture, behavior, social institutions, and social structure over time. We are familiar from Chapter 5 "Social Structure and Social Interaction" with the basic types of society: hunting-and-gathering, horticultural and pastoral, agricultural, industrial, and postindustrial. In looking at all of these societies, we have seen how they differ in such dimensions as size, technology, economy, inequality, and gender roles. In short, we have seen some of the ways in which societies change over time. Another way of saying this is that we have seen some of the ways in which societies change as they become more modern. To understand social change, then, we need to begin to understand what it means for a society to become more modern. We considered this briefly in Chapter 5 "Social Structure and Social Interaction" and expand on it here.

Modernization

Modernization refers to the process and impact of becoming more modern. More specifically, it refers to the gradual shift from hunting-and-gathering societies to postmodern societies, as outlined in Chapter 5 "Social Structure and Social Interaction", and perhaps especially to the changes brought by the Industrial Revolution of the 19th century.

The terms *modern* and *modernization* have positive connotations; it sounds good to modernize and to be modern. Modernization implies that progress has been made and is continuing to be made, and who would not want progress? Yet modernization also has a downside, as we will see in this section and in the later discussion of the environment.

A related problem with the terms and concepts of modern and modernization is that many people think of Western nations when considering the most modern nations in the world today. This implies that Western society is the ideal to which other societies should aspire. While there are many good things about Western societies, it is important to avoid the ethnocentrism of assuming that Western societies are better because they are more modern. In fact, one reason that many people in the Middle East and elsewhere dislike the United States is that they resent the "Westernization" of their societies from the influence of the United States and other wealthy Western nations. When they see Coca-Cola and Pepsi logos and the McDonald's golden arches in their nations, they fear Western influence and the loss of their own beliefs and traditions.

These caveats notwithstanding, societies have become much more modern over time, to put it mildly. We thus cannot fully understand society and social life without appreciating how societies have changed as they have become more modern. Not surprisingly, sociologists have recognized the importance of modernization ever since the discipline of sociology began in the 19th century, and much of the work of sociology's founders—Émile Durkheim, Max Weber, Karl Marx, and others—focused on how and why societies have changed as they became more modern.

We can draw on their efforts and related work by later sociologists and by anthropologists to develop an idea of the differences modernization has made for societies and individuals. Several dimensions and effects of modernization seem apparent (Nolan & Lenski, 2009).

First, as societies evolve, they become much larger and more *heterogeneous*. This means that people are more different from each other than when societies were much smaller, and it also means that they ordinarily cannot know each other nearly as well. Larger, more modern societies thus typically have weaker social bonds and a weaker sense of community than small societies and place more of an emphasis on the needs of the individual.

As societies become more modern, they begin to differ from nonmodern societies in several ways. In particular, they become larger and more heterogeneous, they lose their traditional ways of thinking, and they gain in individual freedom and autonomy.

Thomas Hawk – Big City Turn Me Loose and Set Me Free – CC BY-NC 2.0.

We can begin to appreciate the differences between smaller and larger societies when we contrast a small college of 1,200 students with a large university of 40,000 students. Perhaps you had this contrast in mind when you were applying to college and had a preference for either a small or a large institution. In a small college, classes might average no more than 20 students; these students get to know each other well and often have a lot of interaction with the professor. In a large university, classes might hold 600 students or more, and everything is more impersonal. Large universities do have many advantages, but they probably do not have as strong a sense of community as is found at small colleges.

A second aspect of modernization is a loss of traditional ways of thinking. This allows a society to be more creative and to abandon old ways that may no longer be appropriate. However, it also means a weakening or even ending of the traditions that helped define the society and gave it a sense of identity.

A third aspect of modernization is the growth of individual freedom and autonomy. As societies grow, become more impersonal, and lose their traditions and sense of community, their norms become weaker, and individuals thus become freer to think for themselves and to behave in new ways. Although most of us would applaud this growth in individual freedom, it also means, as Émile Durkheim (1895/1962) recognized long ago, that people feel freer to *deviate* from society's norms and thus to commit deviance. If we want a society that values individual freedom, Durkheim said, we automatically must have a society with deviance.

Is modernization good or bad? This is a simplistic question about a very complex concept, but a quick answer is that it is both good and bad. We see evidence for both responses in the views of sociologists Ferdinand Tönnies, Weber, and Durkheim. As Chapter 5 "Social Structure and Social Interaction" discussed, Tönnies (1887/1963) said that modernization meant a shift from *Gemeinschaft* (small societies with strong social bonds) to *Gesellschaft* (large societies with weaker social bonds and more impersonal social relations). Tönnies lamented the loss of close social bonds and of a strong sense of community resulting from modernization, and he feared that a sense of rootlessness begins to replace the feeling of stability and steadiness characteristic of small, older societies.

Weber (1921/1978) was also concerned about modernization. The hallmarks of modernization, he thought, are rationalization, a loss of tradition, and the rise of impersonal bureaucracy. He despaired over the impersonal quality of rational thinking and bureaucratization, as he thought it was a dehumanizing influence.

Durkheim (1893/1933) took a less negative view of modernization. He certainly appreciated the social bonds and community feeling, which he called **mechanical solidarity**, characteristic of small, traditional societies. However, he also thought that these societies stifled individual freedom and that social solidarity still exists in modern societies. This solidarity, which he termed **organic solidarity**, stems from the division of labor, in which everyone has to depend on everyone else to perform their jobs. This *interdependence* of roles, Durkheim said, creates a solidarity that retains much of the bonding and sense of community found in premodern societies.

We have already commented on important benefits of modernization that are generally recognized: modernization promotes creativity and individual freedom and autonomy. These developments in turn usually mean that a society becomes more tolerant of beliefs and behaviors that it formerly would have disapproved and even condemned. Modern societies, then, generally feature more tolerance than older societies. Many people, undoubtedly including most sociologists, regard greater tolerance as a good thing, but others regard it as a bad thing because they favor traditional beliefs and behaviors.

Beyond these abstract concepts of social bonding, sense of community, and tolerance, modern societies are certainly a force for both good and bad in other ways. They have produced scientific discoveries that have saved lives, extended life spans, and made human existence much easier than imaginable in the distant past and even in the recent past. But they have also polluted the environment, engaged in wars that have killed tens of millions, and built up nuclear arsenals that, even with the end of the Cold War, still threaten the planet. Modernization, then, is a double-edged sword. It has given us benefits too numerous to count, but it also has made human existence very precarious.

Sociological Perspectives on Social Change

Sociological perspectives on social change fall into the functionalist and conflict approaches. As usual, both views together offer a more complete understanding of social change than either view by itself (Vago, 2004). Table 20.1 "Theory Snapshot" summarizes their major assumptions.

Table 20.1 Theory Snapshot

Theoretical perspective	Major assumptions
Functionalism	Society is in a natural state of equilibrium. Gradual change is necessary and desirable and typically stems from such things as population growth, technological advances, and interaction with other societies that brings new ways of thinking and acting. However, sudden social change is undesirable because it disrupts this equilibrium. To prevent this from happening, other parts of society must make appropriate adjustments if one part of society sees too sudden a change.
Conflict theory	Because the status quo is characterized by social inequality and other problems, sudden social change in the form of protest or revolution is both desirable and necessary to reduce or eliminate social inequality and to address other social ills.

The Functionalist Understanding

The functionalist understanding of social change is based on insights developed by different generations of sociologists. Early sociologists likened change in society to change in biological organisms. Taking a cue from the work of Charles Darwin, they said that societies evolved just as organisms do, from tiny, simple forms to much larger and more complex structures. When societies are small and simple, there are few roles to perform, and just about everyone can perform all of these roles. As societies grow and evolve, many new roles develop, and not everyone has the time or skill to perform every role. People thus start to *specialize* their roles and a *division of labor* begins. As noted earlier, sociologists such as Durkheim and Tönnies disputed the implications of this process for social bonding and a sense of community, and this basic debate continues today.

Several decades ago, Talcott Parsons (1966), the leading 20th-century figure in functionalist theory, presented an **equilibrium model** of social change. Parsons said that society is always in a natural state of equilibrium, defined as a state of equal balance among opposing forces. Gradual change is both necessary and desirable and typically stems from such things as population growth, technological advances, and interaction with other societies that brings new ways of thinking and acting. However, any sudden social change disrupts this equilibrium. To prevent this from happening, other parts of society must make appropriate adjustments if one part of society sees too sudden a change.

Functionalist theory assumes that sudden social change, as by the protest depicted here, is highly undesirable, whereas conflict theory assumes that sudden social change may be needed to correct inequality and other deficiencies in the status quo.

Kashfi Halford – More Riot Police – CC BY-NC 2.0.

The functionalist perspective has been criticized on a few grounds. The perspective generally assumes that the change from simple to complex societies has been very positive, when in fact, as we have seen, this change has also proven costly in many ways. It might well have weakened social bonds, and it has certainly imperiled human existence. Functionalist theory also assumes that sudden social change is highly undesirable, when such change may in fact be needed to correct inequality and other deficiencies in the status quo.

Conflict Theory

Whereas functional theory assumes the status quo is generally good and sudden social change is undesirable, conflict theory assumes the status quo is generally bad. It thus views sudden social change in the form of protest or revolution as both desirable and necessary to reduce or eliminate social inequality and to address other social ills. Another difference between the two approaches concerns industrialization, which functional theory views as a positive development that helped make modern society possible. In contrast, conflict theory, following the views of Karl Marx, says that industrialization exploited workers and thus increased social inequality.

In one other difference between the two approaches, functionalist sociologists view social change as the result of certain natural forces, which we will discuss shortly. In this sense, social change is unplanned even though it happens anyway. Conflict theorists, however, recognize that social change often stems from efforts by social movements to bring about fundamental changes in the social, economic, and political systems. In his sense social change is more “planned,” or at least intended, than functional theory acknowledges.

Critics of conflict theory say that it exaggerates the extent of social inequality and that it sometimes overemphasizes economic conflict while neglecting conflict rooted in race/ethnicity, gender, religion, and other sources. Its Marxian version also erred in predicting that capitalist societies would inevitably undergo a socialist-communist revolution.

Key Takeaways

- As societies become more modern, they become larger and more heterogeneous. Traditional ways of thinking decline, and individual freedom and autonomy increase.
- Functionalist theory favors slow, incremental social change, while conflict theory favors fast, far-reaching social change to correct what it views as social inequalities and other problems in the status quo.

For Your Review

1. If you had to do it over again, would you go to a large university, a small college, or something in between? Why? How does your response relate to some of the differences between smaller, traditional societies and larger, modern societies?
2. When you think about today's society and social change, do you favor the functionalist or conflict view on the kind of social change that is needed? Explain your answer.

References

Durkheim, É. (1933). *The division of labor in society*. London, England: The Free Press. (Original work published 1893).

Durkheim, É. (1962). *The rules of sociological method* (S. Lukes, Ed.). New York, NY: Free Press. (Original work published 1895).

Nolan, P., & Lenski, G. (2009). *Human societies: An introduction to macrosociology* (11th ed.). Boulder, CO: Paradigm.

Parsons, T. (1966). *Societies: Evolutionary and comparative perspectives*. Englewood Cliffs, NJ: Prentice Hall.

Tönnies, F. (1963). *Community and society*. New York, NY: Harper and Row. (Original work published 1887).

Vago, S. (2004). *Social change* (5th ed.). Upper Saddle River, NJ: Prentice Hall.

Weber, M. (1978). *Economy and society: An outline of interpretive sociology* (G. Roth & C. Wittich, Eds.). Berkeley: University of California Press. (Original work published 1921).

20.2 Sources of Social Change

Learning Objectives

1. Describe the major sources of social change.
2. Explain cultural lag and provide an example.

We have seen that social change stems from natural forces and also from the intentional acts of groups of people. This section further examines these sources of social change.

Population Growth and Composition

Much of the discussion so far has talked about population growth as a major source of social change as societies evolved from older to modern times. Yet even in modern societies, changes in the size and composition of the population can have important effects for other aspects of a society, as Chapter 19 "Population and Urbanization" emphasized. As just one example, the number of school-aged children reached a high point in the late 1990s as the children of the post–World War II baby boom entered their school years. This swelling of the school-aged population had at least three important consequences. First, new schools had to be built, modular classrooms and other structures had to be added to existing schools, and more teachers and other school personnel had to be hired (Leonard, 1998). Second, school boards and municipalities had to borrow dollars and/or raise taxes to pay for all of these expenses. Third, the construction industry, building supply centers, and other businesses profited from the building of new schools and related activities. The growth of this segment of our population thus had profound implications for many aspects of U.S. society even though it was unplanned and "natural."

Culture and Technology

Culture and technology are other sources of social change. Changes in culture can change technology; changes in technology can transform culture; and changes in both can alter other aspects of society (Crowley & Heyer, 2011).

Two examples from either end of the 20th century illustrate the complex relationship among culture, technology, and society. At the beginning of the century, the car was still a new invention, and automobiles slowly but surely grew in number, diversity, speed, and power. The car altered the social and physical landscape of the United States and other industrial nations as few other inventions have. Roads and highways were built; pollution increased; families began living farther from each other and from their workplaces; tens of thousands of people started dying annually in car accidents. These are just a few of the effects the invention of the car had, but they illustrate how changes in technology can affect so many other aspects of society.

At the end of the 20th century came the personal computer, whose development has also had an enormous impact that will not be fully understood for some years to come. Anyone old enough, such as many of your oldest professors, to remember having to type long manuscripts on a manual typewriter will easily attest to the difference computers have made for many aspects of our work lives. E-mail, the Internet, and smartphones have enabled instant communication and make the world a very small place, and tens of millions of people now use Facebook and other social media. A generation ago, students studying abroad or people working in the Peace Corps overseas would send a letter back home, and it would take up to 2 weeks or more to arrive. It would take another week or 2 for them to hear back from their parents. Now even in poor parts of the world, access to computers and smartphones lets us communicate instantly with people across the planet.

As the world becomes a smaller place, it becomes possible for different cultures to have more contact with each other. This contact, too, leads to social change to the extent that one culture adopts some of the norms, values, and other aspects of another culture. Anyone visiting a poor nation and seeing Coke, Pepsi, and other popular U.S. products in vending machines and stores in various cities will have a *culture shock* that reminds us instantly of the influence of one culture on another. For better or worse, this impact means that the world's diverse cultures are increasingly giving way to a more uniform *global culture*.

This process has been happening for more than a century. The rise of newspapers, the development of trains and railroads, and the invention of the telegraph, telephone, and, later, radio and television allowed cultures in different parts of the world to communicate with each other in ways not previously possible. Affordable jet transportation, cell phones, the Internet, and other modern technology have taken such communication a gigantic step further.

As mentioned earlier, many observers fear that the world is becoming Westernized as Coke, Pepsi, McDonald's, and other products and companies invade other cultures. Others say that Westernization is a good thing, because these products, but especially more important ones like refrigerators and computers, do make people's lives easier and therefore better. Still other observers say the impact of Westernization has been exaggerated. Both within the United States and across the world, these observers say, many cultures continue to thrive, and people continue to hold on to their ethnic identities.

Cultural Lag

An important aspect of social change is cultural lag, a term popularized by sociologist William F. Ogburn (1922/1966). When there is a change in one aspect of society or culture, this change often leads to and even forces a change in another aspect of society or culture. However, often some time lapses before the latter change occurs. **Cultural lag** refers to this delay between the initial social change and the resulting social change.

Discussions of examples of cultural lag often feature a technological change as the initial change. Ogburn (1922/1966) cited one such example from the decades after the American Civil War: the rise of the machine age. The development of factories during the Industrial Revolution meant that work became much more dangerous than before. More industrial accidents occurred, but injured workers were unable to receive adequate financial compensation because the existing law of negligence allowed them to sue only the person—a fellow worker—whose negligence caused the injury. However, negligent workers were typically very poor themselves and thus unable to provide meaningful compensation if they were sued. This meant that injured workers in effect could receive no money for their injuries.

Over time, the sheer number of industrial accidents and rising labor protest movement pressured lawmakers to help injured workers receive financial assistance. Some states began to allow workers to sue the companies whose dangerous workplaces were responsible for their injuries, and juries awarded these workers huge sums of money. Fearing these jury awards, in the early 1900s the manufacturing industry finally developed the process now called *workers' compensation*, which involves fairly automatic payments for workplace injuries without the necessity of lawsuits (Barkan, 2009). The delay of several decades between the rise of factories and industrial accidents and the eventual establishment of workers' compensation is a fine example of cultural lag.

A more recent example of cultural lag involves changes in child custody law brought about by changes in reproductive technology. Developments in reproductive technology have allowed same-sex couples to have children conceived from a donated egg and/or donated sperm. If a same-sex couple later breaks up, it is not yet clear who should win custody of the couple's child or children because traditional custody law is based on the premise of a divorce of a married heterosexual couple who are both the biological parents of their children. Yet custody law is slowly evolving to recognize the parental rights of same-sex couples. Some cases from California are illustrative.

In 2005, the California Supreme Court issued rulings in several cases involving lesbian parents who ended their relationship. In determining custody and visitation rights and child support obligations, the court decided that the couples should be treated under the law as if they had been heterosexual parents, and it decided on behalf of the partners who were seeking custody/visitation rights and child support. More generally, the court granted same-sex parents all the legal rights and responsibilities of heterosexual parents. The change in marital law that is slowly occurring because of changes in reproductive technology is another example of cultural lag. As the legal director of the National Center for Lesbian Rights said of the California cases, "Same-sex couples are now able to procreate and have children, and the law has to catch up with that reality" (Paulson & Wood, 2005, p. 1).

The Natural Environment

Changes in the natural environment can also lead to changes in a society itself. We see the clearest evidence of this when a major hurricane, an earthquake, or another natural disaster strikes. Three recent disasters illustrate this phenomenon. In April 2010, an oil rig operated by BP, an international oil and energy company, exploded in the Gulf of Mexico, creating what many observers called the worst environmental disaster in U.S. history; its effects on the ocean, marine animals, and the economies of states and cities affected by the oil spill will be felt for decades to come. In January 2010, a devastating earthquake struck Haiti and killed more than 250,000 people, or about 2.5% of that nation's population. A month later, an even stronger earthquake hit Chile. Although this earthquake killed only hundreds (it was relatively far from Chile's large cities and the Chilean buildings were sturdily built), it still caused massive damage to the nation's infrastructure. The effects of these natural disasters on the economy and society of each of these two countries will certainly also be felt for many years to come.

As is evident in this photo taken in the aftermath of the 2010 earthquake that devastated Haiti, changes in the natural environment can lead to profound changes in a society. Environmental changes are one of the many sources of social change.

United Nations Development Programme – Haiti Earthquake – CC BY-NC-ND 2.0.

Slower changes in the environment can also have a large social impact. As noted earlier, one of the negative effects of industrialization has been the increase in pollution of our air, water, and ground. With estimates of the number of U.S. deaths from air pollution ranging from a low of 10,000 to a high of 60,000 (Reiman & Leighton, 2010), pollution certainly has an important impact on our society. Climate change, a larger environmental problem, has also been relatively slow in arriving but threatens the whole planet in ways that climate change researchers have already documented and will no doubt be examining for the rest of our lifetimes and beyond (Schneider, Rosencranz, Mastrandrea, & Kuntz-Duriseti, 2010). Chapter 20 "Social Change and the Environment", Section 20.3 "Society and the Environment" and Section 20.4 "Understanding the Environment" examine the environment at greater length.

Social Conflict: War and Protest

Change also results from social conflict, including wars, ethnic conflict, efforts by social movements to change society, and efforts by their opponents to maintain the status quo. The immediate impact that wars have on societies is obvious, as the deaths of countless numbers of soldiers and civilians over the ages have affected not only the lives of their loved ones but also the course of whole nations. To take just one of many examples, the defeat of Germany in World War I led to a worsening economy during the next decade that in turn helped fuel the rise of Hitler.

One of the many sad truisms of war is that its impact on a society is greatest when the war takes place within the society's boundaries. For example, the Iraq war that began in 2003 involved two countries more than any others, the United States and Iraq. Because it took place in Iraq, many more Iraqis than Americans died or were wounded, and the war certainly affected Iraqi society—its infrastructure, economy, natural resources, and so forth—far more than it affected American society. Most Americans continued to live their normal lives, whereas most Iraqis had to struggle to survive the many ravages of war.

Historians and political scientists have studied the effect of war on politics and the economy. War can change a nation's political and economic structures in obvious ways, as when the winning nation forces a new political system and leadership on the losing nation. Other political and economic changes brought by war are subtler. World War I provides an interesting example of such changes. Before the war, violent labor strikes were common in Britain and other European nations. When the war began, a sort of truce developed between management and labor, as workers wanted to appear patriotic by supporting the war effort and hoped that they would win important labor rights for doing so. However, the truce soon dissolved after prices began to rise and wages did not. Labor-management conflict resumed and became very intense by the end of the war.

This conflict in turn forced European political and business leaders to grant several concessions to labor, which thus achieved gains, however limited, in political and economic power. Labor's participation in the war effort helped it win these concessions. As a historian summarized this connection,

> By the end of the war, labor's wartime mobilization and participation had increased its relative power within European societies. As a result, and despite the fact that endeavors to reward labor for its wartime cooperation were, in general, provisional, partial, and half-hearted, it was nonetheless the case that labor achieved some real gains. (Halperin, 2004, p. 155)

Other types of nonobvious social changes have resulted from various wars. For example, the deaths of so many soldiers during the American Civil War left many wives and mothers without their family's major breadwinner. Their poverty forced many of these women to turn to prostitution to earn an income, resulting in a rise in prostitution after the war (Marks, 1990). Some 80 years later, the involvement of many African Americans in the U.S. armed forces during World War II helped begin the racial desegregation of the military. This change is widely credited with helping spur the hopes of African Americans in the South that racial desegregation would someday occur in their hometowns (McKeeby, 2008).

Social movements have also been major forces for social change. Despite African American involvement in World War II, racial segregation in the South ended only after thousands of African Americans, often putting their lives on the line for their cause, engaged in sit-ins, marches, and massive demonstrations during the 1950s and 1960s. The Southern civil rights movement is just one of the many social movements that have changed American history, and we return to these movements in Chapter 21 "Collective Behavior and Social Movements".

Key Takeaways

- Major sources of social change include population growth and composition, culture and technology, the natural environment, and social conflict.
- Cultural lag refers to a delayed change in one sector of society in response to a change in another sector of

society.

For Your Review

1. Write a brief essay in which you comment on the advantages and disadvantages of cell phones for social relationships.
2. The text states that courts are beginning to grant same-sex couples the same parental rights and responsibilities that heterosexual couples have. Do you believe that this is a positive development or a negative development? Explain your answer.

References

Barkan, S. E. (2009). *Law and society: An introduction.* Upper Saddle River, NJ: Prentice Hall.

Crowley, D., & Heyer, P. (2011). *Communication in history: Technology, culture, society* (6th ed.). Boston, MA: Allyn & Bacon.

Halperin, S. (2004). *War and social change in modern Europe: The great transformation revisited.* Cambridge, England: Cambridge University Press.

Leonard, J. (1998, September 25). Crowding puts crunch on classrooms. *The Los Angeles Times,* p. B1.

Marks, P. (1990). *Bicycles, bangs, and bloomers: The new woman in the popular press.* Lexington: University Press of Kentucky.

McKeeby, D. (2008, February 25). End of U.S. military segregation set stage for rights movement. Retrieved from http://www.america.gov/st/peopleplace-english/2008/February/20080225120859liameruoy0.9820215.html.

Ogburn, W. F. (1966). *Social change with respect to cultural and original nature.* New York, NY: Dell. (Original work published1922).

Paulson, A., & Wood, D. B. (2005, August 25). California court affirms gay parenting. *The Christian Science Monitor,* p. 1.

Reiman, J., & Leighton, P. (2010). *The rich get richer and the poor get prison: Ideology, class, and criminal justice* (9th ed.). Upper Saddle River, NJ: Prentice Hall.

Schneider, S. H., Rosencranz, A., Mastrandrea, M. D., & Kuntz-Duriseti, K. (Eds.). (2010). *Climate change science and policy.* Washington, DC: Island Press.

20.3 Society and the Environment

Learning Objectives

1. List two reasons that make the environment an appropriate topic for sociologists to study.
2. Describe two of the environmental problems facing the world today.

At first glance, the environment does not seem to be a sociological topic. The natural and physical environment is something that geologists, meteorologists, oceanographers, and other scientists should be studying, not sociologists. Yet the environment is very much a sociological topic for at least five reasons. First, our worst environmental problems are the result of human activity, and this activity, like many human behaviors, is a proper topic for sociological study. Second, environmental problems have a significant impact on people, as do the many other social problems that sociologists study. Third, solutions to our environmental problems require changes in economic and environmental policies, and the potential impact of these changes depends heavily on social and political factors. Fourth, many environmental problems reflect and illustrate social inequality based on social class and on race and ethnicity: as with many issues in our society, the poor and people of color often fare worse when it comes to the environment. Fifth, efforts to improve the environment, often called the *environmental movement*, constitute a social movement and, as such, are again worthy of sociological study.

All these considerations suggest that the environment is quite fittingly a sociological topic, and one on which sociologists should have important insights. In fact, so many sociologists study the environment that their collective study makes up a subfield in sociology called **environmental sociology**, which refers simply to the sociological study of the environment. More specifically, environmental sociology is the study of the interaction between human behavior and the natural and physical environment.

Environmental sociology assumes "that humans are part of the environment and that the environment and society can only be fully understood in relation to each other" (McCarthy & King, 2009, p. 1). According to a report by the American Sociological Association, environmental sociology "has provided important insights" (Nagel, Dietz, & Broadbent, 2010, p. 13) into such areas as public opinion about the environment, the influence of values on people's environmental behavior, and inequality in the impact of environmental problems on communities and individuals. We will examine some of these insights after first reviewing the serious state of the environment.

To say that the world is in peril environmentally might sound extreme, but the world is in fact in peril. People are responsible for the world's environmental problems, and we have both the ability and the responsibility to address these problems. As sociologists Leslie King and Deborah McCarthy (2009, p. ix) assert,

> We both strongly believe that humans have come to a turning point in terms of our destruction of ecological resources and endangerment of human health. A daily look at the major newspapers points, without fail, to worsening environmental

problems....Humans created these problems and we have the power to resolve them. Naturally, the longer we wait, the more devastating the problems will become; and the more we ignore the sociological dimensions of environmental decline the more our proposed solutions will fail.

A few facts and figures on selected issues will indicate the extent and seriousness of the environmental problem.

Air Pollution

Air pollution probably kills thousands of Americans every year and 2 million people across the planet.

Lei Han – Shanghai – CC BY-NC-ND 2.0.

We have already mentioned that air pollution is estimated to kill at least 10,000 Americans, and possibly as many as 60,000, every year. The worldwide toll is much greater, and the World Health Organization (2008) estimates that 2 million people across the globe die every year from air pollution. These deaths typically result from the health conditions that air pollution causes, including heart disease, lung cancer, and respiratory disease such as asthma. Most air pollution stems from the burning of fossil fuels such as oil, gas, and coal. This problem occurs not only in the wealthy industrial nations but also in the nations of the developing world; countries such as China and India have some of the worst air pollution. In developing nations, mortality rates of people in cities with high levels of particulate matter (carbon, nitrates, sulfates, and other particles) are 15%–50% higher than the mortality rates of those in cleaner cities. In European countries, air pollution is estimated to reduce average life expectancy by 8.6 months. The World Health Organization (2008) does not exaggerate when it declares that air pollution "is a major environmental health problem affecting everyone in developed and developing countries alike."

Global Climate Change

The burning of fossil fuels also contributes to *global climate change*, often called *global warming*, thanks to the oft-discussed *greenhouse effect* caused by the trapping of gases in the atmosphere that is turning the earth warmer, with a rise of almost 1°C during the past century. In addition to affecting the ecology of the earth's polar regions and ocean levels throughout the planet, climate change threatens to produce a host of other problems, including increased disease transmitted via food and water, malnutrition resulting from decreased agricultural production and drought, and a higher incidence of hurricanes and other weather disasters. All these problems have been producing, and will continue to produce, higher mortality rates across the planet. The World Health Organization (2010) estimates that climate change annually causes more than 140,000 excess deaths worldwide.

Water Pollution and Inadequate Sanitation

Water quality in wealthy and developing nations is also a serious problem. Drinking water is often unsafe because of poor sanitation procedures for human waste and because of industrial discharge into lakes, rivers, and streams. Inadequate sanitation and unsafe drinking water cause parasitic infections and diseases such as diarrhea, malaria, cholera, intestinal worms, typhoid, and hepatitis A. The World Health Organization estimates that unsafe drinking water and inadequate sanitation annually cause the following number of deaths worldwide: (a) 1.4 million child deaths from diarrhea; (b) 500,000 deaths from malaria; and (c) 860,000 child deaths from malnutrition. At least 200 million more people annually suffer at least one of these serious diseases resulting from inadequate sanitation and unsafe drinking water (Prüss-Üstün, Bos, Gore, & Bartram, 2008).

Hazardous Waste Sites

Love Canal, an area in Niagara Falls, New York, was the site of chemical dumping that led to many birth defects and other health problems.

Wikimedia Commons – public domain.

Hazardous waste sites are parcels of land and water that have been contaminated by the dumping of dangerous chemicals into the ground by factories and other industrial buildings. The most famous (or rather, infamous) hazardous waste site in the United States is undoubtedly Love Canal, an area in a corner of Niagara Falls, New York. During the 1940s and 1950s, a chemical company dumped 20,000 tons of toxic chemicals into the canal and then filled it in with dirt and sold it for development to the local school board. A school and more than 800 homes, many of them low-income, were later built just near the site. The chemicals eventually leached into the groundwater, yards, and basements of the homes, reportedly causing birth defects and other health problems.

The Superfund program of the U.S. Environmental Protection Agency (EPA), begun about 30 years ago, monitors and cleans up hazardous waste sites throughout the country. Since its inception, the Superfund program has identified and taken steps to address more than 1,300 hazardous waste sites. About 11 million people live within one mile of one of these sites.

Key Takeaways

- The environment is a proper topic for sociological study. Environmental problems have a significant impact on people, and solutions to these problems require changes in economic and environmental policies.
- Air pollution, global climate change, water pollution and inadequate sanitation, and hazardous waste are major environmental problems that threaten the planet.

For Your Review

1. Of the several reasons that the environment is a proper topic for sociological study, which reason do you think is the most compelling? Explain your answer.
2. List one thing you did yesterday that was good for the environment and one thing that was bad for the environment.

References

King, L., & McCarthy, D. (Eds.). (2009). *Environmental sociology: From analysis to action* (2nd ed.). Lanham, MD: Rowman & Littlefield.

McCarthy, D., & King, L. (2009). Introduction: Environmental problems require social solutions. In L. King & D. McCarthy (Eds.), *Environmental sociology: From analysis to action* (2nd ed., pp. 1–22). Lanham, MD: Rowman & Littlefield.

Prüss-Üstün, A., Bos, R., Gore, F., & Bartram, J. (2008). *Safer water, better health: Costs, benefits and sustainability of interventions to protect and promote health*. Geneva, Switzerland: World Health Organization.

Nagel, J., Dietz, T., & Broadbent, J. (Eds.). (2010). *Workshop on sociological perspectives on global climate change*. Washington, DC: National Science Foundation and American Sociological Association.

World Health Organization. (2008). Air quality and health. Retrieved from http://www.who.int/mediacentre/factsheets/fs313/en/index.html.

20.4 Understanding the Environment

Learning Objectives

1. Describe what is meant by the assertion that environmental problems are human problems.
2. Explain the concepts of environmental inequality and environmental racism.

Sociologists emphasize two important dimensions of the relationship between society and the environment: (a) the impact of human activity and decision making and (b) the existence and consequences of environmental inequality and environmental racism.

Human Activity and Decision Making

Perhaps more than anything else, environmental sociologists emphasize that *environmental problems are the result of human decisions and activities that harm the environment.* Masses of individuals acting independently of each other make decisions and engage in activities that harm the environment, as when we leave lights on, keep our homes too warm in the winter or too cool in the summer, and drive SUVs and other motor vehicles that get low gas mileage. Corporations, government agencies, and other organizations also make decisions and engage in activities that greatly harm the environment. Sometimes individuals and organizations know full well that their activities are harming the environment, and sometimes they just act carelessly without much thought about the possible environmental harm of their actions. Still, the environment is harmed whether or not they intend to harm it.

In the examples of environmental problems we reviewed in Chapter 20 "Social Change and the Environment", Section 20.3 "Society and the Environment"—air pollution, climate change, water pollution, and hazardous waste sites—the human factor is obvious: our personal behavior, the actions of corporations, and the weakness of government environmental regulation are all to blame for the serious environmental problems that threaten the planet. Yet we even see the heavy hand of human involvement in certain accidents and "acts of nature" that harm the environment.

A recent example of this "heavy hand" is the BP oil spill that began in April 2010 when an oil rig leased by BP exploded in the Gulf of Mexico and eventually released almost 5 million barrels of oil (about 200 million gallons) into the ocean. Congressional investigators later concluded that BP had made a series of decisions that "increased the danger of a catastrophic well," including a decision to save money by using an inferior casing for the well that made an explosion more likely. A news report paraphrased the investigators as concluding that "some of the decisions appeared to violate industry guidelines and were made despite warnings from BP's own employees and outside contractors" (Fountain, 2010, p. A1).

The April 2010 BP oil spill occurred after BP made several decisions that may have increased the possibility of a catastrophic explosion of the well.

International Bird Rescue Research Center – Gulf Oiled Pelicans June 3, 2010 – CC BY 2.0.

Sociologists McCarthy and King (2009) cite several other environmental accidents that stemmed from reckless decision making and natural disasters in which human decisions accelerated the harm that occurred. One accident occurred in Bhopal, India, in 1984, when a Union Carbide pesticide plant leaked 40 tons of deadly gas. Between 3,000 and 16,000 people died immediately and another half million suffered permanent illnesses or injuries. A contributing factor for the leak was Union Carbide's decision to save money by violating safety standards in the construction and management of the plant.

A second preventable accident was the 1989 *Exxon Valdez* oil tanker disaster, in which the tanker hit ground off the coast of Alaska and released 11 million gallons of oil into Prince William Sound. Among other consequences, the spill killed hundreds of thousands of birds and marine animals and almost destroyed the local fishing and seafood industries. The immediate cause of the accident was that the ship's captain was an alcoholic and left the bridge in the hands of an unlicensed third mate after drinking five double vodkas in the hours before the crash occurred. Exxon officials knew of his alcoholism but let him command the ship anyway. Also, if the ship had had a double hull (one hull inside the other), it might not have cracked on impact or at least would have released less oil, but Exxon and the rest of the oil industry had successfully lobbied Congress not to require stronger hulls.

Hurricane Katrina was a more recent environmental disaster in which human decision making resulted in a great deal of preventable damage. After Katrina hit the Gulf Coast and especially New Orleans in August 2005, the resulting wind and flooding killed more than 1,800 people and left more than 700,000 homeless. McCarthy and King (2009, p. 4) again attribute much of this damage to human decision making: "While hurricanes are typically considered 'natural disasters,' Katrina's extreme consequences must be considered the result of social and political failures." Long before Katrina hit, it was well known that a major flood could easily breach New Orleans levees and have a devastating impact. Despite this knowledge, U.S., state, and local officials did nothing over the years to strengthen or rebuild the levees. In addition, coastal land that would have protected New Orleans had been lost over time to commercial and residential development.

According to sociologist Nicole Youngman (2009, p. 176), this development also "placed many more people and structures in harm's way than had existed there during previous hurricanes." All these factors led Youngman (2009, p. 176) to conclude that Katrina's impact "demonstrated how a myriad of human and nonhuman factors can come together to produce a profoundly traumatic event." In short, the flooding after Katrina was a human disaster, not a natural disaster.

Environmental Inequality and Environmental Racism

A second emphasis of environmental sociology is *environmental inequality* and the related concept of *environmental racism*. **Environmental inequality** (also called *environmental injustice*) refers to the fact that low-income people and people of color are disproportionately likely to experience various environmental problems, while **environmental racism** refers just to the greater likelihood of people of color to experience these problems (Bullard & Johnson, 2009; Mascarenhas, 2009). The term **environmental justice** refers to scholarship on environmental inequality and racism and public policy efforts and activism aimed at reducing these forms of inequality and racism. The "Sociology Making a Difference" box discusses scholarship on environmental racism that contributed to interest in, and concern about, this topic and to public policy aimed at addressing it.

Sociology Making a Difference

Environmental Racism in the Land of Cotton

During the 1970s, people began to voice concern about the environment in the United States and across the planet. As research on the environment grew by leaps and bounds, some scholars and activists began to focus on environmental inequality in general and on environmental racism in particular. During the 1980s and 1990s, their research and activism spawned the environmental justice movement that has since shed important light on environmental inequality and racism and helped reduce these problems.

Research by sociologists played a key role in the beginning of the environmental justice movement and continues to play a key role today. Robert D. Bullard of Clark Atlanta University stands out among these sociologists for the impact of his early work in the 1980s on environmental racism in the South and for his continuing scholarship since then. He has been called "the father of environmental justice" and was named by *Newsweek* as one of the 13 most influential environmental leaders of the 20th century, along with environmental writer Rachel Carson, former vice president Al Gore, and 10 others.

Bullard's first research project on environmental racism began in the late 1970s after his wife, an attorney, filed a lawsuit on behalf of black residents in Atlanta who were fighting the placement of a landfill in their neighborhood. To collect data for the lawsuit, Bullard studied the placement of landfills in other areas. He found that every city-owned landfill in Houston was in a black neighborhood, even though African Americans amounted to only one-fourth of Houston residents at the time. He also found that three out of four privately owned landfills were in black neighborhoods, as were six of the eight city-owned incinerators. He extended his research to other locations and later recalled what he discovered: "Without a doubt, it was a form of apartheid where whites were making decisions and black people and brown people and people of color, including Native Americans on reservations, had no seat at the table" (Dicum, 2006).

In 1990, Bullard published his findings in his book *Dumping in Dixie: Race, Class, and Environmental Quality* (Bullard, 1990). This book described the systematic placement in several Southern states of toxic waste sites, landfills, and chemical plants in communities largely populated by low-income residents and/or African Americans. *Dumping in Dixie* was the first book to examine environmental racism and is widely credited with helping advance the environmental justice movement. It received some notable awards, including the Conservation Achievement Award from the National Wildlife Federation.

More recently, Bullard, along with other sociologists and scholars from other disciplines, has documented the impact of race and poverty on the experience of New Orleans residents affected by the flooding after Hurricane Katrina. As in many other cities, African Americans and other low-income people largely resided in the lower elevations in New Orleans, and whites and higher-income people largely resided in the higher elevations. The flooding naturally had a much greater impact on the lower elevations and thus on African Americans and the poor. After the flood, African Americans seeking new housing in various real estate markets were more likely than whites to be told that no housing was available (Bullard & Wright, 2009).

For more than three decades, Robert D. Bullard has documented environmental racism in the South and elsewhere in the United States. His work alerted the nation to this issue and helped motivate the Environmental Protection Agency in the 1990s to begin paying attention to it. Once again, sociology has made a difference.

For example, almost all of the hazardous waste sites already mentioned are located in or near neighborhoods and communities that are largely populated by low-income people and people of color. When factories dump dangerous chemicals into rivers and lakes, the people living nearby are very likely to be low-income and of color. Around the world, the people most affected by climate change and other environmental problems are those in poor nations and, even within those nations, those who are poorer rather than those who are wealthier.

Global climate change is very likely to have its greatest impact on people in the poorest nations, even though these nations are the least responsible for greenhouse gases.

Hamed Saber – The Nomads' Simple LIfe – CC BY 2.0.

According to the American Sociological Association report mentioned earlier, the emphasis of environmental sociology on environmental inequality reflects the emphasis that the larger discipline of sociology places on social inequality: "A central finding of sociology is that unequal power dynamics shape patterns of social mobility and access to social, political, and economic resources" (Nagel, Dietz, & Broadbent, 2010, p. 17). The report adds that global climate change will have its greatest effects on the poorest nations: "Many of the countries least responsible for the rise in greenhouse gases will be most likely to feel its impacts in changes in weather, sea levels, health care costs, and economic hardships" (Nagel, Dietz, & Broadbent, 2010, p. 17).

An interesting controversy among environmental sociologists is whether social class or race plays a bigger role in environmental inequality. This controversy is called the "race-versus-class debate" (Mascarenhas, 2009). Some sociologists feel that environmental inequality is mostly a matter of social class and economic inequality, and some say that environmental inequality is mostly a matter of race and racial inequality. Taking a middle ground, other sociologists believe that environmental inequality reflects both racial and social class inequality.

Some evidence shows that while low-income people are the most likely to be exposed to environmental problems, this exposure is even more likely if they are people of color than if they are white. As a review of this evidence concluded,

> It would be fair to summarize this body of work as showing that the poor and especially the non-white poor bear a disproportionate burden of exposure to suboptimal, unhealthy environmental conditions in the United States. Moreover, the more researchers scrutinize environmental exposure and health data for racial and income inequalities, the stronger the evidence becomes that grave and widespread environmental injustices have occurred throughout the United States. (Evans & Kantrowitz, 2002, p. 323)

Regardless of the correct answer to the race-versus-class debate, the very existence of environmental inequality shows that social inequality in the larger society exposes some people much more than others to environmental dangers.

Improving the Environment: What Sociology Suggests

We have discussed two major emphases of environmental sociology. First, environmental problems are largely the result of human decision making and activity and thus preventable. Second, environmental problems disproportionately affect the poor and people of color.

These two insights have important implications for how to improve our environment. Simply put, we must change the behaviors and decisions of individuals, businesses, and other organizations that harm the environment, and we must do everything possible to lessen the extra environmental harm that the poor and people of color experience. Many environmental scholars and activists believe that these efforts need to focus on the corporations whose industrial activities are often so damaging to the air, water, and land. The "Learning From Other Societies" box discusses a lesson from Australia about the need for this sort of focus.

Learning From Other Societies

Lead Contamination Down Under

Lead is a toxic chemical that causes much damage, especially in children. Among the problems that lead poisoning causes are brain damage, kidney damage, and developmental disability.

During the 1980s, Australian officials responded to research linking lead to these problems by determining that several behaviors of children contributed to high lead levels. These behaviors included placing objects in one's mouth, nail biting, and not washing one's hands. But for children living in several smelter towns, the most important factor for their lead levels was whether they lived near a smelter.

Rather than focusing on the emissions from the smelter and on addressing the amount of lead that its activities had added to the surrounding land over the years, the Australian government instead advised parents to do a better job of household cleaning and of making sure that their children did not engage in the behaviors just listed, which contributed to their lead levels. A smelter official in the town of Port Pirie in South Australia said that "given reasonable care and hygiene, then you can live with the levels of contamination from past emissions."

Despite this official's assurance, lead blood levels continued to be too high. In 1993, a report by the South Australian Health Commission admitted that the focus on children's hygiene had not worked. Despite this conclusion, government efforts to address lead poisoning in other smelter towns during the 1990s continued to focus on household cleaning and children's personal hygiene. A study of this history of these Australian efforts concluded that the government there did not want to offend the lead companies and that the companies were more concerned with losing profits than with reducing lead pollution.

Because the government was reluctant to antagonize business, its efforts focused on the home and placed the responsibility for protecting children on their parents, especially mothers given their more central role in household work and child care. The Australian experience with lead suggests that efforts to improve the environment need to focus more on the corporations that damage the environment than on the behavior of private citizens. The behavior of private citizens is certainly important, but efforts that do not focus sufficiently on the source of environmental hazards will ultimately fail to improve our environment. From the Australian experience, the United States has much to learn. (Bryson, McPhillips, & Robinson, 2009)

Beyond these general approaches to improving the environment that sociological insights suggest, there are a number of strategies and policies that the United States and other nations could and should undertake to help the environment. Although a full discussion of these is beyond the scope of this chapter, a recent report by the Center for American Progress (Madrid, 2010) recommended a number of actions for the United States to undertake, including the following:

1. Establish mandatory electricity and natural gas reduction targets for utilities.
2. Expand renewable energy (wind and sun) by setting a national standard of 25% of energy to come from renewable sources by 2025.
3. Reduce deforestation by increasing the use of sustainable building materials and passing legislation to protect forests.
4. Reduce the use of fossil fuels by several measures, including higher fuel economy standards for motor vehicles and closing down older coal-fired power plants.
5. In cities, increase mass transit, develop more bicycle lanes, and develop more efficient ways of using electricity and water.

It is not an exaggeration to say that the fate of our planet depends on the successful implementation of these and other policies. Because, as sociology emphasizes, the environmental problems that confront the world are the result of human activity, changes in human activity are necessary to save the environment.

Key Takeaways

- Environmental problems are largely the result of human behavior and human decision making. Changes in human activity and decision making are thus necessary to improve the environment.
- Environmental inequality and environmental racism are significant issues. Within the United States and around the world, environmental problems are more often found where poor people and people of color reside.

For Your Review

1. Pretend you are on a debate team and that your team is asked to argue in favor of the following resolution: *Be it resolved, that air and water pollution is primarily the result of reckless human behavior rather than natural environmental changes*. Using evidence from the text, write a two-minute speech (about 300 words) in favor of the resolution.
2. How much of the environmental racism that exists do you think is intentional? Explain your answer.

References

Bryson, L., McPhillips, K., & Robinson, K. (2009). Turning public issues into private troubles: Lead contamination, domestic labor, and the exploitation of women's unpaid labor in Australia. In L. King & D. McCarthy (Eds.), *Environmental sociology: From analysis to action* (2nd ed., pp. 80–92). Lanham, MD: Rowman & Littlefield.

Bullard, R. D. (1990). *Dumping in Dixie: Race, class, and environmental quality*. Boulder, CO: Westview Press.

Bullard, R. D., & Johnson, G. S. (2009). Environmental justice: Grassroots activism and its impact on public policy decision making. In L. King & D. McCarthy (Eds.), *Environmental sociology: From analysis to action* (2nd ed., pp. 63–79). Lanham, MD: Rowman and Littlefield.

Bullard, R. D., & Wright, B. (2009). Race, place, and the environment in post-Katrina New Orleans. In R. D. Bullard & B. Wright (Eds.), *Race, place, and environmental justice after Hurricane Katrina: Struggles to reclaim, rebuild, and revitalize New Orleans and the Gulf Coast* (pp. 19–48). Boulder, CO: Westview Press.

Dicum, G. (2006, March 14). Meet Robert Bullard, the father of environmental justice. *Grist Magazine*. Retrieved from http://www.grist.org/article/dicum.

Evans, G. W., & Kantrowitz, E. (2002). Socioeconomic status and health: The potential role of environmental risk exposure. *Annual Review of Public Health, 23*(1), 303.

Fountain, H. (2010, June 15). Documents show risky decisions before BP blowout. *The New York Times*, p. A1.

Madrid, J. (2010). *From a "green farce" to a green future: Refuting false claims about immigrants and the environment*. Washington, DC: Center for American Progress.

Mascarenhas, M. (2009). Environmental inequality and environmental justice. In K. A. Gould & T. L. Lewis (Eds.), *Twenty lessons in environmental sociology* (pp. 127–141). New York, NY: Oxford University Press.

McCarthy, D., & King, L. (2009). Introduction: Environmental problems require social solutions. In L. King & D. McCarthy (Eds.), *Environmental sociology: From analysis to action* (2nd ed., pp. 1–22). Lanham, MD: Rowman & Littlefield.

Nagel, J., Dietz, T., & Broadbent, J. (Eds.). (2010). *Workshop on sociological perspectives on global climate change*. Washington, DC: National Science Foundation and American Sociological Association.

Youngman, N. (2009). Understanding disaster vulnerability: Floods and hurricanes. In K. A. Gould & T. L. Lewis (Eds.), *Twenty lessons in environmental sociology* (pp. 176–190). New York, NY: Oxford University Press.

20.5 End-of-Chapter Material

Summary

1. Social change involves the transformation of cultural norms and values, behavior, social institutions, and social structure. As societies become more modern, they become larger, more heterogeneous, and more impersonal, and their sense of community declines. Traditions decline as well, while individual freedom of thought and behavior increases. Some sociologists view modernization positively, while others view it negatively. Tönnies in particular lamented the shift from the *Gemeinschaft* of premodern societies to the *Gesellschaft* of modern societies. Durkheim also recognized the negative aspects of modernization but at the same time valued the freedom of modern societies and thought they retain a good amount of social solidarity from their division of labor.
2. A functionalist understanding of social change emphasizes that it is both natural and inevitable. Talcott Parsons's equilibrium model recognized that gradual change is desirable and ordinarily stems from such things as population growth and technological advances, but that any sudden social change disrupts society's equilibrium. Taking a very different view, conflict theory stresses that sudden social change is often both necessary and desirable to reduce inequality and to address other problems in society. Such social change often stems from intentional efforts by social movements to correct perceived deficiencies in the social, economic, and political systems.
3. Several sources of social change exist. These include population growth and changes in population composition, changes in culture and technology, changes in the natural environment, and social and ethnic conflict.
4. Environmental sociology is the sociological study of the environment. One major emphasis of environmental sociology is that environmental problems are largely the result of human activity and human decision making.
5. A second major emphasis of environmental sociology is that environmental problems disproportionately affect low-income people and people of color. These effects are called environmental inequality and environmental racism, respectively.

Using Sociology

You are in your second year in the public relations department of a medium-sized company that owns and operates three factories along the Mississippi River. Each of the factories is discharging toxic chemicals into the river in violation of federal safety standards, and each of the factories is located near a small town populated mostly by low-income residents. The percentage of African Americans in the three towns ranges from 33% to 55%. Having had an environmental sociology course in college, you are very concerned about the factories' pollution, but you also do not want to lose your job. Do you take any action to try to address this form of pollution, or do you remain silent? Explain your answer.

Chapter 21: Collective Behavior and Social Movements

Social Issues in the News

"N.J. Student Protests Showcase Facebook's Role in Mobilizing Social Movements," the headline said. On April 27, 2010, thousands of high school students across New Jersey walked out of their schools to protest budget cuts for secondary education. The mass protest began with a single Facebook page, "Protest NJ Education Cuts—State Wide School Walk Out," set up by Michelle Ryan Lauto, a first-year student at Pace University, who had graduated a year earlier from a state high school. Her Facebook site quickly attracted 18,000 members as word spread about the walkout. Students used Facebook to discuss news media contacts and other strategies for their protests, and Lauto logged on to tell everyone to keep their walkouts and rallies peaceful. In Newark, New Jersey, students also tweeted and texted to make sure that their citywide walkouts all occurred at the same time.

Lauto recognized how much Facebook and other social media had helped the students' cause: "You can use these social networking tools for very positive things—it's not just about kids putting up photos from their weekend party." She added, "All I did was make a Facebook page. Anyone who has an opinion could do that and have their opinion heard. I would love to see kids in high school step up and start their own protests and change things in their own way." (Heyboer, 2010; Hu, 2010)

Chapter 20 "Social Change and the Environment" noted that protest is an important source of social change. As the student walkouts across New Jersey illustrate, protest often involves mass numbers of individuals united in a cause; they sometimes know each other but often do not. Other kinds of mass behavior also exist, including crowds, riots, and rumors. These forms of mass behavior can also promote social change.

This chapter examines the social phenomena called *collective behavior* and *social movements*. These phenomena are a common feature of modern society and often attract much public attention when they occur. They also often arouse controversy because they tend to "shake things up" by upsetting the status quo. Accordingly, we will discuss the many types of collective behavior and social movements to get a sense of their origins, dynamics, and impact.

References

Heyboer, K. (2010, April 28). N.J. student protests showcase Facebook's role in mobilizing social movements. *Newark Star-Ledger*. Retrieved from http://www.nj.com/news/index.ssf/2010/2004/facebook_student_protest_mobilize.html.

Hu, W. (2010, April 27). In New Jersey, a civics lesson in the Internet age. *The New York Times*, p. A19.

21.1 Types of Collective Behavior

Learning Objectives

1. List the major types of collective behavior.
2. Explain the difference between conventional crowds and acting crowds.
3. Describe the behavior that typically occurs during and after a disaster.

Collective behavior is a term sociologists use to refer to a miscellaneous set of behaviors in which large numbers of people engage. More specifically, **collective behavior** refers to relatively spontaneous and relatively unstructured behavior by large numbers of individuals acting with or being influenced by other individuals. *Relatively spontaneous* means that the behavior is somewhat spontaneous but also somewhat planned, while *relatively unstructured* means that the behavior is somewhat organized and predictable but also somewhat unorganized and unpredictable. As we shall see, some forms of collective behavior are more spontaneous and unstructured than others, and some forms are more likely than others to involve individuals who act together as opposed to merely being influenced by each other. As a whole, though, collective behavior is regarded as less spontaneous and less structured than conventional behavior, such as what happens in a classroom, a workplace, or the other settings for everyday behavior with which we are very familiar.

As just noted, the term collective behavior refers to a miscellaneous set of behaviors. As such, these behaviors often have very little in common with each other, even if their basic features allow them to be classified as collective behavior. Common forms of collective behavior discussed in this section include crowds, mobs, panics, riots, disaster behavior, rumors, mass hysteria, moral panics, and fads and crazes. Of these forms, some (crowds, panics, riots, and disasters) involve people who are generally in each other's presence and who are more or less interacting with each other, while other forms (rumors, mass hysteria, moral panics, and fads and crazes) involve people who are not in each other's presence—in fact, they may be separated by hundreds or thousands of miles—but nonetheless share certain beliefs or concerns.

Another common form of collective behavior is the social movement. The study of social movements exploded in the 1960s and 1970s, and social movement scholarship now dwarfs scholarship on other forms of collective behavior. The second part of this chapter thus focuses solely on social movements.

Crowds

A **crowd** is a large number of people who gather together with a common short-term or long-term purpose. Sociologist Herbert Blumer (1969) developed a popular typology of crowds based on their purpose and dynamics.

The four types he distinguished are casual crowds, conventional crowds, expressive crowds, and acting crowds. A fifth type, protest crowds, has also been distinguished by other scholars.

Casual Crowd

A casual crowd is a collection of people who happen to be in the same place at the same time. It has no common identity or long-term purpose. This gathering of people waiting to cross the street is an example of a casual crowd.

Corey Templeton – Waiting to Walk – CC BY-NC-ND 2.0.

A *casual crowd* is a collection of people who happen to be in the same place at the same time. The people in this type of crowd have no real common bond, long-term purpose, or identity. An example of a casual crowd is a gathering of people who are waiting to cross the street at a busy intersection in a large city. True, they are all waiting to cross the street and to this degree do have a common goal, but this goal is temporary and this particular collection of people quickly disappears once this goal is achieved. As Erich Goode (1992, p. 22) emphasizes, "members of casual crowds have little else in common except their physical location." In fact, Goode thinks that casual crowds do not really act out collective behavior, since their behavior is relatively structured in that it follows conventional norms for behaving in such settings.

Conventional Crowd

A *conventional crowd* is a collection of people who gather for a specific purpose. They might be attending a movie, a play, a concert, or a lecture. Goode (1992) again thinks that conventional crowds do not really act out collective behavior; as their name implies, their behavior is very conventional and thus relatively structured.

Expressive Crowd

An *expressive crowd* is a collection of people who gather primarily to be excited and to express one or more emotions. Examples include a religious revival, a political rally for a candidate, and events like Mardi Gras. Goode (1992, p. 23) points out that the main purpose of expressive crowds

> is belonging to the crowd itself. Crowd activity for its members is an end in itself, not just a means. In conventional crowds, the audience wants to watch the movie or hear the lecture; being part of the audience is secondary or irrelevant. In expressive crowds, the audience also wants to be a member of the crowd, and participate in crowd behavior—to scream, shout, cheer, clap, and stomp their feet.

A conventional crowd may sometimes become an expressive crowd, as when the audience at a movie starts shouting if the film projector breaks. As this example indicates, the line between a conventional crowd and an expressive crowd is not always clear-cut. In any event, because excitement and emotional expression are defining features of expressive crowds, individuals in such crowds are engaging in collective behavior.

Acting Crowd

As its name implies, an *acting crowd* goes one important step beyond an expressive crowd by behaving in violent or other destructive behavior such as looting. A **mob**—an intensely emotional crowd that commits or is ready to commit violence—is a primary example of an acting crowd. Many films and novels about the Wild West in U.S. history depict mobs lynching cattle and horse rustlers without giving them the benefit of a trial. Beginning after the Reconstruction period following the Civil War, lynch mobs in the South and elsewhere hanged or otherwise murdered several thousand people, most of them African Americans, in what would now be regarded as hate crimes. A **panic**—a sudden reaction by a crowd that involves self-destructive behavior, as when people stomp over each other while fleeing a theater when a fire breaks out or while charging into a big-box store when it opens early with an amazing sale—is another example of an acting crowd. Acting crowds sometimes become so large and out of control that they develop into full-scale *riots*, which we discuss momentarily.

Protest Crowd

As identified by Clark McPhail and Ronald T. Wohlstein (1983), a fifth type of crowd is the protest crowd. As its name again implies, a *protest crowd* is a collection of people who gather to protest a political, social, cultural, or economic issue. The gatherings of people who participate in a sit-in, demonstration, march, or rally are all examples of protest crowds.

Riots

A **riot** is a relatively spontaneous outburst of violence by a large group of people. The term *riot* sounds very negative, and some scholars have used terms like *urban revolt* or *urban uprising* to refer to the riots that many U.S. cities experienced during the 1960s. However, most collective behavior scholars continue to use the term riot without necessarily implying anything bad or good about this form of collective behavior, and we use riot here in that same spirit.

Terminology notwithstanding, riots have been part of American history since the colonial period, when colonists often rioted regarding "taxation without representation" and other issues (Rubenstein, 1970). Between 75 and 100 such riots are estimated to have occurred between 1641 and 1759. Once war broke out with England, several dozen more riots occurred as part of the colonists' use of violence in the American Revolution. Riots continued after the new nation began, as farmers facing debts often rioted against state militia. The famous Shays's Rebellion, discussed in many U.S. history books, began with a riot of hundreds of people in Springfield, Massachusetts.

Rioting became even more common during the first several decades of the 19th century. In this period rioting was "as much a part of civilian life as voting or working" (Rosenfeld, 1997, p. 484), with almost three-fourths of U.S. cities experiencing at least one major riot. Most of this rioting was committed by native-born whites against African Americans, Catholics, and immigrants. Their actions led Abraham Lincoln to observe in 1837, "Accounts of outrages committed by mobs form the every-day news of the times…Whatever their causes be, it is common to the whole country" (quoted in Feldberg, 1980, p. 4).

Rioting continued after the Civil War. Whites attacked Chinese immigrants because they feared the immigrants were taking jobs from whites and keeping wages lower than they otherwise would have been. Labor riots also became common, as workers rioted to protest inhumane working conditions and substandard pay.

Race riots again occurred during the early 20th century, as whites continued to attack African Americans in major U.S. cities. A major riot in East St. Louis, Illinois, in 1917 took the lives of 39 African Americans and 9 whites. Riots begun by whites occurred in at least seven more cities in 1919 and ended with the deaths of dozens of people (Waskow, 1967). During the 1960s, riots took place in many Northern cities as African Americans reacted violently to reports of police brutality or other unfair treatment. Estimates of the number of riots during the decade range from 240 to 500, and estimates of the number of participants in the riots range from 50,000 to 350,000 (Downes, 1968; Gurr, 1989).

Types of Riots

Several types of riots may be identified according to the motivation and goals of the participants in the riots. One popular typology distinguishes between protest riots and celebration riots (McPhail, 1994). *Protest riots* express discontent regarding a political, social, cultural, or economic issue, while *celebration riots* express joy or delight over an event or outcome, such as the celebration of a football team's championship that gets out of hand. Protest riots are fundamentally political in nature, while celebration riots are decidedly apolitical.

Another popular typology distinguishes four types of riots: purposive, symbolic, revelous, and issueless (Goode, 1992). *Purposive riots* arise from dissatisfaction regarding a particular issue and are intended to achieve a specific goal regarding that issue. The colonial riots mentioned earlier are examples of purposive riots, as are many of the riots that have occurred in U.S. prisons during the past few decades. *Symbolic riots* express general discontent but do not really aim to achieve a specific goal. The early 20th-century riots by whites, also mentioned earlier, are examples of symbolic riots. *Revelous riots* are the same as the celebration riots already discussed, while *issueless riots* have no apparent basis or purpose. An example of an issueless riot is the looting and general violence that sometimes occurs during a citywide electrical outage.

An important factor in understanding rioting is the type of people who take part in a riot. The "Sociology Making a Difference" box discusses this issue.

Sociology Making a Difference

The "Scum of the Earth" View of Rioters

When a riot occurs, it is almost natural to think that the rioters must be out-of-control, violent individuals who come from and represent the dregs of society. In the study of riots and rioting, this belief is called the "scum of the earth" view. Reflecting this view, about a century ago an Italian scholar called rioters "criminals, madmen, the offspring of madmen, alcoholics, the slime of society, deprived of all moral sense, given over to crime" (Rule, 1988, p. 95). In scholarly circles this view, though often expressed in less extreme terms, was fairly popular from the end of the 19th century, when it was first formulated, through the 1960s.

If scholars and the public have this view of rioters, then it becomes easy to dismiss a riot as the irrational action of people not worthy of our attention and thus to not respond to any possible economic or political conditions that might have given rise to the riot. After the urban riots in U.S. cities began in the 1960s, politicians and the news media often depicted the urban rioters in negative terms that basically reflected a "scum of the earth" view. This depiction helped delegitimize the riots, which were thus seen not as protests against poverty and other conditions affecting U.S. cities but rather as wanton violence by the dregs of society.

Sociologists' research on the social backgrounds of the 1960s urban rioters provided an important corrective to this common view of the rioters. These sociologists found that the rioters were fairly typical of the average resident—in terms of employment, economic status, and other factors—of the areas in which the riots occurred. For example, a study of almost 3,400 people arrested during the large 1965 riot in the Watts district of South Los Angeles found that more than half had no previous criminal convictions and that the remainder had been convicted only of minor offenses. In fact, these offenses were less serious than those leading to the arrests of Los Angeles residents in 1965 for nonriot reasons. Researchers also found that the median educational level of the arrested rioters was the same as that of other residents of South Los Angeles, and their political views were also similar to the views of residents who had not participated in the riot.

An important conclusion from these and other findings on the 1960s urban rioters was that instead of being the "scum of the earth," the rioters were fairly typical and representative of the people in the communities where the riots occurred. These findings indicated that the riots could *not* easily be dismissed as the actions of the dregs of society but instead should be regarded, despite their violence, as protests against urban poverty that deserved to be heeded. By providing this perspective, the work by sociologists helped make a difference. (McPhail, 1971; Oberschall, 1967; Rule, 1988)

Social Movements

A **social movement** is an organized effort by a large number of people to bring about or impede social, political, economic, or cultural change. We have much more to say about social movements later in this chapter, but for now simply identify them as an important form of collective behavior that plays a key role in social change.

Disaster Behavior

A **disaster** is an accident or natural catastrophe that causes many deaths and much property destruction. Hurricanes, earthquakes, tornadoes, fires, and floods are the most common natural disasters, while the sinking of the *Titanic* and the April 2010 BP oil well explosion are among the most well-known accidents that had disastrous consequences. Some disasters, such as plane crashes and the *Titanic* sinking, are very "localized" and affect a relatively small number of people, however tragic the consequences might be for those directly affected. Other disasters, such as hurricanes and earthquakes, affect a much larger geographical area and number of people and thus have far-reaching consequences.

Some sociologists study why disasters occur, but sociologists interested in collective behavior study another aspect of disasters: how people behave during and after a disaster. We call this form of behavior **disaster behavior**.

When disasters occur, people's daily lives and normal routines are disrupted. As David L. Miller (2000, p. 250) observes,

> Disasters often strike without warning, and when they do, people face unexpected and unfamiliar problems that demand direct and prompt action. There is the obvious problem of sheer survival at the moment when disaster strikes. During impact, individuals must confront and cope with their fears while at the same time looking to their own and others' safety. After disaster impact, people encounter numerous problems demanding life-and-death decisions as they carry out rescues and aid the injured.

Over the next several days, weeks, and months, they must make many adjustments as their lives slowly return to normal, or at least as close to normal as can be expected. How do people generally behave while all this is going on?

A common belief is that people look out for themselves after a disaster occurs and that they panic and engage in "wild, selfish, individualistic, exploitative behavior" (Goode, 1992, p. 181). However, sociologists who study disaster behavior generally find that the opposite is true: people stay remarkably calm after a disaster occurs and for the most part do not react with terror or panic. As Goode (1992, p. 181) observes, "People tend to confer with others about the appropriate line of action. They weigh alternatives, consider consequences, and come up with socially and collectively reasoned solutions." In addition, relatively few people experience emotional shock. Friends, relatives, and even strangers tend to help one another and generally display a "high level of concern for and generosity toward disaster victims" (Miller, 2000, p. 274). Grief, depression, and other psychological consequences do occur, but these generally are no more serious than the reactions that follow the deaths of friends and family members caused by reasons other than disasters.

Rumors, Mass Hysteria, and Moral Panics

The types of collective behavior discussed so far—crowds, riots, and disaster behavior—all involve people who are often physically interacting with one another. As mentioned earlier, however, some forms of collective behavior involve people who are much more widespread geographically and who typically do not interact. Nonetheless, these people share certain beliefs and perceptions that sociologists classify as collective behavior. Two broad categories of these beliefs and perceptions have been distinguished: (a) rumors, mass hysteria, and moral panics; and (b) fads and crazes.

Rumors, mass hysteria, and moral panics all involve strongly held beliefs and perceptions that turn out to be not true at all or at least gross distortions of reality. A **rumor** is a story based on unreliable sources that is nonetheless passed on from one person to another person. A rumor may turn out to be true, but it often turns out to be false or at least to be an exaggeration or distortion of the facts. The defining feature of a rumor, though, is that when it arises it is not based on reliable evidence and thus is unsubstantiated (Goode, 1992). In today's electronic age, rumors can be spread very quickly over the Internet and via Facebook, Twitter, and other social media. In October 2010, a rumor quickly spread that Apple was planning to buy Sony. Although there was no truth to the rumor, Sony's stock shares rose in value after the rumor began (Albanesius, 2010).

Mass hysteria refers to widespread, intense fear of and concern for a danger that turns out to be false or greatly exaggerated. Episodes of mass hysteria are relatively rare. One that is often-cited is the "War of the Worlds" episode (Miller, 2000). On October 30, 1938, actor and director Orson Welles aired a radio adaptation of this famous story by H. G. Wells, which involved a Martian invasion of Earth. The show depicted the invasion occurring in New Jersey and New York, and thousands of listeners reportedly thought that an invasion was really occurring. This was decades before the Internet, so they called the police, National Guard, hospitals, and other sources for information and got in touch with friends and family members to share their fears. Although the next day newspapers carried many stories of stampedes in theaters, heart attacks, suicides, and other intense reactions to the radio show, these stories turned out to be false.

A **moral panic** is closely related to mass hysteria and refers to widespread concern over a perceived threat to the moral order that turns out to be false or greatly exaggerated. Often people become very concerned about a moral problem involving such behaviors as drug use and sexual activity. Their concerns may have no basis in reality or may greatly exaggerate the potential and actual danger posed by the problem. In either case, their strongly held moral views about the situation heighten their concern, and they often seek legislation or take other actions to try to battle the moral problem.

Goode and Nachman Ben-Yehuda (2009) describe several moral panics in American history. One of the most important was the concern over alcohol that motivated the Prohibition movement of the early 20th century. This movement was led primarily by rural Protestants who abhorred drinking as a moral and social sin. They thought drinking was a particular problem among urban residents, many of whom were Catholic Irish and Italian immigrants. Their Catholic faith and immigrant status contributed to the outrage that Prohibition activists felt about their alcohol use.

Another moral panic over a drug occurred during the 1930s and led to antimarijuana legislation. Marijuana had been legal before then, but Anglo Americans became concerned about its use among Mexican Americans.

Newspapers began to run articles about the effects of marijuana, which was said to turn its users into rapists and other types of violent criminals. The Federal Bureau of Narcotics provided "facts" about these effects to the news media, which published this misleading information.

As these two examples illustrate, moral panics often center on social groups that are already very unpopular, including the poor, people of color, and religious minorities. Prejudice against these groups fuels the rise and intensity of moral panics, and moral panics in turn reinforce and even increase this prejudice.

Fads and Crazes

Fads and crazes make up the second category of beliefs and perceptions that are considered to be collective behavior. A **fad** is a rather insignificant activity or product that is popular for a relatively short time, while a **craze** is a temporary activity that attracts the obsessive enthusiasm of a relatively small group of people (Goode, 1992). American history has witnessed many kinds of fads and crazes throughout the years, including goldfish swallowing, stuffing people into a telephone booth, and the notorious campus behavior known as streaking. Products that became fads include Rubik's Cube, Pet Rocks, Cabbage Patch dolls, and Beanie Babies. Cell phones were a fad when they first appeared, but they have become so common and important that they have advanced far beyond the definition of a fad.

Key Takeaways

- Collective behavior involves large numbers of people and is relatively spontaneous and relatively unstructured. Its major types include crowds, riots, rumors, and fads.
- Riots have been common in American history since the colonial era. Two major types of riots are protest riots, which are political in nature, and celebration riots, which are apolitical.
- Most disaster behavior is fairly calm and altruistic. Disaster victims generally do not react in a panicky or selfish manner.
- Moral panics often focus on unpopular groups in society, including the poor, people of color, and immigrants.

For Your Review

1. Think of the last time you were in one of the types of crowds discussed in the text. What type of crowd was it? Explain your answer.
2. Think of the last rumor you heard. As far as you know, did it turn out to be true, not true, or partly true but an exaggeration or distortion of the truth?

References

Albanesius, C. (2010, October 26). Apple buying Sony? Probably not. *PC Magazine*. Retrieved from http://www.pcmag.com/article2/0,2817,2371467,2371400.asp.

Blumer, H. (1969). Collective behavior. In A. M. Lee (Ed.), *Principles of sociology* (pp. 165–221). New York, NY: Barnes and Noble.

Downes, B. T. (1968). The social characteristics of riot cities: A comparative study. *Social Science Quarterly, 49,* 504–520.

Feldberg, M. (1980). *The turbulent era: Riot and disorder in Jacksonian America*. New York, NY: Oxford University Press.

Goode, E. (1992). *Collective behavior*. Fort Worth, TX: Harcourt Brace Jovanovich.

Goode, E., & Ben-Yehuda, N. (2009). *Moral panics: The social construction of deviance*. Malden, MA: Wiley-Blackwell.

Gurr, T. R. (1989). Protest and rebellion in the 1960s: The United States in world perspective. In T. R. Gurr (Ed.), *Violence in America: Protest, rebellion, reform* (Vol. 2, pp. 101–130). Newbury Park, CA: Sage.

McPhail, C. (1971). Civil disorder participation: A critical examination of recent research. *American Sociological Review, 36,* 1058–1073.

McPhail, C., & Wohlstein, R. T. (1983). Individual and collective behaviors within gatherings, demonstrations, and riots. *Annual Review of Sociology, 9,* 579–600.

Miller, D. L. (2000). *Introduction to collective behavior and collective action* (2nd ed.). Springfield, IL: Waveland Press.

Oberschall, A. (1967). The Los Angeles riot of August 1965. *Social Problems, 15,* 322–341.

Rosenfeld, M. J. (1997). Celebration, politics, selective looting and riots: A micro level study of the Bulls riot of 1992 in Chicago. *Social Problems, 44,* 483–502.

Rubenstein, R. E. (1970). *Rebels in Eden: Mass political violence in the United States*. Boston, MA: Little, Brown.

Rule, J. B. (1988). *Theories of civil violence*. Berkeley: University of California Press.

Waskow, A. I. (1967). *From race riot to sit-in: 1919 and the 1960s*. Garden City, NY: Anchor Books.

21.2 Explaining Collective Behavior

Learning Objectives

1. Discuss the major assumptions of contagion theory and why this theory is no longer popular.
2. Describe the central views of convergence theory.
3. Explain how emergent norm theory takes a middle ground between contagion theory and convergence theory.

Over the years, sociologists and other scholars have proposed many explanations of collective behavior. Most of these explanations have focused on crowds, riots, and social movements, rather than on rumors, fads, and other collective behaviors that involve less social interaction. Table 21.1 "Theory Snapshot" summarizes these explanations.

Table 21.1 Theory Snapshot

Theory	Major assumptions
Contagion theory	Collective behavior is emotional and irrational and results from the hypnotic influence of the crowd.
Convergence theory	Crowd behavior reflects the beliefs and intentions that individuals already share before they join a crowd.
Emergent norm theory	People are not sure how to behave when they begin to interact in collective behavior. As they discuss their potential behavior, norms governing their behavior emerge, and social order and rationality then guide their behavior.
Value-added theory	Collective behavior results when several conditions exist, including structural strain, generalized beliefs, precipitating factors, and lack of social control.

Contagion Theory

Contagion theory was developed by French scholar Gustave Le Bon (1841–1931) in his influential 1895 book, *The Crowd: A Study of the Popular Mind* (Le Bon, 1895/1960). Like many other intellectuals of his time, Le Bon was concerned about the breakdown of social order that was said to have begun with the French Revolution a century earlier and to have continued throughout the 19th century. Mob violence by the poor was common in the century in cities in Europe and the United States. Intellectuals, who tended to live in relatively wealthy circumstances, were very disturbed by this violence. They viewed it as irrational behavior, and they thought that the people taking part in it were being unduly swayed by strong emotions and the influence of other people in the mobs.

Le Bon's book and its contagion theory reflected these intellectuals' beliefs. When individuals are by themselves, he wrote, they act rationally, but when they are in a crowd, they come under its almost hypnotic influence and act irrationally and emotionally. They no longer can control their unconscious instincts and become violent and even savage. In short, contagion theory argues that collective behavior is irrational and results from the contagious influence of the crowds in which individuals find themselves.

Contagion theory assumes that people in a crowd act emotionally and irrationally because they come under the influence of the crowd's impulses.

Joanna – GREEKS PROTEST AUSTERITY CUTS – CC BY 2.0.

The views of contagion theory were popular well into the 20th century, but scholars came to believe that collective behavior is much more rational than Le Bon thought and also that individuals are not controlled by crowd influences as he thought.

Convergence Theory

Convergence theory is one of the theories that presented this new understanding of collective behavior. According to this theory, crowds do not unduly influence individuals to act in emotional and even violent ways. Rather, crowd behavior reflects the behavior and attitudes of the individuals who decide to join a crowd. Once they converge in a crowd, the behavior of the crowd is a consequence of their behavior and attitude. Instead of the crowd affecting the individuals in it, the individuals in it affect the crowd. Reflecting the adage that "birds of a feather flock together," people who feel a certain way about a particular issue and who wish to act in a certain way tend to find and converge with similar people. The crowd they form then reflects their beliefs and desired activities. As Goode (1992, p. 58) writes, convergence theory says that the way people act in crowds or publics is an expression or outgrowth of *who they are ordinarily*. It argues that like-minded people come together in, or *converge* on, a certain location where collective behavior can and will take place, where individuals can act out tendencies or traits they had in the first place. (emphasis in original)

Convergence theory does not deny that people may do something in a crowd that they would not do by themselves, but it does say that what a crowd does largely reflects the individuals who compose it. If we think of a mob or at least a small group of people who commit a hate crime—for example, gay bashing—we can see an application of convergence theory. The individuals who form this group are people who hate homosexuality and who hate gays and lesbians. The group violence they commit reflects these beliefs.

Emergent Norm Theory

Just after the mid-20th century, Ralph H. Turner and Lewis M. Killian (1957) presented their *emergent norm theory* of collective behavior, which downplayed the irrationality emphasized in earlier decades by Le Bon and other intellectuals. According to Turner and Killian, when people start interacting in collective behavior, initially they are not sure how they are supposed to behave. As they discuss their potential behavior and other related matters, norms governing their behavior emerge, and social order and rationality then guide behavior.

In at least two ways, emergent norm theory takes a middle ground between contagion theory and convergence theory. As should be clear, emergent norm theory views collective behavior as more rational than contagion theory does. But it also views collective behavior as less predictable than convergence theory does, as it assumes that people do not necessarily already share beliefs and intentions before they join a crowd.

Value-Added Theory

According to sociologist Neil Smelser, an important condition for protest is a precipitating factor: a sudden event that ignites people to take action. During the 1960s, several urban riots began when police were rumored to have unjustly arrested or beaten someone.

Anna – Busted… – CC BY 2.0.

One of the most popular and influential explanations of social movements and other forms of collective behavior is Neil Smelser's (1963) *value-added theory* (also called *structural-strain theory*). Smelser wrote that social movements and other collective behavior occur if and only if several conditions are present. One of these conditions is *structural strain,* which refers to problems in society that cause people to be angry and frustrated. Without such structural strain, people would not have any reason to protest, and social movements do not arise. Another condition is *generalized beliefs,* which are people's reasons for why conditions are so bad and their solutions to improve them. If people decide that the conditions they dislike are their own fault, they will decide not to protest. Similarly, if they decide that protest will not improve these conditions, they again will not protest. A third condition is the existence of *precipitating factors,* or sudden events that ignite collective behavior. In the 1960s, for example, several urban riots started when police were rumored to have unjustly arrested or beaten someone. Although conditions in inner cities were widely perceived as unfair and even oppressive, it took this type of police behavior to ignite people to riot. A fourth condition is *lack of social control*; collective behavior is more likely if potential participants do not expect to be arrested or otherwise hurt or punished.

Smelser's theory became very popular because it pointed to several factors that must hold true before social movements and other forms of collective behavior occur. However, collective behavior does not always occur when Smelser's factors do hold true. The theory has also been criticized for being a bit vague; for example, it does not say how much strain a society must have for collective behavior to take place (Rule, 1988).

Key Takeaways

- Contagion theory assumes that individuals act irrationally as they come under the hypnotic influence of a crowd. Collective behavior scholars now believe that collective behavior is much more rational than contagion theory assumed.
- Convergence theory assumes that crowd behavior reflects the preexisting values and beliefs and behavioral disposition of the individuals who join a crowd.
- Emergent norm theory assumes that norms emerge after people gather for collective behavior, and that their behavior afterward is largely rational.
- Value-added theory argues that collective behavior results when several conditions exist, including structural strain, generalized beliefs, precipitating factors, and lack of social control. All these conditions must exist for collective behavior to occur.

For Your Review

1. Which of the four theories of collective behavior presented in this section do you most favor? Explain your answer.
2. If riots are assumed to involve irrational behavior, how and why should that assumption affect perceptions of a particular riot and its possible consequences for public policy?

References

Bon, G. L. (1960). *The crowd: A study of the popular mind*. New York, NY: Viking Press. (Original work published 1895).

Goode, E. (1992). *Collective behavior*. Fort Worth, TX: Harcourt Brace Jovanovich.

Rule, J. B. (1988). *Theories of civil violence*. Berkeley: University of California Press.

Smelser, N. J. (1963). *Theory of collective behavior*. New York, NY: Free Press.

Turner, R. H., & Killian, L. M. (1957). *Collective behavior*. Englewood Cliffs, NJ: Prentice Hall.

21.3 Social Movements

Learning Objectives

1. List the major types of social movements.
2. Provide evidence against the assumption that discontent always leads to social movement activity.
3. Describe the stages of the life cycle of social movements.
4. Discuss examples of how social movements have made a positive difference.

Social movements in the United States and other nations have been great forces for social change. At the same time, governments and other opponents have often tried to thwart the movements' efforts. To understand how and why social change happens, we have to understand why movements begin, how they succeed and fail, and what impact they may have.

Understanding Social Movements

To begin this understanding, we first need to understand what social movements are. To reiterate a definition already presented, a **social movement** may be defined as an organized effort by a large number of people to bring about or impede social, political, economic, or cultural change. Defined in this way, social movements might sound similar to special-interest groups, and they do have some things in common. But a major difference between social movements and special-interest groups lies in the nature of their actions. Special-interest groups normally work *within the system* via conventional political activities such as lobbying and election campaigning. In contrast, social movements often work *outside the system* by engaging in various kinds of protest, including demonstrations, picket lines, sit-ins, and sometimes outright violence.

Social movements are organized efforts by large numbers of people to bring about or impede social change. Often they try to do so by engaging in various kinds of protest, such as the march depicted here.

Glenn Halog – Clampdown, We are the 99% – CC BY-NC 2.0.

Conceived in this way, the efforts of social movements amount to "politics by other means," with these "other means" made necessary because movements lack the resources and access to the political system that interest groups typically enjoy (Gamson, 1990).

Types of Social Movements

Sociologists identify several types of social movements according to the nature and extent of the change they seek. This typology helps us understand the differences among the many kinds of social movements that existed in the past and continue to exist today (Snow & Soule, 2009).

One of the most common and important types of social movements is the *reform* movement, which seeks limited, though still significant, changes in some aspect of a nation's political, economic, or social systems. It does not try to overthrow the existing government but rather works to improve conditions within the existing regime. Some of the most important social movements in U.S. history have been reform movements. These include the abolitionist movement preceding the Civil War, the women's suffrage movement that followed the Civil War, the labor movement, the Southern civil rights movement, the Vietnam era's antiwar movement, the contemporary women's movement, the gay rights movement, and the environmental movement.

A *revolutionary* movement goes one large step further than a reform movement in seeking to overthrow the existing government and to bring about a new one and even a new way of life. Revolutionary movements were common in the past and were responsible for the world's great revolutions in Russia, China, and several other nations. Reform and revolutionary movements are often referred to as *political* movements because the changes they seek are political in nature.

Another type of political movement is the *reactionary* movement, so named because it tries to block social change or to reverse social changes that have already been achieved. The antiabortion movement is a contemporary example of a reactionary movement, as it arose after the U.S. Supreme Court legalized most abortions in *Roe v. Wade* (1973) and seeks to limit or eliminate the legality of abortion.

One type of social movement is the self-help movement. As its name implies, the goal of a self-help movement is to help people improve their personal lives. These tokens are used at meetings of Alcoholics Anonymous, which is an example of a group involved in a self-help movement.

Chris Yarzab – Alcoholics Anonymous – Keep Coming Back – CC BY 2.0.

Two other types of movements are *self-help* movements and *religious* movements. As their name implies, self-help movements involve people trying to improve aspects of their personal lives; examples of self-help groups include Alcoholics Anonymous and Weight Watchers. Religious movements aim to reinforce religious beliefs among their members and to convert other people to these beliefs. Early Christianity was certainly a momentous religious movement, and other groups that are part of a more general religious movement today include the various religious cults discussed in Chapter 17 "Religion". Sometimes self-help and religious movements are difficult to distinguish from each other because some self-help groups emphasize religious faith as a vehicle for achieving personal transformation.

The Origins of Social Movements

To understand the origins of social movements, we need answers to two related questions. First, what are the social, cultural, and other factors that give rise to social movements? They do not arise in a vacuum, and people must become sufficiently unhappy for a social movement to arise. Second, once social movements do begin, why are some individuals more likely than others to take part in them?

Discontent With Existing Conditions and Relative Deprivation

For social movements to arise, certain political, economic, or other problems must first exist that prompt people to be dissastisfied enough to begin and join a social movement. These problems might include a faltering economy; a lack of political freedom; certain foreign policies carried out by a government; or discrimination based on gender, race and ethnicity, or sexual orientation. In this regard, recall that one of the essential conditions for collective behavior in Smelser's value-added theory is *structural strain*, or social problems that cause people to be angry and frustrated. Without such structural strain, people would not have any reason to protest, and social movements would not arise.

Whatever the condition, the dissatisfaction it generates leads to *shared discontent* (also called *shared grievances*) among some or most of the population that then may give rise to a social movement. This discontent arises in part because people feel deprived relative to some other group or to some ideal state they have not reached. This feeling is called **relative deprivation**. The importance of relative deprivation for social protest was popularized by James C. Davies (1962) and Ted Robert Gurr (1970), both of whom built on the earlier work of social psychologists who had studied frustration and aggression. When a deprived group perceives that social conditions are improving, wrote Davies, they become hopeful that their lives are getting better. But if these conditions stop improving, they become frustrated and more apt to turn to protest, collective violence, and other social movement activity. Both Davies and Gurr emphasized that people's *feelings* of being relatively deprived were more important for their involvement in collective behavior than their level of actual deprivation.

Relative deprivation theory was initially very popular, but scholars later pointed out that frustration often does not lead to protest, as people can instead blame themselves for the deprivation they feel and thus not protest (Gurney & Tierney, 1982). Scholars who favor the theory point out that people will ordinarily not take part in social movements unless they feel deprived, even if many who do feel deprived do not take part (Snow & Oliver, 1995).

Although discontent may be an essential condition for social movements (as well as for riots and other collective behavior that are political in nature), discontent does not always lead to a social movement or other form of collective behavior. For example, it might be tempting to think that a prison riot occurred because conditions in the prison were awful, but some prisons with awful conditions do not experience riots. Thus, although discontent may be an essential condition for social movements (and other collective behavior) to arise, discontent by itself does not guarantee that a social movement will begin and that discontented people will take part in the movement once it has begun.

An often-cited study that documented this fundamental point concerned the peace movement in the Netherlands during the 1980s (Klandermans & Oegema, 1987). The movement was trying to prevent the deployment of cruise missiles, and a survey of a town near Amsterdam revealed that about 75% of the town's residents were opposed to the deployment. However, only about 5% of these residents took part in a protest that the peace movement organized against the deployment. Thus, there is a huge drop-off from the number of potential social movement participants (*sympathizers*), in terms of their discontent with an existing problem or concern about an issue, to the number of actual social movement participants (*activists*).

Social Networks and Recruitment

This huge drop-off from sympathizers to activists underscores another fundamental point of social movement scholarship: people are much more likely to participate in social movement activity when they are asked or urged to do so by friends, acquaintances, and family members. As David S. Meyer (2007, p. 47) observes, "[T]he best predictor of why anyone takes on any political action is whether that person has been asked to do so. Issues do not automatically drive people into the streets." Social movement participants tend to have many friends and to belong to several organizations and other sorts of social networks, and these social network ties help "pull" or *recruit* them into social movements. This process of *recruitment* is an essential fact of social movement life, as movements usually cannot succeed if sufficient numbers of people are not recruited into the movement.

Participants in social movement activities are often recruited into the movement by people they know from the many social networks to which they belong.

James Cridland – Crowd – CC BY 2.0.

An interesting development in the modern era is the rising use of electronic means to recruit people into social movement activities and to coordinate and publicize these activities. The "Learning From Other Societies" box discusses a now-famous protest in Iran in which electronic media played a key role.

Learning From Other Societies

Electronic Media and Protest in Iran

Less than a generation ago, the Internet did not exist; cell phones did not exist; and Facebook, Twitter, and other social media did not exist. When activists organized a rally or march, they would typically publicize it by posting flyers (which were mass produced at some expense by using a mimeograph machine or photocopier) on trees, telephone poles, and campus billboards, and they would stand on campuses and city streets handing out flyers. Sometimes phone trees were used: one person would call two people, each of these two people would call two other people, and so forth. Activists would also contact the news media and hope that a small story about the planned rally or march would appear in a newspaper or on radio or TV. Once the event occurred, activists would hope that the news media covered it fully. If the news media ignored it, then few people would learn of the march or rally.

This description of protest organizing now sounds quaint. As the news story about high school protests in New Jersey that began this chapter illustrates, a single Facebook page can ignite a protest involving hundreds and even thousands of people, and other social media and smartphone apps enable us to announce any event, protest or otherwise, to countless numbers of potential participants.

Although social movement scholars have begun to consider the impact of the electronic age on social movement activism and outcomes, the exact nature and extent of this impact will remain unclear until much more research is done. If one needed proof of the potential of this impact, however, events in Iran not long ago provided this proof.

In June 2009, thousands of protesters, most of them young people, took to the streets in Iran to protest a presidential election that was widely regarded as being rigged by and on behalf of the existing regime. When the government tried to stop the protests and prevented newspapers from covering them, the protesters did what came naturally: they tweeted and texted. As a writer for *Time* magazine later observed, because tweets go out over both the Internet and cell phone networks, "this makes Twitter practically ideal for a mass protest movement." The protesters' tweets and texts warned other protesters as well as the rest of the world what Iranian police were doing, and they helped the protesters plan and coordinate their next steps. The protesters also used their cell phones to transmit photos and videos of the protests and the police violence being used to stop the protests; many of the videos ended up on YouTube. When the government tried to electronically block the tweeting and texting, the protesters and their allies outside Iran took electronic countermeasures to help thwart the blocking.

The *Time* writer eloquently summarized what Twitter meant to the Iranian protesters:

> Twitter didn't start the protests in Iran, nor did it make them possible. But there's no question that it has emboldened the protesters, reinforced their conviction that they are not alone and engaged populations outside Iran in an emotional, immediate way that was never possible before. President Ahmadinejad—who happened to visit Russia on Tuesday—now finds himself in a court of world opinion where even Khrushchev never had to stand trial. Totalitarian governments rule by brute force, and because they control the consensus worldview of those they rule. Tyranny, in other words, is a monologue. But as long as Twitter is up and running, there's no such thing.
> In short, the Iranian election protests in June 2009 revealed the power of Twitter and other electronic media to shape the dynamics and outcomes of protest. The day when activists had to stand in the rain on city streets to hand out flyers has long passed. Instead, they can tweet and use other electronic media. Social movement scholars, activists, and governments learned an important lesson from the Iranian protests. (Grossman, 2009)

Resource Mobilization and Political Opportunities

Resource mobilization theory is a general name given to several related views of social movements that arose in the 1970s (McCarthy & Zald, 1977; Oberschall, 1973; Tilly, 1978). This theory assumes that social movement activity is a rational response to unsatisfactory conditions in society. Because these conditions always exist, so does discontent with them. Despite such constant discontent, people protest only rarely. If this is so, these conditions and associated discontent cannot easily explain why people turn to social movements. What is crucial instead are efforts by social movement leaders to mobilize the resources—most notably, time, money, and energy—of the population and to direct them into effective political action.

Resource mobilization theory has been very influential since its inception in the 1970s. However, critics say it underestimates the importance of harsh social conditions and discontent for the rise of social movement activity. Conditions can and do worsen, and when they do so, they prompt people to engage in collective behavior. As just one example, cuts in higher education spending and steep increases in tuition prompted students to protest on campuses in California and several other states in late 2009 and early 2010 (Rosenhall, 2010). Critics also say that resource mobilization theory neglects the importance of emotions in social movement activity by depicting social movement actors as cold, calculated, and unemotional (Goodwin, Jasper, & Polletta, 2004). This picture is simply not true, critics say, and they further argue that social movement actors can be both emotional and rational at the same time, just as people are in many other kinds of pursuits.

Another influential perspective is **political opportunity theory**. According to this view, social movements are more likely to arise and succeed when *political opportunities* for their emergence exist or develop, as when a government that previously was repressive becomes more democratic or when a government weakens because of an economic or foreign crisis (Snow & Soule, 2010). When political opportunities of this kind exist, discontented people perceive a greater chance of success if they take political action, and so they decide to take such action. As Snow and Soule (2010, p. 66) explain, "Whether individuals will act collectively to address their grievances depends in part on whether they have the political opportunity to do so." Applying a political opportunity perspective, one important reason that social movements are so much more common in democracies than in authoritarian societies is that activists feel more free to be active without fearing arbitrary arrests, beatings, and other repressive responses by the government.

The Life Cycle of Social Movements

Although the many past and present social movements around the world differ from each other in many ways, they all generally go through a life cycle marked by several stages that have long been recognized (Blumer, 1969).

Stage 1 is *emergence*. This is the stage when social movements begin for one or more of the reasons indicated in the previous section. Stage 2 is *coalescence*. At this stage a movement and its leaders must decide how they will recruit new members and they must determine the strategies they will use to achieve their goals. They also may use the news media to win favorable publicity and to convince the public of the justness of their cause. Stage 3 is *institutionalization* or *bureaucratization*. As a movement grows, it often tends to become bureaucratized, as paid leaders and a paid staff replace the volunteers that began the movement. It also means that clear lines of authority develop, as they do in any bureaucracy. More attention is also devoted to fund-raising. As movement organizations bureaucratize, they may well reduce their effectiveness by turning from the disruptive activities that succeeded in the movement's earlier stages to more conventional activity by working within the system instead of outside it (Piven & Cloward, 1979). At the same time, if movements do not bureaucratize to at least some degree, they may lose their focus and not have enough money to keep on going.

Stage 4 is the *decline* of a social movement. Social movements eventually decline for one or more of many reasons. Sometimes they achieve their goals and naturally cease because there is no more reason to continue. More often, however, they decline because they fail. Both the lack of money and loss of enthusiasm among a movement's members may lead to a movement's decline, and so might *factionalism*, or strong divisions of opinion within a movement.

Political repression sometimes leads a social movement to decline or end altogether. The mass slaughter by Chinese troops of students in Tiananmen Square in June 1989 ended a wave of student protests in that nation.

Wikimedia Commons – CC BY-SA 3.0.

Government responses to a social movement may also cause the movement to decline. The government may "co-opt" a movement by granting it small, mostly symbolic concessions that reduce people's discontent but leave largely intact the conditions that originally motivated their activism. If their discontent declines, the movement will decline even though these conditions have not changed. Movements also may decline because of government repression. Authoritarian governments may effectively repress movements by arbitrarily arresting activists, beating them up, or even shooting them when they protest (Earl, 2006). Democratic governments are less violent in their response to protest, but their arrest and prosecution of activists may still serve a repressive function by imposing huge legal expenses on a social movement and frightening activists and sympathizers who may not wish to risk arrest and imprisonment. During the Southern civil rights movement, police violence against protesters won national sympathy for the civil rights cause, but arrests and incarceration of civil rights activists in large protest marches looked "better" in comparison and helped stifle dissent without arousing national indignation (Barkan, 1985).

How Social Movements Make a Difference

By definition, social movements often operate outside the political system by engaging in protest. Their rallies, demonstrations, sit-ins, and silent vigils are often difficult to ignore. With the aid of news media coverage, these events often throw much attention on the problem or grievance at the center of the protest and bring pressure to bear on the government agencies, corporations, or other targets of the protest.

As noted earlier, there are many examples of profound changes brought about by social movements throughout U.S. history (Amenta, Caren, Chiarello, & Sue, 2010; Meyer, 2007; Piven, 2006). The abolitionist movement called attention to the evils of slavery and increased public abhorrence for that "peculiar institution." The women's suffrage movement after the Civil War eventually won women the right to vote with the ratification of the 19th Amendment in 1920. The labor movement of the late 19th and early 20th centuries established the minimum wage, the 40-hour workweek, and the right to strike. The civil rights movement of the 1950s and 1960s ended legal segregation in the South, while the Vietnam antiwar movement of the 1960s and 1970s helped increase public opposition to that war and bring it to a close. The contemporary women's movement has won many rights in social institutions throughout American society, while the gay rights movement has done the same for gays and lesbians. Another contemporary movement is the environmental movement, which has helped win legislation and other policies that have reduced air, water, and ground pollution.

Although it seems obvious that social movements have made a considerable difference, social movement scholars until recently have paid much more attention to the origins of social movements than to their consequences (Giugni, 2008). Recent work has begun to fill in this gap and has focused on the consequences of social movements for the political system (*political consequences*), for various aspects of the society's culture (*cultural consequences*), and for the lives of the people who take part in movements (*biographical consequences*).

Regarding political consequences, scholars have considered such matters as whether movements are more successful when they use more protest or less protest, and when they focus on a single issue versus multiple issues. The use of a greater amount of protest seems to be more effective in this regard, as does a focus on a single issue. Research has also found that movements are more likely to succeed when the government against which they protest is weakened by economic or other problems. In another line of inquiry, movement scholars disagree over whether movements are more successful if their organizations are bureaucratic and centralized or if they remain decentralized and thus more likely to engage in protest (Piven & Cloward, 1979; Gamson, 1990).

Regarding cultural consequences, movements often influence certain aspects of a society's culture whether or not they intend to do so (Earl, 2004), and, as one scholar has said, "it is perhaps precisely in being able to alter their broader cultural environment that movements can have their deepest and lasting impact" (Giugni, 2008, p. 1591). Social movements can affect values and beliefs, and they can affect cultural practices such as music, literature, and even fashion.

Movements may also have biographical consequences. Several studies find that people who take part in social movements during their formative years (teens and early 20s) are often transformed by their participation. Their political views change or are at least reinforced, and they are more likely to continue to be involved in political activity and to enter social change occupations. In this manner, writes one scholar, "people who have been involved in social movement activities, even at a lower level of commitment, carry the consequences of that involvement throughout their life" (Giugni, 2008, p. 1590).

Key Takeaways

- The major types of social movements are reform movements, revolutionary movements, reactionary movements, self-help movements, and religious movements.
- For social movements to succeed, they generally must attract large numbers of participants. Recruitment by people in the social networks of social movement sympathizers plays a key role in transforming them into social movement activists.
- Four major stages in the life cycle of a social movement include emergence, coalescence, institutionalization or bureaucratization, and decline.
- Social movements may have political, cultural, and biographical consequences. Political consequences seem most likely to occur when a movement engages in disruptive protest rather than conventional politics and when it has a single-issue focus. Involvement in movements is thought to influence participants' later beliefs and career choices.

For Your Review

1. Have you ever taken part in a protest of some kind? If so, write a brief essay outlining what led you to take part in the protest and what effect, if any, it had on the target of the protest and on your own thinking. If you have not participated in a protest, write a brief essay discussing whether you can foresee yourself someday doing so.
2. Choose any U.S. social movement of the past half-century and write a brief essay that summarizes the various kinds of impacts this movement may have had on American society and culture.

References

Amenta, E., Caren, N., Chiarello, E., & Sue, Y. (2010). The political consequences of social movements. *Annual Review of Sociology, 36*, 287–307.

Barkan, S. E. (1985). *Protesters on trial: Criminal prosecutions in the Southern civil rights and Vietnam antiwar movements*. New Brunswick, NJ: Rutgers University Press.

Blumer, H. (1969). Collective behavior. In A. M. Lee (Ed.), *Principles of sociology* (pp. 165–221). New York, NY: Barnes and Noble.

Davies, J. C. (1962). Toward a theory of revolution. *American Sociological Review, 27*, 5–19.

Earl, J. (2004). The cultural consequences of social movements. In D. A. Snow, S. Soule, & H. Kriesi (Eds.), *The Blackwell companion to social movements* (pp. 508–530). Malden, MA: Blackwell.

Earl, J. (2006). Introduction: Repression and the social control of protest. *Mobilization, 11*, 129–143.

Gamson, W. A. (1990). *The strategy of social protest* (2nd ed.). Belmont, CA: Wadsworth.

Giugni, M. (2008). Political, biographical, and cultural consequences of social movements. *Sociology Compass, 2*, 1582–1600.

Goodwin, J., Jasper, J. M., & Polletta, F. (2004). Emotional dimensions of social movements. In D. A. Snow, S. A. Soule, & H. Kriesi (Eds.), *The Blackwell companion to social movements* (pp. 413–432). Malden, MA: Blackwell.

Grossman, L. (2009, June 17). Iran protests: Twitter, the medium of the movement. *Time*. Retrieved from http://www.time.com/time/world/article/0,8599,1905125,1905100.html.

Gurney, J. N., & Tierney, K. J. (1982). Relative deprivation and social movements: A critical look at twenty years of theory and research. *Sociological Quarterly, 23*, 33–47.

Gurr, T. R. (1970). *Why men rebel*. Princeton, NJ: Princeton University Press.

Klandermans, B., & Oegema, D. (1987). Potentials, networks, motivation, and barriers: Steps toward participation in social movements. *American Sociological Review, 52*, 519–531.

McCarthy, J. D., & Zald, M. N. (1977). Resource mobilization and social movements: A partial theory. *American Journal of Sociology, 82*, 1212–1241.

Meyer, D. S. (2007). *The politics of protest: Social movements in America*. New York, NY: Oxford University Press.

Oberschall, A. (1973). *Social conflict and social movements*. Englewood Cliffs, NJ: Prentice Hall.

Piven, F. F. (2006). *Challenging authority: How ordinary people change America*. Lanham, MD: Rowman & Littlefield.

Piven, F. F., & Cloward, R. A. (1979). *Poor people's movements: Why they succeed, how they fail*. New York, NY: Vintage Books.

Rosenhall, L. (2010, February 28). Education protests on tap this week in California. *The Sacramento Bee*, p. 1A.

Snow, D. A., & Soule, S. A. (2010). *A primer on social movements*. New York, NY: W. W. Norton.

Snow, D. E., & Oliver, P. E. (1995). Social movements and collective behavior: Social psychological dimensions and considerations. In K. S. Cook, G. A. Fine, & J. S. House (Eds.), *Sociological perspectives on social psychology* (pp. 571–599). Boston, MA: Allyn & Bacon.

Tilly, C. (1978). *From mobilization to revolution*. Reading, MA: Addison-Wesley.

21.4 End-of-Chapter Material

Summary

1. Collective behavior refers to a miscellaneous set of behaviors that are relatively spontaneous and engaged in by large numbers of people.
2. Several types of collective behavior exist, including crowds, riots, disaster behavior, social movements, rumors, and fads and crazes.
3. The early contagion theory emphasized that crowds unduly influence individual behavior to be violent and irrational, but more recent theories emphasize that collective behavior is much more predictable and rational.
4. Social movements have been important agents for social change. Common types of social movements include reform movements, revolutionary movements, reactionary movements, and self-help and religious movements.
5. Explanations of social movements address both micro and macro factors. Important issues at the micro level include the question of irrationality, the importance of relative deprivation, and the impact of social isolation. Macro theories address the social, economic, and political conditions underlying collective behavior. Two of the most important such theories are Smelser's structural-strain theory and resource mobilization theory.
6. Most social movements go through a life cycle of four stages: emergence, coalescence, bureaucratization, and decline. Decline stems from several reasons, including internal divisions and repressive efforts by the state.
7. Social movements have political, cultural, and biographical consequences. Research finds that movements are more successful in the political arena when they use more rather than less protest and when they focus on a single issue rather than multiple issues.

Using Sociology

You are 35 years old and living with your spouse and 3-year-old child in a racially integrated neighborhood in a fairly large city. News reports indicate that two young Latino males from your neighborhood, both immigrants, were attacked and beaten the previous evening by a gang of young white (Anglo) males. Several people from the neighborhood organize a meeting to respond to the beatings. At the meeting, the organizers announce that a protest march will take place the following weekend to protest the hate crime that has just occurred. Do you participate in the march?